de Paula's Auditing

de Paula's Auditing

Seventeenth Edition

FRANK A. ATTWOOD
BSc(Econ) FCA ACIS
Partner, Robson Rhodes, Chartered Accountants

NEIL D. STEIN
FCA, ATII
Senior Lecturer in Accounting at
Ealing College of Higher Education

Pitman

PITMAN PUBLISHING
128 Long Acre   London   WC2E 9AN

© FRM de Paula and F Clive de Paula 1970
© F Clive de Paula and Frank A Attwood 1976, 1982
© F Clive de Paula, Frank A Attwood and Neil Stein 1986

Seventeenth edition first published in Great Britain 1986
Reprinted 1989

British Library Cataloguing in Publication Data
De Paula, F. Clive
    De Paula's auditing.—17th ed.
    1. Auditing
    I. Title   II. Attwood, Frank A.   III. Stein,
    Neil D.   IV. De Paula, F. Clive. Auditing
    657'.45 HF5667

ISBN 0-273-02501-5

Typeset by Burgess & Son (Abingdon) Ltd.
Printed and bound in Singapore

Contents

8 The audit 1: General principles – auditing the transactions 135

9 Audit sampling 160

10 The audit 2: Verification of assets and liabilities 185

Preface to the seventeenth edition

Perhaps the most notable feature of this edition, compared with previous ones, is that we have made the book more student-orientated, though without discarding the large amount of practical material of value to practitioners and students alike. Once again this material is based on the audit working papers of Robson Rhodes, whose partners have allowed us to draw freely on their documentation.

The objective of the book is to provide complete coverage of the auditing syllabuses of all the UK professional bodies. The emphasis throughout is on clarity of explanation and informality of style.

Chapter 1 indicates the chapters relevant for each of the main examinations and concludes with a detailed guide to assist in planning study.

Chapters 2–14 deal logically and clearly with the stages of an audit, including discussion of the controversy over the audit of small companies (Chapter 12) and the audit of computer systems (Chapter 13). Chapters 15–19 cover the legal background to auditing and auditors, and Chapters 20–24 deal with matters mainly to be found in the more advanced auditing examinations including investigations (Chapter 24).

Each chapter ends with a set of progress questions designed to test the reader's absorption of its contents.

Since 1980, when the first Auditing Standards and Guidelines were issued by the Auditing Practices Committee of the Consultative Committee of Accountancy Bodies, we have had a steady stream of authoritative material from this source. The study of auditing without the study of the Standards and Guidelines is virtually impossible. We are grateful to the Committee for their permission to reproduce most of the documents in their entirety, and to summarize the remainder. Details of the Standards and Guidelines, and their location in this book, are to be found in Appendix 1.

Frank Attwood has been a member of the Auditing Practices Committee for some six years, but of course the views expressed in this book are not necessarily views which the Committee would share.

We should also like to express our gratitude to the Controller of Her Majesty's Stationery Office for permission to reproduce relevant parts of the

Companies Act 1985, and to Mr John Frew, editor of the Certified Accountants Students' Newsletter, for his permission for us to reproduce in Chapters 10 and 23 extracts from articles by Neil Stein which first appeared in that magazine.

Finally, we should like to acknowledge the continuing debt which we, and all auditing writers, owe to the late F.R.M. de Paula, CBE, FCA, the author of the first and many later editions of this book, and one of the great pioneers of auditing and accountance in this country.

1 How to study auditing

1.1 Introduction

There is no special trick to studying auditing. All that is needed is the application of the general principles to be followed in studying anything, which we may summarize as:

(a) Know what you have to know. Familiarize yourself with the syllabus you are studying.

(b) Plan your work. Identify the time you are going to devote to study each week. If you are attending college the course structure is your overall plan, but you must back this up between sessions with reading, consolidation and working questions.

(c) Make your reading effective.

(d) Build up your own notes—and file them methodically.

(e) Test your knowledge. Get hold of the relevant past examination questions. Remember you must build up speed and this can only come from practice.

(f) Remember that repeated study of material is necessary to master detail.

(g) Allow time for revision.

(h) Study examination technique.

1.2 Know what you have to know

Make sure you know exactly what is in your syllabus.

The table below lists the chapters in this book relevant for the main UK and Irish auditing examinations. It is based on the published syllabuses as at July 1986. *Watch for announcements of changes since this date.*

Institude of Chartered Accountants in England and Wales
Professional Examination 1: Auditing, Systems and Data Processing
The auditing section of the paper (55 per cent of the total) requires study of Chapters 1—12 and 14—20. Note that the syllabus specifically mentions knowledge of SSAPs (Statements of Standard Accounting Practice).

Note also: In the proposed new syllabuses to be examined for the first time in 1988 there will be a whole paper devoted to auditing; it will then be necessary to study Chapters 1—20 for PE1.

Professional Examination 2: Auditing
The whole book. Section 24.4 is strictly outside the syllabus but will provide useful background material for item (*e*) in the Financial Management syllabus (Valuation of shares and businesses). *Note:* The proposed new syllabus for PE2:Auditing will be examined for the first time in 1989. Section 24.4 remains outside the syllabus. The whole of the rest of the book is within the new syllabus, as before.

Chartered Association of Certified Accountants
Level 2, Paper 2.1: Auditing
Chapters 1—20. Note that the syllabus specifically mentions SSAPs.

Chartered Association of Certified Accountants
Level 3, Paper 3.4: Auditing and Investigations
The whole book.

Institute of Chartered Accountants of Scotland
Part I Examination: Auditing I
Chapters 1—8, 10—12, 14—20 and 23. It would be wise to have a general appreciation of the contents of Chapters 9 and 13.

Part II Examination: Auditing II
Chapters 1—22

Institute of Chartered Accountants in Ireland
Professional three examination—Auditing I
Chapters 1—14 and 18, excluding Section 10.10
Final Admitting Examination—Auditing and the General Duties of Professional Accountants
Chapters 1—22 and 24. *Note:* For both of the ICAI examinations the legal requirements relating to audits and auditors are different from the UK requirements presented in the book.

Association of International Accountants
Foundation examination: Auditing and Taxation
Chapters 1—14, 16—18. Appreciation only of some of the contents is all that is required. Chapters 3—8, 10, 14 and 16 should be the main areas studied.

Professional Examination I: Auditing
Chapters 1—20

Professional Examination II: Professional Practice
The whole book. There remain a few topics not fully covered, especially in
the area of practice administration (item 15.4 in the syllabus).

Association of Accounting Technicians (AAT)
Final Examination, Paper 12:Auditing and Taxation
The auditing section of the paper requires study of Chapters 1—14, 16, 17, 18
and 19

In all these syllabuses it is either stated or implied that parallel accounting
knowledge is required in the auditing examination. Auditing is an awkward
subject in this respect, particularly for referred candidates. It obviously
overlaps with accounting and especially with Statements of Standard
Accounting Practice (SSAPs). It also overlaps with company law (statutory
accounting requirements, statutory provisions governing auditors, for
example), computing (computer audits), taxation (verification of taxation and
deferred taxation), and even financial management for aspects of investigations.

Some of the SSAPs are examined more frequently in the auditing paper
than in the accountancy papers—SSAP 17, Accounting for Post Balance Sheet
Events, for example.

It is essential for you to get hold of past examination papers (see Section
1.6) to give you an idea of the depth of study required.

1.3 Plan your work

Most people find it best to set aside regular times for study each week.
Identify leisure commitments and build your study around them.

If you are studying part-time you may be able to spend, say, 12 hours per
week. As a very rough guide you may think in terms of 150 hours of study per
subject in the professional accountancy examinations. This includes time for
practice questions but not for pre-examination revision. That means it is
going to take most part-time students the best part of a year to prepare for
each sitting: certainly the time from announcement of results to the next
examination but one.

Full-time students may be able to work to six-monthly sittings.

If you are attending a college, the course structure will provide your overall
plan, but you must still back up the lecture sessions with reading,
consolidation and practice questions. *Do not expect mere course attendance
to provide all you need for the examination.*

Most people find it productive to break a three-hour study session into
fairly short periods of, say, one hour. Build in short breaks for coffee, etc. As
well as varying your study *topics*, vary your study *methods* during a session.

For example, you may switch from reading about one topic to answering questions on another.

Make use of travel time for reading if you can. This is time that otherwise may be completely wasted.

Every few weeks build in some revision sessions to go over material studied so far in conjunction with your notes.

1.4 Make your reading effective

Have you ever read a page from a book and then suddenly realized that you do not have the faintest idea what it was about? The eyes go through the motions of reading but the brain is busy thinking of something else.

Effective reading means absorbing the material and being able to use it later.

Several features of this book are there to help these processes:

(*a*) Chapter summaries. Each chapter concludes with a paragraph summarizing its contents. Read this *before* you read the chapter as well as at the end. That gives you an overview of the material to be studied before you begin.

(*b*) Section numbering. Each section is numbered and divided into subsections. This is partly to facilitate reference but also to present the material in an orderly way to assist absorption.

(*c*) Progress questions. At the end of each chapter there is a set of progress questions. They are there to enable you to test yourself. Rework them at intervals.

To summarize, your approach to reading this book needs to be something like this:

(*a*) Overview. Read the chapter summary
(*b*) Read the chapter (or section of it that you are studying)
(*c*) Read the chapter again slowly, making orderly notes as you go. (See Section 1.5 below)
(*d*) Read the chapter summary again
(*e*) Work the progress questions (See Section 1.6 below)

1.5 Making notes

Making notes is a vital part of learning. First of all, the act of writing the material down helps you to absorb it, especially if you write it in your own words. Secondly, well written notes provide a valuable revision aid.

Do not cut corners on note-taking material. Buy suitable paper and files and keep all material neat. Be on the look-out for articles or other material to add to your notes.

1.6 Working questions

As already mentioned, each chapter (except this one) concludes with a set of *progress questions*. These are designed to test your absorption of the material in the chapter. Answers are references back to the relevant paragraph.

Such questions are important to test knowledge, but they are not intended to replace or simulate examination questions. You need to buy yourself a book of past examination papers to provide examination level practice. A typical examination question may range over several topic areas and will require thought and preparation before you write the answer.

Whenever questions *with* answers are available to you, the strong temptation is to take a quick look at the answer before attempting it. That is fatal. Any question becomes easy if you have seen the answer. All you will get is delusions of adequacy. Work the question *without* looking at the answer. Then you have earned the right to read it.

Approach to an examination level question is:

(a) READ the question
(b) THINK, and PLAN your answer. This means:
    (1) identifying exactly what your answer will consist of;
    (2) identifying relevant statutory and professional material to be referred to: Companies Act 1985, SSAPs, Auditing Standards and Guidelines, other pronouncements, case law;
    (3) noting the main heads of your answer and arranging them in logical order.
(c) WRITE your answer, based on your plan but including additional material that comes to mind as you write.

1.7 Repetition and revision

If you are to master a complex subject, material needs to be studied using several different methods and with repeated coverage of material. The final repetition before the examination is your revision. The more times you have been through the material before the revision phase the easier and quicker your revision will be.

Your programme for each topic needs to be something like this:

If attending a course of oral tuition	If not attending a course of oral tuition
1 Overview of material to be studied (Chapter summaries)	1 Overview of material to be studied (Chapter summaries)
2 Before a lecture, take a look at the subject briefly	2 Read the chapter
3 Attend lecture	3 Re-read the chapter slowly, making notes as you go
4 Consolidate lecture by reading relevant material, making notes as you go	
5 Answer progress questions	4 Answer progress questions
6 Revision	5 Revision
7 Answer examination questions	6 Answer examination questions
8 Final revision	7 Final revision
9 Sit examination	8 Sit examination

1.8 Examination technique

1.8.1 Before the examination

(a) Get your examination entry in before the deadline!

(b) Ensure you know *exactly* where and when you are to sit the examination and how you are to get there, including contingency plans to cope with a rail strike or other travel difficulties.

(c) Get all necessary equipment together and check it. This means pens, pencils (for graphs), calculators (sometimes useful in the auditing examination) with spare battery, ruler, glucose tablets (for energy during the exam).

(d) Try to get a good night's sleep before the exam but do not take sleeping pills or the like.

(e) A little *light* revision the night before can be a good idea.

(f) Have a good breakfast on the day of the exam. (You'll get nothing to eat or drink for three hours—except your glucose tablets!)

1.8.2 During the examination

An examination is a test of your learning but it is also a time test. At the revision stage you should have built up your speed so that you can cope with the speed requirement.

You may calculate the time available for a question by the formula:

$$\text{Minutes per mark} = \frac{\text{Minutes of examination}}{\text{Marks for examination}}$$

In most examinations this is 180/100 = 1.8 minutes per mark.

(*a*) Read the instructions at the head of the paper, noting how many questions have to be answered.

(*b*) Glance through the paper, deciding which questions you plan to answer. You may leave the final decision for some questions until later, but you must obviously choose one to start with.

(*c*) Calculate the time available (marks×2 less 10 per cent) per question.

(*d*) Most people like to begin with the easiest question on the paper rather than with question 1. This is a matter of taste, but obviously you should not leave the easiest question until last. If you are going to run out of time at the end, let it be while answering the most difficult question.

(*e*) Watch the time constantly: not only the total time for each question but, where marks are broken down for parts of the question, the time spent on each part. Do not leave yourself with no time to do part of the question.

(*f*) Attack each question as outlined in Section 1.6:
READ
THINK and PLAN
WRITE

(*g*) Begin each question on a separate sheet of paper. Also, leave space between parts of the answer and even between paragraphs. This makes it much easier to insert extra material later if you have to.

(*h*) Keep taking the glucose tablets.

(*i*) Keep your work as neat as possible. In particular:
—do not write in the margins
—use a ruler to underline headings
—number your answers clearly

(*j*) Attempt all questions you are required to attempt. If you do not you increase your chances of failure ENORMOUSLY.

(*k*) When you think you have finished, and if time permits, read through your work to make any necessary corrections. You will almost certainly have omitted a word or made some error in spelling or grammar under the pressure of the examination.

1.8.3   After the examination

Outside every examination hall there lurks a know-all eager to explain how you should have mentioned SSAP 74 in your answer to question 3. Steer clear of him and do not be put off. Your objective now is to do well in the next paper. He's probably wrong, anyhow!

1.9 Summary

Effective study means:

(*a*) familiarity with the syllabus;

(*b*) regular planned study over an adequate time period—something like 150 hours of study per subject is needed by the average student;

(*c*) methodical notes based on reading or lectures;

(*d*) regular testing of your knowledge by working questions without prior reference to the answers;

(*e*) periodic revision sessions to consolidate work to date;

(*f*) intelligent technique to ensure that you achieve your full potential in the examination. In particular:

(1) plan optimum use of time by reference to marks per question

(2) READ, THINK, WRITE

(3) Keep your work as neat as possible

(4) Conclude by reading through your script

1.10 A study plan for auditing

Chapter topic	Time guide for reading (hours)	Progress questions	Complete (tick)	Notes
2 Introduction to auditing This chapter sets the scene for studying auditing. Many of the matters covered are dealt with in greater detail later. Note particularly the advantages of an audit in Section 2.6	1	1–6		
3 Auditing—before the work begins The most important material here is the guideline on letters of engagement. Make sure you fully understand the purpose and content of these.	1	1–5		

Chapter topic	Time guide for reading (hours)	Progress questions	Complete (tick)	Notes
4 Audit planning, controlling and recording Everything in this chapter is of great examination importance. It provides essential support for the following seven chapters dealing with the audit itself.	3	1–6		
5 Principles of internal control The quality of the client's system of internal control is of great concern to the auditor.	3	1–7		
Revision Revise all work to date. Rework progress questions to test your retention.	3	As many as time permits		
6 Ascertaining and recording the system of internal control This chapter deals with vital preliminary work by the auditor.	2	1–2		
7 Evaluating the system Do not skip the reading and study of the ICQ in Section 7.7 and the MCC in Section 7.8.	3	1–6		
8 The audit 1: general principles—auditing the transactions	4	1–5		
9 Audit sampling	3	1–7		

Chapter topic	Time guide for reading (hours)	Progress questions	Complete (tick)	Notes
Revision Revise all work to date.	4	As many as time permits		
10 The audit 2: verification of assets and liabilities This long chapter should be split into three parts for study purposes:				
Section 10.1—Section 10.5	4	1–16		
Section 10.6	4	17–30		
Section 10.7—Section 10.14	4	31–52		
11 The audit 3: review of financial statements	7	1–15		
12 Small companies	3	1–5		
13 Computer systems The time you require on this chapter will depend on your level of computer expertise and your practical experience of computers and computer auditing.	5–8	1–15		
Revision A major revision of all work to date, please.	10			
14 Reporting	3	1–8		
15 Special reports required of auditors under the Companies Act 1985 Profit available for distribution (Section 15.2) is probably the most important area here.	2	1–10		

Chapter topic	Time guide for reading (hours)	Progress questions	Complete (tick)	Notes
16 Statutory requirements governing auditors	$2\frac{1}{2}$	1–12		
17 Other statutory requirements of concern to auditors	$2\frac{1}{2}$	1–6		
18 Auditor's independence	2	1–2		
19 Professional liability of accountants and auditors	4	1–7		
20 Audit committees	1	1–4		
21 Auditing consolidated financial statements	3	1–5		
22 Auditing current cost accounts Watch for future developments!	1	1		
23 Special types of audit	6	1–18		
24 Investigations	6	1–19		
Final revision				

2 Introduction to auditing

2.1 What is auditing?

The whole of this book is an attempt to answer that question, but in one sentence auditing is 'checking somebody else's accounting'.

2.2 Historical and legal background in the UK

When businesses were mainly small and conducted by sole proprietors or partnerships, as they were until the development of limited companies in the nineteenth century, there was not much demand or need for audit work, or indeed for complex accounting.

The passing of the first Companies Act, introduced by Gladstone in 1844, set the scene. As soon as there was a separation between the providers of capital for a business (shareholders) and its management (directors) there developed a need for an independent examination of accounts to safeguard shareholders' interests.

At first, a company's auditors were appointed from among its shareholders, but the work they did was probably not very effective.

Under the 1844 Act, registered companies were required to appoint 'one or more auditors', but there was no guidance as to their qualifications or independence. If at the conclusion of the annual meeting of the company no auditor had been appointed, the Board of Trade was directed to appoint an auditor—a requirement that still continues today.

In 1856 the 1844 Act was repealed and replaced by the Companies Act 1856, under which the provision *requiring* auditors to be appointed was replaced by a set of model regulations which a company was not bound to adopt. These included provision for auditors to be appointed.

The 1856 Act introduced the idea that the auditor need not be a shareholder, thus encouraging the development of professional auditors.

The Companies Act 1879 made the appointment of auditors compulsory for banking companies, and this was finally extended to all companies by the Companies Act 1900. All this time the auditor's concern was with the balance sheet, not the profit and loss account, and it was not until the Companies Act

1929 that the auditor's report was extended to cover the profit and loss account, and not until the 1948 Act that extended profit and loss disclosure requirements were introduced. (In fact, many companies produced and had audited accounts which in many cases gave more information than published accounts do today, but there was no legal compulsion to do so until the dates stated above.)

2.3 The professional bodies in auditing and accounting

In the UK today there are four professional bodies whose members are authorized under the Companies Act to audit the accounts of companies:

Institute of Chartered Accountants of Scotland (ICAS), 1854
Institute of Chartered Accountants in England and Wales (ICAEW), 1880
Institute of Chartered Accountants in Ireland (ICAI), 1885
Chartered Association of Certified Accountants (CACA), 1905

With minor exceptions dealt with in Chapter 16, no-one other than a member of one of these four bodies may audit a UK company.

There are other important professional bodies of accountants—the Institute of Cost and Management Accountants (ICMA) formed in 1919, and the Chartered Institute of Public Finance and Accountancy (CIPFA) (1885). Each of these has its specialized areas which lie outside auditing, but which obviously include important aspects of accounting. The six bodies so far mentioned are represented in the Consultative Committee of Accountancy Bodies (CCAB), which exists to promote cooperation among them.

Two committees set up by the CCAB are most important to us:

(a) The Accounting Standards Committee (ASC), set up in 1970, issues Statements of Standard Accounting Practice (SSAPs)—authoritative pronouncements of best practice which members of the bodies concerned are required to follow. (Full details of all SSAPs are not given in this book as they will be covered in your accounting texts, but a good knowledge of them is *essential* for your auditing examinations.)

(b) The Auditing Practices Committee (APC), which was set up in 1976, and which issued its first Discussion Drafts for Auditing Standards and Guidelines in 1978, does for auditing what the ASC does for accounting. The Auditing Standards and Guidelines issued by the APC cover much of the core of the subject and are also *essential* material for auditing students and practitioners. They are reproduced in full and discussed in detail in this book. A list of the topics covered by them so far appears in Appendix 1.

The APC also publishes a bulletin entitled *True and Fair*. This appears about three times a year and contains short articles of use to practitioners and students alike.

The UK professional bodies are also members of international accounting organizations which, in many cases, they played an important part in founding. Such international bodies include:

(a) the International Accounting Standards Committee (IASC), set up in 1973 to issue international accounting standards to promote the world-wide acceptance and observance of basic standards in the presentation of audited accounts and financial statements;

(b) The Union Européenne des Experts Comptables Économiques et Financiers (UEC);

(c) the International Federation of Accountants (IFAC) (1977), which issues International Guidelines on Auditing through the International Auditing Practices Committee.

Other UK bodies concerned with auditing and accounting are:

Institude of Internal Auditors, 1979
Association of International Accountants (AIA), 1928
Society of Company and Commercial Accountants (SCCA), 1923
Association of Accounting Technicians (AAT), 1980

In the closely connected field of company secretarial practice there is the Institute of Chartered Secretaries and Administrators (ICSA), founded in 1891.

2.4 The work of a practising accountant

Although auditing may be an important part of the work of an accountant in practice, other areas of work include the following:

(a) Provision of accounting services

Many firms are too small to employ accountants and rely on professional firms to prepare their financial statements.

Smaller firms still may lack basic accounting records and use the services of professional firms to provide basic accounting information—in other words, the writing up of their books or the maintenance of computerized records which can provide such information.

(b) Taxation

(1) Preparing taxation computations and agreeing them with the Inland Revenue;
(2) Provision of advice to minimize tax liabilities—tax planning;
(3) VAT returns and advice.

(c) Management consultancy

(d) Provision of advice

Accountants may advise on improving efficiency of operation or internal systems of control. This area of work can be particularly important for a client whose business is growing rapidly and needs control systems to grow with it.

(e) Financial advice

Accountants may be called upon to advise on the best way to finance growth and to manage working capital effectively. They may also be useful intermediaries in the operation of the Business Expansion Scheme introduced in 1983 to assist in the provision of finance for smaller businesses.

(f) Investigations

An independent accountant's assistance is frequently sought by the purchaser of a business to investigate its past history and to advise on value.

Another possible subject of accountants' investigation is fraud. Accountants may also be appointed as inspectors under the Companies Act 1985 to investigate the affairs of a company at the instigation of the members or the Department of Trade and Industry. Investigations are covered in detail in Chapter 24.

(g) Prospectuses

Before a company can make an issue of shares to the public it must issue a *prospectus* detailing the terms of the issue and the financial history of the company for the previous five years. The prospectus will usually include an accountants' report on profit figures and details of assets and liabilities contained in this history. See Chapter 24 for further details of this important area.

(h) Profit forecasts

Accountants may be required to report on profit forecasts made in a bid situation.

When one company is attempting to take over another, either of the companies involved may issue forecasts of future profit levels. Such forecasts will usually be reported on by accountants. This matter too is covered in detail later. (See Chapter 24).

(i) Liquidations

Accountants are often appointed as liquidators to wind up the affairs of a company. This involves realising the assets, paying off the liabilities and returning the surplus, if any, to the shareholders.

(j) Receiverships

The terms of a debenture trust deed may entitle the debenture holders to appoint someone to take temporary control of a company, realise the asset which is security for the loan, and pay the proceeds to the debenture-holders. The person so appointed is a *receiver* and is frequently a professional accountant.

2.5 Independence of the auditor

The previous section listed some of the many tasks performed by accountants for their clients. If accountants get involved in several such tasks, could this impair their independence as auditors? For example, what if auditors are responsible for auditing records or accounts that they themselves have prepared? What is the dividing line between the provision of professional advice and participating in the management of a company?

These and other problems have been dealt with by a Guide to Professional Ethics fully detailed in Chapter 18.

For the moment let us simply say that it is essential for accountants to maintain independence and only to accept or continue a professional appointment if they are satisfied that to do so does not reflect adversely upon their integrity and objectivity in relation to that appointment.

2.6 Types of client and advantages of an audit

Although one thinks first of limited companies and other organizations required by law to have auditors as the main audit clients of an accountant, other types of entity may well require an audit.

Sole traders and partnerships, for example, may well wish to have their accounts audited. Why? What are the advantages?

2.6.1 General advantages for all organizations

(*a*) The independent review of internal systems, and the report on them customarily provided each year, is helpful in drawing attention to weaknesses to be corrected.

(b) The knowledge of the client's affairs automatically acquired by the auditor provides a valuable background to the provision of specialized advice when required.

(c) The auditor may be able to assist by providing a fund of expertise and experience when accounts and control systems are to be introduced or extended.

(d) The presence of auditors will inhibit attempts at fraud and make their success less likely.

(e) Errors and fraud are likely to be discovered more quickly.

2.6.2 Advantages for sole traders

(a) Audited accounts are given more weight by banks and others approached to provide finance.

(b) A prospective purchaser of a business will place more confidence in audited accounts as evidence of past profitability.

(c) Audited accounts are likely to have more credibility for the Inland Revenue.

2.6.3 Advantages for partnerships

(a) The interests of a sleeping partner (one providing capital but not active in management) will be protected.

(b) Disputes among partners over such matters as profit-sharing may be less likely to arise when accounts have been audited; and if they do arise their effect may be minimized if partners are prepared to accept the auditor as an independent arbitrator whom all partners can trust.

(c) The financial arrangements on the admission of a new partner or retirement etc., are more soundly based if the accounts themselves are known to be reliable.

In recent years the question has been raised that a full audit may well not be cost-effective for small companies in which the shareholders are also directors. This controversy is discussed further in Chapter 12.

2.7 Objects of an audit

Originally the work of professional accountants was confined largely to the checking of the arithmetical accuracy of the detailed records in books of account, the agreement of the trial balance, and the preparation of accounts; in fact, to what may be described as 'accountancy work', but nowadays a large part of a professional accountant's work is that of auditing. The difference between accountancy and auditing is not always clearly understood, it being thought that if accounts are prepared by a professional accountant, he or she necessarily guarantees their accuracy. This, however, is far from being the case.

If an accountant is instructed merely to prepare accounts from a set of books, the work involved would be that of agreeing the trial balance, and thereafter preparing the profit and loss account and the balance sheet. The accountant would not check the books, except in so far as would be necessary to agree the trial balance, and would not report that the position shown by the balance sheet was a true and fair one. All the accountant could say would be that the balance sheet was in accordance with the books. Accountants are often called upon to deal with figures in this way, but when doing so, they should be particularly careful to point out to their clients that they are not carrying out an audit, for an audit is quite distinct and apart from accountancy.

An audit does not entail the preparation of the accounts at all, but denotes something much wider, namely:

'the independent examination of financial statements of enterprises, where such an examination is conducted with a view to expressing an opinion on whether those statements give a true and fair view and comply with the relevant statutes'.

This then is the main object of an audit in accordance with the Companies Act 1985, to report whether, in the opinion of the auditors, the balance sheet and profit and loss account give a true and fair view.

In the past, the detection of fraud was also regarded as being a major part of an auditor's function, and indeed probably is still so regarded by many of those who employ auditors. However, leading professional opinion, set out by the Auditing Practices Committee in the Explanatory Foreword to 'Auditing Standards and Guidelines', would no longer regard its discovery as being more than a by-product of the proper application of the audit procedures necessary to enable the expression of an opinion on the accounts under examination:

'The responsibility for the prevention and detection of irregularities and fraud rests with the management, who may obtain reasonable assurance that this responsibility will be discharged, by instituting an adequate system of internal control.'

'The auditor should recognize the possibility of material irregularities or fraud which could, unless adequately disclosed, distort the results or state of affairs shown by the financial statements. The auditor should, therefore, plan his audit so that he has a reasonable expectation of detecting major misstatements in the financial statements resulting from irregularities or fraud.'

Whilst an audit cannot be a substitute for internal controls over transactions exercised at the time, nevertheless an assessment of these controls must be made by the auditor so that he or she can determine the volume of detailed checking necessary to enable the discharge of the primary audit function. This also then provides the opportunity for a service to management in pointing out deficiencies in internal control and making recommendations for improvements.

The basic approach to which we shall be returning in later chapters is thus that auditors should aim to reduce their detailed checking to the minimum consistent with the system of internal control and the state in which they find the records. If their inquiries and tests satisfy them that the system is sound in principle and is carried out in practice, then no useful purpose is served by extensive detailed checking. If on the other hand the system is not sound or is not properly carried out, then the auditors must first reach a conclusion as to the nature of the shortcomings before they can decide upon the nature and extent of the detailed checking which they should undertake.

2.8   Auditing Standards and Guidelines

Interestingly, and perhaps surprisingly, in spite of the legislative background to the development of auditing since the nineteenth century, the form and extent of the detailed audit work required to support an audit opinion have never been prescribed. Until recently, this was primarily a question for the individual auditor's professional judgement, and the only recommendations made as to how such judgement should be exercised were contained in Statements on Auditing issued by the Institute of Chartered Accountants in England and Wales. Over the last decade, however, in parallel with the promulgation of Statements of Standard Accounting Practice and with the development of Statements of Auditing Standards in the United States of America, there has been pressure to set auditing standards in the UK. This pressure has been further reinforced during the last five years or so by criticisms of audit procedures expressed by Department of Trade inspectors.

The consequences of these circumstances have been twofold: firstly, the establishment with effect from 1 January 1980 of the Joint Disciplinary Scheme to investigate, in cases of public interest, the competence and conduct of members, and secondly, the publication in April 1980 by the Auditing Practices Committee of the Consultative Committee of Accountancy Bodies of the first Auditing Standards and Guidelines.

Auditing Standards may be seen as having the same objective in relation to audit practice as Accounting Standards to the preparation of accounts: 'the narrowing of areas of difference and variety in practice'.

Previously, as we have said, auditors have developed their practical skills from a number of sources: statements by the professional bodies, formal professional training, case law, Department of Trade reports, practical experience of course, and even from well-known auditing texts!

However, individual auditors had been left to develop their own approach and procedures for all types of audit assignment, and to establish 'good practice' for themselves. The codification arising from the Standards now aims to set out what is best practice.

As the chairman of the Auditing Practices Committee said in an introductory letter to them:

'Auditing Standards and Guidelines are, of course, only the codification of existing best practice, but I believe that they will provide for each member a yardstick by which he may judge not only the general level of his work, but also the suitability of the action he proposes to take in a particular case. That is not to suggest that Auditing Standards and Guidelines can ever replace the judgement of the individual member. Only the member carrying out the audit can decide when he has adequate evidence for the purpose of arriving at the opinion expressed in his audit report.'

The Auditing Standards and Guidelines consist of brief statements of principle (the Standards) each supported by Guidelines dealing with individual aspects. As with the Accounting Standards, the issue of a new auditing Standard or Guideline is preceded by an Exposure Draft on which comment is invited. In this way the greatest possible consensus is obtained and, of course, the combined expertise of the whole profession can contribute to the final form of the pronouncement.

Appendix 1 details the topics so far covered by the Standards and Guidelines and indicates where they are to be found in this book.

2.9 The audit report and the true and fair view

After the audit work is completed the auditors report their findings to the client. A fairly standard form of words has been developed for the report, based on the requirements of the Companies Act 1985 and the Reporting Standard referred to in Section 2.8.

A very similar form of report is used for non-statutory audits of sole traders or partnerships.

The fundamental point of the report is to state whether in the auditor's opinion the financial statements show a *true and fair view* of the profit and state of affairs of the business. It is important to realize that the auditor does not *certify* the accuracy of the figures—he or she proceeds in many cases by *testing* a representative sample of transactions or records as a result of which his or her confidence in the accuracy of the records is built up.

This is not to say that auditors cannot be held liable for damage suffered as a result of their negligence in carrying out the audit. Although the detection of errors and fraud is not the main objective of an audit, auditors may still be liable if, say, they fail to detect a fraud which a reasonably competent audit would have detected.

If auditors are not happy about all the matters they have to report on, they 'qualify' the report; that is, they include a reservation or, in extreme cases, a statement that the accounts do not show a true and fair view or comply with the Companies Act.

Further details on reporting requirements, including the Reporting Standards and Guidelines, are in Chapter 14.

2.10 Summary

An audit may be defined as an 'independent examination of, and expression of opinion on the financial statements of an enterprise by an appointed auditor in pursuance of that appointment and in compliance with any relevant statutory obligations' (Explanatory foreword to Auditing Standards and Guidelines published by the APC in 1980).

Auditing developed in parallel with the growth of limited companies in the second half of the nineteenth century.

With few exceptions, UK companies must have professionally qualified auditors, members of one of four accountancy bodies.

The Consultative Council of Accountancy Bodies, through two committees, the Accounting Standards Committee and the Auditing Practices Committee, issues authoritative statements on accounting and auditing which are of great importance to auditing practitioners and students.

The work of professional accountants covers many areas besides auditing, including accountancy, taxation, consultancy and special reports. In accepting an appointment, accountants must ensure that other work which they undertake for the same client does not jeopardize their independence or integrity in relation to their audit or other appointment.

In addition to being a legal requirement for companies, an audit has many advantages for a business and in many cases will be a very cost effective item of expenditure even when not a legal requirement.

The main object of an audit is to enable the auditor to report as to whether the financial statements under review show a true and fair view of the profit or loss and of the state of affairs of the business at the end of the period covered.

Progress questions

Questions	Reference for answers
(1) What other services may professional accountants offer besides auditing?	Section 2.4
(2) List four advantages of an audit for all organizations.	Section 2.6.1
(3) What further advantages may there be for (a) sole traders, (b partnerships?	Section 2.6.2 Section 2.6.3
(4) Who are primarily responsible for the prevention and detection of fraud and error in a company?	Section 2.7
(5) What is the fundamental point covered by an audit report?	Section 2.9
(6) What does the auditor do if he has a material reservation about some matter in the financial statements he is auditing?	Section 2.9

3 Auditing—before the work begins

3.1 Before appointment

In most business situations an offer to buy goods or make use of services is accepted with alacrity by the provider with no consideration of the effect on any previous provider of similar goods or services to the customer or client.

The acceptance of appointment as auditor cannot, however, be regarded in quite such a light-hearted manner.

It is part of the code of professional conduct set up by the professional bodies that a member should not accept nomination in replacement of the auditor of a company without first communicating with the former or existing auditor to enquire whether there is any professional or other reason for the proposed change of which he or she should be aware when deciding whether or not to accept nomination.

The following extracts from the Code of Professional Conduct of the ICAEW summarize the position.

Changes in a professional appointment

Communication with the existing auditor is not only a question of professional courtesy. The purposes are to enable the member to ascertain whether the circumstances in which a change of auditor is proposed are such that he can properly accept the nomination and also whether he would wish to do so. While it is essential that the legitimate interests of shareholders, including their right to change the company's auditor, if they so wish, should be protected, it is also essential that the independence of the existing auditor should be safeguarded. The member who is invited to replace the existing auditor should therefore endeavour to ascertain the reasons for the proposed change. He cannot effectively do so without direct communication with the existing auditor. The need to communicate exists whether or not the existing auditor intends to make representations to the shareholders, and whether or not he still holds office as auditor.

When a member is first approached he should explain his duty to communicate with the existing auditor *and request authority to do so. If authority is refused, he should not accept nomination.* [our italics]

The member should suggest that the company should inform the existing auditor of the proposed change before the member himself communicates (making it clear that the member has not at that stage accepted nomination) and that, at the same time, the company should give the existing auditor written authority to discuss the company's affairs with the proposed new auditor.

The initiative in the matter of communication rests with the proposed new auditor. The existing auditor should not volunteer information in the absence of any communication.

The legal position of the existing auditor who may have to communicate to a proposed new auditor matters damaging to the company depends not upon whether the proposed new auditor has received the company's authority to communicate with the existing auditor but upon whether the existing auditor has been authorized by the company to discuss the company's affairs with the proposed new auditor. If when the proposed new auditor communicates with him, the existing auditor has not received this authorization, he should ask the company for authority to reply and to protect himself should if possible ensure that the authority is written. If he has this authority, then provided he says what he honestly believes to be true, he can state, so far as he knows them, the reasons for the proposed change in auditors and pass on any relevant information without any fear of an action for either breach of contract or defamation. If he does not have this authorization, the Council is advised that he would nevertheless have a strong measure of protection against an action for defamation in that his communication would be protected by qualified privilege, which means that he would not be liable to pay damages for defamatory statements, even if they turn out to be untrue, if they were made without malice; and provided he stated only what he sincerely believed to be true the chances of his being held malicious are remote. Moreover, although in making a communication without authorization the existing auditor might technically be in breach of contract and although there could be circumstances in which the resulting damages were substantial, the likelihood of an action being brought against him is small and in most cases the damages awarded in such an action would be nominal.

The member should decline to accept nomination if the existing auditor informs him that the company has refused to give the existing auditor authority to discuss the company's affairs with the proposed new auditor.

The existing auditor should answer without delay the communication from the proposed new auditor, whether or not the latter is a member of the Insitute. If there are no reasons for the proposed change of which the new auditor should be made aware, the existing auditor should write to say that this is the case. Subject to the legal constraints described above, and the problem regarding possible tax irregularities in the next paragraph, if there are such reasons he should inform the proposed new auditor of those factors of which the new auditor should be aware; and if he wishes to put forward any professional reason why the proposed new auditor should not accept nomination, it is not sufficient for him merely to state that he has such a professional reason, he should be prepared to state the nature of it. He may prefer to explain orally, so far as he knows them, the reasons for the proposed change and in that event the member who has been approached should be prepared to confer with the existing auditor if the existing auditor so desires.

Where the existing auditor has unconfirmed suspicion but no actual knowledge that the company or its directors or servants have defrauded the Inland Revenue or been guilty of some other unlawful act or default, no general rule can be laid down as to whether and if so in what detail he should communicate his suspicion to a proposed new auditor who communicates with him. It must rest with the individual in the particular circumstances of the case to determine what he considers to be a proper course. Where, however, there has been failure or refusal by the company or its directors or servants to supply him with information properly required by him for the performance of his duties, he should in any event so inform the proposed new auditor who communicates with him.

The member should treat in the strictest confidence any information given to him by the existing auditor. He should give due weight to the reply of the existing auditor and to any respresentations which the latter may inform him he intends to make to the shareholders. Resentment on the part of the existing auditor at the actions taken by those who propose a change or at the possible loss of an audit is not a valid professional reason against the change. The existing auditor should give information as to the professional considerations which arise. This information may indicate, for example, that the ostensible reasons given for the change are not in accordance with the facts. It may disclose that the proposal made to displace the existing auditor is put forward because he has stood his ground and carried out his duties as auditor in the teeth of opposition or evasion on an occasion on which important differences of principle or practice have arisen between him and the directors.

The member who is invited to replace the existing auditor may decline the nomination if he considers that the existing auditor is being treated unfairly; members differ in their views as to the circumstances in which they are prepared, as a matter of personal choice, to accept nomination in the place of another auditor but every member who is approached should consider carefully whether as a matter of professional conduct or as one of personal inclination he can properly accept nomination in the circumstances in which the change is proposed. The communication therefore serves to protect the member from accepting nomination in circumstances of which he was not fully aware and also to protect shareholders who are not fully informed of the circumstances in which the change is proposed as well as the interests of the existing auditor where the proposed change arises from, or is an attempt to interfere with, the conscientious exercise by the existing auditor of his duty as an independent professional man.

Fees—scale of charges

It is not necessarily improper for a member to charge a lower fee than has previously been charged by another auditor for similar work. However, evidence that a member has obtained professional work through having quoted with that object a fee lower than that charged or proposed by the accountant previously carrying out that work could be regarded as cause for complaint and could therefore render the member liable to disciplinary action.

Unpaid fees of previous auditor

The fact that there may be fees owing to the existing auditor is not of itself a professional reason why the member should not accept nomination. If he does accept it may be appropriate for him to assist in any way open to him towards achieving a settlement of the fees outstanding; whether or not he does so is entirely a matter for his own judgement in the light of all the circumstances. He should not seek to interfere with the exercise of any lien which the existing auditor may have.

Transfer of books and papers

The existing auditor should transfer promptly to the new auditor after he has been duly appointed all books and papers of the company which are in his possession, unless he is exercising a lien thereon for unpaid fees.

Business acquired by a new company

When a member is asked to accept appointment as auditor of a new company formed to acquire an existing business and the ownership of the company is substantially the same as it was in the acquired business, the member should communicate with the accountant who acted for that business.

Appointment other than as auditor

The considerations arising on a change of auditor apply to a large extent also where a member is invited to undertake other recurring professional work in place of another accountant.

3.2   Appointment

Professional clearance by communication with a previous auditor is not the only matter to be considered by the prospective auditor. He or she must consider whether it is proper to accept appointment in view of possible conflicts of interest arising because of other appointments or connections. The auditor must also realistically consider whether he or she is technically competent to do the work.

Assuming that all is well, however, the auditor will then signify acceptance by sending an engagement letter to the client.

It is at this point that we meet for the first time in this book the Auditing Standards and Guidelines in detail. A Guideline issued in May 1984 covers the subject of engagement letters and is reproduced in its entirety in the next section.

3.3 Engagement letters

Auditing Practices Committee Guidelines on engagement letters, issued May 1984

Preface

This Guideline gives guidance on one of the procedures to be followed before the commencement of an audit and is written in the context of audit appointments in the United Kingdom and the Republic of Ireland. It is supplementary to and should be read in conjunction with the auditor's operational and reporting standards, and the Explanatory Foreword to the Auditing Standards and Guidelines.

The principles contained in this guideline should also be followed in the case of non-audit engagements. In such a case, if purely accounting services are being provided to a client such as a sole trader or partnership, the engagement letter should make it clear that these services will be performed without any audit work being carried out.

Members are advised that from time to time their professional bodies may issue handbook statements recommending that certain points not mentioned in this guideline be included in engagement letters.

Introduction

(1) The purpose of an engagement letter is to define clearly the extent of the auditor's responsibilies and so minimize the possibility of any misunderstanding between the client and the auditor.

(2) Further, the engagement letter provides written confirmation of the auditor's acceptance of his appointment, the scope of the audit and the form of his report. If an engagement letter is not sent to clients, both new and existing, there is scope for argument about the precise extent of the respective obligations of the client and its directors and the auditor. Furthermore, the auditor may find that he has entered into an implied contract arising either from the Articles of Association or by virtue of conduct arising from practices that he has adopted over a period of time.

Procedures

(3) The agreement of an engagement letter is in the interest of both the auditor and the client. Therefore the contents of an engagement letter should be discussed and agreed with management before it is sent and preferably prior to the audit appointment. In the case of a company incorporated under the Companies Acts, the term management should be taken as meaning the directors of the company and persons acting with similar authority.

(4) The auditor should send an engagement letter to all new clients soon after his appointment as auditor and, in any event, before the commencement of the first audit assignment. He should also consider sending an engagement letter to existing clients to whom no letter has previously been sent as soon as a suitable opportunity presents itself.

(5) Where an auditor is engaged by a client that has subsidiary companies, a separate letter should be sent by the auditor to the board of directors of each company which he is auditing. However, if the terms of the engagements are common, one letter may be sent relating to the group as a whole. In the latter case, the auditor's letter should identify the group companies for which he is appointed auditor, and the directors of the holding company should be requested to forward the letter to the boards of directors of the subsidiary companies concerned. The auditor should request confirmation from each board that the terms of the engagement letter are accepted. Where more than one firm of auditors is involved in the audit of the group, the respective responsibilities of the holding company auditor and the subsidiary company auditors should be clearly defined.

(6) Where there are joint auditors, the audit engagement should be explained in similar terms by each auditor. The auditors should agree whether joint or separate letters should be sent to the client. Separate letters would normally need to be sent where other services are provided.

(7) Once it has been agreed by the client, an engagement letter will, if it so provides, remain effective, from one audit appointment to another, until it is replaced. However, the engagement letter should be reviewed annually to ensure that it continues to reflect the client's circumstances. If a change has taken place, including a significant change in management, which materially affects the scope or understanding of the audit, the auditor should discuss the matter with management and where appropriate send a revised engagement letter.

Contents and form of the letter

Responsibilities and scope of the audit

(8) The letter should explain the principal statutory responsibilities of the client and the statutory and professional responsibilities of the auditor.

(9) In the case of a company, it should be indicated that it is the statutory responsibility of the client to maintain proper accounting records, and to prepare financial statements which give a true and fair view and comply with the Companies Acts and other relevant legislation. It should also be indicated that the auditor's statutory responsibilities include making a report to the members stating whether in his opinion the finanancial statements give a true and fair view and whether they comply with the Companies Act.

(10) It should be explained that the auditor has an obligation to satisfy himself whether or not the directors' report contains any matters which are inconsistent with the audited financial statements. Furthermore, it should be indicated that the auditor has a professional responsiblity to report if the financial statements do not comply in any material respect with Statements of Standard Accounting Practice, unless in his opinion the non-compliance is justified in the circumstances.

(11) The scope of the audit should be explained. In this connection, it should be pointed out that the audit will be conducted in accordance with approved Auditing Standards and have regard to relevant Auditing Guidelines. It should be indicated that:

(a) the auditor will obtain an understanding of the accounting system in order to assess its adequacy as a basis for the preparation of the financial statements;

(b) the auditor will expect to obtain relevant and reliable evidence sufficient to enable him to draw reasonable conclusions therefrom;

(c) the nature and extent of the tests will vary according to the auditor's assessment of the accounting system and, where he wishes to place reliance upon it, the system of internal control;

(d) the auditor will report to management any significant weaknesses in, or observations on, the client's systems which come to his notice and which he thinks should be brought to management's attention.

(12) Where appropriate, reference should be made to recurring special arrangements concerning the audit. These could include arrangements in respect of internal auditors, divisions, overseas subsidiaries, other auditors and (in the case of a small business managed by directors who are the major shareholders) significant reliance on supervision by the directors.

Representations by management

(13) Where appropriate it should be indicated that, prior to the completion of the audit, the auditor may seek written representations from management on matters having a material effect on the financial statements.

Irregularities and fraud

(14) The responsibilty for the prevention and detection of irregularity and fraud rests with management and this responsibility is fulfilled mainly through the implementation and continued operation of an adequate system of internal control. The engagement letter should make this clear. Furthermore, it should explain that the auditor will endeavour to plan his audit so that he has a reasonable expectation of detecting material misstatements in the financial statements resulting from irregularities or fraud, but that the examination should not be relied upon to disclose irregularities and frauds which may exist. If a special examination for irregularities or fraud is required by the client, then this should be specified in the engagement letter, but not in the audit section.

Accounting and taxation services

(15) The auditor may undertake, for the company, services in addition to carrying out his responsibilities as auditor. An engagement letter should adequately describe the nature and scope of those services. In the case of accounting services, the letter should distinguish the accountant's and the client's responsibilities in relation to them and to the day-to-day bookkeeping, the maintenance of all accounting records and the preparation of financial statements. Preferably this should be done in a separate letter but such services may form the subject of a section in the audit engagement letter.

(16) In the case of the provision of taxation services, the responsibilities for the various procedures such as the preparation of tax computations and the submission of returns to the relevant authorities should be clearly set out, either in a section of the main letter or in a separate letter.

(17) Where accounting, taxation or other services are undertaken on behalf of an audit client, information may be provided to members of the audit firm other than those engaged on the audit. If this is the case, it may be appropriate for the audit

engagement letter to indicate that the auditor is not to be treated as having notice, for the purposes of his audit responsibilities, of the information given to such people.

Fees
(18) Mention should normally be made of fees and of the basis on which they are computed, rendered and paid.

Agreement of terms
(19) The engagement letter should include a request to management that they confirm in writing their agreement to the terms of the engagement. It should be clearly understood that when agreed the letter will give rise to contractual obligations, and its precise content must therefore be carefully considered. In the case of a company, the auditor should request that the letter of acknowledgement be signed on behalf of the board.

Form of the letter
(20) Appendix 1 sets out a form of letter generally appropriate for company clients. *It is not intended to be used in relation to every company, as it must be tailored to specific circumstances.* It can also be used as the basis of an engagement letter in respect of an unincorporated client.

Appendix 1: Example of an engagement letter

This form of letter is generally appropriate for client companies. *It is not intended to be used in relation to every company, as it must be tailored to specific circumstances.*

To the directors of ....

The purpose of this letter is to set out the basis on which we (are to) act as auditors of the company (and its subsidiaries) and the respective areas of responsibility of the company and of ourselves.

1 Audit
(1.1) As directors of the above company, you are responsible for maintaining proper accounting records and preparing financial statements which give a true and fair view and comply with the Companies Acts. You are also responsible for making available to us, as and when required, all the company's accounting records and all other records and related information, including minutes of all management and shareholders' meetings.

(1.2) We have a statutory responsibility to report to the members whether in our opinion the financial statements give a true and fair view of the state of the company's affairs and of the profit or loss of the year and whether they comply with the Companies Act 1985 (*or other relevant legislation*). In arriving at our opinion, we are required to consider the following matters, and to report on any in respect of which we are not satisfied:

(*a*) whether proper accounting records have been kept by the company and proper returns adequate for our audit have been received from branches not visited by us;

(*b*) whether the company's balance sheet and profit and loss account are in agreement with the accounting records and returns;

(*c*) whether we have obtained all the information and explanations which we think necessary for the purpose of our audit; and

(*d*) whether the information in the directors' report is consistent with that in the audited financial statements.

In addition, there are certain other matters which, according to the circumstances, may need to be dealt with in our report. For example, where the financial statements do not give full details of directors' remuneration or of transactions with the company, the Companies Acts require us to disclose such matters in our report.

(1.3) We have a professional responsibility to report if the financial statements do not comply in any material respect with Statements of Standard Accounting Practice, unless in our opinion the non-compliance is justified in the circumstances.

(1.4) Our audit will be conducted in accordance with the Auditing Standards issued by the accountancy bodies and will have regard to relevant Auditing Guidelines. Furthermore, it will be conducted in such a manner as we consider necessary to fulfil our responsibilities and will include such tests of transactions and of the existence, ownership and valuation of assets and liabilies as we consider necessary. We shall obtain an understanding of the accounting system in order to assess its adequacy as a basis for the preparation of the financial statements and to establish whether proper accounting records have been maintained. We shall expect to obtain such relevant and reliable evidence as we consider sufficient to enable us to draw reasonable conclusions therefrom. The nature and extent of our tests will vary according to our assessment of the company's accounting system, and where we wish to place reliance on it the system of internal control, and may cover any aspect of the business operations. We shall report to you any significant weaknesses in, or observations on, the company's systems which come to our notice and which we think should be brought to your attention.

(1.5) As part of our normal audit procedures, we may request you to provide written confirmation of oral representations which we have received from you during the course of the audit.

(1.6) In order to assist us with the examination of your financial statement, we shall request sight of all documents or statements, including the chairman's statement and the directors' report, which are due to be issued with the financial statements. We are also entitled to attend all general meetings of the company and to receive notice of all such meetings.

(1.7) (*Where appropriate*) We appreciate that the present size of your business renders it uneconomic to create a system of internal control based on the segregation of duties for different functions within each area of the business. In the running of your company we understand that the directors are closely involved with the control of the company's transactions. In planning and performing our audit work we shall take account of this supervision. Further, we may ask additionally for confirmation in writing that all the transactions undertaken by the company have been properly reflected and recorded in the accounting records, and our audit report on your company's financial statements may refer to this confirmation.

(1.8) The responsibility for the prevention and detection of irregularities and fraud rests with yourselves. However, we shall endeavour to plan our audit so that we have a reasonable expectation of detecting material misstatements in the financial statements or accounting records resulting from irregularities or fraud, but our examination should not be relied upon to disclose irregularities and frauds which may exist.

(1.9) *(Where appropriate)* We shall not be treated as having notice, for the purposes of our audit responsibilities, of information provided to members of our firm other than those engaged on the audit (e.g. information provided in connection with accounting, taxation and other services).

(Where appropriate) It was agreed that we should carry out the following services as your agents and on the basis that you will make full disclosure to us of all relevant information.

2 *(Where appropriate)* Accounting and other services
We shall:

(2.1) prepare the financial statements based on accounting records maintained by yourselves;

(2.2) provide assistance to the company secretary by preparing and lodging returns with the Registrar of Companies;

(2.3) investigate irregularities and fraud upon receiving specific instructions.

3 *(Where appropriate)* Taxation services
(3.1) We shall in respect of each accounting period prepare a computation of profits, adjusted in accordance with the provisions of the Taxes Acts, for the purpose of assesment to corporation tax. Subject to your approval, this will then be submitted to the Inspector of Taxes as being the company's formal return. We shall lodge formal notice of appeal against excessive or incorrect assessments to corporation tax where notice of such assessments is received by us. Where appropriate, we shall also make formal application for postponement of tax in dispute and shall advise as to appropriate payments on account.

(3.2) You will be responsible, unless otherwise agreed, for all other returns, more particularly: the returns of advance corporation tax and income tax deducted at source as required on Forms CT61, returns relating to employee taxes under PAYE and returns of employee expenses and benefits on Forms P11D. Your staff will deal with all returns and other requirements in relation to value added tax.

(3.3) We shall be pleased to advise you on matters relating to the company's corporation tax liability, the implications of particular business transactions and on other taxation matters which you refer to us, such as national insurance, income tax deducted at source, employee benefits, *development land tax, value added tax and *capital transfer tax.

---

* Development land tax was abolished, and capital transfer tax replaced by inheritance tax, in the Finance Act 1986.

4 Fees

Our fees are computed on the basis of the time spent on your affairs by the partners and our staff, and on the levels of skill and responsibility involved. Unless otherwise agreed, our fees will be charged separately for each of the main classes of work described above, will be billed at appropriate intervals during the course of the year and will be due on presentation.

5 Agreement of terms

Once it has been agreed, this letter will remain effective, from one audit appointment to another, until it is replaced. We shall be grateful if you could confirm in writing your agreement to the terms of this letter, or let us know if they are not in accordance with your understanding of our terms of appointment.

Yours faithfully

3.4 Summary

A prospective auditor invited to take up an appointment should first communicate with the previous auditor. The client must give authority to the prospective auditor to communicate, and also give authority to the existing auditor to discuss the client's affairs with the proposed new auditor.

Prospective auditors should also consider their own ability to carry out the work, and whether acceptance of the appointment would give rise to a conflict of interests.

Formal acceptance of an appointment should be made in an engagement letter. The contents of the engagement letter should be discussed and agreed with the client before it is sent.

The letter should:

(a) make it clear that it is the responsibility of management to maintain proper accounting records as laid down by the Companies Act, and to prepare the annual financial statements;

(b) explain the auditor's reporting responsibilities including the requirement normally to qualify the auditor's report if SSAPs are not complied with;

(c) refer to the fact that the audit will be conducted in accordance with approved Auditing Standards;

(d) undertake to report to the client weaknesses in the system of internal control which come to the auditor's notice during the audit;

(e) refer to the auditor's statutory rights to access to all records and information and to receive notice of and attend all general meetings of the company;

(f) refer, for small companies, to the fact that the effectiveness of the system of internal control must be dependent upon the personal involvement of the directors in controlling transactions, and that the auditor will be seeking confirmation that all transactions have been properly reflected and recorded in the accounting records;

(g) refer to the fact that primary responsibility for the detection of errors and fraud rests with the directors, though pointing out that the audit will be planned with a view to giving a reasonable expectation of detecting material misstatements;

(h) refer to other services (for example, accounting work and taxation services) offered;

(i) explain the basis of calculation of fees.

Progress questions

Questions	Reference for answers
(1) Why should a prospective new auditor communicate with the existing holder of the post before accepting nomination?	Section 3.1
(2) What must the prospective auditor do before communicating?	Section 3.1
(3) Is it improper for a new auditor to charge a lower fee than had previously been charged?	Section 3.1
(4) What further matters should be considered by a prospective new auditor before accepting nomination?	Section 3.2
(5) (a) What is an engagement letter? (b) What are the main points covered by an engagement letter?	Section 3.3

4 Audit planning, controlling and recording

4.1 The Guideline 1—Planning

Any activity, if it is to be properly done, needs planning beforehand. The more complex the task, the more planning is required.

Audit planning covers the preparations needed for an individual audit, and its integration with the other work to be completed by the audit firm within the same time-span.

The whole subject of this chapter is dealt with in the first of the Auditing Guidelines issued in April 1980. It is entitled 'Planning, Controlling and Recording'. We shall look at each of these three elements in turn. Here is the introductory paragraph and the section on planning. Original paragraph numbers have been retained to facilitate reference.

Guideline on planning, controlling and recording

Introduction

(1) Paragraph 2 of the Auditing Standard *The auditor's operational standard* states that:

'The auditor should adequately plan, control and record his work.'

This Auditing Guideline, which gives guidance on how that paragraph may be applied, should be read in conjunction with the Explanatory Foreword to Auditing Standards and Guidelines including the Glossary of Terms.

(2) In order to ensure that an audit is carried out effectively and efficiently, the work needs to be planned, controlled and recorded at each stage of its progress. Planning, controlling and recording are considered separately below although they are not mutually exclusive.

(3) The need to plan, control and record audit work exists regardless of the size of the enterprise concerned. Although all of the procedures described in this Guideline need to be considered by the auditor, in the case of smaller enterprises the work involved in implementing them will be less.

Planning

Background

(4) The form and nature of the planning required for an audit will be affected by the size and complexity of the enterprise, the commercial environment in which it operates, the method of processing transactions and the reporting requirements to which it is subject. In this context the auditor should aim to provide an effective and economic service within an appropriate time-scale.

(5) Adequate audit planning:

(*a*) establishes the intended means of achieving the objectives of the audit;
(*b*) assists in the direction and control of the work;
(*c*) helps to ensure that attention is devoted to critical aspects of the audit; and
(*d*) helps to ensure that the work is completed expeditiously.

(6) In order to plan his work adequately the auditor needs to understand the nature of the business of the enterprise, its organization, its method of operating and the industry in which it is involved, so that he is able to appreciate which events and transactions are likely to have a significant effect on the financial statements.

Procedures

(7) The auditor should consider the outline audit approach he proposes to adopt, including the extent to which he may wish to rely on internal controls and any aspects of the audit which need particular attention. He should also take into account in his planning any additional work which he has agreed to undertake.

(8) Preparatory procedures which the auditor should consider include the following:

(*a*) reviewing matters raised in the audit of the previous year which may have continuing relevance in the current year;
(*b*) assessing the effects of any changes in legislation or accounting practice affecting the financial statements of the enterprise;
(*c*) reviewing interim or management accounts where these are available and consulting with the management and staff of the enterprise. Matters which should be considered include current trading circumstances, and significant changes in (i) the business carried on, (ii) the enterprise's management;
(*d*) identifying any significant changes in the enterprise's accounting procedures, such as a new computer-based system.

(9) The auditor should also consider:

(*a*) the timing of significant phases of the preparation of the financial statements;
(*b*) the extent to which analyses and summaries can be prepared by the enterprise's employees;
(*c*) the relevance of any work to be carried out by the enterprise's internal auditors.

(10) The auditor will need to determine the number of audit staff required, the experience and special skills they need to possess and the timing of their audit visits. He will need to ensure that all audit staff are briefed regarding the enterprise's affairs and the nature and scope of the work they are required to carry out. The preparation of a memorandum setting out the outline audit approach may be helpful.

(11) On joint audits there should be consultation between the joint auditors to determine the allocation of the work to be undertaken and the procedures for its control and review.

4.2   Client timetables

While the engagement letter may formalize the auditor's responsibilities to the client, in practice problems will continue to recur regarding the responsibility for specific tasks associated with the preparation of audited accounts. Many of these may be clarified by having a regular planning meeting with the client before starting each year's audit, to deal with such matters as a discussion of the client's current business situation, and any points outstanding from the previous audit, such as a review of accounting systems developments following the previous year's management letter (see below). The opportunity should also be taken to discuss detailed arrangements for the audit visits and any specific audit points likely to cause problems.

An important preparation for such a meeting is to ensure that all specific points requiring attention will be discussed and, rather than relying on general discussion to bring these out, the auditor would be well advised to undertake the necessary preparatory work himself and produce an appropriate agenda for the meeting.

The matters likely to be covered would include the following.

4.3   Agenda for Audit Planning Meeting

1. Consideration of current trading circumstances and business developments since the previous financial statements.
2. Consideration of any problems arising during the previous audit and any recommendations to management made following previous audit.
3. General review of principal accounting systems, state of internal control, and any known areas of difficulty.
4. Consideration of accounting policies generally, and specifically in relation to Statements of Standard Accounting Practice.
5. Consideration of timetable for completion and audit of the financial statements.
6. Agreement of dates for the detailed review and testing of internal controls and the audit of transactions for the year.
7. Agreement of detailed timings for:
   (a) Physical stocktakings;
   (b) Circularization of debtors and creditors for verification purposes;
   (c) Agreement of intra-group balances;

(*d*) Letters of authority to be sent by the client regarding information required from third parties;

(*e*) Inspection of documents (e.g. title deeds, share certificates), statutory books and minutes;

(*f*) Internal certificates to be obtained by the client and made available to the auditors (e.g. cash floats, employee loans);

(*g*) Certificates to be obtained from third parties (e.g. stocks in hands of third parties);

(*h*) Certificates to be obtained from the client (e.g. directors' emoluments);

(*i*) Valuations of specific assets (e.g. properties, unquoted investments), including availability of required additional information.

Such a meeting also provides an opportunity to agree the nature and extent of the audit schedules which will be required and which of them will be prepared by the client rather than the auditors. In that many of the problems of audit planning relate specifically to timing, discussion of a programme of audit schedules provides an opportunity for auditors to influence client work timetables and thereby improve the allocation of audit staff. It should also serve to reduce the overall time spent on the preparation and audit of the accounts by focusing attention on the general extent of tasks to be done, thus enabling these tasks to be marshalled better. Whilst it is recognized that the extent of formalized planning required for the small assignment will be less elaborate than that for the larger one, nevertheless every well-run audit entails some planning.

Set out below is a specimen timetable for the completion of the preparation and audit of a company's accounts; such a timetable should be discussed with the client before starting the audit and then kept under review throughout the audit with all deviations being noted and explained as they occur:

Specimen timetable for the preparation and audit of a company's accounts

Client	Schedule	*Date received*
Job timetable	Prepared by .... Date	(and any comments)
	Reviewed by .... Date	
Accounting date		

General

1 (*a*) Year-end trial balance, before taxation and other adjustments to be available.

(*b*) Company to notify the auditors in writing of any appropriations to reserve or any proposed dividends.

(*c*) Adjustments to trial balance, to include tax provisions, and extension to final trial balance to be complete.

(*d*) First draft of company's accounts to be available.

(*e*) Company to supply the auditors with a draft of the proposed directors' report.

(*f*) Auditors to notify clearance of accounts, or any changes.

(*g*) Final copies of accounts and the auditors' report to be available.

Taxation

2 Company's auditors to compute the tax charge on current profits.

Creditors and accrued expenses

3 (*a*) Bought ledger to be closed.

(*b*) Balances at year-end to be proved with control account and scheduled for the auditors.

(*c*) Detailed schedules of goods received but not invoiced and accrued expenses to be prepared by the company and made available to auditors.

(*d*) Sales-ledger credit balances to be extracted and listed, together with explanations.

(*e*) Balances due to other group companies to be agreed at the year-end and made available to auditors to enable direct confirmation with companies concerned.

Capital commitments and contingent liabilities

4 (*a*) Company to prepare schedules of outstanding capital commitments and other capital sanctions at the end of the year and deliver this to auditors.

(*b*) Company to instruct its solicitors to confirm direct to the auditors any outstanding claims and other litigious matters of which they are aware and in which the company is, or may become, involved.

Fixed assets

5 (*a*) Company to provide schedules of fixed assets, additions and deletions during the year, together with relevant dates.

(*b*) Company to provide summary of fixed assets and depreciation, including movements during year, supported by detailed schedules showing depreciation calculations.

Stock and work-in-progress

6 (*a*) Company to let auditors have a copy of detailed instructions for the counts.

(b) Reconciliations between stock records and financial records to be completed and summary handed to auditors.

(c) Company to review for obsolete and slow-moving items; and a copy of report to management thereon, together with any authorization for disposal or other write-off to be handed to auditors.

Debtors and prepayments

7 (a) Sales-ledger balances at year-end to be proved with control accounts and made available to auditors.

(b) Schedule of bills receivable at year-end to be made available to auditors.

(c) Schedule of miscellenaeous sundry accounts receivable to be made available to auditors.

(d) Schedule of debit balances on bought ledger, together with explanation of each item, to be made available to auditors.

(e) Provision for bad debts to be reviewed at year-end in light of latest information and statement setting out provision and how derived to be made available to auditors.

(f) Balances due from other group companies to be agreed at the year-end and made available to auditors to enable direct confirmation with companies concerned.

Bank balances and cash

8 (a) Cash book to be closed promptly at close of business.

(b) Bank reconciliations to be prepared and made available to the auditors.

Profit and loss account schedules

9 (a) Auditors to inform the company what profit and loss account schedules they need.

(b) Agreement on the responsibility for the preparation of these schedules to be reached before the year-end.

(c) Company to provide such schedules as agreed.

Directors' emoluments

10 Company to prepare a schedule setting out the directors' emoluments in detail for the year and make this available to auditors.

Letter of representation

11 Letter confirming amounts appearing in the accounts to be obtained from the directors at the conclusion of the audit:

(a) auditors to provide suitable draft for consideration.

(b) final letter to be completed, signed by the managing director and the chief accountant, and returned to auditors.

4.4   Audit timetables and budgets

If an audit is to be controlled in an efficient and business-like way, then, besides persuading clients to plan their work, the auditors too must pay sufficient advance attention to the preparation of their own plans.

As a minimum, these plans should document the following points:

(*a*) the overall audit timetable, setting out the dates agreed with the client for the commencement and completion of the work;

(*b*) in general terms, the audit tasks to be undertaken;

(*c*) an assessment of the skill required for each audit task and the level of staff most appropriate, together with arrangements for the supervision of staff and review of their work;

(*d*) an assessment of the time required to complete each audit task by such a member of staff;

(*e*) a summary of the staff required to complete the audit within the given timetable;

(*f*) the allocation of the appropriate members of staff with the requisite experience and special skills;

(*g*) an evaluation of the audit budget;

(*h*) arrangements for adequate briefing of audit staff regarding the company's affairs and the audit work they are to carry out.

The preparation of such a plan enables the early agreement of fees between the auditor and the client, always desirable from the points of view of both parties; and both for this reason and because one year's plan is widely used in the preparation of next year's, any significant variations between budgeted and actual performance should be analyzed. Where such variations are due to poor performance by the client's staff, these should be reported to the client immediately. Where it is due to poor performance of the audit staff, then the appropriate training of the individuals should be initiated.

The timetable prepared for these purposes should also provide for phasing the audit over the year, as an alternative to carrying out the audit all at one time, thus helping to spread the workload, easing time pressures generally, and improving control over audit progress.

The opportunities for phasing an audit are likely to be threefold:

(*a*) Interim audit, generally covering the assessment and testing of internal control, together with detailed checking of transactions. In the case of a large client, such interim audit work may involve several similar visits during a year, or even a continuous attendance by audit staff.

(*b*) Advance year-end work to deal with the verification of certain balance sheet items prior to the end of the financial year. Suitable items, where the client's internal control is adequate, might include debtors, creditors and stocks.

(c) Final audit, largely confined to the audit of the accounts and concentrating on a review of the profit and loss account, together with verification of the balance sheet.

The main danger of audit phasing is likely to be that of insufficient link-up between staff involved in the various phases of such an audit. It is, of course, most important that any balance sheet implications of matters coming to light when checking transactions should be properly taken into account when planning the year-end work. For instance, the testing of sales credit notes during the interim audit may reveal some delay in their issue. This must put the auditors on notice to inquire into parallel circumstances at the year-end. To provide a basis for this follow-through, it is essential that sufficient conclusions are recorded at each stage of the audit, and it is important that their filing within the audit working papers be systematized, so as to ensure that due attention is later given to those conclusions.

4.5   The Guideline 2—Controlling

The section of the 1980 Guideline on controlling the progress of an audit is mainly concerned with the control of an individual audit. It is important also to consider the overall control features in a practice to ensure the maintenance of good standards of audit work. This report is covered by the later Guideline entitled Quality Control (February 1985) and is dealt with in Section 4.8 below.

Let's first take a look at the paragraphs from the 1980 Guideline on control:

Controlling

Background

(12) Management structures vary between firms of auditors and this Auditing Guideline should be interpreted in the context of the particular structure within each firm. The Guideline has, however, been written on the basis that the audit is carried out by a reporting partner and his staff.

(13) The reporting partner needs to be satisfied that on each audit the work is being performed to an acceptable standard. The most important elements of control of an audit are the direction and supervision of the audit staff and the review of the work they have done. The degree of supervision required depends on the complexity of the assignment and the experience and proficiency of the audit staff.

Procedures

(14) The nature of the procedures needed to control an audit and the extent to

which they need to be formalised cannot be precisely specified as they depend on the organisation of the audit firm and the degree of delegation of the audit work. The procedures established should be designed and applied to ensure the following.

(a) Work is allocated to audit staff who have appropriate training, experience and proficiency.

(b) Audit staff of all levels clearly understand their responsibilities and the objectives of the procedures which they are expected to perform. Audit staff should be informed of any matters identified during the planning stage that may affect the nature, extent or timing of the procedures they are to perform. They should be instructed to bring to the attention of those to whom they are responsible any significant accounting or auditing problems that they encounter.

(c) The working papers provide an adequate record of the work that has been carried out and the conclusions that have been reached.

(d) The work performed by each member of the audit staff is reviewed by more senior persons in the audit firm. This is necessary to ensure that the work was adequately performed and to confirm that the results obtained support the audit conclusions which have been reached.

(15) The final stages of an audit require special attention. At this time, when pressures are greatest, control of the audit work is particularly required to ensure that mistakes and omissions do not occur. The use of an audit completion checklist, with sections to be filled in by the reporting partner and his staff, will help to provide such control.

(16) Where matters of principle or contentious matters arise which may affect the audit opinion the auditor should consider consulting another experienced accountant. This accountant may be a partner, a senior colleague, or another practitioner. If another practitioner is consulted, confidentiality of the client's affairs must be maintained.

(17) The auditor should also consider how the overall quality of the work carried out within the firm can best be monitored and maintained.

Note the reference in paragraph 14(c) to working papers. It is absolutely essential for the progress of the audit to be methodically RECORDED. Without records control is impossible. The concluding section of the Guideline, which goes into detail on working papers, is reproduced next.

4.6   The Guideline 3—Recording

Recording

Background

(18) Reasons for preparing audit working papers include the following.

(a) The reporting partner needs to be able to satisfy himself that work delegated by him has been properly performed. The reporting partner can generally only do this by having available to him detailed working papers prepared by the audit staff who performed the work.

(b) Working papers provide, for future reference, details of problems encountered, together with evidence of work performed and conclusions drawn therefrom in arriving at the audit opinion.

(c) The preparation of working papers encourages the auditor to adopt a methodical approach.

Procedures

(19) *Contents of working papers* Audit working papers should always be sufficiently complete and detailed to enable an experienced auditor with no previous connection with the audit subsequently to ascertain from them what work was performed and to support the conclusions reached. Audit working papers should be prepared as the audit proceeds so that details and problems are not omitted.

(20) Audit working papers should include a summary of all significant matters identified which may require the exercise of judgement, together with the auditor's conclusions thereon. If difficult questions of principle or of judgement arise, the auditor should record the relevant information received and summarise both the management's and his conclusions. It is in such areas as these that the auditor's judgement may subsequently be questioned, particularly by a third party who has the benefit of hindsight. It is important to be able to tell what facts were known at the time the auditor reached his conclusion and to be able to demonstrate that, based on those facts, the conclusion was reasonable.

(21) Audit working papers will typically contain:

(a) information which will be of continuing importance to the audit (e.g. Memorandum and Articles of Association);

(b) audit planning information;

(c) the auditor's assessment of the enterprise's accounting system and, if appropriate, his review and evaluation of its internal controls;

(d) details of the audit work carried out, notes of errors or exceptions found and action taken thereon, together with the conclusions drawn by the audit staff who performed the various sections of the work;

(e) evidence that the work of the audit staff has been properly reviewed;

(f) records of relevant balances and other financial information, including analyses and summaries supporting the financial statements;

(g) a summary of significant points affecting the financial statements and the audit report, showing how these points were dealt with.

(22) *Standardisation of working papers* The use of standardised working papers may improve the efficiency with which they are prepared and reviewed. Used properly they help to instruct audit staff and facilitate the delegation of work while providing a means to control its quality.

(23) However, despite the advantages of standardising the routine documention of the audit (e.g. checklists, specimen letters, standard organisation of the working papers), it is never appropriate to follow mechanically a 'standard' approach to the conduct and documentation of the audit without regard to the need to exercise professional judgement.

(24) *Ownership and custody of working papers* Working papers are the property of the auditor and he should adopt appropriate procedures to ensure their safe custody and confidentiality.

4.7 Permanent file and current file

The Guideline does not attempt to lay down detailed requirements as to the form and content of audit working papers.

It is normal for the audit working papers to be split into two files, one containing material relating specifically to the year under review (the current working papers file), and one containing more permanent records likely to be required from year to year (the permanent audit file). It must not be overlooked, however, that the details in the permanent file will change as time goes by, and will require updating each year. Typical contents of the two files are given below.

4.7.1 Contents of the permanent file

General
1. Brief description and history of business, copies of investigation reports, etc.
2. Addresses of Registered Office, other offices and factories, together with note of their size and functions and instructions to staff on how to get to each location.
3. Organization chart of directors, secretary, senior executives, accounting personnel, indicating name and telephone number of primary client contact (updated as necessary from year to year).
4. Copy of letter of engagement and any amendments or additions thereto limiting or increasing the scope of the work undertaken.
5. Copy of memorandum and articles of association, and amending resolutions.
6. Copies of important agreements, service contracts etc.

Group structure
1. Details of parent companies.
2. Details of subsidiary companies.
3. Details of fellow subsidiaries.

4. Details of associated companies.
5. Make-up of consolidation adjustments reflecting above relationships.

Accounting systems
1. Details of accounting policies.
2. List of books of account maintained.
3. Code of accounts.
4. Copy of client's accounting instructions.
5. Accounting systems documentation.
6. Assessment of internal controls.
7. Copies of management letters and notes on subsequent action taken by client.
8. Authorities and specimen signatures.

Share capital, reserves and long-term loans
1. Details of issued share capital.
2. Details of reserves.
3. Copies of loan stock and debenture trust deeds.
4. Details of mortgages and charges.
5. Details of share options.

Fixed assets
1. Details of freehold and leasehold premises.
2. Summary of other fixed assets.
3. Details of depreciation policies.
4. Details of leasing and hire-purchase agreements.
5. Copies of professional valuations.

Financial history
1. Tabulated balance sheets, sources and applications of funds, and profit and loss accounts for recent years, noting significant features.
2. Tabulations of relevant financial ratios for recent years, with explanations of material fluctuations.

Miscellaneous
1. Banking arrangements and facilities.
2. Guarantees held and given.
3. Insurance cover: details of risks and extent of insurance.
4. Pension arrangements.

4.7.2 Contents of the current file

The current working papers files, on the other hand, should relate only to the accounts in respect of the period under review and should contain schedules supporting these accounts and a record of the audit work done. Variations between clients make a rigid system of filing such working papers undesirable in that the constraints so imposed may cause important information to be omitted simply because there was nowhere to file it. However, some degree of standardization is desirable to ensure a methodical approach, and the following is put forward as a comprehensive system of indexing allowing sufficient flexibility.

Current working paper file index

A. General review notes and points forward, including copy of management letter, letter of representation and certificates of directors' emoluments
B. Accounts
C. Analytical review (including forecasts, budgets, etc.)
D. Trial balance, journal entries
E. Minutes
F. Post-balance-sheet events, contingencies and commitments
G. Share capital and statutory books
H. Reserves
J. Taxation, including copy of previous year's computation
K. Debentures, secured loans and unsecured loan stock
L. Creditors and accrued expenses, including direct verifications
M. Fixed assets and depreciation
N. Investments (including subsidiary and associated companies)
P. Inter-company balances (group and associated companies)
Q. Stocks and work-in-progress, including physical stocktaking observation reports
R. Debtors and prepayments, including direct verifications
S. Bank and cash balances (and bank overdrafts), including direct verifications
T. Consolidated accounts
U. Profit and loss account details, including:

> Detailed trading and profit and loss account.
> Internal management accounts, including budget and prior-year comparatives.
> Forecast (budget) for following year and supporting cash flow forecast.
> Details of transaction tests executed.

Z. Other working papers, including sundry notes and minor queries disposed of.

4.7.3   File control schedule and file review checklist

It is essential that working papers contain adequate notes of verifications obtained, work done generally, and the conclusions ultimately derived, thus facilitating review of the audit without need for verbal clarification. The working papers must provide a record of all material aspects of the accounts and they must indicate the means by which constituent figures were derived and the reasons for any decisions taken at the time of the audit.

In this way, should questions arise in the future, the auditors will be in a position to show exactly what work was performed, what queries were raised, what explanations and information were received, and by whom these latter were given. The importance of this will be appreciated later, when the question of an auditor's liability is considered. It must be remembered that, should anything be amiss, it may emerge years after the work was performed, when perhaps those who were in charge are no longer available, so that, if proper records were not kept, auditors might find themselves in a position of considerable difficulty and danger.

To guard against this we would recommend the adoption of a formalized system for evidencing the control and supervision of an audit as it progresses. We set out below a suggested means of achieving this, by the use firstly of a 'file control schedule', and secondly of a 'file review checklist'. By these means the staff undertaking the detailed audit work will be subject to the discipline of reviewing the completeness of their own work, listing outstanding points for further consideration, before passing their working papers through for final review. In turn, that reviewer is provided with an 'aide memoire' of those major aspects of an audit which he should ensure have received adequate consideration.

The degree of day-to-day supervision required by the reporting partner in any particular audit will depend on the complexity of the assignment and the experience and proficiency of the audit staff. It follows that the details of a review will vary from one assignment to another. Nevertheless the final responsibility rests with the reporting partner and accordingly he may wish to adopt a form of audit completion checklist to ensure that all significant audit procedures have been followed.

FILE CONTROL SCHEDULE   Schedule no.

Client:

Accounting date: *Date*   *Intls.*

Before passing for review, senior auditor should indicate as follows:
— File indexes amended to final form
— All audit schedules, working papers and audit programmes complete, including extent of work done and conclusions reached (except for points listed)
— All queries cleared (unless referred to reviewer)
— Audit notes for reviewer's attention listed
— Draft accounts cross-referenced to schedules
— Accounts agreed to trial balance and post-trial balance journal adjustments
— Companies accounts checklist completed
— Review for presentation and disclosure completed
— Analytical review of trading results completed
— All necessary third-party confirmations obtained
— Following certificates drafted:
  (*a*) representation
  (*b*) directors' emoluments
— Management letter drafted
— Time records completed, variances explained, fee/scale comparison prepared
— Permanent file reviewed and updated
— Points forward from last audit cleared
— Points forward to next audit listed

REVIEWED BY

FILE COMPLETION CHECKLIST   Schedule no.

Client:

Accounting date:

Tick as appropriate

	Yes or N/A	Refer to note

Permanent file
— Engagement letter appropriate to the current circumstances of the assignment
— Specimen signatures updated. Notes made of
  changes in business organization, resources, etc.

Current files—interim
— Systems notes/flowcharts updated; ICQs and
  MCCs completed (See Sections 7.7 and 7.8 below)
— Systems properly evaluated; significant strengths
  and weaknesses highlighted
— Compliance/substantive tests tailored to evaluation;
  level of testing appropriate
— Tests recorded in adequate detail as to work done,
  results, and conclusions drawn; signed off for
  completion and review
— Adequate audit coverage of computer procedures

Current files—final
— File control schedule signed off; all matters included
  therein satisfactorily completed
— Balance sheet audit programme suitably adapted;
  signed off for completion and review
— Level of testing appropriate—related to conclusions
  drawn from interim work
— Schedules and working papers initialled and dated;
  clear evidence of work done and conclusions drawn
— Tax position reviewed
— Adequate review of accounts of associates and
  subsidiaries audited by other firms; consolidation
  working papers reviewed
— Trading, profit and loss account schedules adequate
  and not excessive
— Analytical review completed; satisfactory explana-
  tion of trading result in terms of prior year, budgets,
  management accounts, gross profit changes, etc.
— Exchange control position reviewed
— Letter of representation appropriately worded
— Management letter(s) constructive
— Time records reviewed; adverse variances analysed; remedial action noted for next year
— Client Services Review completed; pursued with
  client as necessary

Tick as appropriate

Yes or   Refer
N/A   to note

Financial statements
— Companies Accounts checklist completed
— Reviewed for adequacy of diclosure, propriety of accounting policies, and fairness of presentation
— Post-balance-sheet events reviewed; disclosed as necessary

Financial position
— Future financing requirements reviewed
— Short-term borrowing repayments adequately covered
— Working capital position adequate; bank overdraft facilities reviewed
— Going-concern assumption appropriate

Audit report
— Wording of draft audit report satisfactory
— The expression of any qualification is:
  (a) clear as to the nature and degree of our reservations
  (b) clear as to the effect on the financial statements
  (c) referred, where appropriate, for second opinion or review panel

Completion
— All notes and queries cleared; all outstanding audit matters satisfactorily concluded
— Firm's procedures properly followed; sufficient evidence on file to support audit opinion
— Points forward for next year include notes on
  (a) any areas in which the efficiency or cost effectiveness of audit procedures might be improved
  (b) any respects in which we can improve the planning and organization of this assignment
— Any points of special interest or difficulty notified to technical partner for further discussion or wider dissemination within firm
— Accounts and relevant working papers submitted for Technical Review

Signed off for completion

.... **Date** ....

4.8 Quality control

The introduction of Auditing Standards and Guidelines in 1980 was a major step towards improving the standard of audit work. In February 1985 the

APC issued the following Guideline dealing specifically with the ways in which a practice can work to maintain and improve the quality of its work.

APC Guideline on Quality control

Preface

Para 2 of the Auditing Standard 'The auditor's operational standard' states that the auditor 'should adequately plan, control and record his work'. The Auditing Guideline 'Planning, controlling and recording' gives guidance on how that paragraph may be applied and describes the quality control measures necessary in respect of individual audits. However, para 17 of that guideline states that the auditor 'should also consider how the overall quality of the work carried out within the firm can best be monitored and maintained'.

This guideline is therefore intended to provide guidance on those quality control procedures that relate to audit practices in general and is drafted so as to apply to firms or organisations of all sizes. Without prejudice to the powers of the public sector audit organisations, the principles contained in this guideline apply to all organisations carrying out independent audits whether in the private or the public sector. The word 'firm' has been used throughout simply for ease of reference.

Introduction

(1) The principles of quality control are applicable not only to auditing but to the entire range of professional services provided by a firm. For the purposes of this guideline, however, quality control is the means by which a firm obtains reasonable assurance that its expression of audit opinions always reflects observance of approved Auditing Standards, any statutory or contractual requirements and any professional standards set by the firm itself. Quality control should also promote observance of the personal standards relevant to the work of an auditor, which are described in the ethical statements published by the Accountancy Bodies.

Procedures

(2) The objectives of quality control procedures are the same for all firms. At the beginning of subsequent paragraphs, therefore, a specific objective of quality control, which is considered to be universally applicable, is highlighted. This is followed by a brief description of the procedures that firms may adopt to meet this objective. For each firm the exact nature and extent of the procedures needed will depend on its size and the nature of its practice, the number of its offices and its organisation.

(3) *Each firm should establish procedures appropriate to its circumstances and communicate them to all partners and relevant staff, and to other professionals employed by the firm in the course of its audit practice.* This should normally involve

putting them in writing, although it is recognised that oral communication may be effective in the small closely controlled firm.

The following paragraphs describe the objectives and the basic procedures applicable to each firm.

Acceptance of appointment and reappointment as auditor

(4) *Each firm should ensure that, in making a decision to accept appointment or reappointment as auditor, consideration is given to the firm's own independence and its ability to provide an adequate service to the client.* The firm should determine what information is needed to evaluate prospective clients, and whether the decision to accept appointment or reappointment should be taken by the firm as a whole or by a designated partner or committee.

Professional ethics

(5) *There should be procedures within the firm to ensure that all partners and professional staff adhere to the principles of independence, objectivity, integrity and confidentiality, set out in the ethical statements issued by the Accountancy Bodies.* These procedures include providing guidance, particularly to those staff who are not members of the Accountancy Bodies, resolving questions on the above principles, and monitoring compliance with them. For larger firms in particular, it may be appropriate that the task of guiding staff in these areas should be allotted to a particular partner. If, for example, the firm does not permit staff to hold shares in client companies, the designated partner should ensure that staff are aware of such a policy.

Skills and Competence

(6) *The firm's partners and staff should have attained the skills and competence required to fulfil their responsibilities.* This involves procedures relating to:

    (a) recruitment (paragraph 7);
    (b) technical training and updating (paragraph 8);
    (c) on-the-job training and professional development (paragraph 9).

Staff should be informed of the firm's procedures for example by means of manuals and standardised documentation or programmes. The firm's procedures should be regularly updated.

(7) Effective recruitment of personnel with suitable qualifications including any necessary expertise in specialised areas and industries, involves both planning for staffing needs and determining criteria for recruitment based on such needs. Such criteria should be designed to ensure that cost considerations do not deter the firm from recruitment of audit staff with the experience and ability to exercise the appropriate judgement.

(8) All partners and staff should be required to keep themselves technically up-to-date on matters that are relevant to their work. The firm should assist them to meet this requirement. Such assistance should include:

(*a*) circulating digests or full texts, where appropriate, of professional publications and relevant legislation;

(*b*) maintaining a technical library;

(*c*) issuing technical circulars and memoranda on professional developments as they affect the firm;

(*d*) encouraging attendance at professional courses;

(*e*) maintaining appropriate training arrangements.

The methods of implementing the above procedures may vary according to the size of the firm. For example, a smaller firm can ensure that it has copies of essential reference books relevant to its practice where a fuller technical library would be impracticable. Also manuals and standardised documentation do not need to be produced internally by the smaller firm but can be acquired from various professional bodies and commercial sources; and cooperative arrangements with other firms can help meet training needs.

(9) The Auditing Guideline 'Planning, controlling and recording' relates staff assignment to the needs of the particular audit visit but, in the context of quality control generally, a further factor in staff assignment should be the opportunity for on-the-job training and professional development. This should provide staff with exposure to different types of audit and with the opportunity to work with more experienced members of the team who should be made responsible for the supervision and review of the work of junior staff. It is important that the performance of staff on audits is evaluated and that the results of these assessments are communicated to the staff concerned, giving the opportunity for staff to respond to comments made and for any action to be agreed.

Consultation

(10) *There should be procedures for consultation.* These will include a structured approach to audit file review (so that the review procedures recommended in the Auditing Guideline 'Planning, controlling and recording' are effective for every audit); reference of technical problems to designated specialists within the firm; and procedures for resolving matters of judgement. For smaller firms, and particularly for sole practitioners, consultation at the appropriate professional level within the firm may not be possible. Consultation with another practitioner or with any relevant professional advisory service, may be a suitable alternative, providing confidentiality of the client's affairs is maintained. To provide opportunities for such consultations, practitioners in smaller firms will find it helpful to develop links with other practitioners or with relevant professional associations.

Monitoring the firm's procedures

(11) *The firms should monitor the effectiveness of its application of the quality control procedures outlined above.* This monitoring process should provide reasonable assurance that measures to maintain the professional standards of the firm are being properly and effectively carried out.

(12) This process should include periodic review of a sample of the firm's audit files by independent reviewers from within the firm. The firm should:

(a) have procedures for selection of particular audits for review, and for the frequency, timing, nature and extent of reviews;

(b) set the levels of competence for the partners and staff who are to participate in review activities;

(c) establish procedures to resolve disagreements which may arise between the reviewers and audit staff.

It should be borne in mind that the purpose of this independent review is to provide an assessment of the overall standards of the firm, and so it is quite separate from the purpose of the earlier review procedures referred to in paragraph 10, which are carried out by members of the audit team to provide control over the individual audit.

(13) Where, in the smaller firm, independent review within the firm is not possible, attendance at professional courses and communication with other practitioners can provide the opportunity of comparison with the standards of others, thereby identifying potential problem areas. Alternatively, an independent and objective basis for monitoring the effectiveness of quality control procedures can be achieved by reference to professional practice advisory services, where available.

(14) Whatever action is taken by the firm to monitor the effectiveness of quality control procedures, the firm should ensure that any recommendations for improvement that arise are implemented.

4.9 Summary

Planning is essential to an audit. The manager or partner in charge of the job needs to plan the audit itself and also to integrate it with the other work of the practice.

Vital planning points are:

(a) review of previous year's working papers to pick up points of weakness or difficulty encountered—this will include consideration of the letter reporting weaknesses to the client and action taken by the client as a result to remedy them;

(b) review of the effect of new legislation, SSAPs, etc., on the audit;

(c) review of interim or management accounts;

(d) consideration of any known changes to the client's control systems, such as a new computer-based system;

(e) timing of work, both to suit the client and to optimize efficiency of practice operation;

(f) selection of suitable staff for the audit team;

(g) consultation with client's management accounting and internal audit staff;

(h) consultation with joint auditors, if relevant;

(i) briefing of audit staff regarding the enterprise's affairs and the nature and scope of the work they are required to carry out;

(j) preparation of a memorandum setting out the outline audit approach.

Controlling an individual audit involves:

(a) proper use of audit working papers, including audit programmes, to record the progress of the work;

(b) review of work and of working papers during and towards the end of the audit;

(c) adequate supervision;

(d) use of checklists;

(e) ensuring that audit staff understand the objectives of their work and have the appropriate training, experience and proficiency.

Recording an audit means maintaining adequate *working papers*. These are typically divided into a *permanent file* containing information of continuing importance from one audit to the next, and a *current file* containing the working papers of one year's audit.

Quality control in auditing requires attention to:

(a) communication to all partners and staff of quality control procedures established;

(b) review of the firm's independence and expertise before accepting a new appointment;

(c) ensuring that all partners and staff adhere to principles of independence, objectivity, integrity and confidentiality;

(d) maintaining and improving the technical skills of partners and staff;

(e) monitoring the effectiveness of quality control procedures listed in (a) to (d) above.

Progress questions

Questions	Reference for answers
(1) What are the main matters requiring the auditor's attention at the planning stage of the audit?	Section 4.1—Guideline paragraphs 4–11
(2) List the matters that should appear on the agenda for the audit planning meeting.	Section 4.3
(3) What are the main areas to be covered in controlling an audit?	Section 4.5—Guideline paragraphs 12–17
(4) Why is it important to record the progress of the audit?	Section 4.6—Guideline paragraph 18
(5) What are the main contents of: (a) permanent audit file; (b) current audit file?	Section 4.7.1 Section 4.7.2
(6)(a) What do you understand by the term 'quality control' in relation to an audit?	Section 4.8
(b) What are the main matters requiring attention to ensure the high quality of audit work?	

5 Principles of internal control

5.1 Introduction

With this chapter we begin our examination of the practical work of the audit itself.

The work of the auditor is all directed towards the main object of reporting on the financial statements.

Study the diagram below:

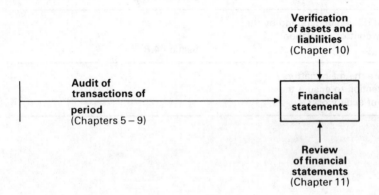

This diagram illustrates the three main directions from which auditors approach their task:

(1) Proving the completeness, accuracy and validity of the financial statements by testing the accuracy of the underlying records on which they are based. (Chapters 5 to 9).

(2) Examining reliable, relevant and sufficient evidence of the existence, ownership and valuation of assets and liabilities (Chapter 10).

(3) Reviewing the overall position shown by the financial statements (Chapter 11).

5.2 The system of internal control as an aid to the auditor

Every business has some kind of accounting system by which transactions are processed, and records of those transactions maintained. That 'system' should incorporate control features and is normally referred to as the system of 'internal control', defined in the Auditing Guideline on the subject as:

'the whole system of controls, financial and otherwise, established by the management in order to carry on the business of the enterprise in an orderly and efficient manner, ensure adherence to management policies, safeguard the assets and secure as far as possible the completeness and accuracy of the records. The individual components of an internal control system are known as "controls" or "internal controls".'

The existence of a reliable system of internal control can be a great help to the auditor, because the objectives of the system should be:

(*a*) ensuring that the records are complete, accurate and properly authorized;

(*b*) detecting errors and fraud.

The auditor's first task in relation to the client's system of internal control is to ascertain, record and evaluate it. That is covered in Chapters 6 and 7.

Secondly, the auditor uses his knowledge of the client's system to plan his audit tests, as explained in Chapter 8.

The purpose of this chapter is to set the scene for these three by describing the principles of internal control.

Let us first of all pick up the main types of internal controls. The Appendix to the Guideline on Internal Control gives us:

Types of internal controls

The following is a description of some of the types of controls which the auditor may find in many enterprises and on some of a combination of which he may seek to place some degree of reliance.

(1) *Organisation.* Enterprises should have a plan of their organisation, defining and allocating responsibilies and identifying lines of reporting for all aspects of the enterprise's operations, including the controls. The delegation of authority and responsibility should be clearly specified.

(2) *Segregation of duties.* One of the prime means of separation of those

responsibilities or duties which would, if combined, enable one individual to record and process a complete transaction. Segregation of duties reduces the risk of intentional manipulation or error and increases the element of checking. Functions which should be separated include those of authorisation, execution, custody, recording and, in the case of a computer-based accounting system, systems development and daily operations.

(3) *Physical.* These are concerned mainly with the custody of assets and involve procedures and security measures designed to ensure that access to assets is limited to authorised personnel. This includes both direct access and indirect access via documentation. These controls assume importance in the case of valuable, portable, exchangeable or desirable assets.

(4) *Authorisation and approval.* All transactions should require authorisation or approval by an appropriate responsible person. The limits for these authorisations should be specified.

(5) *Arithmetical and accounting.* These are the controls within the recording function which check that the transactions to be recorded and processed have been authorised, that they are all included and that they are correctly recorded and accurately processed. Such controls include checking the arithmetical accuracy of the records, the maintenance and checking of totals, reconciliations, control accounts and trial balances, and accounting for documents.

(6) *Personnel.* There should be procedures to ensure that personnel have capabilities commensurate with their responsibilities. Inevitably, the proper functioning of any system depends on the competence and integrity of those operating it. The qualifications, selection and training as well as the innate personal characteristics of the personnel involved are important features to be considered in setting up any control system.

(7) *Supervision.* Any system of internal control should include the supervision by responsible officials of day-to-day transactions and the recording thereof.

(8) *Management.* These are the controls exercised by management outside the day-to-day routine of the system. They include the overall supervisory controls exercised by management, the review of management accounts and comparison thereof with budgets, the internal audit function and any other special review procedures.

5.3 Practical aspects of internal control

Guidance in the detailed application of internal controls is provided by an Appendix to a Statement of Auditing dealing with internal control issued by the ICAEW but which has now been withdrawn. Although it has been withdrawn, in our view it remains an excellent summary of the principles of internal control in the main systems areas. We therefore reproduce it here almost in full.

Practical aspects of internal control

Classification of operations for internal control purposes

(1) A typical classification of operations for internal control purposes is as follows:

(*a*) general financial arrangements
(*b*) cash and cheques received (including cash and bank balances)
(*c*) cheque and cash payments
(*d*) wages and salaries
(*e*) purchases and trade creditors
(*f*) sales and trade debtors
(*g*) stock (including work in progress)
(*h*) fixed assets and investments.

Some of the principal considerations that arise in examining these items from the point of view of internal control are dealt with below.

General financial arrangements

(2) The general financial arrangements involved in instituting a system of internal control include:

(*a*) devising an appropriate and properly integrated system of accounts and records;
(*b*) determining the form of general financial supervision and control by management, using such means as budgetary control, regular interim accounts of suitable frequency, and special reports;
(*c*) ensuring that adequate precautions are taken to safeguard (and if necessary to duplicate and store separately) important records;
(*d*) engaging, training and allocating to specific duties management and staff competent to fulfil their responsibilities; arranging for rotation of duties as necessary; and deputing responsibilities during staff absences.

Cash and cheques received (including cash and bank balances)

Receipts by post and cash sales
(3) The risk of misappropriation of cash and cheques needs no emphasis. Safeguards vary according to the circumstances of each business, but the principles of control may be summarised as follows: the number of persons handling cash and cheques should be restricted; responsibilities should be clearly defined; the principles of division of duties, particularly as between the recording and custodianship functions, should be observed as far as possible; adequate supervision and independent checks should be imposed; and moneys received should be paid into the bank at the earliest opportunity.

(4) Considerations involved in dealing with cash and cheques received by post include:

(*a*) instituting safeguards to minimise the risk of interception of mail between its receipt and opening;

(*b*) wherever possible, appointing a responsible person, independent of the cashier, to open, or supervise the opening of, mail;

(*c*) ensuring that cash and cheques received are (i) adequately protected (for instance, by the restrictive crossing of all cheques, money orders and the like on first handling) and (ii) properly accounted for (for instance, by the preparation of post-lists of moneys received for independent comparison with subsequent records and book entries).

(5) In establishing an adequate system of control over cash sales and collections it should be decided:

(*a*) who is to be authorised to receive cash and cash articles (i.e. whether such items are to be received only by cashiers or may be accepted by sales assistants, travellers, roundsmen, or others);

(*b*) how sales and the receipt of cash and cash articles are to be evidenced, and what checks may usefully be adopted as regards such transactions (for instance, by the use of serially numbered receipt forms or counterfoils, or cash registers incorporating sealed till rolls).

Custody and control of money received

(6) Money received should be subject to adequate safeguards and controls at all stages up to lodgement in the bank. Amongst the matters which may require considerations are the following:

(*a*) the appointment of suitable persons to be responsible at different stages for the collection and handling of money received, with clearly defined responsibilities;

(*b*) how, by whom, and with what frequency cash offices and registers are to be cleared;

(*c*) what arrangements are to be made for agreeing cash collections with cash and sales records (preferably this should be carried out by a person independent of the receiving cashier or employee);

(*d*) according to the nature of the business, what arrangements are to be made for dealing with, recording and investigating any cash shortages or surpluses.

Recording

(7) Incoming cash and cheques should be recorded as soon as possible. Means of recording include, as appropriate, receipt forms and counterfoils, cash registers and post lists. Matters for consideration include the following:

(*a*) who is to be responsible for maintaining records of money received;

(*b*) what practicable limitations may be put on the duties and responsibilities of the receiving cashier particularly as regards dealing with such matters as other books of account, other funds, securities and negotiable instruments, sales invoices, credit notes and cash payments;

(c) who is to perform the receiving cashier's functions during his absence at lunch, on holiday, or through sickness;

(d) in what circumstances, if any, receipts are to be given; whether copies are to be retained; the serial numbering of receipt books and forms; how their issue and use are to be controlled; what arrangements are to be made, and who is to be responsible, for checking receipt counterfoils against (i) cash records and (ii) bank paying-in slips; and how alterations to receipts are to be authorised and evidenced.

Payments into bank

(8) It is desirable that cash and cheques received should be lodged with the bank with the minimum of delay. Adequate control over bank lodgements will involve setting rules as to:

(a) how frequently payments are to be made into the bank (preferably daily);

(b) who is to make up the bank paying-in slips (preferably this should be done by a person independent of the receiving and recording cashier) and whether there is to be any independent check of paying-in slips against post-lists, receipt counterfoils and cash book entries;

(c) who is to make payments into the bank (preferably not the person responsible for preparing paying-in slips);

(d) whether all receipts are to be banked intact; if not, how disbursements are to be controlled.

Cash and bank balances

(9) Questions to be decided in connection with the control of cash balances include:

(a) what amounts are to be retained as cash floats at cash desks and registers, and whether payments out of cash received are to be permitted;

(b) what restrictions are to be imposed as to access to cash registers and offices;

(c) rules regarding the size of cash floats to meet expenses, and their methods of reimbursement;

(d) the frequency with which cash floats are to be checked by independent officials;

(e) what arrangements are to be made for safeguarding cash left on the premises outside business hours;

(f) whether any special insurance arrangements (such as fidelity guarantee and cash insurance) are judged desirable having regard to the nature of the business, the sums handled, and the length of time they are kept on the premises;

(g) what additional independent checks on cash may usefully be operated (for instance, by periodic surprise cash counts);

(h) what arrangements are to be made for the control of funds held in trust for employees, both those which are the legal responsibility of the company and, as necessary, those which are held by nominated employees independent of the company's authority (for instance, sick funds or holiday clubs).

(10) Regular reconciliation of bank accounts by a responsible official is an essential element of control over bank balances. Considerations involve deciding to whom bank statements may be issued, how frequently reconciliations should be performed, by whom, and the detailed procedure to be followed. Special factors include the

treatment of long-standing unpresented cheques, stop-payment notices, examination of the sequence of cheque numbers and comparison of cheque details with details recorded in the cash book. So far as possible the person responsible for carrying out the bank reconciliation should not normally be concerned with handling cash and cheques received or with arrangements for disbursements.

Cheque and cash payments

(11) The arrangements for controlling payments will depend to a great extent on the nature of business transacted, the volume of payments involved, and the size of the company.

Cheque payments
(12) Amongst the points to be decided in settling the system for payments by cheque are the following:

(a) what procedure is to be adopted for controlling the supply and issue of cheques for use, and who is to be responsible for their safe-keeping;

(b) who is to be responsible for preparing cheques and traders' credit lists;

(c) what documents are to be used as authorisation for preparing cheques and traders' credit lists, rules as to their presentation to cheque signatories as evidence in support of payment, and the steps to be taken to ensure tha payment cannot be made twice on the strength of the same document

(d) the names, number and status of persons authorised to sign cheques; limitations as to their authority; the minimum number of signatories required for each cheque; if only one signatory is required, whether additional independent authorisation of payments is desirable; if more than one signatory is required, how it is be ensured that those concerned will operate effective independent scrutiny (for instance, by prohibiting the signing by any signatory of blank cheques in advance); limitations, if any, as to the amount permissible to be drawn on one signature; whether cheques drawn in favour of persons signing are to be prohibited;

(e) safeguards to be adopted if cheques are signed mechanically or carry printed signatures;

(f) the extent to which cheques issued should be restrictively crossed; and the circumstances, if any, in which blank or bearer cheques may be issued;

(g) arrangements for the prompt despatch of signed cheques and precautions against interception;

(h) arrangements for obtaining paid cheques; whether they are to be regarded as sufficient evidence of payment or whether receipts are to be required; and the procedure to be followed in dealing with paid cheques returned as regards examination and preservation

(i) the arrangements to be made to ensure that payments are made within discount periods.

Cash payments
(13) Factors to be considered include the following:

(a) nomination of a responsible person to authorise expenditure, the means of indicating such authorisation and the documentation to be presented and preserved as evidence;

(*b*) arrangements to ensure that the vouchers supporting payments cannot be presented for payment twice;

(*c*) whether any limit is to be imposed as regards amounts disbursed in respect of individual payments;

(*d*) rules as to cash advances to employees and officials, IOUs, and the cashing of cheques.

Cheque and cash payments generally

(14) Arrangements should be such that so far as practicable the cashier is not concerned with keeping or writing-up books of account other than those recording disbursements, nor should he have access to, or be responsible for the custody of, securities, title deeds or negotiable instruments belonging to the company.

(15) Similarly, so far as possible the person responsible for preparing cheques or traders' credit lists should not himself be a cheque signatory; cheque signatories in turn should not be responsible for recording payments.

(16) On the other hand it must be recognised that in the circumstances of smaller companies staff limitations often make it impossible to divide duties in this manner and in such cases considerable responsibility falls on the adequacy of managerial supervision.

Wages and salaries

(17) While in practice separate arrangements are generally made for dealing with wages and salaries, the considerations involved are broadly similar, and for convenience the two aspects are here treated together.

General arrangements

(18) Responsibility for the preparation of pay sheets should be delegated to a suitable person, and an adequate staff appointed to assist him. The extent to which the staff responsible for preparing wages and salaries may perform other duties should be clearly defined. In this connection full advantage should be taken where possible of the division of duties and checks available where automatic wage-accounting systems are in use. *Inter alia*, provision should be made as to:

(*a*) who may authorise the engagement and discharge of employees;

(*b*) who may authorise general and individual changes in rates of pay;

(*c*) how notifications of changes in personnel and rates of pay are to be recorded and controlled to prevent irregularities and errors in the preparation and payment of wages and salaries;

(*d*) how deductions from employees' pay other than for income tax and national insurance are to be authorised;

(*e*) what arrangements are to be made for recording hours worked (in the case of hourly-paid workers) or work done (in the case of piece workers), and for ensuring that the records are subject to scrutiny and approval by an appropriate offical before being passed to the wages department; special supervision and control arrangements may be desirable where overtime working is material;

(*f*) whether advances of pay to be permitted; if so, who may authorise them, what limitations are to be imposed, how they are to be notified to and dealt with by wages and salaries departments, and how they are to be recovered;

(*g*) how holiday pay is to be dealt with;

(*h*) who is to deal with pay queries.

Preparation of payroll

(19) The procedure for preparing the payroll should be clearly established. Principal matters for consideration include the following:

(*a*) what records are to be used as bases for the compilation of the payroll and how they are to be authorised;

(*b*) who is to be responsible (i) for preparing pay sheets, (ii) for checking them and (iii) for approving them (preferably separate persons), and by what means individual responsibility at each stage is to be indicated;

(*c*) what procedures are to be laid down for notifying and dealing with non-routine circumstances such as an employee's absence from work, or employees leaving at short notice in the middle of a pay period.

Payment of wages and salaries

(20) Where employees are paid in cash the following matters are amongst those that require decision:

(*a*) what arrangements are to be made to provide the requisite cash for paying-out (e.g. by encashment of a cheque for the total amount of net wages) and what steps are to be taken to safeguard such moneys during collection and transit and until distributed;

(*b*) what safeguards against irregularities are to be adopted (e.g. by arranging for pay packets to be filled by persons other than those responsible for preparing pay sheets, providing them with the exact amount of cash required, and forbidding their access to other cash), and what particulars are to be given to payees;

(*c*) who is to pay cash wages over to employees (preferably a person independent of those engaged in the preparation of pay sheets and pay packets); how payees' identities are to be verified; what officials are to be in attendance; and how distribution is to be recorded (e.g. by recipient's signature or by checking off names on the pay list);

(*d*) what arrangements are to be made for dealing with unclaimed wages.

(21) Where wages and salaries are paid by cheque or bank transfer the matters to be decided include:

(*a*) which persons are (i) to prepare and (ii) to sign cheques and bank transfer lists (preferably these persons should be independent of each other and of those responsible for preparing pay sheets);

(b) whether a separate wages and salaries bank account is to be maintained, what amounts are to be transferred to it from time to time (preferably on due dates the net amount required to meet pay cheques and transfers), and who is to be responsible for its regular reconciliation (preferably someone independent of those responsible for maintaining pay records).

Deductions from pay

(22) Appropriate arrangements should be made for dealing with statutory and other authorised deductions from pay, such as national insurance, PAYE, pension fund contributions, and savings held in trust. A primary consideration is the establishment of adequate controls over the records authorising deductions. Further points include ensuring, where Inland Revenue tax deduction cards are used for PAYE, that arrangements are made for comparing totals of gross pay and tax deducted as shown on the cards against relevant totals on the payroll, and how frequently this comparison is carried out.

Additional checks on pay arrangements

(23) In addition to the routine arrangements and day-to-day checks referred to above, use may be made, as judged desirable, of a number of independent overall checks on wages and salaries. Amongst those available may be listed the following:

(a) the maintenance, separate from wages and salaries departments, of employees' records, with which pay lists may be compared as necessary;

(b) the preparation of reconciliations to explain changes in total pay and deductions between one pay day and the next;

(c) surprise counts of cash held by wages and salaries departments;

(d) the comparison of actual pay totals with independently prepared figures such as budget estimates or standard costs and the investigation of variances;

(e) the agreement of gross earnings and total tax deducted for the year to 5th April with PAYE returns to the Inland Revenue.

Purchases and trade creditors

(24) The three separate functions into which accounting controls may be divided clearly appear in the considerations involved in purchase procedures. They are buying ('authorisation'), receipt of goods ('custody') and accounting ('recording').

Buying

(25) Factors to be considered include:

(a) the procedure to be followed when issuing requisitions for additions to and replacements of stocks, and the persons to be responsible for such requisitions;

(b) the preparation and authorisation of purchase orders (including procedures for authorising acceptance where tenders have been submitted or prices quoted);

(c) the institution of checks for the safe-keeping of order forms and safeguarding their use;

(d) as regards capital items, any special arrangements as to authorisations required (for a fuller description of this aspect see the section dealing with fixed assets below).

Goods inwards

(26) Factors to be considered include:

(a) arrangements for examining goods inwards as to quantity, quality and condition, and for evidencing such examination;

(b) the appointment of a person responsible for accepting goods, and the procedure for recording and evidencing their arrival and acceptance;

(c) the procedure to be instituted for checking goods inwards records against authorised purchase orders.

Accounting

(27) Factors to be considered include:

(a) the appointment of persons so far as possible separately responsible for: (i) checking suppliers' invoices, (ii) recording purchases and purchase returns, (iii) maintaining suppliers' ledger accounts or similar records, (iv) checking suppliers' statements, (v) authorising payment;

(b) arrangement to ensure that before accounts are paid: (i) the goods concerned have been received, accord with the purchase order, are properly priced and correctly invoiced, (ii) the expenditure has been properly allocated, and (iii) payment has been duly authorised by the official responsible;

(c) the establishment of appropriate procedures in connection with purchase returns, special credits and other adjustments;

(d) arrangements to ensure that liabilities relating to goods received during an accounting period are properly brought into the accounts of the period concerned (i.e. cut-off procedures);

(e) the establishment of arrangements to deal with purchases from companies or branches forming part of the same group;

(f) arrangements to deal with purchases made for employees under special terms;

(g) regular independent checking of suppliers' accounts against current statements, or direct verification with suppliers;

(h) the institution of a purchases control account and its regular checking by an independent official against suppliers' balances.

Sales and trade debtors

(28) The separation of authorisation, custodianship and recording functions described above in respect of purchases and trade creditors applies similarly to sales and trade debtors.

Sales

(29) Considerations include the following:

(a) what arrangements are to be made to ensure that goods are sold at their correct prices, and to deal with and check exchanges, discounts and special reductions including those in connection with cash sales;

(b) who is to be responsible for, and how control is to be maintained over, the granting of credit terms to customers;

(c) who is to be responsible for accepting customers' orders, and what procedure is to be adopted for issuing production orders and despatch notes;

(d) who is to be responsible for the preparation of invoices and credit notes and what controls are to be instituted to prevent errors and irregularities (for instance, how selling prices are to be ascertained and authorised, how the issue of credit notes is to be controlled and checked, what checks there should be on the prices, quantities, extensions and totals shown on invoices and credit notes, and how such documents in blank or completed are to be protected against loss or misuse);

(e) what special controls are to be exercised over the despatch of goods free of charge or on special terms.

Goods outwards

(30) Factors to be considered include:

(a) who may authorise the despatch of goods and how such authority is to be evidenced;

(b) what arrangements are to be made to examine and record goods outwards (preferably this should be done by a person who has no access to stocks and has no accounting or invoicing duties);

(c) the procedure to be instituted for agreeing goods outwards records with customers' orders, despatch notes and invoices.

Accounting

(31) So far as possible sales ledger staff should have no access to cash, cash books or stocks, and should not be responsible for invoicing and other duties normally assigned to sales staff. The following are amongst matters which should be considered:

(a) the appointment of persons as far as possible separately responsible for: (i) recording sales and sales returns, (ii) maintaining customers' accounts, (iii) preparing debtors' statements;

(b) the establishment of appropriate control procedures in connection with sales returns, price adjustments and similar matters;

(c) arrangements to ensure that goods despatched but not invoiced (or vice versa) during an accounting period are properly dealt with in the accounts of the period concerned (i.e. cut-off procedures);

(d) the establishment of arrangements to deal with sales to companies or branches forming part of the same group;

(e) what procedures are to be adopted for the preparation, checking and despatch of debtors' statements and for ensuring that they are not subject to interference before despatch;

(f) how discounts granted and special terms are to be authorised and evidenced;

(g) who is to deal with customers' queries arising in connection with statements;

(*h*) what procedure is to be adopted for reviewing and following up overdue accounts;

(*i*) who is to authorise the writing off of bad debts, and how such authority is to be evidenced;

(*j*) the institution of a sales control account and its regular checking preferably by an independent official against customers' balances on the sales ledger.

Stocks (including work in progress)

(32) Stocks may be as susceptible to irregularities as cash: in some circumstances the risks of loss may be materially higher. Arrangements for the control of stocks should be framed with this in mind.

(33) In summary it may be said that stock control procedures should ensure that stocks held are adequately protected against loss or misuse, are properly applied in the operations of the business, and are duly accounted for. According to the nature of the business separate arrangements may be necessary for different categories of stocks, such as raw materials, components, work in progress, finished goods and consumable stores.

(34) Amongst the main considerations may be listed the following:

(*a*) what arrangements are to be made for receiving, checking and recording goods inwards (see also paragraphs 24 to 27 relating to purchases and trade creditors above);

(*b*) who is to be responsible for the safeguarding of stocks and what precautions are to be taken against theft, misuse and deterioration;

(*c*) what arrangements are to be made for controlling (through maximum and minimum stock limits) and recording stocks (e.g. by stock ledgers, independent control accounts and continuous stock records such as bin cards); who is to be responsible for keeping stock records (preferably persons who have no access to stocks and are not responsible for sales and purchase records); and what procedure is to be followed as to the periodic reconciliation of stock records with the financial accounts;

(*d*) how movements of stock out of store (or from one process or department to another) are to be authorised, evidenced and recorded, and what steps are to be taken to guard against irregularities;

(*e*) what arrangements are to be made for dealing with and accounting for returnable containers (both suppliers' and own);

(*f*) what arrangements are to be made for dealing with and maintaining accounting control over company stocks held by others (for instance, goods in warehouse, on consignment or in course of processing) and goods belonging to others held by the company (e.g. how withdrawals are to be authorised and evidenced, and how goods belonging to others are to be distinguished from own goods);

(*g*) what persons are to be responsible for physically checking stocks, at what intervals such checks are to be carried out, and what procedures are to be followed (for instance, if continuous stocktaking procedures are in use, arrangements should ensure that all categories of stock are counted at appropriate intervals normally at least once a year; counts should preferably be conducted by persons independent of storekeepers; how stock counts are to be recorded and evidenced; and what cut-off procedures are to be operated to ensure that stocks are adjusted to take proper account of year-end sales and purchases invoiced);

(*h*) what bases are to be adopted for computing the amount at which stocks are to be stated in the accounts (these should be in accordance with recognised accounting principles and should be applied consistently from year to year), and which persons are to perform and check the calculations;

(*i*) what arrangements are to be made for the periodic review of the condition of stocks, how damaged, slow-moving and obsolete stocks are to be dealt with and how write-offs are to be authorised;

(*j*) what steps are to be taken to control and account for scrap and waste, and receipts from the disposal of such items.

Fixed assets and investments

Fixed assets

(35) Some of the principal matters to be decided in connection with controls relating to fixed assets are as follows:

(*a*) who is to authorise capital expenditure and how such authorisation is to be evidenced;

(*b*) who is to authorise the sale, scrapping or transfer of fixed assets, how such authorisation is to be evidenced, and what arrangements are to be made for controlling and dealing with receipts from disposals;

(*c*) who is to maintain accounting records in respect of fixed assets and how it is to be ensured that the proper accounting distinction is observed between capital and revenue expenditure;

(*d*) what arrangements are to be made for keeping plant and property registers and how frequently they are to be agreed with the relevant accounts and physically verified;

(*e*) what arrangements are to be made to ensure that fixed assets are properly maintained and applied in the service of the company (e.g. by periodic physical checks as to their location, operation and condition);

(*f*) where fixed assets are transferred between branches or members of the same group, what arrangements in respect of pricing, depreciation and accounting are to be made;

(*g*) how depreciation rates are to be authorised and evidenced, and which persons are to be responsible for carrying out and checking the necessary calculations.

Investments

(36) Arrangements for dealing with investments will involve, *inter alia*, determining:

(*a*) who is to be responsible for authorising purchases and sales of investments, and how such authorisations are to be evidenced (those responsible should preferably have no concern with cash or the custody of documents of title);

(*b*) what arrangements should be made for maintaining a detailed investment register: and who should be responsible for agreeing it periodically with the investment control account and physically verifying the documents of title;

(*c*) what arrangements are to be made for checking contract notes against authorised purchase or sale instructions and for ensuring that charges are correctly calculated: for dealing with share transfers: and for ensuring that share certificates are duly received or delivered and that bonuses, rights, capital repayments and dividends or interest are received and properly accounted for.

Documents of title

(37) Adequate arrangements should be made for the scheduling and safe custody of property deeds, share certificates and other documents of title, with the object of protecting them against loss and irregularities. Preferably they should be deposited in a secure place under the authority and control of at least two responsible persons, and access to or withdrawals of such documents should be permissible only on the authority of such persons acting jointly.

5.4   Internal audit as an element in internal control

A large organization will often set up an internal audit department to exercise an independent appraisal function within the organization to examine and evaluate its activities. From the external auditor's point of view, the work of the internal auditor could be regarded as aspects of the client's overall control system to be appraised and tested. The external auditor is entitled to take the internal auditor's work into consideration in fixing the extent of the necessary tests. There will also be scope for cooperation between them.

Main areas for collaboration are:

(*a*) *Communication*   Periodic meetings between the two auditors are desirable, especially at the stage of planning the external audit, so that the external auditor becomes aware of the internal auditor's planned internal control coverage, and so that a joint plan of operation can be prepared.

(*b*) *Audit working papers*   The external auditor will examine the internal auditor's working papers as part of the process of determining the extent to which the internal auditor's work can be relied upon.

The external auditor may well also make available some of his or her working papers to the internal auditor, though retaining the right to withhold especially confidential material.

It will be helpful if both parties use the same audit documentation, and this could in some cases take the form of a joint file available to either.

(*c*) *Joint procedures*   Where possible the two auditors should agree and make use of common methods. Because of their different objectives, however, it will be necessary to reserve the right for each to develop separate methods in some aspects—the internal auditor to pursue the main objective of reviewing and appraising the system of internal control, the external auditor to pursue the objective of reporting on the truth and fairness of the financial statements.

It must also be recognized that there remain differences between the external auditor and the internal auditor as to:

(a) *Scope*   The extent of the work undertaken by the internal auditor is determined by the management whereas that of the independent auditors arises from the responsibilities placed upon them by statute.

(b) *Approach*   The internal auditor's approach is with a view to ensuring that the accounting system is efficient, so that the accounting information presented to management throughout the period is accurate and discloses material facts. The independent auditor's approach, however, is governed by the duty to be satisfied that the accounts to be presented to the shareholders show a true and fair view of the profit or loss for the financial period and of the state of the company's affairs at the end of that period.

(c) *Responsibility*   The internal auditor's responsiblity is to the management whereas the independent auditor is responsible directly to the shareholders. It follows that the internal auditor, being a servant of the company, does not have the independence of status which independent auditor possesses.

Study the Auditing Guideline on this subject reproduced below.

APC Guideline on reliance on internal audit

Preface

This Guideline gives guidance on the matters that need to be considered and the procedures that need to be followed by external auditors when placing reliance on internal audit. It should be read in conjunction with 'The auditor's operational standard', its related Auditing Guidelines, particularly the Auditing Guideline 'Internal Controls', the Explanatory Foreword to the Auditing Standards and Guidelines and, in the public sector, with 'Statements on Internal Audit Practice in the Public Sector' published by the Chartered Institute of Public Finance and Accountancy.

This Guideline is written in the context of audits conducted within both the commercial sector and the public sector. References in this Guideline to 'management' are to the board of directors in the commercial sector, and to the equivalent body in the public sector.

In certain circumstances the external auditor may have a responsibility to report on the internal audit function. Guidance is not given in respect of such a report, but many of the principles and procedures described in this Guideline will also apply in those circumstances.

Introduction

(1) Internal audit is an element of the internal control system set up by the management of an enterprise to examine, evaluate and report on accounting and other

controls on operations. It exists either because of a management decision or in certain circumstances because of a statutory requirement.

(2) Certain of the objectives of internal audit may be similar to those of external audit, and procedures similar to those carried out during an external audit may be followed. Accordingly, the external auditor should make an assessment of the internal audit function in order to be able to determine whether or not he wishes to place reliance on the work of internal audit. An external auditor may be able to place reliance on internal audit as a means of reducing the work he performs himself in:

(a) the documentation and evaluation of accounting systems and internal controls;
(b) compliance and substantive testing.

(3) The scope of internal audit's work will generally be determined in advance and a programme of work will be prepared. Where reliance is placed on the work of internal audit, the external auditor will need to take into account this programme of work and amend the planned extent of his own audit work accordingly. In addition, the external auditor may agree with management that internal audit may render him direct assistance by performing certain of the procedures necessary to accomplish the objectives of the external auditor but under the control of the chief internal auditor, who would then have to consider the effect on his department's programme of work.

(4) This guideline does not deal with those cases where internal audit staff are seconded to work under the direct supervision and control of the external auditor. This is because the guideline addresses reliance on internal audit as a function, rather than reliance on individuals within that function. The work of seconded internal audit staff should be controlled by the external auditor in accordance with the Auditing Guideline 'Planning, controlling and recording', having regard to the position of internal audit staff as employees of the enterprise.

Background

The internal audit function

(5) The scope and objectives of internal audit vary widely and are dependent upon the responsibilities assigned to it by management, the size and structure of the enterprise, and the skills and experience of the internal auditors. Normally, however, internal audit operates in one or more of the following broad areas:

(a) review of accounting systems and related internal controls;
(b) examination of financial and operating information for management, including detailed testing of transactions and balances;
(c) review of the economy, efficiency and effectiveness of operations and of the functioning of non-financial controls;
(d) review of the implementation of corporate policies, plans and procedures;
(e) special investigations.

(6) Where internal audit staff carry out routine tasks such as authorisation and approval or day to day arithmetical and accounting controls, they are not functioning as internal auditors and these tasks are not dealt with in this guideline; this is because these tasks are recognised as other types of internal controls by the Appendix to the Auditing Guideline 'Internal controls'. Moreover, objectivity may be impaired when

internal auditors audit any activity which they themselves carried out or over which they had authority. The possibility of impairment should be considered when deciding whether to place reliance on internal audit.

The relationship between external and internal audit

(7) Unlike the internal auditor who is an employee of the enterprise or a related enterprise, the external auditor is required to be independent of the enterprise, usually having a statutory responsibility to report on the financial statements giving an account of management's stewardship.

(8) Although the extent of the work of the external auditor may be reduced by placing reliance on the work of internal audit, the responsibility to report is that of the external auditor alone, and therefore is indivisible and is not reduced by this reliance.

(9) As a result, all final judgements relating to matters which are material to the financial statements or other aspects on which he is reporting, must be made by the external auditor.

Procedures

Planning

(10) Before any decision is taken to place reliance on internal audit, it is necessary for the external auditor to make an assessment of the likely effectiveness and the relevance of the internal audit function. The criteria for making this assessment should include the following:

(a) The degree of independence. The external auditor should evaluate the organisational status and reporting responsibilities of the internal auditor and consider any constraints or restrictions placed upon him. Although an internal auditor is an employee of the enterprise and cannot therefore be independent of it, he should be able to plan and carry out his work as he wishes and have access to the highest level of management. He should also be free of any responsibility which may create a conflict of interest when he attempts to discharge his internal audit function, or of a situation where middle management on whom he is reporting is responsible for his or his staff's appointment, promotion or remuneration. Furthermore, an internal auditor should be free to communicate fully with the external auditor, who should be able to receive copies of all internal audit reports that he requires.

(b) The scope and objectives of the internal audit function. The external auditor should examine the internal auditor's formal terms of reference and should ascertain the scope and objectives of internal audit assignments. In most circumstances, the external auditor will regard assignments as likely to be relevant where they are carried out in the areas described in paras 5(a) and (b) above. He will also be interested in internal audit's role in respect of specialist areas and those described in paras 5(c), (d) and (e) above, when it has an important bearing on the reliability of the financial statements or other matters being reported on.

(c) Due professional care. The external auditor should consider whether the work of internal audit generally appears to be properly planned, controlled, recorded and reviewed. Examples of the exercise of due professional care by internal audit are the existence of an adequate audit manual, general internal audit plans, procedures for supervising individual assignments, and satisfactory arrangements for ensuring adequate quality control, reporting and follow-up.

(d) Technical competence. The external auditor should ascertain whether the work of the internal audit is performed by persons having adequate training and proficiency as auditors. Indications of technical competence may be membership of an appropriate professional body or the possession of relevant practical experience, such as computer auditing skills.

(e) Internal audit reports. The external auditor should consider the quality of reports issued by internal audit and ascertain whether management considers, responds to and where appropriate acts upon internal audit reports, and whether this is evidenced.

(f) Level of resources available. The external auditor should consider whether internal audit has adequate resources eg in terms of staff and of computer facilities.

(11) The external auditor's assessment of the likely effectiveness and the relevance of the internal audit function will influence his judgement as to whether he wishes to place reliance on internal audit. Consequently the external auditor should document his assessment and conclusions in this respect, and he should update his assessment year by year. Where the external auditor concludes that the internal audit department is weak or ineffective then it should not be relied upon. Furthermore, the external auditor should inform management in writing of the significant weaknesses in the internal audit function, his reasons for not placing reliance on their work and his recommendations for improvement.

(12) Where the external auditor decides that he may be able to place reliance on internal audit, he should consider in determining the extent of that reliance:

(a) the materiality of the areas or the items to be tested or of the information to be obtained;

(b) the level of audit risk inherent in the areas or items to be tested or in the information to be obtained;

(c) the level of judgement required;

(d) the sufficiency of complementary audit evidence;

(e) specialist skills possessed by internal audit staff.

(13) The external auditor should be involved in the audit of all material matters in the financial statements, particularly in those areas where there is a significant risk of misstatement. High audit risk does not preclude placing some reliance on internal audit, but the external auditor should ensure that the extent of his involvement is sufficient to enable him to form his own conclusions.

(14) Having decided that he may be able to place reliance on the work of internal audit, the external auditor should agree with the chief internal auditor the timing of internal audit work, test levels, sample selection and the form of documentation to be used.

(15) The external auditor should record in his working papers the extent to which he intends to place reliance on internal audit, and the reasons for deciding that extent. Furthermore, the external auditor should consider confirming with management the overall arrangements that have been agreed, either in the engagement letter or in a separate letter.

Controlling

(16) Where the external auditor places reliance on the work of internal audit he should review that work and satisfy himself that it is being properly controlled. In this connection, the external auditor should:

(a) consider whether the work has been appropriately staffed and properly planned, supervised and reviewed;

(b) compare the results of the work with those of the external auditor's staff on similar audit areas or items, if any;

(c) satisfy himself that any exceptions or unusual matters that have come to light as a result of the work have been properly resolved;

(d) examine reports relating to the work produced by internal audit and management's response to those reports.

In addition, the external auditor should determine whether internal audit will be able to complete, on a timely basis, the programme that it has agreed to undertake and, if it will not, he should make appropriate alternative arrangements.

(17) At the conclusion of the audit, the external auditor should review the economy, efficiency and effectiveness of the basis of working and discuss with the chief internal auditor the significant findings and any means of improving the approach.

Recording

(18) The external auditor will need to ensure that all work relating to his audit whether performed by internal audit or the external auditor is properly recorded. He should satisfy himself that the working papers relating to the work of internal audit upon which he is placing reliance are up to an acceptable standard. Consideration should be given to the method of recording so that relevant working papers are available and are of use to both the external auditor and internal audit.

Audit evidence

(19) Where the external auditor places reliance on internal audit whether by means of direct assistance or otherwise, he should satisfy himself that sufficient evidence is obtained to afford a reasonable basis for the conclusions reached by internal audit, and that those conclusions are appropriate to the circumstances and are consistent with the results of the work performed. This may involve him in performing supplementary procedures. The extent of these procedures will depend on his assessment of the internal audit function, the materiality of the area or item to be tested and the risk of misstatement in the financial statements (see para 13). The procedures may include re-examining transactions or balances that internal audit have tested, examining similar transactions or balances, or the performance of analytical review procedures, as well as discussing with internal audit the work they have performed.

Internal controls

(20) Where the work of internal audit reveals weaknesses in internal controls, the external auditor should consider whether it is enough to draw management's attention to a report from internal audit or whether he should also report to

management himself, particularly where he considers management response to internal audit reports is inadequate or where the weaknesses are significant. The external auditor should consider whether his own programme should be amended because of those weaknesses.

5.5 Summary

The auditor's objective of reporting on the financial statements is achieved by three main processes:

(a) establishing the completeness, accuracy and validity of the underlying records;

(b) verification of assets and liabilities;

(c) review of financial statements.

The first of these processes will include the auditor's review of the client's system of control.

Adequate internal controls should exist for all the operational areas of a business.

Internal audit is an important aspect of internal control in larger organizations. The external auditor and the internal auditor may well work closely together, though it remains the responsibility of the external auditor to evaluate the work of the internal auditor as part of an overall review of the system.

Progess questions

Questions	Reference for answers
(1) What are the three directions from which the auditor approaches the task of verifying the financial statements?	Section 5.1
(2) Define 'internal control'.	Section 5.2
(3) Why is the existence of a sound system of internal control important to the auditor?	Section 5.2
(4) What are the main types of internal control?	Section 5.2 Appendix to Guideline on Internal Control
(5) List the main internal control requirements in each of the following areas:	Section 5.3 Appendix to Auditing Statement on Internal Control:
(a) general financial arrangements	Paragraph (2)
(b) cash and cheques received	Paragraphs (3)–(10)
(c) cheque and cash payments	Paragraphs (11)–(16)
(d) wages and salaries	Paragraphs (17)–(23)
(e) purchases and trade creditors	Paragraphs (24)–(27)
(f) sales and trade debtors	Paragraphs (28)–(31)
(g) stock (including work in progress)	Paragraphs (32)–(34)
(h) fixed assets and investments	Paragraphs (35)–(37)
(6) How may the internal auditor and the external auditor collaborate?	Section 5.4
(7) What differences are there between the internal and the external auditor?	Section 5.4

6 Ascertaining and recording the system of internal control

6.1 Techniques for ascertainment

Before the auditor can begin the process of reviewing the client's system of internal control, it is first necessary to *ascertain* that system. (In practice, the work of ascertainment, recording and evaluation may well happen in parallel, but it is convenient for study purposes to consider them separately).

The techniques used should be appropriate to the size of the client's business and the complexity of its system.

In the case of a new audit client, initial ascertainment procedures will inevitably be more time-consuming as the systems record for the permanent file is built up. Systems ascertainment is not a once-and-for-all job, however. At each audit the *changes* in the system since the last visit must be picked up and the systems record in the permanent file amended where necessary.

Possible techniques are:

(a) reference to existing systems notes in the permanent audit file;

(b) discussion with the management/owner;

(c) use of internal control questionnaires (ICQs);

(d) obtaining a copy of the client's systems manual, if such exists;

(e) inspection of the format of accounting records, including obtaining copies of any special forms used;

(f) obtaining a list of staff and their duties, together with an organization chart;

(g) observation of procedures;

(h) discussion with internal auditors, both to obtain their explanation of any points of difficulty and to review their audit programme, which of course will form part of the system.

(i) the final technique is the use of 'walk-through tests' in which one or two representative transactions are traced through each systems area. The object of these tests is to confirm that the auditor has in fact accurately recorded the system.

6.2   The Auditing Guideline: Accounting Systems

Let us pick up the Auditing Guideline on Accounting Systems which deals
with this area. It was issued in April 1980.

APC Guideline on accounting systems

Introduction

(1) Paragraph 3 of the Auditing Standard *The auditor's operational standard* states
that:

'The auditor should ascertain the enterprise's system of recording and processing
transactions and assess its adequacy as a basis for the preparation of financial
statements.'

This Auditing Guideline, which gives guidance on how that paragraph may be applied,
should be read in conjunction with the Explanatory Foreword to Auditing Standards
and Guidelines including the Glossary of Terms.

Background

(2) As part of his audit planning, in particular in determining the nature of his audit
tests, the auditor will need to consider the overall design of the accounting system and
the adequacy of the accounting records from which the financial statements are
prepared.

(3) The auditor will often have a separate and distinct responsibility to form an
opinion as to the adequacy of the accounting records for the purpose of complying
with the legislation or regulations to which the enterprise may be subject. The
Companies Act 1985, the Companies Act (Northern Ireland) 1960, as subsequently
amended, and the Companies Act 1963 set out the requirements concerning
accounting records and books of account for companies incorporated under those
Acts in Great Britain, Northern Ireland and the Republic of Ireland respectively.
Auditors of enterprises such as building societies or trade unions which are subject to
separate legislation will need to consider their specific duties relating to accounting
records.

(4) The management of an enterprise requires complete and accurate accounting
and other records to assist it in:

(*a*) controlling the business;
(*b*) safeguarding the assets;
(*c*) preparing financial statements;
(*d*) complying with legislation.

(5) An accounting system should provide for the orderly assembly of accounting
information and appropriate analyses to enable financial statements to be prepared.
What constitutes an adequate accounting system will depend on the size, nature and

complexity of the enterprise. In its simplest form for a small business dealing primarily with cash sales and with only a few suppliers the accounting system may only need to consist of an analysed cash-book and a list of unpaid invoices. In contrast, a company manufacturing several different products and operating through a number of dispersed locations may need a complex accounting system to enable information required for financial statements to be assembled.

(6) Depending upon the size and nature of the business concerned an accounting system will frequently need to incorporate integral controls to provide assurance that:

(a) all the transactions and other accounting information which should be recorded have in fact been recorded;

(b) errors or irregularities in processing accounting information will become apparent;

(c) assets and liabilities recorded in the accounting system exist and are recorded at the correct amounts.

(7) The evaluation of the internal controls referred to in paragraph 6 is dealt with in a separate Auditing Guideline, but in practice the auditor will probably carry out the work concurrently with his assessment of the accounting system.

Procedures

(8) The auditor will need to obtain an understanding of the enterprise as a whole and how the accounting system reflects assets and liabilities and transactions.

(9) The auditor will need to ascertain and record the accounting system in order to assess its adequacy as a basis for the preparation of financial statements. The extent to which the auditor should record the enterprise's accounting system and the method used will depend on the complexity and nature of the system and on the degree of reliance he plans to place on internal controls. Where the auditor plans to rely on internal controls, the accounting system needs to be recorded in considerable detail so as to facilitate the evaluation of the controls and the preparation of a programme of compliance and substantive tests. The record may take the form of narrative notes, flowcharts or checklists or a combination of them.

(10) As an aid to recording the accounting system, the auditor should consider tracing a small number of transactions (possibly one or two of each type) through the system. This procedure (often known as 'walk-through checks') will confirm that there is no reason to suppose that the accounting system does not operate in the manner recorded. The procedure is particularly appropriate where the enterprise has itself prepared the record of the system which the auditor is to use.

(11) In addition to making an assessment of the adequacy of the accounting system the auditor needs to confirm that the system has operated as laid down throughout the period. Evidence of this may be obtained by means of the compliance tests that the auditor carries out when he chooses to rely an internal controls. Alternatively the evidence may be obtained indirectly from his substantive testing.

6.3   Recording the system

There are for practical purposes three main methods of documenting systems information, and these will be dealt with in turn:

(a) systems notes;
(b) descriptive questionnaires;
(c) flowcharts.

6.3.1   System notes

Systems notes involve the compilation of a narrative description of accounting routines, in itself a simple operation. However, a general criticism of such systems notes as are frequently found on audit files is that they are badly compiled, neither fully detailed nor adequately cross-referenced, with the result that they are difficult to understand subsequently, and it becomes impossible to identify the controls within the systems from the notes—the very purpose for which they were compiled. In addition, it is not always easy to detect if any part of the system has been omitted.

A disciplined approach to writing systems notes does, to some extent, enable these weaknesses to be overcome and the remedy is in the adoption of a formalized method of recording, with standardized layout and, perhaps, symbols. For instance:

(a) The systems should be clearly identified at the head of the page, with a reference number and description, and the date at which operative.

(b) Each operation should be sequentially listed, and numbered for purposes of subsequent identification and cross-referencing.

(c) Each operation should also be categorized, by use of a standard symbol, to indicate its type, for instance, as between an operation, a check and a filing process.

The comprehensive narration can be ensured in a format which facilitates identification of controls.

Alternatively a form may be designed along the following lines:

(a) Descriptions of operations should be listed down the centre of the form.

(b) To the left of the operation description, input documents should be identified, together with their source, volume and frequency.

(c) To the right, output documents should be similarly specified.

(d) In each case, all documents should be cross-referenced.

(e) Each system description should be supported by a note of the personnel concerned with its operation and details of the records retained within the relevant department, their volume, filing sequence, etc.

In this case the control points are less readily identifiable, but the inter-relationship and interdependence of different systems is better highlighted.

6.3.2 Descriptive questionnaires

Questionnaires used for audit purposes are generally referred to as ICQs (Internal Control Questionnaires), and their purpose is to assist in the evaluation of the various types of internal check operating within a company. This function of evaluation will be returned to in the next chapter, but in dealing with recording systems it should be borne in mind that an ICQ can be drafted in such a way as to call for descriptive answers to questions which serve to describe the systems in operation. The preparation of such an ICQ involves the following steps:

(a) Breaking down each section of the system into appropriate sections.

(b) Phrasing questions calling for detailed descriptions of the systems.

(c) Additionally posing questions to assist in the identification of the various controls.

Examples of questions dealing with goods-received procedures for a purchase system, which would be suitable for inclusion in a descriptive questionnaire, are as follows:

(a) Is the receipt of goods at all locations recorded?

(b) By what means is such receipt recorded?

(c) Who prepares receiving records?

(d) How many copies are there of receiving records and to whom are these passed?

(e) Are receiving records prenumbered?

(f) What system is there for ensuring that all goods received have been properly ordered?

(g) How are receiving records controlled to ensure that invoices are obtained for all goods received?

(h) Are goods received examined for quantity and quality?

(i) What evidence is there for such examination?

Although such an ICQ is comprehensive, its very bulk can inhibit the exercise of initiative by its user and, by itself, it does not evaluate the significance of weaknesses.

6.3.3 Flowcharts

Flowcharts probably represent the most satisfactory method of recording important accounting systems, consistent with a disciplined approach to systems audits. A flowchart is a method of representing systems graphically by showing:

(a) A record of documents in existence and their movements.

(*b*) A record of the operations performed and their sequence.

(*c*) A record of check procedures built into internal control systems, at which stage these are performed, and by whom.

(*d*) How staff duties are segregated.

(*e*) How accounting procedures relate to other facets of the business.

The symbols set out on page 87 are suggested as suitable for flowcharting for audit purposes (other than computer systems where certain other symbols have become accepted as standards), and a series of specimen flowcharts for a simple purchasing system is shown to illustrate the above points (pp. 88–95).

The disciplines of this technique ensure that the flowchart will highlight strengths and weaknesses in internal control in a way which systems notes or descriptive questionnaires rarely can. Thus the flowchart, besides fulfilling its primary purpose of providing a record of the accounting system, will assist the auditor in evaluating internal control.

In preparing flowcharts, the following points should be borne in mind:

(*a*) The charts are to feature a movement of documents and information, in space and time:

Horizontal lines indicate movement in space.

Vertical lines indicate movement in time.

(*b*) Each chart should be headed with the name of the client, the general description of the operation, the date and the initials of the person who has prepared the chart.

(*c*) The chart should start in the top left of the paper and finish in the bottom right.

(*d*) A column on the left-hand side of the paper should provide a brief narrative explanation of each operation and the consecutive operation number. The rest of the chart should be divided according to the departments/persons involved.

(*e*) The lines should be:

(i) ————solid: to show the flow of a document.

(ii) – – – – –broken: to indicate a flow of information, which should be horizontal.

It is essential to differentiate between these two flows. Thus information flows include:

—posting of a ledger;

—checking of one document with another, or preparation of one document from information contained in another.

(*f*) The flowcharts should not indicate movements of goods.

(*g*) As an operation is rarely carried out on a document while it is being transferred from one department to another, it follows from (*a*) above that symbols should only appear on a solid vertical or on a broken horizontal flow-line.

(*h*) It is important that not too much information be put on one chart. Where it is necessary to use more than one chart, a connector symbol should be used. Where a document is transferred from one chart to another, it should be 'ghosted' by a broken line symbol, as shown on page 87, to indicate on the new chart what the document is.

(*i*) Copy documents, preferably actual documents, should be attached where necessary.

(*j*) A key should be provided where symbols or abbreviations used on a flowchart are not expressed in generally accepted terminology.

From an audit point of view, the purpose of the flowchart is not only to chart the client's accounting system, but also to highlight the weaknesses in internal control. Consequently, it is essential that a proper distinction be made between:

(1) an operation,
(2) a check.

The greater the preponderance of checking operations, the more appropriate it may be to reduce audit tests or switch them to other areas.

6.4 Summary

Before the detailed work of the audit can begin, the auditor must evaluate the client's system of internal control to enable him to decide upon the type and extent of tests to be applied. As a preliminary to that, it is necessary for the auditor to *ascertain* and *record* the system.   Techniques for ascertainment:

(*a*) reference to systems notes
(*b*) discussion with managers/owner
(*c*) ICQs
(*d*) client's systems manual
(*e*) inspection of records
(*f*) obtaining list of staff and their duties
(*g*) observation
(*h*) discussion with internal auditors, and review of their audit programmes
(*i*) walk-through tests.

Techniques for recording:

(*a*) systems notes
(*b*) descriptive questionnaires
(*c*) flowcharts

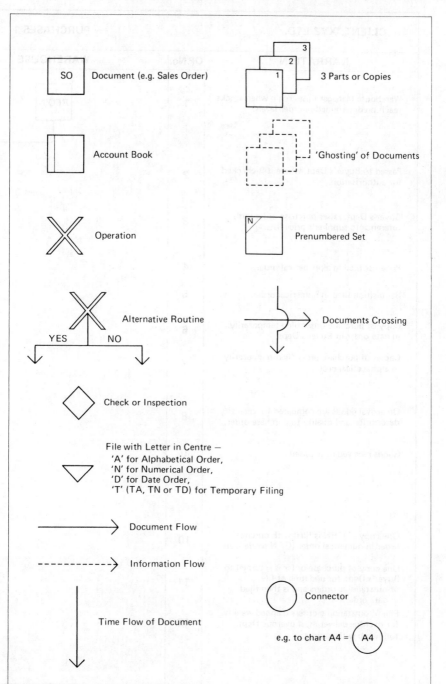

SO Document (e.g. Sales Order)	3 Parts or Copies
Account Book	'Ghosting' of Documents
Operation	Prenumbered Set
Alternative Routine YES NO	Documents Crossing
Check or Inspection	

File with Letter in Centre —
'A' for Alphabetical Order,
'N' for Numerical Order,
'D' for Date Order,
'T' (TA, TN or TD) for Temporary Filing

Document Flow

Information Flow

Connector

e.g. to chart A4 = (A4)

Time Flow of Document

CLIENT: XYZ LTD.		PURCHASES 1
NARRATION	**OP.No.**	**WAREHOUSE**
Warehouse Manager raises req'n when stocks reach predetermined re-order levels.	**1**	REQ'N
Passed to Buyer's Dept. where it is checked for authorisation.	**2**	
Buyer's Dept. raises purchase order with reference to supplier's price lists.	**3**	
Price list filed in alphabetical order.	**4**	
Requisition filed in numerical order.	**5**	
Copy of purchase order filed temporarily in date order in Buyer's Dept.	**6**	
Copies of purchase order filed temporarily in alphabetical order.	**7**	
On arrival goods are compared for quantity, description and quality to purchase order.	**8**	
Goods received note raised.	**9**	
One copy of GRN is filed with purchase order in numerical order (GRN sequence).	**10**	
One copy of purchase order is returned to Buyer's Dept. for updating of file of outstanding orders and is then filed in date order.	**11**	
File of outstanding orders scanned weekly for overdue deliveries, if overdue Dept. follow up with supplier.	**12**	

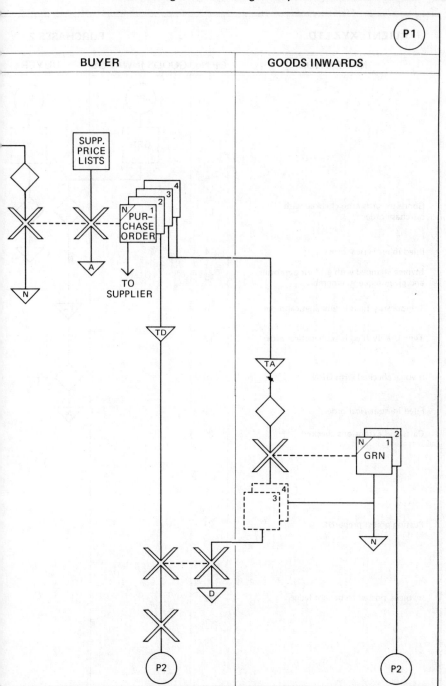

CLIENT: XYZ LTD.		PURCHASES 2	
NARRATION	OP. No.	GOODS INWARDS	BUYER
		P1 → GRN (2)	P1 → PO (2)
Goods inwards note checked with purchase order.	13		
Filed in numerical order.	14		N
Invoice stamped with grid for approvals and given sequential number.	15		
Temporarily filed in alphabetical order.	16		TA
Temporarily filed in alphabetical order.	17		
Invoice checked with GRN	18		
Filed in numerical order.	19		N
Casts and extensions checked.	20		
Posting prelist prepared.	21		
Invoices posted to bought ledger.	22		

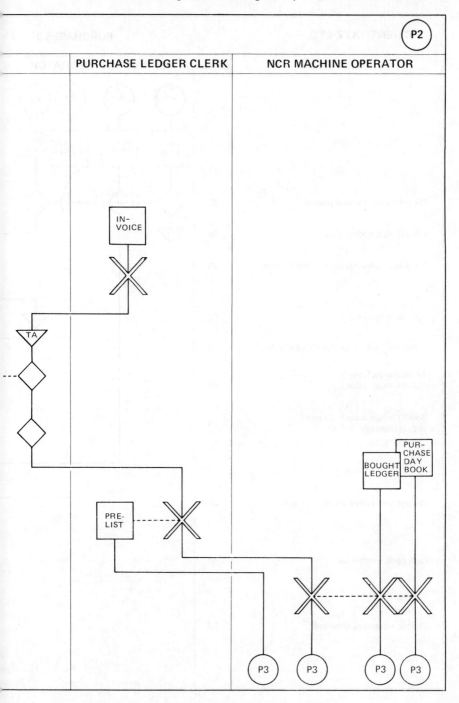

CLIENT: XYZ LTD.		PURCHASES 3

NARRATION	OP. No.	NCR MACHINE OPERATOR
		P2 P2 P2 P2
		PRE-LIST IN-VOICE BOUGHT LEDGER PUR-CHASE DAY BOOK
Pre-list agreed to total posted.	23	
Filed in date order.	24	D
Total purchases posted to general ledger.	25	
Filed in date order.	26	D
Statements sorted to alphabetical order.	27	
Temporarily filed in alphabetical order.	28	
Bought ledger accounts agreed with statements.	29	
Cheque remittance advice prepared.	30	
Cash book written up.	31	
Cheque signatures obtained.	32	P4

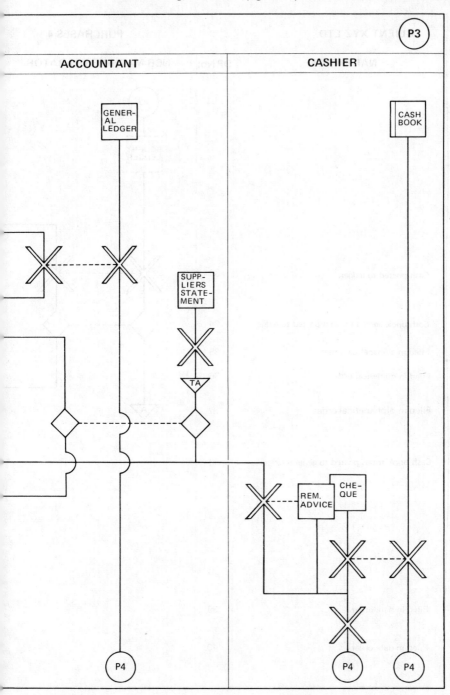

CLIENT XYZ LTD.		PURCHASES 4
NARRATION	**OP.No.**	**NCR MACHINE OPERATOR**

NARRATION	OP.No.
Cash posted to ledger.	33
Cash book agreed to total posted to ledger.	34
Filed in alphabetical order.	35
Filed in numerical order.	36
Filed in alphabetical order.	37
Cash book totals posted to general ledger.	38
Filed in date order.	39
Filed in date order.	40

P3

BOUGHT LEDGER

A

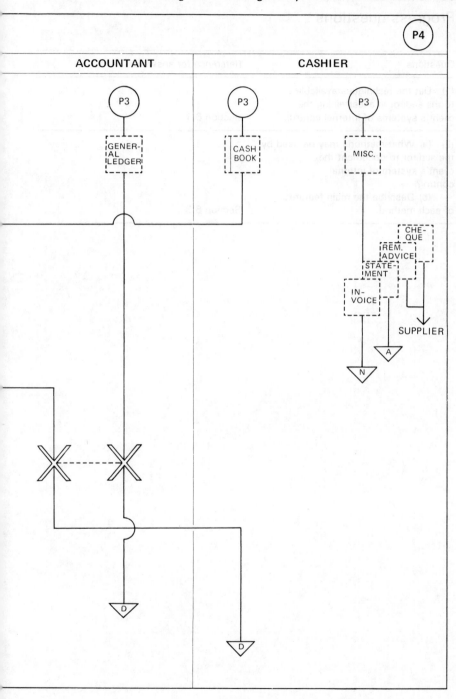

Progress questions

Questions	Reference for answers
(1) List the techniques available to the auditor in ascertaining the client's systems of internal control.	Section 6.1
(2) (*a*) What methods may be used by the auditor to document the client's system of internal control? (*b*) Describe the main features of each method.	Section 6.3

7 Evaluating the system

7.1 Introduction

As already indicated, one main objective of the audit is to prove the completeness, accuracy and validity of the records of the transactions of the period under review. There are two main approaches to this task:

- the systems based approach
- the vouching approach

The systems based approach is used when the system of internal control is strong. It consists of the following stages:

(a) Ascertain the system, using the techniques explained in Section 6.1.
(b) Record the system (Section 6.3).
(c) Evaluate the system in theory.
(d) If the evaluation in (c) leads the auditor to conclude that the system is strong in theory, apply tests to confirm that the system is in fact being followed efficiently in practice. These are *compliance tests*, defined as 'those tests which seek to provide audit evidence that internal control procedures are being applied as prescribed'.
(e) Follow up with a limited programme of *substantive tests*—'those tests of transactions and balances, and other procedures such as analytical review, which seek to provide audit evidence as to the completeness, accuracy and validity of the information contained in the accounting records or in the financial statements'.

The strength of this approach is that it gives the auditor the chance, in stage (d), to establish the accuracy of a large group of transactions with a limited amount of testing. The logic is:

- The system is satisfactory in theory.
- Compliance tests show that the theoretically satisfactory system is functioning properly in practice.
- Therefore all transactions processed through the system have been correctly processed.

It is important to note that the auditor does not rely solely on compliance tests. It remains necessary to corroborate the conclusions based on them by means of substantive tests.

The second audit approach, the vouching audit, is adopted when the systems evaluation shows that the system is poor or non-existent. The auditor then has no alternative but to proceed by extended substantive tests of transactions. This is a more time-consuming and less satisfactory method, in which the examination of the evidence relating to a transaction record verifies that record only, without contributing to the verification of a whole group of transactions as compliance tests do.

More details of the testing techniques are outlined in the next chapter. The purpose of the remainder of this chapter is to explain the process of evaluating the system of internal control which will determine, and must therefore precede, the testing itself.

7.2 The Auditing Guideline—Internal Controls

The Guideline entitled Internal Controls (issued in April 1980) is relevant here and is reproduced below except for the Appendix listing types of control. That part of the Guideline has already been reproduced in Section 5.2.

APC Guideline on internal controls

Introduction

(1) Paragraph 5 of the Auditing Standard *The auditor's operational standard* states that:

'If the auditor wishes to place reliance on any internal controls, he should ascertain and evaluate those controls and perform compliance tests on their operation.'

This Auditing Guideline, which gives guidance on how that paragraph may be applied, should be read in conjunction with the Explanatory Foreword to Auditing Standards and Guidelines including the Glossary of Terms.

Background

(2) At an early stage in his work the auditor will have to decide the extent to which he wishes to place reliance on the internal controls of the enterprise. As the audit proceeds, that decision will be kept under review and, depending on the results of his examination, he may decide to place more or less reliance on these controls.

Management responsibility for internal control
(3) An internal control system is defined as being:

'the whole system of controls, financial and otherwise, established by the management in order to carry on the business of the enterprise in an orderly and efficient manner, ensure adherence to management policies, safeguard the assets and secure as far as possible the completeness and accuracy of the records. The individual components of an internal control system are known as 'controls' or 'internal controls'.'

(4) It is a responsibility of management to decide the extent of the internal control system which is appropriate to the enterprise. The nature and extent of controls will vary between enterprises and also from one part of an enterprise to another. The controls used will depend on the nature, size and volume of the transactions, the degree of control which members of management are able to exercise personally, the geographical distribution of the enterprise and many other factors. The choice of controls may reflect a comparison of the cost of operating individual controls against the benefits expected to be derived from them.

(5) The operating procedures and methods of recording and processing transactions used by small enterprises often differ significantly from those of large enterprises. Many of the internal controls which would be relevant to the larger enterprise are not practical, appropriate or necessary in the small enterprise. Managements of small enterprises have less need to depend on formal internal controls for the reliability of the records and other information, because of their personal contact, with, or involvement in, the operation of the enterprise itself.

Limitations on the effectiveness of internal controls

(6) No internal control system, however, elaborate, can by itself guarantee efficient administration and the completeness and accuracy of the records; nor can it be proof against fraudulent collusion, especially on the part of those holding positions of authority or trust. Internal controls depending on segregation of duties can be avoided by collusion. Authorisation controls can be abused by the person in whom the authority is vested. Management is frequently in a position to override controls which it has itself set up. Whilst the competence and integrity of the personnel operating the controls may be ensured by selection and training, these qualities may alter due to pressure exerted both within and without the enterprise. Human error due to errors of judgement or interpretation, to misunderstanding, carelessness, fatigue or distraction may undermine the effective operation of internal controls.

The auditor's use of internal controls

(7) The auditor's objective in evaluating and testing internal controls is to determine the degree of reliance which he may place on the information contained in the accounting records. If he obtains reasonable assurance by means of compliance tests that the internal controls are effective in ensuring the completeness and accuracy of the accounting records and the validity of entries therein, he may limit the extent of his substantive testing.

(8) Because of the inherent limitations in even the most effective internal control system, it will not be possible for the auditor to rely solely on its operation as a basis for his opinion on the financial statements.

(9) In some enterprises the auditor may be unable to determine whether all the transaction have been reflected in the accounting records unless there are effective internal controls.

(10) The types of internal controls on which the auditor may seek to rely vary widely. An appendix contains a description of some of the main types of internal controls which the auditor may find and on which he may seek to place some degree of reliance. [This appendix has been reproduced in Section 5.2.]

Procedures

Audit procedures in relation to internal controls

(11) The auditor will need to ascertain and record the internal control system in order to make a preliminary evaluation of the effectiveness of its component controls and to decide the extent of his reliance thereon. This recording will normally be carried out concurrently with the recording of the accounting system. As indicated in the guideline on accounting systems the auditor may find it helpful to trace one or two transactions through the system.

(12) The evaluation of internal controls will be assisted by the use of documentation designed to help identify the internal controls on which the auditor may wish to place reliance. Such documentation can take a variety of forms but might be based on questions asking either:

(*a*) whether controls exist which meet specified overall control objectives; or

(*b*) whether there are controls which prevent or detect particular specified errors or omissions.

(13) Where this preliminary evaluation indicates that there are controls which meet the objective which the auditor has identified, he should design and carry out compliance tests if he wishes to rely on them. Where, however, the preliminary evaluation discloses weaknesses in, or the absence of, internal controls, such that material error or omission could arise in the accounting records or financial statements, the auditor will move directly to designing and carrying out substantive tests.

(14) *Compliance tests*   The auditor is not entitled to place any reliance on internal controls based solely on his preliminary evaluation. He should carry out compliance tests to obtain reasonable assurance that the controls on which he wishes to rely were functioning both properly and throughout the period. It should be noted that it is the control which is being tested by a compliance test, and not the transaction which may be the medium used for the test. For this reason the auditor should record and investigate all exceptions revealed by his compliance testing, regardless of the amount involved in the particular transaction. (An 'exception' in this context is an occurrence where a control has not been operated correctly whether or not a quantitative error has occurred.)

(15) If compliance tests disclose no exceptions the auditor may reasonably place reliance on the effective functioning of the internal controls tested. He can, therefore, limit his substantive tests on the relevant information in the accounting records.

(16) If the compliance tests have disclosed exceptions which indicate that the control being tested was not operating properly in practice, the auditor should determine the reasons for this. He needs to assess whether each exception is only an isolated departure or is representative of others, and whether it indicates the possible existence of errors in the accounting records. If the explanation he receives suggests

that the exception is only an isolated departure, then he must confirm the validity of the explanation, for example by carrying out further tests. If the explanation or the further tests confirm that the control being tested was not operating properly throughout the period, then he cannot rely on that control. In these circumstances the auditor is unable to restrict his substantive testing unless he can identify an alternative control on which to rely. Before relying on that alternative control he must carry out suitable compliance tests on it.

Timing and scope of the review and testing of internal controls

(17) If reliance is to be placed on the operation of controls, the auditor should ensure that there is evidence of the effectiveness of those controls throughout the whole period under review. Compliance tests carried out at an interim date prior to the year end need, therefore, to be supplemented by tests of controls for the remainder of the year; alternatively, the auditor will need to carry out other procedures to enable him to gain adequate assurance as to the reliability of the acccounting records during the period which has not been subject to compliance tests. In determining the alternative procedures which are necessary he should consider:

(a) the results of earlier compliance tests;

(b) whether, according to enquiries made, controls have remained the same for the remaining period;

(c) the length of the remaining period;

(d) the nature and size of the transactions and account items involved; and

(e) the substantive tests which he will carry out irrespective of the adequacy of controls.

(18) Where the internal control system has changed during the accounting period under review, the auditor will have to evaluate and test the internal controls on which he wishes to rely, both before and after the change.

Reliance on internal audit

(19) Internal audit is an element of the internal control system set up by management. The extent to which the external auditor is able to take account of the work of the internal auditor will depend on his assessment of the effectiveness of the internal audit function. In making this assessment, the external auditor will be concerned with:

(a) the degree of independence of the internal auditor from those whose responsibilities he is reviewing;

(b) the number of suitably qualified and experienced staff employed in the internal audit function;

(c) the scope, extent, direction and timing of the tests made by the internal auditor;

(d) the evidence available of the work done by the internal auditor and of the review of that work;

(e) the extent to which management takes action based upon the reports of the internal audit function.

(20) Provided that relevant internal audit work has been carried out effectively, the external auditor may be able to reduce the level of his tests.

Reporting to management on internal controls

(21) It is important that the auditor should report, as soon as practicable, significant weaknesses in internal controls which come to his attention during the course of an audit to an appropriately senior level of management of the enterprise. Any such report should indicate that the weaknesses notified are only those which have come to the attention of the auditor during the course of his normal audit work and are not necessarily, therefore, all the weaknesses which may exist.

(22) The fact that the auditor reports weaknesses in internal controls to management does not absolve:

(a) management from its responsibility for the maintenance of an adequate internal control system; or

(b) the auditor from the need to consider the effect of such weaknesses on the extent of his audit work and on his audit opinion.

7.3 The divisions of the system

In recording the systems of the company in whose audit he or she is engaged, the auditor will need to break down the overall accounting routines into appropriate subdivisions for ease of assimilation. It is suggested that for most purposes the following would be suitable, and accordingly these same divisions have been adopted in subsequent chapters:

(1) Organizational and general matters
(2) Purchases and accounts payable
(3) Stocks and costing
(4) Payroll
(5) Sales and accounts receivable
(6) Receipts, payments, bank and cash balances
(7) Investments and investment income.

Some specialist undertakings would, of course, need additional relevant sections.

The purpose of compiling systems information is to enable the auditor firstly to evaluate the adequacy of the systems themselves and, secondly, to evaluate the internal controls built into those systems. These tasks tend to be done concurrently. However, this is not always easy to accomplish. It has already been said that neither systems notes, nor descriptive ICQs even, specifically identify controls; flowcharts do, but it still takes an experienced systems auditor to recognize potential weaknesses and assess the extent to which the basic controls are adequate. Furthermore, even when this is done, the auditor must recognize inevitable limitations on the extent of internal control in at least some areas of every undertaking: as the Auditing Guideline on Internal Controls says, 'management is frequently in a position to override controls which it has itself set up', and, 'any system of internal control is always subject to the possibility of human error'.

However, it seems to us likely that to achieve initial assurance in the accounting system, the auditor will have to be satisfied that there are some effective internal controls in existence, although these may vary widely as to type.

7.4   Management controls

One of the elements of control which the auditor should be looking for is management supervision and review.

An important feature of effective internal control is that directors should review the company's financial operations and position at regular and frequent intervals by means of interim accounts and reports, operating summaries and other appropriate financial and statistical information. Comparison with results for previous periods may indicate discrepancies that call for further examination or, where budgetary control is in use, attention will be drawn to material variances and explanations required. In addition to regular reviews of this nature management may from time to time call for special reviews of particular items such as stocks, or the operation of the wages department; these constitute yet another instrument of control. In smaller firms examinations of the nature indicated may be carried out by the owner or manager personally. Managerial supervision and reviews of this nature are an essential element in any effective internal control system.

To some extent it is possible for management to delegate this function, especially as regards detailed examinations and special reviews; and hence the existence in some large organizations of an internal audit department, made up of specially assigned staff with a principal accounting objective of assuring management of the efficient and effective design and operation of internal checks within accounting systems.

The role of the internal auditor and his or her position *vis-à-vis* the external auditor have already been covered in Section 5.4.

7.5   Organizational controls and segregation of duties

The company's organization chart must be reviewed for the extent to which authority and responsibility has been appropriately allocated in a clear reporting structure to those with sufficient ability to fulfil their function within the internal control system. In particular the auditor will wish to assess the extent to which the division of duties between members of the staff has been arranged in a manner to lessen the risk of errors and defalcations. It is suggested that a segregation of staff duties questionnaire should be drawn up to supplement the flowcharts, thus providing a résumé of 'who does what' and serving to highlight areas of poor organizational control, possible conflict of duties, and areas where family relationships could serve to vitiate the effectiveness of the division of duties.

Using the divisions above, the following specimen questions indicate what is required to serve this purpose.

The more that the functions indicated above can be seen to be separated, then the more effective is the existence of internal check upon which the auditor may still seek to place reliance.

1. Organizational and general matters

	Name and position	Com-pleted by
Who:		
1.1 is responsible for the use of the company seal?		
1.2 is responsible for the custody of the company minute book?		
1.3 ensures that transfer documents are in order?		
1.4 is responsible for the custody and issue of share and loan certificates?		
1.5 is responsible for share and loan registers?		
1.6 checks dividend warrants?		
1.7 signs dividend warrants or controls pre-signed warrants?		
1.8 authorizes the issue of duplicate dividend warrants?		
1.9 prepares dividend bank reconciliations?		
1.10 keeps the nominal ledger?		
1.11 keeps the journal?		
1.12 is authorized to make journal entries?		
1.13 raises requests for capital expenditure?		
1.14 sanctions capital expenditure?		
1.15 maintains records of outstanding sanctions and orders?		
1.16 maintains registers of fixed assets?		
1.17 is responsible for custody of documents of title?		
1.18 determines depreciation rates?		
1.19 authorizes disposals of assets?		

	Yes/ No	Comment/reference to other controls	Com-pleted by
1.20 Are 1.1 to 1.5 above the responsibility of separate individuals?			
1.21 Are 1.6 to 1.9 above the responsibility of separate individuals?			
1.22 Are 1.10 to 1.12 above the responsibility of separate individuals?			

	Yes/ No	Comment/reference to other controls	Com- pleted by
1.23 Are 1.14 to 1.19 above the respon- siblity of a separate individual from 1.17 above?			
1.24 If not, are there adequate compen- sating controls?			

2. Purchases and accounts payable

	Name and position	Com- pleted by
Who:		
2.1 raises requisitions for orders?		
2.2 approves requisitions?		
2.3 places orders with suppliers (i) for goods? (ii) for services?		
2.4 receives goods onto premises?		
2.5 approves invoices?		
2.6 keeps the accounts payable ledgers?		
2.7 checks calculations on invoices?		
2.8 codes invoices?		

	Yes/ No	Comment/reference to other controls	Com- pleted by
2.9 Are 2.2 to 2.8 above the responsi- bility of separate individuals?			
2.10 Is 2.6 above the responsibility of a separate individual from 1.10–1.12?			
2.11 Is 2.5 above the responsibility of a separate individual from 1.14 and 1.17?			
2.12 If not, are there adequate compen- sating controls?			

3. Stocks and costing

	Name and position	Completed by
Who: 3.1 is responsible for custody of stocks? 3.2 is responsible for keeping physical stock control records? 3.3 is responsible for keeping financial stock control records? 3.4 approves stock issues? 3.5 approves scrap sales and other disposals? 3.6 is responsible for periodic counting of stock? 3.7 authorizes the amendment of physical stock records following counts? 3.8 authorizes the amendment of financial stock records following counts? 3.9 reviews stocks and stock levels, etc.?		

	Yes/No	Comment/reference to other controls	Completed by
3.10 Are 3.1 to 3.3 above the responsibility of separate individuals? 3.11 Are 3.4 and 3.5 above the responsibility of separate individuals? 3.12 Are 3.6 to 3.8 above the responsibility of separate individuals? 3.13 Is 3.9 above the responsibility of an individual not involved in the custody of stocks or stock records? 3.14 If not, are there adequate compensating controls?			

Contracts	Name and position	Completed by
Who 3.15 is responsible for authorizing acceptance of a contract? 3.16 is responsible for authorizing amendments to a contract? 3.17 is responsible for keeping the contract cost ledger? 3.18 authorizes cost transfers in the cost ledger? 3.19 is responsible for periodic contract valuations? 3.20 keeps the records of progress monies received?		

	Yes/ No	Comment/reference to other controls	Com- pleted by
3.21 Are 3.15 and 3.16 above the responsibility of the same individuals? 3.22 Are 3.17 and 3.18 above the responsibility of separate individuals? 3.23 Are 3.19 and 3.20 above the responsibility of separate individuals? (*Note:* Normally, 3.15, 3.16, 3.18 and 3.19, will be the collective responsibility of more than one person. It is essential to support the brief answers above with full notes of the precise authorization/checking procedures and of the level of Authorizing Authority of each individual concerned.			

4. Payroll

	Name and position	Com- pleted by
Who: 4.1 keeps records of engagements, terminations, etc.? 4.2 authorizes or approves clock cards, timesheets, etc.? 4.3 calculates the payroll from such supporting documents? 4.4 checks these calculations? 4.5 authorizes changes in rates of pay? 4.6 makes up wages envelopes? 4.7 distributes wages? 4.8 has custody of unclaimed wages? 4.9 approves payrolls before wages distribution?		

	Yes/ No	Comment/reference to other controls	Com- pleted by
4.10 Are 4.1 to 4.7 above the responsibility of separate individuals? 4.11 If not, are there adequate compensating controls?			

5. Sales and accounts receivable

	Name and position	Completed by
Who: 5.1 approves customers' credit limits? 5.2 approves customers' orders? 5.3 dispatches goods? 5.4 raises invoices? 5.5 receives returned goods? 5.6 approves credit notes? 5.7 keeps the accounts receivable ledger? 5.8 is responsible for credit control? 5.9 authorizes writing-off bad debts?		

	Yes/ No	Comment/reference to other controls	Completed by
5.10 Is each of the above the responsibility of a separate individual? 5.11 Are 5.7 and 5.9 above the responsibility of separate individuals from 1.10 to 1.12? 5.12 If not, are there adequate compensating controls?			

6. Receipts, payments, bank and cash balances

	Name and position	Completed by
Who: 6.1 opens the mail? 6.2 makes the first listing of remittances received? 6.3 records receipts in the cash book? 6.4 reconciles the cash book with till rolls, receipt books, etc. for cash sales? 6.5 prepares bank paying-in slips? 6.6 banks receipts? 6.7 approves cash discounts? 6.8 prepares cheques and records payments? 6.9 signs cheques? 6.10 has custody of any facsimile signatures? 6.11 is responsible for custody of petty cash? 6.12 approves petty cash payments? 6.13 carries out checks of petty cash balances? 6.14 prepares bank reconciliations? 6.15 checks bank reconciliations?		

	Yes/ No	Comment/reference to other controls	Com- pleted by
6.16 Is the responsibility for 6.3 and 6.8 above separate from that for 1.11 to 1.18, 2.5, 3.5, 4.1 and 4.5 to 4.8, and 5.7 and 5.9?			
6.17 Is the responsibility for 6.3 and 6.8 above separate from that for 6.11, 6.14 or 6.15 above?			
6.18 Is the responsibility for 6.1 and 6.2 above separate from that for 5.2 and 5.6, and from 6.3, 6.6 and 6.7 above?			
6.19 Is the responsibility for 6.7 above separate from that for 5.7?			
6.20 If not, are there adequate compen- sating controls?			

7. Investments and investment income

	Name and position	Com- pleted by
Who: 7.1 is responsible for authorizing purchases and sales? 7.2 checks prices of transactions? 7.3 has custody of documents of title? 7.4 keeps investment registers? 7.5 keeps financial records of investment income? 7.6 checks to ensure that income is properly received?		

	Yes/ No	Comment/reference to other controls	Com- pleted by
7.7 Are all the above the responsibility of separate individuals?			
7.8 Are 7.5 and 7.6 above the responsi- bility of separate individuals from 6.3 and 1.10?			
7.9 If not, are there adequate compen- sating controls?			

7.6   Accounting controls

These should ensure:

(a) that all transactions have been authorized and approved:
(b) that all those so authorized and approved are then included;
(c) that all transactions are correctly recorded;
(d) that all records have been accurately processed into the accounts.

To assist in their evaluation it is possible to design a shorter form of ICQ than the descriptive one, comprising a checklist of questions pertinent to the identification of controls. It is suggested that such questions in turn be segregated between fundamental 'key' questions and supporting subsidiary questions influencing the answer to each key question. The extent of this influence will vary depending upon the particular circumstances, but most of the key questions should be relevant to most businesses other than some specialist undertakings.

To ensure that the auditor properly understands the system with which he or she is concerned and that it is the auditor rather than the client who critically appraises the internal controls, it is recommended that the auditor personally answers the subsidiary questions and refers to the client's staff only if further clarification then becomes necessary. Having answered questions concerning related detailed internal controls, the auditor is then in a position to give a considered and reasoned answer to the key questions, based on an understanding of the strengths and weaknesses of the system. All answers to key questions should be supported by explanations and appropriate cross-references both to the relevant flowcharts and subsidiary questions, for it is on these that the initial levels of audit testing will be based and it is essential, therefore, to identify those areas requiring particular attention.

For this reason it is also recommended that each system be dealt with comprehensively in turn, rather than adopting a work method whereby, for instance, flowcharts for all systems are prepared before the evaluation of any of them is commenced. Better, having recorded a system, that the auditor should proceed to answer the subsidiary and key questions relating to it and, based on the resultant assessment of the controls, proceed to draw up the programme of audit tests for that area.

However, many of the internal controls which would be relevant to large businesses will be inappropriate or unnecessary in the case of smaller businesses. As a result the ICQ set out below may, for businesses below a given size, prove over-elaborate as a basis for evaluating a limited system of control.

For this reason, and in the interests of an efficient and cost-effective audit, a checklist of Minimum Controls may be preferable in respect of such smaller businesses.

As a general guide, it is suggested that this approach might be appropriate on the audit of businesses which are distinguished by:

(a) a limited number of accounting or office staff (perhaps up to 4 or 5) and, in consequence, the absence of many of the formal internal control duties that would be appropriate in larger businesses; and

(b) the close personal involvement of the manager and/or proprietor in the conduct or supervision of day-to-day transactions.

The Minimum Controls Checklist (MCC) can adopt the same key-question concept as is used in the full Internal Control Questionnaire (ICQ). The difference between the two documents is primarily one of scale: the MCC anticipates a less sophisticated system and is therefore shorter; the subsidiary questions within it are designed to highlight the aspects of control which are of particular relevance to the smaller business. Examples of both the ICQ and MCC are set out below.

7.7 Specimen Internal Control Questionnaire

The following specimen ICQ indicates the form of key and subsidiary questions which will assist the auditor to identify the strengths and weaknesses in a client's systems. Whenever answering a subsidiary question adversely, i.e. acknowledging a weakness in internal control, the auditor should pay particular attention to the possibility of the existence of a compensating control at a different point in the accounting system. It is important that the ICQ should be carefully reviewed, once completed, for it will have an important bearing on the nature and extent of audit testing, which we discuss in the next chapter, and on the matters to be reported in the management letter.

ICQ1. Organizational and general matters

KEY QUESTION
1.1 Is the business effectively managed and properly administered?

SUBSIDIARY QUESTIONS
(a) Are accurate and timely management accounts (and/or other reports of business performance) produced on a regular basis?
   (b) Are financial plans, budgets and cash-flow forecasts maintained?
   (c) Is a comparison made between actual and forecast/budgeted results and are significant variances analysed and explained?
   (d) Do management appear to be fully informed of the performance of the business?

(e) Are management decisions properly minuted?

(f) Are there adequate procedures to ensure that all decisions are implemented?

(g) Are there any non-executive directors on the board and is their function specified?

(h) Is there an audit committee? (If so, obtain copy of its 'constitution' or terms of reference.)

(i) Is there a proper definition of duties and responsibilities at all levels?

(j) Are accounting procedures laid down (by manual, etc.) and how are they monitored?

(k) Is there an internal audit department? If so:

  (i) to whom is it responsible?

  (ii) are regular reports submitted by the department to the Board?

(l) Is an up-to-date organization chart maintained?

(m) Are there adequate stand-by arrangements in force to cover staff sickness, etc. or loss of accounting records (by fire, etc.)?

KEY QUESTION
1.2 Can the secretarial and statutory records be improperly manipulated or misappropriated?

SUBSIDIARY QUESTIONS
(a) Is the company seal kept in safe custody and its use controlled?

(b) Is the supply of blank share certificates controlled?

(c) Is the register of members, debenture holders, etc. agreed with the issued share or loan capital and the dividend/interest payments?

(d) Are share and debenture records subjected to a transfer audit?

(e) Are dividend/interest payments made through a separate account and the balances checked against unclaimed warrants?

(f) Are all registers required by law maintained by the company and up-to-date?

(g) Is the company's file at the Companies' Registry maintained up-to-date?

KEY QUESTION
1.3 Can fixed assets be acquired or disposed of without proper authority or recording?

SUBSIDIARY QUESTIONS
(a) Is capital expenditure over certain limits subject to authority?

(b) Is disposal of fixed assets subject to special authority?

(c) Is there a capital expenditure/disposal budget and, if so, is it regularly compared with actual expenditure authorized and incurred?

(d) Are records maintained for capital works carried out by the company including the allocation of overheads?

(e) Is a register of fixed assets maintained and is this checked regularly against the actual assets?

(*f*) Are records maintained for fixed asset disposal/scrappings, etc.?

(*g*) Is the register of fixed assets regularly reconciled to the nominal ledger?

(*h*) Are rates of depreciation laid down and are they adequate in the particular circumstances? Or excessive?

(*i*) Are profits on disposal of fixed assets within the group segregated?

(*j*) Are documents of title kept in safe custody?

KEY QUESTION

1.4 Does the company maintain adequate insurance cover over all aspects of its business?

SUBSIDIARY QUESTIONS

(*a*) Does the company maintain adequate insurance cover in respect of:

    (i)   consequential loss

    (ii) employer's liability

    (iii) public liability

    (iv) fire, burglary and theft

    (v) cash and goods in transit

    (vi) any other cover relevant to the type of business transacted?

(*b*) Is cover periodically reviewed and updated in the light of current results and values?

(*c*) Have all the required declarations by the company and/or certificates by third parties been submitted to the insurers?

(*d*) Are persons handling cash or high value stocks covered by fidelity bonds?

KEY QUESTION

1.5 Are transactions with related parties (i.e. with group, associated and other affiliated companies or with businesses under common control) undertaken otherwise than at arms length?

SUBSIDIARY QUESTIONS

(*a*) Is there a properly defined group structure?

(*b*) Are there adequate procedures for the disclosure of interests of shareholders, directors and employees in other undertakings?

(*c*) Is the transfer of funds between such undertakings properly authorized and, as regards overseas transfers, in accordance with any exchange controls in the countries concerned?

(*d*) Are trading transactions and transfers of fixed assets between such undertakings in accordance with laid down procedures and on an arms length basis?

(*e*) If transactions are undertaken on other than at arms length basis:

    (i) is their effect on trading results/asset values quantified and assessed?

    (ii) are they approved by the Board?

KEY QUESTION
1.6 Can improper entries be made in the nominal ledger?

SUBSIDIARY QUESTIONS
(a) Is the nominal ledger kept in safe custody?
  (b) Can unauthorized persons make entries in the nominal ledger?
  (c) Is the nominal ledger regularly cast and balanced?
  (d) Are all journal entries subject to authorization by a responsible official?
  (e) Are all journal entries supported by proper documentation?
  (f) Do the nominal ledger accounts provide sufficient analysis over headings appropriate to the business, so as to facilitate the preparation of financial statements and management reports?

ICQ2. Purchases and accounts payable

KEY QUESTION
2.1 Can goods or services (other than occupancy charges) be ordered without being authorized?

SUBSIDIARY QUESTIONS
(a) Are purchase requisitions prepared and approved by responsible officials?
  (b) Are there any limits of authority operating over the ordering of goods/services?
  (c) Are blank purchase orders issued only to personnel responsible for buying?
  (d) Are purchase orders:

  (i)   issued for all purchases of goods and services?
  (ii) pre-numbered, and all numbers accounted for?
  (iii) completed with specifications of prices and terms?

  (e) Are purchase orders valued and compared with existing budgets or other management information?
  (f) Is there adequate control over the recharge of staff purchases?

KEY QUESTION
2.2 Can liabilities for goods or services be incurred but not recorded?

SUBSIDIARY QUESTIONS
(a) Are all goods received at a central receiving point?
  (b) Are goods-received records:

  (i)   made out immediately on receipt of goods?
  (ii) on pre-numbered forms?
  (iii) all accounted for?
  (iv) used to update stock records?

(c) Are goods examined on arrival as to quantity and quality and, if so, how is this evidenced?

(d) Are copies of the goods-received records given to:

(i) purchasing department?
(ii) accounts department?
(iii) stock records department?
(iv) other departments (give details)?

(e) Are there any records prepared for services received?

(f) Are goods-returned records:

(i) made out immediately on return of goods to suppliers?
(ii) on pre-numbered forms?
(iii) all accounted for?
(iv) used to update stock records?

(g) Are returned goods properly authorized?

KEY QUESTION
2.3 Can liabilities be omitted, wrongly recorded or wrongly charged?

SUBSIDIARY QUESTIONS

(a) Are purchase orders regularly reviewed for items for which no invoices have been received and are these investigated?

(b) Are goods-received records regularly reviewed for items for which no invoices have been received and are these investigated?

(c) Does the system ensure that all invoices received and approved are processed through the accounting systems?

(d) Are suppliers' statements reviewed for items which have not been processed into the accounting system?

(e) Are purchase ledger balances regularly reconciled with suppliers' statements and outstanding items investigated?

(f) Are debit balances in the purchases ledger regularly reviewed?

(g) Are goods-returned records regularly reviewed to ensure all credit notes have been received?

(h) Is there an adequate system to ensure that invoices are processed into the correct accounting classification, with particular reference to fixed-asset accounts?

KEY QUESTION
2.4 Can goods or services be paid for without being received?

SUBSIDIARY QUESTIONS

(a) Are suppliers' invoices and credit notes:

(i) serially numbered immediately on receipt?
(ii) all accounted for?
(iii) correlated with purchase order for type, quality and price?

(iv) correlated with goods received (or returned) records for type and quantity?

(v) checked for casts and calculations?

(vi) checked for correct accounting classification?

(vii) initialled for work done?

(viii) approved by a responsible official?

(*b*) Are invoices and credit notes recorded only when authorized?

(*c*) Are the purchase ledger balances regularly agreed with the control account?

(*d*) Is there adequate control over deliveries direct to customers?

ICQ3. Stocks and costing

KEY QUESTION
3.1 Can stocks be misappropriated or mislaid?

SUBSIDIARY QUESTIONS
(*a*) Is there proper security covering the handling and storage of stocks?

(*b*) Are stocks stored in an orderly manner and readily identifiable?

(*c*) Are there satisfactory controls over the documentation covering the receipt and issue of goods? (Refer also to questions dealing with sales and credit procedures.)

(*d*) Are perpetual stock records maintained and if so, is the recording function separated from that for the handling of goods?

(*e*) Are there regular stocktakings and proper control over the adjustment of physical discrepancies?

(*f*) Do the stock records facilitate the identification and reconciliation of physical discrepancies?

(*g*) Is there control over allowances made for shrinkage from whatever cause?

(*h*) Are there adequate procedures for the identification and segregation of obsolete, damaged and slow-moving stocks?

(*i*) Is there control over the disposal of obsolete, damaged and slow-moving stock?

(*j*) Are there adequate controls over stocks held by third parties or on behalf of third parties?

KEY QUESTION
3.2 Can work in progress be overstated or understated?

SUBSIDIARY QUESTIONS
(*a*) Is there an acceptable and consistent basis for charging materials, direct labour and overheads?

(*b*) Are interdepartmental transfers of

(i) materials

(ii) partly finished work

(iii) completed work

all subject to documentary control?

    (c) Do the work-in-progress records properly identify:

    (i) each separate stage of production;

    (ii) the amount of materials, labour and overheads charged to each job?

    (d) Is the work-in-progress subject to periodic physical checks which are reconciled with book records?

KEY QUESTION

3.3 Does the costing system provide adequate controls with the financial records?

SUBSIDIARY QUESTIONS

(a) Is the cost-accounting system integrated with the financial records?

    (b) Are cost variances properly analysed and explained on a regular basis?

    (c) Are standard costs kept under proper review by management and are they reliable?

KEY QUESTION

3.4 Do the stock records adequately segregate raw materials, work-in-progress and finished stocks and do they provide for movements between these categories to be properly recorded?

SUBSIDIARY QUESTIONS

(a) Are there physical counts at points of transfer between areas?

    (b) Is there an acceptable and consistent basis for charging overheads into valuations and does this basis make proper allowances appropriate to the stages of manufacture?

KEY QUESTION

3.5 Does the system ensure that contracts accepted are within the capabilities of the business and are economically viable?

SUBSIDIARY QUESTIONS

(a) Do the methods of estimating and preparing quotations ensure that all the items and/or stages of the contract are correctly costed?

    (b) Is allowance made in the quotation for known or expected price rises?

    (c) Does the company ensure that all contracts make adequate provision for the effects of inflation?

    (d) Are estimates and quotations reviewed by a senior official of the company?

    (e) Is the method of financing contracts sufficient to ensure cash flow is adequate for the duration of contracts?

(*f*) Are specific warranties and indemnities, penalty terms and conditions reviewed and agreed by a senior official(s) as being reasonable and attainable?

(*g*) Do contracts always include specific maintenance periods and conditions of release?

(*h*) Are there any limits to the authority of those responsible for accepting contracts on the company's behalf?

(*i*) Are contract price adjustments (other than those specified in the original contract) and variation orders subject to the same controls and authority as the original contract?

(*j*) Are quotations checked by a senior official to ensure that the proposed work falls within:

   (i) the technical capability of the company?
   (ii) the anticipated capacity of the company at the time when the contract will have to be undertaken?

(*k*) If some of the contract work has to be put to subcontract, are quotations received from subcontractors before the submission of the main quotation; and is there an authorized list of approved subcontractors?

(*l*) Is the procedure for putting names on the list of approved subcontractors subject to authorization by a senior official?

(*m*) Are contracts and contract variations agreed with subcontractors by a senior official?

KEY QUESTION
3.6 Are contract costs correctly allocated, recorded and controlled?

SUBSIDIARY QUESTIONS
(*a*) Are there adequate controls in the following systems to ensure that costs are allocated to the correct contract?

   (i)   Purchase invoice processing?
   (ii) Subcontractors' certificates?
   (iii) Payroll?

(*b*) Is there an acceptable and consistent basis for allocating overheads to contracts?

(*c*) Are the contract cost ledger balances regularly agreed with the control account?

(*d*) Is there written authority for any transfers of costs between contracts or to close contract records?

(*e*) Is the use of plant charged to contracts carefully controlled? If plant is operated as a cost centre, are there procedures for:

   (i)   Physically controlling plant?
   (ii) Calculating the daily rate at which it should be charged to contracts?
   (iii) Recording plant movements between contract sites?
   (iv) Controlling plant operating costs?

KEY QUESTION
3.7 Is contract performance adequately monitored and regularly reviewed?

SUBSIDIARY QUESTIONS
(a) Are valuation procedures carried out regularly and are they adequate with regard to:

 (i)   Measuring procedures adopted for work done and materials on site?
 (ii) Recording of work carried out against variation orders?
 (iii) Recording of rectification work carried out and/or to be carried out?

(b) Are valuations regularly compared to estimated and actual costs to date?
(c) Are 'costs to complete' forecasts regularly prepared and reviewed in relation to contract value?
(d) Are visits arranged to the major contract sites at the financial year-end to ensure that the valuation procedures are being satisfactorily carried out?
(e) Is the work of sub-contractors controlled to ensure that it complies with the terms of the main contract?
(f) Are the procedures adequate for warning senior management if any penalty clauses in a contract are likely to be invoked by the customer?

KEY QUESTION
3.8 Are progress monies receivable adequately controlled and properly recorded?

SUBSIDIARY QUESTIONS
(a) Are there satisfactory procedures for ensuring that monies due in accordance with the contract terms are applied for as and when they become receivable?
(b) Are overdue progress monies followed up promptly?
(c) Is the contract manager/quantity surveyor notified of monies which are seriously overdue?
(d) Are retention monies due recorded separately from monies received?
(e) Are progress monies received recorded in such a way as to be separately identifiable from other amounts due?
(f) Are penalty clause deductions suffered recorded separately from outstanding progress accounts?

ICQ4. Payroll

KEY QUESTION
4.1 Can employees be paid for work not done?

SUBSIDIARY QUESTIONS
(a) Are time clocks supervised by a responsible official?
(b) Are time records and piece-work sheets and other source documents:

    (i) controlled by persons independent of the payroll department,

    (ii) approved by a responsible official before being processed?

(c) Are time records, piecework sheets and other source documents checked before processing by the payroll department for:

    (i) appropriate authorization as to their correctness,

    (ii) casts and calculations?

(d) Are proper controls exercised over adjustments for lateness, sickness and absenteeism (holidays, etc.)?

(e) Are separate payroll bank accounts operated, credited with the exact amount required, and regularly reconciled?

(f) Are adequate safeguards operated over wages and salaries paid to employees in cash, and over unclaimed wages?

(g) Are adequate controls operated over the processing of payrolls into the accounting records?

KEY QUESTION

4.2 Can the payroll be inflated in any way?

SUBSIDIARY QUESTIONS

(a) Are individual personal records (including contracts of employment) maintained independently of the payroll department?

(b) Are written authorizations required for all:

    (i) employees added to the payroll,

    (ii) changes in rates of pay,

    (iii) employees taken off the payroll?

(c) Is the payroll section effectively notified by the personnel department of any changes?

(d) Are payrolls checked:

    (i) with clock cards or other relevant time records,

    (ii) for salesmen's commission based on periodic sales,

    (iii) for correct rates applied,

    (iv) for casts and calculations?

(e) Are payrolls and payroll summaries approved and initialled by a responsible official?

(f) Are all payments for casual labour approved and made against proper documentation?

(g) Are payrolls periodically checked against the independent personal records?

(h) Is written authorization required for overtime, and are the rates clearly laid down?

(i) Are movements between successive payrolls reconciled in terms of numbers and values?

(j) Are wages and salaries regularly compared with budgets, costing records or other management information and significant variances investigated?

(k) Are payroll deductions reconciled with the nominal ledger?

(l) Is the cash for payrolls kept entirely separate from any other sources of cash (e.g. sales, petty cash)? Are all payroll deductions settled by cheques?

KEY QUESTION
4.3 Can other errors occur in payroll calculations?

SUBSIDIARY QUESTIONS
(a) Are there proper authorizations for all payroll deductions other than statutory deductions?

(b) Does the system provide adequate safeguards for dealing with PAYE and other statutory deductions and are these reconciled regularly?

(c) Are the gross wages or salaries and total tax deducted agreed with PAYE returns to the Inland Revenue?

(d) Is the issue of luncheon vouchers satisfactorily controlled?

ICQ5. Sales and trade debtors

KEY QUESTION
5.1 Can goods be dispatched to a bad credit risk?

SUBSIDIARY QUESTIONS
(a) Are orders accepted only from customers whose credit worthiness is acceptable?

(b) Is reference made to the age and amount of debtors' balances prior to further goods being dispatched to them?

(c) Are goods only dispatched against approved orders?

(d) Is there any credit insurance?

KEY QUESTION
5.2 Can goods be dispatched but not invoiced, or vice versa?

SUBSIDIARY QUESTIONS
(a) Can dispatches go unrecorded?

(b) Are there adequate safeguards over the security and access to stores, dispatch areas and other locations where goods are held?

(c) Are dispatch notes:

   (i)   pre-numbered,
   (ii) controlled to ensure that all have been accounted for,
   (iii) checked against goods dispatched?

(d) Does the customer acknowledge receipt of the goods?

(e) Are dispatch notes correlated with:

   (i) sales invoices,
   (ii) stock records?

(f) Can goods be invoiced without a dispatch note?

(g) Is there an adequate system for processing partly completed customers' orders?

(h) Are dispatches in respect of cash sales (including sales to staff) properly controlled?

(i) Is the sale of scrap effectively controlled?

(j) Are modifications made by the customer to his original order properly controlled, and invoiced?

KEY QUESTION
5.3 Can sales be invoiced but not recorded in the accounts?

SUBSIDIARY QUESTIONS
(a) Are invoices pre-numbered?

(b) Is there an independent sequence check of the ledger-posting copies of the invoices?

(c) Are there satisfactory procedures for spoilt and cancelled invoices?

(d) Is there control over 'sale or return' goods?

KEY QUESTION
5.4 Can invoicing errors occur?

SUBSIDIARY QUESTIONS
(a) Are invoices prepared from approved price lists? Is there control over sales or trade discounts on terms different from approved price lists?

(b) Are customers' orders numbered and checked against invoices?

(c) Are invoices checked with dispatch notes?

(d) Are invoices checked arithmetically?

(e) Is there an independent check of amounts recharged for freight, insurance, etc.?

KEY QUESTION
5.5 Can debtors' accounts be improperly credited or returns, etc. not be recorded in accounts?

SUBSIDIARY QUESTIONS
(a) Are credit notes:

(i) prepared from approved price lists and/or checked against original invoice values,

(ii) issued against approved documentation and authorized by a senior official. What are the limits of such authorizations?

(iii) checked with goods returned documents,

(iv) checked arithmetically,

(v) pre-numbered and checked sequentially?

(b) Are cash discounts:

(i) checked to be in accordance with approved terms,

(ii)   checked arithmetically,

(iii)   where found to be excessive, followed up with the customer?

(c) Are transfers between accounts or between sales and purchases ledgers authorized? If so, by whom, and are such transfers and the resulting balances agreed with customers/suppliers?

(d) Are goods-returned documents:

(i)   pre-numbered and checked sequentially,

(ii)   checked to credit notes,

(iii)   checked to stock records, if appropriate?

KEY QUESTION

5.6 Are accounts receivable properly controlled?

SUBSIDIARY QUESTIONS

(a) Are statements sent out on a regular basis?

(b) Is there adequate control over, and identification of, accounts subject to factoring agreements?

(c) Are statements to customers controlled to prevent falsification, suppression or interception prior to mailing?

(d) Are accounts receivable followed up if payment is not received promptly?

(e) Are ledger balances:

(i)   periodically extracted,

(ii)   agreed with an independent control account,

(iii)   aged,

(iv)   reviewed by a responsible official?

(f) Are bad-debt recoveries controlled by a responsible official and bad debts pursued even after being written off?

(g) Are there satisfactory controls over ledger postings covering proof of entries, additions in day books and ledgers, independent control accounts, etc.?

(h) Are any of the sales invoices factored, or pledged as security in any way?

ICQ6. Receipts, payments, bank and cash balances

KEY QUESTION

6.1 Can monies be received but not properly recorded?

SUBSIDIARY QUESTIONS

(a) Is incoming mail controlled to prevent misappropriation between arrival on premises and opening by authorized officials?

(b) Is mail opened in the presence of at least two employees?

(c) Is there rotation of duties on mail opening and are these duties kept strictly separate from cashiers and staff responsible for the maintenance of ledgers, payments of wages, etc.?

(*d*) Are records of over-the-counter cash receipts subject to independent controls?

(*e*) Are all cheques received immediately stamped 'not negotiable—A/C payee only'?

(*f*) Are all remittances received through the post:

(i)   listed in the mail room immediately on receipt,
(ii) entered onto bank paying-in records,
(iii) banked intact as soon as possible?

(*g*) Are remittances received by other employees (e.g. travellers)? If so, are these receipts adequately controlled?

(*h*) Are the remittances to the bank independently scrutinized against the bank statement?

(*i*) Are pre-numbered receipts given for all cash received? If so, is there control over unused receipt books?

(*j*) Are all cash-received sheets and cash books checked to prove that casts and cross casts are correct?

(*k*) Is there adequate control over the accounts classification of receipts?

KEY QUESTION
6.2 Can unauthorized payments be made?

SUBSIDIARY QUESTIONS
(*a*) Are cheques crossed, marked 'A/C Payee' and 'Not Negotiable' before being signed?

(*b*) Are unused cheque books kept in controlled custody?

(*c*) Are at least two signatories required on cheques and are they governed as to authorized limits as to value?

(*d*) Are cheques drawn only against authorized vouchers, remittance advices, etc.?

(*e*) Are supporting documents produced to each cheque signatory before payment is made?

(*f*) Is there adequate check that proper discounts are being obtained where possible?

(*g*) Are the authorized vouchers, etc. immediately stamped 'paid' or otherwise cancelled to prevent duplicate payment?

(*h*) Are cheques mailed without being returned to the drawers of these cheques?

(*i*) Do any cheques carry pre-printed signatures?

(*j*) Are cheques ever signed in blank?

(*k*) If mechanical cheque signers are used, is such use adequately controlled?

(*l*) Is there control over:

(i) cheques drawn for cash,
(ii) payments on account or in advance of delivery?

(*m*) Are all cash payments sheets and cash books checked to prove that casts and cross casts are correct?

(*n*) Are all direct debits and standing orders or bank statements checked for accuracy and authority?

(*o*) Is there adequate control over the accounts classification of payments?

(*p*) Is there proper control of cheques cashed for members of the staff?

KEY QUESTION
6.3 Can cash and bank balances (and negotiable instruments) be misappropriated?

SUBSIDIARY QUESTIONS
(*a*) Are bank reconciliations prepared at least monthly and regularly checked by a senior official other than those responsible for receipts and payments?

(*b*) Are items more than one month old contained in the reconciliation statement thoroughly investigated to establish that they are genuine?

(*c*) Are checks imposed on the sequential numbering of cheques, etc. issued and are all spoiled cheques retained and cancelled?

(*d*) Are transfers between bank accounts authorized by a senior official?

(*e*) Is petty cash subject to an imprest system? Is the float reasonable for the size of business and not excessive?

(*f*) Are all negotiable instruments in hand subject to adequate control?

(*g*) Are petty-cash balances independently counted and reconciled, on an irregular basis?

(*h*) Are cash payments made only against authorized vouchers? Are vouchers then cancelled to prevent duplicate payment?

(*i*) Are IOUs permitted only on the specific authority of a senior official?

ICQ7. Investments and investment income

KEY QUESTION
7.1 Are all purchases and sales of investments authorized, in accordance with the company's policy, and properly recorded in the accounts?

SUBSIDIARY QUESTIONS
(*a*) Are all purchases and sales authorized or approved by responsible officials?

(*b*) Is a proper record maintained of all orders to brokers to buy and sell investments and are brokers' accounts regularly reconciled?

(*c*) Are all records of purchases and sales checked with authorities?

(*d*) Are investment records regularly agreed with the nominal ledger accounts?

(*e*) Are gains or losses on disposal properly calculated?

(*f*) Is the value of securities:

    (i) only written down or off on the authority of a responsible official,

    (ii) reviewed periodically for any changes?

(*g*) Is the company's entitlement to bonus or rights issues properly recorded and checked against other sources (e.g. Extel cards)?

KEY QUESTION

7.2 Can documents of title be lost or misappropriated?

SUBSIDIARY QUESTIONS

(a) Are documents of title physically safeguarded and their location recorded?

(b) Does the system ensure that securities not received promptly are followed up?

(c) Are all investments registered in the name of the client?

(d) Are documents of title subject to periodic physical inspection?

(e) Can documents of title be released other than on authorized written instructions?

(f) Do officials responsible for the purchase or sale of investments or the custody of documents of title have access to the investment records or the nominal ledger?

(g) Are any documents of title pledged as security in any way?

KEY QUESTION

7.3 Is all income due received or otherwise accounted for?

SUBSIDIARY QUESTIONS

(a) Is income mandated directly to a bank account?

(b) Are records of income independently checked with other sources, e.g. published accounts, Extel cards?

(c) Does the system ensure that all income receivable in respect of securities sold 'ex-dividend' is received?

(d) Is all income received in respect of securities sold 'cum dividend' properly accounted for to the purchaser?

(e) Is there a proper system for claiming income on bearer shares?

7.8 Specimen Minimum Controls Checklist

In planning the audit of a small business it will not normally be possible to place so much reliance on internal controls as would be the case for a large business with a more comprehensive system. In the small business, however, the absence of many of the more formal sources of control may be compensated for by the close personal involvement of management on the day-to-day operations.

It is for this reason, in the modified specimen checklist set out below for businesses of this type, the final question in each section requires an assessment as to how far the manager/proprietor supervision effectively compensates for what would otherwise be regarded as weakness in the system. In answering this question it will be necessary to assess *inter alia* whether the manager/proprietor exercises that supervision consistently and with sufficient diligence. This assessment should be made critically, and with an awareness that their close personal involvement in itself makes it easier for management to override controls and to exclude totally from the records transactions which a proper segregation of duties should ensure are included.

MCC1. Supervision, organization and general matters

KEY QUESTION
Is the business conducted in an orderly and profitable manner, including the maintenance of adequate accounting records?

SUBSIDIARY QUESTIONS
1.1   Are the accounting records:
   (a) kept up to date and balanced monthly?
   (b) sufficient to satisfy the minimum requirements of the Companies Act 1985?
   (c) kept in safe custody?
1.2   Are journal entries authorized only by the manager/partner?
1.3   Is a suitable record of fixed assets maintained, periodically checked against assets, and reconciled with the nominal ledger?
1.4   Are investments adequately accounted for and bought and sold only on the authority of the manager/partner?
1.5   Are statutory books and documents of title kept in safe custody?
1.6   Is there adequate insurance cover (particularly fidelity insurance in respect of employees handling cash or desirable goods)?
1.7   Has the division and rotation of duties been developed to the fullest possible extent within the framework of the business?
1.8   Are all staff required to take holidays and are standby arrangements adequate to cover holiday and sickness periods?
1.9   What is the relationship of the manager/partner to the business (e.g. age, length of service, shareholding, relationship to other shareholders/employees, etc.)?
1.10 What is your assessment of the efficiency with which the commercial and accounting aspects of the business are conducted?
1.11 Are budgets used to monitor business performance?
1.12 Are adequate financial statements available to the manager/partner on a regular basis? (Describe form and content: append specimen.)
1.13 Does the manager/partner appear to take a direct and active interest in the financial affairs and reports which are available to him?

MCC2. Purchases and creditors

KEY QUESTION
Is there reasonable assurance that all liabilities are: (a) incurred for the purposes of the business, and (b) fully and properly recorded?

SUBSIDIARY QUESTIONS

2.1   Are all orders evidenced in writing?

2.2   Are purchase orders:
(a) pre-numbered and all numbers accounted for?
(b) approved by the manager/partner?
(c) reviewed for items for which no invoices have been received?

2.3   Is the receipt of goods evidenced in writing?

2.4   Are goods-received records:
(a) pre-numbered and all numbers accounted for?
(b) compared with copy purchase orders?

2.5   Are suppliers' invoices:
(a) checked with purchase orders?
(b) checked with goods-received records?
(c) checked for calculations?
(d) initialled for work done?
(e) approved by the manager/partner and authorized for processing?

2.6   Are purchase ledger balances regularly reconciled with:
(a) suppliers' statements?
(b) the control account?

2.7   Does the extent of manager/partner involvement and/or supervision in this area effectively compensate for any basic control weaknesses noted above?

MCC3. Stocks and work-in-progress

KEY QUESTION
Is there reasonable assurance (a) that stocks cannot be misappropriated or mislaid, and (b) that the records fairly state the cost of all work-in-progress?

SUBSIDIARY QUESTIONS
Stocks

3.1   Are goods stored under proper security and in an orderly manner?

3.2   (a) Are perpetual stock records maintained?
(b) If not, are stocks periodically estimated on the basis of gross-profit tests?

3.3   (a) Is the record (or estimate) of stock periodically checked against physical quantities?
(b) Are material differences always investigated/explained?

3.4   Is the person responsible for the receipt storage and issue of goods independent of any responsibility for the purchases, sales and stock records?

Work-in-progress

3.5   Are interdepartmental transfers of (a) materials, (b) partly finished work, (c) completed work all subject to documentary control?

3.6   Do the work-in-progress records properly identify:
(a) each separate stage of production?

(b) the amount of materials, labour and overheads charged to each job?

3.7 Does the extent of manager/partner involvement and/or supervision in this area effectively compensate for any basic control weaknesses noted above?

MCC4. Wages

KEY QUESTION
Is there reasonable assurance that wages are paid only for work done and that the payroll cannot be inflated?

SUBSIDIARY QUESTIONS
4.1 Are individual personnel records maintained?
4.2 Are adequate time and/or piecework records maintained?
4.3 Is the payroll independently checked for calculations and casts?
4.4 Are all changes in (a) employees and (b) rates of pay authorized only by the manager/partner?
4.5 Is a separate cheque drawn for the exact amount of net pay?
4.6 Does the manager/partner review and approve the payroll before signing the cheque?
4.7 Is the person preparing the payroll independent of any responsibility for the payment of wages?
4.8 Are any amounts being drawn gross, without deduction of PAYE, either through petty cash or the payroll? If so, is it acceptable for Inland Revenue purposes?
4.9 Does the extent of manager/partner involvement and/or supervision in this area effectively compensate for any basic control weaknesses noted above?

MCC5. Sales and debtors

KEY QUESTIONS
Is there reasonable assurance: (a) that all goods leaving the premises are invoiced, (b) that all invoices are recorded and, (c) that debtors' accounts are not improperly credited?

SUBSIDIARY QUESTIONS
5.1 Credit control: does the manager/partner approve all new customers before goods are dispatched to them?
5.2 Are all orders recorded?
5.3 Are delivery notes:
   (a) pre-numbered and all accounted for?
   (b) prepared for all goods leaving the premises?
   (c) correlated with order forms?
   (d) correlated with invoices?

5.4   Are invoices pre-numbered and all accounted for?
5.5   Are credit notes pre-numbered and all accounted for?
5.6   Are discounts, allowances and bad-debt write-offs authorized only by the manager/partner?
5.7   Are statements:
   (a) sent out monthly to all customers?
   (b) reviewed by the manager/partner before mailing?
5.8   Are sales ledger balances listed and reconciled with the control account monthly?
5.9   Does the listing include an age analysis and is this reviewed by the manager/partner?
5.10 Does the extent of manager/partner involvement and/or supervision in this area effectively compensate for any basic control weaknesses noted above?

MCC6. Receipts

KEY QUESTION
Is there reasonable assurance that all monies received are fully and properly recorded?

SUBSIDIARY QUESTIONS
6.1   To what extent does the business:
   (a) sell goods or services for cash?
   (b) deal in 'desirable' products or services which although generally invoiced on credit terms can, in fact, be sold or converted directly for cash)?
6.2   Does the manager/partner open and check the contents of all incoming mail?
6.3   Are all cheques stamped 'A/C payee only'?
6.4   Are over-the-counter takings controlled by cash-register tapes/counter receipts, etc.?
6.5   Are all receipts banked
   (a) regularly?
   (b) intact?
6.6   Is the record of receipts independently checked against bank statements?
6.7   Is the 'cashier' totally independent of any responsibility for the sales or nominal ledger?
6.8   Does the extent of manager/partner involvement and/or supervision in this area effectively compensate for any basic control weaknesses noted above?

MCC7. Payments

KEY QUESTION
Is there reasonable assurance that monies cannot be put to improper use?

SUBSIDIARY QUESTIONS

7.1   Are all payments (except sundry expenses) made by cheque?

7.2   Are all cheques signed:

(a) by the manager/partner?

(b) only after they have been properly completed (i.e. never in blank)?

(c) only on the evidence of supporting documentation?

(d) only after that documentation has been approved and cancelled?

7.3   Are all cheque numbers accounted for?

7.4   (a) Is petty cash subject to an imprest system?

(b) Does the manager/partner approve all items above a set limit?

7.5   Does the manager/partner prepare, or review in detail, regular bank reconciliations?

7.6   Are those responsible for preparing cheques or handling cash totally independent of any responsibility for:

(a) approving or authorizing invoices for payment?

(b) maintaining purchases and nominal ledgers?

7.7   Does the extent of manager/partner involvement and/or supervision in this area effectively compensate for any basic control weaknesses noted above?

Whenever major changes occur in the way a business operates, careful consideration should be given as to whether the use of the MCC will continue to be appropriate. As businesses grow in size, so the level of internal control should correspondingly increase. The position should be appraised afresh each year in order to establish whether the control systems have become sufficiently comprehensive for them to be better assessed by completing a full ICQ. Similarly, a significant expansion in the size of a business which is not matched by an increased level of formal controls should cause a careful reappraisal of the extent to which management supervision can continue to be effective as an alternative.

This assessment of the efficacy of managerial supervision is particularly important, as it follows that failure to comply with the minimum controls specified by the checklist must entail reference in the audit report to accounting inadequacies. This matter of the appropriate form of audit report in the circumstances of the smaller business has been one which has beset the development of Auditing Standards. While we do not believe substantial reliance on managerial supervision automatically has to lead to a form of audit report disclaimer, nevertheless we do not wish to underestimate the number of occasions where such involvement can throw into question the existence of essential and verifiable accounting controls.

In such circumstances the decision may be taken to adopt a non-systems based approach to the audit, i.e. not to rely on internal controls, but rather to follow the 'vouching' approach to the work. This may often be associated with the auditor receiving instructions to undertake extensive accountancy work too, but the audit work must be clearly identifiable as being a separate responsibility.

Annual evaluation and test of internal control
Name of client:
Accounting period:
KEY QUESTION:

Preliminary evaluation			Audit tests					Work done by	
Overall conclusion			C/S†	Sample and population size	Description	Results/conclusions	Audit schedule	Intls	Date
Ref*	Reasons*								

Evaluated by	Date	Tests designed by	Date
Reviewed by	Date	Approved by	Date
		Reviewed by	Date

* List (by reference to supporting documentation) the major strengths and weaknesses of the system which support this conclusion.
† Indicate whether (C)ompliance or (S)ubstantive test.

However, even in these circumstances where the audit concentrates on extensive vouching of transactions and substantiation of year-end balances, the requirement for proper accounting records remains, and this implies the need still to consider a minimum level of controls.

7.9 Evaluation of internal control

The record of the systems and the information obtained from completing either the Internal Control Questionnaire or the Minimum Controls Checklist provides the basis for a preliminary evaluation of the extent of internal control within the system. Such evaluation should be of each key control question. It will be this preliminary evaluation which will determine the nature and extent of the audit tests planned: as such it is critical to the efficiency and effectiveness of the audit and its importance cannot be too greatly emphasized.

Accordingly it should be formally documented, listing—with reference to supporting documentation—the major strengths and weaknesses in a system, and then recording an overall conclusion. Moreover it will be at these major strengths and weaknesses that the subsequent audit testing will be directed, and it may therefore be convenient to devise audit documentation in a manner to facilitate this approach.

A suggested format is set out opposite which combines evaluation of internal control with an audit programme to test the critical areas.

7.10 Summary

If the auditor wishes to rely on the client's system of internal control he or she must first be assured that it is satisfactory in theory, then confirm by testing that it is functioning in practice.

The use of internal control questionnaires is an important and widely used method for the preliminary evaluation of the system, though recent forms of questionnaire introduce the 'key question' concept illustrated in the example in this chapter.

Progress questions

Questions	Reference for answers
(1) Distinguish between the systems based audit approach and the vouching audit approach.	Section 7.1
(2) Define: (a) compliance tests, (b) substantive tests.	Section 7.1
(3) What are the objectives of accounting controls?	Section 7.6
(4) Explain the difference between 'key' and 'subsidiary' questions in an internal control questionnaire (ICQ).	Sections 7.6 and 7.7
(5) List suitable questions for inclusion in an ICQ for the following systems areas, distinguishing clearly between key questions and subsidiary questions: (a) Organizational and general matters (six key questions) (b) Purchases and accounts payable (four) (c) Stocks and costing (eight) (d) Payroll (three) (e) Sales and trade debtors (six) (f) Receipts, payments, bank and cash balances (three) (g) Investments and investment income (three)	Section 7.7
(6) When will the use of a minimum controls checklist be appropriate?	Section 7.8

8 The Audit 1: General principles—auditing the transactions

8.1 Planning audit tests

Having recorded the systems of accounting and internal control and assessed the strengths and weaknesses, the auditor is then in a position to plan the nature and extent of the audit tests he proposes to execute in relation to the company's accounting transactions. The tailoring of the audit programme in this way to the individual demands of different accounting and control systems is fundamental to the concept of systems audits, and again it may be seen how it is dependent upon the care with which the systems evaluation has taken place. A distinction will be drawn between compliance tests, to be applied where internal controls are to be relied upon, and substantive tests. It is important to make this distinction correctly because the nature of the subsequent audit approach may be dependent upon it. In this connection the Planning Audit Tests diagram set out on page 136 may be of assistance as a reminder of the general audit approach already outlined in earlier chapters.

The distinction is also well illustrated in *True and Fair* (Issue 12, Summer 1979, the bulletin of the Auditing Practices Committee), by two examples of the different types of test. Firstly a compliance test: 'to satisfy yourself with reasonable confidence that no goods *can* be dispatched without being invoiced'. This is contrasted with a substantive test: 'to satisfy yourself that no material amounts of goods *have been dispatched without being invoiced*'.

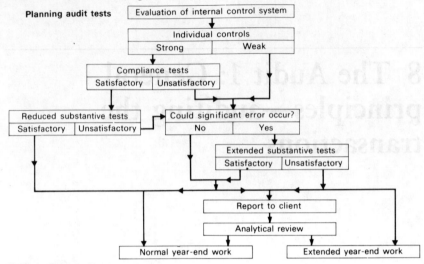

Planning audit tests · Evaluation of internal control system · Individual controls · Strong · Weak · Compliance tests · Satisfactory · Unsatisfactory · Reduced substantive tests · Satisfactory · Unsatisfactory · Could significant error occur? · No · Yes · Extended substantive tests · Satisfactory · Unsatisfactory · Report to client · Analytical review · Normal year-end work · Extended year-end work

8.2 Compliance tests

Compliance tests are explained in the Auditing Guideline on Internal Controls:

'The auditor is not entitled to place any reliance on an internal control based solely on his preliminary evaluation. He should carry out compliance tests to obtain reasonable assurance that the controls on which he wishes to rely were functioning both effectively and throughout the period. It should be noted that it is the control which is being tested by a compliance test, and not the transaction which may be the medium used for the test. For this reason the auditor should record and investigate all exceptions revealed by his compliance testing, regardless of the amount involved in the particular transactions.'

It concludes:

'If compliance tests disclose no exceptions, the auditor may reasonably place reliance on the effective functioning of the internal control tested.'

It is submitted that the auditor will then be able to limit the substantive tests on the relevant accounting information.

Compliance tests are therefore designed to test that the key aspects of the controls have operated so that the auditor is able to rely on the information being produced by the system. For this reason the tests should be concentrated on those aspects of the control system which are fundamental to its efficient and accurate operation. However, if the results of the compliance tests are unsatisfactory—if, for instance, one member of the company's staff is not adequately performing the delegated control function—then the system, notwithstanding the initial evaluation, must be regarded in practice as being weak and, as an alternative, appropriate tests must be designed to evaluate the materiality of that weakness.

The programme of compliance tests will need to be written out by senior staff responsible for the audit because this whole approach of tailoring the work to the different requirements of individual systems precludes the use of any master audit programme suitable for use under a variety of circumstances.

This programme will record the exact details of the work to be performed by the audit staff, columns being provided in order that the persons who are occupied in performing each part of the checking may add their initials as and when they complete it.

If an audit programme is drawn up in this way, the auditor can be certain that all the necessary audit work is planned in a systematic manner after careful consideration of all the circumstances of the case. The auditor may then be certain that the audit staff will cover the whole of the ground, and in future years, the staff engaged upon the audit can see by reference to the programme exactly what work has previously been performed. Further, reporting partners can see at any time what part of the work has been completed, and what remains to be done. In a large practice, unless some such method is adopted, the reporting partners would of necessity lose a very large amount of control, and be very much in the hands of their staff. Then the efficiency of the audit would depend, not upon the skill and competence of such partners, but upon the skill and competency of the member of staff in charge of the particular audit.

An objection to the programming of audit tests is that the staff may lose a sense of responsibility, and consequently carry out the work in a mechanical manner. It should be impressed upon them, therefore, that the programme set out is the basis upon which the audit is to be conducted, and that they must use their intelligence when carrying it out. They should be encouraged to recommend additions and improvements to the audit programme. It should constantly be borne in mind that experience shows that serious discrepancies in accounts are frequency revealed by unprogrammed investigations and inquiries.

The greatest danger in practical auditing is that the work may become mechanical. Most businesses are in a process of continual change, and this process inevitably extends to the accounting system. These changes will be disclosed by the continual review of the system of internal control, and the audit programme must be regularly modified to ensure that it, too, is kept up to date.

For this reason it is important that the audit programme, besides recording the actual test carried out, should be cross-referenced to the appropriate questions in the internal control questionnaire and should clearly identify any errors or weaknesses found during the execution of the tests, as those may affect the overall view taken of the adequacy of the internal control. Thus, if the compliance tests have disclosed exceptions which indicate that the control being tested was not operating properly in practice, the auditor should determine the reasons. He or she needs to assess whether each exception is only an isolated departure or is representative of others, and whether it indicates the possible existence of errors in the accounting records. If the explanation received suggests that the exception is only an isolated departure, then the auditor must confirm the validity of that explanation, for example by carrying out further tests. If the explanation or the further tests confirm that the control being tested was not operating properly throughout the period, then he or she cannot rely on that control. In these circumstances the auditor should determine whether it will be possible to seek to rely on an alternative control and carry out compliance tests on that, or whether the substantive testing cannot be restricted.

8.3 Substantive tests

The Auditing Guideline on Audit Evidence states that:

'Audit test may be classified as "compliance" or "substantive" according to their primary purpose. Both purposes are sometimes achieved concurrently. Substantive tests are those tests of transactions and balances, and other procedures such as an analytical review, which provide audit evidence as to the completeness, accuracy and validity of the information contained in the accounting records or in the financial statements.'

The nature, extent and timing of the substantive tests are determined by the degree of reliance which the auditor can place on the operation of internal controls.

Where there are no contols on which to place reliance, or where the auditor has decided that it will be more efficient to disregard the existence of internal controls, he or she will similarly need to design and carry out substantive tests in such a way as to obtain reasonable assurance that material error or omission has not occurred.

Substantive tests must therefore be adopted in relation to items which are material to the validity of the accounts and may need to be extended where compliance tests have proved the controls to be weak.

Designing substantive tests appropriate to individual circumstances often calls for some ingenuity on the part of the auditor; but the nature of the resultant detailed tests of transactions will generally fall into one or more of the following broad classifications and should be recorded in a programme similar to that used for compliance tests.

8.3.1 Vouching approach

Vouching means the examination of the transactions of a business, together with documentary and other evidence of sufficient validity to satisfy an auditor that such transactions are in order, have been properly authorized, and are correctly recorded in the accounting records. By this means the auditor goes behind the accounting records and traces the entries to their source, and it is in this way that he or she can ascertain the full meaning and circumstances of the various transactions. In the absence of an effective internal control system, the entries in the records may show only such information as the client's accountant chooses to disclose, and such information may be purposely, or unintentionally, contrary to the true facts. Therefore, only by examining external evidence can an auditor possibly ascertain the real state of affairs.

The vouching approach has its place in every audit, but extensive vouching should be restricted to circumstances of weakness and should only be adopted with caution and after careful consideration of what it will achieve. This method of audit testing is very time-consuming and the auditor must always be wary lest, even after extensive vouching, the state of the control systems is such that it is still not possible to derive assurance as to the accuracy of the recording of other transactions which have not been vouched.

8.3.2 Examination of management information

This would include the detailed review of management accounts, together with their comparison with budgeted results and actual financial statements for comparable periods in prior years, from which the auditor would follow up any unusual features disclosed.

Similarly he or she would undertake appropriate ratio analysis of figures connected with the area of weakness, the resultant ratios being compared with those expected and those being achieved by comparable companies within the same industry group.

8.3.3 Extended balance-sheet audit work

Especially in the absence of a satisfactory system of internal control, the auditor may find the most effective form of substantive test, and in some cases the only practicable one, to be an extension of the audit work on the final accounts figures. For instance, if the key control question 'Can goods be dispatched to a bad credit risk?' receives an affirmative answer, then the most effective audit test will be an extension of the year-end balance sheet work necessary to verify the adequacy of the provision for bad and doubtful debts.

Such applications of substantive testing to year-end balances and financial statements will be matters to which we shall return in later chapters.

8.4   The Guideline on Audit Evidence

It is appropriate at this point to introduce the very important Auditing Guideline on Audit Evidence, issued in April 1980. This deals with the qualities audit evidence should have, types of test and techniques of audit testing.

APC Guideline on audit evidence

Introduction

(1) Paragraph 4 of the Auditing Standard *The auditor's operational standard* states that:

> 'The auditor should obtain relevant and reliable audit evidence sufficient to enable him to draw reasonable conclusions therefrom.'

This Auditing Guideline, which gives guidance on how that paragraph may be applied, should be read in conjunction with the Explanatory Foreword to Auditing Standards and Guidelines including the Glossary of Terms.

Background

The nature of audit evidence

(2) Audit evidence is information obtained by the auditor in arriving at the conclusions on which he bases his opinion on the financial statements. Sources of audit evidence include the accounting systems and underlying documentation of the enterprise, its tangible assets, management and employees, its customers, suppliers and other third parties who have dealings with, or knowledge of, the enterprise or its business.

(3) The sources and amount of evidence needed to achieve the required level of assurances are questions for the auditor to detemine by exercising his judgement in the light of the opinion called for under the terms of his engagement. He will be influenced by the materiality of the matter being examined, the relevance and reliability of evidence available from each source and the cost and time involved in obtaining it. Often the auditor will obtain evidence from several sources which, together, will provide him with the necessary assurance.

Sufficiency

(4) The auditor can rarely be certain of the validity of the financial statements. However, he needs to obtain sufficient relevant and reliable evidence to form a reasonable basis for his opinion thereon. The auditor's judgement as to what

constitutes sufficient relevant and reliable audit evidence is influenced by such factors as:

(a) his knowledge of the business of the enterprise and the industry in which it operates;

(b) the degree of risk of misstatement through errors or irregularities; this risk may be affected by such factors as: (i) the nature and materiality of the items in the financial statements; (ii) the auditor's experience as to the reliability of the management and staff of the enterprise and of its records; (iii) the financial position of the enterprise; (iv) possible management bias;

(c) the persuasiveness of the evidence.

Relevance

(5) The relevance of the audit evidence should be considered in relation to the overall audit objective of forming an opinion and reporting on the financial statements. To achieve this objective the auditor needs to obtain evidence to enable him to draw reasonable conclusions in answer to the following questions.

Balance sheet items

(a) Have all of the assets and liabilities been recorded?

(b) Do the recorded assets and liabilities exist?

(c) Are the assets owned by the enterprise and are the liabilities properly those of the enterprise?

(d) Have the amounts attributed to the assets and liabilities been arrived at in accordance with the stated accounting policies, on an acceptable and consistent basis?

(e) Have the assets, liabilities and capital and reserves been properly disclosed?

Profit and loss account items

(f) Have all income and expenses been recorded?

(g) Did the recorded income and expense transactions in fact occur?

(h) Have the income and expenses been measured in accordance with the stated accounting policies, on an acceptable and consistent basis?

(i) Have income and expenses been properly disclosed where appropriate?

Reliability

(6) Although the reliability of audit evidence is dependent upon the particular circumstances, the following general presumptions may be found helpful:

(a) documentary evidence is more reliable than oral evidence;

(b) evidence obtained from independent sources outside the enterprise is more reliable than that secured solely from within the enterprise;

(c) evidence originated by the auditor by such means as analysis and physical inspection is more reliable than evidence obtained from others.

(7) The auditor should consider whether the conclusions drawn from differing types of evidence are consistent with one another. When audit evidence obtained from one source appears inconsistent with that obtained from another, the reliability of each remains in doubt until further work has been done to resolve the inconsistency. However, when the individual items of evidence relating to a particular

matter are all consistent, then the auditor may obtain a cumulative degree of assurance higher than that which he obtains from the individual items.

Procedures

Obtaining audit evidence

(8) Audit evidence is obtained by carrying out audit tests which may be classified as 'substantive' or 'compliance' according to their primary purpose. Both such purposes are sometimes achieved concurrently. Substantive tests are defined as those tests of transactions and balances, and other procedures such as analytical review, which seek to provide audit evidence as to the completeness, accuracy and validity of the information contained in the accounting records or in the financial statements. Compliance tests are defined as those tests which seek to provide audit evidence that internal control procedures are being applied as prescribed.

(9) The auditor may rely on appropriate evidence obtained by substantive testing to form his opinion, provided that sufficient of such evidence is obtained. Alternatively, he may be able to obtain assurance from the presence of a reliable system of internal control, and thereby reduce the extent of substantive testing. The audit procedures which are appropriate when the auditor wishes to place reliance on the enterprise's internal controls are set out in the Auditing Guideline *Internal Controls*.

Techniques of audit testing

(10) Techniques of audit testing fall into the following broad categories:

(a) *Inspection*—reviewing or examining records, documents or tangible assests. Inspection of records and documents provides evidence of varying degrees of reliability depending upon their nature and source (see paragraph 6b above). Inspection of tangible assets provides the auditor with reliable evidence as to their existence, but not necessarily as to their ownership, cost or value.

(b) *Observation*—looking at an operation or procedure being performed by others with a view to determining the manner of its performance. Observation provides reliable evidence as to the manner of the performance at the time of observation, but not at any other time.

(c) *Enquiry*—seeking relevant information from knowledgeable persons inside or outside the enterprise, whether formally or informally, orally or in writing. The degree of reliability that the auditor attaches to evidence obtained in this manner is dependent on his opinion of the competence, experience, independence and integrity of the respondent.

(d) *Computation*—checking the arithmetical accuracy of accounting records or performing independent calculations.

Analytical review procedures

(11) In addition to the above techniques, there are analytical review procedures, referred to in paragraph 8 above. These procedures include studying significant ratios, trends and other statistics and investigating any unusual or unexpected variations. The precise nature of these procedures and the manner in which they are documented will depend on the circumstances of each audit.

(12) The comparisons which can be made will depend on the nature, accessibility

and relevance of the data available. Once the auditor has decided on the comparisons which he intends to make in performing his analytical review, he should determine what variations he expects to be disclosed by them.

(13) Unusual or unexpected variations, and expected variations which fail to occur, should be investigated. Explanations obtained should be verified and evaluated by the auditor to determine whether they are consistent with his understanding of the business and his general knowledge. Explanations may indicate a change in the business of which the auditor was previously unaware in which case he should reconsider the adequacy of his audit approach. Alternatively they may indicate the possiblity of misstatements in the financial statements; in these cicumstances the auditor will need to extend his testing to determine whether the financial statements do include material misstatements.

8.5 Suggested tests for auditing transactions

Set out below are examples of typical audit tests which may be appropriate to the key control questions outlined in Chapter 7. It should now be appreciated that these are merely guidelines, and any selection of these tests will need to be augmented by additional work specifically designed for the precise circumstances under review.

In drawing up detailed tests it will always be helpful to refer to the Auditing Guideline on Audit Evidence. Look back at paragraph 10 of that Guideline reproduced in Section 8.4.

The Guideline further puts forward the following general presumptions concerning the reliability of audit evidence:

'documentary evidence is more reliable than oral evidence;
evidence obtained from independent sources outside the enterprise is more reliable than that secured solely from within the enterprise;
evidence originated by the auditor by such means as analysis and physical inspection is more reliable than evidence obtained from others'.

From this we may conclude that the most effective audit tests will involve the *auditor* obtaining *documentary* evidence from *independent* third parties; the least effective may be those which rely on oral evidence obtained within the company; and accordingly the detailed audit programme should be constructed with this in mind.

8.5.1 Organizational and general matters

General
1. Obtain a copy of organization chart.
2. Consider internal control effected by division of duties.

3. Consider actual results against budget and ascertain reasons for major variances.
4. Examine reports of internal audit department and note points for particular attention.
5. Check that accounting procedures laid down are satisfactory and are being maintained.
6. Test specific areas of laid-down accounting procedures.

Secretarial
1. Check records of use of seal from mintue book and note any points affecting audit.
2. Extract and agree schedules of members and debenture holders to total issued capital, etc.
3. Reconcile unclaimed dividend/interest account.
4. Examine minutes, noting approval and any points affecting audit.
5. Inspect all statutory books and confirm up to date.

Fixed assets
1. Check compliance with rules laid down for authorizing capital expenditure or disposals.
2. Check actual costs, etc. against budgets and ascertain reasons for major variances.
3. Consider correctness of records (including overhead allocation) of capital works carried out by company.
4. Examine asset register, vouch movements and note periodic check by company.
5. Test existence of assets.
6. Check depreciation calculations.
7. Check reconciliation of asset register to nominal ledger.

Insurance
1. Obtain a schedule of insurance policies and the extent of cover, and review for adequacy and completeness.
2. Check that all required declarations and certificates have been submitted.

Group trading
1. Obtain a schedule of all group, associated and other affiliated companies.
2. Enquire into relevant interests in other concerns with which the company has dealings.
3. Check that all transfers of funds have been properly authorized and recorded and that the relevant statutory and other requirements have been complied with.
4. Test transactions and note and inquire into any that appear to be on other than arm's length terms.
5. Inquire into any expenditure made for or by, and income received for or by, such concerns and test with relevant documentation.

Nominal ledger
1. Test nominal ledger casts.
2. Test extraction of trial balance and casts.
3. Examine nominal ledger for unusual entries.
4. Examine journal entries and authorizations.
5. Test journal postings to nominal ledger.
6. Vouch sample of journal entries.

8.5.2 Purchases and accounts payable

COMPLIANCE TESTS
1. Test sequence of purchase orders.
2. Test approval of purchase orders.
3. Test adherence to authority limits.
4. Test sequence of goods-received records.
5. Test sequence of goods-returned records.
6. Test authorization of adjustments to purchase ledger balances.
7. Test that purchase invoices are serially numbered.
8. Test sequence of purchase invoices.
9. Test correlation of purchase invoices with purchase orders and goods-received records.
10. Test correlation of credit notes with goods-returned records.
11. Test that casts and calculations on purchase invoices have been checked.
12. Test that purchase invoices have been coded for accounting classification purposes.
13. Test that VAT has been correctly segregated.
14. Test that purchase invoice 'grid' has been initialled for work done.
15. Test approval of purchase invoices for processing into accounting system.

SUBSTANTIVE TESTS
1. Test purchase orders in relation to nature of company's business.
2. Select sample of goods-received records and:
   (a) note whether goods received have been checked as to quantity and quality;
   (b) check against suppliers' advice notes;
   (c) trace copies of purchasing, accounts, and stock records department.
3. Test goods-returned records to stock records.
4. Review:
   (a) outstanding purchase orders;
   (b) outstanding goods-received records;
   (c) outstanding goods-returned records.
5. Examine reconciliations of purchase ledger balances with suppliers' statements.
6. Review debit balances in purchase ledger.

7. Check purchase invoices to purchase orders and goods-received records for relevant details.
8. Check purchase invoice codings for accounting classification purposes.
9. Test casts and calculations on purchase invoices.
10. Select sample of purchase invoices and test postings to:
    (a) personal account;
    (b) control account;
    (c) nominal account.
11. Agree list of balances to control account.
12. Review nominal accounts for expenses for unusual items.
13. Inquire into procedures for identification of liabilities secured by reservation of title.
14. Test procedures relating to recording purchases subject to reservation of title.

8.5.3 Stocks and costing

COMPLIANCE TESTS
1. Observe physical security over stocks.
2. Test recording of stock movements.
3. Test authority for stock adjustments.
4. Test authority for dumping of stocks.
5. Test recording of stock movements relating to third parties.
6. Test authority for stock movements.
7. Inspect cost-variance analyses.
8. Test identification of stocks held subject to reservation of title.

SUBSTANTIVE TESTS
1. Examine selected stock records, vouch movements and count stock balances.
2. Examine calculations supporting shrinkage allowances.
3. Confirm stock reports from third parties and stock records.
4. Vouch cost records with underlying documentation.
5. Test transfer of information from cost records to financial records.

8.5.4 Wages

COMPLIANCE TESTS
1. Test sample of time records, etc. for:
    (a) approval by responsible official;
    (b) check of casts and calculations.
2. Test authority for payment of casual labour.
3. Observe wages distribution for adherence to procedures.
4. Test authorizations for payroll amendments.
5. Test control over payroll amendments.
6. Examine evidence of checking of payroll calculations.

7. Examine evidence of approval of payrolls by a responsible official.
8. Examine evidence of independent checks on payrolls.
9. Inspect payroll reconciliations.
10. Examine explanations for payroll expense variances.
11. Test authorities for payroll deductions.
12. Inspect reconciliations of payroll deductions.

SUBSTANTIVE TESTS
1. Select sample of time records, etc. and test casts and calculations.
2. Test sample of personnel records for:
   (a) rates of pay;
   (b) authorization of changes in rates of pay;
   (c) leavers' and joiners' personnel details.
3. Select payrolls and:
   (a) check to time records, etc.;
   (b) test to personnel records;
   (c) test casts and calculations;
   (d) vouch deductions.
4. Vouch sample of payroll reconciliations.
5. Test totals of cheques drawn to net pay due.
6. Test controls over unclaimed wages and vouch signatures for receipts to personnel records.
7. Test postings of payrolls to nominal accounts.

8.5.5 Sales and accounts receivable

COMPLIANCE TESTS
1. Test approval of orders for creditworthiness.
2. Test sequence of dispatch notes.
3. Test customer acknowledgements of receipt of goods.
4. Test correlation of dispatch notes with sales invoices.
5. Test correlation of sales invoices with dispatch notes.
6. Test sequence of sales invoices.
7. Test postings of sales invoices to personal and nominal accounts.
8. Test that invoices quote customers' order numbers.
9. Test evidence of arithmetical check on sales invoices.
10. Test that VAT has been correctly segregated.
11. Test sequence of credit notes.
12. Test correlation of credit notes with goods-returned documents.
13. Test authorization of credit notes.
14. Test evidence of arithmetical check on credit notes.
15. Test authority for bad-debts written-off.
16. Test sequence of returned-goods documents to credit notes.
17. Test correlation of returned-goods documents to credit notes.
18. Test postings of credit notes to personal and nominal accounts.
19. Test authorization of transfers between personal accounts.
20. Test debtors ageing analysis.

SUBSTANTIVE TESTS
1. Review selected credit limits.
2. Check that credit limits have not been exceeded.
3. Examine stores and dispatch security.
4. Select sample of sales invoices and:
    (a) check to customer order;
    (b) note whether details agree to dispatch records;
    (c) check prices against independent sources;
    (d) check extensions and casts;
    (e) check postings to personal and nominal accounts.
5. Select sample of credit notes and:
    (a) check to returned-goods documents;
    (b) check prices;
    (c) check extensions and casts;
    (d) check authorization;
    (e) check postings to personal and nominal accounts.
6. Test cash discounts in accordance with approved terms and for arithmetical correctness.
7. Check sample of bad-debts written-off against external evidence.
8. Agree list of balances to control account.
9. Observe procedures for dispatch of statements to debtors.
10. Review follow-up procedures for recovery of bad-debts written-off.

8.5.6 Receipts, payments, bank and cash balances

COMPLIANCE TESTS
1. Attend mail-opening procedures.
2. Test control medium for cash receipts for independent check to bank lodgements.
3. Test sequence of any pre-numbered receipts for cash.
4. Test authority for cash discounts.
5. Test evidence of arithmetical check on cash-received records.
6. Inspect current cheque books for:
    (a) restrictive endorsements;
    (b) sequential use;
    (c) controlled custody;
    (d) any signatures in blank.
7. Test cancellation of paid vouchers.
8. Test evidence of arithmetical check on cash payment records.
9. Examine evidence of authority for current standing orders and direct debits.
10. Examine evidence of regular bank reconciliations.
11. Examine evidence of independent check of bank reconciliations.
12. Examine evidence of follow-up of outstanding items on bank reconciliations.
13. Test petty cash vouchers for approval.
14. Test cancellation of paid petty cash vouchers.

15. Test evidence of arithmetical check on petty cash records.
16. Examine evidence of independent check of petty cash balance.

SUBSTANTIVE TESTS

1. Test mail-room listings of receipts to:
   (a) bank paying-in records;
   (b) cash-received records;
   (c) bank statement; and confirm prompt banking.
2. Test control medium for cash receipts to bank lodgements.
3. Vouch miscellaneous receipts.
4. Test rates and calculations of cash discounts.
5. Test casts and cross casts of cash-received records.
6. Test postings of cash-received to:
   (a) personal account or nominal account;
   (b) control account(s).
7. Vouch miscellaneous cash payments outside purchase ledger system.
8. Test casts and cross casts of cash payment records.
9. Test postings of cash payments to:
   (a) personal account or nominal account;
   (b) control account(s).
10. Vouch sample of returned cheques (if available).
11. Check selected bank reconciliations in detail.
12. Vouch transfers between bank accounts and reimbursements of petty cash.
13. Vouch sample of petty-cash payments and sundry petty-cash payments and sundry petty-cash receipts.
14. Test casts and cross casts of petty-cash records.
15. Count and reconcile petty-cash float.
16. Test petty-cash postings.
17. Test that exchanged cheques are banked promptly.

8.5.7 Investments and investment income

1. Test purchases and sales with evidence of authority and confirm prices with contract notes.
2. Test agreement of investment records with nominal ledger at dates throughout period.
3. Test nominal ledger postings and casts.
4. Test calculation of gains or losses on disposal.
5. Check authority for writing-down or -off investments.
6. Test holdings against external sources for entitlement to bonus and rights issues.
7. Examine security of documents of title.
8. Inspect documents of title to confirm that registered in name of client.
9. Examine evidence of checks carried out by client.
10. Test authorization for release of documents of title.

8.6   Sampling

Having decided on the nature of the audit tests to be applied in the individual circumstances, it remains to decide on the extent of those tests and the method to be adopted for the selection of the given sample. Broadly there are two ways of selecting an audit sample: either by the use of random selection techniques or otherwise by the exercise of personal judgement in a number of ways.

Sampling is a complex matter which needs detailed consideration. It is covered fully in the next chapter.

8.7   Materiality

Our initial description of the first stages of obtaining audit evidence would not be complete without introducing the concept of materiality, as the Auditing Standards contain several references to the subject and references to the materiality or significance of an item also appear with some frequency in the Companies Act and in Statements of Standard Accounting Practice. Moreover its consideration is germane to the ensuing chapters dealing with the audit of the profit and loss account and balance sheet.

A set of financial statements summarizes a mass of facts, and those who prepare and report on them have to extract from all that information those items which have a real bearing on the true and fair view. Not to disclose an important fact or figure may give a misleading view to the financial statement; conversely, the overall view can be obscured by the inclusion of too much detail. A true and fair view can take a variety of forms. There are degrees of latitude involved in the preparation of financial statements, the acceptable parameters of which are dictated by judgements as to materiality. Materiality is fundamental to the whole audit process and it has many aspects from an auditors' point of view. It influences the extent of his or her field work, the scope and thrust of the detailed audit tests, and the way in which he or she will substantiate particular assets and liabilities. It also has a bearing on evaluation of any errors or discrepancies disclosed by the audit work. Thus the extent to which the auditor will increase the substantive tests will depend largely on an evaluation of the significance of the way in which the error has arisen.

We also have to be concerned with materiality in the accounting disclosure and reporting sense, and particularly in so far as it has a bearing on the principles of presentation in financial statements. For this purpose, the English Institute's Statement V.10 (2.206), *The Interpretation of 'Material' in Relation to Accounts,* offers the following definition:

'A matter is material if its non-disclosure, misstatement or omission would be likely to distort the view given by the accounts or other statement under consideration.'

Matters which may require decisions as to materiality in this sense include the following:

—whether an error should be corrected before financial statements are issued;
—whether an item should be separately disclosed;
—whether an accounting policy needs disclosure and explanation;
—whether the fact, and financial effect, of a change in accounting policy needs to be disclosed and explained;
—whether the auditor should draw attention in the report to a departure from acceptable accounting policies.

It should be noted that the English Institute preface their definition of materiality by describing the word as requiring a 'wide interpretation according to the variety of circumstances which can arise' and therefore that it is 'not possible or desirable...to give a precise definition of such an expression'.

In other words, the materiality of an item is relative to the circumstances surrounding it and it is therefore essentially a matter of judgement. That judgement must be based on professional experience, an awareness of the particular circumstances, and with regard for the needs of the readers of the financial statements. As far as the auditor is concerned, his or her judgement as to materiality must be grounded in a sound knowledge of the business of the company upon which he or she is reporting.

The auditor's judgement will always be personal and highly subjective, but there is room for making that judgement more than purely arbitrary. Whilst it must be stressed that the intention throughout is not to eliminate the need for professional judgement—which would be both impossible and undesirable—but merely to guide it, nevertheless attempts have been made to provide specific definitions of materiality in percentage forms.

A percentage limit requires some basis against which to calculate the percentage. If the materiality of an item is to be assessed in the context of the overall view of the financial statements, then in the great majority of cases it will be judged in terms of its impact on profits. In so far as profits are an important indicator of performance, and of primary significance to the readers of financial statements, net profit would seem to be the most appropriate basis against which to measure the materiality of an item.

Profits, however, can be unstable. Consequently, the same amount might—because of a change in profitability—be judged material in one year and immaterial in the next. Similarly, low profits or losses may give rise to unacceptability small materiality limits. A better basis for comparing materiality of an item might therefore be the average or 'normal' profits for a number of years. Normal profits would be before extraordinary items and before taxation.

Perhaps the most useful percentage levels suggested are in the proposals contained in a Statement issued by the Institute of Chartered Accountants in Australia in August 1974. This document might be thought to provide a convenient working guide to practical materiality decisions and can be summarized as follows:

(a) When considering the materiality of an item, it should be compared with an appropriate base amount. The following base amounts should be used:
(1) profit and loss account items should be compared with the operating profit for the current year or with the average operating profit for the last five years, whichever is the more relevant measure of profit having regard to the trend of business over that period;
(2) balance sheet items should be compared with the lower of:
—total share capital and reserves, and
—the appropriate balance sheet class total.
(b) The above comparison should be guided by the following percentage limits:
(1) an amount of 10 per cent or more of the appropriate base amount should be presumed to be material unless there is evidence to the contrary;
(2) an amount of 5 per cent or less of the appropriate base amount should be presumed to be immaterial unless there is evidence to the contrary;
(3) the materiality of an amount which lies between 5 and 10 per cent of the appropriate base amount is a matter of judgement depending upon the circumstances.

In general there are two broad factors relating to the materiality of any item, both of which will usually be considered together, but each of which might have particular bearing on the final decision: firstly, the nature or characteristics of the item in question; secondly, its amount. While percentage guidelines may be helpful, they should neither predicate nor dictate judgement. In the final analysis, the materiality of an item can only be assessed in terms of its impact on the overall view given by the financial statements in the light of existing circumstances. Some of the more general matters which might influence decisions as to materiality are described below.

Recurring or non-recurring: An item of a non-recurring or exceptional nature or arising from unusual circumstances is likely *prima facie* to be of more significance than an item arising out of the ordinary activities of the business.

Statutory requirement: The permissible margin of error on items subject to the disclosure requirements of the Companies Act will often be very small. Indeed for items such as directors' and auditors' remuneration or investment income, there can be very little latitude at all. Matters such as these are believed to be of particular relevance to the readers of financial statements and any error or misstatement might be regarded as material even though its impact on the overall true and fair view may be trivial.

Degree of estimation: The value of an item may be capable of precise measurement (for example debtors, cash balances and monetary amounts in general) or it may be based on estimates and assumptions (such as stock or depreciation). The degree of latitude permissible in the former case is likely to be narrower than in the latter.

Material in principle: Even though the amount involved is significant, it may be necessary to regard an item as material because of a departure from some acceptable accounting policy. For example, describing as extraordinary an item which is manifestly not so might be regarded as a material distortion of the overall view, even if the amount involved is insignificant. Similarly, a change in accounting policy might, in a particular case, be expected to have a major impact on the results of future periods—and may therefore require disclosure—even though the effect on the current year is negligible.

Trend: When assessing the materiality of the amount of an item the overriding test is its effect on the reported earnings or net worth of the business. However, the amount involved should also be judged in the light of the relevant trend, since it might be said that the reported earnings of a company for any one period are *per se* of less importance than the trend of that company's profits over a number of periods. To the extent that readers of financial statements can be said to regard the trend of profits as important, any materiality decision must also be viewed in that context.

Related amounts: The emphasis on the trend of results suggests that the materiality of an item might be assessed in a wider context; it should also, however, be viewed in the narrower context of its relationship with other amounts which appear in the financial statements. Thus the materiality of an item might be judged in terms of the corresponding amount for the previous year or in terms of the caption or class of which it forms part.

Critical points: An item which would otherwise be regarded as insignificant might, if corrected or disclosed, have a critical impact on the overall view. A minor adjustment might have the effect of turning a small profit into a small loss, or of revealing as marginally insolvent what would otherwise have appeared to be marginally solvent. Similarly an amount can assume disproportionate significance and this may have particular bearing on the matter of disclosure, especially where the reader might have expected the amount to be far greater than in fact it is.

Matters such as these go to emphasize that there are many aspects to any one materiality decision; that more is called for than the strict application of percentage guidelines; and that it is the exercise of professional judgement in specific circumstances which is required. Whatever the final decision, the auditor would be well advised to place a well-documented note of his or her conclusion, together with the reasons which support it, on the audit file.

8.8 Reliance on other specialists

In the affairs of some clients there will be technical matters with which the auditor will be unfamiliar—confirming the value of specialized stock, for example. In this situation the auditor may be compelled to seek the assistance of independent specialists.

The APC issued a Draft Guideline on this subject in December 1984:

Auditing Guideline: Reliance on Other Specialists

Preface

Paragraph 4 of the Auditing Standard 'The Auditor's operational standard' states that: 'The auditor should obtain relevant and reliable audit evidence sufficient to enable him to draw reasonable conclusions therefrom'.

This guideline provides guidance on the principles to be followed by the auditor when he wishes to place reliance on audit evidence provided by specialists.

The guideline does not apply to reliance on specialists employed by the auditor, to whom the same considerations apply as with other audit staff. For further guidance in respect of the auditor's employees reference should be made to the Auditing Guideline 'Planning, controlling and recording'.

Reliance on the work of other auditors, both external and internal, will be dealt with in separate guidelines. Additional detailed guidance on the relationship between the auditors and the actuaries of long-term insurance funds is also given separately, and, because of their specialist nature, separate guidance on the audit of pension schemes will be developed.

This guideline is supplementary to and should be read in conjunction with, Auditing Standards and related Auditing Guidelines.

Introduction

(1) The auditor has, through training and experience, a general knowledge of business, but is not expected to have the detailed knowledge and experience of specialists in other disciplines.

(2) For the purpose of this guideline, a specialist is a person or firm possessing special skills, knowledge and experience in a discipline other than accounting or auditing.

(3) During the course of an audit, the auditor may need to consider audit evidence in the form of statistical data, reports, opinions, valuations or statements from

specialists such as valuers, architects, engineers, actuaries, geologists, lawyers, stockbrokers or quantity surveyors. Examples include:

(a) valuations of fixed assets, including freehold and leasehold property, plant and machinery, works of art and antiques;

(b) the measurement of work done on long term contracts;

(c) valuations of certain types of stocks and consumable materials, including the determination of their quantity and composition;

(d) geological determination of mineral reserves and characteristics;

(e) the legal interpretation of agreements, statutes or regulations;

(f) legal opinions on the outcomes of disputes and litigation; and

(g) actuarial advice for the purpose of assessing the cost of pension provision and its disclosure in the employer's financial statements.

(4) The guidance below is presented in the context of reliance on the work of a particular specialist. Where the nature of the business of an enterprise is such that a number of specialists produce reports routinely for management purposes, (for example, regular site valuation reports by quantity surveyors in a contracting company) the scope of the work performed by the auditor will need to take account of the frequent and systematic way that reports are produced and his previous experience of the reliability and objectivity of such information.

Considerations for the auditor

Determining the need for specialist evidence

(5) When planning the audit, the auditor should consider whether specialist evidence may be necessary in order to form his opinion.

(6) When determining the need for specialist evidence regarding information contained in, or relevant to, the financial statements, the auditor should consider:

(a) the materiality of, and the likelihood of significant error in, the information being examined;

(b) the complexity of the information, together with his knowledge and understanding of it and of any specialism relating to it; and

(c) whether there are any alternative sources of audit evidence.

(7) Requests for specialist evidence should be made either by the management of the client, or by the auditor, after obtaining the consent of management.

(8) Where management is unable or unwilling to obtain specialist evidence, the auditor does not have a responsibility to seek that evidence independently by engaging his own specialist. If there is insufficient alternative audit evidence to enable the auditor to draw reasonable conclusions, then he can properly discharge his responsibilities by qualifying his audit report.

Competence and objectivity of the specialist

(9) The auditor should satisfy himself that the specialist is competent to provide the audit evidence he requires. Normally this will be indicated by technical qualifications or membership of an appropriate professional body.

Exceptionally, in the absence of any such indications of his competence, the specialist's experience and established reputation may be taken into account.

(10) The auditor should consider the relationship between the specialist and the client: whether, for example, the specialist or any of his partners or co-directors are closely related to the client, or are directors or employees of the client or its associates. In particular, the auditor should consider whether the specialist's objectivity is likely to be impaired by such a relationship. This may be the case if the specialist has a significant financial interest in the client. He should also consider the extent to which the specialist is bound by the disciplines of his professional body or by statutory requirements to act responsibly, notwithstanding his relationship to the client.

(11) The auditor's assessment of the specialist's competence and objectivity will influence his evaluation of the evidence provided by the specialist, and his decision on the extent to which he can place reliance on that evidence. If the auditor believes that the specialist may not be sufficiently competent or objective to provide the audit evidence which is needed, he should discuss his reservations with the management of the client.

Agreement on scope of the work of the specialist

(12) It is desirable that, where the evidence of a specialist is to be provided, there should be consultation between the auditor, the client and the specialist, in order to establish the specialist's terms of reference. This should take place as soon as is practicable after the specialist has been appointed. The terms of reference should be documented, reviewed annually where applicable, and preferably confirmed in writing, and should include the following:

(a) the objectives, scope and subject matter of the specialist's work;

(b) the sources of information to be provided to the specialist;

(c) the identification of any relationship which may affect the specialist's objectivity;

(d) the assumptions upon which the specialist's report depends, and the bases to be used, and their compatibility with the assumptions and bases used in preparing the financial statements;

(e) where appropriate, a comparison of the assumptions and bases to be used with those used in preceding periods, together with explanations for any changes;

(f) the use to be made of the specialist's findings in relation to the financial statements or other financial information on which the auditor is required to report;

(g) the form and content of the specialist's report or opinion that would enable the auditor to determine whether or not the findings of the specialist constitute acceptable audit evidence.

Where it is not practicable for consultation to take place before the specialist carries out his work, the auditor will nevertheless need to obtain an understanding of the specialist's terms of reference and of the work he has been instructed to carry out.

Evaluating the findings of the specialist

(13) The auditor will need to evaluate the audit evidence provided by the specialist to determine whether it is sufficient, relevant and reliable enough for him to draw reasonable conclusions from it. The procedures which the auditor will apply will

depend upon the nature of the evidence, the circumstances necessitating its preparation, the materiality of the items to which it relates and the auditor's assessment of the specialist's competence and objectivity.

(14) The auditor should make a detailed examination of the specialist's evidence including ascertaining whether:

(a) the data provided by management to the specialist is compatible with that used for the preparation of the financial statements;

(b) the assumptions and bases used by the specialist are compatible with those used in preparing the financial statements, and consistent with earlier years;

(c) the information supplied by the specialist has been prepared and presented in accordance with his terms of reference;

(d) the specialist has qualified his opinion, or expressed any reservations;

(e) the effective date of the specialist's findings is acceptable;

(f) the details of the specialist's findings are fairly reflected in the financial statements.

(15) The specialist is responsible for ensuring that he uses assumptions and bases which are appropriate and reasonable. Where the skills applied by the specialist involve highly complex, technical considerations, then it may be that the level of the auditor's understanding of them can be no higher than that of the informed layman. However, the auditor should obtain a general understanding of the assumptions and bases used by the specialist, and consider whether they appear reasonable, given his knowledge of the client's business, and consistent with other audit evidence.

(16) Where specialist evidence is obtained on a recurring basis, comparison of the key features of the findings with those of prior years may indicate to the auditor whether there are any grounds for doubting the reasonableness of the evidence.

(17) If the auditor concludes that the specialist's evidence is not relevant or reliable enough to assist him in forming an opinion on the financial statements, or that the specialist may not have acted within his terms of reference, the auditor should endeavour to resolve the manner by discussion with the management of the client and with the specialist, and by further examination of the specialist's findings. In rare circumstances it may be necessary to obtain the opinion of another specialist. However, a second opinion might only relate to part of the original specialist's evidence, for example, the appropriateness of the bases used.

Reporting

(18) The auditor should not ordinarily refer in his report to any specialist on whose evidence he has relied. Such a reference might be misunderstood as either a qualification of his opinion or a division of responsibility, when neither of these is intended.

(19) Where the auditor is unable to satisfy himself regarding the specialist's evidence, or where no such evidence is available, and there is no satisfactory alternative source of audit evidence, he should consider qualifying his audit report. The situations in which this may be necessary include:

(a) where management is unable or unwilling to obtain specialist evidence;

(b) where the relevance and reliability of the specialist's evidence remains uncertain;

(c) where management refuses to accept and make use of specialist evidence which is relevant, reliable and material to the financial statements; and

(d) where management refuses to agree to the appointment of another specialist when the auditor considers that a second opinion is needed.

8.9 Summary

The techniques available to the auditor in verifying the transactions of a period are:

(a) *compliance tests*, designed to test the effective practical operation of controls, and hence to enable the auditor to rely on those controls if they prove in fact to be effective;

(b) *substantive tests*, which test transactions or balances individually.

Audit evidence examined in the course of these tests must be reliable, relevant and sufficient.

The auditor usually works to an audit programme—a predetermined list of tests to be carried out. It is important not to define the work too rigidly. Audit staff should be free to extend or shorten tests according to their findings during the audit.

Most audit work is based on examining a sample of items. Sampling may use random selection (statistical sampling) or be based on judgement (judgement sampling).

Materiality affects the amount of audit work done in a given area. The auditor's decision as to what is material involves the use of his or her professional judgement in considering and applying the criteria listed in Section 8.7.

Progress questions

Questions	Reference for answers
(1) Summarize, in diagram form, the process of deciding the level of testing necessary in an audit plan.	Section 8.1
(2) Define: (a) compliance tests (b) substantive tests (You looked at these in the previous chapter, but do you still remember the definitions?).	Sections 8.2 and 8.3
(3)(a) What three qualities should audit evidence possess? (b) Explain each of them in detail.	Section 8.4: Guideline on Audit Evidence Paragraphs (2)–(7)
(4) List and describe the possible techniques of audit testing.	Section 8.4: Guideline on Audit Evidence Paragraphs (10)–(13)
(5) What are the factors determining materiality in relation to audit evidence and reporting?	Section 8.7

9 Audit sampling

9.1 Introduction

In normal circumstances there will be three main sources of audit assurance: internal control, analytical review, and the examination of detailed evidence supporting transactions and balances. In the case of two of them—assessing compliance with internal controls and substantiating the detail of transactions or balances—we usually conduct our audit work on a 'test' basis: we examine a sample of items and based on that examination we draw conclusions about the population as a whole.

The advantage of sampling is that it is cost efficient: it saves time and money. The disadvantage of sampling is that there is a risk that the sample will not be representative of the population from which it is drawn: because we have not examined them, we do not know for certain what the other items are like. In particular, we cannot be sure that the population does not contain errors which have not been revealed in the sample.

The justification for accepting some risk in our audit work rests on two particular characteristics of an audit report. First, the report is given in the form of an opinion and not as a statement of fact. The giving of an opinion must be based on a reasonable level of assurance, but it does not require absolute certainty. Second, the form of opinion ('a true and fair view') implies a sense of materiality, rather than correctness and precision in all details.

The critical questions are therefore what degree of assurance we should look for in our audit work and what degree of precision we should require. The answers to these two questions determine the extent of our detailed audit examination.

It should be noted that any reference to the extent of an audit test implies that a prior decision has been taken that the test in question is necessary and appropriate in the first place. For example, a decision as to the extent of a compliance test assumes that the particular control procedure under examination is one which will be of major importance to our planned reliance on internal control. These decisions as to the scope and purpose of audit tests are a critical part of audit efficiency, and they also form an important part of 'sample design' (see below). Once the need for a particular type of test has been established, however, the decision as to the extent of it is a question of determining an audit sample, which involves three further questions:

How many?—sample size
Which ones?—sample selection
What conclusion?—sample evaluation

When these questions are answered subjectively, the result is a wide variation in the extent of work done in different cases. Sometimes these variations are acceptable because they arise from legitimate differences in circumstances. More often they are due purely to personal differences of opinion in similar circumstances.

Furthermore, when samples are chosen and evaluated on a subjective basis it is not possible to express the level of risk we are accepting or the degree of precision we believe we are working to. Our assessment of these matters is wholly intuitive.

The alternative to pure intuition in the choice and evaluation of samples is to adopt some form of statistical method. Statistical sampling is an attempt to answer these sort of questions (how many? what level of assurance?) in an objective manner. In so doing it helps to establish a degree of uniformity in the amount of work done in similar circumstances. It also provides a means of measuring and expressing the degree of risk inherent in the sampling process. It should be made quite clear, however, that where they are used in audit sampling statistical techniques do not replace professional judgement; they merely help to apply it.

The choice—between intuitive and statistical sampling—will usually rest on an assessment of the costs involved and the benefits to be derived. In some circumstances it may be excessively time consuming to satisfy some of the requirements for statistical evaluation—in particular the requirement that the sample should be selected on a random basis. For this reason, the cost effectiveness of statistical sampling will often depend on the ease with which sample items can be identified and retrieved, which will in turn depend on such practical matters as the manner in which entries are recorded and the sequence in which documents are filed.

Whatever method is used—intuitive or statistical—any sampling application involves three basic steps: design, selection, and evaluation. The following paragraphs offer guidance on the main matters which fall to be considered under each of these three headings, regardless of whether or not statistical methods are adopted. Later sections give guidance on the different procedures which will usually apply according to whether the test in question is a compliance test or a substantive test.

9.2 Designing a sample

The basic requirement in designing a sample is that it should be representative of the population from which it is drawn.

The population under examination must therefore be defined with some care. It must be defined first in terms of the items of which it is made up. This in turn will depend for the most part on the purpose and direction of the audit test. If, for example, the objective is to test debtors for over-statement, the appropriate population will be recorded debtor balances. If the purpose is to test sales for under-statement, the population to be examined might be copy despatch notes.

Defining the population in these terms will also determine the 'sampling unit' which, depending on the audit objective, might be a voucher, an individual entry, or an account balance.

The population should also be defined in terms of its boundaries. A sample which is drawn from one month or from one location can only be evaluated in terms of the population for the particular month or location in question. As far as possible, samples should be designed so that they are representative of the whole of the period under examination or the whole of the amount appearing in the accounts.

The purpose of examining a sample is to identify any which are in error. It is therefore important to predetermine what will constitute an error. For any one sample the particular characteristics which distinguish an error will usually follow from the particular objective of the test. However all errors can be classified into one of two general types, according to whether the audit test in question is substantive or compliance:

—a monetary error
—a compliance deviation

A monetary error is one which affects the amount of any item shown in the accounts. A compliance deviation is a departure from a prescribed internal control procedure. Compliance deviations may or may not give rise to monetary errors but, when designing a compliance test, it is important to recognize that the monetary consequences of any deviation will be irrelevant to our evaluation of whether or not the particular control procedure is reliable.

9.3 Sample size

The key determinant of the size of a sample is the level of assurance we seek: a high level of assurance can only be derived from a relatively large sample, and vice versa. As a general principle, therefore, the tests we apply to important internal controls or critical balance sheet figures should be based on larger samples than those which are used in the testing of secondary controls or less significant balances (if indeed such less material items demand testing at all).

In statistical terms, the level of assurance which is sought can be expressed as a combination of 'reliability' and 'precision'.

'Reliability' is a measure of the confidence with which, having inspected a sample, we can draw conclusions about the population from which it is drawn. Any sample of less than 100 per cent carries the risk that it is not truly representative of the surrounding population. In statistical sampling, that degree of risk is expressed in terms of confidence in the results.

When drawing a conclusion based upon a sample, it is prudent to make allowance for some range of error inherent in the estimate which is made. 'Precision' is a measure of the limits of accuracy within which conclusions can be drawn. For auditing purposes, precision is related to the maximum amount or rate of error which might exist in the population but which would not be regarded as material.

These two factors, reliability and precision, are inter-related. In statistical terms, it is meaningless to design a sample to a given level of reliability without also specifying the required level of precision. A sample can be evaluated to a fine degree of precision and a low level of reliability or vice versa. For example, on an examination of the same sample, the results might be expressed as giving either 90 per cent reliability within the range ±2 per cent or 99 per cent reliability within the range ±10 per cent.

With intuitive sampling the required level of assurance cannot be measured (other than in such general terms as high, medium or low), and sample sizes are arrived at wholly as the result of subjective assessment. With statistical sample, the level of assurance required can be expressed objectively, and sample sizes can be read from statistical tables according to the levels of reliability and precision required. Note, however, that even in statistical sampling the levels of reliability and precision which are adopted are themselves entirely a matter of audit judgement.

In either case, therefore, the size of a sample depends ultimately on professional judgement. In either case, the means by which we have determined the size of a sample, and the decisions and judgements which have been made, must be recorded in our working papers. The principal matters to be considered will usually vary according to whether the test in question is compliance or substantive; guidance on fixing the sample size for each type of test is given in Sections 9.7 and 9.8 below.

9.4 Methods of sample selection

Once the size of the sample has been fixed the next stage in the sampling process is to decide by what method the items which will comprise the sample are to be selected. The method of selection is important because it determines whether or not the results of the sample can be statistically evaluated.

The basic requirement for statistical sampling is that each item in the population should have an equal or otherwise determinable probability of being selected (which means that every form of bias must be eliminated from the selection process).

There are two basic statistical selection methods: random selection and systematic selection.

Random selection is a technical term that implies more than arbitrary, haphazard or impartial selection. It involves the use of random numbers, usually obtained from random number tables. It can be excessively time consuming and is therefore not usually appropriate for audit purposes.

Systematic selection (every nth) provides a statistically valid alternative to random selection. For compliance testing, the method requires calculation of the sampling interval (population size divided by sample size). The first item is selected at random and the remaining items are selected according to the sampling interval. The random starting number must be less than the required interval. A convenient way of choosing it is by referring to the appropriate number of digits in the identification number of a five pound note.

As an example of this techique, assume a population comprising 3000 items and a required sample size of 40. The sampling interval is therefore 75. If the chosen random starting number is 58, the sample would begin as follows: 58th item, 133rd, 208th, 283rd etc., and continue until the population is exhausted.

The one important condition for systematic selection to be valid is that the population does not have any recurring pattern to it which coincides with the sampling interval. For example, the selection of every twentieth item in a series of payrolls each of which comprises 10 employees will result in the same employee being chosen each time, with the consequence that the sample will not be representative.

Systematic selection can also be used in choosing monetary samples for substantive tests. The Cumulative Money Amount (CMA) process, described in Section 9.8 below, is a systematic selection method particularly suited to audit purposes.

The decision as to whether systematic or more arbitrary or judgemental selection methods are to be used will usually depend on the methods of recording and filing within the accounting system. For example, where the sample item is a document, statistical selection methods will be difficult unless each document is given an identifying number. Even pre-numbered documents may be unduly time consuming to locate if they are filed other than sequentially.

Where samples are selected on an arbitrary or intuitive basis the principle remains that the sample should be as representative as possible of the population. 'Block' sampling—for example taking one or more months in total—is to be discouraged as it will usually provide less of a basis from which to draw conclusions about the transactions arising in other months. As far as possible intuitively selected samples should therefore be drawn so as to cover all locations and the whole of the period under review.

9.5 Sample evaluation

Once the sample has been selected and examined, the third and final stage in the process is to evaluate the results. The basic principle of evaluation is that any errors discovered in the sample must be projected for the population as a whole.

Once projected, it is then a matter of audit judgement as to whether the incidence of compliance deviations in a compliance test or the monetary value of errors in a substantive test are acceptable in terms of the particular audit objective. This evaluation provides the core of any conclusions to be drawn from the tests carried out.

For statistical samples (that is those which are designed and selected on a statistical basis) the results should be evaluated by statistical techniques. In the same way as the statistical design of a sample provides an objective measure of the levels of assurance which are sought or planned, so the statistical evaluation of the results of that sample provides an objective measure of the levels of reliability and precision with which conclusions can be drawn. These conclusions will usually be expressed in terms such as 'we are X per cent confident that this item is not overstated by more than £Y'; or 'we are X per cent confident that the population contains not more than Z errors'. It should be emphasised, therefore, that the ultimate decision as to whether those statistically derived conclusions are acceptable for audit purposes will remain a matter of professional judgement; that is, it will still be a matter of judgement to decide whether X per cent provides sufficient confidence, and £Y sufficient precision (or Z a tolerable error rate) for audit purposes.

For intuitively designed samples the results can only be evaluated intuitively. Nevertheless the principle remains that any errors which are discovered in the sample should be projected in terms of the population as a whole. The evaluation and projection of errors requires careful analysis and is discussed further in the following sections—according to whether the test is compliance or substantive.

9.6 Sampling in practice

Many firms will use both intuitive and statistical sampling as acceptable audit procedures. The decision as to which to use—either wholly or in part—on a particular assignment may be at the discretion of the audit partner concerned. The remainder of this section and the three which follow are based on the Robson Rhodes approach to statistical sampling.

Statistical sampling provides a tool for use in the exercise of judgement. It enables us to measure and control the risks involved in sampling. Wherever it is practical to use it, it is to be preferred.

As a matter of principle it should be noted that statistically derived samples will always provide the minimum sample size needed for a given level of assurance. Intuitively derived samples should as far as possible be determined by reference to the same criteria as would apply in statistical samples, and should never be less than the size required if full statistical techniques had been adopted.

Sample sizes for compliance tests should be fixed by reference to the table in Section 9.7.3. Sample sizes for substantive tests of account balances should be fixed by reference to the materiality level established for the assignment and the chosen reliability factor from the table in Section 9.8.4.

Wherever we are carrying out audit work on a test basis—that is, wherever we are designing a sample—the working papers should record:

—a description of the audit objective;
—a definition of the population being examined, and of the sampling unit;
—a description of the characteristics which will constitute an error;
—the sample size and the means by which it was determined;
—the method of selection;
—details of any errors found, and their evaluation;
—the conclusions to be drawn from the work.

For the purposes of recording this work a separate schedule should be completed for each audit test that is performed, along the lines of the examples attached for compliance tests (Section 9.9.1) and substantive tests (Section 9.9.2).

9.7 Compliance Tests

9.7.1 Numeric sampling

In compliance testing we are concerned with the *number* of times a particular control procedure has or has not been applied. The method adopted is numeric sampling. The characteristics of numeric sampling are that the level of precision which is set both in the design of the sample and in the evaluation of the results is expressed in terms of either the number or rate of errors planned for or found. The results of a numeric sample cannot be evaluated in monetary terms: each error is given equal weight, without regard for any monetary consequences.

9.7.2 Sample design

The purpose of a compliance test is to establish whether a particular control procedure has in fact been applied as prescribed. The basic principle bears repetition: compliance testing will only be worth while if we plan to rely on internal control and, as a result of that reliance, to reduce significantly the amount of related substantive work we would otherwise have carried out.

The particular objective of a compliance test will follow from the particular control procedure which is under examination. That control procedure will also determine the definition of an error or deviation.

The population for a numeric sample will usually comprise all the documents or entries for the whole of the period under examination. Particular care should be taken in defining the population where documents or entries are filed or recorded at more than one location, or where there has been a significant change in the system during the period. The design of a numeric sample should be recorded on an appropriate Sample Design Worksheet (in the form suggested in Section 9.9.1 below.)

9.7.3 Sample size

The size of numeric samples used in compliance tests should be fixed by reference to the following table—regardless of whether the sample is to be statistically or intuitively selected and evaluated.

Compliance Tests—Sample Sizes

Degree of Reliance Planned	Sample Size	
	No Errors Expected	Up to 2 Errors Expected
High	45	105
Moderate	30	70
Low	15	35
None	0	0

The size is determined in the first instance by the degree of reliance we plan to place on the particular control. The table provides for alternative sample sizes according to our expectation of finding errors. Where we expect to find more than two errors it will not usually be cost effective to perform a compliance test. Whether our planned degree of reliance proves, in the event, to be warranted will depend on the number of errors which are actually found—as to the evaluation of which see Section 9.7.5 below.

The table has been drawn up on the basis that the reliability level we should seek for any compliance test should be 90 per cent. The alternative sample sizes given in the table derive from alternative levels of precision—wider precision at low levels of planned reliance and increasingly finer precision limits at higher levels of reliance.

Matters affecting the decision as to sample size will include:

—our preliminary evaluation of the system of internal control and the relative importance of the particular control procedure under examination (the more critical the control, the higher should be our degree of planned reliance);
—the existence or otherwise of related or subsidiary controls;
—the possible monetary consequences of errors or deviations (if high we would want a higher degree of assurance);
—our experience in previous years as to the incidence of errors.

If a compliance test has been properly designed it will be based on a control procedure which is critical to the assurance we seek from the system. It follows therefore by definition that we shall want to evaluate it to a high degree of reliance. Sample sizes which anticipate moderate or low reliance will be rare—except perhaps where there are known to be other related controls which will also be tested or where the same sample is to be used also as the basis for a substantive test (in which case the lesser degree of assurance derived from the control procedure will be compensated by the increased assurance that comes from direct substantiation of the accounting entry in question).

9.7.4   Sample selection

Wherever possible, systematic selection methods should be adopted (but see Section 9.4 above for the practical constraints which may apply). Where the selection is arbitrary, every attempt should be made to ensure that the sample is as representative as possible of the population.

9.7.5   Sample evaluation

Numeric samples which have been systematically selected should be evaluated by reference to the table below. Although there will be no statistical basis for it, the same table should be used as a guide for evaluating the results of samples which have been intuitively selected.

Compliance Tests—Evaluation Table

Sample size	Degree of reliance warranted for number of errors in sample						
	0	1	2	3	4-5	6-7	8
15	L	N	N	N	N	N	N
30	M	L	N	N	N	N	N
35	M	L	L	N	N	N	N
45	H	M	L	L	N	N	N
70	H	H	M	M	L	N	N
105	H	H	H	M	M	L	N

H=High M=Moderate L=Low N=None

For a given sample size, and based on the number of errors discovered, the table shows the degree of reliance which can be placed on the particular control under examination. This conclusion will provide the basis for deciding the extent to which related substantive work can be reduced. (The statistical basis for the table is that if the incidence of discovered errors is greater than those planned for, the sample can nevertheless still be evaluated at the same level of confidence: the alternative degrees of reliance warranted are based on evaluations at wider precision limits.)

For example, if no errors are discovered in a sample of 45 items the table shows that we will be justified in placing a high degree of reliance on the particular control procedure under examination. If one error is discovered, only moderate reliance is justified. If more than three errors are discovered, no reliance can be placed on that part of the system at all.

If in designing the test we had expected to find up to two errors, but had nevertheless planned to derive a moderate level of assurance from the system, we would have chosen (from the table in Section 9.7.3.) a sample size of 70. If no more than 3 errors are discovered we shall have achieved our planned level of reliance; 4 or 5 errors and only low reliance is justified; more than 5 errors mean that no reliance can be placed at all. Note therefore that this table can itself also be used for the purposes of planning sample sizes—according to the anticipated number of errors and the desired level of reliance.

Note also, for each sample size, the relatively small number of errors that will reduce the degree of reliance to 'none'. The impact of errors on the conclusions which can be drawn from compliance tests will give even greater cause for consideration at the outset whether audit work which is directed towards deriving assurance from the system will in fact prove to be the most effective approach.

Where, during the examination of a sample, the number of errors exceeds the threshold at which no reliance can be placed, it will usually be appropriate to abandon the test at that point—unless there are other specific reasons for pursuing it (such as client instructions or for the purposes of a management letter).

Where errors occur at an unacceptable rate we should however also consider the following matters:

—whether the sample size should be increased and the subsequent results re-evaluated;
—what alternative auditing procedures might be, or have been, adopted (including tests of other compensating controls, or substantive tests of related transactions);
—the possible monetary effect of errors or deviations. (Although there is no valid basis for translating errors in a numeric sample into monetary terms, it may be possible in some circumstances—particularly where there is some consistency or homogeneity in the value of the related transactions —to estimate some 'average' value for each error detected and to project that value to the population by multiplying by the error rate discovered in the sample);
—most importantly, whether the planned reduction in the related year-end substantive work is justified.

9.8 Substantive tests

9.8.1 Monetary sampling

Numeric sampling leads to conclusions which can only be expressed in terms of the number or rate of errors found in the sample and projected for the population (for example, that not more than three debtors balances are in error). The very distinct advantage of monetary sampling (at least for audit purposes) is that it allows errors and precision limits to be expressed in money amounts, so that conclusions can be drawn in terms which are related directly to materiality (for example, the more helpful conclusion that debtors are not overstated by more than £10,000).

9.8.2 Sample size

The design and size of a monetary sample should be recorded on an appropriate Sample Design Worksheet (in the form suggested in Section 9.9.2 below).

In numeric sampling, the sample size is fixed first and it then dictates the sampling interval (where such an interval is needed for the purposes of systematic selection methods). In monetary sampling, the procedure is reversed: first, the sampling interval—referred to as the Judgement or J Factor—is calculated and it then establishes by reference to the population value, the sample size. The Sample Design Worksheet describes J as coming from the formula MP/R. In other words sample size is determined by the audit decisions which are made regarding precision (MP) and reliability (R) (see below).

9.8.3 Precision limits

Establishing precision limits is a critical decision in the design of a sample. It is a decision which should be made by the reporting partner, based on his assessment of the level of materiality which is appropriate to the particular assignment.

The assessment of what is material is entirely a matter of professional judgement. It is an assessment which can be measured against a number of alternative bases (for example net profit, sales, net assets, or the particular amount of the asset or liability in question) but it is a matter for which it would be entirely inappropriate to prescribe definitive percentages or limits. Nevertheless, materiality is something which must be assessed each time an audit is undertaken.

Once established, the level of overall materiality will usually provide the basis for setting monetary precision in any subsequent sample design. This is because the precision limits which are set in designing samples from different populations are non-cumulative with respect to the combined populations. Thus, if a precision limit of £50,000 is used for sampling both stock and debtors the precision limit with respect to the total of stock and debtors is £50,000, and not £100,000 or any intermediate amount (assuming no errors: if errors are found, their effect is cumulative in computing the 'adjusted' precision limit applicable to the combined population).

The practical advantage of this non-cumulative feature is that a precision limit can be established with respect to the accounts as a whole and then applied directly in designing samples to be taken from particular populations, without the need to consider other populations being examined. This is particularly useful when designing samples which are to be taken at interim dates during the year (when the purpose is to relate the overall precision limit to transactions for the whole year) or when selecting samples from various locations when the required level of precision is related to the combined operations at all locations.

The basic rule, therefore, is that the monetary precision limit used in deciding a particular sample should be set at the maximum amount of error that would be considered not material in relation to the accounts. In practice, and particularly where a degree of error is expected, it will often be expedient to set MP somewhere below the overall materiality level—in order that the adjusted precision level which results from the evaluation and projection of any errors should still fall within acceptable limits.

There is one further feature of monetary precision which should be noted: whereas precision limits used in numeric sampling can be interpreted only in terms of the number or rate of errors, precision limits in monetary sampling are expressed in sterling amounts, and this requires a distinction to be drawn between errors of overstatement and understatement.

Clearly, there is a mathematical limit to the amount by which a balance or population can be overstated: a debtor of £12,000, for example, cannot be overstated by more than £12,000. As a consequence, precision limits in monetary sampling can be interpreted in terms of the maximum potential error of overstatement. This is a feature which makes monetary sampling particularly suitable for audit purposes: for a very large part, audit tests are designed to detect possible overstatements.

Conversely, there is no mathematical limit to the amount by which an item or a population might be understated, whether due to plain understatement or total omission. As a result, it is not possible to interpret precision levels in monetary sampling as placing any upper limit on possible errors of understatement. In practice, this unavoidable restriction as to potential errors of understatement is usually overcome by other audit procedures.

Auditing for the completeness or omission of amounts is typically met by tests which start from originating (and usually non-monetary) documents—such as goods inwards notes—which are then traced into the accounting records. Alternatively, procedures which are designed to test for understatement in the population of primary interest (such as year-end accruals) will often consist of selecting items from the reciprocal population (such as post date payments) and examining them for overstatement—on the basis that any overstatement in the reciprocal population will represent an equivalent understatement in the primary population.

In practice, a statistically based test on, for example, post-date payments will be difficult to apply and limited (because it is entirely dependent on the timing of the audit) in the assurance it provides. The sort of monetary sampling described here will most usefully be applied in the audit of year-end asset balances (debtors, stock, fixed assets) where the primary audit concern is to test for overstatement.

9.8.4 Reliability levels

The second determinant of sample size is the chosen level of reliability (that is, the level of confidence with which we wish to evaluate the results of the sample). For practical purposes the chosen level of confidence is expressed as a 'reliability factor' (R).

Evaluating samples at higher levels of confidence (that is at greater values for R) will require a larger sample than evaluation at lower levels. The following table indicates that the primary consideration in choosing the appropriate reliability factor for a substantive test should be the degree of reliance we have decided to place on internal controls as the result of any related compliance work. Where that reliance is high, the use of a lower reliability factor in the design of related substantive tests will be justified. Where reliance on internal control is low, higher values for R must be used in substantive tests.

Reliability Factors for Monetary Samples

Reliance placed on internal control	Monetary Samples—Substantive Tests	
	Confidence Level	Reliability Factor (R)
High	63%	1
Moderate	86%	2
Low	95%	3

The required level of reliability for substantive tests will also be influenced by the level of any audit assurance which can be obtained from analytical review techniques. In practice, the potential for deriving any significant level of assurance from analytical review will depend largely on the type, timeliness and reliability of data available from the client's accounting and information system. Where that data exists, the assurance thereby gained will itself provide the potential for conducting substantive tests of related detail to a lower level of reliability than would otherwise have been the case.

If a decision has been taken not to rely on internal control, and there is little or no assurance to be derived from analytical review, an R of 3 should be used in substantive tests.

The Sample Design Worksheet demonstrates how the decisions which are made regarding monetary precision and reliability determine the question of sample size. If on a particular assignment monetary precision is set at say £70,000, and if an R of 2 is chosen for a particular audit test, the worksheet shows that these decisions will produce a J factor (or sampling interval) of £35,000 which, for a population value of, say, £1,050,000 would produce an estimated sample size of 30.

9.8.5   Stratification

A feature of monetary sampling, because it refers to sterling values, is that it allows the possibility of 'stratification'. Stratification is no more than a technique for breaking a population into sub-populations, usually on the basis of size. It is therefore a technique which lends itself well to the usual audit preference to look at high value items.

The principle involved in stratification is that each stratum can be viewed as a separate population. A series of samples can be designed which tests top stratum items (see Section 9.8.6 below) to a high level of reliability while attached lesser weight to lower value items. For samples which are selected on a statistical basis, the Cumulative Monetary Amount (CMA) technique, described below, provides a method of selection which is both systematic and one which provides automatic stratification.

9.8.6   Sample selection

The Cumulative Monetary Amount (CMA) technique is a systematic selection method which uses a random start and in which the sampling interval thereafter is measured by the J factor. Its main application will be in those audit areas in which the normal scope of our work would include the need to total the population.

The CMA method has two major audit advantages. First, it produces the minimum sample size necessary for a given level of statistical assurance. Second, the probability of items being selected is directly proportional to their size: the larger the item, the greater the probability of its being selected in the sample.

The CMA selection process involves the following steps:

(a) Calculate the judgement factor (J) from the formula MP/R.
(b) Select a random starting number which is not greater than J.
(c) Insert the random number as the first item in an add-list and progressively add the items in the population to it. Select as the sample those items which cause the cumulative amounts to equal or exceed J, 2J, 3J and further multiples of J.

Assume, for example, that the following is a list of balances extracted from a sales ledger and our purpose is to select a sample for confirmation. Assume that we have calculated J=£5000 and that we have chosen a random number (from a five pound note) of 3564.

The items marked with an asterisk are those which cause the cumulative total to equal or exceed multiples of J (selection amounts). These are the items which would be selected for the sample.

Note that the probability of any item being selected is equal to the ratio

	Amount of item £	Cumulative Amount £	Selection Amount £
		3,564	5,000
1	325	3,889	5,000
2	669	4,558	5,000
3	23	4,581	5,000
4	1,437*	6,018	5,000
5	6,233*	12,251	10,000
6	2,003	14,254	15,000
7	11,422*	25,676	15,000
8	550	26,226	30,000
9	4,010*	30,236	30,000
etc.	etc.	etc.	etc.

Extract from list of balances

which the amount of that item bears to J. Items equal to or greater than J are certain to be selected; they are referred to as 'top stratum' items. When it comes to the analysis of any errors discovered in the sample there are important differences in the evaluation techniques which are adopted according to whether the errors are discovered in top stratum or other strata items.

Note also that whereas sample size can be estimated by the formula MJ, the actual sample size will be reduced to the extent that the population contains items greater than J. CMA therefore produces minimum sample sizes.

For practical purposes, the mechanics of cumulative addition will usually best be conducted by using an adding machine (or computer programmes where they are available). In this case the tape, suitably marked to identify selected items, should be retained on file as audit evidence.

9.8.7 Subsampling

Subsampling is a useful technique which can save time in applying the CMA method of selection. It can also serve useful audit purposes of its own. Where, for example, it is known that a customer's accounting system does not provide for confirmation of the whole balance, subsampling can be used to select a specific invoice instead.

Subsampling will particularly save time where the data to be sampled are in list form totalled at the foot of each page. In a series of stock sheets, for example, the CMA method can be applied first to the totals of whole sheets. A sheet will be selected if it takes the cumulative total past a selection amount (based on the same progressive multiples of J), and items within that sheet will then be randomly selected by subsampling. Sheets not selected at the first level play no further part in the selection.

The process of selecting a subsample is similar to that described earlier, except that the random starting number must not exceed either J or the amount of the sample item, whichever is lower. A convenient way of choosing the random start number is to generate it automatically from the selection of the primary sample—by calculating the excess of the cumulative population total over the selection amount. Using the previous example, the excesses would be calculated as follows:

	Amount of item £	Cumulative Amount £	Selection Amount £	Selection Excess £
		3,564	5,000	
1	325	3,889	5,000	
2	669	4,558	5,000	
3	23	4,581	5,000	
4	1,437*	6,018	5,000	1,018
5	6,233*	12,251	10,000	2,251
6	2,003	14,254	15,000	
7	11,422*	25,676	15,000	10,676
8	550	26,226	30,000	
9	4,010*	30,236	30,000	236
etc.	etc.	etc.	etc	

For each (asterisked) item selected in the primary sample, the excess (of the cumulative total over the selection amount) provides a random start for the selection of a subsample. Provided this excess is less than J, it can be used in selecting the subsample as follows:

ITEM 3:	Amount of sub-item £	Cumulative Amount £	Selection Amount £
	18	18	1,018
	632	650	1,018
	295	945	1,018
	73*	1,018	1,018
	419	1,437	1,018
	1,437		

The amount of £73 would be selected for the subsample since the cumulative amount at that point equals or exceeds the selection amount. In this example there will be no further items in the subsample since the next selection amount (£6,018) exceeds the total of the sub-population.

For item 7 (£11,422) the excess of £10,676 is greater than J and must therefore be reduced by successively subtracting J until the random starting number is less than J. The selection amounts for subsampling item 7 would therefore be £676, £5,676 and £10,676.

9.8.8 Sample evaluation

If a sample contains no errors, no further work is required and an audit conclusion can be drawn in accordance with the planned degree of precision and reliability. Thus, for example, if a sample of debtor balances has been selected for direct confirmation, with an MP of £15,000 and an R of 3, and if the sample contained no errors, the audit conclusions would take the form 'We are 95 per cent confident that debtors are not overstated (for existence) by more than £15,000'.

Where errors are discovered in the sample, it will be necessary to evaluate them (and, for statistical samples, to calculate an adjusted precision limit) before any audit conclusion can be drawn. The evaluation and projection of errors in a monetary sample should for statistical purposes, be carried out by reference to the Error Evaluation Worksheet. (Sections 9.9.3 to 9.9.5 below).

The 'revised MP' referred to in that worksheet provides a measure of the statistical assurance with which audit conclusions can be drawn from the sample which has been examined. If in the earlier example of the debtors' confirmation (MP £15,000, R = 3) errors had been discovered which led to the calculation of a revised MP of, say, £16,300, the initial conclusion which could be drawn would be in terms of 'we are 95 per cent confident that debtors are not overstated (for existence) by more than £16,300'.

It then remains as a matter of judgement whether this level of assurance is acceptable for audit purposes. If it is not, further audit work may be necessary. Any additional work should always start with a qualitative assessment of the errors which have been found, their causes, and the possible effect of those causes on other aspects of our audit work. It may be possible to identify a discernible pattern or feature to the errors (for example, all occurring in one identifiable part of the year, or in documents initiated at one particular department or location) in which case any further work might be concentrated in the corresponding segment of the population.

Where monetary samples have been intuitively selected there will be no basis on which to calculate a revised level of precision. Nevertheless the same qualitative assessment of any errors should be made and the same consideration given to whether further work is necessary.

Where no discernible pattern exists, or where the errors cannot otherwise be isolated, we should consider the level of assurance that might be obtained from any other audit tests which can be applied to the balance or class or transactions in question (and any corroborating evidence which that further work might provide). In any event, and whatever sampling procedures have been applied, the adequacy of that assurance will always be a matter of judgement.

9.9 Specimen statistical sampling worksheets

9.9.1 Sample Design Worksheet–numeric samples–compliance tests

---

Client _____

Accounting Date _____

SAMPLE DESIGN WORKSHEET
(NUMERIC SAMPLES—COMPLIANCE TESTS)

Audit Test Objective _____

Planned Reduction in Substantive Tests _____

Population _____

Description of population _____

Sampling unit _____

Sub-sampling unit _____

Definition of error _____

Sample
Planned degree of reliance   _____
Expected number of errors   _____
Sample size (from table)   _____
Selection
Statistical: Random starting number   _____
Judgemental: Describe basis of selection   _____

_____

_____

Actual sample size   _____

Evaluation
Insert schedule reference on which any errors are listed and
evaluated; otherwise, indicate 'none'   _____

Conclusion

_____

_____

_____

Prepared by _____	**Date** _____
Reviewed by _____	**Date** _____

9.9.2 Sample Design Worksheet–monetary samples–substantive tests

---

Client
_____

Accounting Date
_____

**SAMPLE DESIGN WORKSHEET
(MONETARY SAMPLES—SUBSTANTIVE TESTS)**

Audit Test Objective
_____

Population
Description of population
_____

Sampling unit
_____

Sub-sampling unit
_____

Definition of error
_____

Value of population (M)   £ _____

Sample Size
Monetary precision (MP)   £ _____
Reliability factor (R)   _____
Judgement factor (J=MP/R)   _____
Estimated sample size (M/J)   _____

Selection
Statistical (CMA): Random starting number   _____
Judgemental: Describe basis of selection_____
_____
_____

Actual sample size   _____

Evaluation
If errors are found, insert schedule reference on which they are
listed and evaluated; for statistical samples, complete error
evaluation worksheet. Otherwise, indicate 'none'   _____

Conclusion
_____
_____
_____

Prepared by _____ **Date** _____
Reviewed by _____ **Date** _____

9.9.3 Error Evaluation Worksheet

Client

Accounting Date

ERROR EVALUATION WORKSHEET
(see notes attached for explanation)
(MONETARY SAMPLES)

J Factor (per sample design worksheet) £

1	2	3	4	5	6	7	8	9
Sample item (I)		Top stratum		Other strata errors (I<J)				
Reference	Amount	errors (I>J)	Sample error	Estimated population error		Revised monetary precision		
				Sampling interval	Error blow-up	Error rank	Adjustment factor	Adjusted error
		£			£			£

'Best Estimate' of Errors in Population
Total top stratum errors (column 3)
Add: Total other error blow up (column 6) _____
Less: Adjustments made to accounts to correct errors _____
Best estimate of population errors £

Revised Monetary Precision £
Original monetary precision (MP)
Add: Total top stratum errors (column 3)
Add: Total precision adjusted other errors (column 9)
Less: Adjustments made to accounts to correct errors
Revised MP £

Conclusion

_____

_____

_____

Prepared by _____ **Date** _____
Reviewed and approved by ____ **Date** _____

9.9.4 Error Evaluation Worksheet—notes on completion

ERROR EVALUATION WORKSHEET
NOTES ON COMPLETION

As a first step in the evaluation errors should be distinguished according to whether they are discovered in sample items (I) which rank in the top stratum (I equal to or greater than J) or whether they occur in items ranking in any other strata (wherever I is less than J)—see columns 3 and 4.

The importance of this distinction is that only errors occurring in other strata have to be 'blown-up' in projecting the estimated amount of error in the population as a whole. Errors occurring in top stratum items require no blow-up or projection because it is known with certainty that all items in that stratum (i.e. all items equal to or greater than J) have been included in the sample.

The next step in the evaluation is to calculate the sampling interval (column 5) for each error discovered in other strata items and listed in column 4. The sampling interval is found by the formula J/I and is a measure of the probability of selecting an item whose amount is exactly I.

The estimated error in the population is calculated by multiplying each error listed in column 4 by the corresponding sampling interval. (The 'blow-up' effect of projecting sample errors to the population as a whole arises because, for all errors occurring in other strata items, J/I will always be greater than I; because top stratum items are certain to be selected, the probability of being selected will always equal I and there is no blow-up effect).

The total of the top stratum errors (column 3) together with the total of the blown-up other errors (column 6) provides the best estimate, based on the sample results, of the projected amount of error in the population as a whole. The remainder of the evaluation is concerned to establish the revised level of statistical assurance which the sample results justify. In order to be able to evaluate at the same level of reliability as was planned for in designing the sample, the revised level of statistical assurance is established by calculating a revised precision limit.

The first step in calculating a revised MP is to rank in order of their size the various blown-up errors entered in column 6. Separate rankings should be given for errors of overstatement and errors of understatement. The rankings in column 7 should therefore be entered by designating the largest error of overstatement as I, the next largest as 2 and so on; the largest error of understatement should be designated (I), the next largest (2), etc. The appropriate precision adjustment factor (column 8) for each blown-up error should then be found by reference to the table attached. The precision adjusted error in column 9 is calculated by multiplying the error blow-up in column 6 by the precision adjustment factor in column 8.

The revised MP can then be calculated by adding to the original MP used in designing the sample the total of the top stratum errors in column 3 and the total of the precision adjusted other errors in column 9. Any adjustments which are made to the accounts to correct errors which have been discovered should be deducted before calculating revised MP. It would be quite appropriate to include in these adjustments not only any entries made to correct specific errors but also any provision which is made in respect of estimated population error. For this purpose reference should be made to the 'best estimate' of population error referred to above and described on the evaluation worksheet.

9.9.5   Error Evaluation–Table of Precision Adjustment Factors

MONETARY SAMPLE ERROR EVALUATION
PRECISION ADJUSTMENT FACTORS

Errors of overstatement

	Rank of Error									
R	1	2	3	4	5	6	7	8	9	10
3.0	1.75	1.56	1.46	1.40	1.36	1.33	1.31	1.29	1.28	1.26
2.0	1.51	1.38	1.31	1.27	1.25	1.23	1.21	1.20	1.19	1.18
1.0	1.15	1.12	1.10	1.09	1.08	1.07	1.07	1.06	1.06	1.06

Errors of understatement

	Rank of Error									
R	1	2	3	4	5	6	7	8	9	10
3.0	0.05	0.30	0.46	0.54	0.60	0.64	0.67	0.69	0.71	0.73
2.0	0.14	0.49	0.62	0.69	0.73	0.75	0.77	0.79	0.80	0.81
1.0	0.45	0.82	0.88	0.90	0.91	0.92	0.93	0.93	0.94	0.94

9.10   Summary

In most areas, the audit approach is to test a selection of items rather than make an exhaustive check on every item in a population.

In many cases STATISTICAL sampling is a suitable technique to use. Advantages claimed for statistical sampling are:

(*a*) The sample result may be defended objectively. A properly selected random sample is free from bias.

(*b*) It forces clarification of audit thinking in determination of precision and confidence levels.

(*c*) A careful examination of a properly planned sample may give a more accurate result than the checking of a vast volume of data by possibly overworked staff.

(*d*) A precise measure of the risk that the sample may not be representative is given.

(*e*) Time and money may be saved because sample sizes are fixed at the optimum level to achieve stated audit objectives.

(*f*) The use of judgement is not excluded, since it enters into the determination of precision and confidence levels, and the definition of an error.

Statistical selection methods may be *random*, in which each item is selected using random number tables, or *systematic*, in which a random starting point is determined and then further items taken at regular intervals thereafter, the interval being determined by dividing the population size by the calculated sample size.

In compliance testing we may use *numeric sampling*. The level of precision is expressed in terms of the *number* of errors expected or actually found. This is because the object of compliance testing is to check compliance with the system—the actual monetary value of any errors found is not important in evaluating that compliance.

In substantive testing, on the other hand, we are interested in the materiality of errors found and we use *monetary sampling*. If monetary sampling is used a conclusion incorporating materiality can be formulated using the approach described in Sections 9.8.4 to 9.8.6 above.

Statistical sampling is particularly useful where the following conditions exist:

(*a*) large population to be examined
(*b*) items in the population are homogeneous
(*c*) there is a low expected error rate
(*d*) there is reasonable ease of selection and access to selected items.

Progress questions

Questions	Reference for answer
(1) Distinguish between judgement (intuitive) sampling and statistical sampling	Section 9.1
(2) What are the advantages of statistical sampling?	Sections 9.1, 9.10
(3) a) What two factors are the main determinants of sample size? (b) Explain what each of these two factors are	Sections 9.3, 9.8.3, 9.8.4 Section 9.3
(4) Distinguish between random selection and systematic selection	Section 9.4
(5) What should be recorded in the audit working papers when statistical sampling is being used?	Section 9.6
(6) (a) Explain the terms 'numeric sampling' and 'monetary sampling'. (b) Which of these two methods is used for compliance testing?	Sections 9.7.1 and 9.8.1 Sections 9.7.1
(7) What is stratification?	Section 9.8.5

10 Verification of assets and liabilities

10.1 Introduction

As we saw in Chapter 8, and in particular in the Guideline on Audit Evidence quoted in Section 8.4, a vital part of the audit is obtaining sufficient, relevant and reliable evidence of the ownership, value and existence of the assets and liabilities of the business. Techniques available may include physical inspection, examination of documents of title, obtaining information from individuals inside and outside the organization, and analytical review. We should not forget that the work of confirming the accuracy of the transaction records (as outlined in previous chapters) is also a valuable aid to confirming the assets and liabilities to which those records relate.

We shall go through the satatutory balance sheet format from the top, dealing in turn with each item. There are a number of features common to groups of assets, and where convenient these will be discussed first, followed by items peculiar to individual assets within the group, to avoid unnecessary repetition. Where this is done, each individual paragraph will be cross-referred to the general paragraph, if any, so that nothing is missed by a reader picking up a particular item from the middle of the chapter.

10.2 Fixed assets generally

10.2.1 Regulatory background

Note. This is just a brief synopsis of the requirements—refer to your accounting texts for more details.

(a) Companies Act 1985

Schedule 4 contains a number of provisions governing fixed assets:

(1) Basis of valuation

The basis of valuation required under the historical cost accounting rules is cost less depreciation (paragraph 17). Cost includes incidental costs of acquisition (paragraph 26). If the asset has been produced by the company the cost may also include:

—a reasonable proportion of overhead expenditure, to the extent that it relates to the period of production;
—interest on capital borrowed to finance the production (paragraph 26).

The alternative accounting rules allow the assets to be included at current cost or, in the case of tangible assets, at their market value at the date of their last valuation (paragraph 31). The revised value must be used as the basis for the calculation of depreciation (paragraph 32).

(2) Depreciation

All assets having a finite life must be depreciated (paragraph 18). See also (b)(1) below for the requirements of SSAPs 12 and 19.

(3) Disclosure

For each fixed asset heading the following details must be shown:

—cost or valuation at the beginning and end of the year;
—effect of any revaluation;
—acquisitions during the year;
—disposals during the year;
—transfers of assets to and from the item during the year;
—accumulated depreciation at the beginning and end of the year;
—provision for depreciation in the current year;
—adjustments to depreciation as a result of disposals during the year or for any other reason (paragraph 42);
—where there have been revaluations, the year of revaluation and, for revaluations in the current year, the names or qualifications of the valuers (paragraph 43).

In addition, Schedule 7 (paragraph 1) requires the disclosure in the directors' report of any material difference between the value of land and its balance sheet amount, if the directors believe the difference is significant for members or debenture-holders.

(b) SSAPs

The most important relevant SSAPs are SSAPs 12 and 19, dealing with depreciation, SSAP 21 dealing with leased assets and SSAP 22 with goodwill. SSAP 2 (accounting policies) and SSAP 4 (government grants) must also be considered, as must SSAP 6 and ED 36 when it comes to accounting for disposals.

(1) SSAP 12 and SSAP 19
SSAP 12 requires nearly all fixed assets having a finite life to be depreciated. Exceptions are:

—freehold land;
—investment properties (required by SSAP 19 to be revalued);
—goodwill, covered by SSAP 22;
—development costs (SSAP 13);
—investments, which by their nature do not suffer an automatic loss in value
  with the passage of time.

SSAP 19 presents a problem, because the Companies Act does not allow investment properties to be excepted. It is only possible to comply with SSAP 19 by invoking the 'true and fair' override of S228. (This enables any Companies Act accounting requirement to be disregarded if it is necessary in order for the accounts to show a true and fair view, provided the accounts dislose by note the reasons for the departure and its effect.)

(2) SSAP 21—Accounting for leases and hire purchase transactions
Although there is no provision in the Companies Act formats for the inclusion of leased assets, SSAP 21 requires assets held on finance leases to be disclosed, analysed by each major type of asset.

(3) SSAP 22—Accounting for goodwill
The main provisions of SSAP 22 are summarized in Section 10.3.3 below.

(4) SSAP 2—Disclosure of accounting policies
In the context of asset verification we are interested in the acceptability and disclosure of the company's policies as to:

—capitalization policy (distinction between capital and revenue);
—depreciation.

(5) SSAP 4—The accounting treatment of government grants
SSAP 4 allows government grants to be deducted from the cost of the asset concerned or held as a deferred credit to be released to profit and loss account in step with depreciation.

(6) SSAP 6—Extraordinary items and prior year adjustments, and ED 36
SSAP 6 and ED 36 deal, among other things, with the accounting treatment of profits and losses on asset disposals. A special problem arises when the asset

sold has been revalued. ED 36 proposes that the profit or loss on disposals taken to the profit and loss account should be the difference between proceeds and *depreciated original cost*. ED 16 had previously proposed that the profit or loss should be the difference between proceeds and the *depreciated revalued amount*.

10.2.2 Internal control over fixed assets

The areas of internal control of most relevance for fixed assets are:

(*a*) Custody procedures—the existence of controls over access and unauthorized use, backed up by periodic physical checks by the internal auditors or other designated supervisory staff. Safe custody arrangements for documents of title are also obviously essential.

(*b*) Authorization—for acquisitions, disposals, scrapping or major repairs.

(*c*) Records—including *registers* for each type of fixed asset held.
An asset register will typically contain:

(1) Date of purchase

(2) Supplier's name

(3) Cost, insured value and current valuation

(4) Full description

(5) Manufacturer's serial numbers, if any, and internally allocated identifying numbers

(6) Location

(7) Depreciation rate and planned disposal/scrapping date

(8) Major repairs, extensions or additions

(9) Details of any leasing or hire purchase arrangements.

Such a register is useful both to the client and to the auditor. It provides:

(1) A convenient link between the accounting records and the assets themselves, thus facilitating physical checks by internal and external auditors

(2) a ready source of reference for details of fixed assets which might otherwise entail lengthy searches in records and files

(3) a historical record which may be of value for tax purposes

(4) useful information about planned asset scrapping or disposal dates which will facilitate cash budgeting.

(*d*) Internal audit—the arrangements made for the methodical checking of the other controls, especially by means of a physical check.

10.2.3 The audit approach

What we have to prove is that the asset is there, that it belongs to the client and that it is valued on a reasonable basis—or, to put that in auditing language, we have to obtain adequate evidence as to the existence, ownership and valuation of the assets.

An outline audit programme appears below:

1. Obtain and vouch schedules of additions and disposals during the period, confirming that all are duly authorized at appropriate level. Check calculation of cost of any asset created by the client.
2. Confirm acceptable distinction between capital and revenue expenditure is made.
3. Confirm that all government grants have been duly taken into account.
4. Depreciation:
    (a) Ensure that depreciation is charged on all assets with a finite useful life;
    (b) Check depreciation calculations, noting consistency of rates of depreciation used.
5. Check calculation of profit or loss on disposals.
6. Confirm reconciliation between plant registers and nominal ledger. Review plant registers for obsolete items.
7. Valuation:
    (a) Check whether there is any significant difference between the market and balance sheet values of land and buildings.
    (b) Obtain copies of any valuations during the period.
8. Agree schedules to balance sheet and recorded accounting policies. Check notes concerning any assets revalued in the year.
9. Confirm existence of and title to all fixed assets (by direct confirmation from third parties, if required):

    (a) properties—inspect title deeds, leases, etc. ensuring that *all* properties are covered;
    (b) plant, equipment etc.—confirm client's own inspection procedures and test to plant registers;
    (c) motor vehicles—inspect registration records;
    (d) other material fixed assets—detail method of verification.

10.3 Intangible fixed assets

Under this heading we shall deal with:

—development costs
—concessions, patents, licences, trade marks and similar rights and assets
—goodwill

10.3.1   Development costs

(a) Regulatory background

Schedule 4 contains two points of interest:

(1) research expenditure must *not* be capitalized (paragraph 3)
(2) if development costs are capitalized the following information must be given by note:
—the period over which the amount of these costs originally capitalized is being or is to be written off;
—the reasons for capitalizing the development costs in question (paragraph 20).

In amplification of these requirements SSAP 13 lays down further detailed conditions which must be satisfied before development costs can be capitalized:
there must be:

(1) a defined project with identifiable expenditure, which is technically feasible and commercially viable;
(2) expectation of ultimate profit;
(3) adequate resources, including necessary working capital.

SSAP 13 also requires the amount capitalized to be written off 'systematically' to revenue. If any of the circumstances justifying deferral cease to apply, the development expenditure should be written off immediately. Once written off, development expenditure should not be reinstated even when the uncertainties which had led to its being written off no longer apply.

The amount of development expenditure, and movements on the account during the year, must be disclosed.

(b) Verification procedures

Audit steps will be:

(1) Ascertain the client's procedure for authorizing development projects and for identifying and recording the costs of duly authorized schemes.
(2) Vouch substantial items of cost, including time and materials booked to development schemes from general factory expenditure through the costing system.
(3) Ensure that no research costs are included in the amounts capitalized.
(4) Critically review the technical feasibility by discussion with the client's engineers, scientists or other expert staff.
(5) Critically review the commercial viability by discussion with the client's sales, marketing and finance directors.

(6) Critically review the adequacy of resources, having regard to estimated costs to completion of each project.

(7) Confirm that the rate of amortization is acceptable.

(8) Confirm that all other requirements of SSAP 13 and the Companies Act, including disclosure, have been complied with.

(9) Form an overall view as to whether the company's policy with regard to development expenditure is acceptable in all the circumstances. In cases where the amount involved is substantial, and the decision difficult, it may be necessary to seek independent expert advice.

10.3.2 Concessions, patents, licences, trade marks and similar rights and assets

The Companies Act 1985 (Note 2 to balance sheet format in Schedule 4) only allows the inclusion of assets under this heading if either:

(*a*) the assets were acquired for valuable consideration;
(*b*) the assets were created by the company itself.

There is no direct coverage in SSAPs.

Let us first pick up the two items where there is a standard verification procedure based on the documents of title relating to them.

(a) Patents

Patents are evidenced by *letters patent* issued by the Patent Office, and by the legal *assignment* transferring ownership if they have been purchased. The cost should be written off over the remaining legal life or over the estimated useful life, whichever is shorter. The legal life is 20 years from the date of the patent application.

Any internally incurred development costs should appear in the balance sheet under that heading, so that only the costs of the patent application are included as patents in the balance sheet.

The payment of annual renewal fees should be vouched. (If they are not paid the patent will lapse.) Such fees should be written off to revenue and not capitalized.

(b) Trade Marks

Trade marks are registered at the Patent Office and a certificate is issued by the registrar. If they are acquired by purchase there will be a legal assignment.

Costs which can be capitalized include design fees and registration charges. Annual renewal fees should be written off to revenue as incurred.

(c) Other items

As for the other items, concessions, licences and so on, these will be evidenced by a contract granting the concession, etc. The auditor will verify the authority for the acquisition and confirm that the cost is being written off over the shorter of its legal life and its useful life.

10.3.3 Goodwill

(a) Regulatory background

Goodwill is the subject of SSAP 22 and is also subject to a number of disclosure requirements of Schedule 4. The following table summarizes these references:

	SSAP 22 paragraph	Schedule 4 CA 1985
Accounting policy for goodwill to be explained by note	39	36
Goodwill to be shown separately in balance sheet	30,41	Formats
Accounting policy for goodwill existing at date of introduction of SSAP 22, if different from SSAP 22	42	
Details of goodwill arising on each acquisition in period, if material	40	
When goodwill is amortized, movements during year to be shown	41(a)	42
Period selected for amortization	41(b), Appendix 1, paragraph 4	21(4)
Reason for selecting that period		21(4)
Details of any amount written off as a result of permanent diminution in value	34(a)	19(2)

Both the Companies Act (Schedule 4, paragraph 17) and SSAP 22 are clear that goodwill should only appear in the balance sheet if it has been purchased.

SSAP 22 recommends that goodwill should preferably be written off immediately on acquisition against reserves, but it also allows goodwill to be amortized over its useful economic life through the profit and loss account in arriving at profit or loss on ordinary activities.

(b) Verification procedures

Goodwill arises when the fair value given as consideration for the purchase of a business exceeds the aggregate of the fair value of the separable net assets acquired.

The starting point for verification is therefore the contract for the purchase and a critical review of the values placed on the assets.

If the goodwill is immediately written off no asset remains for verification in future years. If the alternative of amortization is chosen, the auditor will confirm that the period selected is a reasonable one.

10.4   Tangible fixed assets

10.4.1   Land and buildings, freehold and leasehold (see also Section 10.2)

(a) Ownership

Ownership is conclusively demonstrated by the title deeds or the lease, or by the land certificate in the case of registered property. Title deeds and leases should be inspected by the auditor. If they are deposited with a third party as security for an advance, a certificate from that third party may be accepted. If deposited with a bank for safe custody, documents of title will be covered by the standard bank report reproduced and explained in Section 10.8.2 below. Note that a land certificate is not a document of title, but merely a certificate issued by the land registry certifying the ownership on the date concerned.

(b) Existence

The existence of the land is evidenced by the deeds, etc., which establish ownership. Physical inspection of buildings is a necessary means of confirming their continued existence.

(c) Valuation

Valuation of most fixed assets is cost less depreciation. Cost is evidenced by the 'invoice' or other document showing the details of the purchase. In the case of freehold land we have the *conveyance* and for leaseholds, the *assignment,* as the legal documents transferring ownership. In both cases there will also be the *completion statement* showing the full details of the make-up of the purchase price.

SSAP 12 does not require the depreciation of freehold land, but does require buildings to be depreciated, unless they are investment properties revalued annually in accordance with SSAP 19. (See Section 10.2.1(*b*)(1).) The adequacy of the building depreciation must therefore be reviewed.

Freehold and leasehold land and buildings are frequently revalued. If this has been done the auditor needs to confirm that the basis of valuation is acceptable and that the disclosure requirements given in Section 10.2.1(*a*)(3) above have been met.

The cost of self-created assets should be verified by reference to costing records detailing the expenses incurred, ensuring that no profit element has been included.

If there has been a permanent diminution in value then provision should be made for it.

(*d*) Sundry matters

(1) Partly completed buildings

Architects' certificates for work completed to date should be inspected. The amount capitalized should be the gross amount certified, any retentions being treated as creditors. ('Retentions' is the term used for the deduction, often 10 per cent, made from payments to builders and paid after satisfactory completion of the work.) Contracts for such partly completed work will need to be reviewed to verify the amount disclosed by note as the value of contracts for future capital expenditure. (Amounts authorized but not yet contracted for will need to be picked up from the minute book and references to corporate plans and budgets).

(2) Leases

The main points of lease agreements should be recorded in the permanent audit file, and those notes should be updated for acquisitions during the period. Matters to note particularly are restrictive covenants, so that the auditor may confirm that they are being complied with, and any provisions as to dilapidations, which may involve considerable expense. (The term 'dilapidations' means redecoration and reinstatement work which may be required by the lease to be done at the end of it). It is normal to make an annual provision for the estimated cost of such work. This is completely separate from the amortization of the lease itself, of course.

(3) Disclosure requirements

The main disclosure requirements were summarized in Section 10.2.1(*a*)(3). One additional point is the requirement to show separate figures for freeholds, long leases (50 years or more) and short leases (less than 50 years).

(4) Charges over property

The existence of a charge will usually be apparent from the fact that the documents of title are held by the lender. The auditor should confirm that any charges entered into during the year have been entered in the register of charges held by the company and also filed with the Registrar of Companies.

10.4.2 Plant and machinery; fixtures, fittings, tools and equipment

Under this heading we have both factory and office equipment. They are dealt with together because the techniques for verification are virtually the same. The special points relevant for motor vehicles are in Section 10.4.3 below.

(a) Ownership and existence

As there is no document of title, the strict verification of ownership is not possible as it is for landed property. Ownership will be established by reviewing the client's internal control procedures for custody, etc. (See Section 10.2.1(*c*) above), vouching purchases and sales and physical check. The combination of these should build up the necessary confidence in the auditor's mind that there is, for example, no realistic possibility that an item has been sold without authorization and then leased back to conceal its absence. The asset register will be most useful and its absence a systems weakness to be reported to management at the end of the audit.

(b) Valuation

It is frequently the case that office equipment is less carefully controlled than factory plant, and much more liable to loss or unauthorized removal in many cases. When the value of such equipment is material, as it is increasingly becoming, the auditor should pay special attention to this area.

With relatively short-lived assets of this kind, upward revaluation in the historical-cost based accounts is less likely than for landed property. Neverthelesss, it is increasingly encountered. The valuation basis will be either cost less depreciation or valuation less depreciation. Some assets in this category, like loose tools, may be included at a conservative valuation, the annual drop in value being taken as the measure of the depreciation charge.

(The term 'loose' tools is used for small items of equipment not screwed down to the floor—and hence liable to loss through pilferage.)

In reviewing the adequacy of the depreciation charge the possibility of obsolescence must be considered as well as the nominal useful life of the machine, especially in fast-moving technologies such as electronics.

(c) Sundry matters

(1) Assets on financial leases

SSAP 21 requires leased assets to be disclosed separately, analysed by major type of asset. The auditor's responsibility here is to confirm that all leased assets have been identified, correctly classified as operating leases or finance leases, and then the necessary and possibly tortuous calculations called for by SSAP 21 correctly made. (The full requirements of SSAP 21 are obligatory from 1987.) Note that it is very important to identify leased or hired assets in case they are masquerading as owned items.

(2) Items out on hire

These are difficult assets to verify satisfactorily. The contract for the hire should be inspected. The client's policy as to obtaining references before entering into a hire agreement, and the level of loss experienced in previous years, may give a guide to the provision for non-return that is required. In the case of short-term hire, the subsequent return of the asset will obviously be strong evidence of its existence at the balance sheet date. For long-term hire contracts the payment of the rental is some evidence of the continuation of the contract. Sample circularization of hirers, asking for confirmation that the asset is held, will also be apppropiate.

Depreciation rates on such items will often need to be higher than those for similar items in the permanent possession of the company.

(3) Capital/revenue expenditures

The auditor must confirm that the client's policy as to the distinction between capital expenditure and revenue expenditure is both acceptable and being adhered to.

10.4.3 Motor vehicles

All the points listed in Section 10.4.2 for plant apply to motor vehicles. In addition there are the following further ones peculiar to motor vehicles:

(1) Vehicle registration certificates should be inspected. Although they are not documents of title, their absence should put the auditor upon enquiry. The vehicle should be registered in the company's name. Some companies

adopt the policy of registering cars in employees' own names in an effort to improve the eventual resale value. In this case the employees concerned should sign a certificate acknowledging the company's ownership of the vehicle.

(2) Payments for insurance and road tax should be vouched, on a test basis.

(3) It may not be possible for the auditor to physically inspect all cars as some may be operating from remote branches. A certificate from the branch manager covering the car and other assets held at the branch may be accepted and this will be backed up by detailed checks as branches are visited on a rotational basis by the internal and external auditors.

10.5 Investments

10.5.1 Regulatory background

(a) Companies Act 1985

The Companies Act balance sheet format lists seven types of investment under Fixed Assets and another three under Current Assets, the distinction being between those which have some trading significance (fixed assets) and those which are merely temporary investments of surplus funds (current assets).

The techniques for verification are broadly the same for the two categories of investment, though the auditor must confirm that they have been properly classified and disclosed under the appropriate headings. The method of valuation laid down in Schedule 4 is also different as we shall see.

The detailed requirements governing investments are as follows.

(1) Valuation
Under the historical-cost accounting rules, fixed asset investments are valued at cost less any necessary provision for a permanent diminution in value, while current assets will be at the lower of cost and net realizable value (paragraphs 19 and 22–23).

Under the alternative accounting rules, which permit the use of current-cost accounting, fixed asset investments may be included at their market value at the time of the last valuation, or on any other basis which the directors consider appropriate, provided details of that other basis and the reasons for adopting it are disclosed. Current asset investments may be included at their current cost (paragraph 31).

(2) Disclosure

Provision is made in the balance sheet format for the following separate disclosure:

Fixed asset invesments	*Current asset investments*
1 Shares in group companies	1 Shares in group companies
2 Loans to group companies	2 Own shares
3 Shares in related companies	3 Other investments
4 Loans to related companies	
5 Other investments other than loans	
6 Other loans	
7 Own shares	

A breakdown between listed investment and unlisted investments is required for each investment heading, whether fixed or current. (paragraph 45)

For listed investments the market value (and the stock exchange value if lower) must be stated (paragraph 45).

If at the end of the financial year the company owns shares in another company exceeding 10 per cent of that company's allotted share capital, or 10 per cent of the investing company's assets, the acounts must show by note:

—the name of that other company;

—its country of incorporation;

—proportion of allotted share capital of each class of allotted share capital held by the investing company.

The format refers to 'related' companies. These are companies other than subsidiaries, in which the investing company holds 20 per cent or more of the equity voting shares on a long-term basis to obtain a trading benefit or to influence the affairs of that other company.

(b) SSAP 1

The definition which concluded (*a*) above is similar to, but not identical with, that of an 'associated' company in SSAP 1:

'An associated company is a company not being a subsidiary of the investing group in which:

(1) The interest of the investing group is effectively that of a partner in a joint venture or consortium and the investing group or company is in a position to exercise significant influence over the company in which the investment is made; or

(2) The interest of the investing group or company is for the long term and is substantial and, having regard to the disposition of the other shareholdings, the

investing group or company is in a position to exercise a significant influence over the company in which the investment is made' (SSAP 1, para. 13).

If a company in which a shareholding of 20 per cent or more is held is *not* treated as an associate, the accounting treatment adopted and the reason for adopting it must be disclosed (SSAP 1, para. 38).

If a company in which a shareholding of less than 20 per cent is held *is* treated as an associate, the basis on which it is contended that significant influence is exercised should be stated (SSAP 1, para. 38).

The following details of associated companies must be given:

(1) The proportion of the issued share capital held;
(2) An indication of the nature of the business.

10.5.2 Internal control

Internal controls over investments should be similar to those described in Section 10.2.2 above for fixed assets:

(*a*) Custody arrangements for share certificates
(*b*) Authorization for purchases and sales
(*c*) Records—showing full details of each investment and the income etc derived.

10.5.3 The audit approach

The audit approach is again similar to that given in Section 10.2.3 for fixed assets—verifying ownership, existence and valuation.

(a) Ownership and existence

These will normally be covered by inspecting the share certificates, to confirm that they are prima facie valid and in the name of the client. If they are held by a third party as security for an advance, a certificate from that third party may be accepted. If deposited with a bank for safe custody, share certificates will be covered by the standard bank report reproduced and explained in Section 10.8.2 below. Certificates from other third parties are not normally acceptable—see the City Equitable Fire Assurance case in Section 19.2. If, exceptionally, certificates are held by a broker, this should only be because the shares were in the course of being purchased or sold at the balance sheet date. Then a certificate from the broker may be accepted on the basis that confirmation will be available because the share certificate or cash proceeds will have been received after the balance sheet date.

Receipt of dividends, income, bonus shares etc is secondary evidence of ownership and it is obviously important to confirm that such items have been duly received. For listed shares, this is done by reference to Extel cards. For unlisted companies, the annual accounts of the companies concerned will give the information, at least up to the latest balance sheet date. Dividends and other distributions will be tested using the dividend counterfoils. Purchases and sales of investments during the year will be tested with brokers' contract notes, or with correspondence and agreements in the case of unlisted shares. It is important to review the procedure for authorizing such transactions within the company. For sale transactions, the correct calculation of the profit or loss arising, including the tax consequences, must be checked.

(b) Valuation

The statutory requirements as to valuation were listed in Section 10.5.1(a)(1).

For listed securities, the market value at the balance sheet date may be checked by using the Stock Exchange Daily Official List (SEDOL) or the *Financial Times*. The mid-point of the prices in the SEDOL will be taken (*FT* prices are mid-point prices).

For unlisted securities, the main source of information as to market value will be the accounts of the companies. Although the market value does not have to be disclosed for unlisted securities, it is necessary to consider, for current asset investments, whether net realizable value is below cost and for fixed asset investments whether a permanent diminution in value has occurred.

(c) Sundry matters

(1) Inscribed stocks
A few government stocks do not have a share certificate but the records of holders are maintained by the Bank of England. Such stocks are called 'inscribed' stocks. Verification of title is by means of the standard forms issued by the Bank.

(2) Loans
Everything we have said so far has been about investments in the form of shares or securities, including debentures or loan stock. The heading 'investments' in the format also includes loans, which have to be disclosed separately. (Note, by the way, that in answering examination questions on

this subject it is necessary to be clear whether you are to talk about loans made (assets) or loans received (liabilities):)

The procedure for verifying loans (as assets) is:

—review authorization;

—obtain a certificate from the borrower confirming the amount outstanding;

—study the written agreement covering the loan;

—review the possibility of non-repayment, considering particularly any security given, repayment instalments, if any, and changes in the status of the borrower;

—review as possible related party transactions (see Section 11.11.2);

—confirm that disclosure requirements are met;

—confirm, in the case of loans to directors or other officers, that they do not contravene the provisions of the Companies Act 1985 (Section 17.4)

Those steps are also applicable for current asset loans.

10.6   Stock and work in progress

We now turn to what is probably the most important and most difficult task for the auditor—verifying stock and work in progress.

10.6.1   Regulatory background

(a) Companies Act 1985

Under the historical cost accounting rules, stock, like all current assets is required to be valued at the lower of cost and net realizable value. The chart below summarizes possible methods of arriving at cost under the historical cost accounting rules and their allowability under the Companies Act and SSAP 9.

	Acceptable under	
Method	Companies Act	SSAP 9
Unit cost	✓	✓
First in first out (FIFO)	✓	✓
Last in first out (LIFO)	✓	(Note 1)
Base stock	✓	(Note 1)
Weighted average price	✓	✓
Adjusted selling price	✓	✓ (Note 2)
Replacement cost (current cost)	(Note 3)	Not allowed
Selling price	Not allowed	Not allowed
Standard cost	✓ (Note 4)	✓ (Note 4)

Notes

1. The use of the LIFO and base stock methods is barred by SSAP 9 because they are likely not to provide a reasonably close approximation to actual cost. The Companies Act allows their use, but also provides, whichever method of stock valuation is used, that the difference between the valuation shown and replacement price or the latest purchase price should be disclosed, if that difference is material. The LIFO and base stock methods are more likely than other methods to give rise to such a difference.

2. Adjusted selling price (selling price less profit mark-up) is allowed by SSAP 9 provided it can be shown to give a reasonably close approximation to actual cost. The method is not specifically allowed by the Companies Act but qualifies under the heading of 'any other method similar to any of the methods mentioned above'.

3. Replacement cost (current cost) is not allowed by either authority in historical cost accounting, but would, of course, be permitted in current cost accounting under the alternative accounting rules (Schedule 4 paragraph 31(5)).

4. Standard costs are only allowed if they have been reviewed to ensure that they bear a reasonable relationship to actual costs.

The Schedule 4 format requires the separate disclosure of the elements of stocks:

—Raw materials and consumables
—Work in progress
—Finished goods and goods for resale
This analysis can be very significant. Consider the following example:

	Opening (£000)	Closing (£000)
Raw materials	1000	100
Work in progress	200	50
Finished goods	100	1150
	1300	1300

The implications here, in the absence of special factors, are:

—the level of manufacturing output has declined;
—the finished goods won't sell.

These vital conclusions would have been completely hidden if nothing but the total stock figure of £1 300 000 had been available.

(b) SSAP 9

The main provisions of SSAP 9 have been covered in parallel with the Companies Act requirements in (a) above. We shall consider work in progress separately later.

10.6.2 Internal control

Internal controls over stock need to cover:

(a) *Custody.* There must be provision of adequate controls to guard the stock from loss through pilferage, exposure to weather and other hazards.

(b) *Records.* There should be adequate records of all stock movements, periodically reconciled with total accounts and with costing records.

(c) *Authorization.* All stock movements should be properly authorized—purchases by the ordering or reordering procedures, issues by duly signed requisitions, scrappings by special authorization within a defined set of procedures.

(d) *Physical checks.* There should be continuous or periodic agreement of physical stocks with records, and all material differences investigated.

(e) *Cut-off.* Although cut-off is of most significance to the auditor at the year-end, the discipline of establishing consistency of treatment of items in different records is something that should be maintained at all times. Remember that cut-off is not confined to the relationship between purchase and stock.

As the stock moves through the system from purchase to sale, it enters five different record systems:

(1) purchases in the financial accounting system;
(2) raw materials stock record;
(3) costing system;
(4) finished goods stock record;
(5) sales in the financial accounting system.

A cut-off error means a failure of consistency of recording between two of the different record systems. For example, if a purchase is dated in the financial accounting system on the day the invoice is received from the supplier, and the entry for the goods in the stock record is dated when the stock is actually received, a substantial error which directly affects the net profit is introduced. Of course if an integrated accounting system, computerized or not, is in operation, the risk of undiscovered cut-off errors is greatly reduced.

(*f*) *Slow-moving stock.* There should be a regular review to identify and take action to get rid of slow-moving, obsolescent or defective stock.

(*g*) *Supervision.* There should be adequate supervision of all stages of stock handling.

(*h*) *Stocktaking.* Detailed procedures should be established to ensure that stocktaking is done properly. These should include:

(1) ensuring that staff involved are both knowledgeable about the stock and independent of the day-to-day handling or recording of the stock. (This may be difficult to combine in one person but the use of a two-person team, which has other advantages in the counting procedure, makes it easier.)

(2) issue of written stocktaking instructions, laying down counting and re-counting procedures, methods of marking stock when counted and precisely defining the responsibilities of all staff involved.

(3) proper arrangements to ensure that items belonging to third parties are excluded.

(4) attention to cut-off at the time of the count, so that unavoidable movements are accurately reflected.

(5) arrangements to ensure that prices entered on stock sheets are correct and in line with the company's policy as regards valuation (FIFO, average, etc).

(6) computing and checking calculations and additions on stock sheets.

(7) application of overall tests as detailed in Section 10.6.5 below.

(*i*) *Continuous stocktaking.* The system will often include a process whereby stock items are checked throughout the year, so that every item is checked at least once per year, and important or fast-moving items more frequently. Such a process, properly carried out, means that the year-end stock figure can be arrived at from the stock records, which will have been checked against the physical stock throughout the year.

10.6.3 The audit approach

It is to be expected that the client has some useful controls in the area of stock, as outlined in the previous paragraph. Compliance tests on those will be made when reliance is to be placed upon them.

The stock system—with stock records

The use of the system illustrated in our diagram should mean that stock is effectively controlled, and year-end stock can be accurately ascertained. The stock records are absolutely essential—without them we have as little control over stock as we should have over petty cash if no record of movements (the

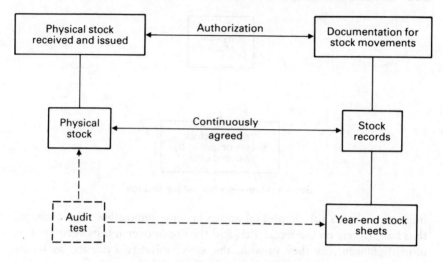

Stock system—with stock records

petty cash book) existed to provide a measure of the money which should be in the cash box.

Against such a background an auditor may proceed as follows:

(*a*) Review system of internal control;

(*b*) Compliance tests on key controls;

(*c*) Physical checks—a test physical check on a sample of stock items, not to be confused with attendance to observe stocktaking;

(*d*) Observation (see Section 10.6.4 below);

(*e*) Substantive tests on accuracy of records;

(*f*) Substantive tests on accuracy of stock sheets (casts and calculations);

(*g*) Check on cut-off procedure (see Section 10.6.2(*e*) above);

(*h*) Overall tests (see Section 10.6.5 below);

(*i*) Check on slow-moving, obsolete and defective items. These should be identified by the client's own procedures. The auditor will be able to scrutinize stock records for items with few entries in the course of the year and be alert to detect such items when carrying out physical checks or observation;

(*j*) Confirm that the valuation of the stock is in line with the Companies Act, SSAP 9 and the company's valuation policy;

(*k*) Obtain certificates from third parties holding the company's stock and, if the amounts involved are material, consider counting the stock at the third parties' premises. The subsequent return of the stock after the year-end, or the receipt of the proceeds of its sale, may lighten the auditor's burden in this respect.

If the client's system is less comprehensive, and in particular if there are no stock records, we may have something like this:

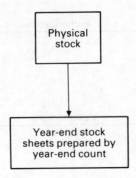

Stock system—without stock records

Important checks (*a*), (*b*) and (*e*) above become impossible. The audit will thus have to rely on the remainder, and the use of overall tests becomes even more significant, as they provide the only objective evidence as to the accuracy of the stock total. The most fundamental of these is the comparison of the gross profit percentage achieved with that which could be expected (see Section 10.6.5 below).

10.6.4 APC Guideline on Attendance at Stocktaking

This important area is covered by an Auditing Guideline issued in October 1983. The full text is reproduced below:

Preface

Paragraph 4 of the Auditing Standard, 'The auditor's operational standard' states that:

'The auditor should obtain relevant and reliable audit evidence sufficient to enable him to draw reasonable conclusions therefrom'.

This Auditing Guideline gives guidance on how that paragraph may be applied in relation to attendance at stocktaking. It is supplementary to and should be read in conjunction with the auditor's operational and reporting standards and related guidelines.

Introduction

(1) The value of stock and work in progress ('stocks') in the financial statements of a trading enterprise will often be material to the profit and loss account and to the balance sheet and, as such, is of great importance to the financial statements. There are three main elements in the audit of stocks: existence, ownership and valuation. This guideline is primarily concerned with the first of these elements.

Responsibilities

(2) It is the responsibility of the management of an enterprise to ensure that the amount at which stocks are shown in the financial statements represents stocks physically in existence and includes all stocks owned by the enterprise. Management satisfies this responsibility by carrying out appropriate procedures which will normally involve ensuring that all stocks are subject to a count at least once in every financial year. Further, where the auditor attends any physical count of stocks in order to obtain audit evidence, this responsibility will not be reduced.

(3) In the case of a company incorporated under the Companies Acts, management also has responsibilities to maintain proper accounting records and to include all statements of stocktakings in those records.

(4) It is the responsibility of the auditor to obtain evidence in order to enable him to draw conclusions about the validity of the quantities upon which are based the amount of stocks shown in the financial statements. The principal sources of this evidence are stock records, control systems, the results of any stocktaking and test counts made by the auditor himself. By reviewing the enterprise's stock records and stock control systems, the auditor can decide to what extent he needs to rely upon attendance at stocktaking to obtain the necessary audit evidence.

Attendance as a means of providing evidence

(5) Where stocks are material in the enterprise's financial statements, and the auditor is placing reliance upon management's stocktake in order to provide evidence of existence, then the auditor should attend the stocktaking. This is because attendance at stocktaking is normally the best way of providing evidence of the proper functioning of management's stocktaking procedures, and hence of the existence of stocks and their condition.

(6) Evidence of the existence of work in progress will frequently be obtained by a stocktake. However, the nature of the work in progress may be such that it is impracticable to determine its existence by a count. Management may place substantial reliance on internal controls designed to ensure the completeness and accuracy of records of work in progress. In such circumstances there may not be a stocktake which could be attended by the auditor. Nevertheless, inspection of the work in progress will assist the auditor to plan his audit procedures, and it may also help on such matters as the determination of the stage of completion of construction or engineering work in progress.

Types of stocktaking

(7) Physical verification of stocks may be by means of a full count (or measurement in the case of bulk stocks) of all the stocks at the year end or at a selected date before or shortly after the year end, or by means of a count of part of the stocks in which case it may be possible to extrapolate the total statistically. Alternatively, verification may be by means of the counting or measurement of stocks during the course of the year using continuous stock-checking methods. Some business enterprises use

continuous stock-checking methods for certain stocks and carry out a full count of other stocks at a selected date.

(8) Paragraphs 9 and 10 set out some special considerations in circumstances where the count is carried out at a date which is not the same as that of the financial statements or where it takes place throughout the year. The principal procedures which the auditor would normally carry out in relation to his attendance at any count of stocks are set out in paragraphs 11 to 21 of this guideline.

(9) The evidence of the existence of stocks provided by the stocktake results is most effective when the stocktaking is carried out at the end of the financial year. Stocktaking carried out before or after the year end may also be acceptable for audit purposes providing records of stock movements in the intervening period are such that the movements can be examined and substantiated. The auditor should bear in mind that the greater the interval between the stocktaking and the year end the greater will be his difficulties in substantiating the amount of stocks at the balance sheet date. Such difficulties will, however, be lessened by the existence of a well developed system of internal control and satisfactory stock records.

(10) Where continuous stock-checking methods are being used, the auditor should perform tests designed to confirm that management:

(a) maintains adequate stock records that are kept up-to-date;

(b) has satisfactory procedures for stocktaking and test-counting, so that in normal circumstances the programme of counts will cover all stocks at least once during the year; and

(c) investigates and corrects all material differences between the book stock records and the physical counts.

The auditor needs to do this to gain assurance that the stock-checking system as a whole is effective in maintaining accurate stock records from which the amount of stocks in the financial statements can be derived. It is unlikely that he will be able to obtain such assurance if the three matters above are not confirmed satisfactorily, in which circumstances a full count at the year end may be necessary.

Procedures

(11) The following paragraphs set out the principal procedures which may be carried out by an auditor when attending a stocktake, but are not intended to provide a comprehensive list of the audit procedures which the auditor may find it necessary to perform during his attendance.

Before the stocktaking: planning

(12) The auditor should plan his audit coverage of a stocktake by:

(a) reviewing his working papers for the previous year where applicable, and discussing with management any significant changes in stocks over the year;

(b) discussing stocktaking arrangements and instructions with management;

(c) familarising himself with the nature and volume of the stocks, the identification of high value items and the method of accounting for stocks;

(d) considering the location of the stock and assessing the implications of this for stock control and recording;

(e) reviewing the systems of internal control and accounting relating to stocks, so as to identify potential areas of difficulty (for example cut-off);

(f) considering any internal audit involvement, with a view to deciding the reliance which can be placed on it;

(g) ensuring that a representative selection of locations, stocks and procedures are covered, and particular attention is given to high value items where these form a significant proportion of the total stock value;

(h) arranging to obtain from third parties confirmation of stocks held by them, but if the auditor considers that such stocks are a material part of the enterprise's total stock, or the third party is not considered to be independent or reliable, then arranging where appropriate either for him or for the third party's auditor to attend a stocktake at the third party's premises; and

(i) establishing whether expert help needs to be obtained to substantiate quantities, or to identify the nature and condition of the stocks, where they are very specialised.

(13) The auditor should examine the way the stocktaking is organised and should evaluate the adequacy of the client's stocktaking instructions. Such instructions should preferably be in writing, cover all phases of the stocktaking procedures, be issued in good time and be discussed with those responsible for carrying out the stocktaking to ensure the procedures are understood and that potential difficulties are anticipated. If the instructions are found to be inadequate, the auditor should seek improvements to them.

During the stocktaking

(14) During the stocktaking, the auditor should ascertain whether the client's staff are carrying out their instructions properly so as to provide reasonable assurance that the stocktaking will be accurate. He should make test counts to satisfy himself that procedures and internal controls relating to the stocktaking are working properly. If the manner of carrying out the stocktaking or the results of the test-counts are not satisfactory, the auditor should immediately draw the matter to the attention of the management supervising the stocktaking and he may have to request a recount of part, or all of the stocks.

(15) When carrying out test-counts, the auditor should select items both from count records and from the physical stocks and should check one to the other to gain assurance as to the completeness and accuracy of the count records. In this context, he should give particular consideration to those stocks which he believes, for example from the stock records or from his prior year working papers, to have a high value either individually or as a category of stock. The auditor should include in his working papers items for subsequent testing, such as photocopies of (or extracts from) rough stocksheets and details of the sequence of stocksheets.

(16) The auditor should determine whether the procedures for identifying damaged, obsolete and slow moving stock operate properly. He should obtain (from his observations and by discussion, e.g. with storekeepers) information about the stocks' condition, age, usage and, in the case of work in progress, its stage of completion. Further, he should ascertain that stock held on behalf of third parties is separately identified and accounted for.

(17) The auditor should consider whether management has instituted adequate cut-off procedures i.e. procedures intended to ensure that movements into, within and out

of stocks are properly identified and reflected in the accounting records. The auditor's procedures during the stocktaking will depend on the manner in which the year end stock value is to be determined. For example, where stocks are determined by a full count and evaluation at the year end, the auditor should test the arrangements made to segregate stocks owned by third parties and he should identify goods movement documents for reconciliation with financial records of purchases and sales. Alternatively, where the full count and evaluation is at an interim date and year end stocks are determined by updating such valuation by the cost of purchases and sales, the auditor should perform those procedures during his attendance at the stocktaking and in addition should test the financial cut-off (involving the matching of costs with revenues) at the year end.

(18) In addition, the auditor should:

(a) conclude whether the stocktaking has been properly carried out and is sufficiently reliable as a basis for determining the existence of stocks;

(b) consider whether any amendment is necessary to his subsequent audit procedures; and

(c) try to gain from his observations an overall impression of the levels and values of stocks held so that he may, in due course, judge whether the figure for stocks appearing in the financial statements is reasonable.

(19) The auditor's working papers should include details of his observations and tests, the manner in which points that are relevant and material to the stocks being counted or measured have been dealt with by the client, instances where the client's procedures have not been satisfactorily carried out and the auditor's conclusions.

After the stocktaking

(20) After the stocktaking, the matters recorded in the auditor's working papers at the time of the count or measurement should be followed up. For example, details of the last serial numbers of goods inwards and outwards notes and of movements during the stocktaking should be used in order to check cut-off. Further, photocopies of (or extracts from) rough stocksheets and details of test-counts, and of the sequence of rough stocksheets, may be used to check that the final stocksheets are accurate and complete.

(21) The auditor should ensure that continuous stock records have been adjusted to the amounts physically counted or measured and that differences have been investigated. Where appropriate, he should ensure also that management has instituted proper procedures to deal with transactions between stocktaking and the year end, and also test those procedures. In addition, he should check replies from third parties about stocks held by or for them, follow up all queries and notifiy senior management of serious problems encountered during the stocktaking.

10.6.5 Overall tests

Once all possible audit tests have been applied to individual stock items, there remains a powerful set of further tests which can be applied to the *total* of the stock. These tests are intended to confirm that the stock total is consistent with other figures in the accounts or available from other sources. The six overall tests given in ICAEW Statement on Auditing U11 (now withdrawn) are:

(a) reconciliation of changes in stock quantities as between the beginning and end of the financial year with records of purchases, production and sales;

(b) comparison of the quantities and amounts of stocks in the various categories with those included at the previous balance sheet date and with current sales and purchases;

(c) consideration of the gross profit ratio shown by the accounts and its comparison with the results shown in previous years;

(d) consideration of the rate of turnover of stocks and its comparison with previous years;

(e) consideration of the relationship of the quantities ready for sale and in course of production with the quantities shown in operating and sales budgets;

(f) where applicable, examination of standard costing records and consideration of the variances shown thereby and their treatment in the accounts.

10.6.6 Finished goods—valuation

It is important to realize that the principles of valuation of finished goods manufactured by the client are different from those for raw materials or items bought ready for sale. The cost of finished goods will include materials and labour *plus an allocation of overhead costs*. SSAP 9 defines cost as 'expenditure incurred in the normal course of business in bringing the stock to its present location and condition'. Related production overheads should be included in cost, as should other overheads attributable to bringing the product or services to its present location and condition. The allocation of overheads should reflect current and expected future levels of activity. Pricing information will be obtained from the costing system.

10.6.7 Work in progress

Most work in progress will be valued and audited according to the principles already explained for stock. Initial information will be obtained from the costing records, backed up by physical measurement by the client and verified by the auditor. The auditor's work will therefore consist of:

(a) compliance and substantive tests of costing records;
(b) physical check;

(c) review against budgets, contract prices and records of other similar jobs to confirm that it is in order to value the work in progress at cost and that no reduction to net realizable value is necessary;

(d) review of completions since balance sheet date to confirm that valuation is acceptable;

(e) review basis for inclusion of overheads;

(f) discussion of individual material jobs with the responsible manager or director to enable the auditor to form a view as to whether the valuation placed upon them is reasonable.

10.6.8 Long-term contract work in progress

The additional problem arising with long-term contract work in progress is that of valuation. SSAP 9 defines a long-term contract as one which will extend for more than one year. This means that the profit on the job, if any, will be attributable to two or more accounting periods. Is it acceptable to take some of this profit each year or should we wait until the job is finished? SSAP 9 requires long-term contract work in progress to be valued at 'cost plus any attributable profit, less any foreseeable losses and progress payments received and receivable'. In other words, profit can be taken as the job proceeds, provided, of course, that a profitable outcome to the contract can be reasonably expected. If a loss is forecast, *the whole loss* should be provided for immediately. The normal basis of valuation *for each contract* will therefore be:

Materials plus labour plus attributable overheads plus attributable profit
OR
Materials plus labour plus attributable overheads *minus full expected loss on completion*

If the expected loss on completion exceeds the costs to date (disastrous but possible) a provision has to be made for the excess.

So what is attributable profit? SSAP 9 defines it as:

'that part of total profit currently estimated to arise over the duration of the contract (after allowing for likely increases in costs so far as not recoverable under the terms of the contract) which fairly reflects the profit attributable to that part of the work performed at the accounting date. (There can be no attributable profit until the outcome of the contract can be assessed with reasonable certainty.)'

Many long-term contracts are civil engineering or building works for which a supervising architect or surveyor issues *certificates* for work completed, on the basis of which payments are made for the work, often with the deduction of a *retention* (5 or 10 per cent of the certificate value) which is not released until the job is completed. These provide important evidence of the amount of work completed, but it will be dangerous to take as the measure of profit:

Why? Because no account is taken of costs to completion, penalties for late completion, or for the fact that the easy part of the job has been done so far.
   A more reliable method is:

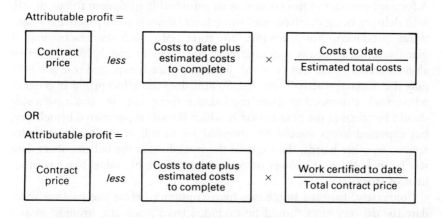

Even these methods cannot be adopted blindly. It is still necessary for the auditor to consider carefully, and discuss with management, factors which may influence the outcome of the contract:

(*a*) size and likelihood of penalties for late completion;
(*b*) difficult or unknown site conditions, especially on overseas contracts;
(*c*) likelihood of strikes or other labour difficulties;
(*d*) the fact that the contract is unusually large compared with the client's normal work, or involves unusual technological problems;
(*e*) possible effect of foreign exchange movements;
(*f*) reliability of subcontractors and others associated with the contract;
(*g*) on the plus side, possible additional payments to be received for contract variations;
(*h*) provision for possible costs of rectification during the maintenance period which often extends for six months after the completion of the work.

   The final problem is the potential clash between the SSAP 9 basis for taking profit explained above and the rule under the Companies Act. It is argued by some that the Companies Act does not allow the taking of profits on long-term contracts. (Paragraph 22 of Schedule 4 requires all current assets to be valued at cost or net realizable value if lower.) We may escape from this problem either by invoking the 'true and fair' override of S228, or by regarding the profit as realized to the extent that the value of work in progress certified to date (and on which payment has been received or is due) exceeds the cost of that work.

10.6.9 Forward contracts for the purchase or sale of stock

A forward contract in this context is an enforceable agreement to buy or sell, with delivery being deferred until some future date. It is the practice for base metal producers, for example, to enter into such contracts, and a manufacturing company requiring large quantities of metals like copper or aluminium may well 'buy forward' when the price is expected to rise by the time the material is actually needed. So how does this affect profit? In general, where such a transaction spans the balance sheet date, any profit on a *sale* should be taken in the next period in which the sale is completed by delivery, but expected losses should be provided for in full in the accounts under review. In other words, the value of the stock held at the balance sheet date will be included at the lower of cost and net realizable value, like any other item of stock.

Conversely, forward *purchases* by a consumer before the balance sheet date for delivery after should be excluded from stock and brought in as a purchase only when the goods are actually received. Any cash paid will simply be regarded as a payment in advance. If the price at the balance sheet date is less than the contracted price, no provision will normally be necessary, unless the reduction is so great that it is expected that the product into which the material is included will show a loss on sale as a result.

10.7 Debtors

The items in the balance sheet format under the general heading of debtors are:

—trade debtors;
—amounts owed by group companies;
—amounts owed by related companies;
—other debtors;
—called up share capital not paid;
—prepayments and accrued income.

Each heading has to be analysed where necessary between those due to be received within one year and those not due for more than one year. The most important of these is probably going to be trade debtors.

10.7.1 Trade debtors

Compliance and substantive tests on the sales ledger will have gone a long way towards establishing the correctness of this figure. Assuming that this work has been completed, the audit work on the debtor balances will be:

(a) Obtain a copy of the *balances*, preferably one analysed according to the number of months each debt has been understanding:

Pre-October	October	November	December	Total

If an 'aged' list is not available the auditor will have to request the client to produce one or prepare one himself.

(1) Check or test the extraction of the balances from the ledger and the additions of the schedule.
(2) Confirm agreement of total of balances with control account.
(3) Review adequacy of provision for doubtful debts and bad-debt write-offs, by examining correspondence relating to older or disputed balances and discussing them with the credit control staff. Any provision will normally be a specific one, as it is then allowable for tax purposes. If general provisions are made their adequacy may be assessed by reference to past experience and to the auditor's listing of debts which he considers should be provided for the in the current year.

(b) *Scrutiny.* Whenever work is being carried out on the ledger (items (1) and (3) above, and tests on transactions) the auditor will be alert for irregular or potentially fraudulent transactions. For example, an apparent increase in the number of payments on account, where payments cannot be matched with specific invoices, may be due to *teeming and lading*, a fraud which works like this.

Suppose a business receives payment of its accounts partly by cash and partly by cheque. Suppose also that the cashier can make entries in the sales ledger, and that he has decided to help himself to all cash receipts where possible, letting the company have the benefit of the cheques:

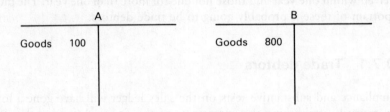

A	B
Goods 100	Goods 800

Customer A pays his £100 in cash, and the cashier embezzles it. He now has the problem of getting a credit into A's account. This he could do by 'splitting' a subsequent cheque from B, crediting £100 to A and £700 to B. The shortage in B's account will be made good out of a cheque received from another customer C, and so on. Such a fraud is called 'teeming and lading', an old phrase meaning taking out (teeming) and putting back (lading). The expression is a particularly happy one as 'teem' means both 'to be full' and 'to empty', while 'lade' means both 'to load' and 'to unload'.

Other possible methods the fraudulent cashier could try are:

(1) passing fictitious credit notes;
(2) writing off the debt as bad;
(3) transferring the balance to another account; or
(4) omitting altogether the recording of an invoice to a customer expected to pay by cash.

Of course, such frauds can only exist without collusion in systems lacking fundamental controls. The discovery of the absence of such controls at an earlier stage of the audit should alert the auditor to the possibility of fraudulent exploitation of the weakness.

(c) *Analytical review.* In the context of trade debtors, analytical review can be useful in drawing attention to poor credit control or to customers' increasing difficulty in paying accounts. The trend may be checked by calculating the number of days' credit sales represented in the annual sales figure. If the business is seasonal it may be better to relate debtors to the sales total of the months immediately before the year-end, or to compare the age analysis of debtor from year to year or from month to month. Care must also be taken here to leave out large sales on which specially extended credit terms have been granted.

Another useful overall test is comparison of monthly sales figures. If sales for the last month of the year are high without being explained by seasonal factors, it may be that sales from the following year have been brought back to boost the profit. If sales for the first month of the new period are exceptionally low this becomes more probable still. The auditor's action here will be to pay special attention to cut-off procedures affecting debtors. This is discussed next.

(d) *Cut-off procedure.* In relation to debtors, cut-off means confirming that all goods sold in the period were actually delivered in the period and are excluded from stock. In some cases, valid sales may have been effected but the goods are not yet delivered pending instructions from the customer. It is only too easy for such goods to be included in stock and the auditor's cut-off check will obviously cover this aspect if relevant.

(e) *Review of credit notes. Credit notes can equal cash (see (b) above).* Procedures for authorization of credit notes will have been covered at an earlier stage of the audit, but it is worth vouching larger ones as part of the check on debtors, especially those issued in the early months of the next period, in case they represent the cancellation of a transaction before the balance sheet date which was included fraudulently or in error.

(f) *Circularization.* Circularization means asking a selection of debtors to confirm their balance directly to the auditor. It is a potentially powerful technique, its major limitation being that increasing numbers of customers fail to cooperate by responding to confirmation requests.

Circularization may be either 'positive' or 'negative'. Positive circularization means that the debtor is asked to reply whether the balance is agreed or not, and negative circularization that the debtor is asked to reply only if the balance is not agreed. Positive circularization obviously gives the auditor greater assurance, but negative circularization has some value, especially when dealing with a large number of small balances. A combination of the two techniques could be used, with positive circularization of large balances and negative circularization of small ones.

Circularization procedure should therefore be as follows:

(1) obtain client's permission
(2) select accounts for circularization. This is an ideal opportunity to use statistical sampling, with stratification so that greater attention is paid to larger balances. In addition it may be appropriate to make a list of accounts which for some special reason need to be confirmed by the debtor, perhaps because the balance is old. Auditing Statement U7 issued by the ICAEW in 1967, offers useful guidance on categories of account and lists as accounts needing special attention:

—old unpaid accounts
—accounts with credit balances
—accounts written off during the period

It also identifies accounts needing some attention but less than the rest:

—accounts with nil balances
—accounts paid after the balance sheet date.

Eliminating these groups of debtor leaves the central group of balances which are neither paid nor particularly old to receive standard attention.

Debtors' confirmation (positive)

Small & Steady Components Ltd

Debtor's name and address

(Address)
Date

Dear Sirs

In accordance with the request of our auditors, Messrs ...., we ask that you kindly confirm to them direct your indebtedness to us at .... which, according to our records, amounted to £ .... as shown by the enclosed Statement.

If the above amount is in agreement with your records, please sign in the space provided below and return this letter direct to our auditors in the enclosed stamped addressed envelope.

If the amount is not in agreement with your records, please notify our auditors direct of the amount shown by your records, and if possible, detail on the reverse of this letter full particulars of the difference.

Yours faithfully

Serial No ....

The amount shown above is in agreement with our records as at ....

Account no .... Signature ....

Date .... Company ....

Title or position ....

Debtors' confirmation (negative)

Small & Steady Components Ltd

Debtor's name and address

(Address)
Date

Dear Sirs

We enclose a statement of your account up to.......

If you do not agree the balance shown on the enclosed statement, we shall be obliged if you will show below the balance appearing in your books and return this direct to our auditors, ...together with, if possible, particulars of the difference.

Yours faithfully

Serial no.......

The balance shown in our books at..............is £ ....

Account no .... Signature ....

Date .... Company ....

Title or position ....

---

(3) send out confirmation requests. These may take the form of a standard letter incorporating authorization from the client for the customer to reply. Customers should be asked to reply direct to the auditor, and a stamped addressed envelope should be enclosed. The letter should ask the customer to indicate the extent of any disagreement, and this may be facilitated if a detailed statement or copy of the ledger account is sent.

(4) Follow up. When the positive method is used, the auditors must follow up with a second request if necessary. When all possible replies are in, the

auditor will classify them as:

—agreed and requiring no further action;
—not agreed by customer but reconciled by auditor;
—not agreed by customer and not reconciled by auditor. Such accounts will need to be discussed with the client's staff and, perhaps in collaboration with the customer, necessary adjustments made. Further action may be necessary if the discrepancy shows failure of, or weakness in, the client's system of internal control.
—non replies. It will be necessary for the auditor to obtain acceptable alternative evidence for such balances. The best possible evidence is the subsequent payment of the account. When the account is still outstanding the paperwork supporting the sale (despatch notes, copy invoices, etc.) should be examined.

The auditor will prepare a working schedule listing all accounts circularized, indicating the response received and summarizing the conclusions drawn from the process.

A list of all accounts not satisfactorily resolved should be passed to a responsible company official, preferably one independent of the sales accounting department, who should arrange for them to be investigated.

If the circularization reveals widespread disagreement and lack of reliability in the client's records the auditor must consider qualifying the audit report.

(g) *Disclosure.* The Companies Act format requires separate disclosure of amounts due to group companies and to related companies. Such balances should have been identified and correctly included in the balance sheet by the client. It is obviously important for the auditor to confirm that this has been done accurately. It is also necessary to separate debtors into those due within one year and those due after more than one year.

10.7.2 Bills of exchange receivable

Amounts due on bills receivable will normally have been received by the time of the audit, and this constitutes pretty convincing evidence of the ownership, value and existence of the bill at the balance sheet date.

This check will be supplemented by test checks on the bills receivable record. It is good auditing practice to inspect the bills themselves *at the year end* (i.e. on the balance sheet date). Any bills held by the client's bankers will be picked up by means of the bank report given in Section 10.8.2 below.

In the case of bills which have not yet matured by the time of the audit, the question of a provision for possible doubtful debts needs to be considered. If any bills have been renegotiated or replaced by another bill with a later maturity, that could indicate financial difficulties.

Bills discounted represent a contingent liability and should be disclosed as such.

10.7.3 Amounts owed by group companies

Amounts owed by group companies will be reconciled in the normal course of preparing and auditing group accounts.

10.7.4 Amounts owed by related companies

These are potentially going to be very large balances because of the trading connection. Related companies should first be identified and then all material balances covered by circularization.

10.7.5 Other debtors, including prepayments and accrued income

This heading can include:

—loans;
—prepayments and accrued income;
—deferred revenue expenditure.

(a) Loans

The verification of loans has already been covered in Section 10.5.3(c)(2). The rules relating to loans to directors and other officers are dealt with in Section 17.4.

(b) Prepayments and accrued income

The client will have produced a schedule of such items in the course of preparing the accounts. The auditor will scrutinize the schedule and vouch supporting evidence for the calculations of the larger items.

(c) Deferred revenue expenditure

The sort of item included here will be heavy advertising expenditure towards the end of the period which is expected to benefit future periods rather than the current one. Carrying forward such expenditure is an obvious way of 'improving' the profit or reducing a loss. The auditor will need to confirm that there is a genuine reason for the treatment adopted, not merely a window-dressing one. Remember that the Companies Act prohibits the carrying forward of:

(1) preliminary expenses;
(2) expenses of, or commission on, any issue of shares or debentures;
(3) research expenditure.

10.7.6 Called up share capital not paid

See Section 10.11.1(*a*)(3) below.

10.8 Cash at bank and in hand

10.8.1 Bank balances generally

Bank balances are easy to verify. Two steps are necessary:

—obtain confirmation of balances from the bank or banks concerned (see Section 10.8.2);
—as the balance confirmed is that according to the bank's records, check the reconciliation of the cash book with the bank statement.

(a) Set-off

The Companies Act bars any set-off between assets and liabilities. An overdraft on one account and a balance on another should not be offset unless there is a legal right of set-off.

(b) Unpresented cheques and receipts after the balance sheet date

Clients with high overdrafts pushing on the agreed limit frequently write and date cheques but do not post them until the overdraft will stand them. This practice is not acceptable and such cheques must be regarded as being paid *on the date they leave the client's premises*. Receipts after the balance sheet date are sometimes included in the cash book as having been received before it.

This is also unacceptable and they must, of course, be entered in the cash book on the actual date of receipt.

(c) The bank reconciliation

(1) Teeming and lading

When checking the agreement between the cash book and the bank statement the auditor should pay particular attention to the dating of the lodgements. A discrepancy in the dates may indicate delay in banking resulting from a form of teeming and lading (see Section 10.7.1(b)) in which a cashier obtains personal use of the client's receipts, making good the embezzled takings of Day 1 from Day 2, and so on.

(2) Outstanding cheques generally

Cheques not presented at the balance sheet date should be checked to the bank statement after date.

(3) Old outstanding cheques

A few cheques issued by a company are never presented. After perhaps six months it becomes necessary for the client to consider reversing the entry for them, restoring the bank balance and reinstating the liability concerned.

(d) Overdrafts

The procedures for verifying overdrafts are the same as those for bank balances. Two further points need to be considered.

(1) Overdraft limit

It will be necessary for the auditor to enquire into the terms and limits of any overdraft facility as part of the going concern review. (The availability of further bank finance, or the lack of it, may be very material factors in assessing the company's viability).

(2) Disclosure requirements

Where an overdraft is secured the fact must be stated in the accounts. The amount of bank loans and overdrafts has to be disclosed separately in the Companies Act format.

(e) Balance with small or obscure banks

Such balances need to be reviewed to confirm that amounts deposited are in fact recoverable and can correctly be described as a bank balance.

10.8.2 Bank balances—the Auditing Guideline: Bank Reports for Audit Purposes

As indicated above, the auditor must obtain a report from the bank confirming the bank balance. The opportunity is taken to pick up a lot more information from the bank at the same time.

The Auditing Guideline, which includes a specimen form of report, was issued in June 1982 and is reproduced below.

Introduction

(1) Paragraph 4 of the Auditor's Operational Standard states that the auditor should obtain relevant and reliable audit evidence. This guideline is designed to assist auditors in complying with this standard with respect to amounts due to and from banks, and assets held by them.

(2) The practice of obtaining independent certificates or reports from banks is an important feature in the proper discharge of auditors' responsibilities. Bank reports assist auditors to ascertain the existence and the amount of liabilities and the existence, amount, ownership and proper custody of assets; they also provide other information relevant to the audit of financial statements.

(3) The standard audit request letter in the Appendix to this guideline has been prepared following discussions with the Committee of London Bankers, and the Committee of Scottish Clearing Bankers. The standard letter has been prepared primarily for the purpose of obtaining information from the clearing banks. Many companies, however, also have dealings with other banks or licenced deposit-taking institutions, and auditors will normally need reports from them. The British Bankers' Association has indicated that the standard letter may not always be appropriate for requests to such organisations, particuarly where specialised or limited services are offered, and that consequently no undertaking can be given by their members to answer every question on every occasion. Separate guidance relating to Ireland will be issued in due course. The standard request letter set out in the guideline should be used for all requests to banks after 1 October 1982.

Background

(4) The information which auditors regularly need from banks is substantially the same for most audits, and can be obtained in a standard letter of request. The use of such a letter, designed to cover all normal banking activity and to facilitate the extraction of information from banking records, should smooth the processing of these audit requests. The answers received should assist in highlighting areas which require particular audit attention.

(5) As the clearing banks keep their customer records in a more or less similar manner, the use of a standard letter should facilitate the efficient preparation of their replies. The banks accept the need for their assistance in these matters, and a standard letter gives them a clearer understanding of auditors' requirements.

(6) Auditors should therefore request information from banks in the form of the

standard letter set out in the Appendix and in accordance with the procedures in paragraph 11 to 13 below. It is intended that this standard letter should be primarily for audit purposes, but if it is used when members are only concerned with the preparation of accounts and not with the audit of, for instance, sole traders, partnerships or other non-statutory organisations, then any reference in it to an audit should be deleted. For certain purposes other than verification at the year-end (for example for work of an accounting nature, interim audits and accountants' reports on solicitors' accounts), it may be necessary to seek confirmation only of selected items from the standard request. In such cases the letter should not be headed 'standard request for bank report'.

(7) The attached standard letter is a revision of the one set out in the Statement issued in 1976, following experience gained in the use of that earlier version. It now includes enough space for the banks to enter their replies on a copy of the letter, which should be sent at the same time as the audit request.

(8) As indicated in paragraph 3 above, in the case of institutions other than clearing banks it may often be more appropriate for the auditor to make a specific request for the information he requires rather than to use the standard letter. If he is unable to obtain any of the information he requires, he must consider the effect of this on his audit opinion.

Authority to disclose

(9) Banks will require the explicit authority of their customers to disclose the requested information. They will always require such authority in writing, and this may be obtained either on each occasion a bank report is requested, or as an authority which continues until further notice. In the former case it is recommended that the authority should be evidenced by the customer's countersignature to the letter of request; in the latter case the letter of request should refer to the customer's written authority given on a specified earlier date. In the case of a joint account, the authority should be given by all parties to the account.

Disclaimers

(10) The introduction to the letter states that there is no contractual relationship between banker and auditor. In addition, the banks may add a disclaimer at the end of their reply, the text of which may be as follows:

'This reply is given solely for the purpose of your audit without any responsibility to you on the part of the bank, its employees or agents, but it is not to relieve you from any other enquiry or from the performance of any other duty.'

Counsel has given the opinion that the inclusion of the introductory statement and of a disclaimer of this nature does not significantly impair the value of the information given as audit evidence. The information given by a reputable bank should not be regarded as inaccurate or likely to be inaccurate simply because the giving of it is not actionable. Accordingly, an auditor can reasonably rely upon information given by a banker, provided it is not clearly wrong, suspicious or inconsistent in itself, ambiguous or in conflict with other evidence gathered in the course of an audit.

Procedures

(11) Auditors should, where appropriate, adopt the following procedures in connection with requests to banks for audit purposes:

(a) The standard letter set out in the Appendix to this guideline should be sent in duplicate on each occasion by the auditor on his own note paper to each bank branch with which it is known that the client holds an account or has had dealings since the end of the previous accounting reference period.

(b) Auditors should ensure that the bank receives the client's authority to permit disclosure. This authority must be evidenced by: (i) the client's countersignature to the standard letter; or (ii) a specific authority contained in an accompanying letter; or (iii) a reference in the standard letter to the client's specific written authority, given on a specified earlier date, which remains in force.

(c) The letter should reach the branch at least two weeks in advance of the date of the client's financial year-end. This should enable the banks to provide the information within a reasonable time after the year-end. It should be borne in mind, however, that many requests arise at the same time and at a period of peak activity for the banks. Special arrangements should therefore be made with the banks in those cases where, because of time constraints on the audit, a reply is required within a few days of the company's year-end.

(d) The dates to be entered on the standard letter are normally the closing dates of: (i) the client's accounting reference period for which the report is requested; and (ii) the client's previous accounting reference period for which a full bank report was compiled. If, exceptionally, audited accounts are produced other than for an accounting reference period, alternative dates should be substituted.

(e) In reviewing the bank's reply, it is important for auditors to check that the bank has answered all questions in full.

(f) Auditors will need to check the authenticity of any letters not received directly from the bank branch concerned. If an auditor receives a bank report without having made a previous request, he should check with the branch concerned that the report has been prepared in compliance with the terms of the standard letter.

(12) The standard letter should be used in its complete form for all audit requests in respect of year-end financial statements and should not normally be altered or extended. In certain circumstances supplementary requests for additional information may be required for audit purposes. For administrative reasons the letter containing these supplementary requests should be submitted where possible at the same time as the standard letter. Where supplementary information is requested the banks will, as indicated above, require authority to disclose this. If the wording of the authority is not sufficiently comprehensive, additional authority may be required. For some information, such as security lodged by a third party, authority from someone other than the customer may be required.

(13) The banks may choose not to reply on the copy standard letter itself, but instead on their own note paper. If this is the case, the auditor should check that the

list of replies corresponds with the questions on the standard letter and that there have been no omissions.

Appendix: Standard letter of request for bank report for audit purposes

(i) *The form of the letter should not be amended by the auditor.*
(ii) *Sufficient space should be left for the bank's replies (two-thirds of each page is recommended).*

The Manager,

.... (Bank)

.... (Branch)

Dear Sir,

.... (Name of Customer)

STANDARD REQUEST FOR BANK REPORT
FOR AUDIT PURPOSES

FOR THE YEAR ENDED...........

In accordance with your above-named customer's instructions given

(1) hereon
(2) in the attached authority
(3) in the authority dated .... already held
    by you

Delete as appropriate

please send us, as auditors of your customer for the purpose of our business, without entering into any contractual relationship with us, the following information relating to their affairs at your branch as at the close of business on............and, in the case of items 2, 4 and 10 during the period since............. . For each item, please state any factors which may limit the completeness of your reply; if there is nothing to report, state 'none'.

We enclose an additional copy of this letter, and it would be particularly helpful if your reply could be given on the copy letter in the space provided (supported by an additional schedule stamped and signed by the bank where space is insufficient). If you find it necessary to provide the information in another form, please return the copy letter with your reply.

It is understood that any replies given are in strict confidence.

Information requested   *Reply*

Bank accounts

(1) Please give full titles of all accounts whether in sterling or in any other currency together with the account numbers and balances thereon, including NIL balances:

(*a*) where your customer's name is the sole name in the title;

(*b*) where your customer's name is joined with that of other parties;

(*c*) where the account is in a trade name.

NOTES
(i) Where the account is subject to any restriction (e.g. a garnishee order or arrestment), this information should be stated.
(ii) Where the authority upon which you are providing this information does not cover any accounts held jointly with other parties, please refer to your customer in order to obtain the requisite authority. If it is not forthcoming please indicate.

(2) Full titles and dates of closure of all accounts closed during the period.

(3) The separate amounts accrued but not charged or credited at the above date, of:

(*a*) provisional charges (including committment fees); and

(*b*) interest.

Information requested	*Reply*

(4) The amount of interest charged during the period if not specified separately in the bank statement.

(5) Particulars (i.e. date, type of document and accounts covered) of any written acknowledgement of set-off, either by specific letter of set-off, or incorporated in some other document or security.

(6) Details of:

(*a*) overdrafts and loans repayable on demand, specifying dates of review and agreed facilities;

(*b*) other loans specifying dates of review and repayment;

(*c*) other facilities.

Customer's assets held as security

(7) Please give details of any such assets whether or not formally charged to the bank.

If formally charged, give details of the security including the date and type of charge. If a security is limited in amount or to a specific borrowing, or if there is to your knowledge a prior, equal or subordinate charge, please indicate.

If informally charged, indicate nature of security interest therein claimed by the bank.

Whether or not a formal charge has been taken, give particulars of any undertaking given to the bank relating to any assets.

Customer's other assets held

(8) Please give full details of the customer's other assets held, including share certificates, documents of title, deed boxes and any other items listed in your Registers maintained for the purpose of recording assets held.

Contingent liabilities

(9) All contingent liabilities, viz:

(*a*) total of bills discounted for your customer, with recourse;

Information requested   *Reply*

(b) date, name of beneficiary, amount
and brief description of any guarantees,
bonds or indemnities given to you by the
customer for the benefit of third parties;

(c) date, name of beneficiary, amount
and brief description of any guarantees,
bonds or indemnities given by you, on
your customer's behalf, stating where
there is recourse to your customer an-
d/or to its parent or any other company
within the group;

(d) total of acceptances;

(e) total sterling equivalent of outstanding forward foreign exchange contracts;

(f) total of outstanding liabilities under documentary credits;

(g) others—please give details.

Other information

(10) A list of other banks, or branches
of your bank, or associated companies
where you are aware that a relationship
has been established during the period.

Yours faithfully

Disclosure authorised

For and on behalf of

. . . .
(Official stamp of bank)

. . . .
(Name of customer)

. . . .
(Authorised signatory)

. . . .

. . . .
(Signed in accordance with the mandate
for the conduct of the customer's bank
account)

. . . .
(Position)

. . . .
(Date)

Notes to the standard letter

(References are to item numbers in the standard letter)

(1) and (2) *Bank accounts:* The phrase 'all accounts" includes details of all current, deposit, loan and foreign currency accounts and other advances or facilities, money held on deposit receipt. The reply should indicate whether the balance is in favour of the bank or customer, and account numbers. Where a number of deposits have been made or uplifted during the year, it is not neccessary to give details of each separate deposit transaction as would be required in the case of the opening and closing of accounts.

(3) *Accrued charges:* These can be quoted only on a provisional basis; the rate for notional allowances will not be fixed until near the end of the charging period.

(4) *Analysis of charges:* For the purposes of profit and loss disclosure requirements it is only necessary to ask for details of interest charged. (But see note 6 (b) below in respect of balance sheet disclosure requirements). The details of the rate of interest applicable to any interest-bearing accounts, or the appropriate formula by which interest is calculated, should only be required exceptionally.

(5) *Set-off:* Auditors will need to have an understanding of the principles governing set-off, but it should not normally be necessary to make enquiries beyond the question as put in the standard letter. Details should be available from the relevant documents. A right of set-off may exist even when there are no written arrangements.

(6) *Loans and other facilities:* The following details are not normally required:

(a) the date term loans were granted if new or renewed during the period:

(b) rate of interest charged or similar form of compensation (which information is only required by the Companies Acts to be disclosed for facilities which are wholly or partly repayable in more than five years' time);

(c) the purpose of the facility;

(d) loan repayment arrangements, where these are included in a written agreement which is available for inspection by the auditor.

(7) and (8) *Customer's assets:*

(a) *Security* includes details of charge, mortgage or other claims or security registered (e.g. debenture, memorandum of deposit); assets charged and, where appropriate, cross reference to facility specifically secured.

(b) *Assets* include bonds, stock and share certificates, investments, bearer or other securities; title deeds relating to freehold, leasehold or other property; certificates of tax deposit, bills of exchange or other negotiable instruments receivable (other than cheques); shipping and other commercial documents; deposits receipts (as distinct from any account represented by the deposit receipt). The names of persons who are able to obtain release of the assets should be acertained from the customer and are usually covered by the bank mandate.

(c) *Lien:* auditors should be aware that any assets held by the bank for safe custody may be subject to some form of banker's lien, although this may only operate under particular conditions. It should be necessary to enquire only in exceptional circumstances.

(d) *Bearer securities:* detailed enquiries on bearer securities should be made of the bank only when evidence cannot be obtained from the customer or his banking records.

(9) *Contingent liabilities:* The liabilities under indemnities given in respect of missing bills of lading do not have an expiry date. From time to time banks take a view on old liabilities and remove some of them from their records. Certain of these old liabilities may not therefore be shown in the figure quoted by the bank, but it cannot be guaranteed that no claim will be incurred subsequently.

(10) *Other information:* Banks are often asked for introductions to other branches or banks for the purpose of establishing new sources of finance. The provision of any available information relating to introductions or new accounts will assist auditors to satisfy themselves that they have information about all of their client's banking relationships.

Notes on matters excluded from the standard letter

Supplementary requests

The standard letter contains all items found to be regularly required for audit purposes. In cases of doubt, or specific requirement, auditors may wish to make supplementary requests regarding other items which are not regularly required. These may include the following:

(a) copies of bank statements;

(b) copies of paying-in slips for specified lodgements on specified dates;

(c) details showing make-up of those lodgements;

(d) any list of securities or other documents of title which have been with its customer as security for deposit with that bank (This particular matter would probably apply only between banking organisations);

(e) interest on any account paid to or by third parties, and the names of those third parties;

(f) receipts for fire and other insurances, and similar documents in the bank's possession;

(g) returned paid cheques;

(h) stopped cheques—these are normally presented through the banking system within the audit period, and therefore there should be no need to seek specific details;

(i) details of third party security, including directors' guarantees; if this information is required, the request must be accompanied by a specific authority from the appropriate third parties;

(j) details of outstanding forward foreign exchange contracts, including the particulars of each contract, the dates of maturity and the currencies concerned.

Notes

(i) The cost of providing audit information falls on the customer and supplementary requests should be kept to a reasonable minimum.

(ii) Depending on the terms of the authority which has been given, it may be necessary to seek specific authorisation for the disclosure of supplementary information.

Bank mandates

Auditors may require supplementary information about bank mandates as independent verification that board resolutions concerning a company's banking affairs have been duly communicated to the bank so that they may ensure that only authorised persons are acting on behalf of the company. Auditors should ensure that they receive copies of all such resolutions from their clients.

10.8.3 Cash balances

Cash balances seldom amount to a material total. Nevertheless, the auditor will frequently be involved in cash counts, perhaps because the client specifically requests them as a deterrent to fraud. It is first of all necessary to review the client's control procedures over cash, including internal checks, distinguishing between floats held to support expenditures (petty cash) and cash generated by the client's business (cash sale receipts).

(a) Petty cash and similar balances

One possibility is to have all such floats banked at the year end and immediately withdrawn again. Another is to rely on counts by a responsible official of the client. If the auditor does get involved the procedures will be:

(1) obtain a list of all floats, their purpose and the member of staff responsible for each;
(2) review amounts for reasonableness;
(3) Select floats for physical check. Count cash in the presence of the official responsible for it, and agree to petty cash book or other record. Confirm due authorization for IOUs and advances;
(4) test vouch supporting record up to the date of the count and check additions;
(5) check transfers from main cash book to petty cash book;
(6) scrutinize record for large or unusual amounts.

   Care should be taken during the count to ensure that it is not possible for a deficiency in one float to be concealed by producing cash from another. This is best achieved by having all cash and other readily realizable items (e.g. luncheon vouchers) under the auditor's control simultaneously.

(b) Cash sale receipts

In a cash-based business the amount of cash being handled is going to be very

substantial and the auditor's review of the controls surrounding it necessarily rigorous.
The audit procedure will be:

(1) review banking arrangements and internal controls over cash handling;
(2) test vouch record with available evidence (till rolls, receipts etc). Continue check to the actual date of the count, to ensure that money is banked promptly. (Here is another opportunity for teeming and lading—delay in banking of takings and using takings of later days to make up the deficiency.);
(3) count any cash unbanked at the time of the check and agree with record.

10.9 Creditors

The standard balance sheet format in Schedule 4 analyses creditors under nine headings. Each of these must then be separated into items falling due within one year and items falling due after more than one year.

The nine headings are:
—debenture loans.
—bank loans and overdrafts.
—payments received on account.
—trade creditors.
—bills of exchange payable.
—amounts owed to group companies.
—amounts owed to related companies.
—other creditors including taxation and social security;
—accruals and deferred income.

10.9.1 Debenture loans

The auditor's work here will largely arise only in years in which fresh debentures are issued or debentures are redeemed. In other years the auditor will merely confirm that the register of debenture-holders has been correctly maintained and that the total agrees with the balance sheet.

(a) Fresh issue of debentures

(1) Authorization
A company's articles of association will probably state the borrowing powers,

and authorize the directors to borrow up to a defined limit without seeking the approval of the members. Authorization will therefore be:

—authority in articles;
—approval of members if necessary;
—borrowing powers in articles not exceeded;
—borrowing limitations imposed by other lenders not exceeded (a debenture trust deed frequently contains a provision limiting further borrowing by the company);
—directors' minute.

The auditor will verify all these stages and also confirm that any charge is entered in the company's register of mortgages and charges and that notice of it has been given to the Registrar if necessary under S395.

(2) Accuracy of records
The procedure here will be as for an issue of shares—see Section 10.11.1(a)(3).

(3) Disclosure requirements
Paragraph 41 requires the disclosure of the date and terms of redemption and, if debentures have been issued during the year:

—the reason for the issue;
—the amount of each class of debenture issued, and the consideration received.

Details of any interests of the directors in the debentures at the beginning and end of the year must be disclosed.

(b) Redemption or purchase of debentures

Redemption will be in accordance with the terms of the trust deed. This could be at a fixed date when all of a particular class of debenture is redeemed, or by drawings. It is also possible for a company to purchase its own debentures on the open market.

There may well be a sinking fund, externally invested, to provide the cash to make the redemption. (That means the auditor will need to brush up that particular piece of bookkeeping which has bedevilled generations of students!)

(1) Redemption
The stages of the redemption will be:

—sales of investments to raise cash (if there is an externally invested sinking fund);

—preparation of redemption lists, advices and cheques;

—postings to register of debenture-holders;

—cancellation of returned stock certificates;

—accounting entries, including the correct treatment of any premium on redemption (allowed by S130 to be debited to share premium account)

The auditor will verify all these stages, the proportion of detailed checking done varying according to the number of holders and the degree of internal control exercised by the client.

(2) Open market purchase

The company's debentures may be purchased for cancellation or purchased and held as an investment.

The transaction may be vouched in exactly the same way as any other investment purchase. The cancellation will be duly minuted by the directors.

(3) Disclosure requirements

Apart from the disclosure requirements for debentures generally as noted in Section 10.9.1(a)(3), particulars must also be given of any redeemed debentures which the company has power to reissue.

10.9.2 Bank loans and overdrafts

See Sections 10.8.1 and 10.8.2.

10.9.3 Trade creditors

Many of the procedures listed in Section 10.7 for trade debtors are applied also to trade creditors.

Compliance and substantive tests on the purchases ledger will provide useful evidence.

Specific audit work on the trade creditors will include the following.

(a) Obtain a copy of the schedule of balances:

(1) check or test the extraction of the balances from the ledger and the additions of the schedule;

(2) confirm agreement of total of balances with control account;

(3) reconcile with suppliers' statements, where possible.

(b) *Analytical review*. With debtors, the analytical review can draw attention to a slow-down in payments from customers. In the case of trade creditors, the ratio of trade creditors to purchases will show the period of credit being taken by the company, and the trend in the ratio over the years will show whether the period is increasing or decreasing. A high and increasing ratio may indicate a shortage of liquid funds and possibly even insolvency. As with the corresponding debtors' ratio, it is necessary to be careful if the business is seasonal. It may then be better to relate creditors to the purchases totals of the months immediately before the year-end. Large special accounts on which extended credit terms have been negotiated must be omitted.

(c) *Cut-off procedure.* We are interested here to confirm that all goods delivered and included in stock have also been included in purchases and, of course, vice versa.

(d) *Circularization.* Circularization of creditors is by no means as universally adopted by the auditor as circularization of debtors. Nevertheless, it must be regarded as a very important technique and its use is increasing. The procedure will be much the same as that outlined in Section 10.7.1(f) for debtors.

(e) *Disclosure.* See Section 7.1(g)—the disclosure for trade creditors is as for trade debtors.

10.9.4 Bills of exchange payable

Bills payable, like bills receivable, will probably have been paid by the time of the audit and thus can be verified by picking up that subsequent payment. If the bills are in fact still outstanding, the amount may be verified via the client's record of bill transactions with supporting documentation. If a liability is covered by a bill then obviously the liability itself must not also be included.

There is one further point that could be relevant to the auditor's going concern review (see Section 11.9)—if a bill payable has been renegotiated or replaced by another bill with a later maturity this could be evidence of the client's difficulty in meeting liabilities as they fall due.

10.9.5 Amounts owing to group companies

See Section 10.7.3 above.

10.9.6   Amounts owing to related companies

See Section 10.7.4 above.

10.9.7   Other creditors including taxation and social security

This heading from the format is difficult to define precisely. The Companies Act itself gives no guidance other than the format headings themselves. Companies may differ in that some may choose to include items under this heading, while others include the same items under 'accruals and deferred income'—see Section 10.9.8.

For the purpose of our coverage in this book, all items relating to expenses and income in the profit and loss account are dealt with under 'accruals and deferred income'. That leaves for 'other creditors including taxation and social security' the following:

—creditors for fixed asset purchases;
—Value added tax (VAT) owing;
—Pay as you earn (PAYE) and National Insurance owing
—mainstream corporation tax on the profits of the year and, if outstanding, the previous year;
—advance corporation tax (ACT) on proposed dividends;
—proposed dividends;
—other unclassifiable creditors.

The first and last of these can be verified by applying an appropriate selection from the techniques already described in Section 10.9.3.

Let's take a close look at verifying the remainder.

(a) VAT

The amount owing will be picked up from the client's ledger account for HM Customs and Excise. This in turn will be agreed with the VAT returns for the year and payments made will be vouched.

The client's routines for identifying recoverable VAT and accuracy in preparing returns generally will be critically reviewed. Compliance tests already carried out on purchases and sales invoices should already have validated these routines.

For retailers it will be necessary for the auditor to be familiar with the special schemes and to consider the appropriateness to the one selected. With VAT, as with all taxes, the audit requires attention to three areas—the accuracy and completeness of the records, consideration of any possible accidental or deliberate breaches of the law by the client and their consequences, and any help that can be provided to reduce the tax liability, perhaps after referral of the problem for the tax department to deal with for a separate fee.

(b) PAYE and National Insurance owing

This should normally be the amount due for the last month of the year, and will have been checked as part of the audit of wages.

Problem (1)—Delay in payment
Companies with a cash flow problem may be tempted to delay payment of PAYE and National Insurance. If this has happened the auditor should register the fact as a 'minus' in his mind in relation to the going concern review.

Problem (2)—Payments without accounting for PAYE
In some trades payments to casual labour are frequently made gross. In other cases directors and other senior employees may submit 'expenses' claims which cannot be justified and which are merely attempts to get money out of the company 'tax free'. The company may be liable to account for PAYE which should have been deducted and was not, and it is probably only a matter of time before the Inland Revenue discovers the irregularity in a routine or other examination of the company's PAYE records. The auditor must draw the directors' attention to the possible additional tax liability and strongly advise them to cease such practices.

(c) Corporation tax and advance corporation tax (ACT)

(1) Regulatory background
The Companies Act 1985 contains provisions governing the disclosure of taxation. SSAP 8 is also relevant. SSAP 15 deals with deferred taxation which appears under the heading 'provisions for liabilities and charges' (Section 10.10 below).

The statutory requirements in Schedule 4 call for disclosure by note of the basis of calculation of UK tax and details of any special circumstances affecting the tax liability. The profit and loss account must disclose separately:

—UK corporation tax
—double taxation relief
—overseas tax

The balance sheet must show figures for taxation and social security separately from other creditors, split of course between liabilities due within one year and those due after more than one year.

SSAP 8 deals with a number of matters:

—Outgoing dividends in the profit and loss account must be shown at the actual amount paid with the ACT regarded as part of the tax charge.
—ACT may be regarded as recoverable (deductible from the corporation tax charge of the current year, the preceding six years or future years) only if the availability of a tax charge against which it can be offset in those years is reasonably certain. Otherwise it must be written off through the profit and loss account as part of the normal tax charge for the year. It will not normally be possible to regard recovery as 'reasonably certain' if it cannot be foreseen taking into account income and dividends up to the end of the next accounting period only.
—Dividends received from other UK companies are exempt from corporation tax. SSAP 8 requires them to be credited gross in the profit and loss account with the related tax shown as part of the tax charge.
—ACT on proposed dividends will be due for payment in the next accounting period and will be deductible from the corporation tax liability of the period in which the dividend is paid. It is not acceptable to allow the liability and the asset to cancel each other out. Apart from the fact that the asset may not be recoverable, there is also the delay before any benefit is obtained from it. The offsetting right is therefore shown as a deferred asset in the balance sheet unless it can be deducted from the deferred tax account (see Section 10.10.2 below);

(2) The audit of taxation

Taxation could be the biggest single liability in the balance sheet and the most complex. In many auditing areas, your accounting knowledge will come in useful. Here, your tax knowledge will. Don't go too far in the auditing paper in displaying tax knowledge, but be prepared to if the question demands it, as some CACA level 3 Auditing questions have. Computations may have been done by the client, by the tax department of the audit firm, or possibly by another firm of accountants. In all cases it will be necessary for the audit team to check them. The detailed programme will be:

—vouch all payments or refunds of tax;
—check in detail, item by item, all tax computations. This will include adjustment of profit, including correct allowance/disallowance of expenses and computation of capital allowances;
—optimum utilization of loss reliefs;
—capital gains;
—accounting for ACT/tax on franked investment income (Form CT61);
—accounting for income tax deducted and suffered;
—small company computation;

—close company computation (including confirmation whether the company is indeed close or not close where necessary);

—utilization and offset of income tax and ACT, including carry-back of ACT;

—group and consortium relief where applicable;

—foreign tax liabilities and consequent double taxation relief;

—surrender of ACT by parent company to subsidiary;

—confirm that ACT may reasonably be treated as recoverable;

—confirm compliance with disclosure requirements of Companies Act and SSAP 8;

—overall review of tax affairs (see (3) below).

(3) Overall review of tax affairs

The following review form is a useful guide for the last matter listed in (2) above.

TAX COMPUTATION CHECKLIST

Name of client _____   Approved—Senior_____   Date _____

Accounting period ___   Approved—Partner/manager _____   Date _____

1. *Profit and Loss Account*
   Ensure that the relevant audit schedules have all been prepared (by client if possible), and check in particular that:

   (a) allowable/disallowable entertaining is detailed, and source of information for allocation is shown.

   (b) depreciation shown in detailed profit and loss account equals that shown on movements on fixed assets. If not reconcile the figures.

   (c) legal and professional charges show name and nature of work done. Consider whether capital allowances or CGT relief available on capital items.

   (d) interest and royalities paid/payable detail opening and closing accruals and whether paid gross or under deduction of tax. Consider nature of interest/royalty and whether to treat as deduction from profit or charge on income.

   (e) interest received/receivable details opening and closing accruals and whether received gross or under deduction of tax.

   (f) subscriptions and donations identify covenants, and whether shown gross or net.

   (g) repairs to land and buildings have been considered for possible capital expenditure.

   (h) there is a full analysis of miscellaneous/general expenses and that disallowable items have been identified.

2. *Balance Sheet—Fixed Assets*
   Ensure the file gives the following information:

(a) additions to each class of fixed asset

   (i) split cost of land and buildings
   (ii) give details of expensive motor cars
   (iii) give an analysis of additions to buildings to ascertain whether FYA or revenue relief on repairs may be claimed.
   (iv) if buildings accquired are secondhand, obtain details of residue of expenditure and remaining tax life from vendor.
   (v) give dates of acquisition if rate of FYA, rate of initial allowance or limit for expensive motor cars changed in period or if period of account longer than 12 months.

(b) disposals from each class of fixed asset

   (i) identify items where proceeds exceed cost
   (ii) ensure adequate information is available for disposals of chargeable assets

(c) transfer value and transferor/ee company for intra-group transfers during the period.
(d) details of grants received and receivable, identifying nature of grants and whether for plant or buildings.
(e) in respect of buildings:

   (i) the uses to which the buildings are put (especially whether the use might be considered for scientific purposes)
   (ii) any changes in use during year
   (iii) confirmation that the buildings are in use at the year end.
(f) where assets are written down in the accounts eg goodwill, shareholdings etc., provide details for possible capital loss claims.
(g) ensure motor cars and leased assets purchased after 31.5.80 are treated as separate pool.

3. *Balance Sheet—Other Items*
(a) *Intangible assets*
   In respect of patents knowhow and goodwill, obtain details of acquisitions and royalty agreements.
(b) *Debtors*
   Give details of both general and specific bad or doubtful debt provisions.
(c) *Current liabilities*
   Give details of any provisions made during the year (eg future losses or liabilities, pension contributions).

(d) Proposed dividend

Several audit implications of dividends paid and proposed are touched upon elsewhere in this book. They are:

(1) Qualified audit report
A company can't pay a dividend *at all* if the audit report is qualified, unless the report is accompanied by a statement from the auditor that the qualification is not material for the purpose of determining whether the distribution is allowable (Section 17.2.2)

(2) First dividend of a newly formed public company.
The auditor must report on the interim accounts out of which the dividend is to be paid before the payment can be made (Section 17.2.2)

(3) Statutory definition of distributable profit.
There are separate definitions for public and private companies (Section 17.2.1)

Apart from these requirements, what must a company have before it can pay a dividend?

(1) profit legally available as explained above;
(2) cash to pay the dividend without difficulty;
(3) authority to make the payment.

The availability of cash requires consideration of the company's cash forecast up to and beyond the payment date.
Authority will be:

—articles of association, normally giving the directors power to pay interim dividends, and perhaps imposing restrictions;

—directors' minute;

—shareholders at AGM (This formal authorization must obviously come after the conclusion of the audit but is necessary before the final dividend is paid).

Audit steps
—review all legal and other factors listed above;

—confirm that no ordinary dividend is paid or proposed until any arrears of cumulative preference dividend have been made up;

—confirm the correctness of dividend calculation in accordance with the directors' minute authorizing it;

—test vouch payments for dividends actually paid. The procedure here is normally for the company to prepare dividend cheques drawn on a special bank account opened for the purpose for the exact total sum required;
—confirm correctness of disclosure requirements in balance sheet and profit and loss account;
—where the company under audit is a subsidiary, and an election under S256 TA 1970 has been made for dividends to the holding company to be paid without ACT, confirm that payment has in fact been so made.

10.9.8 Accruals and deferred income

These will be verified in the same way as the corresponding debtors (see Section 10.7.5(b) above).

10.10 Provisions for liabilities and charges

Items under this heading are:

—pensions and similar obligations
—taxation, including deferred taxation
—other provisions

10.10.1 Pensions and similar obligations

This may be a very important liability in the accounts. We are talking here about a provision in the company's own accounts, not the accounts of the separate pension trust fund which probably exists. The audit of these is discussed in Section 23.6.

Let us first of all summarize the main features of pension schemes. This is also relevant for your later study of the audit of pension trust funds.

The following material is based on an article by Neil Stein in the Certified Accountants Students' Newsletter of June 1985:

Types of Scheme

Pension schemes can be divided into two main classes—those providing benefits based on earnings and years of service (defined benefit schemes), and those providing benefits determined by the contributions paid into the fund plus investment income thereon (defined contribution schemes). Most UK schemes are defined benefit, but they give rise to greater problems because it is impossible to quantify the ultimate future liability of the scheme. Estimations of the solvency of such schemes must be based on reasonable actuarial assumptions, whereas the solvency of a defined contribution scheme is much more readily ascertainable.

Each type may be *contributory* or *non-contributory* (i.e. with or without employee contributions). Further, each type may or may not be insurance-company based. An insurance company based scheme entails paying the bulk of the money flowing into the fund as a premium on a pension policy. Such an arrangement does not shift the risk implicit in a defined benefit scheme to the insurance company—the annual premium demanded is the amount necessary to keep the scheme viable.

In most cases a separate trust fund will be set up, but there is nothing legally to stop a company running an internally financed scheme, in which the benefits are provided directly by the company.

Funding

The majority of UK pension schemes are *funded*—that is to say a fund of cash is built up over the years to pay for the benefits. In an unfunded scheme the benefits are paid out of current income without any attempt to create such a fund. The UK state pension scheme is unfunded, with pensions paid out of annual tax revenue and the pension part of National Insurance contributions.

Calculating the debit to profit and loss account

In principle, the debit to profit and loss account is the amount necessary to increase the value of the fund to cover the end of year actuarial estimate of the future pension liabilities. This would also be the amount of cash transferred to the fund.

In practice, this may be approximated by transferring an agreed percentage of the payroll each year, with adjustments as necessary when an actuarial valuation is carried out. (This may well be every three years, though some funds do in fact have an annual valuation.)

However, a number of factors may influence the profit and loss account debit.

(*a*) Benefit levels may be changed
A change in benefit levels may mean increasing pension benefits relating to past service. This could mean an increased debit in the year in which the change is made, or the company could choose to spread the cost over a number of years, on the basis that the cost is attributable to the remaining working lives of participating employees. Similar considerations apply when a scheme is first introduced. Incidentally, it is generally agreed that it would be incorrect to treat such back-service payments as prior year adjustments,

because the new pensions, or increased rights, are intended to reward future service, not past service.

(b) Actual valuations may reveal a surplus or deficit, or actuarial assumptions about the future may change.

In both of these cases correcting action may be taken by way of a lump sum debit in the current year's profit and loss account or by spreading the charge over a number of years.

The amount of cash to be transferred to the fund

As a completely different exercise from determining the profit and loss account charge, it is necessary to decide how much cash to transfer to the fund. In the long term, profit and loss account debits will equal cash transfers; but there may be short-term or medium-term differences, especially when a scheme is first introduced and the cash contribution necessary to pay for the past service is spread over several years, not always in the same way as profit and loss account debits are spread.

Actuarial valuations

The amount to be transferred to the fund will be based on an actuarial valuation of the fund. Methods of valuation may be prospective or accrued.

(a) *prospective benefit valuation:* This method reflects retirement benefits that are based on service both rendered and to be rendered by an employee as at the date of the actuarial valuation;

(b) *accrued benefit valuation:* This method reflects retirement benefits that are based on service rendered by employees to the date of the valuation.

The elements of a prospective benefit valuation could be as follows:

	£000
Obligations to pay pensions:	
(1) based on service to date and assuming no future salary increases	1000
(2) increase in (i) to reflect estimated future salary increases	800
(3) based on future service until retirement date	3000
Estimated requirement	4800

Present and future assets/receipts:

(1) current value of assets held 1200

(2) estimated future contributions and investment income 3500

4700

Projected deficiency 100

On these figures the scheme shows a projected deficiency of £100 000, not large in relation to the size of the amounts and the degree of approximation inherent in the items included.

The discontinuance actuarial valuation measures the basic solvency of the scheme and on the above figures would be:

	£000
Obligations based on service to date	1000
Current value of assets held	1200
Surplus	200

ED 39 would require the amount of any deficiency on a discontinuance basis to be disclosed, with an indication of the action being taken to deal with it. Note also that the Occupational Pensions Board set up by the UK Department of Health and Social Security to regulate occupational pension schemes requires such deficiencies to be reported to it.

The disclosure requirements proposed in ED 39

The basic disclosure requirements for company accounts under ED 39 are (terms in italics are defined in the next paragraph):

(a) For *defined contribution schemes*

(1) the nature of the scheme (i.e. defined contribution);

(2) the pension cost charge for the period; and

(3) any outstanding or prepaid contributions at the balance sheet date.

(b) For *defined benefit schemes*

(1) the nature of the scheme (i.e. defined benefit);

(2) whether funded or unfunded;

(3) details of accounting and funding policies;

(4) whether the pension cost and liability (or asset) are assessed with the

advice of a qualified actuary, and the date of the latest formal actuarial valuation, with details of the actuarial valuation method used;

(5) pension cost charge for the period, distinguishing between regular costs and any variations. Explanations of the variations and details of the period over which they are to be spread should be given;

(6) details of provisions or prepayments resulting from differences between the amounts recognized as costs and the amounts funded;

(7) expected significant effects on financial statements of any changes which have occurred in any of the above items;

(8) the amount of any deficiency on a *discontinuance·actuarial valuation*, indicating the action, if any, being taken to deal with it in current and future financial statements;

(9) an outline of the results of the most recent formal actuarial valuation, including disclosure in percentage terms of the relationship between the scheme assets and the actuarial value of the accrued benefits.

Definitions

To assist in understanding pension schemes and their audit, the following definitions are reproduced from ED 39.

(*a*) An *accrued benefits method* of actuarial valuation is a valuation method in which the actuarial value of liabilities relates at a given date to:

(1) the benefits, including future increases promised by the rules, for the current and deferred pensioners and their dependants; and

(2) the benefits which the members assumed to be in service on the given date will receive for service up to that date only.

Allowance may be made for expected increases in earnings after the given date, and for additional pension increases not promised by the rules.

The given date may be a current or future date. The further into the future the adopted date lies, the closer the results will be to those of a prospective benefits valuation method. (See (*e*) below.)

(*b*) A *defined benefit scheme* is a pension scheme in which the rules specify the benefits to be paid and the scheme is financed accordingly.

(*c*) A *defined contribution scheme* is a pension scheme in which the benefits are directly determined by the value of contributions paid in respect of each member. Normally the rate of contribution is specified in the rules of the scheme.

(*d*) A *discontinuance actuarial valuation* is a valuation to establish the degree of solvency if a scheme were wound up. The liabilities are calculated as the cost of providing the existing benefits for current and deferred pensioners and accrued benefits (ignoring possible future earnings increases) for active members (i.e. members in service) and their dependants. The assets are taken at market value.

(e) A *prospective benefits method* of valuation is a valuation method in which the actuarial value of liabilities relates to:

(1) the benefits for current and deferred pensioners and their dependants, allowing where appropriate for future pension increases; and
(2) the benefits which active members will receive in respect of both past and future service, allowing for future increases in earnings up to their assumed exit dates, and where appropriate for pension increases thereafter.

(f) A funding plan is the arrangement of the incidence over time of payments with the objective of meeting the future cost of a given set of benefits.

(g) A funded scheme is a pension scheme where the future liabilities for benefits are provided by the accumulation of assets held externally to the employing company's business.

The audit work

The make-up and nature of the amount appearing as a liability in the company's balance sheet, and the consequent audit work, will depend on the organization of the scheme. There are three possibilities to consider:

—unfunded pensions;
—a separate trust fund;
—an internally financed scheme.

(a) Unfunded pensions

A company may have undertaken to provide pensions or benefits to employees out of current profits rather than by setting up a formal fund. Such an arrangement might also exist to supplement a funded scheme.

The problem here is quantifying the future annual liabilities. It should be possible for the company to estimate with reasonable accuracy the liabilities which will be arising in the future, based on expected retirements and levels of benefit to be provided.

The Companies Act requires disclosure (paragraph 50) of provisions for pension liabilities and of any pension commitments for which no provision has been made. It will be necessary for the auditor to ascertain and review the basis of the scheme and confirm that full disclosure is made, as required by statute and SSAPs, of the nature of the scheme, amounts provided for and amounts treated as contingencies.

(b) Separate trust fund

The amount appearing as a liability in the company's accounts will probably be accumulated employees' contributions not yet paid over to the pension fund. In addition there may be further amounts, especially in the early years of the fund, to pay for past service or for improvements in benefits.

The auditor of the employer will obviously need to concern himself with the rules and financial position of the pension fund itself, as the employer will probably have undertaken responsibility for maintaining the fund at a suitable level.

Audit work will be:

(1) Obtain a copy of the pension trust deed and details of contributions and benefits;
(2) Obtain a copy of the pension fund accounts and latest actuarial certificate;
(3) Based on the information from (1) and (2) above, review the solvency of the fund and hence evaluate the possible need for further payments to maintain scheme solvency. This will probably require discussion with the company's directors to find out, among other things, whether there are any plans to increase benefits;
(4) Review the adequacy of employee representation as trustees of the fund;
(5) Test the correctness of employee pension deductions when auditing wages and salaries;
(6) Confirm the accuracy and compleness of refunds received in respect of employees leaving the scheme;
(7) Confirm whether there is a deficiency on the immediate discontinuance basis, and if so confirm that adequate arrangements have been made to eliminate it, and that disclosure is made;
(8) If the scheme is contracred out, confirm that the annual statement required by the Occupational Pensions Board (OPB) has been lodged;
(9) Consider the effect of changes in the scheme or in asset values since the last actuarial valuation which might affect the solvency of the scheme or the computation of costs;
(10) Review the extent of any self-investment by the scheme;
(11) Consider the propriety of any 'related party' transactions by the scheme involving the company or its directors;
(12) If the company makes payments outside the scheme, perhaps on an ex gratia basis, to past employees, confirm the authorization of such payments and confirm the company's system of control ensuring that payments do not continue after the death of the intended recipient;
(13) In the case of payments relating to the retirement of directors, confirm that the prior consent of the members has been obtained, as required by S.312, and that disclosure is made in the accounts as required by paragraph 28 of Schedule 6;

(14) Confirm that the disclosure requirements of the Companies Act and ED 39 have been met.

(c) Internally financed scheme
In this case the liability in the balance sheet will represent the estimated obligation to provide future pensions, and will be balanced by the current value of the assets held.

The example quoted above illustrates the kind of figures that might exist in practice. There should be a surplus on a discontinuance basis (or action taken to eliminate it). A small deficiency on projected benefit valuation need not necessarily be cause for great alarm, as the calculations involve long-range forecasts of future salary increases, future fund income and future capital values of fund assets.

The audit work will include all the steps listed in (*b*) above (except (4)). The assets held for the fund will be verified in the normal way.

The disclosure requirements of SORP 1 Pension scheme accounts should be complied with.

10.10.2 Taxation, including deferred taxation

The verification of the main elements of a company's tax liabilities has already been dealt with in Section 10.9.7 (*c*) above. It now remains to pick up the deferred taxation account.

The following material is based on an article by Neil Stein in the October 1985 issue of the *Certified Accountant's Students' Newsletter*.

(a) What is deferred taxation?

At the very outset we must clarify exactly what deferred taxation is. To understand that it is necessary to examine first the causes of difference between accounting profit and profit for taxation purposes. These can be *permanent,* as when an expense charged in the profit and loss account is simply disallowed for tax purposes, or *temporary,* as when depreciation charged in the profit and loss account is disallowed and replaced by capital allowances which, at the moment, achieve a faster rate of write-off than does depreciation. These temporary differences will correct themselves in the course of time, because over the full life of the asset both depreciation and capital allowances will write off its cost less residual value. Nevertheless, there may be a considerable difference in the timing of the write-off. In most cases these timing differences mean that the profit on which tax is being charged is less than accounting profit, but this is not necessarily so. *Deferred taxation is tax attributable to the difference between accounting profit and taxable profit, to the extent that the difference is caused by timing differences.*

(b) Timing differences

Timing differences may be short-term or long-term. Examples are tabulated below:

Short-term	Long-term
Items arising because financial accounts are prepared on the accruals basis and some expenses and income are treated on a 'cash' basis for tax purposes: —interest and royalties payable —interest receivable —general bad debt provisions —pension costs —provisions for repairs/maintenance All these items normally reverse in the next accounting period.	—Capital allowances *v.* depreciation —Revaluation of assets —Disposals of assets with rollover relief —Leasing of assets

(c) Why deferred taxation?

There are a number of reasons why it is important to reflect deferred taxation in financial statements:

(1) It is an application of the accruals concept. The tax charge relating to the year should be accounted for in that year, regardless of when payable.

(2) The tax deferred will be a liability eventually.

(3) It is relevant for users of financial statements to appreciate the extent to which a company is being financed by deferred taxation, which is not part of shareholders' funds.

(4) Dividend policy could be distorted—an unusually low taxation charge could give the impression that plenty of post-tax profit was available, while in the following year the tax charge could be much greater and profits available for dividend much less.

(5) The distortion of post-tax profit referred to in (4) could seriously distort

the P/E ratio and earnings per share, both important indicators of a company's progress.

(d) Methods of providing for deferred taxation

There are basically two methods of providing for deferred taxation:

(a) *The liability method.* Under this method the amount set aside is revised whenever tax rates change so that the deferred tax balance represents the best estimate of the amounts actually payable or receivable if the relevant timing differences reversed.

(b) *The deferral method.* The deferral method uses the tax rates in operation at the time of the originating timing difference and no adjustment is made for subsequent changes. In the UK the deferral method is rarely used.

Old SSAP 15 allowed the use of either method. New SSAP 15 requires the use of the liability method.

(e) Extent of Provision

It is possible to reflect deferred taxation in the accounts fully, partially or not at all.

(1) *Full provision.* Full provision means that the financial statements recognise the tax effects of all transactions occurring in the period covered.

(2) *Partial provision.* The partial provision concept recognizes that financial statements may be distorted if provision is made for a deferred taxation liability when it is probable that no such liability will crystallize. Both 'old' and 'new' SSAP 15 are based on the partial provision concept, as we shall see.

(3) *Nil provision.* Nil provision, also known as 'flow through', is based on the principle that only the tax payable in respect of a period should be charged in that period. It was, of course, dissatisfaction with this system which led to the development of methods of providing for deferred taxation.

(f) Regulatory background

Deferred taxation has been controversial topic for many years. The first UK pronouncement we need concern ourselves with was ED 11, issued in May 1973. It became a standard (SSAP 11) in August 1975 but was never popular as it required full provision for deferred tax, thought at the time to be leading to excessive provisions for liabilities that would never crystallize. The main cause of deferred taxation at this time was the difference between depreciation and capital allowances, and the argument against full provision was that new capital expenditure was continually generating new capital allowances, leading to an indefinite postponement of the tax liability.

As a result of this dissatisfaction the ASC delayed the implementation date of SSAP 11 and issued a new Exposure Draft (ED 19) in May 1977. This modified SSAP 11 by not requiring a provision if it 'can be demonstrated with reasonable probability' that a tax reduction arising from a timing difference will continue for 'the foreseeable future'. ED 19 became SSAP 15 in October 1978 and the criterion for deferral was changed somewhat from that in the ED, though remaining in substance the same. The old SSAP 15 requirement was that deferred tax should be accounted for in respect of the tax effects arising from:

(1) All short-term timing differences—that is, timing differences arising from the use of the receipts and payments basis for tax purposes and the accruals basis in financial statements. They normally reverse in the next accounting period;

(2) All long-term timing differences UNLESS:

—it can be demonstrated with reasonable probability that the timing difference will not reverse within a reasonable time (at least three years), AND
—there is no indication of any likely change in the position after that period, AND
—the company is a going concern.

Applying these conditions to each of the main types of long-term timing difference, we are saying:

—Capital allowances will exceed depreciation each year,
—Revalued assets will continue in use,
—Rollover relief (capital gains tax) will continue.

As can be seen old SSAP 15 was based on the partial provision concept. It still required the disclosure of the full potential liability by note, and this requirement is continued in new SSAP 15.

The next development was the issue of ED 33 in June 1983. ED 33 left unchanged the basic concept of SSAP 15—that partial provision for deferred taxation is acceptable if certain criteria are met, but it changed the criteria somewhat.

Finally, new SSAP 15 appeared in May 1985 and made changes to the ED.

The table below summarizes the differences between old SSAP 15 and new SSAP 15. Obviously the new provisions are of greater examination importance, but the old requirements are also shown to assist those who have already studied them and need to update the new provisions.

(g) The provisions of old SSAP 15 and new SSAP 15

Old SSAP 15	New SSAP 15
(1) *Method* Use liability method or deferral method.	Use liability method only.
(2) *Criteria for partial provision* Provide on all short-term differences Provide on all long-term differences unless it can be shown with reasonable probability that no liability will crystallize: —for at least three years, with no indication of a change after this period. (Going concern status assumed)	Provide on all timing differences if 'probable that a liability will will crystallize', AND do NOT provide to the extent that it is probable that a liability will not crystallize. In each case directors are required to make reasonable assumptions, including assumptions regarding future plans. Note that new SSAP 15 makes no distinction between long and short term differences. New SSAP 15 also deals with the question of accelerated taxation—where the profit for tax purposes exceeds that for accounting purposes— and applies the same criteria for the recognition of the resultant asset as those listed above for liabilities.
(3) *Debit balances* Debit balances arising from timing differences or ACT payments should be carried forward only if recovery is 'reasonably certain'.	Debit balances should not be carried forward as assets, except to the extent that they are expected to be recoverable without replacement by equivalent debit balances. Debit balances arising for ACT on dividends should be carried forward to the extent that offset is expected to be possible in the next accounting period. Debit balances arising for ACT other than on dividends should be written off unless recovery is assured beyond reasonable doubt.

Old SSAP 15	New SSAP 15

(4) *Trading losses*

No recognition of relief until profits available—BUT—credit on deferred tax account may be released to P & L to the extent that it is attributable to income available for offset. (Reversed when profit made and loss used).

May be recognized if expected to be recoverable without replacement by equivalent debit balances.

May be treated as recoverable if:
—cause of loss is identifiable and non-recurring;
—previous history shows consistent excess of profits over losses;
—recovery is assured beyond reasonable doubt within any limitation in tax legislation on carry-forward period.

(5) *Capital losses*

Not specifically mentioned.

May be treated as recoverable if the company has decided to dispose of an asset not essential to the company's future operations, the sale of which will realize a gain sufficient to offset the loss.

(6) *Disclosure requirements*

(*a*) Profit and loss account

(1) Deferred tax shown separately as component of total tax charge. Deferred tax relating to extraordinary items shown separately as part of such items.

As old SSAP 15, except that deferred tax on extraordinary items to be shown separately as part of tax on extraordinary items.

(2) Show extent of reduction in tax charge through accelerated capital allowances, stock appreciation relief and other timing differences.

No such requirement (but see (*b*)(1) below).

(3) Show adjustments for changes in rate of CT as separate element of tax charge—extraordinary if associated with fundamental change in basis of taxation.

as old SSAP 15.

(*b*) Balance sheet

(1) Deferred taxation shown separately and described as such with note explaining method of calculation.

(2) Not to be shown as part of shareholders' funds.

(3) Analysis of major elements.

(4) Movements attributable to movements on reserves disclosed.

Deferred tax balance, and its major components, should be disclosed in the balance sheet or notes. Transfers to or from deferred tax should be disclosed by note. Covered by Companies Act 1985. (See (*h*) below.)

As old SSAP 15—see (*b*)(1) above.

As old SSAP 15

Old SSAP 15	New SSAP 15
(5) Where the value or an asset is shown in a note because it differs materially from its book amount, the tax implications of its sale at the revalued amount should be shown by note.	As old SSAP 15
(6) Potential amount for all timing differences disclosed by note, with analysis among principal categories.	Unprovided deferred tax disclosed by note, analysed into its major components, plus details of any unprovided deferred tax relating to the period under review.

(h) Statutory disclosure requirements for deferred taxation

Sechedule 4 to the Companies Act 1985 now contains the disclosure requirements for deferred taxation.

Deferred taxation provisions should appear in the balance sheet under the heading 'Provisions for liabilities and charges' as part of the provision for 'Taxation including deferred taxation'.

Any deferred tax carried forward as an asset should be included under the heading of 'Prepayments and accrued income' either within 'Current Assets/Debtors', if it is current, or separately under main heading D. In the former case, any amount due after more than one year should be shown separately.

Paragraph 50(2) of Schedule 4 requires the disclosure of contingent liabilities not provided for. The ASC has obtained legal advice to the effect that unprovided deferred tax is a contingent liability, except where the prospect of it becoming payable is so remote that it does not amount to a contingent liability at all.

(i) Comment

The new SSAP 15, or its precursor ED 33, has been criticized for continuing to advocate partial provision, on the grounds that this may be imprudent and create difficulties for companies without fully developed plans or projections. The emphasis in SSAP 15 on the need to be prudent in assessing the deferred tax provision should meet this criticism.

The current US Standard (APB 11) requires companies to make full provision for deferred tax using the deferral method. The US Financial

Accounting Standard Board (FASB) currently has APB11 under review, mainly because of dissatisfaction with the 'full provision' requirement. It remains to be seen how far the revised US standard follows the new UK standard, if at all.

(j) Audit work on deferred taxation

The audit work on deferred taxation is largely implicit in the requirements listed in (a)–(h) above—in a nutshell the auditor has to confirm that all these have been met.

The problem for the auditor is deciding whether the directors are justified in their application of the criteria set up in SSAP 15 to determine whether or not 'a liability will crystallize'. This leads the auditor into considering future capital expenditure plans and the likelihood of sale of revalued assets and of the continuation of rollover relief.

Debit balances are more likely to arise on deferred taxation, partly because of the change in the treatment of the tax effect of trading losses in the revised version of SSAP 15 issued in May 1985. The criteria for recognizing debit balances are somewhat subjective.

The auditor's job, then, is to obtain from the directors their reasons for adopting the treatment they have used and consider their validity. Discussion with the directors will be necessary to enable the auditor to do this.

Once the amount which should reasonably be provided for has been agreed, the auditor will check the correct calculation under the liability method stipulated in revised SSAP 15—that is, with adjustments for alterations in the rates of corporation tax.

10.11 Capital and reserves

10.11.1 Called-up share capital

The auditor will only have limited work to do in this area if there have been no shares issued or redeemed during the year. If that is the case the work will be limited to testing the correctness of the entries in the share register. (This is not a detailed share transfer audit, which is outside the scope of the audit and will be carried out only if required by the client.) The auditor will also, of course, confirm that the balance sheet continues to disclose the unchanged authorized and issued share capital.

Events which give rise to the need for more action from the auditor are:
—fresh issue of shares;
—redemption of shares;
—purchases by a company of its own shares.

(a) Fresh issue of shares

The special reports required of auditors in certain types of share issue are covered in Sections 17.3 and 17.4. In this chapter we are considering the verification of the share issue in the context of the audit itself.

We are interested in verifying the legality and authorization of the issue, confirming the accuracy of the records and seeing that all disclosure requirements have been met.

(1) Legality
The legal requirements governing share issues are complex. A selection of the more important points appears below:

—The amount issued must not take the share capital above the authorized capital as stated in the memorandum or any resolution increasing it.
—Only a public company may offer shares to the public.
—The issue of shares at a discount is prohibited.
—Any prospectus must have complied with the provisions of Schedule 3 and SS56–79 and the requirements of the Stock Exchange if relevant.
—A public company may only allot shares on which at least 25 per cent of the nominal value and the full amount of any premium have been paid up (S101).
—A public company must first offer any proposed new shares pro rata to existing members.

(2) Authorization
The initial authorization will be a duly minuted resolution of the directors. The approval of the members is required (special resolution) if the offer is to be made otherwise than by a rights issue to them (S95).

(3) Accuracy of records
The stages in the issue will broadly be as follows:
—invitation made (e.g. by a prospectus);
—applications received;
—directors decide on basis of allotment and minute it;
—excess cash returned to unsuccessful or partially sucessful applicants;
—allotment letters sent to successful applicants;
—entries made in share register;
—share certificate issued;
—calls (if necessary) made.

The auditor's job will be to confirm that all cash received has been duly accounted for, that shares have been allotted, entries made in the share register, and share certificates issued, in accordance with the terms of the issue and the directors' minute.

The totals of the share register should agree with the revised total of share capital in the balance sheet.

Calls in arrear are required to be shown separately in the balance sheet. By the time of the audit the amount due will probably have been received, or the shares forfeited. If neither event has happened, the auditor should raise the matter with the directors to find out what they propose to do. A note explaining the position may be necessary if the number of shares concerned is large.

(4) Disclosure requirements
These are contained in paragraphs 38–40 of Schedule 4:

—amount of authorized share capital;
—number and aggregate nominal value of shares allotted;
—for redeemable shares, earliest and latest dates of redemption, details of any premium on redemption and whether redemption is at the company's option or not;
—reasons for any allotment during the year and details of shares allotted;
—details of any share options.

Details of directors' share interests at the beginning and end of the period must also be given.

(b) Redemption of shares and capital redemption reserve

Redemption of shares may be of redeemable preference shares or, exceptionally, redeemable ordinary shares which it became possible for companies to issue in 1981. The auditor must confirm that the redemption is in accordance with the terms of issue and with the requirements of SS159–181. Redemption will normally be out of distributable profits or out of the proceeds of a fresh issue. *Private* companies may redeem out of capital, provided the strict statutory safeguards are complied with. These include an auditor's report, more details of which are given in Section 17.7.

A capital redemption reserve must be created to the extent that redemption is *not* out of the proceeds of a fresh issue or out of capital.

The total of payments to shareholders must be agreed with the reduction in the balance sheet figure of share capital.

10.11.2 Share premium account

All movements in the share premium account must be verified. Credits to the account will be checked in the course of verifying share issues. Debits to the account must be within the permitted uses listed in S130:

—issuing fully paid bonus shares;
—writing-off preliminary expenses;
—writing-off commission or discount on any issue of shares or debentures (note that shares may no longer be issued at a discount);
—providing for the premium on redemption of debentures.

In addition, S160 allows the share premium account to be used to cover the premium on redemption of redeemable shares.

10.11.3 Revaluation reserve

A revaluation reserve comes into existence when an asset is revalued. The credit to the account will be verified when the asset revaluation is agreed. (See Section 10.2.1(b)(6) above.)

An amount may only be transferred from revaluation reserve to the profit and loss account if it represents realized profit, or had previously been charged to the profit and loss account.

10.11.4 Profit and loss account

The amount carried forward under this heading will simply reflect the profit and loss account itself. One point that can arise is the need to confirm that any prior year adjustments are within the definition in SSAP 6.

10.11.5 Other reserves

All movements in reserves must be disclosed and must be verified by the auditor. 'Other reserves' could include, apart from the headings already dealt with, a reserve for increased cost of replacement of assets.

The auditor's task is to confirm that the items comprising reserves are all in the nature of reserves and could not be regarded as provisions, and vice versa.

10.12 Letter of representation

As the final stage of verifying the assets and liablities, and indeed of confirming the accuracy of the profit and loss account, the auditor may wish to seek corroboration of oral representations made to him or her during the audit by the directors. This is frequently done by asking the directors to sign a *letter of representation* dealing particularly with points on which the auditor is unable to obtain independent corroborative evidence. An Auditing Guideline on the subject was issued by the APC in July 1983.

APC Guideline on representations by management

Preface

This Guideline should be read in conjunction with the operational and reporting Standards, their related Guidelines and, where applicable, legislation relating to the disclosure of information to auditors. In this context, section 393 of the Companies Act 1985 provides that an officer of a company will be guilty of an offence where he knowingly or recklessly makes a statement (orally or in writing) to the company's auditor which is misleading, false or deceptive in a material particular.

Introduction

(1) Paragraph 4 of the Auditing Standard 'The auditor's operational standard' states that 'the auditor should obtain relevant and reliable audit evidence sufficient to enable him to draw reasonable conclusions therefrom'. This evidence will be obtained from many different sources. Representations by management are one such source.

(2) Oral representations will be made throughout the audit in response to specific enquiries. Whilst representations by management constitute audit evidence, the auditor should not rely solely on the unsupported oral representations of management as being sufficient reliable evidence when they relate to matters which are material to the financial statements.

(3) In most cases, oral representations can be corroborated by checking with sources independent of the enterprise or by checking with other evidence obtained by the auditor, and therefore do not need to be confirmed in writing.

(4) However, in certain cases, such as where knowledge of the facts is confined to management or where the matter is principally one of judgement and opinion, the auditor may not be able to obtain independent corroborative evidence and could not reasonably expect it to be available. In such cases, the auditor should ensure there is no other evidence which conflicts with the representations by management and he should obtain written confirmation of the representations.

(5) Where written representations are obtained, the auditor will still need to decide whether in the circumstances these representations, together with such other audit evidence as he has obtained, are sufficient to enable him to form an unqualified opinion on the financial statements.

(6) In circumstances where the auditor prepares the financial statements for the company it may be appropriate for the directors to acknowledge their responsibility for the financial statements when confirming their representations in writing. This is because the directors have the ultimate responsibility for ensuring the completeness and accuracy of the enterprise's accounting records and for the view shown by the financial statements.

Procedures

(7) Where oral representations by management are uncorroborated by sufficient other audit evidence and where they relate to matters which are material to the financial statements, they should be summarised in the auditor's working papers. The auditor should ensure that these representations are either formally minuted as being approved by the board of directors or included in a signed letter, addressed to the auditor, known as a "letter of representation'.

(8) Because the representations are those of management, standard letters of representation may not be appropriate. In any event, management should be encouraged to participate in drafting any letter of representation or, after review and dicussion, to make appropriate amendments to the auditor's draft, provided that the value of the audit evidence obtained is not thereby diminished.

(9) A letter of representation should be signed by persons whose level of authority is appropriate to the significance of the representations made—normally by one or more of the executive directors (for example by the chief executive and the chief financial officer), on behalf of the whole board. The signatories of the letter should be fully conversant with the matters contained in it. The auditor should request that the consideration of the letter and its approval by the board for signature be minuted. He may request that he be allowed to attend the meeting at which the board is due to approve the letter. Such attendance may also be desirable where the representations are to be formally minuted, rather than included in a letter.

(10) Procedures regarding written representations should be agreed at an early stage in order to reduce the possibility of the auditor being faced with a refusal by management to co-operate in providing such representations. However, management may at the outset indicate that they are not willing to sign letters of representation or to pass minutes requested by the auditor. If they do so indicate, the auditor should inform management that he will himself prepare a statement in writing setting out his understanding of the principal representations that have been made to him during the course of the audit, and he should send this statement to management with a request for confirmation that his understanding of the representations is correct.

(11) If management disagrees with the auditor's statement of representations, discussions should be held to clarify the matters in doubt, and, if necessary, a revised statement prepared and agreed. Should management fail to reply, the auditor should follow the matter up to try to ensure that his understanding of the position, as set out in his statement, is correct.

(12) There may, however, be circumstances where the auditor is unable to obtain the written representations which he requires. This may be because of a refusal by management to co-operate, or because management properly declines to give the representations required on the grounds of its own uncertainty regarding the particular matter. In either case, if the auditor is unable to satisfy himself, he may have

to conclude that he has not received all the information and explanations that he requires, and consequently may need to consider qualifying his audit report.

Groups

(13) Because the directors and auditors of holding companies have responsibilities to prepare and audit respectively group financial statements auditors should, where appropriate, obtain written representations for those financial statements as well as for the financial statements of the holding companies themselves. The way in which the auditor of a holding company obtains these representations will depend upon the pattern of delegation of managerial control and authority which can vary both between and within different groups of companies. For instance, the auditor of a holding company may be able to obtain the written representations that he requires, regarding the group financial statements, from the directors of the holding company by virtue of their involvement in the management of the subsidiaries. Alternatively, there will be circumstances where the management structure of a group dictates that the auditor of the holding company will wish to have sight of appropriate written representations made by the directors of subsidiary companies to the auditors of those subsidiaries.

Dating

(14) The formal record of representations by manangement should be approved on a date as close as possible to the date of the audit report and after all other work, including the review of events after the balance sheet date, has been completed. It should never be approved after the audit report since it is part of the evidence on which the auditor's opinion, expressed in his report, is based.

(15) If there is a substantial delay between the approval of the formal record of representations by management and the date of the audit report, the auditor should consider whether to obtain further representations in respect of the intervening period and also whether any additional audit procedures need to be carried out, as described in the Auditing Guideline 'Events after the balance sheet date'.

Contents and wording

(16) The precise scope of the formal record of representations should be appropriate to the circumstances of each particular audit. The representations will be necessary where there are matters which are material to the financial statements, in respect of which the auditor cannot obtain independent corroborative evidence and could not reasonably expect it to be available, as indicated in pararaph 4 above. Set out in the appendix is an example of a letter of representation together with examples of additional paragraphs which may appropriate for inclusion in a letter of representation or in board minutes.

Appendix: Examples of representations by management

Set out below is an example of a letter of representation which relates to matters, which are material to financial statements prepared by an auditor for the company, and to circumstances where the auditor cannot obtain independent corroborative evidence and could not reasonably expect it to be available (see pagagraph 4 of the guideline above). It is not intended to be a standard letter because representations by management can be expected to vary not only from one enterprise to another, but also from one year to another in the case of the same audit client.

Dear Sirs,

We confirm to the best of our knowledge and belief, and having made appropriate enquiries of other directors and officials of the company, the following representations given to you in connection with your audit of the company's financial statements for the year ended 31st December............

(1) We acknowledge as directors our responsiblity for the financial statements, which you have prepared for the company. All the accounting records have been made available to you for the purpose of your audit and all the transactions undertaken by the company have been properly reflected and recorded in the accounting records. all other records and related information, including minutes of all management and shareholders' meetings, have been made available to you.

(2) The legal claim by Mr G. H. .... has been settled out of court by the company paying him £38000. No further amounts are expected to be paid., and no similar claims by employees or former employees have been received or are expected to be received.

(3) In conjunction with deferred tax not provided, the following assumptions reflect the intentions and expectations of the company:

(a) Capital investment of £260 000 is planned over the next three years.
(b) There are no plans to sell revalued properties.
(c) We are not aware of any indications that the situation is likely to change so as to necessitate the inclusion of a provision for tax payable in the financial statements.

(4) The company has had at no time during the year any arrangement, transaction or agreement to provide credit facilities (including loans, quasi-loans or credit transactions) for directors nor to guarantee or provide security for such matters, except as disclosed in note 14 to the financial statements.

(5) Other than the fire damage and related insurance claims described in note 19 to the financial statements, there have been no events since the balance sheet date which necessitate revision of the figures included in the financial statements or inclusion of a note thereto. Should further material events occur, which may necessitate revision of the figures included in the financial statements or inclusion of a note thereto, we will advise you accordingly.

Yours faithfully,

Signed on behalf of the board of directors.

The paragraphs included in the example letter relate to a specific set of circumstances. Set out below are some examples of additional paragraphs which, depending on the circumstances, may be appropriate for inclusion in a letter of representation or in board minutes. It is not expected that the auditor will obtain all these written representations as a matter of routine.

—There have been no breaches of the income tax regulations regarding payments to subcontractors in the construction industry which may directly or indirectly affect the view given by the financial statements.
—Having regard to the terms and conditions of sale imposed by major suppliers of goods, trade creditors include no amounts resulting from the purchase of goods on terms which include reservation of title by suppliers, other than £96544 due to ABC plc.
—With the exception of the penalties described in note 17, we are not aware of any circumstances which could produce losses on long-term contracts.
—DEF Ltd, an associated company, is about to launch a new product which has received excellent test results. As a result, the amount of £155000 outstanding since 6th January............, is expected to be fully recoverable.
—The company has guaranteed the bank overdraft of its subsidiary A Ltd, but has not entered into guarantees, warranties or other financial commitments relating to its other subsidiary or associated companies.
—The transaction shown in the profit and loss account as extraordinary is outside the course of the company's normal business and is not expected to recur frequently or regularly.
—Since the balance sheet date, the company has negotiated a continuation of its bank overdraft facilities with a limit of £200000. There have been no other events which are likely to affect the adequacy of working capital to meet foreseeable requirements in the year following the adoption of the financial statements.
—The indices used in the current cost financial statements for the year ended............ are, in our opinion, appropriate to the business of the company and have been properly applied on a consistent basis to assets and liabilities.

10.13 Reservation of title

10.13.1 Legal background

In a normal contract for the sale of goods, ownership in the goods passes as soon as they are in a deliverable state and there exists an unconditional contract for their sale. If the buyer defaults in paying for the goods after delivery, the only remedy available to the seller is to sue for the debt.

In other words, the seller has no right to reclaim the goods unless there is a clause in the contract for sale entitling him to do so. Such a clause is called a *reservation of title* clause and it may take several forms, not all of which achieve the effect desired.

Although the concept has existed for many years, the matter first came into prominence in the UK in 1976 in the Romalpa case (*Aluminium Industrie Vaassen BV v. Romalpa Aluminium Ltd*).

In this case the contract contained a clause providing that the purchaser obtained no title to the goods until they were paid for. The seller succeeded in reclaiming the goods when the purchaser failed to pay.

If the purchaser becomes insolvent, such a clause improves the position of the unpaid seller at the expense of the other creditors, including preferential creditors and those with a floating charge.

In the Romalpa case the unpaid seller succeeded because ownership in the goods had not passed. Suppose the contract gave the seller a *charge* over the goods. This was the position in re Bond Worth (1979)—the Monsanto case. Here the seller was unsuccessful because it was held that the charge had to be registered under what is now S395 Companies Act 1985 if it was to be enforceable.

There is a third possibility. The contract for sale contains a Romalpa-type clause under which ownership does not pass until the goods are paid for. But—by the time the claim is made the goods have been used to manufacture something else. Can the seller succeed in a claim against those new goods? This was attempted in *Borden (UK) Ltd v. Scottish Timber Products Ltd* (1979). It was held that the claim could not succeed as the goods sold no longer existed. Specific provision in the agreement to 'trace' the goods in this way was necessary.

To summarize then, we have:

(*a*) Clause in contract that ownership in goods does not pass until they are paid for: seller can claim back goods (Romalpa) but not goods into which they have been manufactured (Borden) unless there is specific agreement to that effect.

(*b*) Clause in contract establishing charge over goods: effective only if registered under S395 (*Re* Bond Worth).

10.13.2 Accounting treatment

The accounting bodies issued a statement in 1976 indicating the accounting treatment to be adopted for goods subject to a reservation of title clause. Its provisions are:

(*a*) The commercial substance of a transaction should prevail over its legal form. That means that a sale with reservation of title should be treated in the same way as a sale without such a condition—the seller should immediately subtract them from stock and include them in sales and debtors; and the purchaser should include them in stock, purchases and creditors.

(*b*) In the accounts of the purchaser, the liability to creditors with reservation of title should be disclosed by note.

(c) Where the accounts are materially affected by the accounting treatment adopted in relation to sales or purchases subject to reservation of title, the treatment should be disclosed by note.

(d) If a legal charge exists that fact must also be disclosed.

10.13.3 Auditing implications

(a) Client as purchaser of goods subject to reservation of title.

Here we shall potentially have such goods included in stock, and their value in purchases and creditors. The most relevant figure is the amount included in creditors, since this is the measure of the extent to which the supplier has a potential advantage over other creditors in the event of liquidation.

Audit steps will be:
(1) ascertain what steps the client takes to identify suppliers selling on terms which reserve title, by enquiring of those responsible for purchasing and of the board of directors.
(2) obtain a list of such suppliers from the client and verify it by reference to the terms of trading of major suppliers.
(3) ascertain what steps are taken to quantify the liability to such suppliers for balance sheet purposes, including liabilities not yet reflected in the creditors' ledger.
(4) where there are material liabilities to such suppliers, review the accuracy of the amounts of such liabilities as disclosed in the accounts.
(5) consider whether the matter should be covered in the letter of representation (see Section 10.12 above).

(b) Client as seller of goods subject to reservation of title.

At this end of the transaction the audit implications affect only one item, the debtors, though the effect could be dramatic if the amounts involved were large.

If the seller has the right to reclaim the goods, this could be a major factor in determining the need for and amount of any provision for doubtful debts—subject of course to confirmation that the reservation of title clause is a valid one having regard to the legal background outlined in 10.13.1 above.

10.14 Summary

The verification of assets and liabilities is the second of the three stages of the audit process identified in Section 5.1.

As noted in the Auditing Guideline on Audit Evidence, verification means obtaining sufficient, relevant and reliable evidence of the ownership, valuation and existence of each material asset and liability.

Possible evidence available includes:
—documents of title;
—physical inspection;
—certificates or other confirmation from persons outside the organization;
—information supplied by persons inside the organization;
—analytical review.

The client's system of internal control provides essential safeguards over the assets, and all aspects must be reviewed by the auditor:

—custody arrangements;
—records (including, in this context, asset registers);
—authorization procedures—for purchases, sales and scrappings;
—internal audit checks.

Work done on verifying the transactions of the year, like vouching purchases and sales, may also contribute powerfully to verification.

The disclosure requirements of the Companies Act are also important and will frequently be called for in auditing examinations, as will the provisions of relevant SSAPs.

Other areas generally requiring audit attention are:
Fixed assets
—adequacy of depreciation;
—distinction between capital and revenue;
—basis of valuation.
Current assets and liabilities
—basis of valuation;
—cut-off;
—observation of procedures (stock);
—circularization (debtors and creditors);
—overall tests and analytical review.

The letter of representation obtained from the directors may provide additional evidence, especially concerning matters for which independent corroboration is not available.

The verification of creditors has another dimension added to it because of the possibility that amounts owing for goods covered by reservation of title clauses may be included. The disclosure of the existence of material amounts of this kind could be important to other creditors of the company, and must therefore be verified by the auditors.

Progress Questions

Questions	Reference for answers
(1) What are the main disclosure requirements for fixed assets in Schedule 4, Companies Act 1985?	Sections 10.2.1(a) and 10.3.1(a)
(2)(a) Which SSAPs are relevant for fixed assets? (b) Summarize their relevant requirements.	Sections 10.2.1(b),10.3.1 10.3.3
(3) What internal control arrangements are particularly important for fixed assets?	Section 10.2.2
(4) What detailed information will normally be found in an asset register?	Section 10.2.2(c)
(5) What are the main steps in the verification of fixed assets?	Section 10.2.3
(6) List the requirements of the Companies Act and SSAP 13 concerning development costs. (Refer back to your answer to Questions 1 and 2 above.)	Section 10.3.1
(7) How will you set about verifying development costs?	Section 10.3.1
(8) How will you verify: (a) patents; (b) trade marks?	Section 10.3.2(a) Section 10.3.2(b)
(9) List the requirements of the Companies Act and SSAP 22 concerning goodwill. (Refer back to your answers to questions 1 and 2 above.)	Section 10.3.3(a)
(10) How will you verify goodwill?	Section 10.3.3(b)

Questions	Reference for answers
(11) How will you verify freehold and leasehold land and buildings?	Section 10.4.1
(12) What are the requirements of SSAPs 12 and 19 regarding depreciation of land and buildings? Do the provisions of SSAP 19 create a problem for accountants? Explain. (Refer back to your answers to Questions 1 and 2 above.)	Sections 10.2.1(b) and 10.4.1
(13)(a) List the steps necessary to verify plant and machinery.	Section 10.4.2
(b) What additional matters arise in the case of motor vehicles?	Section 10.4.3
(14) Distinguish between the methods of valuation laid down in the Companies Act for (a) fixed asset investments, (b) current asset investments.	Section 10.5.1
(15) How may investments be verified? Cover both listed and unlisted investments.	Section 10.5.3
(16) How will you verify loans made by the client?	Section 10.5.3(c)(2)
(17) What is the general rule for valuing stock as laid down in the Companies Act 1985 and SSAP 9?	Section 10.6.1
(18)(a) What methods of arriving at cost of stock are accepted by (1) Companies Act 1985; (2) SSAP 9? (b) Why are the unacceptable methods rejected?	Section 10.6.1
(19) Why is it important for the breakdown of stock into raw materials, work in progress and finished goods to be disclosed?	Section 10.6.1

Questions	Reference for answers
(20) Explain how each major type of internal control applies to stock.	Section 10.6.2
(21) What is meant by cut-off procedure? Explain how cut-off errors may arise and how they will affect the accounts.	Section 10.6.2(e)
(22) Explain in detail the internal control procedures which should be applied in stocktaking.	Section 10.6.2(h)
(23)(a) Draw a diagram to illustrate the stock system with stock records. (b) Why is it so important for stock records to be maintained?	Section 10.6.3
(24) List the main audit steps in verifying stock.	Section 10.6.3
(25)(a) Why is it important for the auditor to attend to observe the stocktaking?	Section 10.6.4: Auditing Guideline—Attendance at Stocktaking: Paragraphs (5)–(6)
(b) What tests should the auditor carry out when continuous stocktaking methods are being used? (c) List the audit procedures necessary in connection with attendance at stocktaking: (1) before the stocktaking—planning; (2) during the stocktaking; (3) after the stocktaking.	Paragraph (10) Paragraphs (12)–(13) Paragraphs (14)–(19) Paragraphs (20)–(21)
(26) List six overall tests used in verifying stock and explain their value.	Section 10.6.5
(27) What additional valuation problems arise with finished goods stocks?	Section 10.6.6

Questions	Reference for answers
(28) How will you verify work in progress? (Omit reference to long-term contract work in progress.)	Section 10.6.7
(29)(a) What is 'long-term contract work in progress'? (b) What is the basis on which SSAP 9 requires long-term contract work in progress to be valued? (c) How should profit on long-term contract work in progress be calculated? (d) Explain how the provisions of SSAP 9 with regard to long-term contract work in progress may clash with the provisions of the Companies Act. How may the conflict be resolved?	Section 10.6.8
(30) On what basis should forward contracts be included in accounts?	Section 10.6.8
(31) What is meant by 'ageing' trade debtors?	Section 10.7.1
(32) How will you verify trade debtors? List the main audit tasks and go into detail about circularization.	Section 10.7.1
(33) What is teeming and lading? Give three different situations in which it may be encountered.	Sections 10.7.1(b)10.8.1(c) and 10.8.3(b)(2)
(34)(a) What is deferred revenue expenditure? (b) When may an item properly be treated as deferred revenue expenditure? (c) What items are prohibited by the Companies Act 1985 from being carried forward in this way?	Section 10.7.5(c)
(35) What two steps are necessary to verify bank balances?	Section 10.8.1

Questions	Reference for answers
(36)(*a*) A bank report for audit purposes covers several other matters besides confirmation of balance. List these other matters.	Section 10.8.2: Auditing Guideline—bank reports for audit purposes. Appendix— paragraphs (7)–(10) and Notes thereto
(*b*) What supplementary information may the auditor seek to obtain from the client's bank in case of doubt?	Appendix—Notes on matters excluded from the standard letter
(37) Explain the audit procedures necessary to verify cash balances.	Section 10.8.3
(38) What audit work is required when (*a*) a fresh issue of debentures is made in the period under review; (*b*) debentures are redeemed or purchased on the open market?	Section 10.9.1(*a*) Section 10.9.1(*b*)
(39) How will you verify trade creditors?	Section 10.9.3
(40) How will you verify: (*a*) value added tax (VAT) outstanding; (*b*) pay as you earn tax (PAYE) and National Insurance outstanding?	Section 10.9.7(*a*) Section 10.9.7(*b*)
(41) Taxation may be one of the largest single liabilties in the balance sheet. (*a*) What are the disclosure requirements for taxation in the Companies Act and SSAP 8 (*b*) What are detailed audit steps necessary for taxation? (Omit reference to deferred taxation.)	Section 10.9.7(*c*)(1) Section 10.9.7(*c*)(2)

Questions	Reference for answers
(42)(*a*) What must there be before a company can pay a dividend? (*b*) What audit steps are necessary in connection with dividends?	Section 10.9.7(*d*)
(43) Summarize the main features of pension schemes.	Section 10.10.1
(44) List the work necessary in the audit of the employing company when a separate pension trust fund exists.	Section 10.10.1
(45) State the disclosure requirements of the Companies Act 1985 and SSAP 15 (as revised in 1985) regarding deferred taxation.	Section 10.10.2
(46) List the audit work necessary on deferred taxation.	Section 10.10.2
(47)(*a*) What legal requirements must be complied with in making a share issue? (*b*) What audit work is required in a period in which a share issue is made?	Section 10.11.1
(*c*) What are the disclosure requirements of the Companies Act 1985 governing share capital?	
(48) What purposes may the share premium account be used for?	Section 10.11.2
(49)(*a*) Why is it important for the auditor to obtain a letter of representation from the client? (*b*)What types of matter will the letter of representation deal with?	Section 10.12
(50)(*a*) What is a reservation of title clause?	Section 10.13.1

Questions	Reference for answers
(b) Indicate the types of clause included in contracts for sale in the following cases and state whether they were effective:	
(1) the *Romalpa case;*	
(2) *re Bond Worth;*	
(3) *(Borden (UK)* v. *Scottish Timber Products Ltd.*	Section 10.13.1
(c) What accounting treatment should be adopted for goods subject to a reservation of title clause?	Section 10.13.2
(d) What audit steps are necessary in the audit of:	
(1) the supplier;	
(2) the purchaser, of goods subject to a Romalpa clause?	Section 10.13.3

11 The Audit 3: Review of financial statements

11.1 Introduction

The third stage of our audit is to look at the financial statements as a whole to confirm that they do indeed 'show a true and fair view of the company's state of affairs as at...and of the profit and sources and application of funds for the period then ended'.

This review involves us in many different aspects, with some of which we have useful assistance from Auditing Guidelines. The main elements of our review are:

(*a*) compliance with the Companies Act 1985 and other relevant statutes;

(*b*) for listed companies, compliance with Stock Exchange requirements;

(*c*) compliance with SSAPs;

(*d*) review of company's stated accounting policies to confirm that they are appropriate for the company's business, in accordance with SSAPs in areas covered by SSAPs and with generally accepted accounting principles in areas not covered;

(*e*) confirmation that the financial statements do in fact comply with the stated policies;

(*f*) comparisons with figures for previous years and with budgets, to discover whether there are discrepancies requiring further investigation;

(*g*) a going-concern review;

(*h*) a review of events after the balance sheet date;

(*i*) a review of non-routine transactions, or any problem areas to confirm that a true and fair view of them is shown;

(*j*) confirmation that the financial statements are consistent with the directors' report (as required by S237(6) of the Companies Act 1985) and with the chairman's statement;

(*k*) consideration whether proper accounting records have been kept, and adequate returns received from branches not visited;

(*l*) audit of funds flow statement;

(*m*) audit of current cost accounts, if prepared;

(*n*) consideration whether the company, if private, is within the definition of 'small' or 'medium-sized' in S248 of the Companies Act 1985 for the purpose of the disclosure exemptions in Schedule 8 of the Act;

(o) review of amounts derived from the preceding financial statements;

(p) review of financial information issued with the financial statements;

(q) confirmation that the view presented by the financial statements is in accordance with the information and explanations obtained and conclusions reached on particular aspects of the audit.

Each one of these aspects will be dealt with in turn, referring where necessary to relevant Auditing Guidelines.

We might first ask ourselves when the review should be done, and by whom. Much of the work can only be done at a late stage of the audit, and of course only after the financial statements themselves have been prepared. It is useful to bear in mind, however, that the earlier some of these tasks are done, the more effective the auditor's work on transactions and on asset verification will be. For example, a comparison with figures of previous years could bring to light a discrepancy in the gross profit percentage which would add a new dimension to the planning of tests on trading account items.

The review must obviously be carried out by a senior member of the audit team, equally obviously by someone with knowledge and experience of the client and its industry.

11.2 The Auditing Guideline on review of financial statements

One of the first five Operational Guidelines issued in April 1980 deals with the review of financial statements and is reproduced below:

APC Guideline on review of financial statements

Introduction

(1) Paragraph 6 of the Auditing Standard *The auditor's operational standard* states that:

'The auditor should carry out such a review of the financial statements as is sufficient, in conjunction with the conclusions drawn from the other audit evidence obtained, to give him a reasonable basis for his opinion on the financial statements.'

This Auditing Guideline, which gives guidance on how that paragraph may be applied, should be read in conjuction with the Explanatory Foreword to Auditing Standards and Guidelines including the Glossary of Terms.

Background

(2) The auditor is required to form an opinion on the enterprise's financial statements as a whole. Having accumulated audit evidence about individual items or groups of items, he should therefore carry out an overall review to determine whether in his opinion:

(a) the financial statements have been prepared using acceptable accounting policies which have been consistently applied and are appropriate to the enterprise's business;

(b) the results of operations, state of affairs and all other information included in the financial statements are compatible with each other and with the auditor's knowledge of the enterprise;

(c) there is adequate disclosure of all appropriate matters and the information contained in the financial statements is suitably classified and presented;

(d) the financial statements comply with all statutory requirements and other regulations relevant to the constitution and activities of that enterprise;

and ultimately whether:

(e) the conclusions drawn from the other tests which he has carried out, together with those drawn from his overall review of the financial statements, enable him to form an opinion on the financial statements.

(3) Throughout the review the auditor needs to take account of the materiality of the matters under review and the confidence which his other audit work has already given him in the accuracy and completeness of the information contained in the financial statements.

(4) Skill and imagination are required to recognise the matters to be examined in carrying out an overall review and sound judgement is needed to interpret the information obtained. Accordingly the review should not be delegated to someone lacking the necessary experience and skill.

(5) An overall review of the financial statements based on the auditor's knowledge of the business of the enterprise is not of itself a sufficient basis for the expression of an audit opinion on those statements. However, it provides a valuable support for the conclusions arrived at as a result of his other audit work. In addition apparent inconsistencies could indicate areas in which material errors, omissions or irregularities may have occurred which have not been disclosed by other auditing procedures.

Procedures

Accounting policies

(6) The auditor should review the accounting policies adopted by the enterprise to determine whether such policies:

(a) comply with Statements of Standard Accounting Practice or, in the absence thereof, are otherwise acceptable;

(b) are consistent with those of the previous period;

(c) are consistently applied throughout the enterprise;

(d) are disclosed in accordance with the requirements of Statement of Standard Accounting Practice No. 2 *Disclosure of Accounting Policies.*

(7) When considering whether the policies adopted by management are acceptable the auditor should have regard, *inter alia,* to the policies commonly adopted in particular industries and to policies for which there is substantial authoritative support.

General review

(8) The auditor should consider whether the results of operations and the state of affairs of the enterprise as reported in the financial statements are consistent with his knowledge of the underlying circumstances of the business.

(9) In addition to any analytical review procedures carried out during the course of the audit, the auditor should carry out an overall review of the information in the financial statements themselves and compare it with other available data. For such a review to be effective the auditor needs to have sufficient knowledge of the activities of the enterprise and of the business which it operates to be able to determine whether particular items are abnormal. This background information should be available in the auditor's working papers as a result of his planning and earlier audit procedures.

Presentation and disclosure

(10) The auditor should consider the information in the financial statements in order to ensure that the conclusions which a reader might draw from it would be justified and consistent with the circumstances of the enterprises's business. In particular, he should bear in mind the need for the financial statements to reflect the substance of the underlying transactions and balances and not merely their form. He should consider also whether the presentation adopted in the financial statements may have been unduly influenced by management's desire to present facts in a favourable or unfavourable light.

(11) The auditor should also consider whether the financial statements adequately reflect the information and explanations obtained and conclusions reached on particular aspects of the audit.

(12) The auditor should consider whether his review has disclosed any new factors which affect the presentation or accounting policies adopted. For example it may become apparent, as a result of his review of the financial statements as a whole, that the enterprise has liquidity problems and the auditor should consider whether or not the financial statements should have been prepared on a going concern basis.

Compliance with regulations

(13) In reviewing the financial statements to ensure compliance with the requirements of statutes, Statements of Standard Accounting Practice and other applicable regulations, the auditor may find it helpful to use a checklist or other *aide-mémoire.*

11.3   Compliance with Companies Act 1985 and other relevant statutes

The accounting requirements of the Companies Act 1985 are matters more appropriate for an accounting book than for an auditing one, and they are not dealt with in detail here.

The audit approach will probably be the use of a checklist of the requirements of Schedules 4 and 5 and, if relevant, of Schedule 9 which gives the form and content of 'special category' accounts—banking, shipping and insurance companies.

The auditor has the responsibility under S237(5) of the Act to give in his or her report, if not appearing elsewhere in the financial statements, those details of directors' and employees' remuneration, and loans to officers, called for in Schedules 5 and 6. These requirements are given in the next chapter where all the provisions governing the auditor's report are dealt with.

Special types of company, or other entities such as building societies, may be subject to the requirements of separate statutes. These are dealt with in Chapter 23.

11.4   Compliance with Stock Exchange requirements (listed companies)

The Stock Exchange 'Yellow Book' (*Admission of Securities to Listing*) gives details of additional matters required by the Stock Exchange for listed companies. The auditor will confirm that these have been complied with, once again using a checklist. The main requirements are given below:

(a) a statement by the directors of the reasons for any significant departure from applicable standard accounting practices;

(b) an explanation of the reason for a material difference between actual results and any previously published forecast;

(c) a geographical analysis of turnover and contribution to trading results;

(d) the name of the principal country in which each subsidiary operates;

(e) for companies other than subsidiaries in which the group has an equity interest of 20 per cent or more:

   (1) the principal country of operation,

   (2) particulars of its issued capital and debentures,

   (3) the percentage of each class of loan securities attributable to the company's interest;

(f) an analysis of borrowings showing amounts repayable:

   (1) within one year,

   (2) between one and two years,

(3) between two and five years,

(4) in five years or more;

(g) details of any interest capitalized;

(h) directors' share interests, including options, not only at the balance sheet date as required by S324, but also at a date not more than one month before the annual general meeting;

(i) holdings of 'substantial shareholders' (5 per cent or more of nominal value) at a date not more than one month before the annual general meeting;

(j) a statement as to whether the company is a close company for taxation purposes;

(k) details of any interest by a director, or a corporate substantial shareholder, in any contract of significance with the company or a subsidiary;

(l) details of any contract by a substantial shareholder to provide services to the company or a subsidiary;

(m) details of any waiver of directors' remuneration;

(n) details of any waiver of dividend by a shareholder;

(o) details of any shareholders' authority for the purchase by the company of its own shares.

11.5   Compliance with SSAPs

Like the Companies Act, SSAPs are really matters of accountancy, and their detailed coverage would need a separate book.

The audit approach will normally be as for the Companies Act requirements—the use of a checklist of all SSAPs currently in force.

The detailed requirements of some SSAPs are dealt with elsewhere in this book where they are of particular auditing relevance. The following review checklist deals with the more important SSAPs.

Review of financial statements—presentation and disclosure

(1) Companies Act checklist completed and reviewed?

(2) Items in the financial statements properly classified and grouped to avoid unnecessary detail?

(3) (a) Information essential to the true and fair view presented prominently (and not relegated to a note which may obscure its impact)? (b) Does balance sheet clearly show ability of company to meet current indebtedness?

(4) Chairman's Statement/Directors' Report reviewed for consistency with accounts?

(5) Accounts reviewed for consistency with any previously published forecast and (for listed companies) interim announcements?

(6) (a) Income from associated companies (SSAP 1) brought in (i) in the company's own accounts, on the basis of dividends received and receivable; (ii) in the group's accounts (or in the accounts of a company with no subsidiaries), on the basis of the group's share of the associates' profits/losses? (b) Investments in associated companies stated at cost (less any amounts written off) plus share of post-acquisition retained profits and reserves?

(7) (a) Full disclosure of any respects in which the assumptions on which the accounts are based do not conform with the fundamental concepts (SSAP 2) of (i) going concern (ii) accruals (iii) consistency (iv) prudence? (b) All significant accounting policies (SSAP 2): (i) clearly disclosed and explained; (ii) consistent with the previous year; (iii) prudent?

(8) (a) For listed companies, calculation of earnings per share (SSAP 3) based on consolidated results (after minority interests and preference dividends but before extraordinary items) divided by the number of shares in issue and ranking for dividend in respect of the period? (b) Any future obligations regarding share capital accounted for by calculating fully diluted earnings per share?

(9) Government grants (SSAP 4) credited to revenue over the useful life of the asset by either (i) reducing the cost of the fixed assets; or (ii) setting up a deferred credit, a portion of which is transferred to revenue each year?

(10) (a) 'Extraordinary' items (SSAP 6) limited to those which derive from events or transactions outside the ordinary activities of the business and which are both material and non-recurring? (b) Prior-year adjustments (i) limited to items arising from the correction of fundamental errors or from changes in accounting policy; (ii) accounted for by restating prior year? (c) 'Exceptional' items limited to those which arise from ordinary activities of the business which are abnormal in their size and incidence? (d) Unrealized surpluses on revaluations of fixed assets credited direct to reserve?

(11) (a) Basis of valuation of stock and work-in-progress (SSAP 9) (other than long-term contract work-in-progress) based on the lower of cost or net realizable value? (b) Value of long-term (more than 1 year) contract work-in-progress (i) based on cost plus attributable profit and less foreseeable losses and progress payments received and receivable; (ii) provision made for excess where anticipated losses exceed cost less progress payments to date?

(12) (a) Depreciation (SSAP 12) provided on all fixed assets (including buildings) which have a finite useful life? (b) Where assets revalued, depreciation based on the revalued amount?

(13) (a) Expenditure on pure and applied research (other than on fixed assets) written-off as incurred? (b) Development expenditure (SSAP 13) (other than contract) (i) written-off as it is incurred; or (ii) only deferred if there is a clearly defined project for which the expenditure is separately indentifiable and of which the feasibility and viability have been assessed with reasonable certainty?

(14) Deferred taxation accounted for in accordance with SSAP 15 as revised?

(15) Current cost accounts drawn up in accordance with SSAP 16?

(16) Where an accounting policy is not the subject of an SSAP, we are (and

there is evidence that we are) satisfied that the adopted policy is appropriate to the circumstances of the business?

(17) Where a change of accounting policy has occurred: (a) adequate disclosure of the fact of the change and the reasons for it; (b) effect of the change properly disclosed and quantified (see 10(b) above); (c) are we satisfied that the new policy produces a fairer presentation of the results and financial position of the business?

(18) Significant post-balance-sheet events either adjusted for in the accounts or disclosed and explained as necessary?

(19) Nature (and, if practicable, an estimate of the amount) of any contingent profit or loss disclosed?

(20) Disclosure of any long-term commitments (e.g. under leases) sufficient in circumstances ?

(21) Borrowing powers not exceeded?

(22) Adequate disclosure of all matters which require disclosure is such as to make the accounts not misleading?

11.6 Review of company's stated accounting policies

With this item we turn to something far more of a problem than the three we have looked at so far. With the Companies Act, Stock Exchange requirements and SSAPs, we are dealing with clearly stated external regulations, compliance with which is relatively easily confirmed.

We now have to step outside this defined framework and consider the appropriateness and validity of accounting policies in other areas. Sometimes we may have Exposure Drafts or International Accounting Standards to refer to, or pronouncements by accountancy bodies in other countries. If all else fails we may even refer to accountancy textbooks! This is certainly an area where consultation with partners, colleagues or another practitioner will be helpful. Confidentiality of the client's affairs must obviously be maintained if another practitioner is consulted.

11.7 Confirmation of compliance with stated accounting policies

Once the accounting policies themselves have been approved, it is a relatively simple matter to confirm that they have been complied with in the preparation of the financial statements. It is by no means a negligible matter, however, not least because the auditor's interpretation of the policy may not agree with the client's.

11.8 Analytical review and comparison with figures for previous years and with budgets

Some of this work has already been mentioned in the previous chapter as one of the overall tests applied as part of the process of verifying stock. It can assist by drawing attention to anomalies requiring investigation in every area, however.

The purpose of a general analytical review within the overall review of financial statements is to examine critically the inter-relationship between items on balances contained within the financial statements to ensure that they are consistent with one another, with known trends and with the auditor's knowledge of the business. Its roles are emphasized by the Auditing Guideline 'Review of Financial Statements'.

Whilst an analytical review is not of itself a sufficient basis upon which to express an audit opinion, it can nevertheless provide additional assurance in areas where the result of other audit work has been inconclusive. Investigation of apparent inconsistencies revealed by analytical review may disclose errors, irregularities or omissions which would not have been disclosed by other audit procedures.

If the review is to be effective, it is essential that the auditor should have a sound background knowledge of the activities of the business and of the markets and environment in which it operates. This information should be on record in the permanent file which should be updated as necessary when each review takes place.

A review calls for the exercise of skill and judgement. Whilst the assembly of comparative figures, ratios, etc., may be delegated, it is essential that the conclusions derived from the review are subjected to overview by an experienced auditor.

The scope of the review will vary with the circumstances of each audit in order to concentrate the review effort in material and relevant areas. In general terms, however, an analytical review will comprise:

Comparison
—between specific items in the financial statements and corresponding amounts for the previous period;
—between budgets, management accounts and actual results;
—between monthly or periodic totals or ratios, to establish trends;
—between the performance of the business under review and similar businesses in the industry.

Review
—of the amounts contained in financial statements for their consistency with available non-financial data (e.g. sales, production and inventory quantities; employment statistics, etc.);

—of inter-relationships between specific items in the financial statements (ratios).

Investigation
—of unusual or unexpected variances;
—of expected or anticipated variances which do not occur.

The precise scope and content of the analysis can only be determined when the auditor has established:

(*a*) the financial data, ratios, or other statistics which are of significance to the business, and

(*b*) the nature and relevance of other data which are available for the purposes of comparison.

The most important aspect of the review is the interpretation of its results and in particular the investigation of any unexpected variations or anticipated variations which fail to occur. The results of the review should be interpreted against the auditor's background knowledge of the business and its environment. Factors to be considered include:
—the rate of inflation;
—changes in buying and selling prices;
—seasonal factors affecting the pattern of trade;
—any planned expansion or contraction, or major contracts or customers gained or lost;
—changes in the level of activity in the industry and in the economy as a whole;
—technological advances, industrial disputes and government regulations affecting the business' operations.

The explanations obtained should be assessed in the light of the conclusions drawn from other areas of the audit work. Where the results of the review indicate the possibility of errors or misstatements in the financial statements, it will be necessary to consider the extent to which substantive testing must be increased in order to provide an acceptable level of audit assurance.

The following is a list of some of the amounts and ratios which it will often be appropriate to include in an analytical review. The list below would cover the main areas in relation to analysing the profit and loss account and balance sheet for most companies, but it is not intended to be exhaustive as it must always be capable of adaptation to individual circumstances.

11.8.1 Profit and loss account analysis

Turnover
Amount in £
  % annual increase
Quantity/volume (if available)
  % increase
Selling prices: % increase
Discounts as a % of sales
Returns/allowances as a % of sales
Cost of sales
Amount in £
  % material content
  % labour content
  % overhead content
Gross profit
Amount in £
  as % of sales
Expenses
Advertising (as % of sales)
Selling expenses (as % to sales)
Administrative expenses (£ amount)
Financial expenses (£ amount)
Payroll
Average number of employees
Aggregate remuneration
Average payroll cost per employee
Wage settlements made during period (% increase)
Plant
Repairs/maintenance (amount)
Depreciation charge for period (amount)
Interest
Total interest charge as % of total debt
Net profit
as % of:
  sales
  shareholders' funds
  capital employed

11.8.2 Balance sheet analysis

Liquidity
Current ratio (current assets divided by current liabilities: shows ability of
  company to meet current debt)

Quick ratio (current monetary assets divided by current liabilities: shows immediate solvency of the business)

Capital structure

Borrowing ratio (fixed-interest loans divided by capital employed: measures proportion of capital employed raised by fixed-interest debt)

Gearing ratio (fixed-interest loans plus preference capital divided by capital employed: measures proportion of capital employed not financed by ordinary shares)

Interest cover (profit before interest and taxation divided by interest indicates to lenders the security of interest payments)

Dividend cover (profit after interest and tax, divided by ordinary dividends: shows amount of profit cover for the ordinary shareholder's dividend)

Creditor/purchaser ratio (creditors divided by average purchases per day indicates amount of credit taken from suppliers)

Use of assets

Stock turnover (cost of sales divided by stocks: indicates number of times stock turned over in year)

Stock holding period (number of days in year divided by the result of above expresses average length of time stock is held)

Debtors/turnover (sales divided by debtors: expresses relationship between volume of business and outstanding debtors)

Debtors: average collection period (debtors divided by average sales per day: indicates effectiveness of the credit control of the company).

11.9 Going concern review

This matter is covered completely by an Auditing Guideline—the auditor's considerations in respect of going concern. The full text is reproduced below. Please study it carefully.

Auditing Guideline on the auditor's considerations in respect of going concern

Preface

This Guideline gives guidance on the auditor's considerations as to whether or not it is appropriate for an enterprise to prepare financial statements on a going concern basis, i.e. on a basis which assumes that the enterprise is able to continue in operational existence for the foreseeable future. It is supplementary to, and should be read in conjunction with, the auditor's operational and reporting Standards and related Guidelines.

This Guideline is written in the context of the audit of companies incorporated under the Companies Acts. However, in the absence of specific provisions to the contrary, the principles embodied in this Guideline apply also to the audit of other enterprises.

Introduction

(1) The directors of a company have a statutory responsibility to prepare financial statements which give a true and fair view and comply with the Companies Act. This means that the directors are responsible for the appropriateness of the basic assumptions underlying the financial statements.

(2) Schedule 4 of the Companies Act 1985 provides that items shown in the financial statements of a company should be determined in accordance with the principle that it is presumed to be carrying on business as a going concern. Departures from this principle may be made if it appears to the directors that there are special reasons for doing so. Disclosures of the departure, the reasons for it and its effect are required to be made in the financial statements.

(3) SSAP 2 identifies going concern as one of the fundamental accounting concepts and provides that if financial statements are prepared on the basis of assumptions which differ materially from that concept the facts should be explained in the financial statements.

(4) The going-concern concept identified in SSAP 2 is 'that the enterprise will continue in operational existence for the foreseeable future. This means in particular that the profit and loss account and the balance sheet assume no intention or necessity to liquidate or curtail significantly the scale of operation'.

(5) Where the going concern basis is no longer appropriate, adjustments may have to be made to the values at which balance sheet assets and liabilities are recorded, to the headings under which they are classified and for possible new liabilities.

(6) The auditor of a company has a statutory responsibility to express an opinion as to whether the financial statements give a true and fair view and comply with the Companies Acts. When forming his opinion, the auditor needs to consider whether there are reasonable grounds for accepting that the financial statements should have been prepared on a going concern basis. The auditor should therefore be satisfied when planning, performing and evaluating the results of his audit procedures that the going concern basis is appropriate. If, during the course of his audit, the auditor becomes aware of any indications that the going concern basis may no longer be valid, he should carry out the additional procedures outlined in this Guideline. If the auditor's procedures reveal no such indications, it will be reasonable for him to accept that the going concern assumption is appropriate.

(7) It is implicit in assessing the foreseeable future that a judgement must be made about uncertain future events. No certainty exists nor can any guarantee be given that any enterprise will continue as a going concern. Hence the auditor's judgement will always involve an assessment, made at the time that the audit is signed, of the risk that liquidation or enforced substantial curtailment of the scale of operations will occur.

(8) While the foreseeable future must be judged in relation to specific circumstances, it should normally extend to a minimum of six months following the date of the audit report or one year after the balance sheet date, whichever period ends on the later date. It will also be necessary to take account of significant events which will or are likely to occur later.

Background

(9) A company rarely ceases to carry on business without any prior indications, either of inability to meet debts as they fall due or of other problems that raise questions about the continuation of business. The indications may vary in importance depending upon specific circumstances. They may be interdependent and some may only have significance as audit evidence when viewed in conjunction with others. Further, their significance may diminish because they are mitigated by other audit evidence. Paragraphs 10 and 11 below list examples of such indications and paragraphs 12 and 13 list examples of mitigating evidence. The lists are not intended to be exhaustive.

(10) Indications that a company may be unable to meet its debts as they fall due include recurring operating losses, financing to a considerable extent out of overdue suppliers and other creditors (for example, VAT, PAYE, National Insurance), heavy dependence on short-term finance for long-term needs, working capital deficiencies, low liquidity ratios, over-gearing in the form of high or increasing debt to equity ratios, and under-capitalisation, particularly if there is a deficiency of share capital and reserves. Other matters that could indicate difficulty would include borrowings in excess of limits imposed by debenture trust deeds, default on loan or similar agreements, dividends in arrears, restrictions placed on usual trade terms, excessive or obsolete stock, long overdue debtors, non-compliance with statutory capital requirements, deterioration of relationship with bankers, necessity of seeking new sources or methods of obtaining finance, the continuing use of old fixed assets because there are no funds available to replace them, the size and content of the order book and potential losses on long-term contracts.

(11) Indications of problems that raise questions about the continuation of a business and which might lead to an inability to meet its debts might include internal matters; for example, loss of key management or staff, significantly increasing stock levels, work stoppages or other labour difficulties, substantial dependence on the success of a particular project or on a particular asset, excessive reliance on the success of a new product and uneconomic long-term commitments. Alternatively, indications may relate to external matters; for example, legal proceedings or similar matters that may jeopardize a company's ability to continue in business, loss of a key franchise or patent, loss of a particular supplier or customer, the undue influence of a market dominant competitor, political risks, technical developments which render a key product obsolete, and frequent financial failures of enterprises in the same industry.

(12) Indications that the company may be unable to meet its debts might be mitigated by factors relating to alternative means for maintaining adequate cash flows. Such factors include, for example, the ability to dispose of assets or to postpone the replacement of assets without adversely affecting operations, to lease assets rather than purchase them outright, to obtain new sources of finance, to renew or extend loans, to restructure debts, to raise additional share capital, and to obtain financial support from other group companies.

(13) Similarly, indications of problems that raise questions about the continuation of business might be mitigated by factors relating to the company's capacity to adopt alternative courses of action; for example, the availability of suitable persons to fill key positions, the likelihood of finding alternative sales markets when a principal customer is lost, the ability to replace assets which have been destroyed and the

possibility of continuing the business by making limited reductions in the level of operations or by making use of alternative resources.

Audit procedures and reports

Procedures

(14) In performing the preparatory procedures identified in the Auditing Guideline 'Planning, controlling and recording', the auditor should consider whether any of the indications of the nature described in paragraphs 10 and 11 above are present.

(15) Such procedures would not generally encompass any specific additional procedures, since the matters identified above would normally be known to the auditor as a result of his other audit procedures. However, in this context the auditor will be particularly concerned with interim accounts or management information, and consulting with the directors and staff of the company. Such consultations should address not only the current situation but also the future. Where formal forecast and budget systems exist, they should be considered. Where they are not formalized, discussions should be directed to the directors' outline plans, including a comparison of anticipated needs with borrowing facilities and limits.

(16) The auditor should continue this consideration to the date of the audit report, although early identification of evidence that the company may be unable to continue in business will give the directors more time to consider their response and to obtain suitable professional advice.

(17) Where as a result of these procedures, evidence comes to the auditor's attention that suggests that the company may be unable to continue in business, he should review any factors that may counterbalance that evidence. The review should include further discussions with the directors and may also embrace other work as described in the following four paragraphs. These paragraphs are only indicative of the matters to be considered and are not intended to be exhaustive.

(18) Where the directors have developed plans to overcome the company's problems, the auditor should consider the bases on which they have been prepared, consider whether they conform with facts already known to him and compare them with such independent evidence as is available. If such plans are to have value for audit purposes, they should be specific rather than general and above all be feasible courses of action. The auditor should be aware that the relevance of such plans generally decreases as the time period for planned actions and anticipated events increases. A company which does not provide adequate forecasts and budgets as a matter of course will need to develop such information if it is facing difficulties, although small companies need not be expected to provide the same amount and quality of evidence as large companies.

(19) In certain circumstances (for example, where finance is to be provided by third parties or where there are detailed plans to dispose of assets, borrow, restructure debt or increase share capital) the auditor may need to obtain written confirmations from banks or other third parties in order to be able to assess the degree of their commitment.

(20) The auditor should consider any professional advice obtained by the directors as to the extent of the company's difficulties and the practicalities of overcoming them. The directors are responsible for obtaining such professional advice and, in addition to advice which the auditor himself may be able to provide, may need to

consult others such as bankers, qualified insolvency practitioners and solicitors. In particular, it may be necessary for the directors to obtain legal advice on the consequences of the company continuing to trade while it is known by the directors to be insolvent.

(21) Where the company is a member of a group, the auditor should consider the implications of any obligations, undertakings or guarantees which exist between the company and other group members. Consideration should be given both to undertakings or guarantees given by the company and to those received by it. There are many different ways of providing support within a group and a proper understanding of complex agreements may not be possible without legal advice. When considering whether to place reliance on such agreements the auditor has to judge the probability that, in the event that support becomes necessary, it will be forthcoming. He should consider whether the agreements are prima facie legally binding or merely expressions of intent, whether they have been formally approved and minuted, and whether the supporting company is in a position to provide support. He may need to examine the financial statements of other group companies, consult with the management of such companies and, where appropriate, liaise with their auditors. Similar considerations arise where a company is dependent upon the support of another entity, even if no group relationship exists.

(22) Having carried out the procedures and review referred to in paragraphs 14 to 21, the auditor can then consider whether he has sufficient evidence on which to reach a decision as to whether it is appropriate that the financial statements should have been prepared on a going-concern basis.

Unqualified audit reports

(23) Where the auditor is satisfied that it is proper that the financial statements have been prepared on a going concern basis, no mention of any matters relating to the application of that basis will normally be required in the audit report.

(24) There may, however, be circumstances where the reader will obtain a better understanding of the financial statements, and of the appropriateness of the basis on which they are prepared, if his attention is drawn to important matters. Examples might include events or conditions, such as operating trends, borrowing facilities or financing arrangements, awareness of which is fundamental to an understanding of the financial statements. In such circumstances, the auditor may decide to refer to these matters in his report as an emphasis of matter in accordance with the Auditing Standard 'The audit report'.

Qualified audit reports

(25) Where there is uncertainty about the appropriateness of the going concern basis, the auditor should consider the effect of that uncertainty upon the view given by the financial statements. In doing so, he should consider both the adequacy of the disclosure of the uncertainty in the financial statements and the extent of the adjustments that might need to be made to the financial statements in the event that they were not to be prepared on a going-concern basis.

(26) In particular, the auditor should consider the recoverability and classification of assets, the classification of liabilities and the possibility of new liabilities were the company to cease to be a going concern. For example, there may be a need for

provisions or amounts to be written off in respect of stocks and debtors, reclassification of long-term liabilities which become due immediately, provisions in respect of redundancy payments and revaluations of assets at their market values. While it will not normally be practicable to quantify precisely the extent of the adjustments that would be necessary were the financial statements not to be prepared on a going-concern basis, the auditor should form an opinion as to their likely impact on the financial statements.

(27) Where the auditor considers that the uncertainty as to the appropriateness of the going concern assumption materially affects the view given by the financial statements, he should qualify his audit report giving a 'subject to' opinion. Materiality should be judged in terms of the extent of the adjustments that would need to be made to the financial statements in the event that they were not to be prepared on a going concern basis. The audit report should refer to the going concern assumption upon which the financial statements have been based, the nature of the related uncertainty and the nature of the adjustments that may have to be made to the financial statements.

(28) Set out below is an example of a qualified audit report which would be appropriate when uncertainty about the appropriateness of the going concern assumption materially affected the view given by the financial statements.

The example illustrates a form of wording which might be appropriate when the circumstances giving rise to the uncertainty were that the company was loss-making, current liabilities exceeded current assets, negotiations about vital financing arrangements had not been successfully completed at the date of the audit report, adequate disclosure of these facts had been made in the notes to the accounts, and adjustments would be needed to the financial statements were they not to be prepared on a going concern basis. In practice, the circumstances necessitating a qualified report may be different from those of the example, and the form of wording will need to be amended to fit the particular circumstances.

AUDITORS' REPORT TO THE MEMBERS OF ....

We have audited the financial statements on pages .... to .... in accordance with approved Auditing Standards.

The financial statements have been prepared on a going concern basis. This basis may not be appropriate because the company incurred a loss after taxation of £...... during the year ended 31 December 19... and at that date its current liabilities exceeded its current assets by £...... The company is currently negotiating for long-term facilities to replace the loan of £...... which is repayable on ...... These factors, which are explained to note ......, indicate that the company may be unable to continue trading.

Should the company be unable to continue trading, adjustments would have to be made to reduce the value of assets to their recoverable amount, to provide for any further liabilities which might arise, and to reclassify fixed assets and long-term liabilities as current assets and liabilities.

Subject to the company being able to continue trading, in our opinion the financial statements, which have been prepared under the historical cost convention, give a true and fair view of the state of affairs of the company at 31 December 19... and of its loss and source and application of funds for the year then ended and comply with the Companies Act 1985.

(29) Where the uncertainty about the appropriateness of the going concern assumption is so fundamental as to prevent the auditor from forming an opinion on the financial statement, he will need to disclaim an opinion.

(30) In rare cases, the auditor may conclude that the evidence indicating that the company is unable to continue in business is so overwhelming that he will wish to qualify on grounds of disagreement. In such cases, he should give an 'except for' or 'adverse' opinion depending on the extent of the adjustments that would be necessary were the financial statements not to be prepared on a going concern basis.

(31) As discussed in paragraphs 2 and 3, there is a presumption in both law and accounting standards that the financial statements are prepared on a going concern basis. Where there is significant uncertainty about the enterprise's ability to continue in business, this fact should be stated in the financial statements even when there is no likely impact on the carrying value and classification of assets and liabilities. Where this is not stated in the financial statements, the auditor should refer to it in his report.

(32) The auditor should not refrain from qualifying his report if it is otherwise appropriate, merely on the grounds that it may lead to the appointment of a receiver or liquidator.

11.10   Review of events after the balance sheet date and contingencies

11.10.1   Post balance sheet events

The audit does not stop with the balance sheet date. Events after the balance sheet date must be considered. SSAP 17 defines such events as 'those events, both favourable and unfavourable, which occur between the balance sheet date and the date on which the financial statements are approved'. They may be *adjusting events* (those providing additional evidence of conditions existing at the balance sheet date, including events which because of statutory or conventional requirements are reflected in financial statements) or *non-adjusting events* (those which concern conditions which did *not* exist at the balance sheet date).

As the financial statements are to be prepared on the basis of conditions existing at the balance sheet date, adjusting events must be reflected in the financial statements. Non-adjusting events are *not* reflected *unless* they indicate that the going concern concept may not be appropriate.

The fact that non-adjusting events are not allowed for by adjusting the figures does not mean that they are simply ignored. SSAP 17 requires a material non-adjusting event to be disclosed by note if 'its non-disclosure would affect the ability of the users of the financial statements to reach a proper understanding of the position, or it is the reversal or maturity after the year-end of a transaction entered into before the year-end, the substance of which was primarily to alter the appearance of the balance sheet'.

Post balance sheet events for the purpose of SSAP 17 are those occurring between the balance sheet date and the date the financial statements are approved by the directors.

The auditor will be actively concerned to review events up to his signing of the audit report, and it is therefore desirable that there should be as small a gap as possible between the two approvals. Also, the auditor still has a responsibility to consider the effect of further events up to the date of the annual general meeting—see Section 11.10.3 below.

Examples of adjusting and non-adjusting events

Adjusting events	Non-adjusting events
(a) *Fixed assets.* The subsequent determination of the purchase price or of the proceeds of assets purchased or sold before the year end.	(a) Mergers and acquisitions.
	(b) Reconstructions and proposed reconstructions.
(b) *Property.* A valuation which provides evidence of a permanent diminution in value.	(c) Issues of shares and debentures.
	(d) Purchases and sales of fixed assets and investments.
(c) *Investments.* The receipt of a copy of the financial statement or other information in respect of an unlisted company which provides evidence of a permanent diminution in the value of a long-term investment.	(e) Losses of fixed assets or stock as a result of a catastrophe such as fire or flood.
	(f) Opening new trading activities or extending existing trading activities.
(d) *Stocks and work in progress:* (1) the receipt of proceeds of sales after the balance sheet date or other evidence concerning the net realisable value of stocks (2) the receipt of evidence that the previous estimate of accrued profit on a long-term contract was materially inaccurate.	(g) Closing a significant part of the trading activities if this was not anticipated at the year end.
	(h) Decline in the value of property and investments held as fixed assets, if it can be demonstrated that the decline occurred after the year end.
	(i) Changes in rates of foreign exchange.
(e) *Debtors.* The renegotiation of amounts owing by debtors or the insolvency of a debtor.	(j) Government action such as nationalization.
(f) *Dividends receivable.* The declaration of dividends by subsidiaries and associated companies relating to periods prior to the balance sheet date of the holding company.	(k) Strikes and other labour disputes.
	(l) Augmentation of pension benefits.

Adjusting events	Non-adjusting events

(g) *Taxation.* The receipt of information regarding rates of taxation.

(h) *Claims.* Amounts received or receivable in respect of insurance claims which were in the course of negotiation at the balance sheet date.

(i) *Discoveries.* The discovery of errors or frauds which show that the financial statements were incorrect.

11.10.2 Contingencies

SSAP 18 Accounting for Contingencies defines a contingency as 'a condition which exists at the balance sheet date, where the outcome will be confirmed only on the occurrence or non-occurrence of one or more uncertain future events. A contingent gain or loss is a gain or loss dependent on a contingency'.

A useful table summarizing the disclosure requirements of SSAP 18 was published in *True and Fair* No. 17 in 1980/81:

Likelihood of occurrence	Contingent asset	Contingent liability
Remote	No disclosure	No disclosure
Possible/probable	No disclosure	Disclosure by note
Highly probable	Disclosure by note	Provision
Virtually certain	Accrual	Provision

11.10.3 The audit of post balance sheet events and contingencies—the Auditing Guideline

An Auditing Guideline on events after the balance sheet date was issued in November 1982 and is reproduced below.

Preface

This Guideline is intended to clarify the responsibilities of the auditor for examining and reporting upon events which occur after the date of the balance sheet. It also gives guidance on the procedures for the audit of events after the balance sheet date, and on the dating of the audit report. Counsel's opinion on the dating of audit reports was obtained before the Guideline was developed. Counsel has subsequently confirmed that this Guideline is in accordance with the relevant statutory provisions and legal principles and that he approves it accordingly.

The Guideline is supplementary to and should be read in conjunction with the auditor's operational and reporting Standards and related Guidelines.

Introduction and scope

(1) This Guideline is written in the context of the audit of limited companies. However, its principles apply to the audit of other enterprises whose financial statements are intended to give a true and fair view. In other circumstances, the auditor will be guided by the terms of his particular appointment or by relevant legislation.

(2) In the absence of specific provisions to the contrary, either in legislation or in the auditor's terms of appointment, the general principle holds that the auditor's responsibility to his client extends to the date on which he signs his audit report. Further, he may retain some responsibility after that date as described in this Guideline. It is for this reason that the auditor should not confine himself to those events after the balance sheet date which are defined in Statement of Standard Accounting Practice No. 17 as 'post balance sheet events', i.e. those events both favourable and unfavourable which occur between the balance sheet date and the date on which the financial statements are approved by the board of directors.

Dating of the audit report

(3) The auditor should always date his audit report. The date used should, generally, be that on which he signs his report on the financial statements. The auditor should plan his work so that, wherever possible, his report is dated as close as possible to the date of approval of the financial statements by the directors. If, for administrative reasons, final copies of the financial statements are not available at the date that the auditor declares, to the directors, that he is willing to sign his audit report, he may use that date, provided the delay in the preparation of final copies is only of short duration. An example of such administrative reasons would be the non-availability, through illness or overseas location, of directors to sign the financial statements on behalf of the company.

(4) The auditor's responsibility is to report on the financial statements as presented by the directors. Legally, such statements do not exist until they have been approved by the directors. It follows that the auditor can never date his report earlier than the date on which the complete financial statements were approved by the directors. Before signing his report, the auditor should obtain evidence that the financial statements have been approved by the directors. Statement of Standard Accounting Practice No. 17 requires disclosure of the date on which the directors approved the financial statements.

(5) At the date on which the financial statements are approved by the directors, they do not have to be in the precise printed or typewritten form submitted to members. However, the auditor should satisfy himself that the approved financial statements are

complete in all material respects. Accordingly, the financial statements approved by the directors should not leave unresolved any matters which require exercise of judgement or discretion (although they may omit items which merely require mechanical calculation: for example, the provision of a dividend at a rate already agreed by the directors). As compliance with the Companies Act and Statements of Standard Accounting Practice may require the exercise of judgement or discretion, financial statements which do not take account of these matters cannot be regarded as complete in all material respects.

Action up to the date of the audit report

(6) The auditor should take steps, as described in paragraph 13, to obtain reasonable assurance in respect of all significant events up to the date of his report. He should ensure that any such significant events are, where appropriate, accounted for or disclosed in the financial statements. If not, he should consider whether to qualify his report.

Action after the date of the audit report

(7) After the date of the audit report the auditor does not have a duty to search for evidence of post balance sheet events. However, if before the General Meeting at which the financial statements are laid before the members the auditor becomes aware of information, from sources either within or outside the company, which might have led him to give a different audit opinion had he possessed the information at the date of his report, he should discuss the matter with the directors. He should then consider whether the financial statements should be amended by the directors. If the directors are unwilling to take action which the auditor considers necessary to inform the members of the changed situation, the auditor should consider exercising his rights under section 387 of the Companies Act 1985 to make a statement at the General Meeting at which the financial statements are laid before the members. He should also consider taking legal advice on his position. The auditor does not have a statutory right to communicate directly in writing with the members. (Where he wishes to resign or where it is proposed to remove him, sections 390 and 391 of the Companies Act 1985 enable him to communicate in writing with the members via the company.)

(8) If the directors wish to amend the previously approved financial statements after the auditor has signed his report but before they have been sent to the members, the auditor will need to consider whether the proposed amendments affect his report. His report, revised if necessary, should not be dated before the date on which the amended financial statements are approved by the directors. The auditor should take steps, as described in paragraph 13, to obtain reasonable assurance in respect of all significant events up to the date of his report on the amended financial statements.

(9) Where, after the financial statements have been sent to the members, the directors wish to prepare and approve an amended set of financial statements to lay before the members in General Meeting, the auditor should perform the steps described in paragraph 13 before making his report on the amended financial statements. In this latter report he should refer to the original financial statements and his report on them.

(10) If after the General Meeting the auditor becomes aware of information which suggests that the financial statements which were laid before that meeting are wrong, he should inform the directors. He should ascertain how the directors intend to deal with the situation, in particular whether they intend to communicate with the members. Where, in the auditor's opinion, the directors are not dealing correctly with the situation, he should consider taking legal advice on his position.

Procedures for the audit of events after the balance sheet date

(11) Certain events and transactions occurring after the balance sheet date are examined by the auditor as part of his normal verification work on the balance sheet. For example, he may check cash received from certain debtors or the amounts realized from the sale of stock after the year-end. In addition, the auditor should carry out audit procedures which are described as a 'review of events after the balance sheet date'.

(12) The objective of the review of events after the balance sheet date is to obtain reasonable assurance that all such material events have been identified and, where appropriate, either disclosed or accounted for in the financial statements.

(13) The review should consist of discussions with management relating to, and may also include consideration of:

(a) procedures taken by management to ensure that all events after the balance sheet date have been identified, considered and properly evaluated as to their effect on the financial statements;

(b) any management accounts and relevant accounting records;

(c) profit forecasts and cash flow projections, for the new period;

(d) known 'risk' areas and contingencies, whether inherent in the nature of the business or revealed by previous audit experience;

(e) minutes of shareholders', directors' and management meetings, and correspondence and memoranda relating to items included in the minutes;

(f) relevant information which has come to his attention, from sources outside the enterprise including public knowledge, of competitors, suppliers and customers.

This review should be updated to a date as near as practicable to that of the audit report by making enquiries of management and considering the need to carry out further tests.

Contingencies

(14) As part of his review of events after the balance sheet date, the auditor should consider the existence of contingencies and their treatment in the financial statements. Statement of Standard Accounting Practice No. 18 *Accounting for contingencies* requires accrual, or except where the possibility of loss is remote, the disclosure of material contingent losses, and disclosure of material contingent gains only if it is probable that the gain will be realized. The auditor will need to use his judgement in determining 'remoteness' and 'probability' in individual cases. He should pay particular regard to the different treatment required by the Standard, on grounds of prudence, for contingent gains on the one hand and contingent losses on the other.

Working papers and management representations

(15) The audit working papers should contain a record of the work carried out to identify events after the balance sheet date. Where discussions have taken place with the management regarding matters arising from the review of events after the balance sheet date, a note of the discussion should be retained by the auditor. The auditor may wish to obtain formal management representations about events after the balance sheet date or the fact that there have not been any. If such representations are obtained, they should be dated as close as possible to the date of the audit report.

Groups

(16) When the review of events after the balance sheet date is made in respect of consolidated financial statements, the auditor of the holding company will need to have regard to the work carried out in this area by the auditors of subsidiaries. In normal circumstances, audited financial statements of the subsidiaries will be available to him at the time he signs his report on the consolidated financial statements, and the auditors of the subsidiaries will have carried out a review of the events up to the date of their reports. The auditor of the holding company will need to ensure that appropriate audit procedures are carried out to identify events after the balance sheet date which are of significance to the group between the dates of the reports of the auditors of subsidiaries and the date of his own report. Such audit procedures can include the performance by him of the steps, described in paragraph 13, in the context of the group as a whole. They may also include the performance of updated reviews by the auditors of subsidiary companies.

(17) The auditor of the holding company may wish to obtain management representations from its directors, not only in respect of the company but also in respect of the group. It is conceivable, for instance, that the holding company may be aware of, or have instigated, events which have not been communicated to the management of the subsidiaries.

Suggested audit programme and checklist

(1) Audit programme
1. Peruse:
   (a) board minutes and any other sources of authorization;
   (b) outstanding purchase orders;
   (c) contracts and other relevant documentation, including progress reports from outside contractors for approved capital expenditure, and check to or prepare schedules thereof, differentiating between that which has and that which has not been contracted for, at the balance sheet date. Consider adequacy of amounts on long-term contracts, where final price is not fixed.
2. Complete the 'Review of post-balance events and contingencies' checklist.

(2) Checklist for review of post-balance sheet events and contingencies

	Initials	Date
Completed by		
Reviewed by		

A. Review, for the period since the year-end:

	Comments/ref. to further notes
• All books of prime entry, for individually material or unusual items. • Nominal ledger balances, for material variations in individual balances. • Operating results; investigate unusual variations. • Statutory books and minutes.	

B. Discuss with officers of the company the following matters relating to the period since the year-end:

	Notes on discussion
1. Matters which, although not giving rise to adjustments, may require disclosure • Destruction or expropriation of major assets. • Acquisition or disposal of material assets or investments. • Significant reversal of sales or profit trends. • Reasons for any suspension or interruption of operations, or discontinued products. • Loss of major customers or contracts; new contracts entered into. • Forward dealing in materials or commodities; potential losses on forward contracts. • Forward order position. • Major exchange-rate movements. • Imposition of exchange controls. • Major changes in market price of investments. • Acquisition, or withdrawal, of short-term borrowing facilities; cash-flow position. • New issues of shares or acquisition of loan capital. • Effect of any new legislation or government regulations.	

	Notes on discussion

2. Matters which may give rise to adjustments (but only require disclosure if exceptional or extraordinary)

- Subsequent evidence as to cost of acquisition, or proceeds of realization, of fixed assets or investments (contracted pre-balance-sheet date).
- Subsequent evidence as to the value, at the B/S date, of fixed assets or investments.
- Stock and work-in-progress: subsequent sale proceeds; evidence as to NRV at B/S date.
- Long/term contracts; subsequent information affecting estimated final result.
- Adequacy of bad debt provision; evidence as to collectability of debts.
- Dividends payable/receivable declared after balance sheet date.
- Taxation: changes affecting accounting period under review.
- Subsequent information regarding any contingent liability (see below) which makes it reasonably certain that loss will arise.

C. Ascertain from officers of the company whether there is any contingent liability regarding the following matters (whether arising prior or subsequent to the year-end)

	Notes on discussion

- Claims under costed contracts.
- Claims for faulty goods, or for failure to implement guarantees or warranties.
- Claims for damages.
- Claims for branch of contract.
- Claims for guarantees given by the company on behalf of others.
- Discounted bills receivable.
- Taxes in dispute: Inland Revenue enquiries.
- Assets pledged as security for any liability.
- Purchase commitments in excess of normal requirements or at prices in excess of prevailing market rates.
- Commitments to sell products forward at prices below prevailing selling prices.
- Commitments or options given or taken by the company for the purchase, sale, or repurchase of any securities.

Notes on discussion

- Options on the company's own capital; bonus or profit-sharing arrangements.
- Defaults or breaches of covenant—relating to principal interest funding, or redemption provisions—under any loan or credit agreement or share issue.
- Any other commitments, contracts or leases which might adversely affect the company.
- Any other liabilities in dispute, pending law suits, proceedings or unsettled litigation.

11.11   Review of non-routine transactions or problem areas

Much of this work will be covered as part of the review of compliance with SSAP 6. It is not possible to give an exhaustive list of areas to be examined, as it is to the unusual that the auditor is directing his or her attention in this case. What is required is an imaginative appraisal of items like the following:

(1) exceptional or extraordinary items;
(2) related party transactions;
(3) questionable payments by client.

Each of these is considered in turn below.

11.11.1   Exceptional or extraordinary items

SSAP 6 defines and lays down the accounting disclosure requirements for these items. As they may represent some of the most significant transactions of the year they require careful consideration from the auditor.

As part of normal audit procedures applied to transactions, assets and liabilities, many if not all such items will have been identified and checked.

At the review stage this will be confirmed to ensure that all exceptional and extraordinary items have been identified, and that the auditor fully understands the nature of the item and its effects, if any, on other items in the financial statements. Reference to the matter in the letter of representation would probably be necessary.

The auditor must then confirm that the items are correctly disclosed and explained by note according to SSAP 6, with an appropriate degree of emphasis.

11.11.2 Related party transactions

(a) What is a related party?

This is an area not yet covered by UK accounting and auditing standards, but IAS 24 states that 'parties are considered to be related if one party has the ability to control the other party in making financial and operating decisions'.

(b) What are the legal requirements?

S317 of the Companies Act requires directors to disclose any interest they may have in contracts or proposed contracts entered into or to be entered into by a company.

S320 requires the approval by the company in general meeting before a director may acquire a 'substantial' non-cash asset from the company or sell one to it. ('Substantial' means over £50000 or over 10 per cent of the company's asset value.)

SS103 to 109 place restrictions on the issue of shares by a public company in exchange for a non-cash asset and on the transfer by a public company to a member of a non-cash asset. Details of these requirements are in Sections 16.3 and 16.4 below.

SS232 to 234 and Schedule 6 place restrictions on and require much disclosure of loans by a company to its directors or other officers. More details are given in Chapter 17.

S312 requires the prior approval of the members before any compensation for loss of office or lump sum on retirement is paid to a director.

(c) How is the auditor affected?

Audit evidence from third parties is normally regarded as more reliable than evidence from inside the organization. If there is, in fact, some relationship between the client and the third party, then clearly the reliability of the evidence is impaired.

(d) The audit approach

It must not be thought that every related party transaction is automatically suspect. Most larger organizations have many subsidiaries with which transactions take place daily. What the auditor must confirm is that such transactions are genuine, and do not prejudice the interests of minority shareholders. Consideration must also be given to whether the transactions might give rise to claims by the Inland Revenue or other Government authorities.

(e) Identifying related parties

The first step is to identify related parties. This should be done at the planning stage of the audit.
Possible related parties are:

—other group companies;
—companies under common control;
—associated companies;
—members with substantial shareholdings;
—directors, shadow directors and senior management;
—major suppliers or customers;
—a company pension fund.

The following ascertainment steps are based on US Statement on Auditing Standards No. 6 (SAS6) (1975) and IFAC Auditing Guideline No. 17 (1984):

(1) Evaluate the company's procedures for identifying and properly accounting for related party transactions;
(2) Inquire of appropriate management personnel as to the names of all related parties and whether there were any transactions with those parties during the period;
(3) Review annual returns for details of other directorships held by the company's directors;
(4) Review shareholder records for details of principal shareholders (a public company must, under S211, maintain a register of holders of more than 5 per cent of its share capital, and such holders have a duty to inform the company of their holding);
(5) Determine the names of all pension funds or other trusts for the benefit of employees;
(6) Review minutes of meetings of directors and shareholders;
(7) Review prior years' working papers for the name of known related parties;
(8) Enquire of other auditors currently involved in the audit, or predecessor auditors, as to their knowledge of additional related parties. This would, of course, include auditors of subsidiaries.
(9) Review tax returns.
(10) Review material investment transactions during the period under review to determine whether the nature and extent of such transactions created related parties.

In addition to these specific search and review procedures, the auditor may become aware of the existence of related parties during the normal course of audit procedures. In this context the following matters are of particular relevance:

(1) review of large unusual transactions or balances, especially those at or near the end of an accounting period;
(2) transactions which have abnormal terms of trade, such as unusual price, interest rates, guarantees, and repayment terms;
(3) transactions which appear to lack a logical reason for their occurrence;
(4) transactions in which substance differs from form;
(5) transactions processed in other than the normal way for processing similar transactions;
(6) high-volume or significant transactions with certain customers or suppliers.

In addition, the auditor should consider whether related party transactions have occurred that are not recorded, such as the receipt or provision of management services at no charge.

(f) Types of related party transaction

Related party transactions may be of two types:

(1) those entered into in the ordinary course of business;
(2) those not entered into in the ordinary course of business.

Transactions in the first group are likely to be large in number but individually small, though the total may be highly significant. The type of transaction envisaged here is routine supply of components by one group company to another. A major aspect of concern here is the company's pricing policy, which may prejudice the interests of minority shareholders, and give rise to claims from the Revenue or other Government authorities.

Transactions in the second group are likely to be small in number and individually large and thus require individual audit attention. In fact all large and unusual transactions of the period should be examined for evidence of related party involvement. It is with such transactions that the auditor's most difficult problems may arise.

(g) The auditor's action

The auditor has to give his or her opinion as to whether financial statements show a true and fair view. This must include forming an opinion as to whether related party transactions have been fairly dealt with.

In some cases, perhaps most cases, full disclosure of the nature of the transactions will be sufficient. The auditor may wish to insist on fuller disclosure in the financial statements than that which the directors propose.

There remains the hard core of related party transactions which go far beyond the normal course of business and may include management fraud. In such cases the auditor may well feel compelled to qualify his or her report, first taking legal advice as to the position.

11.11.3 Questionable payments by client

Here we are considering bribes or other payments of dubious legality which the company has made.

Auditors are under no obligation to report or disclose such payments, but they do have an audit responsibility to confirm that payments have in fact been made, and made for the purpose of the client's trade. By the nature of such payments, it may be difficult to achieve formal verification (there probably won't be a receipt, for example!) but it will be possible to confirm whether the directors were aware of and authorized the payment. It may be appropriate to obtain a certificate to that effect, signed by the directors. Auditors should also consider whether such transactions might give rise to a contingent liability if action was taken against the company by a Government or any other aggrieved party.

If the company has an audit committee (see Chapter 20) these are matters which should be closely scrutinized by that committee, and it would be appropriate for the auditors to discuss the matter fully with the chairman of the committee.

11.12 Audit of funds flow statements

Any company with a turnover over £25 000 is required by SSAP 10 to produce a funds flow statement or statement of source and application of funds. SSAP 10 requires the auditor to report on the sources and application of funds as shown in the funds flow statement. There is no guidance as to the form of the statement, but some general principles are laid down:

(a) Profit or loss for the period should be shown, with adjustment for items not involving a flow of funds.

(b) There should be separate disclosure of:

(1) dividends paid;
(2) acquisitions and disposal of fixed and other non-current assets;
(3) issues or redemptions of shares or debentures;
(4) increase or decrease in working capital, subdivided into its components.

(c) There should be a minimum of 'netting off' (e.g. the proceeds of sale of one fixed asset against the cost of purchase of another).

(d) Details should be given to enable the figures in the funds flow statement to be reconciled with those in the profit and loss account, balance sheet or notes.

(e) For companies with subsidiaries, funds statement should be based on the group accounts.

As the funds statement is prepared from the profit and loss account and balance sheet, the audit of the funds flow statement requires no audit work apart from checking the figures from one to the other. An audit programme for work could be:

(*a*) Obtain client's working papers for the funds flow statement and check all items against:

(1) agreed profit and loss accounts and balance sheets;
(2) funds statement.

(*b*) In the course of (*a*), confirm that all items in the opening and closing balance sheets are accounted for.

(*c*) Check all costs and calculations in the working papers and the funds flow statement.

(*d*) Review all adjustments made and confirm that they are correctly calculated, and that sufficient information is given to permit the funds flow statement to be reconciled with profit and loss account and balance sheet.

(*e*) Confirm compliance with SSAP 10 requirements as set out above.

(*f*) Confirm that the statement overall shows a true and fair view of the sources and application of funds for the year.

11.13 Audit of current cost accounts

This subject is covered in detail in Chapter 22.

11.14 Size of company

A company within the size criteria of S 248 may lodge modified accounts with the Registrar, containing the reduced disclosure specified in Schedule 8. It is part of the review of financial statements for the auditor to decide whether the company is entitled to the disclosure exemption. See Chapter 16 for more details.

11.15 Review of amounts derived from the preceding financial statements

This is a topic covered by an Auditing Guideline issued in November 1982 and reproduced below.

APC Guideline on amounts derived from the preceding financial statements

Preface

This Guideline gives guidance to the auditor with regard to his responsibility for amounts taken from the preceding period's financial statements used in the current period's financial statements on which he is expressing an opinion. Operational aspects relating thereto are not considered to present any particular problems for the auditor and consequently this Guideline does not consider these matters in detail. Counsel's opinion on the interpretation of the Companies Acts in relation to corresponding amounts was obtained before this Guideline was developed. Counsel has subsequently confirmed that its contents do not conflict with his opinion.

The Guideline is supplementary to and should be read in conjunction with the auditor's operational and reporting Standards and related Guidelines.

Introduction

(1) Consideration of the financial statements of the preceding period is necessary in the audit of the current period's financial statements in relation to the following three aspects, namely:

(a) the opening position: obtaining satisfaction that those amounts which have a direct effect on the current period's results or closing position have been properly brought forward;

(b) accounting policies: determining whether the accounting policies adopted for the current period are consistent with those of the previous period; and

(c) corresponding amounts: determining that the corresponding amounts, which are commonly known as comparative figures, are properly shown in the current period's financial statements.

(2) Financial statements of companies incorporated under the provisions of the Companies Act are required to disclose corresponding amounts for all items in a company's balance sheet and profit and loss account. In other cases, financial statements usually contain corresponding amounts as a matter of law, regulation or good practice. Their purpose, unless stated otherwise, is to complement the amounts relating to the current period and not to re-present the complete financial statements for the preceding period.

(3) The auditor is not required to express an opinion on the corresponding amounts as such. His responsibility is to ensure that they are the amounts which appeared in the preceding period's financial statements or, where appropriate, have either been properly restated to achieve consistency and comparability with the current period's amounts, or have been restated due to a change of accounting policy or a correction of a fundamental error as required by SSAP 6.

Auditor's procedures

(4) If the author himself has issued an unqualified report on the preceding period's

financial statements and his audit of the current period has not revealed any matters which cast doubt on those financial statements, he should not need to extend his audit procedure beyond:

(*a*) satisfying himself that balances have been correctly brought forward and incorporated in the accounting records of the current period; and

(*b*) ensuring that the amounts from the preceding period's financial statements are consistently classified and properly disclosed as corresponding amounts.

If he is satisfied with the results of these procedures, it should not be necessary for him to make any reference to amounts taken from the preceding period's financial statements in his report on the current period's financial statements.

(5) Additional considerations may apply in the following circumstances:

(*a*) the opening position and corresponding amounts are derived from financial statements which have not been audited by the present auditor; or

(*b*) the audit report on the financial statements of the preceding period was qualified.

Preceding period not audited by the present auditor

(6) The new auditor will have to satisfy himself as to the opening position as disclosed by the preceding period's balance sheet in order to express an opinion on the current period's profit or loss and source and application of funds. He will need also to ensure that there is consistency in accounting policies and classification of balances. His lack of prior knowledge of the preceding period's financial statement will require him to apply additional procedures to them in order to obtain the necessary assurance on these matters.

(7) The additional procedures that should be performed by the auditor may include any of the following:

(*a*) consultations with the client's management;

(*b*) review of the client's records, working papers and accounting and control procedures for the preceding period, particularly in so far as they affect the opening position;

(*c*) audit work on the current period, which will usually provide some evidence regarding opening balances; and

(*d*) in exceptional circumstances, substantive testing of the opening balances, if he does not consider the results of procedures (*a*) to (*c*) to be satisfactory.

(8) In addition, the auditor may be able to hold consultations with the previous auditor. Whilst outgoing auditors can normally be expected to afford reasonable co-operation to their successors, neither ethical statements nor the law place them under a specific obligation to make working papers or other information available to these successors. Consultations would normally be limited to seeking information concerning the previous auditor's examination of particular areas which are important to his successor and to obtaining clarification of any significant accounting matters which are not adequately dealt with in the client's records. If, however, such consultations are not possible or alternatively, if the preceding period's financial statements were unaudited, the only evidence about the opening position available to the auditor will be that generated by procedures such as those set out in paragraph 7 above.

(9) Under normal circumstances the auditor will be able to satisfy himself as to the opening position by performing the work set out in paragraphs 7 and 8. If he is not able to satisfy himself in any material respect he will need to qualify his report for the possible effect on the financial statement. A form of report is set out below which might be suitable where the area of difficulty was material but not fundamental.

AUDITORS' REPORT TO THE MEMBERS OF ....

We have auditied the financial statements on pages ... to ..., which have been prepared under the historical cost convention. Our audit was conducted in accordance with approved Auditing Standards, except that the scope of our work was limited by the matter referred to below.

We were not appointed auditors of the company until ... and in consequence did not report on the financial statements for the year ended .... It was not possible for us to carry out the auditing procedures necessary to obtain our own assurance as regards certain stock and work in progress, appearing in the preceding period's financial statements at £.... Any adjustment to this figure would have a consequential effect on the profit for the year ended 31 December 19....

In our opinion the balance sheet gives a true and fair view of the state of the company's affairs at 31 December 19... and, subject to the effect of any adjustment which might have been necessary in respect of the foregoing, the financial statements give a true and fair view of its profit and source and application of funds for the year then ended, and comply with the Companies Act 1985.

If the area of difficulty was fundamental then the auditor would need to consider whether to disclaim an opinion on the profit and source and application of funds.

Preceding period's qualifications

(10) If the audit report on the preceding period's financial statements was qualified, but the matter giving rise to the qualification has been resolved and properly dealt with in the financial statements, then normally no reference need be made to the previous qualification in the current period's audit report. If, however, the matter which gave rise to the qualification remains unresolved and is material in relation to the current period's financial statements, the audit report should be qualified. In such a case, the notes to the financial statements should adequately disclose the circumstances surrounding the qualification. The auditor may consider it advisable to refer to the previous qualification so as to make it clear that the matter giving rise to the qualification did not arise in the current period.

One possible form of report which includes a reference to a previous qualification is set out below:

AUDITORS' REPORT TO THE MEMBERS OF ....

We have audited the financial statements on pages ... to ... in accordance with approved Auditing Standards.

As indicated in note ... to the financial statements debtors include an amount of £... which is the subject of litigation but against which no provision has been made. We have not been able to satisfy ourselves that this amount will be recoverable in full. We qualified our audit report on the financial statements at 31 December 19... (date of preceding financial statements) with regard to this same uncertainty.

Subject to the adjustment, if any, that may be required when the litigation is resolved, in our opinion the financial statements, which have been prepared under the historical cost convention, give a true and fair view of the state of the company's affairs at 31 December 19... and of its profit and source and application of funds for the year then ended and comply with the Companies Act 1985.

Misstated corresponding amounts

(11) The auditor should refer in his audit report to an actual or possible material misstatement in the corresponding amounts even though the misstatement does not directly affect the current period's figures. Such a misstatement may result from:

(a) uncertainty affecting the preceding period's profit and loss account, but not the balance sheet;

(b) misclassification of amounts in the preceding period's financial statements; or

(c) restatement of the preceding period's figures where the auditor does not concur with the restatement, or if in his opinion a restatement is necessary but has not been made.

If corresponding amounts are required by law or by regulations, the reference in the audit report should be in the form of a qualification on the grounds of non-compliance with that requirement. If corresponding amounts are presented solely as good practice, the audit report reference should be made as an 'emphasis of matter'.

(12) The following is an example of an audit report on the financial statements, which has been qualified on these grounds:

AUDITORS' REPORT TO THE MEMBERS OF ....

We have audited the financial statements on pages ... to ... in accordance with approved Auditing Standards.

The corresponding amounts in the current period's financial statements are derived from the financial statements for the year ended 31 December 19.... In our report on those financial statements we stated that we were unable to express an opinion on the profit and source and application of funds for the year ended on that date because we were unable to substantiate the amount of stock at 1 January 19... (preceding year). Accordingly the corresponding amounts shown for the profit and source and application of funds may not be comparable with the figures for the current period.

In our opinion the financial statements, which have been prepared under the historical cost convention, give a true and fair view of the state of the company's affairs at 31 December 19... and of its profit and source and application of funds for the year then ended and, subject to any effects of the matter set out above, comply with the Companies Act 1985.

11.16 Review of financial information issued with audited financial statements

S237(6), Companies Act 1985 requires the auditor to consider whether the information given in the directors' report is consistent with the accounts.

Normal audit practice extends this duty to the chairman's statement also, and indeed to other statements such as the value added statement or a summary of past results.

The statutory contents of the directors' report are in Schedule 7, Companies Act 1985:

(a) Any significant changes in the fixed assets of the company of any of its subsidiaries;

(b) Any significant differences between balance sheet value and market value of the company's interests in land;

(c) Directors' holding of shares and debentures at the beginning and end of the financial year;

(d) Details of any political and charitable gifts if the total of such gifts exceeds £200;

(e) Particulars of any 'important events' which have occurred since the end of the financial year;

(f) Likely future developments;

(g) Indication of research and development activities;

(h) Details of any purchase by the company of its own shares;

(i) Average number of employees if over 250;

(j) For companies employing over 250 a statement of the company's policy in employing disabled persons;

(k) Details of arrangements to secure health, safety and welfare at work of employees;

(l) For companies employing over 250 people, a statement detailing the company's action to give the employees information about the company's affairs and involve them in the company's performance.

Much of this information is financial and thus capable of being compared with the information in the company's detailed profit and loss account and balance sheet, its accounting records or statutory books.

An Auditing Guideline deals with the auditor's responsibility in this area.

Draft Auditing Guideline on financial information issued with audited financial statements

Preface

This Guideline is intended to clarify the statutory responsibilities of the auditor in connection with the directors' report and to explain his non-statutory role with regard to the directors' report and other financial information contained in an annual report of which audited financial statements form a part. The Guideline is supplementary to and should be read in conjunction with the auditor's operational and reporting Standards and related Guidelines.

Introduction and scope

(1) This guideline is written in the context of the audit of companies incorporated under the Companies Acts. The auditor of an enterprise other than such a company will be guided by the terms of his particular appointment or by relevant legislation or other requirements. However, in the absence of specific provisions to the contrary, the general principles embodied in this Guideline should be followed.

(2) This Guideline is structured so as to set out the auditor's responsibilities under statutory and non-statutory requirements. In performing the procedures outlined here, whether required by statute or not, the auditor's main aim is to ensure that the credibility of the financial statements has not been undermined.

(3) It is recognized that in the majority of cases the auditor will be able to achieve the elimination of any inconsistent or misleading item through discussions with the directors and senior management. Accordingly, further action as described in this Guideline should rarely be necessary.

(4) Financial information contained in annual reports is not confined to the statements encompassed by the auditor's report. Other financial information may be included in the directors' report or in other unaudited statements such as a chairman's statement, a report on operations, a value added statement or a summary of past results.

Statutory responsibilities

(5) Section 237(6) of the Companies Act 1985 sets out one of the statutory responsibilities of auditors as follows:

'It is the auditors' duty to consider whether the information given in the directors' report for the financial year for which the accounts are prepared is consistent with those accounts; and if they are of opinion that it is not, they shall state that fact in their report.'

(6) It should be noted that auditors of companies (i.e. banks, insurance and shipping companies) which have availed themselves of the right to prepare accounts under Schedule 9 to the Companies Act 1985 are not required to follow Section 237(6) of the Companies Act 1985. As a result, such auditors should, except where Section 261(3) of the Companies Act 1985 applies, regard directors' reports as being on the same footing as other financial information contained in annual reports, and they should where appropriate follow the procedures described in paragraphs 12 to 18 below. However, Section 237(6) of the Companies Act 1985 does apply to the directors' reports of holding companies which prepare accounts in compliance with the requirements of Schedule 4 even if some or all of the subsidiaries have availed themselves of the right to prepare accounts under Schedule 9.

(7) The above statutory responsibilities of an auditor do not require him to form an opinion on the directors' report itself. The auditor should, to fulfil his statutory responsibilities, confine his work to satisfying himself whether or not the directors' report contains any matters which are inconsistent with the financial statements. His responsibilities and recommended procedures regarding any other matters in the directors' report are explained in paragraphs 12 to 18 of this Guideline.

(8) Matters which may give rise to inconsistency include the following:

(a) an inconsistency between actual figures or narrative appearing in, respectively, the financial statements and the directors' report;

(b) an inconsistency between the bases of preparation of related items appearing in the financial statements and the directors' report, where the figures themselves are not directly comparable and the different bases are not disclosed;

(c) an inconsistency between figures contained in the audited financial statements and a narrative interpretation of the effect of those figures in the directors' report.

This list is not intended to be exhaustive. Care needs to be exercised in identifying inconsistencies in each particular case.

(9) The auditor should consider the implications of any inconsistency which, in his opinion, has not been eliminated following discussions with senior members of management and/or written communication with directors of the company. His course of action will depend on whether he believes that an amendment is required to the directors' report or to the financial statements.

(10) If, in his opinion, it is the directors' report which requires amendment, the auditor should refer in his report to the inconsistency in order to comply with Section 237(6) of the Companies Act 1985. An example of such a report is set out in Appendix 1.

(11) Since the identification of such inconsistencies will normally occur only when the audit has been largely completed, it would be exceptional if in the auditor's opinion, it was the financial statements which required amendment. On such rare occasions, if no amendment is made to the financial statements, he will need to consider qualifying his report on those financial statements and in these circumstances, the auditor should refer to the Auditing Standard 'Qualifications in audit reports' and the Auditing Guideline 'Audit report examples'. The auditor will also have to make reference in his report to the inconsistency between the financial statements and the directors' report as it will still exist.

Non-statutory responsibilities

(12) The auditor has no statutory responsibilities in respect of items in the directors' report which in his opinion are misleading but not inconsistent with the financial statements (for example there may be a statement given in the directors' report for which there is no corresponding financial information in the financial statements but which is nevertheless misleading), or in respect of other financial information contained elsewhere in the annual report.

(13) However, where information of this kind is published as part of, or in conjunction with, the annual report, the auditor should review that information. The auditor does this as part of his overall professional responsibility to ensure that the

credibility of the financial statements is not undermined, and in so doing meets the expectations of those to whom the information is directed.

(14) Where the auditor considers that there is a material inconsistency between the financial statements and other financial information or that an item is misleading in some other respect, he should consider its implications and hold discussions with directors, or other senior members of management, and may also make his views known in writing to all the directors in order to achieve its elimination. Where communication with directors and their representatives does not result in the elimination of the problem, he should consider whether an amendment is required to the financial statements, the directors' report or the other financial information.

(15) If, in the auditor's opinion, it is the financial statements which require amendment, he should follow the guidance given in paragraph 11 above.

(16) Assuming it is not the financial statements which require amendment, there is no statutory requirement for the auditor to comment in his report. However, there may be occasions when a matter is potentially so misleading to a reader of the financial statements that it would be inappropriate for the auditor to remain silent. In these circumstances the auditor should seek legal and other professional advice on what action may be appropriate.

(17) If the auditor decides that he should refer to the matter in his report, he should be aware that Counsel has advised that the qualified privilege (i.e. the defence to an action for defamation) which an audit report normally enjoys may not extend to comments on:

(a) an item in the directors' report which, while not inconsistent with the financial statements, is misleading in some other respect; or

(b) financial information contained elsewhere in an annual report which is inconsistent with the financial statements or otherwise misleading.

(18) The auditor may make use of his right under Section 387 of the Companies Act 1985 to be heard at any general meeting of the members on any business of the meeting which concerns him as auditor. This includes the right to draw attention to those matters described in paragraph 17.

Other considerations

(19) The directors' report and the other financial information contained in the annual report do not normally form part of the financial statements on which the auditor is reporting. Therefore the pages of the annual report to which the audit report refers should not include the directors' report and the other financial information. However, in the case of accounts prepared under Schedule 9 to the Companies Act 1985 some information otherwise required to be included in the financial statements may be given in the directors' report, in which case the audit report will need to refer to that information.

(20) The auditor should urge the company not to publish its annual report until after he has completed his review of the other financial information and he should make arrangements to see, prior to publication, any documents in which the financial statements are to be included. The auditor should deal with these procedures in the audit engagement letter. Where, notwithstanding this, the auditor is not given an

opportunity to complete his review before the date of issue, he should complete it before the general meeting at which the financial statements are laid before the members. In the event that there is something with which he disagrees, the auditor should take legal and other professional advice and consider taking the course of action set out in paragraph 18.

Appendix 1: Auditor's report arising from Section 237(6) of the Companies Act 1985—inconsistency between the directors' report and the financial statements

This sample audit report is not considered to be a qualified report for the purposes of Section 271(4) of the Companies Act 1985 or for the purposes of Section 255(3)(d) of the Companies Act 1985.

AUDITORS REPORT TO THE MEMBERS OF ....

We have audited the financial statements on pages ... to ... in accordance with approved Auditing Standards.

In our opinion the financial statements, which have been prepared under the historical cost convention, give a true and fair view of the state of the company's affairs at 31 December 19... and of its results and source and application of funds for the year then ended and comply with the Companies Act 1985.

In our opinion, the information given in paragraph 7 of the directors' report is not consistent with these financial statements. That paragraph states without amplification that the company's trading resulted in a profit before tax of £X. The profit and loss account, however, states that the company incurred a loss before tax for the year of £Y and, as an extraordinary item, a profit from the sale of land of £Z.

11.17 Conformity of financial statements with information obtained during the audit

The last stage of the audit before the report is drafted is the review by the manager and partner responsible. That review must deal with the financial statements and with the audit itself.

11.17.1 The partner's review of the financial statements

This Chapter has so far been concerned with detailed review procedures which will normally have been carried out by senior staff below partner level. The final review by the partner will be concerned with any matters referred to him by the audit staff but should not be confined to such matters. The partner will need to scrutinize all aspects of the financial statements, in conjunction with the audit file, to confirm that nothing has been overlooked and that the financial statements are in conformity with the information obtained during the audit.

11.17.2 The partner's review of the audit

This is partly a quality control procedure and partly the application of the partner's expertise to provide a final check on the work.

The quality control aspect may be dealt with by having the audit files reviewed by another partner after completion.

The partner's final check on the work will involve a close scrutiny of the audit files in conjunction with the responsible audit staff. The 'file completion checklist' in Section 4.7.3 lists the points that will need to be covered.

11.18 Summary

The review of financial statements is the final stage of the audit and comprises all audit steps in which the financial statements as a whole are considered.

For examination purposes it is necessary to be aware of the main stages of the review and with the details of the more extensive ones, especially those dealt with in Auditing Guidelines.

The following areas are singled out as being of particular examination importance:

(a) going concern review (Section 11.9);

(b) post balance sheet events and contingencies (Section 11.10);

(c) review of related party transactions (Section 11.11.2);

(d) review of questionable payments by client (Section 11.11.3);

(e) review of amounts derived from the preceding financial statements (Section 11.15);

(f) review of financial information issued with the financial statements (Section 11.16).

Progress questions

Questions	References
(1) What is the purpose of the review of financial statements?	Sections 11.1 and 11.2
(2) What audit technique will often be used in the review when compliance with a number of detailed requirements is to be confirmed?	Section 11.3

Questions	References
(3) List ten matters normally covered as part of the auditor's review of financial statements.	Section 11.1
(4) What are the main disclosure requirements of the Stock Exchange 'Yellow Book' (Admission of Securities to Listening)?	Section 11.4
(5) Where may the auditor seek information when reviewing a company's stated accounting policies?	Section 11.6
(6)(a) What is meant by the term 'analytical review'? (b) List ten ratios or percentages which may usefully be computed in the analytical review.	Section 11.8
(7)(a) What is meant by the term 'going concern review'? (b) What audit steps should be carried out in the course of this review?	Section 11.9
(8)(a) Define 'post-balance-sheet event'. (b) Distinguish between adjusting and non-adjusting events, giving eight examples of each.	Section 11.10.1
(9)(a) What is a contingency? (b) Summarize the disclosure requirements for contingencies.	Section 11.10.2
(10)(a) How do the dates up to which the auditor needs to consider events after the balance sheet date differ from the relevant date for the directors? (b) How does the difference in date affect the dating of the audit report? (c) What audit steps must the auditor take in his review of post balance sheet events?	Section 11.10.3 Auditing Guideline on Events after the balance sheet date: Paragraphs 3–5 Paragraphs 3–5 Paragraph 13
(11) Draw up a detailed audit programme for post balance sheet events and contingencies, and a checklist for their review.	Section 11.10.3 (pages 300–302)

Questions	References
(12)(a) What is a related party?	Section 11.11.2(a) (p. 304)
(b) What significance do related parties have for the auditor?	Section 11.11.2(c) (p. 304)
(c) List as many possible related parties as you can.	Section 11.11.2(e) (p. 304)
(d) How may the auditor ascertain the existence of related parties?	Section 11.11.2(e) (p. 305–306)
(e) What possible courses of action must the auditor consider in connection with substantial related party transactions?	Section 11.11.2(g) (p. 306)
(13) How may the auditor confirm a bribe made by the client to a customer.	Section 11.11.3
(14) Draw up a list of work to be done in the audit of the funds flow statement.	Section 11.12
(15)(a) Why is it important for the auditor to review amounts derived from the preceding financial statements?	Section 11.15: Auditing Guideline on Accounts Derived from Preceding Financial Statements Paragraph 1
(b) Explain the auditor's procedures for each of the following situations: (1) auditor himself issued an unqualified report on preceding period's financial statements	Paragraphs 4–5
(2) Preceding period was audited by another who gave an unqualified report	Paragraphs 6–9
(3) audit report on previous period was qualified	Paragraph 10
(4) corresponding amounts were misstated	Paragraphs 11–12
(16)(a) What are the statutory contents of the directors' report? (b) What should the auditor do if there is an inconsistency between the financial information in the directors' report and that in the financial statements?	Section 11.16 Section 11.16: Auditing Guideline on Financial Information issued with Audited Financial Statements Paragraph 5

12 Small companies

12.1 Introduction

There are two problems we need to consider here. Should small companies have an audit? If they should, what is the audit approach? Perhaps there is also a third question—What is small? Let us begin by dealing with this third question, which is easily answered, and then get on to the others.

These are the definitions of 'small' and 'medium sized' in S248 of the Companies Act, based upon the EEC 4th Directive:

	Current limits	Proposed increase
'Small' companies:		
Turnover	£1 400 000	£2 000 000
Balance sheet totals	£ 700 000	£ 975 000
Employees	50	50
'Medium-sized' companies:		
Turnover	£5 750 000	£8 000 000
Balance sheet totals	£2 800 000	£3 900 000
Employees	250	250

To qualify, a company must meet at least two of the three criteria.

The only privilege granted to small and medium-sized companies at the moment is the right to file modified accounts with the Registrar—a minor concession which many qualifying companies do not bother to take advantage of because of the cost of preparing the modified accounts.

It is arguable whether all small companies should be exempt from an audit requirement. A consultative document issued in 1985 by the Department of Trade and Industry (DTI), 'Accounting and audit requirements for small firms', lists three main options:

(*a*) *abolish the audit requirement for small companies all of whose members are directors*—perhaps subject to a requirement that the decision to dispense with an independent audit must be unanimous and subject to annual confirmation in general meeting;

(b) *abolish the requirement for all small companies below a certain size, though not for all small companies as presently defined*—again subject to restrictions designed to protect the rights of minority shareholders;

(c) *abolish the requirement for all small companies and leave it to members to decide the company's policy on auditing of accounts in the light of its particular circumstances*—companies would then be free to decide for themselves whether to commission an audit from a qualified accountant or to circulate and file their accounts unaudited.

A possible variant in each case would be to follow practice in other countries, particularly the USA, and require an independent review of the accounts as opposed to an audit. This would obviously be less rigorous than the present audit but, depending on the precise report provided, it would give shareholders and creditors some assurance as to the value of the accounts. Costs should be correspondingly reduced, but the person carrying out the review would still be expected to take the same degree of responsibility for the review report as the auditor takes for the contents of the audit report.

In considering these options, account should be taken of the potential implications for company directors once the Insolvency Bill becomes law. Under the Bill, directors can be made personally liable to make a contribution to the assets of the company if they are found to have been responsible for the company's wrongful trading. A director would be so responsible if he or she knew or ought to have concluded that there was no reasonable prospect of the company avoiding going into insolvent liquidation and failed to take every possible step with a view to minimizing the potential loss to the company's creditors. A director of an insolvent company may also be disqualified if his or her conduct as a director is judged to be such as to make him or her unfit to be involved in the management of a company.

12.2 Should small companies have an audit?

To answer this question we need to consider the interests of the parties concerned:

—shareholders
—banks and other lenders
—trade creditors
—tax authorities
—employees
—management.

12.2.1   Shareholders

Historically, auditors were appointed to protect the interests of shareholders, who had provided finance without the right to participate in the day-to-day control of a company. Wherever such a separation between members and management exists it would be difficult to justify the abolition of the audit requirement, at least without the consent of all shareholders.

However, there are many companies in which all the shareholders are also directors actively involved in the management, or in which 'outside' shareholders have complete confidence in the integrity of the directors, perhaps because of close kinship or long association.

From the shareholders' point of view we may suggest the following tentative conclusions:

(*a*) it would be reasonable to exempt from the compulsory audit requirement those small companies in which all shareholders are directors;

(*b*) shareholders in small companies other than those in (*a*) could have the right to resolve that the audit may be dispensed with, provided all shareholders (or perhaps 90 per cent) agreed.

12.2.2   Banks and other lenders

Lenders may place considerable importance on audited accounts, but they are not the only source of information for them. They frequently also require the personal guarantees of directors before making an advance. In the USA, banks do on occasion require an independent audit as a condition for extending credit, but this does not necessarily justify making an audit obligatory for all companies.

It would seem that the removal of the statutory audit obligation would not seriously affect bankers and other lenders, since it would remain open to them to require an audit when it seemed necessary to protect their interests.

12.2.3   Trade creditors

Trade creditors do make use of accounts filed at Companies House, and may also rely on reports from credit agencies based on them. Other information like trade references and personal knowledge is at least as important, however, and it is difficult to see how the position of trade creditors would be seriously affected if the audit requirement were to be withdrawn.

12.2.4 Tax authorities

Inland Revenue for corporation tax

A company's corporation tax computation must obviously be based upon its accounts. An independent audit opinion will increase the reliability of those accounts. Having said that, it is clear that the Inland Revenue relies, perforce, on unaudited accounts for most sole traders and partnerships. As the Audit Brief on the audit of small companies issued by the APC in 1979 commented:

'It is questionable whether the Inland Revenue places greater reliance on audited financial statements of small companies than on the unaudited statements received from sole traders and partnerships. Inspectors of Taxes tend to be more influenced by the reputation of the accountant or firm of accountants associated with the information than with the expression of a particular form of opinion, or even of no opinion at all. Certainly, the recently instituted "in depth" enquiries have not been confined to unincorporated businesses'.

12.2.5 Employees

There has been a trend over the past ten years for listed companies to provide employees with copies of the accounts and to prepare versions of the accounts especially for them. Small companies do not do so to the same extent but their accounts, albeit in 'modified' form, are available for inspection by employees or by trade unions representing them.

Whether audited or not, the profit reported in the accounts of small companies is frequently a meaningless figure because directors' remuneration may be raised or lowered to reflect profit levels. Directors may also be providing loans at low interest, also affecting reported profit.

Employees obtain little benefit from the statutory audit requirement.

12.2.6 Management

Management may benefit from the audit by having the auditor's independent check on the adequacy of the accounting and control procedures, and a report on the weaknesses in that system through the annual letter of comment.

Against this it may be argued that the auditor, acting in the role of accountant and financial advisor, may have assisted in the creation of the system itself, and may be able to give a more valuable service by emphasizing the 'non-auditing' aspect of his work for the client.

12.2.8 Conclusions

The conclusion seems to be that although some small companies need an audit all the time, and all may need one some of the time, there is no compelling reason for any of the parties concerned why all small companies should be required to have an annual audit.

If the audit requirements were to be dropped this need not mean that there would be no examination of small company accounts at all. An alternative is to provide for a *review* of the financial statements. The possible scope of such a review and a suitable form of report based on it are indicated in the next section.

12.3 Review of financial statements

12.3.1 Matters covered by a review

Appendix 3 to the Audit Brief, 'Small companies: the need for audit', gives an example of a review check list which is reproduced below:

Example of a review check list

These initial questions are designed so that the replies may be evaluated to determine whether or not further enquiries or procedures are required. This illustrative check list is not intended to be exhaustive or to be followed slavishly. The circumstances of each engagement should be considered carefully.

Preliminary considerations

(1) Are the services to be provided mutually agreed and has an engagement letter been issued?
(2) Nature of business
    (*a*) What kind of business is carried on?
    (*b*) Has the company complied with the statutory requirements for exemption from audit?
    (*c*) Where is business carried on?
(3) What are the significant
    (*a*) assets and liabilities?
    (*b*) sources of revenue?
    (*c*) costs and expenses?
(4) Has consideration been given to matters arising from:
    (*a*) prior period financial statements?
    (*b*) prior period working papers and related files?

    (c)   prior period accounting problems?

(5)   What books and records are kept

    (a)   general ledger?
    (b)   cash book?
    (c)   petty cash book?
    (d)   purchase day book?
    (e)   sales day book?
    (f)   wages salary book?
    (g)   nominal ledger?
    (h)   sales ledger?
    (i)   purchase ledger?
    (j)   costing records?

Items in the financial statements

(6)   Cash and bank

    (a)   Has a bank reconciliation been prepared?
    (b)   Have old or unusual outstanding items in the bank reconciliation been reviewed and adjusted where necessary?
    (c)   Has cash been counted and agreed with records?

(7)   Debtors

    (a)   Is the sales ledger control account in agreement with the listing of debtor accounts?
    (b)   Has provision been made for doubtful debts?
    (c)   What method was used to determine the provision?
    (d)   How has the cut-off with sales been effected?
    (e)   Have subsequent receipts been reviewed?
    (f)   Has aged analysis of debts been provided?
    (g)   Have material credit balances been reviewed and appropriately classified?
    (h)   Has VAT been reconciled with returns?

(8)   Stock and work in progress

    (a)   When was stock counted?
    (b)   Are procedures designed to arrive at a proper and consistent count?
    (c)   Have stock sheets been reviewed as to quantities, prices, calculations, etc.?
    (d)   Have consignment stock, stock held for others or stock held by others been considered?
    (e)   What is the basis of valuation? Is such basis consistent?
    (f)   Have provisions for obsolescence been considered?
    (g)   How has the cut-off of purchases stock, sales, goods in transit, returned goods, etc., been effected?

(9)   Prepaid expenses
Have all significant prepayments been set up?
(10)   Investments (loans, mortgages, investments, etc.)

    (*a*) Have opening balances been reconciled to closing balances?
    (*b*) Have gains and losses on disposal been recorded?
    (*c*) Has investment income been accounted for?
    (*d*) Has current/non-current classification been made?
    (*e*) Has value been considered?

(11) Fixed assets

    (*a*) Have opening balances of fixed assets and accumulated depreciation been reconciled to closing balances?
    (*b*) What significant changes have occurred in owned or leased fixed assets?
    (*c*) Have gains or losses on disposal been recorded?
    (*d*) Have fixed assets been capitalised on a consistent basis?
    (*e*) Has the repairs and maintenance account been reviewed?
    (*f*) Are fixed assets stated at cost?
    (*g*) What are the depreciation methods and rates? Are they consistent?
    (*h*) Is property mortgaged or otherwise encumbered?

(12) Other assets

    (*a*) What is the nature and amount of other assets?
    (*b*) What is the amortization policy? Is it consistent?
    (*c*) Has current/non-current classification been made?
    (*d*) Are the assets realisable at their stated value?

(13) Creditors and accruals

    (*a*) Is the purchase ledger control account in agreement with the listing of creditors?
    (*b*) What procedures have been followed which are designed to result in all major creditors being recorded?
    (*c*) Are suppliers' statements reconciled with ledger accounts?
    (*d*) Are there any undisclosed short-term liabilities?
    (*e*) Have all significant accruals been set-up?
    (*f*) Are secured liabilities appropriately described?
    (*g*) Have subsequent payments been reviewed?
    (*h*) Have VAT, PAYE and NHI been reconciled with returns?

(14) Long-term liabilities

    (*a*) Has current/non-current classification been considered?
    (*b*) Is interest payable recorded?

(15) Tax

    (*a*) Has the relationship between the tax provision and pre-tax result been considered?
    (*b*) To what extent are past tax liabilities agreed?
    (*c*) Have assessments and computations been reviewed?
    (*d*) Has deferred taxation been considered?

(16) Other liabilities

(a) What is the nature and amount of other liabilities?
(b) Has current/non-current classification been made?
(c) Have contingent liabilities and capital commitments been considered?

(17) Statutory requirements

(a) Maintenance of statutory books?
(b) Annual return filed?

(18) Overall review—has appropriate consideration been given to:

(a) the inter-relationship of items in the financial statements?
(b) a comparison of significant components of the profit and loss account (in light of current operating and economic conditions) with budgets and/or figures for preceding periods?
(c) significant operating ratios?
    (i) gross profit
    (ii) debtors to sales

(19) Are there any events which occurred after the end of the financial period which would have a significant effect on the financial statements or would be significant to readers of the financial statements?
(20) Has trial balance been agreed?
(21) Have opening balances been agreed with last year's financial statements?
(22) To what extent are there differences? Quantify and indicate treatment.
(23) To what extent have significant estimates been included?

Final consideration for the accountant

(24) Have the financial statements and 'Accountants' Report' been discussed with the client?
(25) Is the client satisfied that the financial statements are complete and accurate?
(26) Are there are representations by the client regarding full disclosure which should be documented?
(27) Do the financial statements comply with the appropriate disclosure requirements of the Companies Act and the Accounting Standards?
(28) Are the financial statements in accordance with the accounting records?
(29) Have the accounting policies adopted been disclosed and are they in accordance with Accounting Standards?
(30) Based on the information provided and the review performed and so far as you know, are the accounting concepts and policies adopted in respect of material items in the financial statements appropriate to the organisation?
(31) Is the form and content of the 'Accountants' Report' appropriate to this assignment and in particular are you aware of any respects in which the financial statements do not give a true and fair view or in which there has been a failure to comply with law?
(32) **Additional questions**

12.3.2 Report based on a review

A possible form of *accountant's* report following a review is suggested in the brief quoted in Section 12.3.1 above:

Accountants Report to the Members of XYZ Limited
'We have reviewed the accompanying financial statements set out on pages ... to ... in accordance with the approved review standards and have obtained the information and explanations which we required for this purpose.

Our review, which consisted primarily of enquiries, comparisons and discussions, was substantially less in scope than an audit, and in particular did not include the independent verification of information supplied to us. It is, therefore, inappropriate for us to express an audit opinion on the financial statements.

Having carried out our review, we report that the financial statements are in accordance with the underlying records. We are not aware of any material respects in which the financial statements do not show a true and fair view of the state of the company's affairs at 31 December 19.. and of its profit for the year ended on that date or fail to comply with the Companies Act.'

12.4   A small company audit programme

In previous sections we have considered the need for a small company to have an audit, and reached a tentative conclusion that many did not in fact need one.

It was stipulated that some companies *will* still need an audit, the largest such group probably being companies in which there is a separation between shareholders (owners) and directors (managers). In many cases the work will consist of a combination of accounting work and audit work. The following programme provides a guide to such work.

SMALL WORK AUDIT/ACCOUNTANCY PROGRAMME (SWAP)

CLIENT ....

ACCOUNTING PERIOD ....

	Initials	Date
'Overview' completed by (partner/manager)		
Programme amended by		
Use of amended programme authorized by (partner/manager)		
Completed programme reviewed by (partner/manager)		

INSTRUCTIONS FOR USE

This programme has been designed for:

(1) the preparation of accounts, whether from wholly incomplete records or from records brought to various stages of completion by the client, and

(2) audit work (including balance sheet audit work) of a statutory or non-statutory nature on assignments where only a vouching approach can establish the reliability of the accounting records.

As far as its auditing content is concerned, this programme should only be used on assignments which are distinguished by such an absence of internal accounting controls as precludes the use of the Minimum Controls Checklist (see Section 7.8).

The programme is intended as a guide, and will invariably require amendment to suit the particular circumstances of each engagement. The programme as adapted should be approved by the partner/manager before work commences.

Each part of the programme is divided into an 'accountancy' and an 'audit' section. All sections require the person responsible for the work to initial for completion, to indicate the date completed, and, where appropriate, to cross reference to supporting schedules. Where accountancy work has been completed by the client, that fact should be indicated by a tick in the appropriate column, initialled by a member of the audit staff to indicate that the work has been completed to the auditor's satisfaction.

For each section of the audit programme, consideration should be given as to whether the task has been adequately covered by our involvement in accountancy work (For example, where the auditor has written up and agreed the Cash Book, there will be no need to carry out audit tests of casts and cross-casts therein). In such cases the 'Details of Sample' column should be cross referenced to the relevant section of the accountancy programme, but care should be taken to ensure (1) that all aspects of the audit test have been covered in the course of the accountancy work and (2) that there is adequate evidence on file to support any audit conclusions. Otherwise, the details of the test should be summarized in the appropriate column and elaborated on supporting schedules.

SMALL WORK AUDIT/ACCOUNTANCY PROGRAMME (SWAP)

SWAP OVERVIEW	NB. TO BE COMPLETED BY PARTNER/MANAGER

Comments

1. What is the relationship of the proprietor to the business?

● Age

● Length of service

● Shareholding

● Relationship to other shareholders/employees

● Other information

2. Itemize the types (and approximate annual amounts) of personal expenditure met out of business funds.

3. By what means are we able to ensure that personal expenses are not charged to the business?

4. Does the amount of the proprietor's drawings appear sufficient to support his style of living?

5. What is your assessment of the efficiency with which the commercial and accounting aspects of the business are conducted?

SWAP OVERVIEW CONTD.	NB. TO BE COMPLETED BY PARTNER/MANAGER

Comments

6. In view of the fact that controls rest primarily on the personal supervision of the proprietor, to what extent are we satisfied that he exercises that supervision with sufficient diligence for us to rely on it as a point of control?

7. To what extent does the business:

   (a) sell goods or services for cash?

   (b) deal in "desirable" products or services (which although generally invoiced on credit terms, can in fact be sold or converted directly for cash)?

   (c) enter into cash transactions with suppliers, sub-contractors, casual employees etc.?

8. What is our basis for believing that all the income of the business is reflected in the records?

COMPLETED BY .... Date ....

SWAP 1 RECEIPTS AND PAYMENTS	Completed by client	Initials & date	Sch. ref.

1.1
Accountancy Programme

1.1.1 Inspect previous period's trading and profit and loss account, noting headings of items listed to ascertain extent of analysis required.

1.1.2 Write up the following records, analysing them into the headings determined in 1.1.1 above:

    (a) cash payments—by reference to cheque stubs, bank advice notes etc.;

    (b) cash receipts —by reference to paying-in-slips, bank advice notes;

    (c) petty cash —by reference to cash payments book and petty cash vouchers etc.

    (Note: In all cases ensure that VAT is correctly extracted)

1.1.3 Cast and cross-cast receipts and payments analyses.

1.1.4 Prepare appropriate sub-analyses where analysis columns are not sufficient to meet trading and profit and loss account headings.

1.1.5 Post receipts and payments, as appropriate, to:

    (a) Purchase ledger
    (b) Sales ledger
    (c) Nominal ledger.

SWAP 1 RECEIPTS AND PAYMENTS CONT.	Details of sample	Initials & date	Sch. ref.

1.2   *Audit Programme*

1.2.1   Check receipts and payments to bank statements.

1.2.2   Check casts, cross-casts, and analyses in the:
(a) cash payments book
(b) cash receipts book
(c) petty cash book.

1.2.3   For a selected sample of receipts:
(a) check cash receipts to original documents (i.e. till rolls, cash receipt slips)
(b) check to paying-in-slips to ensure prompt and intact banking.

1.2.4   Scrutinize cash book and check that there are no unexplained or abnormal fluctuations in daily/ weekly receipts, or any unusual payments.

1.2.5   Check postings from cash and petty cash books to:
(a) purchase ledger
(b) sales ledger
(c) nominal ledger.

1.2.6   For a selected sample of payments:
(a) verify authorization and cancellation when paid;
(b) ensure that they are correctly analysed (inc. VAT);
(c) observe whether they appear to be for bona fide business purposes;
(d) verify prices with orders or agreements;
(e) check additions and calculations.

1.2.7   Vouch a sample of returned cheques when available ensuring that:
(a) the cheques run in sequence and spoilt and cancelled cheques are accounted for;
(b) cheques are only signed by authorized signatories.

SWAP 1 RECEIPTS AND PAYMENTS CONT.	Details of sample	Initials & date	Sch. ref.
1.2.8 Check payments for petty cash to petty cash book.			
1.2.9 Vouch a sample of petty cash payments ensuring that: (a) the vouchers are authorized and cancelled; (b) the expenditure is correctly analysed.			
1.2.10 Obtain/prepare a bank reconciliation statement at the balance sheet date and: (a) check casts; (b) trace through all outstanding items, noting those uncleared at time of audit; (c) agree balance with nominal ledger.			
1.2.11 Obtain direct confirmation of all bank balances at balance sheet date.			
1.2.12 Count and record all cash holdings and: (a) agree them to the nominal ledger; (b) reconcile back to year-end balances.			
REVIEWED BY			

SWAP 2 PURCHASES AND CREDITORS	Completed by client	Initials & date	Sch. ref.
2.1 *Accountancy Programme*			
2.1.1 Enter all invoices in purchase day book in chronological order and analyse as appropriate. (Note: Ensure VAT is correctly extracted).			
2.1.2 Cast and cross-cast.			
2.1.3 Post all items from purchase day book to purchase ledger.			
2.1.4 Prepare purchase ledger control account from day book and cash book totals.			
2.1.5 Extract balances from purchase ledger and agree to control account.			
2.1.6 Post purchase day book totals to nominal ledger.			
2.1.7 Prepare detailed schedules of other creditors and accruals by reference to invoices, after-date payments, previous year's working papers etc.			
2.1.8 Prepare creditors summary schedule.			

	Details of sample	Initials & date	Sch. ref.
2.2 *Audit Programme*			
2.2.1 Vouch a sample of purchase day book entries with suppliers invoices and credit notes ensuring that: (a) invoices and credit notes are authorized (b) day book is correctly analysed (c) purchases appear to be for bona-fide business purposes.			

SWAP 2 PURCHASES AND CREDITORS CONT.	Details of sample	Initials & date	Sch. ref.
2.2.2 Check casts and cross-casts of purchase day book.			
2.2.3 Check postings from purchase day book to: (a) purchase ledger (b) nominal ledger			
2.2.4 Check extraction of balances from purchase ledger and agree with control account.			
2.2.5 Agree a sample of individual purchase ledger accounts with suppliers' statements.			
2.2.6 Enquire into any old outstanding balances, and debit balances, on the purchase ledger.			
2.2.7 Examine after-date invoices, previous year's working papers etc. to ensure all creditors and accruals at the balance sheet date are brought into account.			
2.2.8 Review procedures adopted for goods received up to balance sheet date but not invoiced and ensure they are taken up in purchases and stocks (including stocks held by third parties).			
2.2.9 Reconcile balance on VAT control account with VAT due or recoverable for last 1 to 3 months.			

SWAP 3 SALES AND DEBTORS	Completed by client	Initials & date	Sch. ref.
3.1 *Accountancy Programme*			
3.1.1 Enter all sales invoices (sequentially) in sales day book, analysing as appropriate. (Note: Ensure VAT is correctly extracted)			
3.1.2 Cast and cross-cast.			
3.1.3 Post day book to sales ledger.			
3.1.4 Prepare sales ledger control account from the sales day book and cash book totals.			
3.1.5 Extract list of balances from sales ledger and agree with control account.			
3.1.6 Post sales day book to nominal ledger.			
3.1.7 Prepare a schedule of prepayments, deposits and other amounts receivable.			
3.1.8 Prepare summary schedule of debtors and prepayments.			
	Details of sample	Initials & date	Sch. ref.
3.2 *Audit Programme*			
3.2.1 For a selected sample of day book entries: (a) vouch with invoices and credit notes; (b) compare prices with price lists etc.; (c) check additions and calculations; (d) check correct analysis in sales day book.			
3.2.2 Check casts and cross-casts of sales day book.			

SWAP 3 SALES AND DEBTORS CONT.	Details of sample	Initials & date	Sch. ref.
3.2.3 Check authorization and supporting correspondence/documentation for a sample of credit notes.			
3.2.4 Test a sequence of sales invoices, to ensure all accounted for.			
3.2.5 Check postings to: (a) sales ledger (b) nominal ledger			
3.2.6 Scrutinize day books for any unusual items throughout the period.			
3.2.7 Test extraction and casts of balances in sales ledger and agree total of balances with control account.			
3.2.8 For a selected sample of individual accounts: (a) ensure balance represents specific invoices; (b) test casts; (c) peruse for unusual entries.			
3.2.9 Check ageing of list of balances and enquire into: (a) any old outstanding balances; (b) adequacy of bad debt provision.			
3.2.10 Examine after-date credits for items relating to the period under review.			
3.2.11 Review procedures adopted for goods invoiced prior to the balance sheet date but not despatched (or vice versa) and ensure proper cut-off.			
3.2.12 Obtain/check details of prepayments and other amounts receivable at balance sheet date.			

SWAP 4 STOCKS AND WORK IN PROGRESS	Completed by client	Initials & date	Sch. ref.
4.1 *Accountancy Programme* Where stocks are counted, but not valued, by the client:			
4.1.1 Segregate stock sheets, identifying raw materials, work in progress and finished goods.			
4.1.2 Price stock quantities on stock sheets by reference to purchase invoices or other cost data.			
4.1.3 Extend/value stock sheets (quantity×price).			
4.1.4 Cast stock-sheet values and summarize totals.			

	Details of sample	Initials & date	Sch. ref.
4.2 *Audit Programme*			
4.2.1 Review client's stock-taking procedures and, where the amount is material, attend.			
4.2.2 Check final stock sheets for: (a) quantities—with rough stock sheets, stock records, and/or by reference to test counts; (b) costs—with purchase invoices or other cost data; (c) casts and extensions.			
4.2.3 Check stocks are valued: (a) on an appropriate and consistent basis; (b) in accordance with disclosed accounting policies; (c) at net realizable value where lower than cost.			

SWAP 4 STOCKS AND WORK IN PROGRESS CONT.	Details of sample	Initials & date	Sch. ref.
4.2.4 Check year-end cut-off with: (a) despatch notes, sales records; (b) goods received notes, purchase invoices.			
4.2.5 Check that adequate provision has been made for obsolete and slow-moving stock by: (a) comparing with previous years' stock sheets; (b) checking usage during the year.			
4.2.6 Where practicable, reconcile closing stock quantities by reference to opening stock plus purchases less sales.			
4.2.7 Obtain direct confirmation of any stock held by third parties.			
4.2.8 Review/prepare stock summary ensuring that: (a) approval of the summary by the client is evidenced by signature, or by way of Stock Certificate or letter of representation; (b) the stock valuation appears reasonable in the context of the previous period's stock levels, the year's turnover and anticipated gross profit.			

SWAP 5 PAYROLL	Completed by client	Initials & date	Sch. ref.
5.1 Accountary Programme			
5.1.1 Prepare a summary of the wages and/or salaries book(s) in a form appropriate for posting, and showing totals for gross pay, net pay, PAYE, NI and other deductions.			
5.1.2 Post totals to nominal ledger and agree control account.			
5.1.3 Distinguish gross pay between directors and employees.			

	Details of sample	Initials & date	Sch. ref.
5.2 Audit Programme			
5.2.1 Check gross pay with contracts of employment, authorized increases, etc.			
5.2.2 Check total net wages and PAYE, NI deductions with amounts drawn per cash book.			
5.2.3 For wages paid by cash, inspect receipts given by employees.			
5.2.4 Check casts, cross-casts and calculations on payroll.			
5.2.5 Check the summary of wages from the wages book.			
5.2.6 Check postings from the wages summary to the nominal ledger.			
5.2.7 Reconcile consecutive payrolls for a chosen week/month and obtain explanation of changes.			
5.2.8 Check authorization of payroll.			
5.2.9 Check year-end creditor/accrual for any unpaid wages, holiday pay, and any PAYE or NI deducted not yet paid over.			
5.2.10 Ascertain whether any amounts are drawn gross, without deduction of PAYE, and, if so, whether such treatment is acceptable for Inland Revenue purposes.			

SWAP 6 INVESTMENTS	Completed by client	Initials & date	Sch. ref.
6.1 Accountancy Programme			
6.1.1 Prepare schedules of investments held at the year end distinguishing between quoted and unquoted and showing: (i) cost (ii) market value (quoted) or directors' valuations (unquoted) (iii) income received/receivable during the period, and related tax credits.			
6.1.2 Prepare schedule of additions and disposals including details of rights or scrip issues, and calculate profit/loss on disposal.			
6.1.3 Prepare summaries of any building society investment accounts.			

	Details of sample	Initials & date	Sch. ref.
6.2 Audit Programme			
6.2.1 Check additions/disposals to contract notes and check calculation of profit/loss on disposal.			
6.2.2 Check income and rights/bonus issues with divident warrants, Extel etc.			
6.2.3 Verify existence of and title to all investments by inspection of certificates or by way of third party confirmations.			
6.2.4 Check valuations with SE Official list (quoted) and other available evidence (unquoted).			
6.2.5 Reconcile building society investment accounts with pass book and with building society certificate(s).			

SWAP 7 FIXED ASSETS	Completed by client	Initials & date	Sch. ref.
7.1 *Accountancy Programme*			
7.1.1 Prepare schedules of fixed assets showing, for each category: (a) cost and/or valuation, and accumulated depreciation at the beginning of the period; (b) additions during the period; (c) the cost and accumulated depreciation on disposals during the period.			
7.1.2 For assets disposed during the year, calculate the profit/loss on disposal.			
7.1.3 Calculate depreciation charge for the year.			
7.1.4 Cast and cross-cast schedules, to show cost (and/or valuations), accumulated depreciation and NBV at the end of the period.			
7.1.5 For fixed assets acquired under hire purchase terms, prepare schedules detailing the full HP liability, distinguishing capital and future interest, and calculate interest expense for the period.			
	Details of sample	Initials & date	Sch. ref.
7.2 *Audit Programme*			
7.2.1 Obtain schedules of additions and vouch with supporting documentation			

SWAP 7 FIXED ASSETS CONT.	Details of sample	Initials & date	Sch. ref.
7.2.2 Check depreciation calculations and consider the consistency and adequacy of the rates used.			
7.2.3 Check calculations of profit/loss on disposals.			
7.2.4 Obtain copies of any revaluations during the period.			
7.2.5 Confirm existence of and title to fixed assets by: (a) Physical inspection; (b) Examination of title deeds/ lease agreements for properties; (c) Examination of registration documents for motor vehicles.			
7.2.6 For fixed assets acquired under HP terms: (a) check liability with HP agreements; (b) check calculations of interest charge for period.			

SWAP 8 OTHER MATTERS	Completed by client	Initials & date	Sch. ref.
8.1 **Accountancy Programme**			
8.1.1 *Journal* (a) Prepare journal entries as necessary, giving a comprehensive narrative and reference to supporting documentation. (b) Post entries to nominal ledger.			
8.1.2 *Trial balance* (a) Extract initial trial balance. (b) Enter journal adjustments required. (c) Enter debtors and creditors and ensure totals are in agreement with the relevant summary schedules. (d) Extend trial balance, cast and cross-cast.			
8.1.3 Prepare tax computations (liaising with manager and/or tax department) together with detailed analyses of appropriate revenue and expense accounts.			
8.1.4 Consider final adjustments for: (a) Additional directors' remuneration; (b) Bonuses; (c) Dividends to be declared.			
8.1.5 *Current Accounts* Prepare analysis of the proprietors/directors current accounts.			

SWAP 8 OTHER MATTERS CONT.	Completed by client	Initials & date	Sch. ref.
8.1.6 *Financial Statements* (a) Prepare detailed trading and profit and loss account and balance sheet by reference to the trial balance and post TB journals. (b) Where required, prepare statutory accounts to include: (i) Directors' report (ii) Statutory profit and loss account (iii) Balance sheet (iv) Notes (v) Source and application of funds statements. (c) Once the accounts have been approved, complete posting of nominal ledger, close off the accounts and extract an opening trial balance.			

	Details of sample	Initials & date	Sch. ref.
8.2 *Audit Programme*			
8.2.1 Scrutinize Minute Book, take copies of important items and, where relevant, cross reference to working papers.			
8.2.2 Check completion of previous annual return.			
8.2.3 Check entries in the following statutory registers and, where necessary, prepare schedules detailing extracts from: (a) Register of members; (b) Register of directors, and their shareholdings; (c) Register of charges.			

SWAP 8 OTHER MATTERS CONT.	Details of sample	Initials & date	Sch. ref.
8.2.4 Examine Memorandum and Articles of Association and: (a) note any amendments on permanent file; (b) agree conformity with details in 8.2.3 above; (c) check compliance with borrowing powers.			
8.2.5 Consider any capital commitments and contingent liabilities.			
8.2.6 Consider any significant post balance sheet events.			
8.2.7 *Trial balance/Journal/Nominal Ledger* (a) Vouch journal entries with available documentation and test postings to nominal ledger. (b) Test casts in nominal ledger, and scrutinise for abnormal items. (c) Test extraction of balances. (d) Test cast and extensions in trial balance.			
8.2.8 *Current Accounts* (a) Obtain proprietors/directors' agreement and signature on analysed summary of current accounts. (b) Ensure that PAYE procedures have been correctly applied as regards credits to these accounts.			
8.2.9 *Financial Statements* (a) Where relevant, check compliance with statutory and SSAP requirements by completing Companies Accounts checklist. (b) Prepare analytical review of trading results. (c) Draft appropriate Accountants Report or Audit Report.			

12.5 Summary

In the UK few concessions are granted to smaller companies. The audit requirement is exactly the same for the huge listed multinational as for a small private company.

The climate of opinion is currently changing towards the idea that not all small companies need have an audit, though the audit safeguard may need to continue for companies in which there are shareholders not participating in the management of the company.

If the audit requirement is dropped there may well be a requirement for a *review* of the financial statements without a detailed audit. The review checklist in Section 12.3.1 is important—study it carefully.

In cases where the audit continues to be necessary it will frequently be combined with accounting work. The accountancy/audit programme in Section 12.4 illustrates what is likely to be necessary.

Progress questions

Questions	Reference for answers
(1) What three options were identified by the Department of Trade and Industry for modifying the requirements for the audit of small companies?	Section 12.1
(2) Summarize the arguments for and against continuation of the statutory audit of small companies from the point of view of: (a) Shareholders; (b) Banks and other lenders; (c) Trade creditors; (d) Tax authorities; (e) Employees; (f) Management.	Section 12.2.1 Section 12.2.2 Section 12.2.3 Section 12.2.4 Section 12.2.5 Section 12.2.6
(3) Prepare a review checklist suitable for use when a limited review of the financial statements of a small company is undertaken (Main headings only).	Section 12.3.1
(4) Draft a suitable form of report based on the type of review considered for Question 3 above.	Section 12.3.2
(5) Draft a suitable accountancy/audit programme covering any two major areas in the work.	Section 12.4

13 Computer systems

13.1 Introduction

The first thing that all the books say about computer audits is that the audit approach is exactly the same as for any other audit and only the methods change. This is true, of course, but the methods can be so different that computer audits must really be regarded as a separate study. For the purpose of this chapter we are assuming that you have a basic knowledge of computers and the terminology of the subject.

Let us first of all take a look at internal controls in a computerized system.

13.2 Computer internal controls

The principles of internal control continue to apply. That is to say, we shall need to have:

(a) custody arrangements;
(b) records;
(c) plan of organization;
(d) segregation of duties;
(e) staff competence;
(f) authorization procedures;
(g) supervision;
(h) internal checks;
(i) arithmetical and accounting controls.

In a computer context, internal controls may be divided into *general controls*, covering the general organization and operation of the department, and *application controls*, set up for each separate function carried out.

Note: The remainder of Section 13.2 relates to a large data processing installation. The special problems of small computers are dealt with in Section 13.5.

13.2.1 General controls

The Auditing Guideline on computer auditing defines general controls as 'controls, other than application controls, which relate to the environment within which computer-based accounting systems are developed, maintained and operated, and which are therefore applicable to all the applications. The objectives of general controls are to ensure the proper development and implementation of applications, and the integrity of program and data files, and of computer operations.' General controls may be either manual or programmed.

(a) *Controls over personnel*
(1) the existence of a coherent plan of organization for the data processing department;
(2) segregation and definition of duties;
(3) control over access;
(4) the existence of a control section;
(5) librarian exercising control over file storage.

(b) *Systems development controls*
(c) *Other general controls*
(1) authorization;
(2) supervision;
(3) reconstruction procedures;
(4) breakdown procedures;
(5) maintenance;
(6) security;
(7) fire precautions.

13.2.2 Plan of organization

A typical plan of organization for a medium to large sized computer installation as shown in the diagram on p. 354.

Systems analysts and programmers are responsible for the development of new systems and systems amendments. The control section is the interface with user departments and supervises routine operations. Alongside we have maintenance and security. The internal auditors, if any, will be working in the department but will not, of course, be responsible to the data processing (DP) manager.

The plan reminds us of the importance of segregation of duties, dealt with in the next paragraph.

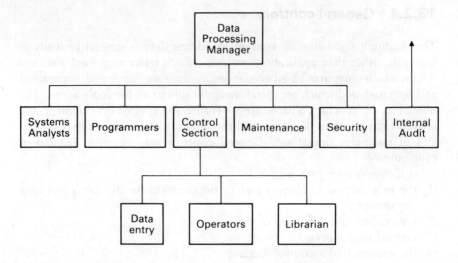

13.2.3 Segregation and definition of duties

The plan of organization in the previous section tells us something about the necessary segregation of duties within the computer department and helps in defining those duties.

In any system, whether it is computerized or not, there must be a fundamental segregation of duties which seeks to place the following responsibilities with independent officials:

(a) initiation and authorization of transactions;
(b) recording of transactions;
(c) custody of assets.

To achieve this division of responsibilities, it is clear that the DP department, when used to maintain accounting records, must be independent of the users who initiate and authorize transactions and who have custody of assets. Historically, in traditional batch-type mainframe installations, this segregation has been relatively easy to achieve. However, two major developments have threatened the isolation of the DP department:

(a) The development of on-line/real-time systems where data entry is performed directly by the user departments via terminals. In some installations, the effective segregation of duties should be enforced by a system of software checks (e.g. passwords) which restrict terminals to those functions and responsibilities applicable to the department(s) which use them (see below).

(b) The emergence of small business computers which are fully integrated within the user organization and specifically preclude the existence of a separate DP department. Problems specific to small business computers are discussed in Section 13.5.

Internally, the DP department should be organized so that the three major disciplines of operations, development and control are undertaken by independent personnel. This segregation would normally involve separating:

(a) data control;
(b) data preparation and conversion;
(c) job scheduling and review;
(d) operations;
(e) program/file library maintenance;
(f) software maintenance;
(g) systems;
(h) programming.

It should be emphasized that the full division of duties as listed above will usually be found in large installations only. Smaller installations, for example, rarely employ a file librarian, and frequently combine the activities of system development and programming. However, the above division of duties should be borne in mind since it represents the optimum definition of theoretical control in a traditional DP environment. Note, however, that the distinction between some of these functions does not exist in many on-line/real-time systems.

Division of duties separates the important DP functions and should minimize the risk of fraudulent manipulation of computer-based records. Additionally, it is essential that the organizational structure be designed to ensure that there is adequate review of all departmental activities. This review function is discussed in more detail below, but its importance must be emphasized since it is the fundamental control which ensures that installation standards (i.e. the prescribed procedures and controls) are adhered to.

Given an adequate number of staff, the internal segregation of DP functions has been generally easy to achieve in the batch-type mainframe installation. In such cases, for example, all processing work is undertaken within the computer area. Thus, by controlling physical access to this area, and ensuring that the operators only accept work via the operations manager, it is a relatively easy task to ensure that only authorized jobs are processed through the machine, thus preventing unauthorized activities. However, with the introduction of on-line terminals, operation of the computer cannot be so easily isolated. Thus, a user could process data, or a programmer may be able to effect program amendments, through terminals located in their own offices.

Where there is an ineffective segregation of duties, DP and user management must resort to other compensating procedures to restrict the use of terminals, control computer operations through review techniques and monitor the validity of the data processed through the installation.

13.2.4   Control over access

Control over access can mean restrictions on access to the computer room and on the operation of computers and terminals.

(a) Restrictions on access to the computer room

The physical layout of the department can control access. Large installations will have security guards posted at entrances to check badges issued to those with authority to pass. An alternative is to use electronic card/key devices. The issue of badges and cards must obviously be strictly controlled.

It is not sufficient to prevent outsiders from entering. 'Insiders' too must be controlled. Programmers, data control staff and other non-operators should not be allowed in the computer room except when necessary, for example for program testing.

(b) Restrictions on operation of computers and terminals

Physical restrictions on access are of limited value when on-line terminals are located in other areas. It may still be possible to place some terminals in secure locations but the whole object may be to make the computer facility available to staff. There are, however a number of methods which can be used to control their use including: (i) physical on/off key devices; (ii) keyboard covers; (iii) password procedures.

Access to computer facilities is controlled by passwords which 'unlock' sections of the computer only. In one firm of accountants for example (not connected with the authors) the lowest level of access available to the most junior staff is that for computer games (available only from 1.00 pm to 2.00 pm, naturally) with nine higher levels of access available to progressively smaller numbers of staff.

The password structure in such systems should reflect the logical segregation of duties within the company so that, for example, passwords to sales ledger programs are only available to sales ledger staff. Additionally, 'sensitive' routines (e.g. resetting credit terms) should be protected by a second level of password to further restrict their use. Note that passwords should not be displayed on entry and should be changed on a frequent and random basis to limit knowledge of them.

Software routines should be used to restrict the capabilities of terminals. For example, specific terminals may not be allowed to access payroll applications, even though the operator may have gained knowledge of the payroll passwords.

13.2.5 The control section

The control section exists to receive input, determine priorities, allocate work to operators and distribute output. It fulfils an important function in the internal control of the DP department. Detailed control section functions are:

(a) receipt and logging of input data;
(b) maintaining records of control information;
(c) determining priorities and monitoring progress of work;
(d) reconciliation of control totals;
(e) distribution of output;
(f) correction of errors in consultation with user departments;
(g) scrutiny of error listings, and maintenance of error reports.

13.2.6 Librarian

The librarian's job is to provide safe storage and control over data files and program files. It is not realistic to expect a full-time librarian in a smaller installation, and the work might be handled by a control clerk.

13.2.7 Systems development controls

The term 'systems development' refers to the creation of new systems and programs. The controls here are exercised over the systems analysts and programmers responsible for development, and cover the development, implementation and maintenance of all systems and application software.

Fundamental to these controls is the use of 'standards', which establish the procedures to be followed in order to ensure a measured approach to each phase of development and maintenance projects. Standards in themselves imply a system of review since only by reviewing the work performed can an assessment be made as to whether the prescribed standards have been adhered to.

(a) Control to ensure proper and accurate systems development

The following steps, explained in detail below, should be undertaken for each major development project.

(1) *Feasibility studies* should be carried out before new systems are authorized and undertaken to:
—define the problem;
—evaluate alternative procedures;
—estimate likely cost and cost savings;
—establish a realistic time for project completion.

The basic objective of this phase is to establish that the proposed solution is viable and also the most suitable to the business.

(2) *System specifications* should be produced to confirm user requirements and to act as a guide for programming staff. Their contents will include:

—an overview of the system;
—a description of each processing step;
—file layouts;
—specimen input documents;
—specimen output reports.

In the detailed specification (which must be complemented by outline or 'functional' specifications for user understanding and review), the system analyst sets out his or her answer to the problem at hand.

(3) *Program specifications* should be created (by reference to the detailed system specification) to establish the purpose of each constituent program and to describe the processing logic used (usually with the aid of logic flowcharts).

(4) *Program coding* represents the detailed set of instructions which will be used to process information within the computer. It should be written with reference to program specifications and reviewed to ensure that the installation's standards are adhered to (e.g. the inclusion of standard control procedures, such as verification of record counts and control totals, and descriptive information where required).

(5) *Test procedures* should be used to verify the accuracy of the development phase before implementation. Standards must be established to determine the method of selecting the test data to be used, and should stipulate:

—the extent of user involvement in the creation and review of test data;
—the extent of test data used within the DP department. (Typically, the programmer may undertake his own initial testing of each program to satisfy himself that the logic used is correct, by a combination of desk checking and program testing. At this point the analyst, an independent person, would perform system tests, e.g. processing test data through the full sequence of events.);
—assigned responsibilities.

(6) It is essential that *review procedures* be performed on the completion of each significant development phase. Thus:

—feasibility studies and system specifications should be reviewed by senior DP and user management;

—program specifications and source listings should be reviewed by the systems analyst or, if applicable, the senior programmer. (In practice, formal review of program coding is normally applicable to large installations only, although it represents an effective control to ensure that recognized techniques are used in problem solving);

—test results must be reviewed by user and DP management and formal user approval must be obtained.

Additionally, the system of review should ensure that established timetables are maintained and that any delays are analyzed for future references and reflected in timetable revisions.

The extent to which auditors should be involved in the development of new systems is discussed in detail below. However, the general premise is that when the auditor seeks to place reliance on system controls, then his or her involvement should start before the programming phase is undertaken in order to ensure that the basic system design is not deficient for the purposes.

(b) Control over software maintenance

Failure to control the software maintenance function undermines the effectiveness of those development procedures which should exist within the installation. Thus, for example, whilst test procedures for a given system may have been adequately performed, failure to subject amendments to similar procedures may result in the implementation of erroneous logic routines.

In addition to the procedures outlined, controls must be exercised as follows:

(1) Development routines must be isolated from operational programs and data files (where used in testing) to ensure that the 'production' system is not disrupted. This control normally involves establishing, for example, separate disc areas, and retaining programs and data files in accordance with test name conventions (e.g. prefixing all program names with 'TEST').

(2) Amendments should be authorized and sequentially controlled, e.g. by entering amendment details on pre-numbered documents. This procedure helps management to ensure that only authorized amendments are undertaken and to determine the progress made to date on each project.

The controls listed above monitor the development of 'authorized' system amendments. It is also essential to establish controls which prevent or detect the implementation of unauthorized amendments where such amendments bypass the recognized procedures laid down with the installation. This area is dependent primarily on an effective segregation of duties between operations and development staff, on the procedures used to control the operation of the computer and on specific controls relating to program maintenance (see below).

Amendments to software packages acquired by the client are usually undertaken by the software house responsible for its development. Therefore, whilst any amendments should be subject to internal test and review procedures by the client himself, it is important that the package is supported by a formal maintenance contract with such a software house.

(c) Implementation controls—conversion of data files

Data-file conversion may be undertaken by a program which forms part of the regular processing cycle (e.g. setting up records on a customer file by means of a maintenance program which can add, change or delete records) or via a special program (e.g. loading cumulative pay details when implementing a payroll system part way through a tax year).

Strict control must be exercised over this phase of development since conversion errors may have a serious impact on subsequent processing cycles. Thus:

(1) Establish a timetable for data conversion and identify the exact point in time at which the converted data files will commence (e.g. a new tax year for a payroll system, or a given month-end for ledger systems). In doing so, due regard must be given to the additional work involved in this process, and, where necessary, provision made to employ additional resources.

(2) Reconcile the results of data conversion to the manual or previous computer system records. In broad terms, reconciliation of transaction files would normally be restricted to transaction totals (e.g. loading an open item ledger file would be controlled by agreeing the total value of transactions on an 'account by account' basis). However, significant master-files (e.g. selling-price information held on a stock file) should be checked on a record by record basis.

(3) Ensure, where data conversion is performed using special 'one-off' programs, that programs are developed in accordance with the controls set out above and contain validation routines to detect all input errors. This is particularly important if conversion can give rise to an error condition which is not envisaged in the main processing cycle: e.g. an open item ledger system, which also summarizes each account balance on a separate master-file, must contain a check to ensure that each account balance is equal to the sum of the open items on the transaction file. (Note that such conditions should also be reviewed to determine whether they should be incorporated into the main production system.)

(4) Test the operational programs against the converted data files. Normally, this involves processing the new system in parallel with the old manual (or computer) system. Parallel running verifies that the new system is functioning properly, and may detect errors which had not been tested for during the earlier test phases. However, although it represents the safest option, full parallel running may prove impractical given data volumes or other circumstances. (In such cases, parallel running against a small section of the new system should be considered.) Where a new computer system represents a significant advance such that it is not possible to run in parallel, procedures should be used to pilot-test the new system in a controlled environment.

(d) Implementation of operational programs

There should be formal procedures to monitor the transfer of programs into the operational libraries, i.e. transfers should only take place after the new system/programs have been authorized by both user and DP management.

Approval should be evidenced (e.g. by authorization of an implementation checklist) and the implementation routines reviewed by management to ensure that they have been undertaken properly (e.g. by reviewing library contents or by controlling program generation numbers assigned by the system software).

Note that the transfer to production libraries will usually involve both source- and object-coded programs which must represent the same version of the program. The proper transfer of source code is essential since it may be used to recompile the object code of an 'operational' program and because the source version may be used for further program maintenance. Compilation procedures provide source-code listings which should therefore be reviewed to ensure that the appropriate version of the program has in fact been compiled and transferred.

Controls to ensure that only authorized (and approved) amendments are transferred into the production libraries of a typical batch-type mainframe should include authorization checks by operations staff over all amendments submitted for processing. In this instance, however, the classic problem is to ensure that amendments are not themselves changed after they have been authorized. In general, this may be achieved by physically restricting access to amendments by development staff after authorization, or, more normally, by reviewing compilation listings. (It is also worth emphasizing that this problem is essentially one of fraud and deliberate intent. As such, the auditor should have regard to it although the detection or prevention of fraud is not the primary audit objective).

Password procedures within the system software should be used to restrict access to production libraries in an installation with on-line terminals located in the user and DP development departments.

Further controls over this area are referred to in the section dealing with computer operations (particularly the review of work performed and the isolation of development staff from the machine itself, i.e. to minimize 'hands on' testing by development staff).

(e) Documentation of new and amended software

Adequate documentation is essential to minimize the risk of error during the subsequent operation, control and maintenance of a system. Additionally, it reduces the reliance which is otherwise placed on the continued employment of key personnel and provides a better understanding of the system's objectives and methodology. Accordingly, it is important that documentation is issued to assist the following functions:

(1) *system maintenance*
—specifications/flowcharts;
—file layouts;
—record of all amendments;
—test documentation.

(2) *Program maintenance*
—specifications/logic flowcharts;
—source listings;
—details of all codes/tables used;
—test documentation.

(3) *Data preparation/control*
—preparation instructions (for each type of input form);
—authorization checks (by data control);
—input/output reconciliations;
—output distribution.

(4) *Computer operations*
—standard run procedures (often in flowchart form and detailing the files used and the sequence in which jobs should be processed);
—run parameters (e.g. month-end dates, payroll week numbers);
—switch selection (to select 'optional' logic routines within a program, e.g. month-end statements);
—message responses;
—halt and restart procedures, indicating which point the operator should return to (if at all) to restart the processing cycle.

(5) *User operation and control*
—instructions on the completion of forms;
—interpretation of output, including error messages and response;
—recommended user control procedures.

Finally it should be emphasized that the development controls outlined above are applicable to all software used by the installation, i.e. both applications and the operating system; and, since system software is usually beyond the experience of the user departments, the control process will be exercised primarily by DP management itself.

13.2.8 Other general controls

(a) *Authorization.* As in any system, proper authorization procedures are essential. Particular aspects of authorization are:

(1) intial authorization and staged approval by users and computer management of new systems for development;
(2) authorization of all systems and program amendments;
(3) authorization of work before processing;
(4) authorization of access to files.

(b) *Supervision.* All aspects of the work of the DP department require adequate supervision.

(c) *File reconstruction procedures.* Back-up copies of important files should be stored at a location entirely separate from the computer, so that if files are lost they can be replaced. Regular and frequent updating and inspection of these files is obviously essential if they are to fulfil their function.

In addition, there should be a file reconstruction capability. Data on disc should, for example, be 'dumped' (transferred to another magnetic storage medium—tape or disc) at intervals so that reconstruction can proceed from that point if it becomes necessary.

(d) *Breakdown procedures.* It is customary to make arrangements with another user or with a computer service bureau to carry out essential work if the computer breaks down.

(e) *Maintenance.* Regular maintenance must be provided for.

(f) *Security.* Precautions against unauthorized entry, vandalism and even sabotage are necessary. Files need protection against static electricity and magnetic interference. (See also Sections 13.2.6 and 13.2.8(c) above.)

(g) *Fire precautions.* The computer should be sited away from possible hazards and suitable fire fighting equipment provided. Smoke detectors should be used.

13.2.9 General controls and their objectives summarized

In 1984 the APC published a Guideline entitled 'Auditing in a computer environment', and this is reproduced in Section 13.4 below. It does not deal with computer internal control, but the Exposure Draft which preceded it did so. It is useful to reproduce here the section dealing with general controls.

Appendix 2: General controls

Introduction

(1) General controls cover the environment within which applications are developed, maintained and operated and within which application controls operate. The objectives of general controls are to ensure the integrity of application development and implementation, program and data files, and computer operations. To achieve this controls are required:

(a) over application development;
(b) to prevent or detect unauthorised changes to programs;
(c) to ensure that all program changes are adequately tested and documented;
(d) to prevent or detect errors during program execution;
(e) to prevent unauthorised amendments to data files;
(f) to ensure that systems software is properly installed and maintained;
(g) to ensure that proper documentation is kept; and
(h) to ensure continuity of operations.

Controls over application development

(2) The auditor might consider the adequacy of such matters as: system design standards, programming standards, documentation controls and standards, testing procedures, approval of development stages by users and computer management, internal audit involvement, segregation of duties for systems design, programming and operations, training and supervision.

Controls to prevent or detect unauthorized changes to programs

(3) This covers both accidental and fraudulent corruption of program logic during program maintenance or program execution. In addition to such matters as the segregation of duties and the training and supervision of staff for program maintenance, the auditor would consider such matters as: authorisation of jobs prior to processing, the record of program changes and its review to detect unauthorised changes, password protection of programs, emergency modification procedures, integrity of back up copies of programs, physical protection of production programs and programs stored off-line, and comparison of production programs to controlled copies. For program execution, the auditor would consider: the operations manual, procedures to prevent access to programs during execution, controls over use of utility programs, restricted access to the computer and remote terminals, review of job accounting reports and investigation of unusual delays, and rotation of duties.

Controls to ensure that all program changes are adequately tested and documented

(4) As program changes may range from a small alteration of an output report to a major redesign, most installations will have more than one set of standards for testing and documenting changes. The auditor would consider the adequacy of such matters

as: testing procedures, documentation controls and standards, approval of changes by users and computer management, internal audit involvement, and segregation of duties, training and supervision of the staff involved.

Controls to prevent or detect errors during program execution

(5) The auditor might consider the adequacy of operations controls included in the systems software, use of job control procedure libraries, an operation manual detailing set up and execution procedures, job scheduling, emergency back up procedures and training and supervision. These procedures should provide protection against errors such as incorrect data files, wrong versions of production programs, running programs in the wrong sequence, incorrect response to a program request, and job control errors.

Controls to prevent unauthorised amendments to data files

(6) Controls to prevent unauthorised amendments to data files are dependent upon the application controls over the file, the manner in which the file is maintained and the file management software, used. The auditor might consider the adequacy of such general control procedures as: authorisation of jobs prior to processing, procedures to detect unauthorised amendments, password protection and procedures for recording and investigating unauthorised access attempts, emergency modification procedures, integrity of back up files, physical protection of data files, restricted use of utility programs, and the segregation of duties.

Controls to ensure that systems software is properly installed and maintained

(7) Systems software includes the operating system, teleprocessing monitors, data base management systems, spooling systems and other software used to increase the efficiency of processing and to control processing. The auditor should consider not only the controls exercised by the software but also the controls over the software, such as: frequency of amendments, amendment procedures, access controls and the segregation of duties.

Controls to ensure that proper documentation is kept

(8) Proper documentation aids efficient and accurate operations by users and computer personnel, setting up and amendments to applications, and recovery from disaster. The auditor would consider such matters as: quality of documentation, quality of standards used, enforcement of standards, internal audit involvement and updating procedures.

Controls to ensure continuity of operation

(9) As part of his overall assessment of the enterprise, the auditor might consider the back up procedures, testing of back up facilities and procedures, protection of equipment against fire and other hazards, emergency and disaster recovery procedures, maintenance agreements and insurance.

13.2.10 Application controls

To quote from the Auditing Guideline reproduced in full in Section 13.4, applications controls

'relate to the transactions and standing data appertaining to each computer-based accounting system and are therefore specific to each application. The objectives of application controls, which may be manual or programmed, are to ensure the completion and accuracy of the accounting records and the validity of the entries made therein resulting from both manual and programmed processing.'

Application controls need to cover:

—input;
—processing;
—output;
—files.

(a) Input controls

The definition of application controls emphasize that the objective is to ensure completeness, accuracy and validity, and that these objectives may be achieved by manual or programmed processing.

(1) Completeness
Techniques to ensure completeness:

—batch control totals;
—hash totals;
—xsequence check on pre-numbered documents;
—'one-for-one' checks—checking each input document with a list of items processed (As this is a manual check it is suitable for low volumes only);
—computer matching of input with master file;
—document counts;
—line counts.

Items rejected as inaccurate (see (2) below) need special attention. An important aspect of ensuring completeness is ensuring that all rejected data are resubmitted for processing after correction.

'Re-entry' controls involve clerical work by the control section, who will receive the error report resulting from the edit run. They will review the cause of rejection, make the necessary corrections, possibly after reference back to the user department, and arrange for re-entry of the corrected data in such a way that they are again subject to the same input controls as the original data.

(2) Accuracy
Techniques to ensure accuracy:

—edit checks;
—check digit verification of code numbers: an extra digit or digits is added to a code number so that the number conforms to a predetermined mathematical formula which the computer can check;
—reasonableness checks: the computer confirms that data submitted lie within a predetermined range;
—existence checks: data codes are compared with a file of valid codes;
—dependency checks: frequently one item has a logical relationship with another. The computer can check whether the relationship actually exists;
—format check: the computer can check that data takes the form it should. (For example, a code number might consist of two alphabetic and three numeric characters. The format check will reject any that do not conform to this pattern.)

(3) Validity
Authorization may be evidenced by a stamp or signature, either on individual documents or on batches of documents.

It is possible for transactions to be authorized after processing by reviewing the transaction output, paying particular attention to larger items.

Authorization problems with on-line/real-time systems are dealt with in Section 13.6.

(b) Processing controls

Much of the work described in (a) above for input contributes to the completeness, accuracy and validity of processing.

It is also necessary to consider the controls over computer operator activities. Whilst it is true to say that many operational errors should be detected by subsequent user checks outide of the DP department, operator controls minimize the occurrence of such errors and ensure that the company's records are processed in a proper environment. In addition, they should prevent other errors which could pass undetected by users.

(1) Control and supervision of operator activities
Job assembly procedures (which contain job control statements, parameter cards, run instructions, run dependencies and restart procedures) should be controlled by persons independent of the operating staff. This minimizes the risk of error during the assembly phase, and should be complemented by a review of the computer-log/job-control statements after processing has taken place.

Retrospective control over operator activities should involve a review by

DP management of the computer log which is produced by most operating systems. (This log normally identifies each job processed and each time the various computer files are accessed.) This review confirms not only the accuracy of operator actions, but also the authorization of processing (i.e. it should detect unauthorized jobs). In addition, it should bring to management's attention all abnormal processing errors (e.g. re-runs, hardware failures, etc.), including instances where operators have bypassed automatic software checks. However, review of the computer log is subject to a number of problems, which the auditor must take into account:

—Logs are usually voluminous documents, with the result that DP management may be unable to review them in full. (One solution to this problem is to install software which will summarize machine activities.)
—In many cases, the printing of computer logs is optional or utilizes spooling files, which are in themselves open to amendment. As a result, there is no guarantee that management are in receipt of all logs unless they contain control information which would indicate missing sections (e.g. time details or the sequential numbering of log sheets by the operating system).
—An effective review usually involves a high degree of technical expertise which, in practical terms, may be restricted to operations management or include those personnel which the review is designed to control.

Thus whilst management review of such logs represents an effective control over operations, the effort it requires is such that many installations (particularly smaller ones) do not use it as a prime control.

In many cases, management rely on manual logs created by the operators themselves. Depending on the extent of these records, such logs can provide management with useful information to analyse 'abnormal' events, although they would not necessarily highlight the processing of unauthorized jobs (particularly where these are initiated by the operators themselves).

In larger installations, operations control may be achieved by the physical presence of more than one operator; thus, operators act as a check to prevent errors by other operating staff, and collusion would be required before deliberate manipulation of computer records could be undertaken. Where this form of control is relied upon, it is important to establish whether adequate provision has been made for holidays, shift working, rest periods and staff holidays. The employment or more than one operator also allows management to rotate processing duties so that no single operator is responsible for running the same application from cycle to cycle.

Finally, in assessing this area of control, the auditor should evelute the software routines which can be used to ensure that the correct data files and programs are used in processing.

(2) Use of comprehensive operating instructions
Standard instructions should be used to guide the operators through each job

step and thus minimize the risk of error. As noted above, it is essential that such documentation be kept up-to-date (to reflect all subsequent development work), and reviewed by operations management to ensure its adequacy.

(c) Output controls

It is the control section's job to supervise the despatch of output to users. Manual controls applied by the control section will include:

(1) scrutiny of output before despatch;
(2) ensuring that output only reaches authorized recipients and is securely despatched to them;
(3) clerical checks of output against input (on a test basis), and agreement of input and output control totals.

Programmed controls may be made to test the reasonableness of output by comparisons with predetermined limits.

(d) File controls

(1) File labelling procedures
Software routines should, where possible, verify file (internal) labels to ensure that the most recent version of the file is processed. Conversely, labelling techniques can be used to ensure that files are not accidentally overwritten before their usefulness has expired. Normally this is achieved by the use of retention dates, which warn operators that a file is about to be updated before the retention date has expired.

External labelling of 'portable' file devices (i.e. exchangeable disc packs and tape reels) should be used physically to identify each device and its contents. This minimizes the risk of the operator loading the wrong version of the file.

(2) Off-line storage
Proper storage arrangements (e.g. tape and disc-rack) help to minimize the risk of confusion or loss of file devices. Larger installations may segregate the custody of off-line file devices from the operating staff by creating a separate librarian function. The responsibilities of this function would include:

(a) authorization checks to ensure that files are only issued with the appropriate authorization;

(b) logging of all devices and contents;

(c) procedures to account for all files and to ensure that they are returned after use.

Where a separate librarian function is created, access to the library area should be restricted to authorized personnel only (i.e. the librarian and senior operations management), and provision made to ensure that the library is controlled at all times (e.g. through night-shift operations). Environmental storage conditions (temperature, humidity, etc.) should be suitable for device storage, thereby reducing the possibility of read/write errors and prolonging the usable life of a file device.

(3) Access to programs and data files

Access to programs and data files can be controlled by a number of procedures, many of which have been discussed in earlier sections:

(a) Review of the computer log by DP management acts as a detective control to highlight unauthorized access.

(b) Restricting the access to, and use of, on-line terminals prevents unauthorized personnel from manipulating computer-based information.

(c) Controlling any standard utility programs which the installation may possess, since these programs can be used to copy or edit computer files without leaving any hard-copy evidence (or audit trail). If used fraudulently, such activities may give rise to a breach of company security (there have been several cases of DP staff selling copy master-files to competitors) or to the manipulation of clients' records.

Edit programs are particularly significant since they do not contain the strict controls normally found in specific applications programs and because they do not necessarily give a hard-copy audit trail of the amendments processed. Thus, for example, an audit utility may be used to amend an employee's rate of pay, which may pass undetected by the user section (particularly if control totals, such as a hash total of all rates of pay used, are obtained from control records and not by adding each individual rate of pay held on file). Control over utilities should include a combination of:

—password protection;
—off-line storage of utilities;
—restricting the files which such utilities are allowed to access;
—management review of each occasion on which such utilities are used. (Details thereof will normally be contained within the main computer log, or, in some instances, may be given on logs specific to the utility in question.)

Let us conclude this section on application controls with the relevant section from the draft guideline.

Appendix 1: Application controls

Introduction

(1) Application controls cover the transactions and the standing data used by each application and are, therefore, specific to each application. However, the basic

controls are common to each type of application, and these are discussed below. The objectives of application controls are to ensure the completeness and accuracy of processing (both computer and manual processing) and to ensure the validity of the resulting accounting entries. The specific requirements to achieve this are:

(a) controls over the completeness, accuracy and authorisation of input;

(b) controls over the completeness and accuracy of processing;

(c) controls over the maintenance of master files and the standing data contained therein.

Controls over input

(2) Control techniques for ensuring the completeness of input in a timely fashion include:

(a) manual or programmed agreement of control totals;

(b) one for one checking of processed output to source documents;

(c) manual or programmed sequence checking;

(d) programmed matching of input to a control file, containing details of expected input;

(e) procedures over resubmission of rejected data.

(3) Controls over the accuracy of input are concerned with the data fields on input transactions. Control should be exercised not only over value fields, such as invoice amounts, but also important reference fields, such as account number or date of payment. Some of the completeness control techniques, such as a batch total, will also control accuracy but others, such as sequence checks, will not. Additional techniques to ensure accuracy include:

(a) programmed check digit verification;

(b) programmed reasonableness checks, including checking the logical relationship between two or more files;

(c) programmed existence checks against valid codes;

(d) manual scrutiny of output.

(4) Controls over authorisation involve checking that all transactions are authorised and that the individual who authorised each transaction was so empowered. This will generally involve a clerical review of input transactions, although a programmed check to detect transactions that exceed authorisation limits may be possible. The clerical review should be done either after a control total has been established or after processing to ensure that unauthorised transactions cannot be introduced after the review.

Controls over processing

(5) Controls are required to ensure that:

(a) all input data is processed;

(b) the correct master files and standing data files are used;

(c) the processing of each transaction is accurate;

(*d*) the updating of data, and any new data generated during processing, is accurate and authorised;

(*e*) output reports are complete and accurate.

(6) The control techniques used to ensure the completeness and accuracy of input may also be used to ensure the completeness and accuracy of processing provided the techniques are applied to the results of processing, such as a batch reconciliation produced after the update and not the one produced after the initial edit. Another technique for ensuring the completeness and accuracy of processing is summary processing, such as a depreciation calculation based on total asset value being compared with the sum of depreciation calculations based on individual asset values.

Controls over master files and the standing data contained therein

(7) Techniques for ensuring the completeness, accuracy and authorisation of amendments to master files and standing data files and for ensuring the completeness and accuracy of the processing of these amendments are similar to the techniques for transaction input. However, in view of the greater importance of master files and standing data, there is often sufficient justification for using the more costly control techniques such as one for one checking. It may also be appropriate for users to check all master file and standing data, perhaps on a cyclical basis.

(8) Controls are also required to ensure the continuing correctness of master files and the standing data contained therein. Frequently control techniques such as record counts or hash totals for the file, are established and checked by the user each time the file is used.

13.3 Audit systems review

We discuss computer audit techniques in Section 13.4. The purpose of this section is to deal with the auditor's review of the system of internal control in operation.

The stages of the review are the same as those outlined in earlier chapters for non-computer systems:

—ascertainment;

—recording;

—evaluation.

These three stages may in practice overlap to some extent, but for clarity are considered separately below.

13.3.1   Ascertainment

The following matters need to be covered:

(a) computer hardware in use and its capabilities;

(b) organization of the computer department;

(c) work performed by the computer, including volumes and timing;

(d) details of general and application controls, including systems development controls;

(e) the possibility of file interrogation by the auditor;

(f) controls in force in user departments.

Techniques used for ascertainment will include ICQs, user manuals, study of systems and program specifications, discussion with computer staff, and inspection of documentation.

13.3.2   Recording

Recording the system will involve ICQs, flowcharts and narrative notes.

The information will need to be assembled in a manner which will facilitate an evaluation of the system on the 'key question' principle. Clearly, no hard-and-fast rules can be laid down, but it will normally be convenient to use the outline system flowchart as the principal record of the system, and to supplement this flowchart with the following three main schedules.

(a) Schedule of input types

This can be drawn up in the form of a columnar schedule, and should record, in respect of each type of input document or magnetic file, the following information:

(1) the name and purpose of the document or file;

(2) the source of the file, or the person or department responsible for input document preparation and authorization;

(3) the volume and frequency of transactions;

(4) the principal fields of data used (e.g. in the case of a sales invoice, the sales amount, the VAT amount, the invoice number and the account number);

(5) the primary input program to the system and edit program, if this is a different program;

(6) details of the audit trail (i.e. the report where individual transactions and control totals next appear);

(7) the principal program and user controls over input, including controls over the resubmission of rejections.

It is useful to obtain specimen copies of input documents and details of the record layouts for magnetic files.

(b) Schedule of files

Files may be categorized as either:

(1) *Master files.* These are files which permanently hold data. They may be further subdivided between those which hold *standing data* (e.g. a customer name and address file in a sales ledger system, or a file of employee records in a payroll system); or *balance data*, which is updated at regular intervals (e.g. monthly sales ledger balances, or cumulative totals of sales).
(2) *Transaction files.* These are files which hold data temporarily during processing and which do not therefore retain data beyond the processing cycle (e.g. a sales ledger transaction file which accumulates during a month prior to a monthly update of sales ledger balances, after which it is erased).

The auditor should draw up a schedule, again in columnar form, recording the following details in respect of each file:

—the name and purpose of the file;
—a brief description of its contents;
—file organization, record type and length (i.e. details of the manner in which data are stored on the file);
—record layouts, including header and trailer records, highlighting important fields within each record (e.g. employee gross pay and tax deducted, in a payroll system).

File descriptions are important to the auditor, since by reviewing them, the auditor can identify potential control problems.

(c) Schedule of output reports and files

This schedule should record, in respect of each output report or file, the following information:

(1) the name and a brief description of the output report or file;
(2) the name of the output system;
(3) the frequency and distribution of reports and the frequency and purpose of output files;
(4) the detailed records output and the sequence in which these records appear (e.g. customer code, customer name, sales invoice number and sales invoice amount by customer code);
(5) the totals output (e.g. total sales for each customer, plus grand total) and

the method used for arriving at these totals (e.g. through accumulation or by using trailer records);

(6) details of the audit trail (this will be a record of the data to which either individual transactions or control totals reported can be reconciled and in many cases will provide a direct link with the information contained in the schedule of input types);

(7) the controls exercised by users over output reports.

Again it is useful to obtain example copies of output reports.

The outline system flowchart, together with the three main supporting schedules outlined above, should provide the auditor with the bulk of the information which he or she requires for an evaluation of the system. However, further information may be required in certain cases where the system has special or unique characteristics (e.g. a formula for calculating average stock prices in a stock records system). Organizational controls which are particular to a system (e.g. details of password controls in a terminal-based on-line system) should also be recorded. Such characteristics clearly cannot be categorized, not can standard methods of recording those characteristics be evolved. However, the auditor must be satisfied that his or her notes record adequate details of these special features.

At this stage it is also appropriate to review the flowcharts relating to the work carried out in the user areas, both on input documents prior to submission for processing, and on output reports when they have been received after processing. This will then link with information recorded on the schedules of input types and output reports and to ensure that the general system review and the computer system review interface correctly and that the overall evaluation covers all procedures, whether manual, mechanized or computerized.

13.3.3 Evaluation

Having completed the documentation of the system, the auditor can undertake an evaluation of the internal controls operating within the system.

Usually, this evaluation involves an internal control questionnaire, which should seek to review the following key control areas:

(*a*) the authorization of data;
(*b*) the accuracy of input data;
(*c*) the completeness of input data;
(*d*) the correct maintenance and updating of master-files.

The internal controls which should be present to achieve these control objectives have been discussed in Section 13.2.

The object of the review is to determine the strengths and weaknesses of the general and application controls to enable audit tests to be planned. Methods will include:

—detailed examination of documentation;
—discussions with internal auditors and computer staff;
—observation of operations;
—review of ICQs.

At the conclusion of the review the auditor will be in a position to plan compliance and substantive tests.

13.4   Audit techniques

Computer audit techniques may be divided into 'manual' techniques, in which the computer is not directly involved, and 'computer-assisted audit techniques' (CAATs).

13.4.1   Manual techniques

Tests in this area could include the following.

(a) Authorization controls

(1) Check a sample of input to ensure that it has been authorized by an appropriate official. Where data are entered via on-line terminals, tests should be performed to determine the effectiveness of terminal controls (e.g. dummy passwords, etc.).

(2) Where the system generates transactions or data ensure that these have been subsequently reviewed and authorized.

(b) Controls over completeness and accuracy of processing

(1) Transaction data
—Trace a sample of input to the update and other appropriate reports (and vice versa) for each type of transaction.
—Test check any fundamental calculations performed by the system.
—Agree a sample of batch totals to the reported batch totals. In the case of on-line systems this may involve document totals or daily transaction totals.
—Follow through the actions taken to correct any rejected transactions and ensure that their final treatment is correct.

(2) Standing data

—Check a sample of master-file amendment details from the input forms to the amendment report.

—Reconcile the movements in any significant standing data control totals to the amendements, insertions and deletions processed in the period.

(c) File maintenance

For a selected period, reconcile the movement in control totals over balance data by reference to the input transactions processed in the period. This should be done by reference to any input registers, batch slips or other independent controls over input.

13.4.2 Computer-assisted audit techniques

The main categories of test in this area are the use of test packs and audit software—computer programs devised to examine the contents of the files. These and other CAATs are dealt with in detail below.

(a) Test packs

A test pack consists of selected data which are processed through the client's programs and the output compared with predetermined results. In this way, the auditor can establish that:

(1) the client's programs are functioning correctly (e.g. correct control totals are obtained, or depreciation rates are calculated accurately);
(2) the program controls are functioning as specified, i.e. they react properly to error conditions.

The method of selecting test data may involve preparation of the data by the auditor, which enables him or her to test those program controls he or she wishes to place reliance on. Alternatively, data may be selected from the client's own data, or by a combination of both client and test data.

The comparison of output results involves checking output reports to manual records independently prepared by the auditor.

In general terms, the advantages and disadvantages of using test packs may be defined as follows:

Advantages

(1) They provide an assurance that program checks are functioning properly and therefore can be relied upon.

(2) They can be used on a continuing basis (assuming that the system does not radically change).

(3) Once set up, running costs can be relatively cheap.

(4) It is relatively easy to add on more tests, or vary the testing to include different controls.

Disadvantages

(1) They require a detailed knowledge of how the system works.

(2) They may require special programs to set up computer files or bypass earlier processing steps which do not need to be tested.

(3) Initial set up costs can be expensive.

(4) They may give rise to processing halts, with their attendant effects on the computer department operations.

(5) Processing time will be required to perform a test pack.

The considerations listed above are expressed in general terms, and their real impact will depend on whether auditors use test packs in isolation or whether they integrate the procedure within the client's operational system (known as the integrated test facility or ITF).

Isolated test packs usually involve processing test data through copy files, often using a copy of the operational program itself. The main problem with this approach is that by isolating the test from the production 'environment', auditors cannot be sure that they are testing the operational version of a client's programs. Thus, it is easily possible for the computer department to process the test data using a modified version of the operational program. (To some extent, this assurance can be obtained by requesting copies on a surprise basis, or by comparing the program used to a secure copy of the operational version.)

ITF involves establishing a dummy set of records within the client's operational system/data files, and processing test data alongside actual data. This approach reduces the risk of not testing the operational version of the client's programs, since test and production runs are now combined. It also obviates the need for arranging special computer runs and facilitates testing on an on-going cycle-to-cycle basis. However, extreme care must be taken to isolate the test records within the production files and to adjust the 'operational' output results by the value of the test data. (In general terms, this would involve creating a separate 'unit' within the system, e.g. a division, company, department, etc.) The isolation of test data is perhaps the biggest disadvantage of using ITF, particularly in integrated and other complex systems where a single transaction can have an effect on several aspects of the system.

The procedure for the use of test packs would incorporate the following steps:

(1) Review the system and be sure of what the system does.
(2) Identify program checks and the functions to be tested.
(3) Discuss the operation with the client.
(4) Agree the format of input and output reports.
(5) Prepare the data to be tested.
(6) Manually predict the results of the exercise.
(7) Attend the running of the program.
(8) Evaluate the results.
(9) Summarize the results.

(b) Computer audit programs

Computer audit programs are those used by the auditor to:

—read computer-based files and extract specified information for subsequent audit work (e.g. to select from a disc file all personnel having a gross wage in excess of £300 per week, or to perform random selections);
—carry out audit work on the contents of the files (e.g. to add up balances, or to compare files against each other).

This type of program is often known as an 'enquiry' or 'interrogation' program. Such programs can be written by the auditor, either in any of the programming languages available (this requires a great deal of technical expertise), or using a standard 'information retrieval package'. On occasions, use can be made of interrogation programs already written by the client.

These programs can be used to assist in audit work as follows:

(a) To select representative types of transactions for audit tests; the selection basis will depend on the auditor, but may include, e.g. the use of random-number or stratification techniques.

(b) To scrutinize files and select exceptional items for examination; for example, interrogation of a customer file may be used to select all customers with excessive discount rates.

(c) To compare two files and select normal or exceptional changes.

(d) To stratify data as an aid to its investigation.

(e) To carry out certain detailed tests and calculations, thereby simulating client reports, for example, checking the arithmetic accuracy and principles of the client's stock obsolescence provision.

Advantages
(a) They can be used to examine data faster and more accurately than clerical audit tests.

(*b*) They may provide the only practical method for scrutinizing large amounts of data.

(*c*) They can continue to be used until the file layouts are changed.

(*d*) They can be made flexible by leaving the parameters (e.g. the amount above which all balances are to be printed out) to be set each time the program is used.

(*e*) Once set-up, the 'running' costs from year to year are relatively low, and offer considerable overall time-savings.

Disadvantages

(*a*) Technical skill and expense are required to develop a program which works. In particular, it is essential that adequate testing of such program is performed, since errors may have a material impact on the audit procedures used and the conclusions drawn.

(*b*) Greater knowledge of the system is required than for conventional audit tests. (Needed by the auditor in any case!)

(*c*) The program needs to be changed to take account of any system amendments.

(*d*) Difficulties may be experienced in obtaining adequate computer time for testing. An alternative to using the client's installation is to arrange for machine time at an independent computer bureau, in which case, arrangements will have to be made with the client to procure copies of the files to be interrogated.

As with test packs, the benefits and drawbacks listed above are expressed in general terms, and their real impact will depend on how computer audit programs are used by the auditor. Again a division can be made between audit software which is used in 'isolation' and that which is used as an integral part of the client's system (known as systems control audit review file or SCARF).

Where the computer audit programs are run in isolation, i.e. on a 'once-off' per year basis, auditors will be dependent for their results on the data files supplied by the computer department. Therefore, they are at risk that these files are modified in some way before copies are made available for their purposes. To minimize this risk, they may request files on a 'surprise' basis, and should build into their own software sufficient control totals which enable them to agree to the client's own output reports. For example, when performing selection routines over a sales ledger file, the audit software should accumulate the total number of accounts and the total value of balances held on file; clearly any disagreement between these and the corresponding client totals should alert the auditors to further investigation.

The SCARF technique involves integrating an audit program within an operational system, so that each transaction processed through that system is analyzed by the audit software and, where it satisfies certain parameters, is captured for subsequent audit review. (Note that the transaction is not otherwise affected and will continue to be processed through the system in the normal fashion.) The main advantage of this approach is that it can be used to review all transactions through the system during the audit period, and not simply those which are outstanding at the time when an 'isolated' audit program is run. As such, it also minimizes the auditors' dependence on the computer department for the files which they wish to interrogate. Against this, the resident audit software risks manipulation by the client's own computer department, with the result that the auditors should employ additional procedures (such as program code comparison) to guarantee their audit objective.

The main problem with special complete audit programs is that a suitable period of time has to be allowed for program testing before a working version is developed and the required output produced. This observation, however, is not necessarily applicable to all specially written programs, especially those written in a very simple language, e.g. RPG II. With such programs, it is quite possible to write a simple interrogation and totalling program that will work and give correct results at the first attempt.

However, to combat this difficulty generalized audit packages are much more widely used in the complex type of file interrogation and system duplication exercises where a great deal of information in a standard format is required. The criteria for such model audit packages are as follows:

(*a*) the ability to access any files, however organized and on whatever device from any computer;

(*b*) the ability to handle any form of data manipulation; this should include:

Arithmetic
Summarization and calculation
Logical
Selection
Error detection
Comparison
Categorization
Stratification and analysis
Sampling
Statistical routines
Sorting

(*c*) the availability of flexible output data with control reports and data reports in flexible format;

(*d*) the facility for production of other files for future reference or interface with the client's systems;

(*e*) it should be easy to use and run, and also be economical;

(*f*) the demands for computer time and assistance from client's staff should be minimal;

(*g*) the package should be reliable.

To summarize the main advantages of such a package, it can theoretically be used, with only minor alterations, at different installations and on different applications, accessing different types of files. In practice, however, this is not always the case, as packages are not always as adaptable as their creators claim. The final choice between the use of a special program or a generalized package will depend to a large extent upon the machine in use and the type of files to be interrogated.

(c) Other techniques

Appendix 4 to the draft Auditing Guideline, listing other techniques for computer auditing, is reproduced below.

Introduction

(1) Various other CAATs are in less frequent use than audit software, and test data. Generally, they have been developed for purposes other than audit and require considerable data processing expertise. The CAATs listed in the following paragraphs should not be regarded as a complete list as new techniques continue to be developed. In all cases it will be necessary properly to plan, control and record the use of the techniques when they are carried out, and to consider the degree of independence achieved.

Embedded audit facilities

(2) Embedded audit facilities consist of program code or additional data provided by the auditor, and incorporated into the computer element of the enterprise's accounting system.

(3) Program code designed to perform audit functions is incorporated into the computer-based accounting system at points determined by the auditor who also controls its detailed working. Audit software is often required to extract the output from the embedded facilities for subsequent manual work.

(4) Embedded facilities may be used during both compliance and substantive tests, although their main use has been in the compliance testing of application controls. By using embedded facilities the auditor may examine a large volume of data without incurring the cost of processing these transactions separately.

(5) During compliance testing the auditor may, for example, re-perform validation checks to assist in obtaining reasonable assurance that the controls over the accuracy of input data are functioning properly. As the tests are being performed concurrently with production programs, any failures of controls will be detected promptly.

(6) Any analytical review may be performed using embedded facilities at the same time as the enterprise's figures are being computed. For example, the auditor may prepare his own profile of payroll payments whilst the detailed data is still available.

(7) The extended records technique involves the inclusion within the enterprise's

accounting system of data for the auditor's use. This may involve adding a history portion to a record in order to provide evidence of transaction up-dates or it may involve the addition of data directly by the auditor, such as the results of the auditor's attendance at physical stocktaking.

Systems software data analysis
(8) Systems software data analysis involves the examination of data concerning computer operations from the records maintained by systems software. Most systems software, including operating systems and data base management systems provide facilities for logging information relating to computer activity. The examination of this data incorporates both the logging process and the analysis of that data, often using audit software.

(9) Systems software data analysis is generally used during the compliance testing of general controls. For example, many operating systems will write to a history file details of attempts to gain unauthorised access to data files and the identification of users who have submitted invalid passwords may be provided.

Application program examination
(10) Application program examination comprises an examination of program code within the enterprise's computer based accounting system. It involves examination either by the computer, or on a manual basis, of selected code within the application software.

(11) Application program examination is sometimes used during compliance testing of application controls. By examining application program code the auditor may gather evidence to ascertain that certain programmed routines are correctly implemented. For example, the program code performing a complex discount calculation may be examined to ensure that discounts are properly computed by the program examined.

(12) The auditor may also choose to examine application programs during compliance testing of general controls. For example, in testing the controls that ensure that all program changes are adequately tested and documented, he may use software to compare two versions of the program in the production library before and after the changes and check them against the program change documentation.

Tracing
(13) Tracing is an extension of application program examination where the auditor uses computer software to trace the program instructions executed during the processing of a specified transaction. Tracing software may be provided within some compilers or by specialised tracing software packages.

(14) Tracing may be used during compliance testing of application controls. Specific transactions may be traced through an application, for example, to provide evidence of the working of a programmed control. During the compliance testing of general contols, tracing may assist in the testing or program testing procedures.

Flowcharting
(15) Flowcharting software produces a diagrammatic representation of the code

from a source program. This assists in examining the program logic to identify control points and assess the impact of system changes.

(16) When recording a computer-based accounting system, a computer-produced flowchart may provide part of the necessary documentation. Whilst compliance testing general controls, it may assist during an examination of program code to ensure that installation standards have been applied.

Mapping
(17) Mapping uses specialist software to monitor the execution of program instructions. Analysis of this data may provide details of program logic not executed and therefore help to detect possible unauthorised program execution.

13.4.3 The Auditing Guideline—Auditing in a computer environment

We conclude this Section with the 1984 Auditing Guideline—

Preface
This Guideline describes how the principles of an external audit should apply in a computer environment, including that relating to smaller computers.

Auditors unaccustomed to auditing in a computer environment are advised to obtain detailed practical guidance on the particular processing situations which they might meet and on the techniques which they might have to employ. Such auditors are also advised to use the detailed guidance available through their Accountancy Body and to attend appropriate training courses.

Introduction

(1) Auditing Standards prescribe the basic principles and practices to be followed in the conduct of an audit. 'The auditor's operational standard' and the Guidelines on planning, controlling and recording, accounting systems, audit evidence, internal controls and review of financial statements apply irrespective of the system of recording and processing transactions. However, computer systems do record and process transactions in a manner which is significantly different from manual systems, giving rise to such possibilities as a lack of visible evidence and systematic errors. As a result, when auditing in a computer environment, the auditor will need to take into account additional considerations relating to the techniques available to him, the timing of his work, the form in which the accounting records are maintained, the internal controls which exist, the availability of the data and the length of time it is retained in readily useable form, as further described below.

(2) Computers have a wide range of capabilities and changes continue to be made as a result of new technology. With the introduction of smaller computers, there is a greater likelihood of weak internal controls. This will normally lead to greater emphasis being placed on substantive testing of transactions and balances, and on

other procedures such as analytical review, rather than on compliance testing. Furthermore, where smaller volumes of transactions are processed, substantive testing may in the circumstances be the more efficient method of obtaining audit evidence.

Background

(3) Audits are performed in a computer environment wherever computer-based accounting systems, large or small, are operated by an enterprise, or by a third party on behalf of the enterprise, for the purpose of processing information supporting the amounts included in the financial statements.

(4) The nature of computer-based accounting systems is such that the auditor is afforded opportunities to use either the enterprise's or another computer to assist him in the performance of his audit work. Techniques performed with computers in this way are known as Computer-Assisted Audit Techniques ('CAATs') of which the following are the major categories:

(a) use of 'audit software'—computer programs used for audit purposes to examine the contents of the enterprise's computer files;
(b) use of 'test data'—data used by the auditor for computer processing to test the operation of the enterprise's computer programs.

(5) Where there is a computer-based accounting system, many of the auditor's procedures may still be carried out manually. For instance, the ascertainment of the accounting system and assessment of its adequacy will normally be performed manually, and in appropriate circumstances the auditor may also decide to select manual audit techniques.

Knowledge and skills

(6) When auditing in a computer environment, the auditor should obtain a basic understanding of the fundamentals of data processing and a level of technical computer knowledge and skills which, depending on the circumstances, may need to be extensive. This is because the auditor's knowledge and skills need to be appropriate to the environment in which he is auditing, and because ethical statements indicate that he should not undertake or continue professional work which he is not himself competent to perform unless he obtains such advice and assistance as will enable him competently to carry out his task.

Planning, controlling and recording

(7) Paragraph 2 of 'The auditor's operational standard' states that 'the auditor should adequately plan, control and record his work'. The principles relating to planning, controlling and recording are the same in a computer environment as in

other circumstances, but there are additional considerations that need to be taken into account.

Planning

(8) In order to plan and carry out an audit in a computer environment, the auditor will need an appropriate level of technical knowledge and skill. As part of his additional planning considerations, he should decide at an early stage what effect the system itself, and the way it is operated, will have on the timing of and the manner in which he will need to perform and record his work. In this respect, he may have had the opportunity to consider these matters during the development and implementation of the system.

(9) The auditor should also consider the use of CAATs, as this may have a significant effect on the nature, extent and timing of his audit tests. As indicated in paragraph 10 below, in certain circumstances the auditor will need to use CAATs in order to obtain the evidence he requires, whereas in other circumstances he may use CAATs to improve the efficiency or effectiveness of his audit. For example, the availability of audit software may mean that substantive tests can be performed more economically or quickly than substantive tests performed manually, which may persuade him to place less reliance on internal controls and to reduce his compliance testing accordingly.

(10) In choosing the appropriate combinations of CAATs and manual procedures, the auditor will need inter alia to take the following into account:

(*a*) Computer programs often perform functions of which no visible evidence is available. In these circumstances it will frequently not be practicable for the auditor to perform tests manually.

(*b*) In many audit situations the auditor will have the choice of performing a test either manually or with the assistance of a CAAT. In making this choice, he will be influenced by the respective efficiency of the alternatives, taking into account: (i) the extent of compliance or substantive testing achieved by both alternatives; (ii) the pattern of cost associated with the CAAT; (iii) the ability to incorporate within the use of the CAAT a number of different audit tests.

(*c*) In some cases, the auditor will need to report within a comparatively short time-scale. In such cases it may be more efficient to use CAATs because they are quicker to apply, even though manual methods are practicable and may cost less.

(*d*) There is a need before using a CAAT to ensure that the required computer facilities, computer files and programs are available. Furthermore, given that enterprises do not retain copies of computer files and programs for an indefinite period, the auditor should plan the use of any CAAT in good time so that these copies are retained for his use.

(*e*) The operation of some CAATs requires frequent attendance or access by the auditor. The auditor may be able to reduce the level of his tests by taking account of CAATs performed by the internal auditors, but the extent to which he can do this in any given situation will depend, amongst other things, on his assessment of the effectiveness and relevance of the internal audit function.

(*f*) Where the enterprise's accounting records include computer data, the auditor will need to have access to that data. Further, where the auditor wishes to perform a

CAAT, it is often necessary for the enterprise to make computer facilities available to the auditor to enable him to discharge his responsibilities.

Controlling

(11) Whether or not the audit is being carried out in a computer environment, audit procedures should always be controlled to ensure that the work has been performed in a constant manner. Where CAATs are used, however, particular attention should be paid to:

(a) the need to co-ordinate the work of staff with specialist computer skills with the work of others engaged on the audit;

(b) the approval and review of the technical work by someone with the necessary computer expertise.

(12) It is acceptable for an auditor to use a CAAT on copies of computer records or programs, provided he has taken steps to gain reasonable assurance that the copies are identical to the originals.

Recording

(13) The standard of the audit working papers relating to computer-based accounting systems, and the retention procedures in respect of them, should be the same as those adopted in relation to other aspects of the audit. Where the technical papers differ materially from the other working papers, for instance where they consist of computer output or magnetic media, it may be convenient to keep these separate from the other working papers.

(14) Where a CAAT is used, it is appropriate that the working papers indicate the work performed by the CAAT, the results of the CAAT, the auditor's conclusions, the manner in which any technical problems were resolved and may include any recommendations about the modification of the CAAT for future audits.

Accounting systems

(15) Paragraph 3 of 'The auditor's operational standard' states that 'the auditor should ascertain the enterprise's system of recording and processing transactions and assess its adequacy as a basis for the preparation of financial statements'. The principles relating to this are the same in a computer environment, but it should be borne in mind that many computer-based accounting systems are specified in far greater detail than non-computer-based accounting systems. In assessing the adequacy of the accounting system as a basis for the preparation of financial statements, the auditor is likely to receive a more detailed record of the enterprise's system than would otherwise be the case.

Audit evidence

(16) Paragraph 4 of 'The auditor's operational standard' states that 'the auditor should obtain relevant and reliable audit evidence sufficient to enable him to draw reasonable conclusions therefrom'. The principles relating to the obtaining of audit

evidence do not change because the audit is being carried out in a computer environment.

(17) However, the availability of computer facilities results in opportunities for auditors to use computers. CAATs may be used at various stages of an audit to obtain audit evidence. For instance where the auditor chooses to place reliance on internal controls, he may use a CAAT to assist in the performance of compliance tests. Furthermore, he may also use CAATs to perform substantive tests, including analytical review procedures.

Internal controls

(18) Paragraph 5 of 'The auditor's operational standard' states that 'if the auditor wishes to place reliance on any internal controls, he should ascertain and evaluate those controls and perform compliance tests on their operation'. The principles relating to internal controls are the same in a computer environment as in any other environment, but there are additional considerations which are discussed in paragraphs 19 to 24 below.

(19) Internal controls over computer-based accounting systems may conveniently be considered under the following two main headings:

(a) Application controls. These relate to the transactions and standing data appertaining to each computer-based accounting system and are therefore specific to each such application. The objectives of application controls, which may be manual or programmed, are to ensure the completeness and accuracy of the accounting records and the validity of the entries made therein resulting from both manual and programmed processing.

(b) General controls. Controls, other than application controls, which relate to the environment within which computer-based accounting systems are developed, maintained and operated, and which are therefore applicable to all the applications. The objectives of general controls are to ensure the proper development and implementation of applications, and the integrity of program and data files, and of computer operations. Like application controls, general controls may be either manual or programmed.

(20) Application controls and general controls are inter-related. Strong general controls contribute to the assurance which may be obtained by an auditor in relation to application controls. On the other hand, unsatisfactory general controls may undermine strong application controls or exacerbate unsatisfactory application controls.

(21) As with controls in other circumstances, the evaluation of application controls and general controls will be assisted by the use of documentation designed to help identify the controls on which the auditor may wish to place reliance. Such documentation can take a variety of forms but might consist of questions asking whether there are controls in a system which meet specified overall control objectives, or which prevent or detect the occurrence of specified errors or omissions. For application controls, an integrated set of internal control questions may be used covering controls over both the manual part and the programmed part of the application, and the impact of relevant general controls.

(22) Where preliminary evaluation of the application controls and general controls discloses the absence of, or uncompensated weaknesses in, controls, and therefore the auditor cannot rely on the controls, he should move directly to substantive tests which may be assisted by the use of CAATs.

(23) However, where preliminary evaluation reveals application controls or general controls which may meet the auditor's objectives, he should design and carry out compliance tests if he wishes to rely on those controls. In determining whether he wishes to place reliance on application controls or general controls, the auditor will be influenced by the cost effectiveness and ease of testing and by the following matters:

(a) Where application controls are entirely manual the auditor may decide to perform compliance tests in respect of the application controls only, rather than to place any reliance on general controls. However, before he can place reliance on application controls which involve computer programs, the auditor needs to obtain reasonable assurance that the programs have operated properly, by evaluating and testing the effect of relevant general controls or by other tests on specific parts of the programs.

(b) Sometimes a programmed accounting procedure may not be subject to effective application controls. In such circumstances, in order to put himself in a position to limit the extent of his substantive testing, the auditor may choose to perform his compliance tests by testing the relevant general controls either manually or by using CAATs, to gain assurance of the continued and proper operation of the programmed accounting procedure. Where as a result of his compliance tests the auditor decides he cannot place reliance on the controls, he should move directly to substantive tests.

(c) As indicated in paragraph 1, there is in a computer environment the possibility of systematic errors. This may take place because of program faults or hardware malfunction in computer operations. However, many such potential recurrent errors should be prevented or detected by general controls over the development and implementation of applications, the integrity of the program and data files, and of computer operations. As a result, the controls which the auditor may evaluate and test may include general controls.

(d) On the other hand, the extent to which the auditor can rely on general controls may be limited because many of these controls might not be evidenced, or because they could have been performed inconsistently. In such circumstances, which are particularly common where small computers are involved , if he wishes to limit his substantive tests, the auditor may obtain assurance from compliance tests on manual application controls or by tests on specific parts of the programs.

(24) In performing compliance tests on application or general controls, the auditor should obtain evidence which is relevant to the control being tested. Procedures the auditor may consider include observing the control in operation, examining documentary evidence of its operation, or performing it again himself. In the case of programmed application controls, the auditor may test specific parts of the programs, or re-perform them, by taking advantage of CAATs. He may also obtain evidence by testing relevant general controls.

Review of financial statements

(25) Paragraph 6 of 'The auditor's operational standard' states 'the auditor should

carry out such a review of the financial statements as is sufficient, in conjunction with the conclusions drawn from the other audit evidence obtained, to give him a reasonable basis for his opinion on the financial statements'. CAATs (particularly audit software) may be of assistance to auditors in carrying out certain aspects of this work.

Third party service organisations

(26) Where enterprises use a third party service organisation such as a computer service bureau or a software house for the purpose of maintaining part or all of their accounting records and procedures, the auditor still has a responsibility to follow 'The auditor's operational standard'. However, the auditor may encounter practical obstacles, as the enterprise may be placing some reliance on the proper operation of internal controls exercised by the third party. Consequently, where the auditor finds it impracticable to obtain all the information and explanations that he requires from the enterprise itself (because the enterprise may not be maintaining sufficient controls to minimise that reliance) he should perform other procedures. These may include taking the steps he considers necessary to enable him to rely on the work performed by other auditors or carrying out procedures at the premises of the third party.

13.5   Problems in auditing small computers

13.5.1   Introduction

As its name suggests, a small business computer (or 'mini', or 'micro') is a computer which is used to process comparatively low volumes of data using relatively straightforward business applications. However, it is difficult to provide an exact technical definition since there is no broad agreement within the computer industry as to what is a 'mini' or 'micro', and because technological advances have blurred the distinction between 'minis' and mainframes in terms of memory size, access speeds, complexity of operation, and costs. It is perhaps more meaningful to discuss the characteristics of housing, software and staffing which generally apply to this type of machine and which have a direct impact on the audit approach thereto.

   Whilst the following is aimed primarily at 'stand-alone' small business installations with little or no in-house DP expertise, it must be emphasized that minicomputers are used in many different business applications. Thus, they can be installed as front-end processors to a large mainframe computer or as part of a distributed network of computers servicing user requirements for separate geographical locations while maintaining accounting information for the business as a whole. In these cases, it is probable that the computer function will be supported by in-house DP expertise, although it remains commonplace to use outside software houses for system development work.

Where in-house DP expertise is used, the controls over computer departments are similar to those in the section of installation controls.

13.5.2 Housing

The environmental requirements are probably the most tangible difference between 'minis' and mainframe. Typically, minicomputers are located in the accounts department or in the general office of a company; mainframes, however, are nearly always sited in separate offices. Mainframes also require special housing considerations which do not apply to minicomputers. Indeed, one of the great 'plus' factors of minicomputers is that the cost of installation, in terms of these special considerations, is almost nil, although in practical terms some means of controlling the operating environment (e.g. elementary air-conditioning units) should be established.

13.5.3 Software

All system and program development is normally undertaken by third-party software houses, who usually offer standard packages to satisfy customer requirements. Where the package does not meet these requirements, it is usual for the software house to amend the 'standard' package or, in extreme cases, to write bespoke software for the client. In any event, in-house software development is unusual in the 'mini' environment.

System software may offer fewer control procedures than mainframes, e.g. label checking. This is particularly true of some of the new low-cost microprocessors which were initially developed in a non-commercial environment.

13.5.4 Staffing

Mainframes are serviced by specialist staff employed by the company and usually grouped within a distinct department, i.e. the DP department. These specialists include operators, systems analysts and programmers, whose jobs and responsibilities do not extend outside the department. Minicomputers, however, are staffed by a minimum number of in-house personnel, mainly involved in operating the machine on a day-to-day basis. Such personnel may also perform bookkeeping functions, and usually receive only a limited amount of DP training.

13.5.5   The audit impact of small business machines

Given that the main audit objective is not affected by the introduction of computerized systems, the auditor need have regard only to the procedures used to satisfy his or her audit opinion. In general terms, the approach adopted should be similar to that used in the audit of mainframe installations, described above. However, small business installations have their own unique problems which are inherent in the characteristics of such machines, and which must be taken into account by the auditor during his evaluation of internal control.

The major problems which the auditor will be faced with are in the area of installation controls.

(a) Lack of an effective segregation of duties

This is a fundamental problem in most small business installations, and arises not only out of the small number of DP staff employed but also from the integration of the DP functions within a larger unit, usually the accounts department. Specifically, problems may arise in terms of:

(1) The DP 'department' may be the responsibility of the chief accountant, who is also responsible for the authorization and custody of assets.

(2) There is no segregation between the functions of operations and control. Typically, the same clerk may be responsible for creating input documentation, operating the machine and controlling output results. Note, however, that one 'plus' factor of this type of installation is that the level of DP knowledge within the user business is usually so restricted that the company itself cannot undertake program amendments. As such, there may be an effective segregation of duties between the development and operating/control disciplines.

(b) Lack of control over software development and maintenance

Inexperience and the lack of DP knowledge within senior management often leads to inadequate control over project development and maintenance. Specifically, this problem can give rise to:

(1) *Inadequate definition of system objectives*, including feasibility studies of cost effectiveness, system design and future growth capacities. As a result, the system may not correspond with user requirements, and indeed may not represent the 'optimum' solution to the problem. Additionally, system constraints (including maximum storage capacities and data entry times) must be assessed fully when selecting the appropriate systems, to avoid premature amendments/enhancements, in themselves often extremely expensive.

To overcome these problems, management must be fully involved in development work and ensure that all factors are identified and taken into account before selection is finalized. This, in turn, may involve the use of independent consultants, including early personal participation of the auditor. Additionally, management must ensure that it alone has the authority to approve systems before implementation is undertaken and the project completed.

(2) *Development being usually undertaken wholly by an outside software house*, which tends to reduce management's ability to control timetables (and often costs) and assess the adequacy of amendment procedures. As a result, projects can experience considerable delays, and implementation may occur without adequate testing of the final design (thus allowing program errors to pass undetected until after the system is operational).

To resolve this problem, management must define a timetable and insist on regular project meetings to review progress to date. Where possible, fixed-price contracts should be negotiated to prevent the 'blank cheque' problem. Responsibilities must be defined exactly, so that each party (and member of staff) knows what is expected. It is also essential that their own staff be involved in system testing and that provision is made, where appropriate, for file conversion and a period of parallel running. It is worth noting that the general tendency is to minimize user involvement (particularly in system testing) and to avoid parallel runs on the basis that client staff cannot be spared from their operational duties within the business.

(3) *Program maintenance difficulties*, since this is again outside management's direct control, unless provision is made for maintenance support. To this end, management must ensure that a support contract is established with the software house responsible for system design. Whilst such contracts should guarantee support facilities, they are subject to:

—The financial viability of the software house. Clearly, support will not be guaranteed if the software house ceases to trade, and, to this end, management should build into the contract provisions which clarify ownership of, or rights to, the underlying system and programming documentation (including source code listings).
—Unless amendments are undertaken by the software house or its recognized agent, there is also a danger that the support service will be nullified; i.e. where an amendment is undertaken by, for example, the chief accountant (who may have an elementary knowledge of the programming language used), the software house may disclaim responsibility for support should a subsequent software error arise.

Finally, support arrangements should extend to all aspects of software, i.e. both applications and operating system.

(4) *Inadequacies of system and programming documentation* (including

amendment procedures), since it is usually 'transparent' to management's main objectives, i.e. it often appears to have no immediate impact on the operation of the system. However, good documentation is essential for orderly development and maintenance and helps to reduce the otherwise total reliance which is placed on the software house. Thus, management should ensure that such documentation is kept up to date and is accurate, either by relying on their own review or, where appropriate, by using independent consultants/auditors.

(5) *Inadequacies of procedures to control program amendments*, and therefore to ensure the integrity of operational programs, in view of a lack of management control over the operation of the computer, and, in many cases, inadequate restrictions preventing access to the computer and to source program codes. This weakness is also compounded by the relative ease which some of the more popular languages (e.g. BASIC) can be learnt, and made available on the machine.

To overcome this problem, a number of controls can be introduced, including:

—password control to restrict use of the computer;
—restricting access to programs, either through further password control or by removing the compiler off-line. (Note that interpretative languages, which maintain programs in source code and interpret them during execution time, do not use compilers, and so this control does not apply);
—removal of source-code off-line. (Many packages are only supplied with object code, which is difficult to change and so helps to prevent unauthorized amendments);
—storage of programs in 'read-only memory' (ROM), which prevents any amendments to the programs stored therein. In these cases, amendments are undertaken by physically replacing the ROM unit (e.g. a chip) with one containing the amended program versions.

Other techniques for detecting unauthorized program amendments (for example, software to compare two versions of the same program) are not common to the small business machine. However, the most significant control to prevent unauthorized amendments is perhaps the system of user procedures which independently verify the results of each processing run.

13.5.6 Lack of control over the operation of the computer

Many of the traditional procedures which can be used to control the operation of mainframe installations are not feasible (or indeed practicable) in the small business organization. Specifically:

(*a*) computer logs may not be produced, with the result that management cannot review machine activities or determine whether essential operations (e.g. back-up procedures) have been completed successfully.

(*b*) to resolve this problem, management should establish a system of manual recording for all salient machine activities and recognize the (emphasized) importance of other procedures such as password controls.

(*c*) there may be inadequate control to prevent unauthorized use of the computer. Specifically:

(1) the computer and its terminals may not be located in a protected area.

(2) to overcome this problem, management should consider the use of physical on/off key devices attached to the computer itself and ensure that it is standard procedure to log-off terminals when not in use. File devices should be stored in secure areas (e.g. safes) when not in use. Where possible, the machine should be located in a lockable room, or, as a minimum, not sited in areas which experience large volumes of pedestrian traffic.

(3) standard software routines may not be sufficient to restrict access to sensitive programs and utilities (particularly edit routines).

Management must consider security routines during machine selection and determine whether these could be enhanced, where necessary, by password controls within specific application programs. Utilities may be subject to similar password routines or controlled by off-line storage procedures.

(*d*) documentation for all operating and data entry routines may not be comprehensive nor supported by adequate staff training. As a result, operators may not understand the significance of processing errors, nor handle error situations correctly.

Management must ensure that such documentation is available before acceptance of the system, and that adequate provision is made with the software house for user understanding training. Note that it is essential to establish back-up personnel for the DP supervisor and operators to cover in the event of sickness, holidays, etc.

13.5.7 Lack of control over computer data files

Standard software routines may not perform internal label checking, nor verify the reading or writing of data files through control (e.g. trailer) records. Additionally, the standard of program checks built into each 'standard' package varies considerably. As a result, incorrect files could be used in processing or errors may occur in handling input data and master-file records.

To resolve these problems, management should:

(*a*) recognize the importance of software controls during the selection process and insist that internal label checking and other controls are performed within the machine to minimize operator error;

(b) where the level of software controls is poor, greater reliance is placed on external labelling procedures, which must, therefore, be sufficient to clearly identify each 'portable' file device used in the installation. Where appropriate, logs should be used to monitor the contents of each device;

(c) enforce a system of independent user controls, to monitor the accuracy of each processing run.

13.5.8 Physical control over the computer facilities

Although the scale of operations is usually smaller in a minicomputer installation than in a traditional mainframe, many of the physical controls over the computer environment are no less important. Specifically:

(a) measures should be taken to protect the machine from unauthorized personnel.

(b) the environment of the computer area should be controlled to avoid extremes of temperature.

(c) security copies of data files and programs must be taken on a regular basis and stored in locations which are remote from the machine area. In this respect, software houses tend to act as a good back-up for system and application software, since they normally retain their own copies; however, special arrangements may be required if amendments have been undertaken which are unique to the business.

(d) hardware maintenance contracts should be established to facilitate recovery from machine failure.

(e) insurance cover should be arranged to minimize the cost of the business should its computer systems be disrupted for any reason.

In principle, there is no difference in the audit approach to small business systems *vis à vis* those run on mainframe installations. Thus, the auditor will seek to determine a system of internal control which will verify:

(a) the authorization of data;
(b) the accuracy of input data;
(c) the completeness of input data;
(d) the correct maintenance and updating of master-files.

However, the general tendency is for the author to place less reliance on the program controls within small business systems since the level of control over the computer is, in general terms, likely to be less effective. (Thus, for example, the auditor may not be able to rely on file maintenance controls, because software routines do not perform internal label checks.)

As is the case with installation controls, the fundamental problem of small business systems is the lack of an effective segregation of duties. Where this cannot be improved without an impractical increase in the number of staff employed by the client, the auditor must determine the degree to which management supervize and control output data.

On a practical level, the auditor may find that the necessary technical information is not available from the client. Therefore, it will be necessary to visit the software house responsible for the particular application, although many software houses are unwilling to divulge this information. In such cases, auditors should inform management that they are unable to obtain the necessary information, and request that management attempt to do so directly. Alternatively, they may choose to rely on their evaluation of the manual control procedures (to the exclusion of any computer-based controls), or, where these are insufficient, to abandon a systems-based approach to their audit and concentrate on substantive testing of the items shown in the client's account.

To summarize the main points which emerge from the above, it is essential that management be involved in all aspects of computer development, and control of subsequent operation. During the selection and development phases in particular, they may need to consult independent DP specialists including the auditor, who can provide valuable assistance in evaluating the standard of software controls. The fundamental weakness of any small installation is the lack of an effective segregation of duties which tends to weaken control over computer operations. Where this factor is combined with inadequate software controls within the machine, the auditor will normally place less reliance on installation procedures, and switch his attention to the independent system of user control and management review of the 'end result'. Should this area also prove inadequate, the auditor may need to abandon the system-based approach, and concentrate his effort on substantive testing of the client's assets and liabilities.

13.6 On-line/real-time systems

The diagram on the next page illustrates the differences between the various methods of processing.

The characteristics of on-line and real-time are that input devices (terminals) are continuously connected to the central processor, and transactions are updated as they occur. In an on-line system without real-time processing, transactions are batched at the central computer and the files updated later. In a real-time system, the central files are updated simultaneously with the keying of the details of the transaction at the terminal.

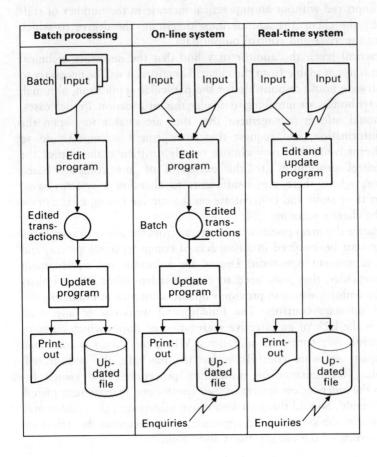

Batch processing	On-line system	Real-time system

Problems for the auditor of such systems are:

(a) loss of the audit trail;
(b) the danger of unauthorized input;
(c) the danger of unauthorized access to files via terminals.

The internal control procedures which will reduce these dangers have already been outlined in Section 13.2, and Subsection 13.2.4(b) is particularly relevant.

It is essential for the auditor to be involved at the system design stage so that necessary audit features can be incorporated in the system. For example, establishing embedded audit facilities (see Draft Guideline Appendix 4 reproduced in Section 13.4.2(c) can really only be done at this early stage.

13.7 Computer bureaux

The same audit principles and procedures should be applied by the auditor where the client uses a computer service bureau (rather than an in-house computer). Thus, where the auditor seeks to place reliance on computer-based controls, he or she must review the installation and system controls operating both within the bureau and at his or her client's.

Before discussing the audit points which are unique to bureaux organizations, it is important to remember that the auditor has no direct relationship with the bureau itself. As a result, it may be difficult to gain access to the bureau and evaluate their control procedures. Where access is refused, the auditor may have recourse to third-party audit reports, since the bureau may have other customers using the same system or, indeed, may have been reviewed by its own auditors. Failing this, the auditor must rely on a review of the client's own control procedures, and where these are ineffective, resort to substantive test procedures. In any event, where the auditor is unable to review the bureau controls, he or she should report to management to this effect, and consider the audit implications of those areas which it has not been possible to review.

An evaluation of installation controls within a bureau should cover the principal areas of operations, system development and maintenance, safeguarding the client records and ensuring the continued existence of DP facilities. Additional points to which the auditor should have regard include:

(a) *Financial stability of the bureau.* Clearly, DP facilities will be disrupted should the bureau cease to trade. The auditor should therefore research the financial stability of the bureau and determine whether the client has made arrangements for alternative facilities (including manual systems).

(b) *Protection of client files.* The nature of any bureau is such that the accounting records for a number of clients are held within the same organization. It is therefore essential that there are controls to ensure that the client's data are adequately separated from data for other bureau customers, and properly protected. Such controls will include:

—software procedures, such as client codes to identify the client's files. (Where the client is linked to the bureau by on-line terminals, controls should be implemented to control the use thereof);
—physical measures to protect confidentiality of data (for example, storage of data in protected areas not accessible by unauthorized peronnel or visitors to the bureau).

(c) *Physical movement of data.* It is often appropriate to retain a copy on microfilm of documents sent to the bureau.

(d) *Contractual relationship.* A formal contract between the client and bureau is essential to define the respective responsibilities and liabilities of the two parties. *Inter alia* the contract should stipulate:

(1) Liability of the bureau for any loss incurred by the user as a result of processing errors or disclosure of confidential information within the bureau (Current practice, however, tends to minimize the bureau's responsibility in this respect);
(2) Processing schedules and charges;
(3) Ownership of data files and file devices. Note that where these belong to the bureau, the user may incur heavy file set-up costs should he choose another form of computerization at a later date

(*e*) *Segregation of duties.* The tendency of a bureau operation is to establish an effective segregation of duties between the user departments (i.e. the client) and the DP function (i.e. the bureau). However, this division of responsibility is less effective in many time-sharing systems where the user is linked to the mainframe by terminal, and, indeed, can undertake program development and amendment work. In any event, there must be a clearly defined liaison between bureau and user, and it is normal for a senior member of the user's staff to be made responsible for this work. Within the bureau itself, the segregation of duties should be similar to any other mainframe computer installation, so as to facilitate the system of internal control.

The objectives of system controls remains as before, i.e. to ascertain the validity, accuracy and completeness of processing. Additional points specific to bureau-based systems include:

(*a*) *Definition of the responsibilities* (and therefore control procedures) of the bureau staff. As mentioned above, these should be defined on a contractual basis, and should extend to authorization checks and any balancing controls which would detect the bureau's own processing errors. It is essential that the client does not rely on these procedures to the extent that he discontinues his own system of control over data.

(*b*) *Carefully planned rejection procedures.* The bureau must provide sufficient documentation for the users to identify any errors. It remains the users' responsibility to ensure the prompt correction and resubmission of rejections to meet the bureau's processing schedules.

(*c*) *Output distribution controls.* In particular there should be procedures in the user company to ensure that all exception/error reports are received from the bureau.

(*d*) *The need for users to exercise effective control*, with input/output reconciliations and run-to-run controls. This is emphasized in the bureau environment, since user management has little influence over the bureau operations and control procedures.

13.8   Summary

The basic principles of internal control and auditing in a computer environment are the same as those in a non-computer system. Implementation of those controls and auditing techniques used are, however, completely different in many respects.

Internal controls in a computer-based system are normally divided into *general controls*, relating to the general organization of the department, and *application* controls set up for each separate function carried out.

General controls include those relating to the systems design stage (systems development controls).

13.8.1   General controls summarized

(*a*) Controls over personnel

(1) plan for organization;
(2) segregation and definition of duties;
(3) control over access;
(4) use of control section;
(5) use of librarian in charge of file storage.

(*b*) Systems development controls
(*c*) Other general controls

(1) authorization;
(2) supervision;
(3) reconstruction procedures;
(4) breakdown procedures;
(5) maintenance;
(6) security;
(7) fire precautions.

13.8.2   Audit procedures

The auditor will first ascertain, record and evaluate the system of internal control. This work will be much the same as that performed in a non-computerized system.

Techniques of audit testing will be:
(*a*) *manual techniques*
(*b*) *computer assisted audit techniques (CAAT)*

(1) test packs;
(2) audit software;
(3) embedded audit facilities;
(4) systems software data analysis;
(5) application program examination;
(6) tracing;
(7) flow charting;
(8) mapping.

13.8.3 Audit of small computers

The normal method of accounting now encountered in quite small businesses is a small computer. The problems outlined in this section are thus constantly encountered by the auditor. It is fundamental to a small computer installation that there cannot be effective segregation of duties.

Other problems which can arise are:

(*a*) lack of control over software development and maintenance.

(*b*) inadequate controls over operation and access. In this connection, the basic controls covered in Section 13.2.4 for larger installations could be appropriate.

13.8.4 On-line/real-time systems

The diagram in Section 13.6 illustrate clearly the differences in processing techniques involved with these systems. The key point is that controls over access *to* terminals and controls limiting access *via* terminals must be present.

13.8.5 Computer bureaux

Points to note particularly are:

(*a*) financial stability of bureaux;

(*b*) procedure to protect client files and to ensure their confidentiality;

(*c*) controls to ensure that data is not lost in transit to the bureau. Retention of a microfilm copy may be useful;

(*d*) need for adequate error correction procedures.

Progress questions

Questions	References for answers
(1) How, if at all, does the auditor's approach to the audit differ if the client's records are maintained on a computer?	Sections 13.1 and 13.2
(2) Define and distinguish between general controls and application controls.	Section 13.2
(3) List (a) ten general controls and (b) ten application controls likely to be found in a large computer installation.	Sections 13.2.1 and 13.2.10
(4) Draw up a typical plan of organization for a large computer installation.	Section 13.2.2
(5) How may controls on access to the computer be imposed?	Section 13.2.4
(6) What are the normal duties of the control section	Section 13.2.5
(7) What is meant by systems development controls?	Section 13.2.7
(8)(a) What three objectives are application controls designed to achieve? (b) Explain in detail the techniques which may be applied in each of these three areas.	Section 13.2.10(a)
(9) How may controls over computer operators by applied?	Section 13.2.10(b)
10(a) What matters need to be ascertained by the auditor before the testing process can begin? (b) How will details of the system be recorded by the auditor?	Section 13.3.1 Section 3.2

Questions	References for answers
(11)(a) What is the difference between manual testing techniques and programmed testing techniques? (b) List three of each type.	Sections 13.4.1 and 13.4.2
(12) What are the advantages and disadvantages of (a) test packs (b) computer audit programs?	Section 13.4.2
(13) What problems may be encountered in auditing small computers?	Section 13.5
(14) Define and distinguish between (a) batch processing (b) on-line processing (c) real-time processing	Section 13.6
(15) What problems may arise if a client's data is processed by a computer bureau?	Section 13.7

14 Reporting

14.1 Introduction

All the work of an audit is directed towards the final objective – the report to the members of a company client or to the owner(s) of an unincorporated one.

In addition to these reports, however, the auditor also reports to the management in a *letter of comment*—offering constructive criticism of the client's control systems.

We therefore have four areas to deal with:

—the unqualified audit report;
—qualifications in audit reports;
—special points for non-corporate reports;
—the letter of comment (also known as letter of weakness or management letter).

14.2 The unqualified audit report

The statutory matters to be covered by the auditor's report are to be found in S237, Companies Act 1985. The audit guideline reproduced later in this chapter adds a number of other requirements, and SSAP 10 requires the report to cover the funds statement. Some of the matters have to be referred to in the report, others are merely implied—that is, reference is only required if the auditor is not satisfied about them.

The chart on page 406 summarizes all the requirements.

Additional disclosure

S237(6) requires the auditor to include in his or her report all the disclosure requirements of Schedule 5 and Schedule 6 relating to directors' and employees' remuneration and loans to directors and other officers, if this information has not been disclosed elsewhere in the accounts (as it almost certainly will have been.

Unqualified audit report for company without subsidiaries

Matters to be stated	Matters implied to be in order if no reference is made

---

S237 Companies Act 1985

(1) Whether accounts show a true and fair view of: (a) profit or loss; (b) state of affairs. (2) Whether accounts comply with the Companies Act 1985.	(1) Proper accounting records kept. (2) Proper returns received from branches not visited. (3) Accounts in agreement with accounting records and returns. (4) All information and explanations necessary for the audit have been obtained. (5) Directors' report consistent with accounts.

Auditing Standards and SSAP 10

(3) Documents reported on and addressees identified. (4) Approved Auditing Standards complied with. (5) Statement of source and application of funds true and fair (SSAP 10). (6) Accounting convention used (if necessary to state it to avoid misunderstanding.)	(6) SSAPs complied with (unless the auditor concurs that compliance is impracticable or gives a misleading view). (7) Comparative figures true and fair (see Section 11.15).

Now take a look at the Auditing Standard on the subject. This was issued in April 1980.

APC Standard on the audit report

This Auditing Standard should be read in conjunction with the Explanatory Foreword to Auditing Standards and Guidelines including the Glossary of Terms. Qualifications in audit reports are dealt with in the Auditing Standard *Qualifications in Audit Reports*. Examples of audit reports which will conform to this Standard are given in the Auditing Guideline *Audit Report Examples*. The considerations which arise when reporting on financial statements not required to give a true and fair view will be dealt with subsequently.

PART 1—STATEMENT OF AUDITING STANDARD
(1) This Auditing Standard applies to all reports in which the auditor expresses an opinion on financial statements intended to give a true and fair view of the state of

affairs, profit or loss and, where applicable, source and application of funds. The Standard is not intended to override the statutory exemptions granted in respect of certain types of enterprise but is intended to apply to the audit reports relating to such enterprises in other respects.

(2) The audit report should identify those to whom it is addressed and the financial statements to which it relates.

(3) The auditor should refer expressly in his report to the following:

(*a*) whether the financial statements have been audited in accordance with approved Auditing Standards;

(*b*) whether in the auditor's opinion the financial statements give a true and fair view of the state of affairs, profit or loss and, where applicable, source and application of funds; and

(*c*) any matters prescribed by relevant legislation or other requirements.

Effective date

(4) This Auditing Standard is effective for the audit of financial statements relating to accounting periods starting on or after 1st April 1980.

Compliance with approved Auditing Standards

(5) The auditor should comply with approved Auditing Standards and it is appropriate that his report should refer to this fact in arriving at his opinion. Approved Auditing Standards are defined as those Statements of Auditing Standards which are approved for issue by the Councils of the accountancy bodies listed in the Explanatory Foreword and which are effective for the period covered by the financial statements on which the auditor is reporting.

True and fair

(6) The majority of audit reports are issued under the Companies Acts which normally require the use of the words 'true and fair view'. For the purpose of this Standard, therefore, the phrase 'true and fair view' has been retained. When expressing an opinion that financial statements give a true and fair view the auditor should be satisfied, *inter alia*, that:

(*a*) all relevant Statements of Standard Accounting Practice have been complied with, except in situations in which for justifiable reasons they are not strictly applicable because they are impracticable or, exceptionally, having regard to the circumstances, would be inappropriate or give a misleading view; and

(*b*) any significant accounting policies which are not the subject of Statements of Standard Accounting Practice are appropriate to the circumstances of the business.

Reference to accounting convention

(7) The auditor should refer in his report to the particular convention used in

preparing the financial statements if he considers it necessary in order to avoid misunderstanding.

Emphasis of matter

(8) As a general principle the auditor issuing an unqualified opinion should not make reference to specific aspects of the financial statements in the body of his report as such reference may be misconstrued as being a qualification. In rare circumstances, however, the reader will obtain a better understanding of the financial statements if his attention is drawn to important matters. Examples might include an unusual event, accounting policy or condition, awareness of which is fundamental to an understanding of the financial statements.

(9) In order to avoid giving the impression that a qualification is intended, references which are intended as emphasis of matter should be contained in a separate paragraph and introduced with a phrase such as 'We draw attention to . . .' and should not be referred to in the opinion paragraph. Emphasis of matter should not be used to rectify a lack of appropriate disclosure in the financial statements, nor should it be regarded as a substitute for a qualification.

Compliance with relevant legislation or other requirements

(10) The auditor should comply with any reporting requirements imposed by legislation and any other reporting requirements relevant to the financial statements. It should be noted that the Companies Acts of Great Britain, Northern Ireland and the Republic of Ireland contain different reporting requirements.

Wording of report

(11) Set out below is a form of audit report appropriate to a company incorporated in Great Britain which meets the requirements of this Standard where the auditor is able to report affirmatively on all the matters contained in paragraph 3 above.

AUDITORS' REPORT TO THE MEMBERS OF ....

We have audited the financial statements on pages......to......in accordance with approved Auditing Standards.

In our opinion the financial statements, [which have been prepared under the historical cost convention as modified by the revaluation of land and buildings], give a true and fair view of the state of the company's affairs at 31st December 19......and of its profit and source and application of funds for the year then ended and comply with the Companies Act 1985.

(12) An example of an unqualified audit report appropriate to a company incorporated in Ireland is given, together with other examples of audit reports, in the Auditing Guideline *Audit Report Examples*.

One further matter is the dating of the audit report. Until a few years ago it was not unusual for the auditor's report to be dated *before* the date of the directors' report. The implications of the date on the auditor's report were the subject of Counsel's opinion taken by the APC and reported in *True and Fair* No. 16 (1980). The clear opinion stated was that auditors cannot date their report before the date on which the directors approve the accounts, because until then no accounts exist on which the auditors can report. Note that SSAP 17 (paragraph 26) requires disclosure in the financial statements of the date the directors approved them.

14.3   Qualifications in audit reports

If the auditor is unhappy about any of the matters referred to in Section 14.2, it will be necessary to consider *qualifying* the report. The Auditing Standard 'Qualifications in audit reports' deals with this. It was issued in April 1980.

APC Standard on qualifications in audit reports

This Auditing Standard should be read in conjunction with the Explanatory Foreword to Auditing Standards and Guidelines including the Glossary of Terms and the Auditing Standard *The Audit Report*. Examples of audit reports which will conform to this Standard are given in the Auditing Guideline *Audit Report Examples*. The considerations which arise when reporting on financial statements not required to give a true and fair view will be dealt with subsequently.

PART 1—STATEMENT OF AUDITING STANDARD
(1) When the auditor is unable to report affirmatively on the matters contained in paragraph 3 of the Auditing Standard *The Audit Report*, he should qualify his report by referring to all material matters about which he has reservations. All reasons for the qualification should be given, together with a quantification of its effect on the financial statements if this is both relevant and practicable. Additionally, reference may need to be made to non-compliance with relevant legislation and other requirements.

(2) A qualified audit report should leave the reader in no doubt as to its meaning and its implications for an understanding of the financial statements. To promote a more consistent understanding of qualified reports the forms of qualification described in this standard should be used unless, in the auditor's opinion, to do so would fail to convey clearly the intended meaning.

(3) The nature of the circumstances giving rise to a qualification of opinion will generally fall into one of two categories:

(*a*) where there is an uncertainty which prevents the auditor from forming an opinion on a matter (uncertainty); or

(*b*) where the auditor is able to form an opinion on a matter but this conflicts with the view given by the financial statements (disagreement).

Each of these categories gives rise to alternative forms of qualification depending upon whether the subject-matter of the uncertainty or disagreement is considered to be fundamental so as to undermine the view given by the financial statements taken as a whole.

(4) The forms of qualification which should be used in different circumstances are shown below.

Nature of circumstances	Material but not fundamental	Fundamental
Uncertainty	'Subject to' opinion	Disclaimer of opinion
Disagreement	'Except' opinion	Adverse opinion

—In a 'subject to' opinion the auditor effectively disclaims an opinion on a particular matter which is not considered fundamental.

—In an 'except' opinion the auditor expresses an adverse opinion on a particular matter which is not considered fundamental.

—In a disclaimer of opinion the auditor states that he is unable to form an opinion as to whether the financial statements give a true and fair view.

—In an adverse opinion the auditor states that in his opinion the financial statements do not give a true and fair view.

Effective date

(5) This Auditing Standard is effective for the audit of financial statements relating to accounting periods starting on or after 1 April 1980.

PART 2—EXPLANATORY NOTE

Introduction

(6) There are occasions when, in order to convey clearly the results of his audit, the auditor needs to depart from the form of wording normally used for unqualified audit reports. Such departures are generally referred to as qualifications. The principles set out in this Standard are intended to make qualified audit reports more understandable by developing a consistent use of language to distinguish the types of qualification appropriate to different circumstances.

Reasons for qualification

(7) As indicated in Part 1, circumstances which give rise to a qualification of opinion in an audit report may be in the nature of uncertainty or disagreement.

(8) Circumstances giving rise to uncertainties include the following:

(a) *Limitations in the scope of the audit.* Scope limitations arise if the auditor is unable for any reason to obtain all the information and explanations which he considers necessary for the purpose of his audit; for example, inability to carry out an audit procedure considered necessary, or the absence of proper accounting records.

(b) *Inherent uncertainties.* Inherent uncertainties result from circumstances in which it is not possible to reach an objective conclusion as to the outcome of a situation due to the circumstances themselves rather than to any limitation of the scope of audit procedures. This type of uncertainty may relate to major litigation, the outcome of long-term contracts or doubts about the ability of the enterprise to continue as a going concern. Inherent uncertainties will not normally include instances where the auditor is able to obtain adequate evidence to support estimates and use his experience to reach an opinion as to their reasonableness; for example as regards collectability of debts or realisability of stock.

(9) The wording in expressing the audit opinion describes the effect of uncertainties on that opinion and does not distinguish those arising from a limitation of scope from those which are inherent. The cause of the uncertainty will be described elsewhere in the audit report.

(10) Circumstances giving rise to disagreement include the following:

(a) departures from acceptable accounting practices where:

   (i) there has been failure to comply with a relevant Statement of Standard Accounting Practice (SSAP) and the auditor does not concur;

  (ii) an accounting policy not the subject of an SSAP is adopted which in the opinion of the auditor is not appropriate to the circumstances of the business; or

 (iii) exceptionally, an SSAP has been followed with the result that the financial statements do not present a true and fair view;

(b) disagreement as to the facts or amounts included in the financial statements;

(c) disagreement as to the manner or extent of disclosure of facts or amounts in the financial statements;

(d) failure to comply with relevant legislation or other requirements.

Small enterprises

(11) The auditor needs to obtain the same degree of assurance in order to give an unqualified opinion on the financial statements of both small and large enterprises. However, the operating procedures and methods of recording and processing transactions used by small enterprises often differ significantly from those of large enterprises. Indeed, many of the controls which would be relevant to the large enterprise are not practical, appropriate or necessary in the small enterprise. The most effective form of internal control for small enterprises is generally the close involvement of the directors or proprietors. This involvement will, however, enable them to override controls and purposely to exclude transactions from the records. This possibility can give rise to difficulties for the auditor not because there is a lack of controls but because of insufficient evidence as to their operation and the completeness of the records.

(12) In many situations it may be possible to reach a conclusion that will support an

unqualified opinion on the financial statements by combining the evidence obtained from extensive substantive testing of transactions with a careful review of costs and margins. However, in some businesses such as those where most transactions are for cash and there is no regular pattern of costs and margins, the available evidence may be inadequate to support an opinion on the financial statements.

(13) There will be other situations where the evidence available to the auditor is insufficient to give him the confidence necessary for him to express an unqualified opinion but this uncertainty is not so great as to justify a total disclaimer of opinion. In such situations the most helpful form of report may be one which indicates the need to accept the assurances of management as to the completeness or accuracy of the accounting records. Such a report should contain a 'subject to . . .' opinion. It would only be appropriate to use this form of report if the auditor has taken steps to obtain all the evidence which can reasonably be obtained and is satisfied that:

(a) the system of accounting and control is reasonable having regard to the size and type of the enterprise's operations; and is sufficient to enable management to give the auditor the assurances which he requires;

(b) there is no evidence to suggest that the assurances may be inaccurate.

Disclosure of reasons for qualification

(14) The audit report should include a brief recital of the reasons for a qualification and should quantify the effects on the financial statements if this is relevant and practicable. Whilst reference may be made to relevant notes in the financial statements such reference should not be used as a substitute for a description of the basic circumstances in the audit report.

(15) The auditor should refer in his report to all material matters about which he has reservations. Thus, a qualification on one matter should not be regarded as a reason for omitting other unrelated qualifications which otherwise would have been reported.

(16) The manner in which the reasons for qualifying are disclosed is for the auditor to decide in the particular circumstances of each case, but the overall objective should be clarity. The inclusion of a separate 'explanatory' paragraph before the paragraph in which the auditor gives his opinion is likely to be the clearest method of outlining the facts giving rise to the qualification.

Statutory requirements

(17) The auditor will also need to consider whether the circumstances which give rise to his qualification impinge on his statutory duties to report. For instance, shortcomings in the sales records which give rise to a qualified opinion on the financial statements will generally mean that proper accounting records have not been maintained. Similarly, limitations in scope may mean that the auditor has not obtained all the information and explanations he considers necessary.

Omission of statements of source and application of funds

(18) SSAP 10 requires, with certain specified exceptions, that financial statements should include a statement of source and application of funds. Omission of such a statement from financial statements to which SSAP 10 applies present a particular problem to the auditor in that the omission of a funds statement does not justify, on this ground alone, a qualified report on the profit and loss account and balance sheet.

(19) It is considered that the standards set out in this statement will be met if the auditor reports the omission of a funds statement by adding a separate paragraph which follows his opinion. An example of the manner in which this matter could be reported is set out below:

'The financial statements do not specify the manner in which the operations of the company (group) have been financed or in which its financial resources have been used during the year as required by Statement of Standard Accounting Practice No. 10.'

Materiality

(20) In deciding whether to qualify his audit opinion, the auditor should have regard to the materiality of the matter in the context of the financial statements on which he is proposing to report. In general terms a matter should be judged to be material if knowledge of the matter would be likely to influence the user of the financial statements. Materiality may be considered in the context of the financial statements as a whole, the balance sheet, the profit and loss account, or individual items within the financial statements. In addition, depending upon the nature of the matter, materiality may be considered in relative or absolute terms.

(21) If the auditor concludes that, judged against the criteria he believes to be most appropriate in the circumstances, the matter does not materially affect the view given by the financial statements, he should not qualify his opinion.

(22) Where the auditor has decided that a matter is sufficiently material to warrant a qualification in his audit report, a further decision is required as to whether or not the matter is fundamental, so as to require either an adverse opinion or a disclaimer of opinion on the financial statements as a whole. An uncertainty becomes fundamental when its impact on the financial statements is so great as to render the financial statements as a whole meaningless. A disagreement becomes fundamental when its impact on the financial statements is so great as to render them totally misleading. The combined effect of all uncertainties and disagreements must be considered.

(23) It is emphasised that the adverse opinion and the disclaimer of opinion are the extreme forms of the two main categories of qualification of opinion arising from disagreement and uncertainty. In most situations the 'except' or 'subject to' form of opinion will be the appropriate form to use; the adverse opinion and the disclaimer should be regarded as measures of last resort.

14.4 Audit report examples

An Auditing Guideline—'Audit report examples'—goes on to provide a set of examples of qualified audit reports.

APC Guideline on audit report examples

This Auditing Guideline gives examples of audit reports which will meet the requirements of Auditing Standards—*The audit report* and *Qualifications in audit reports*. It should be read in conjunction with the Explanatory Foreword to Auditing Standards and Guidelines including the Glossary of Terms.

The examples are intended merely to illustrate possible forms of wording for use in different circumstances. Since qualifications must be expressed in terms chosen to fit the particular circumstances to which they relate, it is impracticable, and could be misleading, to suggest standard forms of qualification. The examples are fictitious and deliberately simplified. In practice, if circumstances call for a qualified audit report they will often be far more complex than the illustrations given, and may necessitate explanation at length to make the position clear. For the purposes of the examples it is assumed throughout that the matters in question are judged to be material.

LIST OF EXAMPLES

Forms of unqualified audit report

1 Companies without subsidiaries and complying with Companies Acts (Great Britain)

2 Companies submitting group accounts and complying with Companies Acts (Great Britain)

3 Companies without subsidiaries and complying with Companies Acts (Ireland)

4 Emphasis of matter—transactions with a group company.

Forms of qualified audit report

Note: Examples are based on legislation applicable to Great Britain. Modifications will be necessary if the audit report is required to comply with legislation applicable to Ireland.

Form	Circumstances
Uncertainty—material but not fundamental;	
5 Subject to—scope	No stock count at a branch
6 Subject to—scope	Acceptance of management assurances (small business)
7 Subject to—inherent uncertainty	Going concern
8 Subject to—inherent uncertainty	Major litigation

Form	Circumstances

Uncertainty—Fundamental;

9 Disclaimer—scope — Accounting breakdown

10 Disclaimer—scope — Inability to substantiate cash transactions

11 Disclaimer—inherent uncertainty — Valuation of long-term construction contracts

Disagreement—material but not fundamental;

12 Except—departure from Statement of Standard Accounting Practice — Failure to apply SSAP 4

13 Except—disagreement as to facts — No provision for doubtful debt

14 Except—non-compliance with legislation — Company omitted information on overseas associated companies and at date of issue of financial statements has not obtained Department of Trade agreement

Disagreement—Fundamental;

15 Adverse—departure from Statement of Standard Accounting Practice — Long-term contracts carried at cost with no provision made for losses in accordance with SSAP 9

16 Adverse—disagreement as to facts — Goodwill no longer justified at balance sheet amount

Multiple qualification;

17 Subject to and except — Based on Examples 5 and 13

EXAMPLE 1: UNQUALIFIED AUDIT REPORT

Companies without subsidiaries—Great Britain

AUDITORS' REPORT TO THE MEMBERS OF ....

We have audited the financial statements on pages ...... to ...... in accordance with approved Auditing Standards.

In our opinion the financial statements, which have been prepared under the historical cost convention as modified by the revaluation of land and buildings, give a true and fair view of the state of the company's affairs at 31 December 19... and of its profit and source and application of funds for the year then ended and comply with the Companies Act 1985.

EXAMPLE 2: UNQUALIFIED AUDIT REPORT

Companies submitting group accounts—Great Britain

AUDITORS' REPORT TO THE MEMBERS OF ....

We have audited the financial statements on pages ...... to ...... in accordance with approved Auditing Standards.

In our opinion the financial statements, which have been prepared under the historical cost convention as modified by the revaluation of land and buildings, give a true and fair view of the state of affairs of the company and the group at 31 December 19... and of the profit and source and application of funds of the group for the year then ended and comply with the Companies Act 1985.

EXAMPLE 3: UNQUALIFIED AUDIT REPORT

Companies without subsidiaries—Ireland

AUDITORS' REPORT TO THE MEMBERS OF ....

We have audited the financial statements on pages ...... to ...... in accordance with approved Auditing Standards and have obtained all the information and explanations we considered necessary.

In our opinion proper books of account have been kept by the Company and the financial statements, which are in agreement therewith and have been prepared under the historical cost convention as modified by the revaluation of land and buildings, give a true and fair view of the state of the company's affairs at 31 December 19... and of its profit and source and application of funds for the year then ended and comply with the Companies Act ....

EXAMPLE 4: UNQUALIFIED AUDIT REPORT

Emphasis of matter: transactions with a group company

AUDITORS' REPORT TO THE MEMBERS OF ....

We have audited the financial statements on pages ...... to ...... in accordance with approved Auditing Standards.

We draw attention to note ... which outlines a number of transactions with the parent company during the year without which the company would have incurred a loss.

In our opinion the financial statements, which have been prepared under the historical cost convention, give a true and fair view of the state of the company's affairs at 31 December 19... and of its profit and source and application of funds for the year then ended and comply with the Companies Act 1985.

Notes

1 The explanatory paragraph may appear before or after the opinion paragraph.
2 It should be noted that the opinion paragraph does not refer to the explanatory paragraph. The use of words such as 'with this explanation' or similar phrases would in effect 'qualify' the opinion.

EXAMPLE 5: QUALIFIED AUDIT REPORT

Uncertainty—subject to: no stock count at a branch

AUDITORS' REPORT TO THE MEMBERS OF ....

We have audited the financial statements on pages ...... to ...... Our audit was conducted in accordance with approved Auditing Standards except that the scope of our work was limited by the matter referred to below.

One branch of the company did not carry out a physical count of stock at 31 December 19... and there were no practicable alternative auditing procedures that we could apply to confirm quantities. Accordingly, we have been unable to obtain all the information and explanations considered necessary to satisfy ourselves as to the existence of stock valued at £... at 31 December 19... which is included as part of the total stock of £... in the balance sheet. In our opinion, in the case of the stocks referred to above, proper accounting records have not been kept as required by Section 221, Companies Act 1985.

Subject to the effects of any adjustments which might have been shown to be necessary had a physical count of the branch stock been carried out, in our opinion the financial statements, which have been prepared under the historical cost convention, give a true and fair view of the state of the company's affairs at 31 December 19... and of its profit and source and application of funds for the year then ended and comply with the Companies Act 1985.

EXAMPLE 6: QUALIFIED AUDIT REPORT

Uncertainty—subject to: acceptance of management assurances (small business)

AUDITORS' REPORT TO THE MEMBERS OF ....

We have audited the financial statements on pages ...... to ...... Our audit was conducted in accordance with approved Auditing Standards having regard to the matters referred to in the following paragraph.

In common with many businesses of similar size and organisation the company's system of control is dependent upon the close involvement of the directors/managing director, [who are major shareholders]. Where independent confirmation of the completeness of the accounting records was therefore not available we have accepted assurances from the directors/managing director that all the company's transactions have been reflected in the records.

Subject to the foregoing, in our opinion the financial statements, which have been prepared under the historical cost convention give a true and fair view of the state of the company's affairs at 31 December 19... and of its profit and source and application of funds for the year then ended and comply with the Companies Act 1985.

Notes

1 Paragraphs 11 to 13 of the Auditing Standard *Qualifications in Audit Reports* outline the circumstances where this form of report might be appropriate.
2 The auditor should consider referring to the specific areas of the financial statements in which he has had to rely on assurances.
3 Where the lack of evidence of the operation of internal controls coupled with the inability to adopt alternative auditing procedures to compensate is regarded as so fundamental as to prevent an effective audit being carried out, a disclaimer such as that set out in Example 10 will be appropriate.

EXAMPLE 7: QUALIFIED AUDIT REPORT

Uncertainty—subject to: going concern (See also p.293)

AUDITORS' REPORT TO THE MEMBERS OF ....

We have audited the financial statements on pages ...... to ...... in accordance with approved Auditing Standards.

As stated in note ...... the company is currently negotiating for long-term facilities to replace the loan of £...... which becomes repayable on [a date early in the next financial year]; continuation of the company's activities is dependent upon a successful outcome to these negotiations. The financial statements have been drawn up on a going concern basis which assumes that adequate facilities will be obtained.

Subject to a satisfactory outcome of the negotiations referred to above, in our opinion the financial statements, which have been prepared under the historical cost convention, give a true and fair view of the state of affairs of the company and the group at 31 December 19... and of the profit and source and application of funds of the group for the year then ended and comply with the Companies Act 1985.

Note

Where there is uncertainty as to an enterprise's ability to continue as a going concern a 'subject to' opinion will generally be the more appropriate form of qualification, provided that the going concern assumption upon which the financial statements have been based is made clear together with the nature of the related uncertainty.

EXAMPLE 8: QUALIFIED AUDIT REPORT

Uncertainty—subject to: major litigation

AUDITORS' REPORT TO THE MEMBERS OF ....

We have audited the financial statements on pages ...... to ...... in accordance with approved Auditing Standards.

As more fully explained in note ...... to the financial statements a claim has been lodged against a subsidiary company in respect of one of its major contracts. The claim calls for rectification and for substantial compensation for alleged damage to the customer's business. The directors have made provision for the estimated cost of rectification but no provision for compensation as that part of the claim is being strongly resisted. At this time it is not possible to determine with reasonable accuracy the ultimate cost of rectification and compensation, if any, which may become payable.

Subject to the adjustment, if any, that may be required when the claim referred to above is determined, in our opinion the financial statements, which have been prepared under the historical cost convention, give a true and fair view of the state of affairs of the company and the group at 31 December 19... and of the profit and source and application of funds of the group for the year then ended and comply with the Companies Act 1985.

EXAMPLE 9: QUALIFIED AUDIT REPORT

Uncertainty—disclaimer: accounting breakdown

AUDITORS' REPORT TO THE MEMBERS OF ....

We have audited the financial statements on pages ...... to ...... Our audit was conducted in accordance with approved Auditing Standards except that the scope of our work was limited by the matter referred to below.

As stated in note .... a fire at the company's computer centre destroyed many of the accounting records. The financial statements consequently include significant amounts based on estimates. In these circumstances we were unable to carry out all the auditing procedures, or to obtain all the information and explanations we considered necessary.

Because of the significance of the matter referred to in the preceding paragraph, we are unable to form an opinion as to (i) whether the financial statements give a true and fair view of the state of the company's affairs as at 31 December 19... and of its profit and source and application of funds for the year then ended, (ii) whether proper accounting records have been kept, or (iii) whether the financial statements comply in all respects with the Companies Act 1985.

Notes

1 This disclaimer of opinion would apply irrespective of the accounting convention adopted. Reference to an accounting convention should therefore be omitted from the opinion paragraph because such a reference might imply that a different form of opinion could be given under a different accounting convention. In order to distinguish the financial statements from statements prepared under an alternative convention, it may be appropriate to include a reference to the accounting convention in the first paragraph of the report viz '. . . the financial statements on pages ...... to ......, which have been prepared under the historical cost convention. Our audit was conducted in accordance with approved Auditing Standards except that . . .'.

2 The notes to the financial statements would clearly identify which amounts are estimates.

EXAMPLE 10: QUALIFIED AUDIT REPORT

Uncertainty—disclaimer: inability to substantiate cash transactions

AUDITORS' REPORT TO THE MEMBERS OF ....

We have audited the financial statements on pages ...... to ...... Our audit was conducted in accordance with approved Auditing Standards except that the scope of our work was limited by the matter referred to below.

A major part of the company's income comprises cash sales. There was no system of control over such sales upon which we could rely for the purpose of our audit and there were no satisfactory procedures which we could adopt to verify the completeness of the income. We were therefore unable to obtain all the information and explanations we considered necessary. Consequently, we were unable to satisfy ourselves as to the completeness and accuracy of the accounting records.

Because of the significance of the matter referred to in the preceding paragraph, we are unable to form an opinion as to (i) whether the financial statements give a true and fair view of the state of the company's affairs at 31 December 19... and of its profit and source and application of funds for the year then ended, (ii) whether proper accounting records have been kept, or (iii) whether the financial statements comply in all respects with the Companies Act 1985.

Notes

1 In this particular case the lack of evidence of the operation of internal controls coupled with the inability to adopt alternative auditing procedures to compensate has been regarded as so fundamental as to prevent an effective audit being carried out.

2 If the system of internal control over the major areas of the company's affairs is considered to be adequate and the limitations are confined to non-fundamental areas, it might be appropriate to describe the areas in which there are limitations and to give a 'subject to' opinion. See Example 5 for a method of reporting when a scope limitation is confined to a specific area.

3 This disclaimer of opinion would apply irrespective of the accounting convention adopted. Reference to an accounting convention should therefore be omitted from the opinion paragraph because such a reference might imply that a different form of opinion could be given under a different accounting convention. In order to distinguish the financial statements from statements prepared under an alternative convention it may be appropriate to include a reference to the accounting convention in the first paragraph of the report viz '. . . the financial statement on pages ...... to ......, which have been prepared under the historical cost convention. Our audit was conducted in accordance with approved Auditing Standards except that . . .'.

EXAMPLE 11: QUALIFIED AUDIT REPORT

Uncertainty—disclaimer: valuation of long-term construction contracts

AUDITORS' REPORT TO THE MEMBERS OF ....

We have audited the financial statements on pages ...... to ...... in accordance with approved Auditing Standards.

As indicated in note ...... the estimates of losses to completion of long-term construction contracts depend on a number of assumptions including those relating to substantially increased production and productivity which have yet to be achieved. In view of these uncertainties we are unable to confirm that the provision of £...... is adequate.

Because of the significance of this matter, we are unable to form an opinion as to whether the financial statements give a true and fair view of the state of the company's affairs at 31 December 19... and of its profit and source and application of funds for the year then ended.

In other respects the financial statements in our opinion comply with the Companies Act 1985.

Notes

1 It is assumed for the purpose of this example that the amount of the provision for losses on long-term construction contracts is of overwhelming significance in relation to the net assets of the company.

2 In this case the area of uncertainty is well defined so that the auditor is able to reach an opinion as to whether the financial statements in other respects comply with the Companies Act. Such a conclusion would not normally be possible where wide ranging scope limitations are involved as instanced in Examples 9 and 10.

3 This disclaimer of opinion would apply irrespective of the accounting convention adopted. Reference to an accounting convention should therefore be omitted from the opinion paragraph because such a reference might imply that a different form of opinion could be given under a different accounting convention. In order to distinguish the financial statements from statements prepared under an alternative convention, it may be appropriate to include a reference to the accounting convention in the first paragraph of the report, viz. 'We have audited the financial statements on pages ...... to ......, which have been prepared under the historical cost convention. Our audit was conducted in accordance with approved Auditing Standards'.

EXAMPLE 12: QUALIFIED AUDIT REPORT

Disagreement—except: failure to apply SSAP 4

AUDITORS' REPORT TO THE MEMBERS OF ....

We have audited the financial statements on pages ...... to ...... in accordance with approved Auditing Standards.

As explained in note ...... regional development grants have been credited in full to profits instead of being spread over the lives of the relevant assets as required by Statement of Standard Accounting Practice No. 4; the effect of so doing has been to increase group profits before and after tax for the year by £...... (19... £......).

Except for the effects of accounting for regional development grants in the manner described in the preceding paragraph, in our opinion the financial statements, which have been prepared under the historical cost convention, give a true and fair view of the state of affairs of the company and the group at 31 December 19... and of the profit and source and application of funds of the group for the year then ended and comply with the Companies Act 1985.

Note
It might also be appropriate to indicate the cumulative effect on retained profits where the amount is significant.

EXAMPLE 13: QUALIFIED AUDIT REPORT

Disagreement—except: no provision for doubtful debt

AUDITORS' REPORT TO THE MEMBERS OF ....

We have audited the financial statements on pages ...... to ...... in accordance with approved Auditing Standards.

No provision has been made against an amount of £...... owing by a company which has been placed in liquidation since the year end. The liquidator has indicated that unsecured creditors are unlikely to receive any payment and in our opinion full provision should be made.

Except for the failure to provide for the amount described above, in our opinion the financial statements, which have been prepared under the historical cost convention, give a true and fair view of the state of the company's affairs at 31 December 19... and of its profit and source and application of funds for the year then ended and comply with the Companies Act 1985.

Note
This is an example of a simple qualification. More explanation might be required in the middle paragraph if there were additional complications such as a consequential material overstatement of the tax provision.

EXAMPLE 14: QUALIFIED AUDIT REPORT

Disagreement—except: information not disclosed

AUDITORS' REPORT TO THE MEMBERS OF ....

We have audited the financial statements on pages ...... to ...... in accordance with approved Auditing Standards.

As explained in note ...... the information concerning overseas investments acquired during the year has not been disclosed in accordance with para. 7, Schedule 5, Companies Act 1985.

In our opinion the financial statements, which have been prepared under the historical cost convention, give a true and fair view of the state of the affairs of the company and the group at 31 December 19... and of the profit and source and application of funds of the group for the year then ended and except for the omission of the disclosure concerning overseas investments referred to above comply with the Companies Act 1985.

Notes
1 The note to the financial statements might explain that to give the information as to the identity and shareholdings of the new investments would harm the company's business and that application would be made to the Department of Trade for exemption in accordance with para. 10, Schedule 5 of the Companies Act 1985.
2 The lack of disclosure in this case does not impair the true and fair view shown by the financial statements.

EXAMPLE 15: QUALIFIED AUDIT REPORT

Disagreement—adverse opinion: contract losses not provided for in accordance with SSAP 9

AUDITORS' REPORT TO THE MEMBERS OF ....

We have audited the financial statements on pages ...... to ...... in accordance with approved Auditing Standards.

As more fully explained in note ...... no provision has been made for losses expected to arise on certain long-term contracts currently in progress because the directors consider that such losses should be offset against expected but unearned future profits on other long-term contracts. In our opinion provision should be made for foreseeable losses on individual contracts as required by Statement of Standard Accounting Practice No. 9. If losses had been so recognised the effect would have been to reduce the profit before and after tax for the year and the contract work in progress at 31 December 19... by £......

In view of the significant effect of the failure to provide for the losses referred to above, in our opinion the financial statements do not give a true and fair view of the state of the company's affairs at 31 December 19... and of its profit and source and application of funds for the year then ended.

In other respects the financial statements in our opinion comply with the Companies Act 1985.

Notes
1 If the effect of the departure is considered to be fundamental to the profit and loss account and balance sheet but not to the funds statement, the final two paragraphs should be modified along the lines used in Example 16.

2 It has been assumed in this example that the need to provide for losses arose during the year and comparative figures are not affected.
3 This adverse opinion would apply irrespective of the accounting convention adopted. Reference to an accounting convention should therefore be omitted from the opinion paragraph because such a reference might imply that a different form of opinion could be given under a different convention.

In order to distinguish the financial statements from statements prepared under an alternative convention, it may be appropriate to include a reference to the accounting convention in the first paragraph of the report, viz. 'We have audited the financial statements on pages ...... to ...... which have been prepared under the historical cost convention. Our audit was conducted in accordance with approved Auditing Standards.'

EXAMPLE 16: QUALIFIED AUDIT REPORT

Disagreement—adverse opinion: goodwill

AUDITORS' REPORT TO THE MEMBERS OF ....

We have audited the financial statements on pages ...... to ...... in accordance with approved Auditing Standards.
Goodwill included in the consolidated balance sheet at £...... relates to a subsidiary which has incurred material losses during the year. In our opinion there are insufficient grounds to support the directors' contention that the subsidiary can be expected to become profitable in the foreseeable future. Accordingly we consider that goodwill should be written off in the consolidated financial statements and the investment in the subsidiary should be written down by a similar amount in the holding company's financial statements.
Because of the significance of the foregoing matter, in our opinion the financial statements do not give a true and fair view of the state of affairs of the company and the group at 31 December 19... and of the profit of the group for the year then ended.
In our opinion, the financial statements give a true and fair view of the source and application of funds of the group for the year ended 31 December 19..., and, except for the matter set out above, comply with the Companies Act 1985.

Notes
1 In this case it has been assumed that, as the writing off of goodwill does not affect the total funds generated from operations, the statement of source and application of funds has not been affected. The validity of this assumption will need to be considered in the light of individual circumstances.
2 This adverse opinion would apply irrespective of the accounting convention adopted. Reference to an accounting convention should therefore be omitted from the opinion paragraph because such a reference might imply that a different form of opinion could be given under a different convention. In order to distinguish the financial statements from statements prepared under an alternative

convention, it may be appropriate to include a reference to the accounting convention in the first paragraph of the report, viz. 'We have audited the financial statements on pages ...... to ...... which have been prepared under the historical cost convention. Our audit was conducted in accordance with approved Auditing Standards.'

EXAMPLE 17: QUALIFIED AUDIT REPORT

Multiple qualification—based on Examples 5 and 13

AUDITORS' REPORT TO THE MEMBERS OF ....

We have audited the financial statements on pages ...... to ...... Our audit was conducted in accordance with approved Auditing Standards except that the scope of our work was limited by the matter referred to below.

One branch of the company did not carry out a physical count of stock at 31 December 19... and there were no practicable alternative auditing procedures that we could apply to confirm quantities. Accordingly, we have been unable to obtain all the information and explanations considered necessary to satisfy ourselves as to the existence of the stock quantities valued at £...... at 31st December 19... and included as part of the total stock of £...... in the balance sheet. In our opinion in the case of the stocks referred to above proper accounting records have not been kept as required by Section 221, Companies Act 1985.

No provision has been made against an amount of £...... owing by a company which has been placed in liquidation since the year end. The liquidator has indicated that unsecured creditors are unlikely to receive any payment and in our opinion full provision should be made.

Subject to the effects of any adjustments which might have been shown to be necessary had a physical count of the branch stock occurred and except for the failure to make provision against an amount receivable, in our opinion the financial statements, which have been prepared under the historical cost convention, give a true and fair view of the state of the company's affairs at 31 December 19... and of its profits and source and application of funds for the year then ended and comply with the Companies Act 1985.

14.5 Reporting on accounts of sole traders and partnerships

If a full audit of the accounts of a sole trader or partnership has been carried out, it is perfectly correct for the auditor to report in 'true and fair' terms. If on the other hand the accounts have been prepared without an audit, the report should make quite clear exactly what the position is. A suitable form of report would be:

ACCOUNTANTS' REPORT

In accordance with instructions given to us we have prepared, without carrying out an audit, the accounts set out on pages ......, from the accounting records of .... and from information and explanations supplied to us.

Of course, the engagement letter sent to the client will have made the extent and nature of the work quite clear. It may have established a full audit; and if so then the audit report can properly deal with all matters specified in Section 14.2 above with the exception of compliance with the Companies Act 1985.

14.6 Reports to management

From the client's point of view, one important by-product of the audit is the independent appraisal of the system of internal control. The main purpose of the letter of comment is to draw the attention of management to areas of weakness requiring rectification. It is also possible for the auditor to suggest areas where economies or improved efficiency are possible.

Such a letter is, of course, no substitute for a qualification in the audit report. It will usually deal with matters not serious enough to justify an audit qualification.

The APC issued an Exposure Draft on the subject in 1985 and this is reproduced below.

Draft Auditing Guideline on reports to management

The purpose of this Guideline is to provide guidance on the procedures involved in making a report to management.

Introduction

(1) Reports to management are known by various names, for example management letters, post audit letters and letters of weaknesses. The report should preferably take the form of a letter. Occasionally, the volume or nature of the auditor's comments may be such that this form of report is either unnecessary or inappropriate. In these circumstances the report will consist of a record of a discussion with management, forming part of the auditor's working papers. The principles outlined in this Guideline should be followed whatever method is used to report to management on matters which have arisen during the audit.

(2) The auditor's primary duty is to express an opinion on the financial statements and this responsibility is not reduced by any report made to management.

Purpose

(3) The principal purpose of a report to management is to enable the auditor to give his comments on the accounting records, systems and controls that he has examined during the course of his audit. Significant areas of weakness in systems and controls that might lead to material errors should be highlighted and brought to management's attention.

(4) There is usually no requirement for the auditor to make a report to management where no significant weaknesses have come to his attention. However the auditor should be aware that in certain cases, for example in local authority, Stock Exchange firms and housing association audits, there is a specific requirement to make a report to management.

(5) As a secondary purpose, a report to management may also be used to provide management with other constructive advice. The auditor might, for example, be able to suggest areas where economies could be made or where resources could be used more efficiently.

(6) A report to management is also a useful means of communicating matters that have come to the auditor's attention during the audit that might have an impact on future audits.

Timing

(7) A report to management will normally be a natural by-product of the audit, and the auditor should incorporate the need to report in the planning of the audit.

(8) To be effective, the report should be made as soon as possible after completion of the audit procedures giving rise to comment. Where the audit work is performed on more than one visit, it will often be appropriate to report to management after interim audit work has been completed as well as after the final visit. If there are procedures that need to be improved before the financial year-end the auditor should raise them in a letter or in discussion at an interim stage. As soon as an accounting breakdown is identified or serious weaknesses are apparent senior management should be informed without delay.

Contents

(9) Generally the following matters, arising out of the audit, will be included in a report to management:

   (*a*) weaknesses in the structure of accounting systems and internal controls;
   (*b*) deficiencies in the operation of accounting systems and internal controls;
   (*c*) unsuitable accounting policies and practices;
   (*d*) non-compliance with accounting standards or legislation.

An auditor may have a specific duty to form an opinion as to whether proper accounting records have been kept. For example, this duty is laid upon the auditor of a company incorporated under the Companies Acts. In such a case, if a qualified audit report is necessary because of (b) above, a report to management is no substitute for a qualified audit report.

(10) Reports to management should explain clearly the risks arising from internal control weaknesses. The use of specific examples discovered in the audit to illustrate the potential effects of weaknesses helps readers to understand the nature of the problems which require rectification.

(11) The auditor may also include comments on inefficiencies as well as weaknesses which have come to his attention.

(12) It is normally helpful for the auditor to make recommendations for improvements so that weaknesses can be eliminated. This should not however delay the issuing of any report. It should be borne in mind that determination of appropriate improvements in systems and the assessment of the cost-effectiveness of additional controls may be complex issues that in any event are management's responsibility.

(13) Points made in previous years' reports should be reviewed. Where they have not been dealt with effectively the auditor should enquire why appropriate action has not been taken. If the auditor considers the points still to be significant, they should be included again in his current report. In addition, recommendations made by internal audit which have not been implemented by management may need to be included.

Format and presentation

(14) The report should be clear, constructive and concise. Careful presentation will help the recipient to understand the significance of the comments and devise corrective actions. The following factors should therefore be borne in mind.

(15) It is important that matters of concern should be discussed and recorded as they arise to ensure that the auditor has properly understood the situation. These discussions may take place with members of staff at an operating level as well as with executives concerned solely with finance and accounting. When the points in the report are drafted they should be cleared for factual accuracy with the client's staff concerned.

(16) The auditor should explain in his report to management that it only includes those matters which came to his attention as a result of the audit procedures, and that it should not be regarded as a comprehensive statement of all weaknesses that exist or all improvements that might be made.

(17) The report may contain matters of varying levels of significance and the inclusion of detail may make it difficult for senior management to identify points of significance. The auditor can deal with this by giving the report a 'tiered' structure so that major points are dealt with by the directors and minor points are considered by less senior personnel. Alternatively, by agreement with the client, this objective might best be achieved by preparing separate reports for different levels of management, and reporting that this has been done.

(18) Where different members of management are responsible for different regions, branches or functions, the report may have separate sections relating to the various areas of responsibility.

(19) When submitting his report the auditor should use his best endeavours to ensure that its contents reach those members of management who have the power to act on the findings. It is usually appropriate to address the report, or that part of the report containing the major points, to the Board of Directors or equivalent body even if the receipt of a report of less important points is delegated by the Board.

(20) If the auditor chooses not to send a formal letter or report but considers it

preferable to discuss any weaknesses with management, the discussion should be minuted or otherwise recorded in writing. Management should be provided with a copy of this note to ensure the discussion has been fairly reflected. The written record of any such discussions should be filed with the audit working papers.

Management response

(21) The auditor should request a reply to all the points raised, indicating what action management intends to take as a result of the comments made in the report. It should be made clear in the report that the auditor expects at least an acknowledgement of the report or, where he considers it appropriate, the directors' discussion of the report to be recorded in the board minutes.

(22) Where weaknesses have been discussed with client staff as and when they arise, the responses made by staff should be embodied where possible in the final form of a report. This will be particularly useful where, say, senior management receive the report and need to be informed of the action taken by their staff.

(23) Where the report to management takes the form of a record of the auditor's discussions with management, this record should include management's response and intended action.

Groups of companies

(24) The management of a holding company may wish to be informed of significant points arising in the reports to the management of the subsidiaries. Where the auditor is responsible for the audit of all the companies in the group, the management of the holding company may request that an additional report be addressed to the holding company summarising points of significance to the group that were made in the individual reports to the management of the subsidiaries. The auditor may agree to this request. However, as the report to management is a confidential matter between the auditor and the management of the company concerned, he should first obtain permission from the management of the subsidiary companies to disclose the contents to the holding company.

(25) The auditor of a holding company is not under any obligation to report to the management of the holding company on matters contained in the reports to the management of subsidiaries not audited by him. But he may do so provided he takes adequate precautions to ensure that the management of the subsidiary companies concerned and their auditors both agree to this procedure, and that no breach of confidence takes place.

(26) Where other auditors are involved, in order to fulfil his responsibilities regarding the group financial statements, the auditor of the holding company will usually request copies of reports sent to the management of subsidiary companies, so that he is aware of any significant internal control weaknesses or accounting weaknesses in those companies.

(27) All these arrangements for groups should be established at the outset, and may be agreed in the engagement letters.

Third parties interested in reports to management

(28) Any report made to management should be regarded as a confidential communication. The auditor should therefore not normally reveal the contents of the report to any third party without the prior written consent of the management of the company.

(29) In practice the auditor has little control over what happens to the report once it has been despatched. Occasionally management may provide third parties with copies of the report, for example, their bankers or certain regulatory authorities. Therefore care should be taken to protect the auditor's position from exposure to liability in negligence to any third parties who may seek to rely on the report. Accordingly the auditor should state clearly in his report that it has been prepared for the private use of his client. However the auditor should recognize that the report may be disclosed by management to third parties, and in certain cases it may be appropriate for the auditor to request that the report is not circulated to any third parties without his prior consent.

(30) Reports to management may contain comments which are critical of members of the client's management or staff, and could lay the auditor open to a charge of defamation. The auditor should therefore ensure that his comments are factually accurate, and do not include any gratuitous remarks of a personal nature.

14.7 Summary

The end-product of the audit is the report to the members or owners. In the case of a company, the matters to be covered in the audit report are laid down in S237 of the Companies Act 1985.

Two things have to be *stated* in an unqualified report under the Companies Act are:

—whether the accounts show a true and fair view of the profit or loss and of the state of affairs of the company;
—whether the accounts comply with the Act.

Five more things are *implicit*—referred to only if the auditor is not satisfied about them:

—proper accounting records kept;
—proper returns received from branches not visited;
—accounts in agreement with accounting records and returns;
—all information and explanations necessary for the purpose of the audit have been obtained;
—directors' report consistent with the accounts.

The Auditing Standards add more requirements:

—documents reported on and addressees must be identified;
—the report must state whether approved Auditing Standards have been complied with;
—the statement of source and application of funds is also covered (SSAP 10);
—accounting convention used must be stated if failure to do so could cause misunderstanding;
—any material departure from SSAPs must result in a qualification in the report, unless the auditor agrees with the departure.

It may sometimes be necessary for the auditor to include an *emphasis of matter* in his report. This must not be used as a substitute for a qualification but can be necessary when awareness of an unusual event, accounting policy or condition is fundamental to an understanding of the financial statements.

The audit report should be signed and dated *after* the directors have approved the financial statements.

The auditor may find it necessary to *qualify* the audit report if he is unhappy about some material matter among those tabulated in Section 14.2 above.

Qualification may be for *uncertainty* or for *disagreement*. Each of these may be *material* or *fundamental* (see the table in paragraph 4 of 'Qualifications in audit reports').

The fundamental forms of qualification should be used sparingly. Note the explanation of this point in paragraphs 22 and 23 of the Standard.

Confidence in deciding on the appropriate form of qualification to use in varying circumstances will come from careful study of the examples of qualified audit reports in the Guideline on the subject reproduced in Section 14.3.

If a full audit is *not* carried out the report must make this quite clear. If the work has merely been the preparation of accounts then the report must be headed as an accountants' report, not as an auditors' report.

The auditor also reports to management on the system of controls in force, drawing attention also to any unsuitable accounting policies and practices, or non-compliance with accounting standards or legislation. Reports to management are known by various names—management letters, letters of weakness, post-audit letters, letters of comment.

Where the audit work is performed on more than one visit, it may be appropriate to report after the interim audit and again after the final visit.

It is important that the letter results in *action* by the directors to remedy the weakness reported.

Progress questions

Questions	Reference for answers
(1) Draw up a chart showing the matters covered by an unqualified audit report, clearly separating matters which must be stated and those which are referred to only in the case of a qualification.	Section 14.2
(2) What additional matters have to be included in the audit report if not disclosed elsewhere in the financial statement?	Section 14.2
(3) What is an emphasis of matter?	Section 14.2; Paragraph 8 of Auditing Standard— The Audit Report
(4) When should the audit report be signed?	Section 14.2
(5) What are the general grounds for qualifying an audit report?	Section 14.3; Paragraph 4 of Auditing Standard— Qualifications in Audit Reports
(6) Get a friend to read out to you the qualifying paragraph (the second paragraph in each report) from each of the reports in the Auditing Guideline—Audit Report Examples. You have to say what type of qualification is appropriate.	Section 14.4: Auditing Guideline— Audit Report Examples
(7) Can the audit report on a sole trader be made in 'true and fair' terms? When?	Section 14.5

Questions	Reference for answers
(8)(*a*) When should a report to management be made by the auditor?	Section 14.6: Reports to management— Paragraph 8
(*b*) What types of matter will such a report normally deal with?	Paragraph 9
(*c*) What is the auditor's object in writing the letter?	Paragraphs 3 to 6 and 21

15 Special reports required of auditors under the Companies Act 1985

15.1 Introduction

The Companies Act 1985 calls for reports from auditors connected with several special matters:

(*a*) profit available for distribution;

(*b*) public company allotting shares otherwise than for cash;

(*c*) non-cash asset being transferred to a public company by a member in the initial period;

(*d*) private company re-registering as a public company;

(*e*) report to directors confirming company's compliance with limits permitting the filing of modified accounts;

(*f*) redemption of shares or purchase of own shares;

(*g*) provision by a company of financial assistance for the acquisition of its own shares.

15.2 Profit available for distribution (SS263–281)

It is obviously important for the protection of creditors that a company's right to pay dividends is clearly defined. Until the Companies Act 1980 we had to rely on some rather unsatisfactory case law. The position is now stated in SS263–281 of the Companies Act 1985. The auditor is involved in two respects, as we shall see in Section 15.2.2 below.

15.2.1 Definition of distributable profit

SS263 and 264 first define profit available for distribution, with separate rules for private companies and for public companies.

(*a*) Rule for all companies, private and public (S263)

Profit available for distribution is:

> accumulated realized profits *less*
> accumulated realized losses.

Obviously previous distributions or capitalization of profit must be allowed for.

S269 provides that any amount shown as development costs in the balance sheet must be treated as a realized loss in the calculation. This is subject to an important proviso, however. If there are 'special circumstances' justifying the directors in deciding that the amount should not be treated as a realized loss in the calculations the restriction will not apply, as long as the note to the accounts showing the reasons for capitalizing the expenditure also explains these special circumstances.

Distributions in kind (non-cash distributions) are permitted, subject to the basic rule indicated above. If the distribution is of an asset which has been revalued, so that the balance sheet value includes an element of unrealized profit, that unrealized profit may be treated as realized. In other words, the unrealized profit is treated as being realized by the distribution (S276).

Where an asset has been revalued upwards, depreciation will be based on the revalued amount. However, in calculating distributable profit, the depreciation attributable to the revaluation increase may be added back, so that only depreciation based on the original cost of the asset is charged for this purpose (S275).

(*b*) Additional rule for public companies (S264)

Profit available for distribution is:

> net assets *minus*
> called-up capital *plus*
> undistributable reserves.

The effect of the additional rule for public companies is that *unrealized* losses have to be brought in as well as realized ones, and thus public companies may distribute the amount that private companies can *minus any excess of UNrealized losses over UNrealized profits.*

Of course, any further restrictions imposed by the company's memorandum or articles, or other statutes, must be complied with.

15.2.2   The auditor's role

So where does the auditor come in?

There are two problems that could involve the auditor. First of all, what is the distributable profit if the audit report is qualified? It could be that the area of doubt causing the qualification is so great that the profit shown by the accounts should not reasonably be distributed at all.

The solution to this one is to require (S271) that NO distribution can be made if the auditor's report is qualified UNLESS the auditor states in writing that his or her qualification is not material for the purpose of determining whether the distribution is allowable. This statement by the auditor can either be a special report or incorporated as a paragraph in the main audit report. A suitable form of separate report could be:

AUDITOR'S STATEMENT TO THE MEMBERS OF XYZ LIMITED UNDER S271, COMPANIES ACT 1985

We have audited the financial statements of XYZ Limited for the year ended 31 December 19... in accordance with approved Auditing Standards and have expressed a qualified opinion thereon.

In our opinion that qualification is not material for the purpose of determining, by reference to those financial statements, whether the distribution proposed by the company is permitted under S271 of the Companies Act 1985.

The second problem is that of the first distribution of a company—that is, an interim dividend being paid out of its first year's profits before there has been an audit of the first year's financial statements. In this case, FOR PUBLIC COMPANIES ONLY, the auditor has to report on the interim financial statements, referred to in the Act as 'initial accounts', confirming that they have been 'properly prepared' (S273). They must also, of course, be approved by the directors and delivered to the Registrar of Companies.

It may also happen that a public company wishes to pay a dividend out of the profits of the current year when the accumulated profits of earlier years are insufficient to cover it. In this case interim accounts must be 'properly prepared', approved by the directors and lodged with the Registrar (S272), but *no* auditor's report is required.

15.2.3 Investment companies

An investment company is defined in S266 as a public company which has given notice to the Registrar of its intention to carry on business as an investment company and complies with the following requirements:

(*a*) The business of the company consists of investing its funds mainly in securities, with the aim of spreading investment risk and giving members the benefit of the results of the management of its funds.

(*b*) None of the company's holdings in other companies represent more than 15 per cent of the total invested.

(*c*) Distribution of the company's capital profits is prohibited by its memorandum of articles of association.

(*d*) Not more than 15 per cent of its income from securities is retained.

Such companies are entitled to distribute realized revenue profits provided that the distribution does not reduce the amount of its assets below *one and a half times* the aggregate of its liabilities (S265). Any development costs are required under S269 to be treated as a realized revenue loss in the calculation, unless the directors consider there are 'special circumstances' as described in paragraph 2.1 above.

15.3 Public company allotting shares otherwise than for cash (SS103 and 108)

A company may well be in the position of allotting shares otherwise than for cash in connection with a merger or takeover. In these situations there are already safeguards to ensure that assets are not being bought at an inflated price, in the form of the prospectus requirements of the Companies Act and the reports required from accountants and merchant bankers in accordance with those requirements.

SS103 and 108 cover allotments of shares *by public companies* otherwise than for cash except in the context of mergers or acquisitions. They require a report from an independent accountant on the value of the assets to be received in exchange. The independent accountant has to be a person qualified to act as auditor of the company and will frequently be the auditor.

An accountant will not necessarily be competent to make a valuation of the assets concerned and it is acceptable for him to rely on an 'independent specialist', perhaps a chartered surveyor. The accountant remains responsible for the report itself. The object is to protect the assets of the company and the interests of the existing shareholders.

The detailed requirements are that a report by a qualified accountant must be made within the six months preceding the allotment. The report must state:

(a) the nominal value of the shares in question;

(b) any premium payable on them;

(c) description of the asset concerned;

(d) extent to which shares are to be treated as paid up;

(e) method of valuation used and reason for adopting it;

(f) date of valuation;

(g) details of extent of participation of any specialist in the valuation.

Additional matters which must be stated in the report or in a note accompanying it are:

(a) that it appeared to the reporting accountant reasonable to accept the valuation;

(b) that the method of valuation was reasonable in all the circumstances;

(c) that there appears to have been no material change in the value of the asset since the valuation;

(d) that on the basis of the valuation, the value of the asset together with any cash to be paid is not less than the total amount to be treated as paid up on the shares to be issued.

A copy of the report embodying these requirements has to be sent by the company to the allottee.

If the auditor cannot give such a report because he or she is not satisfied with the value of the assets it will be necessary to qualify the report. If the company still proceeds with the transaction the *allottee* may be liable to pay the company an amount up to the value of the shares he has received.

15.4 Non-cash asset transferred to a public company by a member (SS104 and 109)

A somewhat similar situation to that covered by S103 could exist if a company buys an asset at an inflated price. Once again the interest of creditors or existing shareholders could be prejudiced. S104 protects them by requiring a similar report on the value of the asset and the consideration given, WHEN A PUBLIC COMPANY BUYS AN ASSET FROM A SUBSCRIBER TO THE COMPANY'S MEMORANDUM IN THE 'INITIAL PERIOD'—within two years of the issue to the company of its certificate to commence business under S117. The provisions DO NOT apply if:

(1) the consideration for the asset transferred is less than one tenth of the issued share capital; OR

(2) it is part of the company's ordinary business to deal in the assets concerned; OR

(3) the transaction is entered into under the supervision of the court.

If the transaction is outside one or more of these exemptions, the company in general meeting must approve the transaction, and the detailed requirements are similar to those covered in Section 15.3. The report must be circulated to the members of the company and to the person selling the asset, and must state:

(a) description of asset and method of payment;

(b) method and date of valuation of the asset;

(c) whether the value of the asset to be received is not less than the value of the payment to be made;

(d) whether the method of valuation was reasonable in all the circumstances;

(e) whether there has been a material change in the value of the asset since the valuation;

(f) if the valuation has been delegated to another person, whether it appeared to the reporting accountant reasonable for it to be delegated.

15.5 Private company re-registering as public company (S43)

When a private company re-registers as public it becomes subject to the stricter rules on distribution applied to public companies. As part of its application it must submit a statement from its auditors that in their opinion the latest balance sheet (dated not more than seven months before the application) shows that at that date the company's net assets were not less than its called-up share capital and undistributable reserves.

15.6 Auditor's report on modified accounts (Sch. 8 para. 10)

The Companies Act 1985 allows smaller companies to file 'modified accounts' with the Registrar, omitting some of the detailed disclosure requirements of the Act.

It is the duty of the auditors to provide the directors with a report stating whether in their opinion the requirements for exemption are satisfied. Also, the auditors' report on the accounts must state that in their opinion the requirements for exemption are satisfied, and reproduce the full text of their main report.

15.7   Redemption of shares or purchase of own shares (SS159–181)

The Companies Act 1981 extended the power of private companies to buy their own shares or issue and redeem redeemable shares, and contained a new power for them to do so out of capital (that is, without covering the amount required by a new issue, or by profits available for distribution). The provisions governing this are now in SS159–181 of the 1985 Act. Such actions could prejudice the interests of creditors and careful safeguards to prevent this are included in the legislation.

One important safeguard is the requirement that the directors have to make a declaration that any redemption or purchase of the company's own shares can be made without jeopardizing the company's ability to pay its debts, and continue to be able to do so in the year following the payment. This declaration of the directors must be accompanied by a report *from its auditors to the directors* as to whether they consider the directors' statement to be reasonable (S173).

15.8   Financial assistance by a company for the acquisition of its own shares (SS151–158)

S151 prohibits a company from providing financial assistance for the acquisition of its own shares, or shares in its holding company, subject to exceptions which are more extensive for private companies.

(*a*) Circumstances in which a *public* company may lend money for the acquisition of its own shares (SS153–154):

(1) if the giving of the assistance is incidental to a larger purpose which is in the interests of the company;
(2) if the lending of money is part of the ordinary business of the company and the loan is the ordinary course of that business, or the loan is for employees or part of an employee's share scheme, provided that the amount advanced is covered by distributable profits.

(*b*) Circumstances in which a *private* company may lend money for the acquisition of its own shares (SS155–158):

These provisions are somewhat similar to those enabling private companies to redeem shares or purchase their own shares. A loan may be made if:

(1) the directors make a statutory declaration that the company will be able to pay its debts as they fall due during the following year. The auditor must give a report that they have examined the company's affairs and that

they are of the opinion that the directors' statement is not unreasonable in all the circumstances;

(2) the company approves the assistance by special resolution.

There are further provisions governing the timing for giving the assistance.

15.9 Summary

(a) Distributable profits (SS263–281)

Perhaps the most important requirement in this chapter is the one about distributable profits. Both the calculation of distributable profit and the effect of audit qualifications are important.

Remember the two profit definitions:

(1) *All companies* (and therefore the normal one for private companies) – S263:

accumulated realized profit *less* accumulated realized losses

(2) *Public companies* – S264

net assets minus called up share capital *plus* undistributable reserves

The effect of an audit qualification is that no distribution can be made unless the auditor states that the qualification is not material in considering the validity of the distribution.

For public companies only, the auditor must report on the first interim accounts if the company intends to pay an interim dividend based on those accounts.

(b) Public company allotting shares otherwise than for cash (SS103 and 108); non-cash asset transferred to a public company by a member (SS104 and 109)

In these two situations the auditor is required to report confirming that the value of the assets concerned and of the shares were reasonable.

(c) Private company re-registering as public (S43)

The auditor's involvement here is to confirm that the balance sheet shows that the company's net assets totalled not less than the aggregate of the called up share capital plus undistributable reserves.

(d) Auditor's report on modified accounts (Schedule 8, paragraph 10)

The auditors must confirm that the company is entitled to avail itself of the reduced disclosure requirements applied to small and medium sized companies.

(e) Redemption of shares or purchase of own shares (SS159–181)

Redemption of shares and purchase of own shares are actions which could seriously prejudice the interests of creditors. The directors have to make a declaration that the purchase or redemption can be made without jeopardizing the company's ability to pay its debts. As an additional safeguard the auditors are required to give a report to the directors stating whether they consider the directors' declaration to be reasonable.

(f) Financial assistance by a company for the acquisition of its own shares

This is generally prohibited for PUBLIC companies but allowed for PRIVATE companies.

It is only allowed for public companies if:

(1) part of a larger purpose; or
(2) in the ordinary course of business; or
(3) for employees.

It is allowed for private companies if directors make a declaration, supported by the auditors, that the company will be able to pay its debts as they fall due during the following year.

Progress Questions

Questions	Reference for answers
(1)(a) Define distributable profit for: (i) all companies, (ii) public companies.	Section 15.2
(b) What is the difference between the definitions?	
(2) What happens to a company's right to distribute if the auditor's report is qualified?	Section 15.2.2

Questions	Reference for answers
(3) What has to happen before a public company can pay an interim dividend in its first year of operation before audited accounts have been prepared?	Section 15.2.2
(4) How is the distributable profit of an investment company defined?	Section 15.2.3
(5) What has to happen before a public company can issue shares otherwise than for cash and not in the course of a merger or takeover?	Section 15.3
(6)(*a*) List the resrictions that may be placed on a public company's power to buy an asset from a member. (*b*) After how long will these restrictions no longer apply?	Section 15.4
(7) How and why is the auditor involved when a private company wishes to re-register as public?	Section 15.5
(8) How is the auditor involved when a company wishes to file modified accounts with the Registrar?	Section 15.6
(9) How is the auditor involved when a private company wishes to redeem shares or buy its own shares?	Section 15.7
(10) Explain (*a*) when a public company may provide financial assistance for the acquisition of its own shares; (*b*) what a private company must do to enable it to provide such assistance.	Section 15.8

16 Statutory requirements governing auditors

16.1 Introduction

It is now time to take a look at the statutory requirements governing auditors of limited companies. The Companies Act 1985 lays down rules covering:

(a) Appointment and remuneration (SS384–385);
(b) Removal (SS386 and 388);
(c) Rights and duties (SS237, 387, 392);
(d) Qualifications (S389);
(e) Disqualifications (S389);
(f) Resignation (SS390–391);
(g) Auditor's liability under statute (SS624–631);
(h) False statements to auditors (S393);
(i) Dormant companies (SS252–253).

16.2 Appointment and remuneration (SS384–385)

S384 requires every company (except dormant companies, see Section 16.9.2 below) to appoint an auditor at each annual general meeting, to hold office until the conclusion of the next AGM. This important requirement ensures that it is normally the *members* who appoint, and that the auditor's position is subject to annual confirmation by the members. Nevertheless, the members have no right of direct communication with the auditor. They only have the right to receive the audit report.

The directors can appoint the first auditors at any time before the first AGM, and can also appoint someone to fill a 'casual' vacancy—one arising during the year, perhaps because of the death of an existing auditor.

If at the conclusion of the AGM no auditor has been appointed, the Secretarty of State for Trade may appoint. The company has to give notice to the Secretaty of State within one week of the meeting, if no auditors have in fact been appointed, to enable the Secretary of State to do so. (This power of the Secretary of State is rarely used but exists to ensure that a company always has an auditor.)

The persons appointing the auditor (members, directors or Secretary of State) have the power under S385 to fix the auditor's remuneration. This is something the auditors themselves also have a hand in, of course! The members may delegate this responsibility to the directors.

16.3   Removal (SS386 and 388)

It is possible to remove an auditor, and the procedures to be followed are designed to ensure that the auditor has plenty of opportunity to communicate with the members who will normally have appointed him or her and to whom his or her primary duty lies.

Removal is normally at the AGM, by simply proposing the appointment of a different auditor. It is also possible to remove the auditor during his or her term of office by convening an extraordinary general meeting. The basic point is that only the MEMBERS can remove the auditor.

The procedure has to go like this:

(a) *Special notice*
Special notice (28 days) has to be given for any resolution at a general meeting:

(1) appointing a different auditor in place of a retiring auditor,
(2) removing an auditor before the end of his term of office.

(Special notice is also required for a resolution filling a casual vacancy in the office of auditor or reappointing an auditor appointed by the directors to fill a casual vacancy).

(b) *Inform the auditor*
Immediately on receipt of the notice the company must send a copy to the auditor concerned.

(c) *Auditor's representations*
The auditor may require the company to circulate his representations to the members. If they are received too late for this to happen, the auditor may have the representations (his side of the case) read out to the meeting.

(d) *At the meeting, a simple majority of members will then remove the auditor.*

(e) *Within 14 days of the meeting the company must inform the Registrar of Companies of the removal.*

The auditor who has been removed retains the right to receive notice of, attend and be heard at the general meeting at which his or her appointment would have ended AND any meeting at which a replacement auditor is to be appointed to fill the casual vacancy arising.

There is the usual proviso that the auditor's representations do not have to be circulated or read out if, on application, the Court considers that the provisions are being abused to secure needless publicity for defamatory matter.

16.4 Rights and duties (SS237, 387, 392)

The auditor's main statutory rights and duties are defined in S237. The auditor is given the necessary rights to carry out his or her duties. Let us take a look at the duties first.

16.4.1 Duties

(a) To report on the accounts. The auditor's main duty is to REPORT to the members on the accounts, covering the matters specified in S237. These points were detailed in Chapter 14.

(b) To qualify the report. The auditor's second duty is to QUALIFY the report if he is not happy about one or more of the matters listed in S237.

(c) To report to directors of small or medium-sized companies. Before small or medium-sized companies can take advantage of the concession to file modified accounts with the Registrar, their auditors must provide a report to the directors that they qualify for the exemption from the requirement to file full accounts (Schedule 8, paragraph 10).

(d) To include additional information in the report in connection with directors' or employees' remuneration, or loans to officers, where not provided in the accounts.

In addition to these duties in connection with the financial accounts, the auditor may have to provide special reports or statements in certain circumstances. These were explained in Chapter 15.

16.4.2 Rights

The auditor's rights, in connection with the statutory audit, enable him or her first to do the work and then to deliver a report to the members. These rights are:

(a) access to books, accounts and vouchers of the company at all times (S237)

(b) entitlement to any information and explanation from the company's officers which the auditor thinks necessary for the performance of his or her duties (S237)

To do the work

(c) to receive notice of all general meetings
   of the company (S387)

(d) to attend such meetings and be heard at them
   on any matter concerning him or her as an
   auditor (S387)

⎫
⎬
⎭
To deliver
the report

The auditor of a holding company is entitled to require reasonable information and explanation from the subsidiary and its auditors (S392). In addition to these rights concerning the audit itself, the auditor has the right to resign (see Section 16.7 below) and has rights in connection with any possible attempt to remove him (see Section 16.3 above).

16.5 Qualifications (S389)

In general, the auditor must be professionally qualified. At the moment there are four UK bodies whose members are automatically qualified for appointment:

—Institute of Chartered Accountants of Scotland
—Institute of Chartered Accountants in England and Wales
—Institute of Chartered Accountants in Ireland
—Chartered Association of Certified Accountants.

The Department of Trade will also authorize holders of equivalent overseas qualifications, provided the country concerned grants similar rights to UK accountants.

In addition to the above, it surprisingly remains possible for unqualified auditors to be appointed. To be eligible, they must be individually authorized by the Department of Trade as having met one of two criteria:

(a) Having been in practice as a public accountant before 6 August 1947;
(b) Having obtained sufficient experience as an acountant and auditor in the 12 months ended 3 November 1966, and been, on that date, auditor of at least one company.

Auditors authorized by the Department of Trade under these provisions have formed their own professional body, the Association of Authorized Public Accountants. No fresh application for authorization under these provisions are now accepted by the Department of Trade, so the number of members of this unusual body will eventually drop to zero. Once authorized, those in practice at 6 August 1947 ((a) above) may be appointed auditors of any company, but those qualifying by experience up to 3 November 1966 may only audit unquoted companies.

16.6   Disqualifications (S389)

A person is not eligible for appointment as auditor of a company if he or she is:

(a) an officer or servant of the company in some capacity other than as an auditor;

(b) a partner or employee of an officer or servant;

(c) disqualified under (a) or (b) above in respect of any other company which is the company's subsidiary or holding company.

A body corporate is also ineligible for appointment as auditor.

These very basic statutory requirements ensuring the independence of the auditor are greatly amplified by the requirements of the professional bodies themselves. These are explained in Chapter 18.

16.7   Resignation

The auditor may resign at any time by giving notice to that effect to the client company. The notice must contain either:

(a) a statement that there are *no* circumstances connected with his or her resignation that should be brought to the attention of members *or creditors*; or

(b) a statement of any such circumstances.

The company must, within 14 days, send a copy of the notice to the Registrar of Companies and, if the auditor has detailed circumstances that should be brought to the attention of members or creditors, to every member and every debenture-holder.

In addition to the right to resign, the auditor has, under S391, the right to requisition an extraordinary general meeting to consider the circumstances of his resignation. The directors then have 21 days to give notice of a meeting to be held within 28 days of that notice. The company, or any other person affected, may make application to the Court for an order not to send out the statement, or not to requisition the meeting, if it considers that the procedure is being used to obtain needless publicity for defamatory matter.

The resigning auditor retains the right to receive notice of, attend and be heard at the next AGM at which his or her appointment would have terminated.

If the auditor does decide to resign in order to bring the attention of members to some matter, it will normally only be after having attempted to persuade the directors to alter their policy to eliminate the matter causing the problem, and possibly after taking legal advice.

The use of the power to resign is not a gesture of weakness. In fact, it may be the only way an auditor can bring important matters to the attention of the members, as this is the only way he can convene a meeting of members to communicate directly with them before the AGM.

16.8 Auditor's liability under statute (SS624–631)

The extent of the auditor's liability to members and third parties is determined by common law, the contract with the client, and by case law. All this is explained in a later chapter.

As an officer of the company, however, the auditor may be liable to civil and even criminal penalties for offences in connection with the winding up of the company.

First of all, S631 imposes a civil liability on all *officers* of a company who can be shown to have made a personal gain by misfeasance, breach of trust or by misapplying property of the company. (Misfeasance means, briefly, doing a lawful act in a wrongful manner.)

The Court may compel an officer guilty of such an act to restore the property or account for any gain, or to compensate the company to the extent the Court thinks just.

S727 empowers the Court to relieve the auditor (or indeed any other officer) if it considers that he or she ought fairly to be excused for acting honestly and reasonably.

Then we have SS624 to 630. These impose *criminal* penalties on a company's officers (including auditors). Offences possibly relevant for auditors include:

(*a*) Within 12 months before liquidation (S624):

(1) concealing, destroying, mutilating or falsifying any books or papers;
(2) making false entries in books or papers;
(3) fraudulently parting with, altering or making any omission in any document.

(*b*) in the course of winding up (S626–628)

(1) failing to disclose details of a company's assets to the liquidator;
(2) failing to deliver to the liquidator any books or papers in his or her possession and which he or she is required by law to deliver up;
(3) preventing the production of any book or paper after the commencement of the winding up;
(4) falsifying records with intent to defraud;
(5) making a material omission in any statement relating to the company's affairs.

It is a defence against all of these charges (except, of course, (b)(4) above), for the auditor to prove that there was no intent to defraud.

16.9 Sundry matters

16.9.1 False statements to auditors (S393)

S393 makes it a criminal offence for any officer of a company to give misleading, false or deceptive statements in response to an auditor's request for information or explanation.

16.9.2 Dormant companies (SS252–253)

Until the Companies Act 1981 all companies without exception were required to have auditors. Since 1981 'dormant' companies are exempt from the requirement. A dormant company is a private company which has had no 'significant accounting transaction' during the period concerned.

The procedure is for the company to pass a special resolution at the AGM at which the company's accounts are presented to the members, making itself exempt from the obligation to appoint auditors in accordance with S384. A company required to prepare group accounts, or one not entitled to the small company exemption, cannot take advantage of the concession, nor can a public company or a banking, shipping or insurance company. The unaudited accounts must still be laid before the company in general meeting, and lodged with the Registrar, but incorporating a statement by the directors immediately above their signature on the balance sheet that the company was dormant throughout the financial year.

16.10 Summary

Appointment

Auditors may be appointed by:

   (a) members at each AGM;
   (b) directors (first auditors or casual vacancy);
   (c) Secretary of State for Trade (if at conclusion of AGM no appointment has been made).

Removal

An auditor may be removed provided the proper procedure is followed:

(a) special notice (28 days);
(b) auditor informed (forthwith);
(c) auditor's representations circulated;
(d) vote at general meeting (simple majority suffices);
(e) Registrar informed within 14 days.

A removed auditor retains the right to receive notice of, attend and be heard at the general meeting at which his appointment would have ended.

Rights and duties

(a) Rights
(1) access to books, accounts and vouchers at all times;
(2) to receive information and explanation from the company's officers;
(3) to receive notice of general meetings, and to attend and be heard at them.

(b) Duties
(1) to report;
(2) to qualify the report if necessary;
(3) to include additional information in the report (directors' and employees' remuneration, loans to officers).

Qualifications

Auditors must be professionally qualified or individually authorized by the Department of Trade if unqualified or a member of a foreign body.

Disqualifications

An auditor must *not* be:

—an officer or servant of the company;
—a partner or employee or an officer or servant.

Resignation

The auditor may resign by giving notice to the company and may requisition an extraordinary general meeting to consider the circumstances of the resignation.

Auditor's liability under statute

As an officer of the company, the auditor may incur civil and criminal penalties for offences in connection with the winding up of a company.

False statements to auditors

It is a criminal offence for an officer of a company to make a deceptive statement to the auditor.

Dormant companies

A company which does not have a 'significant accounting transaction' in a financial year may declare itself 'dormant' by special resolution and thus become exempt from the requirement to appoint auditors.

Progress questions

Questions	Reference and answers
Quote section references in your answers if you can.	
(1) Who may appoint the auditor of a company?	Section 16.2
(2) Is the auditor subject to annual re-appointment?	Section 16.2
(3)(a) Who must initiate the procedure to remove an auditor?	Section 16.3
(b) What are the steps in the procedure to remove an auditor?	Section 16.3
(4)(a) What are the duties of the auditor?	Section 16.4.1
(b) What are the rights of the auditor?	Section 16.4.2
(5) What professional qualifications must the auditor of a company normally hold?	Section 16.5

Questions	Reference and answers
(6) What persons are not eligible for appointment as auditor under the Companies Act?	Section 16.6
(7) What must an auditor do if he resigns?	Section 16.7
(8) What must the company do if its auditor resigns?	Section 16.7
(9) What rights does an auditor who has resigned retain?	Section 16.7
(10) In what circumstances may an auditor be liable to (a) civil penalties (b) criminal penalties under the Companies Act?	Section 16.8
(11) Why is it dangerous for a company's officers to make false statements to auditors?	Section 16.9.1
(12) What is a dormant company?	Section 16.9.2

17 Other statutory requirements of concern to auditors

17.1 Proper accounting records

The requirements of SS221–223 governing proper accounting records are:

(a) The accounting records must show and explain the company's transactions in such a way as to (i) disclose, with reasonable accuracy, the company's financial position at any time, and (ii) enable the directors to ensure that any financial statements comply with the provisions of the Companies Act as to the form and content of company accounts.

(b) Details must be given of:

(1) cash received and paid;
(2) assets and liabilities;
(3) sales and purchases;
(4) stocktaking statements.

The auditor must consider whether the records do in fact meet these requirements, and will qualify the report if in his or her opinion they do not.

The records must be kept at the company's registered office, 'or such other place as the directors think fit', and must be open to inspection at all times by the company's officers.

Private companies must retain these records for at least three years and public companies for at least six years.

17.2 Accounting reference periods

A company is required by S224 to give notice to the Registrar, within six months of incorporation, stating its proposed regular accounting date.

This is known as the company's *accounting reference date*, and the period ending on that date is the company's accounting reference *period*. If such a notice is not given, the company's accounting reference date becomes 31 March.

The accounting reference date may vary by up to seven days each year, to allow for companies wishing to make up their accounts for an exact number of weeks instead of for a calendar year (S227).

A company's first accounting reference period must begin on the date of its incorporation and be for a period of more than six months and not more than eighteen months: this allows a company to get around to the date it proposes to adopt for the future. Later accounting reference periods are of twelve months unless the company changes its date as provided by S225.

S225 allows a company to change its regular accounting reference date by informing the Registrar of its intention to adopt an accounting period other than a year, as long as the accounting period concerned does not exceed eighteen months. Notice must be given to the Registrar before the end of the accounting reference period. If the change is effected by means of a period of more than one year, this is only acceptable if there has been at least five years since a previous extended period, though the Secretary of State has the power to waive this rule.

A company may, however, extend its accounting period at any time regardless of the five-year rule if the purpose is to cause the accounting dates of group companies to coincide.

S242 lays down the period allowed after the accounting reference date within which accounts must be laid before the members and delivered to the Registrar. These periods are:

—private companies with no overseas interests: ten months;
—private companies with overseas interests: thirteen months;
—public companies with no overseas interests: seven months;
—public companies with overseas interests: ten months.

A company must inform the Registrar if it intends to take advantage of the concession extending the period for three months for overseas interests.

For the first accounts of a company the periods are shortened by one month for every month by which the accounting reference period exceeds twelve months, subject to a minimum period of three months.

These provisions are important to company directors because S243 makes them guilty of an offence and liable to a fine and, for continued contravention, a daily default fine. In practice these penalties are rarely invoked.

17.3   Publication of accounts

(a) Publication of full accounts (S254)

If a company publishes its full accounts (whether modified under the provisions of SS247–251 or not), it must publish with them the relevant auditor's report. If the company is also required to prepare group accounts it must publish these group accounts along with the individual accounts and auditor's report.

(b) Publication of abridged accounts (S255)

'Abridged' accounts mean any summarized version of the accounts, omitting parts of the statutory disclosure requirements. In this case the company must publish with the accounts a statement indicating:

(1) that the accounts are not full accounts;
(2) whether full accounts have been lodged with the Registrar;
(3) whether the auditor's report on these accounts was unqualified.

When a company publishes abridged accounts it must *not* publish the auditor's report with them.

Note the distinction between *abridged accounts*—accounts omitting certain disclosure requirements—and *modified accounts*, which are accounts embodying the reduced disclosure requirements applicable to small or medium-sized companies.

17.4   Loans to directors and other officers

The requirements governing loans to directors and other officers are to be found in SS232–234 and SS330–347, and Schedule 6.

What follows is a somewhat abridged version of the full requirements which occupy just over 20 pages of the Companies Act 1985! There are firstly rules applicable to all companies, then a stricter set of rules applicable to 'relevant' companies only. A relevant company is a public company or a private company which is a member of a group which includes a public company.

17.4.1   Rules applicable to all companies

S330 prohibits loans by a company to a director or to a director of its holding company subject to certain exceptions. It also prohibits the provision of guarantees or security for a loan to such a director. The exceptions are:

(a) loan etc. not exceeding £2500 (S334);

(b) loan by a company to its holding company (S336);

(c) loan to enable a director to perform his or her duties or to meet expenditure to be incurred on behalf of the company (S337). In order to qualify for exception under this heading the loan has to have the approval of the company in general meeting either before the loan is made or at the next general meeting. If approval is sought retrospectively at the next general meeting and is not given, the loan has to be repaid within six months;

(d) loan by a money-lending company in the ordinary course of the company's business and on terms no more favourable than would be accorded to an unconnected person of the same financial standing (S338).

Note that these rules do not prohibit a loan to a director's wife or other connected person—that is only prohibited for a 'relevant' company. (See 17.4.2(d) below).

17.4.2 Further rules for relevant companies

(a) A limit of £10 000 is placed on loans to enable a director to perform his duties (17.4.1(c) above) (S337);

(b) A limit of £50 000 is placed on loans by a money-lending company (17.4.1(d) above) (S338). This limit does not apply if the company is a recognized bank, unless the loan is for housing purposes when the £50 000 limit is imposed.

(c) The prohibition is extended to 'quasi-loans' (S330). A quasi-loan is defined in S331 as a transaction in which the company agrees to pay a third party on behalf of a director. S332 allows small quasi-loans not exceeding £1 000 and repayable by the director within 2 months.

(d) The prohibition is extended to 'persons connected with a director' (S330). S346 defines these as:

(1) spouse, minor child or step-child;

(2) company with which the director is 'associated'; (A director is 'associated' with a company if he or she, together with other connected persons, holds 20 per cent or more of the equity share capital or controls 20 per cent or more of the voting power).

(3) trustees of trust (other than a share scheme or pension scheme) for the benefit of the director or persons connected with the director under rules (1) and (2) above;

(4) partner of the director or partner of any person connected with the director under rules (1) to (3) above.

(*e*) The prohibition is extended to cover 'credit transactions' exceeding £5000 (S330). S346 defines these as:

(1) hire purchase tranactions;
(2) leasing or hiring contracts;
(3) any other arrangement by which payment for land, goods or services is deferred.

Credit transactions entered into in the normal course of the company's business and on terms no more favourable than would be offered to an unconnected person of the same financial standing are not affected (S335). Credit transactions entered into for the company's holding company are also excluded from the prohibition (S336).

17.4.3   Disclosure requirements

The disclosure requirements are to be found in paragraph 9 of Schedule 6 and they are:

(*a*) details of contract for loan etc.;
(*b*) name of person concerned and, if that person is not a director, the name of the director with whom the person is connected;
(*c*) amount of loan at beginning and end of year;
(*d*) maximum amount of loan;
(*e*) amount of new unpaid interest;
(*f*) any provision for non-payment;
(*g*) details of any guarantee or security;
(*h*) details of any agreement to provide a loan or similar facility.

Paragraph 11 of Schedule 6 exempts credit transactions not exceeding £5000 from these disclosure requirements.

Finally, the aggregate of all loans, etc., to officers other than directors must be disclosed (Paragraph 16), together with the number of officers receiving them. Loans not exceeding £2500 to any one officer do not have to be disclosed.

17.5   Maintenance of capital—public companies

If the net assets of a *public* company are half or less of its called-up share capital, the directors are required by S142 to convene an extraordinary general meeting to consider what steps should be taken to deal with the situation.

The meeting has to be called within 28 days of the fact of the loss of capital becoming known to a director, and has to be held within a period not exceeding a further 28 days (56 days in all).

The auditor is involved in two respects. First of all the auditor must be satisfied that the section does not apply, and if it does he or she must remind the directors of their duty under the section. Secondly, the auditor may be asked to advise on the situation, and particularly on the basis of valuation of the assets. The Act is silent on this vital matter and there may, of course, be a substantial difference between the going concern value and the possible break-up value.

If the loss in value is such that the going concern value is less than half the called-up share capital, then clearly the section applies. If the going concern basis is more than 50 per cent but the break-up value is less than 50 per cent we have a grey area in which the directors have to watch the company's position closely and take all possible action to improve matters, though probably without calling the extraordinary general meeting at that time. If it appears that the company's affairs are irretrievable it can do no harm to have the extraordinary meeting without delay. The auditor should advise the directors to take legal advice at an early stage.

17.6 Summary

(a) Proper accounting records (SS221–223)

These must show:

(1) explanation of transactions;
(2) cash received and paid;
(3) assets and liabilities;
(4) sales and purchases;
(5) stocktaking statements.

and they must be retained for at least

—three years for private companies and
—six years for public companies.

(b) Accounting reference periods (SS224–225 and SS242–243)

A company must inform the Registrar of its regular accounting date and of any changes in it. Changes involving extending the accounting period are not allowed more than once every five years unless the Secretary of State gives consent, or the purpose is to cause accounting dates of group companies to coincide.

Accounts must be laid before the members and lodged with the Registrar within ten months (private companies) or seven months (public companies), with an extension of three months if the company has overseas interests.

(c) Publication of accounts

If accounts complying with the full disclosure requirements of the Companies Act are published, the auditor's report must be published with them.

If abridged accounts are published, the auditor's report must *not* be published with them, but they must be accompanied by a statement indicating that they are not full accounts, and stating whether full accounts have been lodged with the Registrar and whether the auditor's reports was qualified.

(d) Loans to directors and other officers

(1) Rules for all companies—no loans except:

—loan not exceeding £2500;
—loan to holding company;
—loan in ordinary course of business;
—loan to enable director to carry out duties (subject to approval at AGM).

(2) Further rules for relevant companies

—loans for duties not to exceed £10 000;
—loans in ordinary course of business not to exceed £50 000; (unless the company is a bank and the loan is not for housing)
—quasi-loans (payment to third party on behalf of directors) over £1000 prohibited;
—loans to connected persons also covered;
—credit transactions exceeding £5000 prohibited.

(3) Full details of loans must be disclosed in the accounts.

(e) Maintenance of capital—public companies

If the net assets of a public company fall to half or less of the called-up share capital, the directors must convene an extraordinary general meeting to consider the situation. The meeting must be called within 28 days and held within a maximum of a further 28 days.

Progress questions

Questions	Reference for answers
(1)(*a*) What constitutes proper accounting records for a company? (*b*) What is the minimum time for which such records must be retained?	Section 17.1
(2) What is a company's accounting reference period and how is it determined?	Section 17.2
(3) How long after a company's accounting reference date is allowed for it to file accounts with the Registrar?	Section 17.2
(4) What are the rules concerning the publication by a company of its accounts?	Section 17.3
(5) Summarize briefly but completely the rules relating to loans to directors of (*a*) all companies (*b*) public companies (relevant companies).	Section 17.4
(6) What must the directors of a public company do if the value of the net assets of the company falls to half or less of the called-up share capital?	Section 17.5

18 Auditor's independence

18.1 Introduction

The auditor's independence was briefly mentioned in Chapter 1, and the statutory requirements which contribute to it were dealt with in Chapter 16. It is now time to examine the whole question of independence in detail.

18.2 Statutory requirements

The Companies Act 1985 contains a number of provisions to ensure the independence of the auditor. The areas concerned are listed below. Full details of these requirements were given in Chapter 16.

(a) S384: Auditor must be reappointed annually *by the members*.

(b) S386–388: Special procedure involving the approval of members is necessary to remove the auditors.

(c) S389: Auditor must be professionally qualified, thus bringing him within the control of professional bodies with high ethical standards.

(d) S389: Auditor must not be an officer or servant of the company, or a partner or employee of an officer or servant.

18.3 The Ethical Guide

The statutory requirements merely scratch the surface of the question. In 1979 the professional bodies each issued to their members a *Guide to Professional Ethics*, which dealt with independence and with some other matters such as the extent to which members may advertise their services. This statement became known as *The Ethical Guide*, and the main matters it deals with are summarized in Sections 18.3.1 and 18.3.4.

18.3.1 Fees

It is recognized that a practice drawing a large part of its total fee income from one client might be thought to have its independence impaired as regards that client. The *Guide* therefore states that a practice 'should endeavour to ensure that the recurring fees paid by one client or group of connected clients do not exceed 15 per cent of the gross fees of the practice'. If the fees from one client exceed 15 per cent of the gross recurring fees of a branch office of the practice, it is suggested that a partner from another office should take final responsibility for any report made on the affairs of that client. Exceptions are made for new practices being built up and old practices being run down.

Note the reference to *recurring fees*. A single assignment which causes the 15 per cent limit to be breached in one year does not count.

18.3.2 Personal relationships

Close personal relationships could obviously impair independence. The *Guide* mentions 'close friendship or relationship by blood or marriage' between partners or audit staff and clients. It even suggests that problems may arise if the same partner remains for a number of years responsible for the same audit, thus implying that partners should be rotated from time to time.

18.3.3 Financial involvement with or in the affairs of clients

In this area a distinction is drawn between audit clients and other clients. Note too that some possible financial involvements are barred for all partners, their spouses and minor children, and staff, while others apply only to personnel actually engaged in the work.

(a) Beneficial shareholdings—audit clients

As we saw in Chapter 1, the auditor was originally chosen from among the shareholders, and some old Articles of Association still require the auditor to have a qualifying shareholding. The *Guide* now imposes a strict ban on such holdings: 'A practice should ensure that it does not have as an audit client a company in which a partner in the practice, the spouse or minor child of such partner, is the beneficial holder of shares'. In addition, it should not employ on the audit any member of staff who is a beneficial shareholder.

There are the inevitable necessary exceptions:

(1) Where the company's Articles of Association or an Act of Parliament require the auditor to have a minimum shareholding, it is in order for the auditor to hold that minimum number of shares.

(2) Where the shares are acquired involuntarily—as when a partner inherits them, marries a shareholder, or receives them as a result of a takeover—such holdings should be disposed of at the earliest practicable date, as should any shares already held in a company becoming an audit client.

The number of any shares held by the auditor because of the above exceptions should be disclosed in the directors' report or, if not so disclosed, in the audit report.

(b) Beneficial shareholdings—clients other than audit clients

The rules here are less strict. It is merely necessary to ensure that no partner or member of staff engaged on the assignment, or the spouse or minor child of such a partner, has any beneficial interest in the company.

(c) Trustee shareholdings—public companies

For audit clients, trustee holdings or a partner in the practice or the spouse of a partner, should not exceed 10 per cent of the issued share capital of the company or 10 per cent of the total assets comprised in the trust.

Even when holdings are below this limit, the partner concerned should not participate in the audit, and the shareholding should be disclosed in the directors' report, or failing that in the audit report.

(d) Trustee shareholdings—private companies

No formal restriction is placed on trustee holdings in private company audit clients, except a requirement that they should be disclosed. Where possible a review of the files in such a case should be undertaken by another partner.

(e) Loans to and from clients—practice loans

Not surprisingly, loans to and from clients are barred, as are guarantees of such loans.

There is one exception. It is acceptable for the practice to have a current account in credit or a deposit account with a client bank.

(f) Loans to and from clients—individual loans

These loans are also out, including any to or from the spouse or minor child of a partner. This time there are two exceptions:

(1) a current or deposit account with a clearing bank is in order, including a loan or overdraft;

(2) loans between close relations in fulfilment of family obligations are in order.

(g) Goods and services

The suggested rule here is that partners, their spouses and minor children, and staff, should not accept goods or services on terms more favourable than those available to the client's employees. This could apply, perhaps, to the purchase of goods at a discount.

(h) Commission

The receipt of commission on a transaction the client is advised to enter into is not debarred. However, the client should be informed in writing of the fact that commission will be received and, if possible, the amount of it. Also, special care should be taken so that the advice is in the best interests of the client.

18.3.4 Conflicts of interest

There can be a conflict of interests between the personal affairs of an accountant and those of his client, and between the interests of two clients. The accountant's attitude may be summed up as: 'disclose, discuss and (probably) decline'!

Detailed guidance is offered for a variety of situations:

(a) Competing clients

A firm should avoid becoming involved in providing advice to one client on a matter on which the firm is already advising another client. The example given in *The Ethical Guide* is that of a firm advising one client on figures for inclusion in a tender for a contract. Clearly it would be impossible for the firm to provide advice to another client tendering for the same contract.

(b) Clients in dispute

It may be perfectly proper for a firm to be financial adviser to a company and also deal with the personal affairs of its directors. If a dispute should develop between the company and a director it would be difficult for the firm to continue to advise both sides, unless all parties were prepared to accept the firm's assistance in putting forward proposals to end the dispute.

(c) Provision of other services to audit clients

Historically, UK accountants have provided a comprehensive package of financial services for many clients, especially smaller ones. In other words, the audit is accompanied by accounting, taxation and management consultancy services. It was at one time feared that the EEC Eighth Directive would bring an end to this and ban auditors from providing any other service to clients. The final form of the Eighth Directive omitted any provision to this effect, though the European Commission may return to the point and impose stricter rules at some time in the future.

For the moment, at any rate, the practice of providing other services can continue, subject to the following limits imposed by *The Ethical Guide*:

(1) The auditor must take care not to be involved in executive functions or make executive decisions. There is a difference between offering advice to management as to a course of action and participating in the decision-making process itself.

(2) For public companies, the auditor should only be involved in the preparation of accounting records in exceptional circumstances.

(3) For private companies no such limitation is imposed, but the auditor should ensure that the client accepts full responsibility for the records and that objectivity in carrying out the audit is not impaired.

(d) Current appointment in a company reported on

A practice should not accept appointment as auditor of a company if a partner or employee of the practice is an officer or servant of that company. (In the UK this is, of course, barred by S389 of the Companies Act 1985. *The Ethical Guide* covers the point to ensure that the requirement is followed for audit appointments in countries where such a statutory restriction does not exist.)

(e) Previous appointment in a company reported on

No-one should personally take part in the exercise of the reporting function on a company if he or she has, during the period reported on, or in the previous two years, been an officer (other than auditor) or employee of that company.

(f) Liquidations following receiverships

Where a partner or employee of a practice is, or in the previous two years has been, receiver of any of the assets of the company, no partner in or employee of the practice should accept appointment as liquidator of the company.

(g) Liquidations generally

(1) Insolvent companies
An appointment as liquidator of an insolvent company should be declined if a partner or member of staff has had a continuing professional relationship with the company within the previous two years.

(2) Solvent companies
An appointment should be accepted only after carefully considering the implications of acceptance.

(h) Receiverships

No appointment as receiver should be accepted if a partner or member of staff has had a continuing professional relationship with the company within the previous two years.

(i) Audit following receiverships

No appointment as auditor should be accepted if the period to be reported on is one during which a partner or member of staff had acted as receiver.

(j) Independence

Before accepting a new appointment, the accountant should satisfy himself that his independence will not be jeopardized.

18.4 The audit committee's contribution to independence

The existence of an *audit committee* can be a powerful contributor to the auditor's independence. Audit committees are fairly rare in the UK, however, and really confined to large companies. Audit committees are fully covered in Chapter 20.

18.5 Summary

It is essential for an audit to be conducted from a position of independence. There are some statutory requirements contributing to the auditor's independence but the details are mainly covered by the *Guide to Professional Ethics* issued by the professional bodies and often referred to as The Ethical Guide.

Relevant statutory requirements are:

S384   —auditor reappointed annually by members
S386–388—auditor may only be removed if the special procedure laid down in these sections is followed
S389   —auditor must be professionally qualified
S389   —auditor must not be an officer or servant of the company or a partner or employee of an officer or servant.

Ethical Guide requirements cover:

(a) *Fees*: recurring fees from one client not normally to exceed 15 per cent of total
(b) *Personal relationships*: close friendship or blood relationships between auditor and client must impair independence
(c) *Beneficial shareholding—audit clients*: barred for all partners and their spouses and minor children; audit staff who are shareholders should not be engaged in the work
(d) *Beneficial shareholdings—clients other than audit clients*: No one engaged in the work should be a shareholder
(e) *Trustee shareholdings*: limited to 10 per cent for public companies, no limit for private companies
(f) *Loans to and from clients*: barred subject to minor exceptions
(g) *Goods and services*: should not be obtained from clients on terms more favourable than those available to client's own staff
(h) *Commission*: existence and amount must be disclosed
(i) *Conflicts of interest*:

(1) Conflicts of interest between client and auditor and between two clients must be avoided
(2) The auditor should not become involved in executive decisions
(3) The auditor of a public company should not generally become involved in the preparation of accounting records.

An accountant who has, within the previous two years had another appointment in the company is subject to the following limitations:

Is or has been	Cannot accept appointment as
Officer other than auditor	Auditor
Receiver	Auditor, if period to be reported on overlaps with that of receivership
Receiver	Liquidator
In a continuing professional relationship	Receiver
In a continuing professional relationship	Liquidator of an insolvent company

Finally, the existence of an audit committee can make an important contribution to the auditor's independence.

Progress questions

Questions	Reference for answers
(1) What provisions of the Companies Act contribute to the auditor's independence?	Section 18.2
(2)(a) What are the areas covered by *The Ethical Guide* to ensure independence? (b) Give brief details of each.	Section 18.3

19 Professional liability of accountants and auditors

19.1 Introduction

An audit is a professional service to a client. If the work is negligently done and damage ensues, can the client claim damages? Suppose the plaintiff (claimant) is not the client but a third party. Does the auditor still have a liability?

To answer these questions we must look at statute law, case law and professional pronouncements.

Let us consider first the liability to clients.

19.2 Liability to clients

A claim by a client is often based on an alleged failure of the auditor to carry out a competent audit, thus resulting in financial loss to the client perhaps through a fraud which remains undiscovered.

Such a claim could be made in *contract* (failure to fulfil a contractual obligation) or in *tort*, but it would probably be made in contract because the position is likely to be more clear-cut as the contract would provide evidence of the obligations undertaken.

Our starting point in considering the position under contract law is the specimen engagement letter provided as Appendix 1 to the Auditing Guideline on engagement letters published in May 1984. This contains the following:

'The responsibility for the prevention and detection of irregularities and fraud rests with yourselves (the directors). However, we shall endeavour to plan our audit so that we have a reasonable expectation of detecting material misstatements in the financial statements or accounting records resulting from irregularities or fraud, but our examination should not be relied on to disclose irregularities or frauds which may exist.'

That, then, is likely to be the substance of the contract evidenced by an engagement letter.

We must also consider the statutory duties of the auditor as stated in S237 (see Section 16.4). Failure by the auditor to satisfy himself or herself of the matters needed to be covered in the report is evidence of negligent completion of the audit.

Interpretation of the auditor's statutory responsibility by the Courts goes back to that of Lopes LJ *in re Kingston Cotton Mills Co. (1896)*, the classic case on the subject:

'It is the duty of an auditor to bring to bear on the work he has to perform that skill, care and caution which a reasonable, careful and cautious auditor would use. What is reasonable skill, care and caution must depend on the particular circumstances of each case. An auditor is not bound to be a detective or to approach his work with suspicion or with a foregone conclusion that something is wrong. He is a watchdog, but not a bloodhound.'

This dictum is as true today as it was in 1896, but this is not to say that the *Kingston Cotton Mills* decision still holds good. Auditing case law needs to be interpreted in the light of current practice—the 'skill, care and caution which a reasonable, careful and cautious auditor would use' in the 1980s are very different from those applying in the 1890s. Every time a new Auditing Guideline is issued, the Court's interpretation of the meaning of 'reasonable standard of audit work' required is likely to be raised.

In the *Kingston Cotton Mills* case the auditor was held not to have been negligent in accepting a certificate from the managing director as to the value of stocks, which had in fact been fraudulently inflated by the managing director. Today, the audit of stock, including observation of the stocktaking, is a central feature of the audit, and it would be impossible for the same decision to be reached by the Court in the present day.

Let us take a look at some other cases affecting liability to clients.

Re City Equitable Fire Insurance Co. Ltd (1924) is of great interest to all auditors, and is worthy of close study. Extensive frauds had been perpetrated by the chairman of the company, and the Official Receiver took action against several of the directors and the auditors.

As regards the auditors, the charges were that they were guilty of negligence in respect of the audit by them of the balance sheets of the company for the years ending 28 February 1919, 1920 and 1921. The charges of negligence and breach of duty came under three heads:

(1) That the debt due to the company from Ellis & Co., the stockbrokers of the company—Mr Bevan, the chairman, being a partner in that firm—and the debt due from Mr Mansell the general manager, were misdescribed by being included under 'loans at call or short notice' or 'loans', or, in the case of part of Ellis & Co.'s debt, under the heading of 'cash at bank and in hand'.

Further, that the auditors failed to disclose to the shareholders the existence of these debts.

(2) Their failure to detect the fact that much larger sums were in the hands of Ellis & Co. at the date of each balance sheet than were so included.

(3) Their failure to detect and report to the shareholders the fact that a number of the company's securities which were in the custody of Ellis & Co. were being pledged by that firm to its customers.

Generally speaking, the Judge found that the auditors had displayed great skill, care and industry.

As regards the first charge, the position was that the balances owing to the company from Ellis & Co., in 1919, amounted, according to the books, to £51 423 and rose in 1921 to £423 650. The amount due from Mansell was £6225 in 1919 and in 1921 had increased to £96 233. In the 1919 balance sheet these sums were included under the heading of 'loans at call or short notice', and in the 1921 balance sheet £350 000 owing by Ellis & Co., and the £96 233 owing by Mansell, were included under the heading 'loans', and £73 650 owing by Ellis & Co., on investment account, was included as 'cash at bank and in hand'.

His Lordship held that it was not the duty of the auditors specifically to draw the attention of the directors and the shareholders to these debts. Even if these items were incorrectly described in the balance sheet—and in the case of the debt of £73 650 classified as 'cash at bank and in hand', the Judge held that this was a misdescription—any such misdescription did not involve damage to the company.

The auditor, however, must not include at its face value a debt that is not a good one; but in this case the credit of Ellis & Co. at that time was good, and, further, the company held collateral security. As regards the debt due from Mansell, at that time there was no reason to suppose that this was not a good debt. In this case, however, the auditors were informed that security had been given and Bevan certified that he held that security. As regards the acceptance of this certificate by the auditors, the Judge held, as will be seen later, that they should have called for the production of these securities.

As regards the second and third charges, these involved 'window dressing' operations carried out by Bevan each year, the charge being that the auditors should have detected these and thus have discovered the extensive frauds.

The 'window dressing' operations were carried out each year by a pretended purchase of Treasury Bonds just before the date of the balance sheet, followed by a pretended sale just after that date. In this way, at the date of the balance sheet, the debt due from Ellis & Co. was materially reduced, and the gilt-edged securities shown in the balance sheet increased.

These operations were effected by Ellis & Co. giving an order on their own behalf to another firm of brokers for the purchase of the bonds; at the same time they arranged for the brokers to advance to Ellis & Co. the sum involved, the bonds being given as security for the loan. A few days afterwards Ellis & Co. gave an order for the sale of the bonds, when the loan would be repaid.

Upon the purchase of the bonds, Ellis & Co. debited the company, and in the books of the company the corresponding entries were made.

Part of the charge was that the auditors should have noticed from year to year that the bonds purchased just before the date of the previous balance sheet were sold immediately afterwards in the succeeding financial year, when it would have been obvious that these were 'window dressing' operations. This part of the charge failed.

The second part of the charge was that the auditors should have called for the production of the Treasury Bonds shown by the company's books to be held at the date of the balance sheet; in fact, the auditors accepted certificates from year to year from Ellis & Co. that they held these bonds for the company. His Lordship held that the auditors *should have called for these securities and that they were not entitled to accept the certificate of the company's stockbrokers.* If the auditors had called for these securities the fraud must have been revealed, as Ellis & Co. could not have produced the bonds, as they were charged to the brokers against the loan by them to Ellis & Co. It was held, therefore, that in this direction the auditors were guilty of a breach of duty and of negligence, and they would have been held liable for damages, except for the fact that one of the company's articles of association provided that the directors, auditors and officers of the company should be held indemnified by the company, except in the case of wilful negligence. His Lordship held, therefore, that as the negligence of the auditors did not amount to wilful negligence, they were protected by the article and therefore escaped liability. Auditors can no longer be protected by a similar article.

In the course of the evidence it was established that in cases where the securities of a client were held by a bank of standing, it was the custom for auditors to accept the certificate of the bank as verification of such securities. His Lordship referred to this custom and questioned its soundness. This point, however, was not decided in this case, but his Lordship appeared to be of the opinion that in all cases an auditor should personally inspect all securities, wherever or by whomsoever held.

Armitage v. *Brewer & Knott (1932).* In this case damages were claimed against the auditors in consequence of frauds committed by an employee, and judgment for £1259 was given against the auditors. This case is worthy of detailed study. The frauds were perpetrated by a Miss Harwood, who had complete charge of the books, and the payment of wages; there was no system of internal check. The main point of the case was whether or not the auditors had exercised reasonable care and skill.

Part of His Lordship's summing up reads:

'However much it might be wrapped up, the defendant's case came to this, that systematic fraud for two and a half years by one person could not be detected by the exercise of reasonable care on the part of the accountants. His Lordship did not like to use strong language, but that appeared to him to be bordering closely on nonsense. On the evidence it was an allegation which did not bear a moment's examination.'

In fact, another firm of professional accountants had been called in to investigate the frauds, and Miss Harwood was prosecuted at the Central Criminal Court and pleaded guilty. The importance of an auditor following up small discrepancies is clearly brought out in this case. His Lordship stated:

> 'It was doubtless true that to detect required minute examination of a large number of documents, but that was exactly what the defendants undertook to do ... As to the suggestion that some things were too trivial to notice, audits differed greatly as to scope and special instructions. A 6s. 1d. had been altered to 16s. 1d. That was passed in what purported to be a meticulous examination. The most casual inspection would detect the discrepancy on the voucher; both figures were there. His Lordship was struck by the audacity with which many of these frauds were committed. It looked as though Miss Harwood had found that she had nothing very formidable to fear in the way of audit. It was the duty of the auditor to bring that 10s.—which was indicative not only of fraud but of forgery—at once to the notice of the principal. That one piece of paper raised a grave suspicion. It was of critical importance. It was by little things like that the forgeries and frauds were found out.'

The main part of the fraud arose in connection with the falsification of wages sheets and it was clear that had these wages sheets been examined thoroughly the fraud must have been disclosed. His Lordship stated: 'It was no use looking at such documents as were found here unless one did it with scrupulous accuracy'. And, further, that: 'When there was something to make one uneasy His Lordship thought that defendants should have been doubly vigilant.' And also that 'it was clear that a good many documents were suspicious on their face and called for inquiry'.

This case brings out clearly the vital importance of the exercise of vigilance and care in the vouching of documents.

Re S. P. Catterson & Sons Ltd (1937). In this case the liquidator of the company brought a summons against the auditor.

The facts of the case were that in the showroom of the company the system was that upon cash sales being effected a cash invoice was made out in an invoice book, these invoices being serially numbered. One copy of the invoice was receipted and handed to the customer and the counterfoil remained in the invoice book. Subsequently from the counterfoils the cash sales were entered in a daily cash sales book, the serial numbers being recorded and the total cash handed to the manager who was one of the directors of the company.

From time to time sales were effected on short credit terms when the same invoice book was used. The system was that in those cases where credit had been given the counterfoils were turned up or 'dog-eared'. When the customer paid, the system was that the counterfoils should be turned down. The utilization of this same cash invoice book for both cash and credit transactions at once destroyed the system as the regular consecutive numbering of the counterfoils being accounted for in cash was broken. The clerk in charge of the showroom effected the defalcation by misappropriating cash paid by short credit customers and, therefore, on receipt of the cash did not turn down the counterfoils. In this connection His Lordship stated:

'Now the evidence to my mind is clear that that system of using the invoice book for ready money transactions as well as for short credit transactions had been going on for years, and it is equally clear to me that that system and the so-called system of keeping a record of the transactions done on credit by turning up the invoice was also known to the directors and had been known to them for years'.

The auditors pointed out to the directors that the system was not a satisfactory one and they recommended improvements, but these recommendations were disregarded.

His Lordship stated:

'It is clear that the unsatisfactory system employed in the showroom was clear to the mind of the auditor and that it was called by him to the attention of the directors, and that notwithstanding that fact they preferred, for some reason or another, to continue the system as it was. I am not prepared to hold in those circumstances and on those facts that there was any duty upon the auditors to insist upon that system being changed. It is not their business to tell the directors how to carry on and conduct their accounting system; they make their recommendations and, if they are not acceded to, the responsibility is not the auditor's responsibility, but it is the responsibility of the directors.'

In reviewing the responsibility of the auditors generally. His Lordship stated:

'The first fact which seems often to be lost sight of is that the primary responsibility for the accounts of a company is with those who are in control of the company, that is to say, the directors, and in the case of the directors of this company, they were not a satisfactory team.'

His Lordship stated that:

'I have no doubts as to where the primary responsibility for finding out the defalcation of this man Spicer lies. It lies upon the shoulders of the man whose duty it was as a director of this company to collect from Spicer the cash that he received. If that man had done his duty in any degree at all the frauds could not have been perpetrated in the way in which they were perpetrated.'

His Lordship concluded by stating that, in his opinion, the auditor was an honest man trying to do his duty and that in view of all the facts of the case and the audit notes, the applicant had 'quite failed to satisfy me in respect of the matters charged that there was any negligence. The result is that the application fails and must be dismissed.'

McKesson & Robbins Case (1939). This American case arose out of the operation at the Bridgeport offices of McKesson & Robbins Inc. of a wholly fictitious foreign crude drug business shown in the books of the Connecticut division of the corporation and McKesson & Robbins Ltd (Canada), one of its subsidiaries.

To accomplish the deception, purchases were pretended to have been made by the McKesson companies from five Canadian vendors who were purported to retain the goods at their warehouses. Sales were pretended to have been made on McKesson's account by W. W. Smith & Co. Inc., and the goods shipped directly by the latter from Canadian warehouses to the customers. Payments for goods purchased and collections from customers were pretended to have been made by the Montreal banking firm of Manning & Co. Invoices, advices and other documents prepared on printed forms in the names of these firms were used to give an appearance of reality to these transactions.

The foreign firms to whom the goods were supposed to have been sold were real but had done no business of the type indicated with McKesson. W. W. Smith & Co. Inc., Manning & Co. and the five Canadian vendors were either entirely fictitious or merely blinds used to support the fictitious transactions.

The fraud was engineered by Frank Coster, president of the corporation; George Dietrich, assistant treasurer; Robert Dietrich, head of the shipping, receiving and warehousing department at Bridgeport; and George Venard, who managed the offices, mailing addresses, bank accounts and other activities of the dummy concerns with whom the McKesson companies supposedly did business. In reality these four men were brothers whose real name was Musica.

In 1937, the last year for which a financial statement was issued to stockholders before discovery of the fraud, fictitious sales exceeded $18 000 000, and included in the balance sheet at 31 December 1937 were fictitious assets amounting to some $19 000 000. These consisted of inventories (approximately $10 000 000), accounts receivable (approximately $9 000 000) and bank balance (approximately $75 000). At the time of the exposure of the fraud in December 1938, these fictitious assets had increased to approximately $21 000 000.

In a summary of its findings and conclusions on the case, published in 1941, the American Securities and Exchange Commission stated:

'Investigations of new clients
The facts of this case suggest that for new and unknown clients some independent

investigation should be made of the company and of its principal officers prior to undertaking the work. Such an inquiry should provide a valuable background for interpreting conditions revealed during the audit or, in extreme cases, might lead to a refusal of the engagement.

Review of the client's system of internal check and control

We are convinced by the record that the review of the system of internal check and control at the Bridgeport offices was carried out in an unsatisfactory manner. The testimony of the experts leads us to the further conclusion that this vital and basic problem of all audits for the purpose of certifying financial statements has been treated in entirely too casual a manner by many accountants. Since in examinations of financial statements of corporations whose securities are publicly owned by the procedures of testing and sampling are employed in most cases, it appears to us that the necessity for a comprehensive knowledge of the client's system of internal check and control cannot be over-emphasized.

Cash

The record is clear that the cash work performed on this engagement by Price, Waterhouse & Co. conformed in scope to the then generally accepted standards of the profession. It is unusually clear to us that prior to this case many independent public accountants depended entirely too much upon the verification of cash as the basis for the whole auditing programme and hence as underlying proof of the authenticity of all transactions. Where, as here, during the final three years of the audit, physical contact with the operations of a major portion of the business was limited to examinations of supposed documentary evidence of transactions carried on completely off-stage through agents unknown to the auditors save in connection with the one engagement, it appears to us that the reliability of these agents must be established by completely independent methods. Confirmation of the bank balance under these circumstances was proven in this case to be an inadequate basis for concluding that all the transactions were authentic.

Accounts receivable

Viewed as a whole the audit programme for accounts receivable as used by Price, Waterhouse & Co. conformed to then generally accepted procedures for an examination of financial statements although confirmation of the accounts was not included in the programme. The facts of this case, however, demonstrate the utility of circularization and the wisdom of the profession in subsequently adopting confirmation of accounts and notes receivable as a required procedure '... wherever practicable and reasonable, and where the aggregate amount of notes and accounts receivable represents a significant proportion of the current assets or of the total assets of a concern ...'.

Inter-company accounts

The record indicates that it is not enough for auditors to reconcile inter-company balances and that valuable insight into the company's manner of doing business may be gained by a review of the transactions passed through such accounts during the year. Best practice we believe requires the latter procedure. In this case the recommended procedure, although employed to some extent, was not applied in a thorough-going and penetrating manner.

Inventories
Price, Waterhouse & Co.'s audit programme for the verification of inventories was essentially that which was prescribed by generally accepted auditing practice for the period. However, we find that a substantial difference of opinion existed among accountants during this time as to the extent of the auditors' duties and responsibilities in connection with physical verification of quantities, quality and condition. Price, Waterhouse & Co., in common with a substantial portion of the profession, took the position that the verification of quantities, quality and condition of inventories should be confined to the records. There was, however, a substantial body of equally authoritative opinion which supported the view, which we endorse, that auditors should gain physical contact with the inventory by test counts, by observation of the inventory taking, or by a combination of these methods. Meticulous verification of the inventory was not needed in this case to discover the fraud. We are not satisfied, therefore, that even under Price, Waterhouse & Co.'s view other accountants would condone their failure to make inquiries of the employees who actually took the inventory and to determine by inspection whether there was an inventory as represented by the client. We commend the action of the profession in subsequently adopting as normal, procedures requiring physical contact with clients' inventories.

Other balance sheet accounts
(a) The testimony in respect to the auditing of plant accounts suggests that some accountants, including Price, Waterhouse & Co. could, with advantage, devote more attention to physical inspection than has been general practice with them in the past.

(b) The work in respect to liabilities was in accord with generally accepted practice, but suggests the desirability of independent inquiry when large purchases are made from a very few otherwise unknown suppliers.

(c) The record demonstrates the necessity of a thorough understanding of the client's tax situation, which apparently was not obtained by Price, Waterhouse & Co., in regard to the application of Canadian law.

Profit and loss accounts
We are of the opinion that such analyses of profit and loss accounts as were made were applied to improper combinations of departments, with the result that significant relationships were concealed. It is our conclusion that the independent accountant is derelict in his duty if he does not insist upon having proper analyses available for his review. It is our opinion that best practice supports this view.

In *Fomento (Sterling Area) Ltd* v. *Selsdon Fountain Pen Company Ltd (1958)* the old auditing adage was again quoted: 'The auditor was a watchdog, not a bloodhound; his duty was not detection but verification. But gagging the dog and locking him in his kennel at the bottom of the garden is not the best way to let him keep watch.'

This case, in fact, provided a good illustration of the manner in which the Courts expect an auditor to pursue his enquiries beyond merely taking someone's word as to the facts, and in turn to derive acceptable audit evidence.

A chartered accountant carried out an inquiry for clients, the appellants, to ascertain royalties payable to the clients by a company, the respondents, under a document called a 'deed of terms'. By this agreement, and a sub-licence, the respondents were licensed to make and sell ball-point pens and refills which were protected by letters patent in favour of the licensors, the appellants. The respondents produced to the accountant documents giving details of transactions in ball-points and refills described as 'type A', which were within the patent field, and also referring to sales of similar articles, described as of 'type B' and 'type C', stated not to have been included in the returns because outside the patent field. The accountant asked to be supplied with specimens or specifications of types B and C so as to satisfy himself that they were indeed outside the range of the patent. The respondents refused, saying they were not obliged to give information of their business outside the patent.

By a clause of the deed of terms the respondents were bound to keep all necessary books containing entries necessary for computing the royalties payable to the licensors; to produce the books to the licensors' auditors; and to give all such other information as might be necessary or appropriate to enable the royalties to be ascertained, provided that, if so required by the respondents, the auditors should undertake to treat all such information as condidential and disclosed only for the purpose of verifying the amount of the royalties.

Lord Morton of Henryton said that the auditor could not ascertain the royalties payable without ascertaining whether types B and C were within or outside the patent. The word 'verifying' in the agreement afforded a strong indication that the auditor need not accept the statement of the respondents: that was merely a statement of their opinion. The use in the agreement of the words 'all such other information' meant that the auditor was entitled to receive information not appearing in the respondent's books of account, and there was inserted a clear limitation on the extent of that other information: it must be necessary or appropriate to enable the amount of the royalties to be ascertained. The information sought by the auditor fell within that limitation. Lord Keith of Avonholm and Lord Denning concurred. Lord Denning said that an auditor was not to be confined to the mechanics of checking vouchers and making arithmetical computations; he was not to be written off as a professional 'adderupper and subtractor'.

The lesson regarding audit evidence was re-emphasized in the Australian case *Pacific Acceptance Corporation Ltd* v. *Forsyth and Others (1971)*, which concerned allegations that the auditors were negligent in failing to discover fraudulent and irregular features in connections with certain loans, supposedly against security. The judgement also provided a reminder of the need for proper control and supervision of the audit:

> '*Prima facie* the auditors' job is to check material matters for himself from available documents, and he does not ordinarily do his job ... if he merely seeks the assurance of another as to the check that the other has made or as to his views as to the effect of documents .... The essence of an audit ... is for the auditor to check material documents or matters for himself, subject to exception on reasonable grounds.
>
> An auditor may properly rely a great deal on inquiries made and explanations sought of the company's staff and management at the appropriate level, but *prima facie* this is in aid of his vouching and checking procedures and not in substitution for them.
>
> If a material document ought to be inspected by an auditor the fact that inspection might put the auditor to some inconvenience is normally no excuse for not inspecting it.
>
> Upon any matter of substance ... both the decision to make the inquiry, the making of the inquiry and the consideration of the answer would call for the attention of a person of experience and seniority .... If clerks are allowed to make enquiries which may turn out to be material, at least close supervision is called for in order to counteract his inexperience .... If the irregularities are numerous it is quite unreasonable to continue to be satisfied by explanations of the branch manager and assurances from him that there is nothing wrong because for this reason or that things are in order or he thinks they are. If in this kind of situation an inexperienced clerk is left to make decisions on such matters and he uncritically accepts what the manager says without more inquiry, lack of care on the part of the auditors is likely to be inferred.
>
> Reasonable care and skill calls for changed standards to meet changed conditions or changed understanding of dangers .... If there are shortcomings in the work of the audit clerks or of the reviewers in the area of omission from the work programme, and undiscovered error or fraud occurs in that area, then any failure by the auditors to amend the programme will tend to indicate that the shortcomings were due to negligence.'

Re Thomas Gerrard and Sons Ltd (1968). The facts of this case were that the managing director had been defrauding the company for several years, mainly by altering dates on purchase invoices and sales invoices. Purchases near the end of the financial year were deferred until the next year, and sales early in the next year were brought forward. The audit staff had noticed the alterations and queried them with the managing director. He explained that they were 'end of period adjustments' and that it was 'more convenient' to exclude the invoices concerned. The auditors accepted that explanation without further investigation.

In addition, he had inflated the stock by including non-existent items. Over the years 1957 to 1962, dividends of £26 254 were paid (partly to the defrauding managing director who was also a substantial shareholder) as well as excessive tax amounting to £56 659. In the end the company collapsed, the managing director was prosecuted and convicted, and the liquidator brought an action against the auditors.

The auditors sought to rely on the Kingston Cotton Mills decision discussed above—that they were entitled to trust the word of a responsible official of the client company.

However, Mr Justice Pennycuick rejected this contention since even in the 1896 case the full decision was that the auditor 'is not guilty of negligence if he accepts the certification of a responsible official *in the absence of suspicious circumstances*'. Clearly in the Thomas Gerrard case there were suspicious circumstances—the altered invoices—which were picked up by the auditor but not adequately investigated. The auditors were accordingly held to be liable even under the criteria set up in 1896, though the judge also commented that the Kingston Cotton Mills case could be distinguished on grounds that 'standards were now more stringent'.

The amount of the damages awarded against the auditors was the loss suffered by the company in paying excessive dividends and tax, less an amount of £7100 recovered from the managing director and a substantial refund of tax obtained from the Inland Revenue.

19.2.1 Conclusions

The conclusions to be drawn from the various cases upon this subject would appear to be as follows:

(1) Auditors must carefully examine their client's system of accounting and of internal control and must test it with vouchers and original records and make proper inquiries.

(2) They must verify the existence of assets as far as reasonably possible and cannot absolve themselves from this duty by accepting the certificate of an official.

(3) They are entitled to rely upon the opinion of experts where special knowledge is required.

(4) They will not be held liable for not tracking down ingenious and carefully laid schemes of fraud, where there is nothing to arouse their suspicion and the frauds have been perpetrated by trusted servants of the concern.

(5) They need not necessarily be suspicious, but when their suspicions are aroused they must exercise all reasonable care and skill before they satisfy themselves that all is in order.

(6) As to what is reasonable care and skill depends on the circumstances of the case and the general standard adopted by the profession.

(7) If auditors are not satisfied on any material points, they must report clearly to the shareholders.

(8) If auditors are negligent they may be held liable to damages if their client or third parties have suffered damage which otherwise would have been prevented.

(9) If auditors wilfully certify accounts, knowing them to be false, they may be held criminally liable.

(10) The conduct of the directors of a company is no answer to any breach of duty by the auditors, although it is a circumstance which will be taken into consideration by the Court.

This question of the auditors' legal responsibilities is one of supreme importance to every practising accountant. It is, however, a most difficult one. The auditors' responsibilities are not clearly defined in the Acts and the principles evolved by case law are in several directions conflicting.

In conclusion, it may be said that it is very unlikely that auditors will be held personally liable provided they are possessed of the requisite professional skill, and that they honestly exercise such skill in all cases, taking every reasonable precaution to satisfy themselves upon every point before they certify the accounts. In the event of their being dissatisfied upon any material point, they must report clearly in their audit report to this effect. It is thought that no better short definition of an auditor's duties can be given than the following, which is an extract from the judgment in *re London and General Bank* (1895):

> 'Such I take to be the duty of the auditor; he must be honest—that is, he must not certify what he does not believe to be true, and he must take reasonable care and skill before he believes that what he certifies is true.'

19.3   APC Draft Auditing Guideline on fraud and other irregularities

In 1985 the APC issued a Draft Auditing Guideline which throws further light on the subject. This is now given in full.

Draft Auditing Guideline on fraud and other irregularities

Preface

This Guideline sets out the responsibilities of the auditor with regard to the detection of fraud and other irregularities and the impact this may have on the planning and design of an audit. It also gives guidance on the extent to which the auditor's findings should be reported to management, shareholders and third parties.

Whilst the responsibilities described in this Guideline are consistent with the responsibilities of auditors operating in the public sector, in certain respects the duties of the auditor in the public sector with regard to irregularities are somewhat greater than those of his private sector counterpart. In any event, the auditor should have regard to any statutory, constitutional or contractual requirements in addition to his general responsibilities.

Introduction

(1) The word ERRORS is used to refer to unintentional mistakes in financial statements, whether of a mathematical or clerical nature, or whether in the application of accounting principles, or whether due to oversight or misinterpretation of relevant facts.

(2) The word IRREGULARITIES is used to refer to intentional distortions of financial statements, for whatever purpose, and to misapppropriations of assets, whether or not accompanied by distortions of financial statements. Fraud is one type of irregularity. In this Guideline the word FRAUD is used to refere to irregularities involving the use of criminal deception to obtain an unjust or illegal advantage.

Responsibilities for the prevention and detection of errors and irregularities

Management

(3) The primary responsibility for the prevention and detection of errors and irregularities rests with management. This responsibility may be partly discharged by the institution of an adequate system of internal control including, for example, authorisation controls and controls covering segregation of duties. (See the Auditing Guideline: 'Internal controls' and paragraphs 18–21 of this Guideline.)

(4) Management have particular responsibilities for ensuring that a strong system of internal control exists where assets are held in a fiduciary capacity on behalf of the public or a third party. In such circumstances, management may consider it appropriate to agree with the auditor that additional work be performed by him.

(5) In addition to the contractual duty of care owed to an enterprise by those engaged to manage it, the directors of a company (or others in a similar executive position within the public sector) are regarded at law as acting in a stewardship capacity concerning the property which is under their control and consequently have a duty to take steps to ensure the safety of the enterprise's assets.

(6) The auditor may therefore consider it appropriate to remind management of their responsibility to maintain a proper system of internal control as an adequate deterrent to errors or irregularities. He can do this either in the audit engagement letter (see paragraph 14) or by other communication during the audit. In addition, the auditor may ask management to provide details of any irregularities that have come to their attention during the period under examination.

(7) An officer of a company is guilty of an offence where he knowingly or recklessly makes a statement which is misleading, false or deceptive in a material particular (Section 393 of the Companies Act 1985). An auditor is therefore entitled to accept representations as truthful in the absence of any indication to the contrary and provided these are consistent with other audit evidence obtained. [See Auditing Guideline 'Repesentations by management'.]

The nature of an audit and the responsibilities of the auditor
(8) The explanatory foreword to Auditing Standards and Guidelines defines an audit as 'the independent examination of, and expression of opinion on, the financial statements of an enterprise by an appointed auditor in pursuance of that appointment and in compliance with any relevant statutory obligation'. The auditor's responsibility is to fulfil that function.

(9) The auditor's responsibility towards errors and irregularities is limited to designing and evaluating his work with a view to detecting those errors or irregularities which might impair the truth and fairness of the view given by the financial statements. In certain circumstances, statutory obligations include a requirement to report on the adequacy of the system of internal control (e.g. building societies).

(10) Accordingly, in obtaining sufficient appropriate audit evidence to afford a reasonable basis of support for his report, the auditor seeks reasonable assurance, through the application of procedures that comply with Auditing Standards, that errors or irregularities which may be material to the financial statements have not occurred or that, if they have occurred, they are either corrected or properly accounted for in the financial statements.

(11) The duty of an auditor, when reporting upon financial statements, is to act with the skill and care that a reasonably competent auditor would employ in the circumstances. This duty can be expected to be determined by reference to the current standards generally applied by the accountancy profession in the proper and competent conduct of an audit.

The impact on the audit

Knowledge of the enterprise
(12) The nature of the business undertaken by an enterprise and its circumstances affect the auditor's approach to his work and may affect the

type and extent of work performed. The auditor's appraisal of the risk that a material error or iregularity could occur should therefore take into account problems facing the enterprise and the actual operations of the enterprise itself.

(13) In addition, the auditor should be aware that the internal control environment of the enterprise may facilitate errors and irregularities (see paragraphs 18-21).

Planning

(14) Having decided to accept an audit assignment, the auditor should normally send a letter setting out the terms of his engagement. The Auditing Guideline 'Engagement letters' recommends that this letter should contain a description of the nature of an audit, the responsibilities of management and the duties of an auditor with regard to the prevention and detection of irrecularity and fraud. That guideline also recommends that the letter 'should explain that the auditor will endeavour to plan his audit so that he has a reasonable expectation of detecting material misstatements in the financial statements resulting from irregularities or fraud, but that the examination should not be relied upon to disclose irregularities and frauds which may exist. If a special examination for irregularities or fraud is required by the client, then this should be specified in the engagement letter, but not in the audit section'.

(15) It is not normal practice in certain parts of the public sector for an auditor to send a letter to his client setting out his terms of engagement. In such circumstances it is more usual for the terms of engagement to be laid down by, for example, statute or a code of practice. In the case of local authority audits the terms of employment include adherence to a Code of Practice (in England and Wales) and the Standards and Guidelines (in Scotland), which have been issued respectively by the Audit Commission for Local Authorities in England and Wales and the Commission for Local Authority Accounts in Scotland. Such codes should be consulted with regard to any special guidance on the responsibilities of the auditor in regard to irregularities.

(16) When planning the audit, the auditor should consider the likelihood of irregularities in the following stages:

Business environment
—nature of the business, its services (e.g. assets held in a fiduciary capacity) and its products (e.g. assets readily susceptible to misappropriation);
—circumstances which may exert undue influence on management (e.g. the desire to retain the confidence of depositors or creditors may encourage overstatement of results);
—company performance (e.g. the deliberate distortion of the financial statements to meet a profit forecast, to increase profit related remuneration

or to avoid the appearance of insolvency).

Control environment
—the strength, quality and effectiveness of management;
—management's overall controls (e.g. degree of supervision);
—general segregation of duties;
—existence and effectiveness of any internal audit function;
—information technology environment.

Account areas
—susceptibility to fraud;
—significance of each account area in the context of overall materiality;
—accounting methods;
—related party transactions;
—unusual transactions.

This assessment may also assist the auditor in his preliminary determination as to whether the accounting and other records assist management in safeguarding the enterprise's assets.

(17) In reaching his decision as to the areas to be tested and the number of balances and transactions to be examined, the auditor will need to consider information available from prior experience, where available, and knowledge of the client's business and accounting systems. More specifically, the procedures adopted by the auditor for the purpose of detecting material errors and irregularities in conducting an audit will depend on his judgement as to:

(*a*) the types of errors or irregularities that are likely to occur (or have occurred previously);
(*b*) the relative risk of their occurrence;
(*c*) the likelihood that a particular type of error or irregularity could have a material effect on the financial statements; and
(*d*) the relative effectiness of different audit tests.

The auditor's planning procedures should be designed to assist him in making this judgement. [See Auditing Guideline 'Planning, controlling and recording'.]

Internal controls
(18) The Auditing Guideline 'Internal controls' states that the auditor will need to 'ascertain and record the internal control system in order to make a preliminary evaluation of the effectiveness of its component controls and to decide the extent of his reliance thereon'. This recording might be carried out concurrently with the recording of the accounting system, as the auditor will need to assess this latter system to ensure it forms an adequate basis for the

preparation of financial statements. Although an effective system of internal control is one of management's main methods of preventing errors and irregularities, the auditor does not have a specific responsibility to rely on it, and therefore to test it, except where required by specific legislation.

(19) In considering the risk of irregularities, the auditor may wish, when assessing internal controls, to place additional emphasis on the following control aspects:

—segregation of duties;
—authorisation (particularly of expense items and new ledger accounts);
—completeness and accuracy of accounting data;
—safeguard procedures (e.g. signing cheques);
—comprehensiveness of controls (e.g. including all relevant sub-systems).

In addition, where accounting procedures are computerised, the auditor should be concerned to ensure that a lack of computer controls cannot be exploited to suppress evidence that an irregularity may exist or indeed to allow an irregularity to occur. [See Auditing Guideline 'Auditing in a computer environment'.]

(20) Internal audit, when present and effective, is an important element of a system of internal control and should be a deterrent to irregularities. If he intends to place reliance on the internal audit function, the auditor will need to assess its effectiveness and degree of independence. This will involve reviewing reports made by the internal audit department for evidence of possible irregularities and assessing the extent to which management takes action based upon such reports. [See Auditing Guideline 'Reliance on internal audit'.]

(21) If weaknesses in internal controls are identified, either from his preliminary evaluation or after compliance tests have been performed, the auditor should take into account the possible effect of these weaknesses when planning his substantive testing. Significant weaknesses in internal controls identified during the audit should be promptly reported to management. (A draft Auditing Guideline 'Reports to management' will, when published, give further guidance in this area.)

Design of tests

(22) The decisions that the auditor makes during the planning phase of the audit and, where appropriate, when evaluating the system of internal control will help him to design his tests to obtain relevant and reliable audit evidence sufficient to enable him to draw reasonable conclusions.

(23) In carrying out his procedures, the auditor may discover circum-

stances that could be indicative of irregularities. Examples of such circumstances include:

—missing vouchers or documents;
—evidence of falsified documents;
—unsatisfactory explanations;
—figures, trends or results which do not accord with expectations;
—unexplained items on reconciliations or suspense accounts;
—evidence of disputes;
—evidence of unduly lavish life styles by officers and employees;
—unusual investment of funds held in a fiduciary capacity;
—evidence that the system of internal control is not operating as it was believed or intended to.

The auditor's programme of work needs to be sufficiently flexible to follow up any such points arising and any irregularities or errors detected.

(24) Many substantive tests normally performed by the auditor may assist in isolating irregularities, if they are occurring. For example, tests performed on the debtors ledger may be aimed at revealing overstatement or bad debts, but the design of such tests also assists with cash understatement objectives and may reveal irregularities such as 'teeming and lading'.

(25) In addition to detailed substantive tests, analytical review procedures should be used, during field work and in the auditor's review of the financial statements, to isolate account areas which merit further investigation or trends which seem unusual. For example, in some businesses, the reconciliation of purchases, sales and stock by volumes or quantities can be a useful technique. Where doubts exist about the appropriateness of an enterprise preparing its financial statements on a going-concern basis, the auditor should be aware, particularly when carrying out his analytical review, that there is an increased risk of irregularities. (The Auditing Guideline 'The auditor's considerations in respect of going concern', when published, will suggest procedures to be followed where the going concern basis is under question.)

Action to be taken on the discovery of potential errors and irregularities

(26) If during the course of his work, the auditor obtains information (such as circumstances outlined in paragraph 23) indicating the possible existence of errors or irregularities, the following action should be taken.

(27) Unless it is possible to conclude without additional testing that the circumstances encountered could not give rise to an irregularity or error having a material effect on the financial statements, the auditor should perform appropriate additional tests.

(28) If, after additional testing has been performed, it appears that an error or irregularity has occurred, the auditor should consider its nature, cause and

likely effect on the financial statements, analysing and projecting the results of his tests as appropriate. Any changes necessary to ensure that the financial statements give a true and fair view should be agreed with management on a timely basis. If such changes are not made or there is an uncertainty which prevents the auditor from forming an opinion he should qualify his audit report accordingly.

(29) Where the auditor is satisfied that irregularities are not material to the financial statements, he should discuss nevertheless his concerns with an appropriate level of management, in order to determine what further action should be taken. For example an amendment to the system of internal control may be appropriate in order to reduce or eliminate such errors or irregularities in the future.

Reporting

To members and management
(30) In addition to his statutory duty to report to the members of the enterprise on the truth and fairness of the financial statements, the auditor should report to the management of that enterprise if the audit has brought to light any irregularities. The auditor should ensure that management are informed promptly and that, in the case of a company, a report is made to the board of directors or, if appropriate, the audit committee. It is particularly important that the auditor reports to a suitably senior level within the enterprise if he suspects that management may be involved in or are condoning irregularities. Legal advice may be required if he believes that his report may not be acted upon or is unsure as to whom he should report (see paragraph 33).

(31) In his report to management, the auditor may consider it appropriate in formulating his recommendations to mention, in addition to irregularities and material errors found, matters of good practice such as restrictive crossing of incoming cheques and the prohibition of signing cheques in blank or of opening crossed cheques for encashment.

(32) If after taking account of any adjustments made, an irregularity materially affects the view given by the financial statements the auditor should qualify his opinion on those statements accordingly. However, except in certain parts of the public sector, he has no specific responsibility to report an irregularity in his audit report if the financial statements give a true and fair view despite the occurrence of the irregularity.

To third parties
(33) In the course of his audit the auditor may discover a fraud or other irregularity perpetrated by his client. Normally the auditor's duty of confidentiality debars him from reporting any matters to third parties without his client's permission. He should therefore have careful regard to the

contents of any guidance issued by his accountancy body and obtain legal advice as to whether this duty of confidentiality should be disregarded and the information disclosed to the appropriate authorities.

(34) In certain circumstances the auditor is not bound by his duty of confidentiality. For example the auditor may be legally bound to make disclosure of the commission of a criminal offence if ordered to do so by a Court or a Government Officer empowered to request such information.

(35) Where there is a 'public duty' to make disclosure, an auditor may elect to disclose information voluntarily. A public duty arises where an auditor possesses information of any intended criminal offence, or a serious criminal offence even if it has already been committed, if it is likely to cause serious harm to an individual or if it may affect a large number of people.

(36) In some cases, the reporting procedures to be followed on discovery of an irregularity will be set out in statute. For example, the auditor of a local authority in Scotland who discovers a loss caused by wilful misconduct must report to the Controller of Audit who in turn has his own specific reporting responsibilities. The auditor of a local authority in England and Wales is required to certify that the loss is due from the person responsible and seek to recover the sum from him.

Other considerations

(37) In most instances the auditor has the right of access at all times to the books and accounts and vouchers of the business and is entitled to seek such information and explanation from management as he thinks necessary to perform his duties. If the auditor is unable for any reason to obtain all necessary information and explanations then the scope of his audit has been limited and his audit opinion should be qualified accordingly. [See Auditing Standard 'Qualifications in audit reports'.]

(38) If the auditor feels that he has been frustrated in the execution of his work to such an extent that he is unable to report on the financial statements, he should resign. In these circumstances he should ensure that the reasons for his resignation are made known to shareholders under the provisions of Sections 390 and 391 of the Companies Act 1985. If a resolution to remove the auditor is proposed, he has the right to make a similar statement to shareholders under the provisions of Section 388.

19.4   Liability to third parties

In claims by third parties no contract exists and the claim is therefore in tort. Until 1963 it was clear in English law that no third party could succeed in respect of a negligent statement unless fraud existed. For example, in *Candler v. Crane, Christmas and Co. (1951)* a firm of accountants who did not deny that they had been negligent in preparing accounts were held not to be liable to a third party who suffered financial loss through relying on the accounts. (As we shall see later, however, Denning LJ's dissenting judgment in this case has formed the basis for decisions in the opposite direction.)

In 1963 everything changed as a result of what is possibly the legal case best known to accountants and accountancy students—*Hedley Byrne and Co. Ltd v. Heller and Partners Ltd.*

In *Hedley Byrne* it was recognized that a liability to third parties can exist. Such liability may arise whenever a professional person does work for a client in circumstances where *he or she knows or ought to know*:

(a) that his or her work is likely to be relied upon by a third party; and

(b) that the third party may suffer financial loss if the work in question has been done negligently.

Liability will arise when the work in question is of a kind which it was reasonable for the third party to rely on for his particular purpose.

The facts of *Hedley Byrne* were that the appellants asked their bank to ascertain from the respondents the financial position of Easipower Ltd. The respondents replied, 'without liability', that they considered Easipower to be a respectably constituted company considered good for its ordinary business engagements. Relying on this reply Hedley Byrne allowed Easipower credit of £17 000 before the latter company went into liquidation. In an action for negligence when replying to the enquiry, it was held (House of Lords) that, because of the respondents' disclaimer, they were not liable, but without the disclaimer a duty of care would have existed despite the absence of a contractual relationship. During his judgment Lord Morris said: 'I consider...that if someone possessed of a special skill undertakes, quite irrespective of contract, to apply that skill for the assistance of another person who relies on such skill, a duty of care will arise . . .. Furthermore if, in a sphere in which a person is so placed that others could reasonably rely on his judgment or his skill or on his ability to make careful enquiry, a person who takes it on himself to give information or advice to, or allows his information or advice to be passed on to, another person who, as he knows or should know, will place reliance on it, then a duty of care will arise.'

Although not directly concerned with accountants, Counsel's opinion obtained by ICAEW after the case confirmed that a liability for accountants could exist and defined its extent.

In 1981 the *JEB Fasteners* case (*JEB Fasteners Ltd v. Marks, Bloom and Co.*) involved accountants more directly. The judge in that case, while quoting and relying heavily on the judgment in the *Hedley Byrne* case and on Denning LJ's dissenting judgment in *Candler v. Crane, Christmas and Co.*, held that the appropriate test for establishing whether a duty of care existed was whether the auditors knew *or should reasonably have foreseen* at the time the accounts were prepared that a third party might rely on those accounts.

The importance of the *JEB Fasteners* case means that it is useful to study Mr Justice Woolf's judgment in detail.

The facts of the case were that in 1975 the defendants, a firm of accountants, prepared an audited set of accounts for a manufacturing company for the year ended 31 October 1974. The company's stock, which had been purchased for some £11 000, was shown as being worth £23 080, that figure being based on the company's own valuation of the net realizable value of the stock. The defendants nevertheless described the stock in the accounts as being 'valued at lower of cost and net realisable value'. On the basis of the inflated stock figure the accounts showed a net profit of £11.25, whereas if the stock had been included at cost with a discount for possible errors the accounts would have shown a loss of over £13 000. *The defendants were aware when they prepared the accounts that the company faced liquidity problems and was seeking outside financial support from, among others, the plaintiffs*, who manufactured similar products and were anxious to expand their business. The accounts prepared by the defendants were made available to the plaintiffs, who, although they had reservations about the stock valuation, decided to take over the company in June 1975 for a nominal amount. *In discussions between the plaintiffs and the defendants during the take-over the defendants failed to inform the plaintiffs that the stock had been put in the accounts at an inflated value.* The plaintiffs' take-over of the company proved to be less successful than they had anticipated and they brought an action for damages against the defendants alleging that the defendants had been negligent in preparing the company's accounts, that they had relied on the accounts when purchasing the company, and that they would not have purchased the company had they been aware of its true financial position. The plaintiffs contended that an auditor when preparing a set of accounts owed a duty of care to all persons whom he ought reasonably to have foreseen would rely on the accounts. The defendants contended that if a duty of care existed it was only owed to persons who made a specific request for information.

Held

(1) Whether the defendants owed a duty of care to the plaintiffs in regard to their preparation of the accounts of the company depended on whether they knew or ought reasonably to have foreseen at the time the accounts were prepared that persons such as the plaintiffs might rely on the accounts for the purpose of deciding whether to take over the company and might suffer loss if the accounts were inaccurate. Since the defendants knew at the time the accounts were prepared that the company needed outside financial support and ought reasonably to have foreseen that a take-over was a possible means of obtaining finance and that a person effecting a take-over might rely on those accounts, it followed that the defendants owed the plaintiffs a duty of care in the preparation of the accounts. The

defendants were in breach of that duty by negligently including in the accounts stock at a value of some £13 000 over the discounted cost without appending a note in the accounts to that effect.

(2) However, even though the plaintiffs had relied on the accounts, they would not have acted differently had they known the true position, since they knew the company was in financial difficulties, their reason for taking over the company was to obtain the services of its directors and the consideration paid for the company was only nominal. Accordingly, the defendants' negligence in preparing the accounts was not a cause of any loss suffered by the plaintiffs as a result of taking over the company. The plaintiffs' action would therefore be dismissed.

The same test was applied in the Scots cases *Twomax Ltd* v. *Dickson, McFarlane and Robinson (1983)*, and *Gordon* v. *Dickson, McFarlane and Robinson (1983)*. The plaintiffs in these cases alleged that the accountants had negligently prepared accounts of Kintyre Knitwear Ltd, of which they were auditors. The plaintiffs said that they had relied on these accounts in buying a controlling interest in Kintyre. Later, Kintyre went into liquidation and their whole investment was lost.

The auditors' negligence in this case was established on the grounds that they had failed to circularize debtors or attend stocktaking.

The remaining point is whether the auditors could reasonably foresee that the accounts would be seen and acted upon by the plaintiffs. The judge decided that the auditors were aware that the company was in need of capital and that financial accounts would be available to potential lenders or investors.

What conclusions should be drawn from these two cases? In spite of one's possible first impression, probably the most important conclusion we should draw is that we should be careful before drawing any conclusions. It is important to note that neither of these cases imposes an unlimited liability as regards an unlimited group of people. In order for a liability to exist the auditors must know, or be able reasonably to foresee, that a third party might rely on those accounts for a particular purpose. Note especially in considering this point the two italicized passages from Mr Justice Woolf's judgment quoted above. From these it is clear that the accountants did have knowledge of the possible involvement of the plaintiff third party.

We might deduce that the Courts would be reluctant to find an auditor liable to a third party who had merely visited Companies House and consulted a company's file. Nevertheless, we should be cautious in categorically asserting this. It might be argued that auditors should be able to foresee that such a person would wish to inspect the accounts and would rely upon them! If the Courts ever take this view we shall be close to the point at which the liability does extend to an unlimited group of people.

An auditor of a company in financial difficulties, or obviously in need of fresh capital, will have to be particularly careful on general auditing principles, since the directors might be tempted to try to put the best possible face on things. The possible involvement of a third party invited to provide the fresh capital puts further pressure on the auditor.

Before leaving this subject we should note a rather cheeky development reported in *True and Fair* No. 13 (1979). At this time several firms of accountants received letters from potential investors who were considering takeover bids for companies of which the firms concerned were auditor. These letters contained the following sorts of statements:

(*a*) 'We are writing to let you know that we are contemplating making a substantial investment in X Limited.'

(*b*) 'We have not commissioned an independent report relating to the financial position of X Limited.'

(*c*) 'We will place material reliance upon the audited accounts of X Limited when making a decision as to whether or not to proceed with such an investment.'

Do you see the point? They were trying to put in the knowledge, so that the auditors could not afterwards claim that they did not know that this particular third party was going to see and act upon the accounts!

True and Fair suggested that such a letter should not be left unanswered. The reply should point out that:

(*a*) The accounts are prepared and audited under the requirements of the Companies Act and may therefore not be suitable for the purposes of a potential investor who intends to acquire a substantial interest rather than a small shareholding.

(*b*) The audit report expresses to the members an opinion on the truth and fairness of the accounts; it is not an acquisition or investigation report for which it cannot be a substitute.

(*c*) In preparing the accounts, management has included estimates which the auditor has accepted in the context of the overall financial position shown by the accounts: events may turn out differently.

(*d*) The views of management in certain judgmental areas and in regard to appropriate accounting policies may not coincide with the views of a potential investor.

(*e*) Therefore, although the statutory accounts contain much information of use to a potential investor they are only one part of the information which any investor contemplating a substantial investment should have about the company concerned. Such an investor should be in possession of detailed and up-to-date financial information available to management: normally the most satisfactory way of obtaining this information is for such an investor to carry out his own investigation to satisfy himself as to the suitability of the investment and to assess its inherent risks.

The *True and Fair* report concluded by suggesting that if the auditors were in any doubt they should seek legal advice.

19.5   The ICAEW statement

The most recent official pronouncement on the subject was the issue in November 1983 of a statement by the ICAEW entitled 'Professional liability of accountants and auditors'. This is reproduced below.

ICAEW statement on professional liability of accountants and auditors

(Issued November 1983 replacing Statements 1.305 (V8) *Accountants' liability to third parties—the* Hedley Byrne *decision* and 1.308 (V18) *Professional liability of accountants and auditors*).

The Council of The Institute of Chartered Accountants in England and Wales draws the attention of members to the principal areas in which actions for negligence may be brought against them by clients or third parties and suggests steps which they may properly be able to take to reduce the risk of such claims. The expressions of law included in this statement have the approval of Counsel. This statement does not deal with the position under the law of the Republic of Ireland.

Introduction

(1) This statement is concerned only with the liability for professional negligence which a member may incur because of an act or default by him or by one of his employees or associates which results in financial loss to a person to whom a duty of care is owed. It does not deal with liability arising from other causes (for example criminal acts, breaches of trust, or breaches of contract other than the negligent performance of its terms, and certain heads of liability arising by statute independently of contract).

(2) Negligence in this statement therefore means some act or omission which occurs because the person concerned has failed to exercise that degree of professional care and skill, appropriate to the circumstances of the case, which is expected of accountants and auditors. It would be a defence to an action for negligence to show:

(*a*) that there has been no negligence; or
(*b*) that no duty of care was owed to the plaintiff in the circumstances; or
(*c*) in the case of actions in tort that no financial loss has been suffered by the plaintiff.

The third defence would not be available to a claim in contract, but only nominal damages would be recoverable and in those circumstances it is unlikely that such an action would be brought.

(3) In recent years there have been a number of cases where substantial sums have

been claimed as damages for negligence against accountants and auditors. In a number of cases it appears that the claims may have arisen as a result of some misunderstanding as to the degree of responsibility which the accountant was expected to assume in giving advice or expressing an opinion. It is therefore important to distinguish between (a) disputes arising from misunderstandings regarding the duties assumed and (b) negligence in carrying out agreed terms.

The use of engagement letters

(4) There is a contractual relationship between an accountant and his client. Unless an express agreement is made between them to the contrary, the standard of work required of an accountant is defined by section 13 of the Supply of Goods and Services Act 1982: in a contract for the supply of a service.where the supplier is acting in the course of a business, there is an implied term that the supplier will carry out the service with reasonable skill and care. The degree of skill and care required will depend principally on the nature of the work undertaken. An accountant who undertakes work of an unusually specialized nature, or work of a kind whose negligent performance is particularly liable to cause substantial loss, will usually be taken to have assumed a duty to exercise a higher degree of skill and care than would be appropriate for less demanding work. This will, especially, be the case if he holds himself out as being experienced in the kind of work in question. In no case, however, is the duty likely to be absolute. Opinions expressed or advice given will not give rise to claims merely because in the light of later events they prove to have been wrong.

(5) The accountant should ensure that at the time he agrees to perform certain work for the client the scope of his responsibilities is made clear, preferably in writing, and the terms of his contract with his client are properly defined. Wherever possible, a letter of engagement should be prepared setting out in detail the actual services to be performed and the terms of the engagement should be accepted by the client so as to minimize the risk of disputes regarding the duties assumed. It may also be helpful for the avoidance of misunderstanding to indicate any significant matters which are not included in the scope of responsibilities undertaken, although it will rarely be possible to provide a comprehensive list of matters excluded.

Excluding or restricting liability to a client

(6) It should be borne in mind that an agreement with a client designed to exclude or restrict a member's liability will not always be effective in law. The following are the main relevant considerations.

Auditors under the Companies Acts

(7) Section 310 of the Companies Act 1985 makes void any provision in a company's articles or any contractual arrangement purporting to exempt the auditor from or to indemnify him against any liability for negligence, default, breach of duty or breach of trust. Although section 727 of the Companies Act 1985 empowers the court in certain circumstances to grant relief either wholly or in part from any of such liabilities, it appears that these powers have seldom been exercised and it would be prudent to assume that an auditor might not be relieved of liability.

Other cases
(8) Appropriate reference should be made in the letter of engagement to any exclusion or restriction of liability (other than as auditor of a limited company) because if an attempt is made to introduce such a provision into an existing relationship or in relation to a transaction for which instructions have already been accepted, difficulty may be experienced in showing that there is any legal consideration for the client's agreement to submit to the exemption provisions.

The Unfair Contract Terms Act 1977
(9) This Act introduces extensive restrictions upon the enforceability of exclusions of liability for negligence and breaches of contract. Section 2 of the Act, which applies in England, Wales and Northern Ireland makes void any contractual exclusion or restriction of liability for negligence, even in a case where the client has agreed to it and where legal consideration exists, unless the person seeking to rely on that exclusion or restriction can show that it was reasonable. Part II of the Act contains somewhat similar provisions applying as part of the law of Scotland. There is, at present, little case law which affords guidance as to what exclusions or restrictions of liability for negligence will be regarded as reasonable. However, unless the work undertaken presents unusual difficulties or is required to be carried out in unusually difficult circumstances, it would be prudent to assume that an exclusion of liability for neglegence may be treated by the courts as unreasonable. A limitation of liability for negligence to a particular sum will more readily be treated by the courts as reasonable, particularly if the accountant relying upon it can show that he would have difficulty in obtaining professional indemnity insurance for any greater sum.

(10) An exclusion or restriction of an accountant's liability will not generally avail him against a third party. Third party liability is dealt with separately in paragraphs 14 to 28 below.

Advice on limited information

(11) Besides reporting under the Companies Act 1985, accountants are called upon to give opinions and advice, including financial advice, in connection with many other matters, for example, investigation or management consultancy assignments, the preparation or audit of the accounts of sole traders, partnerships and charities, and in the field of taxation. A member undertaking to carry out work of this nature should make clear to his client the extent of the responsibility he agrees to undertake, making particular reference to the information supplied to him as a basis for his work and to those areas (if any) to be excluded from his examination. In particular, if the client requires a 'snap' answer to a complicated problem, a member would be well advised to record in writing (or alternatively to state orally and forthwith confirm in writing) that the problem is a complicated one, that he has been given a very limited time in which to study it, that further time is required in order to consider it in depth and that the opinion or advice tendered might well be revised if further time were available to him. He should also state that the client is responsible for the accuracy of the information supplied to the accountant. Except in the case of a genuine emergency, the client should be warned against acting on the 'snap' advice tendered before further investigation has been carried out.

(12) Statements and warnings of the kind considered in the preceding paragraph are not exclusions or restrictions of liability, but definitions of the work undertaken, and will protect an accountant from a claim for negligence based on the contention that his enquiries should have been more extensive than those so defined.

(13) There is an increasing tendency for accountants to be required to express an opinion on financial statements relating not to past (and therefore ascertainable) results but to the expected results of future periods. The specific considerations which arise in such circumstances are set out in the Council's Statement **3.918**(S23) *Accountants' reports on profit forecasts* to which reference should be made [See Chapter 24.]

Liability to third parties

(14) An accountant may be liable for negligence not only in contract, but in tort if a person to whom he owed a duty of care has suffered loss as a result of the accountant's negligence. An accountant will almost always owe a duty of care to his own client, but that duty is likely to be co-extensive with his contractual duty. In practice, the possibility of liability in tort will be important mainly in the context of claims by third parties.

(15) Recent decisions of the courts, including three important decisions of the House of Lords, have expanded the classes of case in which a person professing some special skill (as an accountant does) may be liable for negligence to someone other than his own client: *Hedley Byrne & Co. Ltd* v. *Heller & Partners* [1964] A.C. 465, *Anns* v. *Merton London Borough Council* [1978] A.C. 728, and *Junior Books Ltd* v. *Veitschi Co. Ltd* [1982] 3 W.L.R. 477. Such liability may arise whenever a professional person does work for his client in circumstances where he knows or ought to know (*a*) that his work is liable to be relied upon by a third party and (*b*) that that third party may suffer financial loss if the work in question has been done negligently. Liability will arise when the work in question is of a kind which it was reasonable for the third party to rely on for his particular purpose. If these conditions are satisfied, the third party is a person whom in the eyes of the law the professional man ought to have in mind in applying his skills to the work in question.

(16) The implications are important for all accountants who produce or report upon financial statements of various kinds (whether for a fee or not) which are liable to be relied upon by persons other than those for whom they were originally prepared.

(17) An accountant may sometimes be informed, before he carries out certain work, that a third party will rely upon the results. An example likely to be encountered in practice is a report upon the business of a client which the accountant has been instructed to prepare for the purpose of being shown to a potential purchaser or potential creditor of that business. In such a case it would be prudent for an accountant to assume that he will be held to owe the same duty to the third party as to his client.

(18) It is, however, important that members should appreciate that a duty of care to a third party may also arise when an accountant does not know that his work will in fact be relied upon by a third party, but only knows that it is work of a kind which is liable in the ordinary course of events to be relief upon by a third party. For this purpose it is immaterial whether the third party be identifiable in advance or not. In *JEB Fasteners* v. *Marks Bloom & Co* [1981] 3 All E.R. 289, the plaintiffs, who had

acquired a company, contended that they had done so in reliance on accounts which had been negligently audited by the defendant accountants. The judge decided that the appropriate test for establishing whether a duty of care existed was whether the auditors knew *or should reasonably have foreseen* at the time when the accounts were audited that a person *might* rely on those accounts for the purpose of deciding whether or not to acquire the company. That was a question which depended principally on the ordinary practice of persons acquiring companies. The same test has more recently been applied in Scotland in *Twomax Ltd* v. *Dickson McFarlane & Robinson* [1983] S.L.T. 98. In both cases it was held that the auditors owed a duty of care to the plaintiff. In the English case, the auditors escaped liability only because on the facts of that case it was proved that the plaintiff would have bought the company even if the accounts had revealed its true financial position. In the Scots case, substantial damages were awarded the plaintiff.

Avoiding liability to third parties

(19) In many cases there are no steps which an accountant can reasonably take to limit the circulation of his work or the use which is made of it. Some documents, such as the reports of auditors of public companies, are by their nature incapable of being restricted in this way. In other cases, however, there may be steps which an accountant can take to reduce his exposure to the claims of third parties. These cases cannot be exhaustively defined but the following are some of the more important examples of them.

Documents published generally

(20) An accountant may publish a document which is prepared neither in response to the instructions of a particular client nor for any statutory or public purpose: e.g. a text book or a newsletter. In such cases, there will often be no circumstances which would enable a third party to assume that it had necessarily been prepared with all due skill and care, and substantial reliance upon it would not be reasonable. An accountant can reinforce his legal position in relation to documents of this kind by including a disclaimer of liability in the document itself. The form of the disclaimer will depend upon the nature of the document. In many cases a disclaimer along the following lines will be found appropriate:

'While every care has been taken in the preparation of this document, it may contain errors for which we cannot be responsible.'

Work done for special purposes

(21) An accountant may be instructed to prepare or report upon financial material for some particular purpose. He will not usually be liable to a third party who relies on it for any other purpose for which it is or may be unsuitable. In such a case, the accountant would usually have no reason to suppose that such reliance would be placed upon it. Moreover, it would be unreasonable for a third party to rely on it for such a purpose. Members would, however, be well advised to make the position clear by including in the document itself a short statement of the purpose for which it was prepared, if that is not apparent.

Confidential reports

(22) Certain reports or statements may appropriately include a rubric specifically restricting its circulation. For example:

'Confidential

This report (statement) has been prepared for the private use of X (the client) only and on condition that it must not be disclosed to any other person without the written consent of Y (the accountant).'

Current practice is that clients will respect a rubric of this kind. Accordingly, when a document is so marked but is nevertheless relied upon by a third party without the accountant's consent, the accountant will as a general rule be able to resist liability on the basis that the third party was not a person whom he should have had in mind as being likely to suffer loss by his negligence. Such a rubric should be introduced only where the circumstances warrant it, as it would tend to be devalued by indiscriminate use in connection with documents which by their nature must receive a wide distribution. Where a document is prepared in the first instance for discussion with, or approval by, the client or others, and is liable to be altered before it appears in its final form, this fact should be made clear so as to prevent persons from placing undue reliance upon it. This may be done by overstamping the document on each page: 'Unrevised draft'.

Documents intended to be checked; accounts prepared for tax purposes

(23) An accountant may prepare a report or statement to be issued by his client in circumstances where he can reasonably expect his client to check it for fairness or accuracy before any use is made of it involving third parties. Accounts prepared for the purpose of being submitted to the Inland Revenue for the assessment of taxation will frequently, although not invariably, fall within this category. In such cases, the effective cause of any loss suffered by a third party will ordinarily be the negligence of the person in whose name it was issued and who ought to have checked the document, and not that of the accountant.

Disclaimers of liability to third parties

(24) A disclaimer of liability to third parties may sometimes be made in circumstances where liability would or might otherwise arise. Such a disclaimer might, for example, be introduced along the following lines:

'This report is prepared for the use of X (the client) only. No responsibility is assumed to any other person.'

Members should, however, be aware that such a disclaimer will often be inappropriate or ineffective. Disclaimers will be inappropriate in circumstances where their use will tend to impair the status of practising accountants by indicating a lack of confidence in their professional work. It would not, for example, be proper to endorse copies of accounts filed in accordance with section 227 of the Companies Act 1985 with a disclaimer by the auditor of liability to persons other than shareholders.

(25) The following paragraphs deal with those cases in which there are no

professional objections to the use of disclaimers, but in which reservations must be made as to their effectiveness.

Information prepared for the client and passed to third parties
(26) Where a statement or report is prepared by an accountant for his client, which is not confidential and can be expected in the ordinary course to be relied upon by third parties, a disclaimer which purports to apply only as against the third parties presents particular difficulties as a matter of law. By it, the accountant seeks in effect to assume a dual standard of care, the one applicable insofar as his work is read by the client and the other insofar as it is read by the third party. Since the third party will normally rely on the report because he expects the accountant to have performed his duty to the client, and since that expectation will normally be reasonable, the attempt to assume such a dual standard is unlikely to succeed.

Information passed directly to third parties
(27) Where an accountant (necessarily with the authority of his client) passes information directly to a third party, there is no question of a dual standard of liability because the third party is generally the only person who is intended to rely on the accountant's work. In such a case, the effectiveness of a disclaimer will depend upon the nature of the information. For example, when giving references or assurances regarding creditworthiness or similar matters, the normal commercial practice is to state that although the reference or assurance is given in good faith, the accountant accepts no financial responsibility for the opinion he expresses. Such disclaimers will generally be effective because such references or assurances are not information of the kind which is expected to be the result of extensive research by the accountant. Sometimes, however, an accountant may supply directly to a third party information of a kind which the third party (unless he is told otherwise) can reasonably expect to be the result of research of a more or less extensive kind. As applied to such information, a disclaimer will generally be ineffective in England (although not in Scotland) because of section 2 of the Unfair Contract Terms Act 1977 (see the following paragraph).

Unfair Contract Terms Act 1977, Section 2
(28) The effect of this provision is that where a person is in principle liable for negligence, he cannot exclude that liability by a reference to a notice, except where the notice is reasonable. If an accountant prepares a report or statement in circumstances where it can reasonably be expected that a third party may rely on it, a notice excluding liability to him would only exceptionally be regarded as reasonable. The law on this point is different in Scotland, because the equivalent section of the Act which applies as part of Scots law, section 16, does not refer to notices but only to terms of contract. Accordingly, in Scotland an appropriately worded disclaimer may be effective to exclude liability to third parties whether or not it is reasonable.

Inclusion of the accountant's name on a document issued by a client

(29) Members should endeavour to ensure that no statement or document issued

by their client (other than unabridged accounts which have been reported on by them as auditors) will bear their name unless their prior consent has been obtained. It is often desirable for a suitable paragraph to be included in the engagement letter.

(30) There have been occasions when the use of a member's name in a document (other than accounts reported on by him as auditor) has been interpreted by third parties as implying that the company is financially sound and well conducted, whether or not this is in fact the case. If a member learns that a client proposes to cite his name, he should inform the client that his permission must first be obtained and in appropriate cases he should withhold his permission.

Specialist advice

(31) In expressing an opinion or giving advice on difficult and complicated matters (for example in the field of taxation), members should bear in mind the magnitude of the financial consequences for their client should the advice tendered be incorrect or misconceived and the implications for them of a possible result in financial loss. An accountant in general practice is deemed by the law only to undertake to bring a fair and reasonable degree of skill and competence to the problem on which he is required to advise, and in appropriate circumstances he may wish to obtain the approval of his client for consulting another person with specialist experience of the matter in question. Occasions may also arise when a member may wish to consider declining a particular assignment because, for example, he is of the opinion that the matter on which his advice is sought does not fall within the normal scope of a professional accountancy practice and the client would therefore receive better assistance from a member of another profession.

Receiverships, trust and secretarial work

(32) A member acting as a receiver incurs personal liability for his acts and may, in particular, incur liability under commercial contracts irrespective of negligence on his part. Accordingly, if a member appointed by a debenture holder to act in this capacity has to manage a business, he should endeavour to ensure that he is fully indemnified by the person who appoints him against all loss and damage arising out of his management. If such an indemnity cannot be obtained, he should endeavour to ensure that contracts into which he enters on behalf of that business include a clause to the effect that he assumes no personal liability thereunder.

(33) It is often prudent for a member who is appointed to act as a trustee or asked to carry out certain secretarial work, such as cheque signing, to obtain an appropriate indemnity. In the former case, an instrument creating a trust can give a wide form of indemnity if the settlor is willing to approve its inclusion in the deed; in the latter, the member should arrange for an indemnity to be obtained from his client.

Conclusions

(34) Although it is not possible to guard against every circumstance in which an accountant or auditor may run the danger of incurring liability for professional negligence, the following matters should be borne in mind:

(*a*) before carrying out any work for a client, a member should ensure that the exact duties to be performed and in particular any significant matters to be excluded have been agreed with the client in writing by a letter of engagement or otherwise. If the accountant is asked to perform any additional duties at a later date, these should also be defined in writing (paragraph 5);

(*b*) in giving 'snap' advice at the request of a client or advice which must necessarily be based on incomplete information, a member should make it clear that such advice is subject to limitations and that consideration in depth may lead him to revise the advice given (paragraph 11);

(*c*) when publishing documents generally, a member may find it advantageous to include in the document a clause disclaiming liability (paragraph 20);

(*d*) when submitting unaudited accounts or other unaudited financial statements or reports to the client, a member should ensure that any special purpose for which the statements or reports have been prepared is recorded on their face, and in appropriate cases should introduce a clause recording that the report or statement is confidential and has been prepared solely for the private use of the client (paragraphs 21 and 22);

(*e*) it should be recognized that there are areas of professional work (for example, when acting as an auditor under the Companies Act) where it is not possible for liability to be limited or excluded, and that there are other areas of professional work (for example, when preparing reports on a business for the purpose of being submitted to a potential purchaser) where although such a limitation or exclusion may be included, its effectiveness will depend on the view which a court may subsequently form of its reasonableness (paragraphs 24 and 25);

(*f*) when giving references to a third part with regard to future transactions (e.g. payment of rent) a member should state that his opinion is given without financial responsibility on his part (paragraph 27);

(*g*) where the circumstances appear to warrant it because of the complexity of an assignment or otherwise, a member should advise his client that he considers it desirable to take specialist advice. In certain circumstances it may be appropriate for a member either to consult another accountant or to suggest to his client that the advice of a member of another profession should be sought (paragraph 31);

(*h*) where a member acts as receiver, he should endeavour to ensure that the person appointing him executes an appropriate letter of indemnity in his favour or should include appropriate exclusions of his personal liability in contracts with third parties. A member should also arrange for additional professional indemnity insurance cover of a realistic amount and should ascertain from his brokers whether or not cover is provided for the special risks involved (paragraph 32).

19.6 Default or unlawful acts by clients

19.6.1 Introduction

An auditor can only act for a client on the basis of full disclosure of all relevant information. It is an offence under S393 for an officer of a company to make misleading, false or deceptive statements to the auditor.

19.6.2 Confidentiality

It is important to realize, however, that the accountant has a duty of confidentiality and will not, as a general rule, disclose information about a client's affairs without the client's consent. This means that information acquired while auditing one client cannot be disclosed, even by implication, to another client.

As an example, let us assume that we know from the audit of A Limited that the company is in serious financial difficulties. In the course of the audit of B Limited, we find that the company is owed a considerable sum by A Limited, and is not contemplating making a provision for it. What do we do? The guidance note issued by ICAEW in 1980 says:

'The member must first do his best to make sure that the information that he has acquired is valid. Thereafter, the member should use every endeavour to obtain from within the records of the second client evidence to substantiate independently the information acquired from the first client. In the absence of any such evidence the member should, in appropriate cases, consider seeking the second client's consent to obtaining direct confirmation of the information concerned. If the member is seeking confirmation in connection with his work as auditor of the second client and consent is refused he should consider qualifying his report or resigning, and, where relevant, making an appropriate statement under the Companies Act 1985, Section 390, without revealing the name of the first client. In other cases where consent is refused the member should consider ceasing to act.'

19.6.3 Unlawful acts by client

Even if the client has committed a criminal offence or civil wrong, the auditor is under no legal obligation to disclose what he knows to the proper authority, except as explained in Section 19.6.4 below.

19.6.4 Exceptions to the rule as to confidentiality

(a) Obligation to disclose

The auditor or accountant is *bound* to disclose information if:

(1) the offence concerned is treason (perhaps trading with the enemy in time of war). Immediate disclosure is required in this case.
(2) disclosure is compelled by process of law

(b) Freedom to disclose

The auditor or accountant may be *free* to disclose if:
(1) authorized by the client;
(2) the accountant's own interests require it. This might be necessary, for example,

—to enable the member to defend himself or herself against a criminal charge or to clear himself from suspicion; or
—to resist proceedings under S99 Taxes Management Act 1970 where it is suggested that the member assisted or induced a client to make incorrect returns or accounts; or
—to resist an action for negligence brought by the client or a third party; or
—to enable the member to put up a defence against disciplinary proceedings brought by his professional body; or
—to enable him or her to sue for fees.

(3) the client *intends* to commit any criminal act or serious civil wrong, or if
(4) it is clear that non-disclosure of a past offence is likely to cause public harm, for example by enabling an offence to be repeated with impunity or by enabling the perpetrator of some serious fraud to go unpunished.

The ICAEW guidance notes suggest that an accountant should not necessarily disclose merely because he is free to disclose. Disclosure should only be made in the above cases if the potential damage to the public is likely to be very serious. Legal advice should be taken before disclosure.

19.6.5 Prosecution of client

Where a member is approached by the police, the Inland Revenue, the Customs and Excise authorities or any other authority making enquiries which may lead to the prosecution of a client or former client for an offence (other than treason), the member should act with caution. He or she should first ascertain whether or not the person seeking information has a statutory right to demand it. Secondly, he or she should seek legal advice before giving information. Thirdly, the nature of the alleged offence should be considered to decide whether, if the information were given he or she would be in breach of a contractual duty of confidence or acting contrary to professional standards.

Unless ordered by the Court or acting under a statutory authority, the member should decline to give information without having first obtained the client's authority or advice from a solicitor that the information should be given with or without the client's consent. In the meantime the member should declare inability to discuss the client's affairs, and should keep in close touch with his or her solicitor on the legal aspects of the position.

A member should not normally appear in Court as a witness for the Crown in a case against a client or former client, without first being served with a lawful summons to do so. A member cannot lawfully refuse to produce in Court any documents in his or her ownership or possession which the Court may direct to be produced. If the persons in charge of the prosecution have indicated that they will call upon the member to produce certain documents in court, he or she should have the documents ready to hand, but the power to order their production rests with the court.

19.6.6   Offences by the accountant personally

A member himself commits a criminal offence if he or she:

(*a*) incites a client to commit a criminal offence, whether or not the client accepts his advice; or

(*b*) helps or encourages a client in the planning or execution of a criminal offence which is committed; or

(*c*) agrees with a client or anyone else to pervert or obstruct the course of justice by concealing, destroying or fabricating evidence or by misleading the police by statements which he knows to be untrue; or

(*d*) impedes the arrest or prosecution of a client by some positive act; or

(*e*) accepts a bribe for concealing information.

19.6.7   Tax frauds

Perhaps the most likely area of difficulty for the accountant in connection with unlawful acts is that of tax fraud by the client. We may identify two main situations:

—the accountant has prepared accounts later found to be defective, or has acted in tax matters;
—the accountant has not previously acted for the client.

Each of these is dealt with in detail below.

(a) Accounts prepared by accountant later found to be defective, or the accountant has acted in tax matters

The action to be taken is:

(1) Advise the client to obtain legal advice if criminal charges are likely.

(2) Advise full disclosure to the Inland Revenue.

(3) If the client agrees to full disclosure, the client, or the accountant with the client's permission, should write to the Revenue giving details.

(4) If the client does not agree, the accountant should explain the possibly serious consequences of failure to disclose, and that it will be necessary for him or her to write to the Revenue explaining that the accounts can no longer be relied on, but giving no further information.

(5) If the client is still unwilling to disclose, the accountant should cease to act and inform the Revenue that he or she has done so and that the accounts can no longer be relied on.

(6) On receipt of an enquiry from a prospective successor, the accountant will, on receipt of the client's permission, discuss the matter freely. (If the client does not give such permission, the prospective successor should not, of course, take up the appointment.)

(b) Accountant has not previously acted in tax matters

Stages 1 to 3 of (a) above are the same. At stage 4, however, the accountant is not now required to inform the Inland Revenue that the accounts can no longer be relied on, merely that he or she has ceased to act. This is because the accountant was not responsible for the previous accounts. The letter to the Revenue (stage 5 of (a)) will now be notice that the accountant has ceased to act, with no further information. The position with regard to communication with a prospective successor remains broadly as in stage 6 above.

19.7   Summary

An auditor may become liable for damages for negligence to the client or to a third party.

A *client* has to show:

(a) duty of care based on contract or tort

(b) negligence

(c) damage resulting from that negligence.

A *third party* has to show:

(a) duty of care in tort based on whether the auditors knew or ought reasonably to have foreseen that a third party might rely on the accounts

(b) negligence

(c) damage resulting from that negligence.

For examination purposes and for practical purposes it is more important to know the principles involved than to know the details of decided cases, especially as the standards expected of auditors are constantly advancing.

Nevertheless, it is important for you to be familiar, *as a minimum*, with the following cases:

(a) Re *Kingston Cotton Mills Co.*
(b) Re *City Equitable Fire Insurance Co. Ltd.*
(c) Re *Thomas Gerrard and Sons Ltd.*
(d) *Hedley Byrne and Co. Ltd* v. *Heller and Partners Ltd.*
(e) *JEB Fasteners Ltd* v. *Marks, Bloom and Co.*
(f) *Twomax Ltd* v. *Dickson, McFarlane and Robinson.*

The auditor's duty, and possible liability, to clients in respect of fraud is dealt with in a Draft Auditing Guideline issued in 1985.

Although the primary duty to prevent and detect errors and fraud lies with the management, the auditor has the responsibility to design and evaluate his or her work with a view to detecting material errors and irregularities. Failure to detect errors and irregularities which a reasonably competent auditor would have discovered can be the basis for a claim by the client for negligence. The auditor must therefore plan and carry out the audit alert to the possibility of fraud and error.

In the UK, liability to third parties is based on the 1963 case of *Hedley Byrne and Co. Ltd* v. *Heller and Partners Ltd.* The 1981 *JEB Fasteners* case and the *Twomax* case which followed shortly after it clarified the definition of the persons likely to be successful with a claim.

In 1983 the ICAEW issued a statement entitled 'Professional liability of accountants and auditors' which was reproduced in Section 19.5.

Progress questions

Questions	Reference for answers
(1) What must a client show to substantiate a claim for negligence against an auditor?	Section 19.2
(2) Explain the important point established in *re City Equitable Fire Insurance Co. Ltd*	Section 19.2
(3)(a) Where does the primary responsibility for the prevention and detection of fraud lie?	Section 19.3: Draft Guideline—Fraud and other Irregularities— Paragraph 3
(b) How may the responsibilities of the auditor be defined in this area?	Draft Guideline Paragraph 11
(c) What should the auditor do on discovering substantial errors or fraud in the course of the audit?	Draft Guideline Paragraphs 26–32
(d) Is it ever appropriate for the auditor to report fraud or other irregularities to third parties?	Draft Guideline Paragraphs 33–36
(5) What must a claimant prove to succeed in a third party action against an auditor?	Section 19.4
(6) Summarize the facts and decision in the case of *JEB Fasteners Ltd* v. *Marks, Bloom and Co.*	Section 19.4
(7) To what extent is it possible for auditors to avoid liability to third parties?	Section 19.5: ICAEW Statement Professional Liability of Accountants and Auditors Paragraphs 19–28

20 Audit committees

20.1 Historical background

Before considering the role of audit committees in modern business management, it is salutary to remind ourselves that the very first auditing of joint stock companies was undertaken by committees of shareholders who checked the accounts of the company on behalf of their fellow shareholders. Then gradually these audit committees of 'amateurs' were replaced by 'professionals' who did the work on behalf of the shareholders—as they still do in the UK. It is interesting, however, that in the USA, where there is no statutory audit, the auditor works not on behalf of the shareholders but on behalf of the board.

Likewise the directors of the original joint stock companies in the UK were themselves a committee of members who directed the company for their fellow shareholders—whereas today it is often not necessary for a director to be a shareholder at all, and most of them are full-time executive managers of the company together with some part-time non-executive directors.

Currently this whole relationship between the company, its shareholders, its executive and non-executive directors, and the auditor is the subject of public discussion and practical development within business. In this climate of change there has developed an important role for the independent non-executive outside director, who may or may not be a shareholder, and one of whose important tasks is seen as being that of ensuring that the shareholders' interests are adequately taken into account in the policy debates and decisions of the board. Whilst, of course, all members of a unitary board share the responsibility equally, and no doubt have the same loyalties to the company, nevertheless the full-time executive director does have additional responsibilities which can, and do, colour his or her viewpoint. For example, the executive has a direct responsibility for the workforce, whose interests do not always coincide with those of the shareholders. A strong desire on the part of the executive to maintain harmony in industrial relations can militate against the shareholders' interests, on whose behalf the independent outside director may consisder himself as holding a watching brief. Similarly, the current responsibilities of the full-time executive director tend to focus his attention on the present and the short-term, so the view has developed that the independent outside director has a useful monitoring role to perform on behalf of the general long-term interests of the company, its shareholders, and those who work for it.

20.2   Development

Against this background, the audit committee can be seen as a practical mechanism for enabling the independent outside directors to fulfil their role effectively, although it was originally conceived as having a somewhat narrower role. Audit committees were first publicly endorsed in 1940 in the aftermath of the *McKesson & Robbins* scandal in the USA, to which reference is made in Chapter 19, when both the Securities and Exchange Commission (SEC) and the New York Stock Exchange (NYSE) advocated the creation of audit committees.

It took some twenty years for much development to take place, and it was not until 1976 that the NYSE introduced a requirement for audit committees into its listing agreement. Likewise the SEC has stepped up its campaign to get audit committees introduced in all listed companies; and in some cases, as a result of enforcement proceedings, has obliged individual corporations to establish audit committees with specific duties. The result of these pressures has been that the audit committee, composed of outside directors, has become established as a normal part of the structure of corporations in the USA.

Similar developments took place in Canada, where the Business Corporations Act of 1975, and the provincial company laws, require that corporations offering securities to the public must have an audit committee of no fewer than three directors. Some provinces stipulate that the majority of the audit committee must be outside directors.

In the UK, development of the idea has been much slower, and has sometimes been resisted by different parties on what appear to be 'ideological' grounds. Sight seems to have been lost of the fact that it can be developed as a useful adjunct to good company management. It can also serve to plug an odd gap in UK company law—namely, that the shareholder, who legally appoints the auditor and to whom the auditor officially reports, has no right of communication with the auditor, other than to receive his report. An audit committee of outside directors, with the shareholders' interest in the forefront of their minds, can have effective communication with the auditor to discuss and probe the detailed matters which are of concern to the shareholders, and which the shareholders might have themselves wished to discuss with the auditor were they permitted to do so.

Nevertheless, development will depend, in practice, on factors which are peculiar to each individual company. In any event, for the small company, an audit committee might be an organizational sledgehammer—even if the company did have any independent outside directors, which is normally not the case. In the medium- and large-sized companies, actual development will vary from company to company according to:

—the character and personality of the chairman of the board of directors;
—the attitude of the managing director, or chief executive;
—the personalities and experience of the outside directors on the board;
—the history and character of the company itself, and its management.

20.3 Objects of committees

Against this background, the development of audit committees should be seen as having the object of developing auditing in the broadest sense—as compared with the external audit which has the relatively 'narrow' objective of enabling the auditor to express an opinion on the accounts. In this broad sense, the Auditing Practices Committee of the Consultative Committee of Accountancy Bodies (CCAB) has published a booklet on audit committees written by Richard Buckley (1979) in which the view is expressed that audit committees can

—help directors to fulfil their responsibilities;
—strengthen the role of non-executive directors;
—strengthen the objectivity and credibility of financial reporting;
—strengthen the independence of the audit function;
—improve the quality of the audit and accounting functions;
—improve communication between directors, auditors and management.

In addition, if the directors and management wish to do so, the audit committee can be developed as a useful mechanism by which the board can monitor the running of the business. Of course, both the chairman of the board and the chief executive of the company have important and direct responsibilities in this area, which are in no way diminished by the role of the audit committee. But the fact remains that the board carries ultimate responsibility, which its audit committee can assist it to discharge, without impinging on the responsibilities of its chairman, or of the chief executive, any more than does the board in the normal execution of its duties. Indeed some chief executives have found in practice that the audit committee can provide them with valuable support and reassurance.

Purely from a management point of view, then, the audit committee can be given the objective of helping the board by carrying out what is, in effect, a management audit, in order:

(a) to see whether the board policies, in the different areas of management, appear to be properly implemented in practice;

(b) to appraise the company's style of management, and of business conduct, particularly in sensitive areas;

(c) to assess the strengths and weaknesses of the organization, and the manner in which it is reacting to the opportunities and pressures which surround it;

(d) to see how management performance is evaluated at different levels, and to assess whether management succession is being adequately provided to meet the board's plans for the future.

If the audit committee is seen as a means of helping the board of directors to discharge its responsibilities more effectively, then it follows that the audit committee should not generally take decisions. It should report to the board, with recommendations where appropriate, and leave decisions to be taken by the board and the management structure below it.

Such a view of audit committees was endorsed by Mr Gordon Richardson, Governor of the Bank of England, in a speech to the Institute of Directors in November 1978, in which he spoke of the experience of the Bank of England that

'in a number of problem cases with which the Bank had been involved, the likelihood of troubles being identified in good time might have been increased had an audit committee been in existence to help outside directors perform their function.'

He went on to express the view that the inclusion of outside directors in company boards was highly desirable to ensure:

(1) that management's plans were subjected to independent scrutiny;
(2) that management succession was less incestuous:
(3) that management was seen to be accountable.

20.4   Setting up the audit committee

As indicated above, the audit committee would normally be a non-executive subcommittee of the board, working with the full authority of the latter. Its composition will depend on the circumstances of the particular company, and preferably should consist entirely of independent outside directors. However, in many companies this may not be practicable, but even then a majority of members should be non-executive directors. When executive directors are appointed to the committee, it is preferable that they be independent of any responsibility for financial management within the company. This latter requirement is particularly important as regards the chairman of the audit committee, upon whom will probably depend the success or otherwise of the committee.

It must inevitably take time for a newly appointed committee to develop its own skill and experience, and indeed to define more precisely the job which it it trying to do. It is therefore important to achieve a reasonable continuity of experience among the committee members, whilst balancing this against the desirability of achieving some rotation of membership in order to strengthen the independence of the committee. Each company will have to solve this problem in its own way.

In setting up an audit committee and establishing the basis on which it operates, the company must seek to ensure that

(a) the audit committee is seen to have the full authority and backing of the board;

(b) the committee is seen to be independent, both in the make-up of its membership, and in actual practice; and in particular that it is not under the influence of the chief executive;

(c) the committee has clear terms of reference, and all levels of management understand what the board expects it to do; and in particular that the committee does not create conflict by encroaching on the executive responsibility and authority of management at any level;

(d) the committee establishes a clear working relationship with financial management, the internal auditor, and the external auditor.

The precise means of achieving these ends must depend on the circumstances of each individual company, but the first step would normally be a resolution of the board which formally establishes the audit committee. An example of such a resolution is given below.

Board resolution

Audit Committee
1. After consideration of board paper No ...., dated ...., the board *agreed* to establish a permanent non-executive subcommittee of the board to be called the Audit Committee.
2. It was *agreed* that the chairman of that committee shall be one of the outside directors of the company and shall serve for a period of five years but shall be eligible for reappointment. The committee shall have four other members, of whom at least two shall be outside directors of the company. Initially, one of the ordinary members shall retire each year in succession, but shall be eligible for reappointment. Thereafter, each ordinary member shall retire after three years.
3. The following are hereby *appointed* to the Audit Committee:
   Mr ....   Chairman
   Ms ....,   to retire in 19...
   etc. ....,   to retire in 19...

4. It was *agreed* that the terms of reference of the Audit Committee should be as follows:

(*a*) To make recommendations to the board concerning the appointment and remuneration of the external auditors of the group and of each of its subsidiary and associated companies.

(*b*) To review with the external auditor his terms of engagement and his proposed plan for the annual audit, and discuss with him any significant problems which he can foresee, or to which the committee may wish to draw his attention, and to consider whether the auditor's terms of reference should be extended in any respect beyond the field of his statutory audit.

(*c*) In consultation with the chief internal auditor, the finance director of the group, and the external auditor, to review the scope and effectiveness of internal audit procedures, to review the reports and findings of the internal audit department and, where considered appropriate by the committee, to make recommendations.

(*d*) To keep under review the group's systems of accounting and internal control, and the system of reporting to management and to the boards of directors of the subsidiary companies, and of the group.

(*e*) To review the auditor's evaluation of the system of internal control and accounting.

(*f*) To review with the auditor the results of his audit and discuss with him any matters which he may wish to raise, or on which the committee may require further information or explanation either from the auditor or from management; also to review the letter of representation, and any other certificates or matters of confirmation provided by the group to the auditor in connection with the annual accounts.

(*g*) To review the interim and annual financial statements before their submission to the board for approval.

(*h*) To review the share registers in respect of dealings in the shares of the group by employees, officers and directors of subsidiary or associated companies and of the group.

(*i*) To meet either at the request of the external or internal auditor, or on the committee's own initiative, to consider any matter which either the auditor or the committee believes should be brought to the attention of the directors or shareholders.

(*j*) To review the procedures adopted throught the group for implementing the policies of the board, to assess whether there are any weaknesses in those procedures, and, where considered appropriate by the committee, to make recommendations.

(*k*) To monitor the group's business conduct generally and particularly in sensitive areas; to appraise whether the style of management in different parts of the group is best suited to achieve the objectives of the board; and where appropriate, to make recommendations.

(*l*) To assess the strengths and weaknesses of the organization; and assess whether it is reacting successfully to the opportunities and pressures which surround it.

(*m*) To see how management performance is evaluated at different levels; and to assess whether management succession is being adequately provided to meet the board's plans for the future.

(*n*) To make recommendations to the board regarding any change in these terms of reference which the committee considers desirable.

5. Within the group the Audit Committee has the authority of the group board to call for any documents, or other evidence, which it may require, and for explanations from any employees, officers or directors of the group and of any of its subsidiaries, or associated companies.

6. The Audit Committee should report to the group board either formally in writing, or verbally, as it considers appropriate on the matters within its terms of reference at least once a year, but more frequently if it so wishes. It shall report to the group board on any specific matters referred to it by the board for investigation and report.

7. The Audit Committee has the authority of the group board to incur reasonable expenses in carrying out its responsibilities, including the out-of-pocket, hotel and travelling expenses of its members. It is also authorized to incur fees for the services of outside professional advisers or consultants up to an initial budget of £.... The members of the Audit Committee shall be entitled to a *per diem* fee of £... pro rata for the work undertaken. The total of its annual expenditure shall be included in its annual report to the group board.

8. It was *agreed* that the group managing director will circulate a memorandum to all heads of departments at group headquarters and to all managing directors of subsidiary and associated companies explaining the setting up of this committee, together with a copy of its terms of reference.

The audit committee's style of operating will depend critically upon the individuals concerned, but it is essential that it establish a spirit of mutual cooperation and trust with all parts of the organization. This is particularly important as regards the chairman of the board and the chief executive of the company, on whose executive responsibility and authority the audit committee must not trespass in any way. However, it has been found in practice that an audit committee can relieve the chief executive of what might be termed the approbrium of simply checking up on line management, and he or she can largely leave to the committee the task of monitoring the whole system of internal control.

From the point of view of the external auditor it provides, of course, a channel of communication with the board, though only the audit report can provide a channel of communication to the shareholders. If the external auditor is faced with a difficult or delicate situation, particularly if it involves the chief executive or other senior directors or managers, then the audit committee can be most valuable. It is for this reason that clause 4(i) above of the terms of reference gives the auditor the right to approach the chairman of the audit committee to request a meeting with the committee.

As regards the internal auditor, much will depend on the particular circumstances as to how a relationship with the audit committee is built up. Much will depend on the internal audit department's size, the scope of its responsibility and authority, and its established reporting procedures. However, since the audit committee should have a strong non-executive bias, it would be entirely wrong for the internal audit department to be put directly under the control of the audit committee. Nevertheless, clause 4(i) of the above terms of reference gives the internal auditor the same right of direct access to the audit committee as it gives to the external auditor. In practice, this should help to strengthen the position of the internal auditor, and provide an effective channel of communication between the internal auditor, the board, and the external auditor.

20.5 Method of operation

It will be found in practice that the timing of meetings of the audit committee needs to be scheduled well in advance in order to fit in with what is normally a very tight timetable for the production of the company's interim and final accounts. Likewise the audit committee may want to plan meetings with different departments and subsidiary companies, so that over a period of years it covers the whole of the area included in its terms of reference.

It will almost certainly find it useful to keep minutes of its meetings, but this may present problems if its terms of reference include matters such as clause 4(j) above. Discussion between the audit committee and senior directors and managers may be inhibited if it takes place in the knowledge that the matters raised will be minuted and those minutes circulated. There is also the problem of finding an individual of sufficient seniority and confidentiality to do the minute-taking.

The committee will have to decide on the extent to which its minutes are circulated beyond its own membership. It may well decide that some, or all, minutes should go to:

—members of the main board;
—the external auditor;
—the internal auditor;

—where appropriate, the heads of main departments such as the finance department;

—where appropriate, the managing directors of subsidiary companies or associated companies.

However, internal distribution of the committee's minutes below the level of the main board should be made through the chief executive.

Above all, minutes are useful in order to ensure that there is a proper follow-up of the matters on which the audit committee decides that action is needed. Although the committee has no executive authority itself, it will probably find it sufficient if a copy of the appropriate minute is sent as a recommendation to the managing director, or chief executive. More important matters may have to go as a recommendation to the board of directors. Subsequent meetings of the audit committee will need to follow up on whether or not the recommended action was taken. If there is no adequate explanation as to why no action has been taken, then the audit committee will have to take the matter up with the chief executive or the chairman of the board.

20.6 Audit committee questionnaire

As the audit committee tackles its job, it will help to focus the thrust of its inquiries if it prepares in advance of each meeting a list of questions which it proposes to discuss. It may circulate these questions only to its own members, or it may decide to send some of them in advance to those concerned, so as to give time for the information to be prepared, and so as to avoid meetings of the audit committee taking on too much of the air of an inquisition.

Likewise the preparation of a set of detailed questions can help the audit committee to ensure that, over a period of time, it covers the whole of the ground in its terms of reference; for the committee would not attempt to cover the whole of an extensive questionnaire in the course of each year's work.

Section 1

Questions for discussion with management before the year's audit starts

1.1 Is there any reason for making any change of auditor, either for the group as a whole, or for any of the subsidiary or associated companies?

1.2 Are any problems expected regarding the fees likely to be charged by the external auditors?

1.3 Are there any points which need to be raised with the auditor before he starts the audit of this year's accounts?

Section 2

Questions for discussion with the external auditor before the year's audit starts

2.1 With reference to his original letter of engagement, does the auditor see the need for any change in the terms of his engagement?

2.2 What is the auditor's time budget for the audit work to be undertaken in the coming year?

2.3 What are the rates to be charged for the different grades of staff and what is the budget of fees to be charged for auditing the year's accounts?

2.4 What other services does the auditor perform for the group, and how are these charged and to whom?

2.5 Does the auditor perform any personal services for any of the people employed in the group, and are any of the audit personnel employed on such work?

2.6 Does the auditor do audit, tax, or accountancy work for any other activities, or funds, related to the group, such as sports or social clubs?

2.7 What degree of continuity from previous years will there be in the audit staff?

2.8 Who is the second audit partner concerned with the audit and what role is it proposed he or she play during the forthcoming assignment?

2.9 What is the scope of the audit in terms of UK subsidiary companies and locations visited? What is omitted and why? Are any other firms of independent auditors involved, and if so, how?

2.10 What arrangements are being made to audit the overseas subsidiaries? Is another firm of overseas auditors involved? If so, what are the terms of relationship with those other auditors? How frequent, and in what form, is the contact with the other auditors? To what extent does the auditor review the work performed by the other auditors?

2.11 Are any changes expected in:

(a) the levels of materiality used during the audit;
(b) the emphasis of the audit;
(c) the timing of the different parts of the audit

2.12 Is the scope of the audit likely to be affected by changes in:

(a) accounting standards;
(b) generally accepted accounting principles;
(c) auditing standards;
(d) reporting requirements instituted by regulatory authorities such as the Stock Exchange, EEC, etc.?

2.13 Can the auditor foresee any particular developments either within the business, or outside it, which are likely to cause the auditor problems in the future?

2.14 Are any prospective changes of personnel within the group likely to cause the auditor problems, or on the contrary, facilitate his task?

2.15 Are there any significant problems which the auditor can foresee arising in the near future? Or in the distant future?

2.16 What is the basic approach to the proposed audit, and is it to be systems oriented or by detailed testing of transactions?

2.17 Has the auditor staff with the necessary training and experience to audit the computer operations?

2.18 What is the proposed timing of the audit, and if verification steps are carried out prior to the year-end, how does the auditor propose to cover transactions between the verification date and the year-end?

2.19 Is there any work which could be undertaken by the internal audit or other staff of the group which would simplify the auditor's task, and reduce the time spent by him and his staff on the audit?

Section 3

Questions for discussion with the external auditor after the interim audit

3.1 What is the level of experience of the staff who have been employed on the audit, and will there be any changes at the time of the year-end audit?

3.2 To what extent was the work of the internal auditors integrated with the work of the external auditor? Is there any scope for further integration? Is the auditor satisfied with the level of experience, skills, and general effectiveness of the internal auditors?

3.3 Does the auditor have any comments to make on:

   (a)   the quality of the internal accounting records;

   (b)   internal accounting policies;

   (c)   the timeliness, relevance and completeness of the accounting information provided to management for the running of the business?

3.4 Are there any areas where the auditor considers that the advantages of better internal control would be sufficient to warrant the cost of additional controls?

3.5 Are there any changes of any other kind within the group which the auditor would advocate?

3.6 Did the auditor encounter any problems in connection with computer systems?

3.7 Is the auditor satisfied that the computer equipment, programs and data are:

   (a)   adequately controlled to prevent improper use;

   (b)   secured against fire risk;

   (c)   duplicated, or otherwise protected, against risk of accidental loss or damage?

3.8 Are there any matters of internal control which the auditor raised in his management letters in the course of past years' audits, which have not been dealt with?

Section 4

Questions for discussion with management at the time of the interim audit

4.1 What steps has management taken to correct deficiencies in internal control:

(a) brought to their notice by the auditor;

(b) of which they became aware, independently of the auditor?

4.2 What points have been raised by the auditor in his management letter, and what has management done about them?

4.3 Does management consider that physical security of plant, premises and other assets is adequate?

4.4 What steps are taken to control personal transactions going through the books, such as purchases at trade prices?

4.5 Are there any grounds for thinking that any significant amount of business is being done in any part of the group with, or through, the relative of an employee of the group?

4.6 Are there any unusual features in the half-yearly statement being submitted to the board for subsequent distribution to shareholders; and how do these results compare with the monthly management accounts to the same date?

4.7 Is there any reason to doubt the value of stock and work-in-progress at the date of the half-yearly statement?

4.8 Are there any other special provisions or reserves which ought to be made at the date of the half-yearly statement?

4.9 Are the subsequent half-year's results expected to differ very markedly from those now being published?

Section 5

Questions for discussion with management when appropriate
Audit

5.1 Are there any matters which might require special investigation by the auditor, beyond the field of his statutory audit, in particular any potentially sensitive subjects such as:

(a) conflicts of interest;

(b) incompetent or inadequately trained staff in any departments;

(c) inaccurate budgeting, or estimating;

(d) inadequate security of assets;

(e) potential areas of defalcation, or fraud;

(f) transactions of dubious legality (including bribery);

(g) any other matters of concern to management although not directly related to the audit function?

Board policies

5.2 What steps are taken by subsidiary company directors to disseminate, and ensure compliance with, resolutions of the group board or subsidiary company board?

Reporting procedures

5.3 Does management have any comments to make on the timeliness, relevance and completeness of reports to:

(a) members of management;
(b) directors of subsidiary companies;
(c) the group board?

Operating procedures
5.4 What operating procedures have been reviewed by management with a view to making them more effective and less expensive?

Environmental pollution
5.5 Do any of our activities pollute the environment in any way? If so, what would be the cost of eliminating the pollution?

Products
5.6 What products or services have been studied by management with a view to reducing their cost and increasing their profit?

5.7 What steps are subsidiary companies taking regarding:

(a) developing new products;
(b) developing new markets for existing products?
(c) investigating competitors' action in these fields?

5.8 Do any of our products involve a significant product risk? If so, what would insurance cover cost?

Cash, etc.
5.9 What explanation is there for any major divergence during the year between the actual bank (+cash) balance and the projected cash flow for the year?

5.10 Who authorizes transfers between current account and deposit account or short-term investments? In what is he authorized to invest funds? Have any losses (or profits) been made on any such investments?

5.11 Are any such deposits, or investments, pledged or encumbered in any way? Who holds the certificates?

5.12 Who is authorized to accept bills of exchange? To what amount? On the other hand, do we ever draw bills of exchange on customers? Have any been dishonoured?

5.13 Have we ever cashed a cheque for an employee, and had it 'bounce'? Or been asked for loans by any employees? Did we make any such loans? Have they been repaid?

5.14 How much actual cash do we have on different premises? Do we really need to?

5.15 How are foreign exchange transactions handled, and are there any forward dealings? What is our open position?

Sales
5.16 Who fixes selling prices, and how? How often do we get it wrong? How do we take account of inflation?

5.17 How are estimates prepared for contracts, and who is authorized to fix the price at which a tender is submitted?

5.18 If we win the contract, do the works check the budgeted cost against the estimate? What mistakes has this brought to light recently? What about subsequent actual costs?

5.19 If delivery is a long time ahead, who takes what steps to cover us against rising costs of bought in materials and components and wages?

5.20 A contract having been taken at an agreed price, the customer may subsequently agree additions, or modifications, to the original contract. How do we ensure that this gets properly recorded, and that cash payments therefor do not get misappropriated?

Debtors

5.21 Have any sales invoices been factored, or pledged in any way? If so why?

5.22 How are credit levels fixed for different customers? How often are they breached and what was done about it?

5.23 Do we have any special arrangements for providing finance for stocks of our goods in the hands of customers? If so, are we entirely satisfied that each customer can meet his commitments? Does title to such goods remain ours until sold by the customer?

5.24 How are debts 'aged', reviewed, chased and recovered?

5.25 What large debts have been written-off recently? Are any substantial current debts probably uncollectable? What is the trend of our bad-debt experience over recent years?

5.26 Are any debts outstanding from directors or employees of the group?

Purchases

5.27 How are levels of authority fixed as to who can commit the group, for purchases or services, up to what amount? When did somebody last exceed their authorization limit, and what was done about it?

5.28 How do we control modifications to contracts which we have put out to suppliers to ensure that payment is not made for goods or services which we have not received?

5.29 Can any forward commitments be entered into? Are there any?

5.30 What regulations are there about suppliers and others sending presents to purchase officers and other employees? When did it last happen and what was done about it? How do we know that it is not still happening?

5.31 Where repeat orders are regularly needed for goods or services are purchase orders correctly issued each time?

5.32 Are procedures for obtaining competitive tenders for purchases properly carried out?

Creditors

5.33 Do we pay all our creditors promptly, and how promptly? If not, who authorizes the delay, and why?

5.34 Are there any disputes, or pending writs, in respect of amounts we owe to suppliers or others? What are the largest amounts which have recently been in dispute, and how were the disputes settled?

Stocks and work-in progress

5.35 What different treatment is given to high-value and low-value items?

5.36 Is the physical security of high-value items adequate? What have we recently lost?

5.37 Have we undertaken strategic stock-piling of any materials? If so, what material, why, how many months' usage, and of what total value?

5.38 How do we control stock and plant out on sites? What have we recently lost? What about loose tools in the works?

5.39 How much slow-moving and obsolete stock have we as a proportion of the total stock of each class?

5.40 Of what important items have we recently run out of stock? If none, are we holding unnecessarily large stocks?

5.41 How are stock levels, and re-order quantities, fixed? How and when were they last reviewed? With what result?

5.42 How do we control the disposal of unwanted stock, scrap, etc? How did the price we got for it compare with the book write-off?

Guarantees and insurance

5.43 What guarantees have been given within the group, and what is the potential liability thereunder?

5.44 Does the Group itself carry any part of any insured risk? If so, what is the potential liability? Have we ECGD cover on all our exports?

5.45 What insurance cover is maintained, of what risks, and is it reviewed regularly to ensure adequacy in times of inflation, and in the light of changes in trading patterns?

Assets

5.46 What asset registers are maintained, and by whom? How is the physical existence of the asset checked against the register? When did we last find that we had lost an asset? What? Could it happen again? What about office equipment, typewriters, pocket calculators?

5.47 For whom do we provide cars? Who authorizes each purchase? Do we provide anything else, or any other perks, or benefits?

5.48 Do we lease any cars, or plant, or other equipment? How are these identified on the asset registers? Do we capitalize the lease commitment, or else how do we account for these items? Do the asset and capitalized liability on the lease both appear in the accounts?

5.49 How do we capitalize plant made in our own works? Do we take out any patents on this?

5.50 Do we take out patents on designs from our own design office? Can we earn 'outside' revenue from any of our patents?

5.51 How do we account for trade marks, goodwill or other intangible assets?

5.52 What idle, and unused, plant or equipment have we got? Or empty buildings or land? How is this accounted for? What are we going to do about it? Will there be any losses to write off? Or profits to be made on realization?

5.53 How do we decide when plant is obsolete? What new technology are we investigating? Shall we be ready to install new technology before the current methods become obsolete? Can our projected cash flow support the investment?

5.54 Is any property mortgaged or pledged in any way as security for loans or other commitments?

5.55 Have our insurers placed any special limits or conditions on the insurance cover of any buildings, plant or equipment?

Personnel

5.56 How do our rates of pay compare with those in the area? Can we recruit the skilled employees we need? And the right type of youngsters?

5.57 How do we identify 'high fliers' and what steps do we take to train them and give them opportunities to rise?

5.58 What senior, skilled or key personnel have we had to dismiss recently, and why, and who authorized it?

5.59 Who has recently left of their own accord—and we wished they had not? How could we prevent this happening again?

5.60 How do we assess management performance at different levels and what mistakes have we made in promotions? Can we correct them?

5.61 Are we satisfied that, in the light of inflation, we have fulfilled all our moral obligations to all our pensioners, their widows and families? If not, what might the liability be?

5.62 Have any recommendations been made regarding health and safety at any of our places of work by Factory Inspectors, trades union safety representatives, fire officers, police authorities, health or medical authorities, which we have not yet put into effect? What might the cost be?

Share transactions

5.63 Have any material dealings in the shares of the group been undertaken by the relatives of, or the individuals themselves, who are:

(a) employees;
(b) officers;
(c) directors;
of a subsidiary company or of the group?

5.64 Has any such person requested permission to deal in the shares of the group and been refused such permission?

5.65 Does the auditor, or any member of his staff, hold any shares in the group?

5.66 Do any important competitors, suppliers or customers, hold shares in the group?

5.67 Have any shareholders substantially increased their holdings during the year?

Section 6

Questions for discussion with management before the accounts are finalized

6.1 Is management reasonably satisfied that:

      (a) the auditor and his staff carried out their work satisfactorily;

      (b) covered all aspects adequately?

6.2 What has the auditor required in the way of:

      (a) letters of representation;

      (b) other certificates?

      In what respects do these differ from those required in previous years? Did management have any doubt, or reservations, about any of the figures provided? How were those doubts resolved?

6.3 Are any subsidiary companies not consolidated? Why not?

6.4 Did any unusual and significant event occur during the year, such as:

      (a) the acquisition of a new business;

      (b) the commissioning of new plant;

      (c) the purchase, or erection, of new buildings;

      (d) the leasing of substantial assets;

      (e) the disposal of significant segments of the business?

      If so, how were these transactions treated in the financial statements? And, how does it affect comparability with last year's figures.

6.5 Has any new capital been raised, or substantial borrowing undertaken? If so, is it correctly shown? And, does it affect comparability with last year's figures?

6.6 What have been the limits on overdrafts or other forms of fluctuating borrowings, and have these limits ever been breached during the year? Or substantially changed? If so, why?

6.7 Are there any unusual items in the financial statements such as:

      (a) prior period adjustments;

      (b) extraordinary items;

      (c) transfers direct to, or from, reserves;

      (d) capital profits, or losses, or special write-offs;

      (e) transfers between subsidiary companies?

      If so, what accounting treatment has been given them? And, what alternative treatments were there?

6.8 Has adequate provision been made for contingencies? Do the financial statements adequately disclose other unusual uncertainties?

6.9 Has the group or any subsidiary company entered into contracts or agreements involving long-term or unusual commitments, which have not been disclosed in the financial statements?

6.10 Were there any items which were on the threshold of materiality which it was decided not to disclose separately in the financial statements? If so, what were they? And, what would the separate disclosure have been?

6.11 Are the financial statements significantly affected by transactions which were not at arm's length? If so, what was the impact of such transactions on the statements?

6.12 To what extent do the financial statements take account of post-balance-sheet events? Are there any omissions in this respect?

6.13 How does the total of debtors and amounts due to the group compare with previous years, and with the current level of trading?

6.14 Is management satisfied about the cut-off procedure at the year-end in connection with goods and services and current liabilities? When did the procedure last go wrong?

6.15 How did the physical stocktake compare with the book figure? How did the year-end stock adjustment compare with previous years?

6.16 What is the basis of year-end stock valuation; and who fixes, and how, the cost or realizable value?

6.17 How does the group depreciation policy compare with the actual physical life of the assets? How do we treat assets which have been written-off but are still in use—in the annual accounts; in costs and in the management accounts? What are we doing about inflation accounting?

6.18 What items are in dispute with the Inland Revenue in connection with our tax assessments? Is there any likelihood of a material increase, or reduction, in our liability?

6.19 Is it possible to determine with reasonable accuracy how much of the deferred tax liability is likely to be paid in cash in the near future? Are we satisfied that the amount provided for deferred tax reflects a realistic assessment of future developments?

6.20 Have we met all our obligations to our debenture holders or other providers of long-term loans? Will any of these fall due for repayment in the near future?

6.21 How does the trend of sales of different products and services compare with previous years, and with what was budgeted? How is the difference explained, and can we separately identify the separate effects of price changes and volume changes?

6.22 Do we have any overseas contracts running in countries with a high political risk? Or countries where exchange control regulations are liable to change?

6.23 Have we any major disputes with customers over which we may incur a material liability?

6.24 How do we cover ourselves against fluctuations in exchange rates? Both for sales, and also any purchases abroad? What is the extent of our exposure?

6.25 Do we have personnel, or investments, in countries where there is a danger of expropriation, or loss? If so, what is our potential write off, and what might be the cost of our responsibilties to our personnel in voluntary or other compensation?

6.26 Does the source and application of funds statement include any significant transactions which have been netted one against another? Are all non-recurring, or unusual, items fully disclosed?

6.27 What undisclosed provisions were brought forward from last year's trading and how were these disposed of? What undisclosed provisions are we making in these financial statements?

6.28 In the case of our long-term trade investments, what do we assess to be their current value in the light of earnings and asset values, as compared with their book value?

6.29 Are any of our quoted investments not readily marketable?

6.30 Is there any doubt as to whether any of our associated companies, or trading partners, will have the liquid funds to pay us on the due dates what they owe us under loan or trading agreements?

6.31 Are there any restrictions on what can be distributed, or remitted, in the way of profits by any of our subsidiary or associated companies in the UK or overseas?

6.32 In view of the impact of inflation on the cash resources of the group, should any restriction be imposed on the amount of dividend distribution, either by the group or any of its subsidiaries?

6.33 Are there any legal actions pending either in the UK or overseas in which substantial claims might be made against us? If the claim has to be noted on the accounts as a contingent liability, how can this be done without prejudicing our position in the courts?

Section 7

Questions for discussion with the external auditor after the year-end audit, but before the accounts are finalized

7.1 What is the wording which the auditor proposes for his report, and what is the significance of any deviation from the normal form, or from the wording used in previous years?

7.2 Are there any particular problems which the auditor encounters now, which he used not to encounter?

7.3 Has the auditor identified any matters which in his view merit special investigation either by management or by the internal auditor, or by the external auditor himself outside the field of his statutory audit?

7.4 Did the auditor receive full cooperation from all personnel in the group?

7.5 Was there any attempt, either overt or covert, to restrict the scope of the auditor's work in any way?

7.6 To what extent has the auditor had to rely on the professional opinion of experts, with regard to such matters as:

(a) the valuation of properties;
(b) the valuation of plant and machinery;
(c) the valuation of stocks, or work-in-progress;
(d) actuarial valuations of pension, or other funds or liabilities?

7.7 Was the auditor satisfied with regard to the working of cut-off procedures in connection with:

(a) services and supplies;
(b) goods-inwards, stocks, and current liabilities;

(c) finished stocks, goods-outwards, and debtors?

7.8 Were there any differences of opinion with management relating to judgement items such as:

(a) depreciation;
(b) slow moving, or obsolete, stock;
(c) bad, or doubtful, debts;
(d) warranty provisions;
(e) contract terms?
How were such differences resolved?

7.9 What audit steps were taken regarding any significant transactions out of the ordinary course of business, such as:

(a) investment in new plant;
(b) new business activities?

7.10 Have any of the group's funds been placed under the personal control, or discretionary use, of any director or employee of the group?

7.11 To what extent has the auditor tested different ratios disclosed by the financial statements, and do any of these disclose significant fluctuations?

7.12 To what extent has the auditor tested the financial statements against the management accounts, and did this disclose any significant differences?

7.13 Are there any covenants, or requirements, of trust deeds, bankers, or other lenders which must be met in the preparation of these financial statements, and which do not appear to have been met, or which need to be disclosed?

7.14 Have there been any changes in the accounting principles used during the year, or changes in the method of applying those principles? If so, why? What has been the effect? Does the auditor agree that, in the circumstances, the changes are:

(a) appropriate;
(b) preferable to what was done before?

7.15 Did the auditor have any significant disagreements with management as to:

(a) accounting policies;
(b) disclosures in financial statements?

7.16 To what extent do the accounting principles used now by the group conform with those currently being developed for *future* use:

(a) in business generally;
(b) in this industry in particular?

7.17 How do these financial statements compare with those of companies in similar situations and industries as to:

(a) extent, and
(b) method of disclosure?

7.18 Do the statments fail in any way to meet statutory requirements? To
      what extent do the statements fail to conform to the best professional
      standards of disclosure?
7.19 Should there be incorporated now in these financial statements any
      changes pending, or in prospect, in statutory, contractual, or
      professional requirements, or standards, which might affect future
      disclosure?

Of course, it is not envisaged that every audit committee would discuss all
the above questions every year. Some committees will in any case have more
restricted terms of reference, whilst others may be given a wider field to
cover. Nor are the questions necessarily exhaustive. In particular circumstances there will be important matters to consider which are not included
above. The above questions are set out as an indication of the sort of ground
which an audit committee ought to cover. Some questions it will discuss
every year. Other parts of the questionnaire it will aim to cover bit by bit as
the years go by.

20.7 Problems

Any innovation is bound to run into objections and problems. It has been
suggested that an audit committee might create divisions within a board and
conflicts with the executive management of the company. Of course it could,
but there is no reason why it should. Any board can create subcommittees for
any purpose without causing itself problems, so long as the subcommittee
remains clearly subordinate to its board. There is, therefore, no reason why
an audit committee should create problems if its members behave sensibly,
and remember the collective responsibility of the whole board.

It is for this same reason that it is considered that an audit committee must
not report directly to the shareholders, as some people advocate that it
should. Were it to do so, it must automatically tend to create divisions within
a board. An audit committee which reported to the shareholders would take
on the nature of a supervisiory body, along the lines of the two-tier board
practised in some countries. The collective responsibility of the board is
better preserved by keeping the audit committee strictly as a non-executive
subcommittee of that board.

In the same vein, there is no reason for a non-executive audit committee to
create conflicts with executive management. All the questions suggested for
discussion above are ones about which any board of directors is entitled to
obtain reassurance. In this case it is envisaged that the audit committee will

satisfy itself about these matters on behalf of the whole board. Having more time to do so, the audit committee is more likely to arrive at a sensible conclusion than would a full board of directors with all the other day-to-day matters which must occupy the time of its meetings.

However, it is important that the audit committee avoids springing surprises on executive management, as for example could happen if the auditor raised with the committee a matter which he had not discussed with management. Only if the matter were one of supreme personal sensitivity should this ever happen, if management are not to feel that the auditor is going 'behind their backs'. For the same reason, the committee will probably invite the relevant members of management to attend those parts of their meetings at which the managers' responsibilities are being discussed. Or, if they do not attend the meetings, arrange through the chief executive that they receive the relevant extracts of the minutes.

20.8 Advantages

The advantages obtained from setting up an audit committee will depend on how the whole operation is undertaken, from setting up, to selecting its members, to it doing its job. Experience demonstrates that it can be a useful instrument in helping a board to see that the company is run in the way in which the board are seeking to run it.

It can assist the board, particularly the independent non-executive outside directors, to achieve a much better understanding of the company's affairs. Indeed it could prove to be one of the best ways of increasing the usefulness and effectiveness of outside directors within a business. Discussion of the sort of questions outlined above will improve their knowledge and understanding of the way the company operates, and its problems and opportunities. But, of course, it requires time—time of the outside director to attend the discussions of the committee.

Perhaps of more importance is the opportunity it provides for the directors on the committee to meet and get to know the subsidiary company directors and line managers at lower levels within the organization, in the course of discussing the questions outlined above. As time goes by this could be of great help to the committee members when assessing proposals to the main board for promotion to senior management, or to subsidiary company boards, or even to the group board.

On the other hand, practice shows that the discussions of the audit committee with directors and managers of subsidiary companies or departments can be very beneficial to the morale of the whole organization. Admittedly, junior managers may find it a gruelling test of their knowledge of their own business; but at the same time they find it encouraging that senior directors of the group are prepared to spend time to discuss in detail the operations of the subsidiary companies and departments for which the junior managers are responsible.

20.9   Summary

The development of audit committees has been slow in the UK. Nevertheless they can be a useful adjunct to good company management. Their objects are:

(*a*) to help directors fulfil their responsibilties;
(*b*) to strengthen the role of non-executive directors;
(*c*) to strengthen the objectivity and credibility of financial reporting;
(*d*) to strengthen the independence of the audit function;
(*e*) to improve the quality of the audit and accounting functions;
(*f*) to improve communications between directors, auditors and management;
(*g*) to assist the board of directors in monitoring the running of the business.

If the audit committee is to function properly, it must be seen to have the full authority and backing of the board while also retaining its independence. It must have clear terms of reference and channels of communication with the finanancial management and internal and external auditors.

It may be useful for the audit committee to use a questionnaire, answers to which it attempts to establish (see Section 20.6 above).

One problem is that the committee might have a divisive effect on the board, and in particular lead to a split between the executive directors and the non-executive directors. This can be avoided if all directors understand and appreciate the benefits for the company as a whole of the existence of the audit committee.

The advantage of the use of an audit committee, successfully operated, is the achievement of the objectives discussed in Section 20.3.

Progress questions

Questions	References for answers
(1) What are the objects of audit committees?	Section 20.3
(2) Explain how an audit committee may operate within a company?	Section 20.5
(3) Use your knowledge of the audit committee questionnaire in Section 20.6 to summarize the main areas which will be of concern to the audit committee.	Section 20.6
(4) What are the advantages and disadvantages of the use of audit committees?	Sections 20.7 and 20.8

21 Auditing consolidated financial statements

21.1 Introduction and legal background

When a company has subsidiaries it is required by S229, subject to some exceptions, to prepare group accounts which combine the accounts of the company with those of the subsidiaries.

The circumstances giving rise to the holding company/subsidiary company relationship are defined in S736:

A company is deemed to be a subsidiary of another company if that other company:

(a) is a member of it and controls the composition of its board of directors, or

(b) holds more than half in nominal value of its equity share capital.

A company is also treated as a subsidiary of its holding company's own holding company; that is, when it is a sub-subsidiary.

The exceptions from the requirement are given in S229. Group accounts are not required if:

(a) It is impracticable, or would be of no real value to the company's members, in view of the insignificant amounts involved, or

(b) It would involve expense or delay out of proportion to the value to members, or

(c) The result would be misleading, or harmful to the business of the company or any of its subsidiaries, or

(d) The business of the holding company and that of the subsidiary are so different that they cannot reasonably be treated as a single undertaking;

and, if the directors are of that opinion about each of the company's subsidiaries, group accounts are not required.

The approval of the Secretary of State for Trade is required if exemption is claimed on the ground that the result would be harmful or on the ground of difference between the business of the holding company and that of the subsidiary.

Note that the term 'group accounts' does not mean only consolidated accounts. S229 allows a company to submit:

(a) More than one set of consolidated accounts, each set dealing with a different section of the group, or

(b) Separate accounts for each subsidiary, or

(c) Statements expanding the information about the subsidiaries in the holding company's individual accounts.

The Act also requires all group companies to have the same financial year, unless the directors consider that there are good reasons against it.

If group companies do not have the same financial year, the accounts for a non-conformist subsidiary ending last before the holding company's accounting date must be used, unless the Secretary of State agrees to a modification of that requirement.

21.2   SSAP 14—Group Accounts

Note. This is a brief summary of the requirements of SSAP 14. Refer to your accounting books for more detail.

Obviously the provisions of SSAP 14 cannot override those of the Companies Act 1985. What SSAP 14 does, however, is to require subsidiaries to be excluded in four situations, for each of which a different treatment is laid down. The four situations are:

(a) The activities of the companies are dissimilar. This is the same as the exemption under S229(3) given above. In this case SSAP 14 states that separate financial statements for any excluded companies should be included.

(b) The holding company, although owning more than half the equity share capital, does not control more than half of the votes, or has restrictions imposed on its ability to appoint a majority of the board of directors. SSAP 14 requires such a company to be included in the consolidated financial statements under the equity method of accounting* if in all other respects it satisfies the criteria for treatment as an associated company under SSAP 1 or, if these conditions are not met, as an investment at cost or valuation less any provision required. In addition, separate financial information about the company should be included in the group accounts to meet the requirements of the Companies Act.

(c) The subsidiary operates under severe long-term restrictions which

---

* A method of accounting under which the investment in a company is shown at the cost of that investment plus the investing company's share of the post-acquisition profits and reserves of the company.

significantly impair the holding company's control over the subsidiary's assets or operations. Here the group's investment in the subsidiary should be stated in the consolidated balance sheet at the amount at which it would have been included under the equity method of accounting at the date the restrictions came into force.

(*d*) Control is intended to be temporary. The temporary investment should be included in the consolidated balance sheet as a current asset at the lower of cost and net realizable value.

21.3   The auditor's responsibility

S236 requires the auditor of a company preparing group accounts to report on the state of affairs of the group, and its profit or loss so far as concerns the members of the company.

The auditor of the holding company thereby acquires a responsibility for accounts embodying those of other companies of which he may not be the auditor: that can cause problems. The APC has issued an Exposure Draft dealing with the extent of the holding company auditor's reliance on the work of other auditors, and this is reproduced in Section 21.4.3 below.

The auditor of the holding company is referred to as the primary auditor and other auditors responsible for subsidiaries are secondary auditors.

21.4   Auditing group accounts

The work of auditing group accounts may be broken down into five main stages:

—obtaining preliminary information;
—detailed work in checking consolidation working papers;
—review of secondary auditors and their work;
—review of group financial statements;
—audit report.

21.4.1   Obtaining preliminary information

The initial information required is:

(*a*) a copy of group accounting policies and instructions;
(*b*) a list of subsidiaries including any excluded from consolidation, with reasons;
(*c*) details of subsidiaries entering and leaving the group during the period (dates, shares acquired or sold, costs, any special contract provisions);

(d) for each subsidiary:

(1) name and address of registered office and places of operation;
(2) name of auditor;
(3) country of incorporation;
(4) accounting date and financial period;
(5) types of business conducted;
(6) issued share capital and debentures and proportion held by group;
(7) copy of detailed financial statements and auditor's report;
(8) names of directors who have held office in subsidiaries during the period.

At this early stage it will be necessary to set up a channel of communication with subsidiary company auditors through the directors of the holding company and directors of subsidiaries.

21.4.2 Detailed work in checking consolidation working papers.

The consolidation schedules provide the link between the separate company accounts and the consolidated accounts. The auditor will critically review the schedules, confirm that the figures are arithmetically correct and have been correctly extracted.

Special attention must be paid to:

(a) Companies entering the group:
(1) the effective date for accounting in accordance with SSAP 14 (earlier of date on which consideration passes and date on which offer became unconditional);
(2) whether allocation of consideration among net assets other than goodwill is on the basis of fair value to the acquiring company;
(3) correct calculation and treatment of:

—goodwill or reserve arising on consolidation;
—minority interest;
—pre-acquisition profits and losses;
—dividends paid out of pre-acquisition profits.

(b) Companies leaving the group
(1) inclusion in consolidated profit and loss account of subsidiaries' results up to the date of disposal (date taken as in (a) (1) above);
(2) correct calculation and disclosure of gain or loss on sale.
(c) Agreement of inter-company balances
(d) Elimination of unrealized profit on stock purchased from other group companies

(*e*) Cancellation of other inter-company transactions (e.g. management fees or interest charged)

(*f*) Adjustments to allow for transactions between accounting dates when these differ

(*g*) Confirmation that all group taxation reliefs have been claimed where applicable

(*h*) Correctness of exchange rates used for translation of financial statements of foreign subsidiaries, and compliance with SSAP 20

(*i*) Associated companies included in accordance with the provisions of SSAP 1.

21.4.3 Review of secondary auditors and their work

A draft Auditing Guideline on this subject has been issued by the APC and this is reproduced below:

Draft Auditing Guideline on reliance on the work of other auditors

Preface

This Guideline is intended to clarify the duties, responsibilities and practice of the auditor when reporting on group financial statements that include amounts derived from the accounts of subsidiaries or of associated companies which have been audited by other auditors. It should be of use to auditors who act as either primary or secondary auditors.

For the purposes of this Guideline, the term 'primary auditor' refers to an auditor who is responsible for the audit opinion on group financial statements. A 'secondary auditor' is an auditor of a subsidiary or associated company who is not the primary auditor and is responsible for his own audit opinion on the secondary company's financial statements. All other definitions of terms used in the Guideline are included in the Appendix.

The relationship between primary and secondary auditors is not the same as that between the auditors involved:

(*a*) in a joint audit; or

(*b*) where a company has operations based at several locations or branches, and local auditors acting as agents work on behalf of the primary auditor.

Accordingly, neither of these situations is covered by this Guideline.

Introduction

(1) This Guideline is written in the context of companies and company legislation,

which imposes on the directors of a holding company the responsibility to prepare accounts which give a true and fair view so far as concerns the members of the holding company. The auditor of any other form of enterprise is guided by the terms of his particular appointment and by the relevant legislation, but in the absence of specific provisions to the contrary, the general principles embodied in this guideline should be followed.

(2) The primary auditor is required to express an opinion on the group financial statements and has sole responsibility for this opinion even where those group financial statements include amounts derived from accounts which have not been audited by him. As a result, he cannot discharge his responsibility to report on the group financial statements by an uninformed acceptance of secondary companies' financial statements, whether audited or not.

(3) As explained below, however, the primary auditor can take account of the extent of work and the report of other (secondary) auditors through carrying out certain procedures. The extent of these procedures will be determined by the materiality of the amounts derived from the financial statements of secondary companies, and the level of risk that the auditor is willing to accept that such statements contain material errors.

The relationship between the primary and the secondary auditor

(4) The relationship between a primary and a secondary auditor is not that between a principal and an agent. If, however, the secondary company is a subsidiary, and both the primary company and the secondary company are incorporated in Great Britain, the secondary company and its auditor have a statutory duty under section 392(1)(a) of the Companies Act 1985 to give to the primary auditor such information and explanations as that auditor may reasonably require for the purposes of his duties as auditor of the primary company. Similarly, legislation in Northern Ireland imposes this obligation on a subsidiary company and its auditor, when both the holding and subsidiary companies are incorporated in Northern Ireland. (There is no equivalent legislation in the Republic of Ireland.)

(5) Where the statutory duty described in the previous paragraph does not exist, the primary company has a statutory duty under section 392(1)(b) of the Companies Act 1985 to take all steps reasonably open to it to obtain from the subsidiary such information and explanations as the primary auditor may reasonably require for the purposes of his duties as auditor of the primary company.

(6) Even where his responsibilities in this regard are not set down by statute, the secondary auditor should appreciate that the secondary company's financial statements will ultimately form a part of the group financial statements. In principle, the secondary auditor should therefore be prepared to cooperate with the primary auditor and make available such information as the primary auditor may require in order to discharge his duties as auditor of the group financial statements.

(7) The primary auditor should as a matter of courtesy inform the directors of the primary company of his intention to communicate with the secondary auditor. The nature of the instructions which are to be given to the secondary auditor, and the information required from him, should be discussed by the primary auditor with the directors of the primary company at the planning stage. Where the primary auditor has

no statutory right to approach the secondary auditor, he should arrange for the secondary auditor to be instructed to cooperate by the directors of the secondary company, in order to ensure that the duty of confidentiality owed by the secondary auditor to his client is maintained. This may not be possible where the secondary company is an associated company, as the directors of the primary company may have less control than in the case of a subsidiary company.

(8) The primary auditor should inform the secondary auditor in advance of the standard and scope of work required and any reporting deadlines that are to be met. For effective co-operation to take place, the primary and secondary auditors should communicate with each other as early as possible in the planning stage of the audit. The secondary auditor should discuss problems that may lead to delay in reporting or qualification of his opinion as soon as they arise.

Operational procedures

Materiality

(9) In deciding what audit procedures are necessary, the primary auditor should consider the audit risk involved and the materiality of the amounts in the context of the group financial statements. This will involve an evaluation of the significance of each secondary company and also of each account area or item of disclosure, as it is possible that a particular area (e.g. stock or fixed assets) will be considered material in the context of the group as a whole.

(10) A secondary company which is not itself material in the context of the group financial statements may, when taken together with other non-material secondary companies, result in a combination which is material. When this occurs, the primary auditor should proceed as if those secondary companies were material when considered individually.

(11) Any decisions taken regarding materiality should be reassessed each year.

General procedures

(12) The scope and nature of the primary auditor's procedures will vary depending on the particular circumstances of each case. Judgements will need to be made in the light of factors such as the scope of work of the secondary auditor, specific audit problems encountered in the past, and the likely degree of change in the secondary company's results and state of affairs. At the planning stage the primary auditor should assess the risk inherent in the assignment and the related likelihood of audit problems. The information relevant to this preliminary assessment will include the financial statements for earlier periods for both the group and the secondary company.

(13) The primary auditor should obtain and read the financial statements of the secondary company for the period under consideration at the earliest opportunity. This, when taken in conjunction with other information which the primary auditor has, may enable him to determine that the secondary company is immaterial in the context of the group financial statements. In all other cases the primary auditor should then, as a minimum, consider and be satisfied about the general scope of the work of the secondary auditor and in particular:

(a) the terms of the secondary auditor's engagement and any limitation placed on his work;

(*b*) the standard of work of the secondary auditor and the nature and extent of his audit examination;

(*c*) any differences between the auditing, accounting and other professional standards governing the secondary auditor's work and those applicable in the UK and Ireland, and any steps taken by the secondary auditor to conform to UK and Irish standards; and

(*d*) the independence of the secondary auditor.

(14) These matters may be dealt with by means of a questionnaire. The completed questionnaire should be reviewed by the primary auditor who should evaluate the reasonableness of the information provided in the light of his knowledge of the business and follow up any matters which require further explanation.

(15) Frequently the secondary company will be of such significance that the primary auditor will supplement the above procedures by a review of the secondary auditor's working papers.

(16) The principal objective of such a review is to ensure that it is reasonable for the primary auditor to rely on the work of the secondary auditor when expressing an opinion on the group financial statements. He is not expressing his own opinion on the financial statements of the secondary company, and he is not required to re-perform the secondary auditor's work or re-evaluate the audit evidence examined by the secondary auditor. The primary auditor should instead satisfy himself that the audit has been carried out in accordance with approved Auditing Standards and that the conclusions reached by the secondary auditor are both reasonable and reliable.

(17) In the circumstances described in paragraph 10, the review of the secondary auditors' working papers may be carried out on a periodic basis.

(18) In addition, any qualification in the secondary auditor's report should be considered by the primary auditor to ascertain whether it affects his report on the group financial statements.

Additional procedures

(19) If as a result of the above procedures the primary auditor is not satisfied for the purpose of reporting on the group financial statements, he should discuss the problem with his client. If necessary, he should arrange for the secondary auditor to conduct additional audit tests (either alone or jointly with the primary auditor). In exceptional circumstances only, the primary auditor may need to conduct his own tests independently of the secondary auditor. The secondary auditor is fully responsible for the standard of his own work and for his report on the secondary company's financial statements. Therefore any additional tests are required solely for the audit of the group financial statements.

Further considerations

Availability of information

(20) Primary company directors need to secure sufficient information to satisfy themselves that the group financial statements give a true and fair view, and disclose all the information required by statute and other appropriate regulations. Problems due to the lack of necessary information are likely to arise in two specific situations: where the primary and secondary companies are incorporated in different countries,

and are not subject to the same legislation, or where secondary companies' year-ends differ from that of the primary company.

(21) If the primary auditor finds that the directors of the primary company lack information about the accounting policies, items for disclosure, or consolidation adjustments relating to the financial statements of secondary companies, he should ask for the omission to be made good. Occasionally it may be necessary for the primary auditor, after obtaining permission, to obtain the additional information directly from the secondary companies concerned or from their auditors. The primary auditor may need to arrange for such additional information to be audited by the secondary auditor.

Accounting policies

(22) The primary auditor should discuss with the primary company's directors, or other responsible officials, the accounting policies in force throughout the group in order to ensure that these are, in his opinion, appropriate to and consistent with the proper preparation of the group financial statements.

(23) Consistent accounting policies will normally be adopted throughout the group. However, in certain exceptional cases this may not be possible because financial statements of secondary companies are the responsibility of their directors who will have to consider the interests of minority shareholders and comply with local legislation or practice. Where the use of differing accounting policies results in adjustments being necessary to arrive at consolidated figures, the primary auditor should both ensure that the primary company's directors have obtained all the information necessary to make these adjustments, and satisfy himself that any adjustments are appropriate.

(24) Where adjustments are impracticable and material figures based on different accounting policies are included in the group financial statements, the primary auditor should ensure that the policies adopted are fully explained and, where possible, the effects of the different policies are quantified.

Events after the balance sheet date

(25) The Auditing Guideline 'Events after the balance sheet date' requires the primary auditor to ensure that appropriate audit procedures are carried out to identify events after the balance sheet date which are of significance to the group between the dates of the reports of the secondary auditor and the date of his own report. These audit procedures may include the performance of updated reviews by secondary auditors. The primary auditor should contact the secondary auditor to ensure that all necessary further work has been performed.

Reporting

(26) Where there are material subsidiary or associated companies not audited by the primary auditor, the primary company may find it helpful to indicate this in the notes to the group financial statements. However, whether or not this information is given, the primary auditor should not ordinarily refer in his report to the name of any secondary auditor, or to the fact that secondary companies have been audited by other auditors. This is because the primary auditor cannot delegate the responsibility

for his opinion and any such reference might mislead the reader into believing otherwise.

(27) In the event of any restriction in the scope of his audit of the group financial statements the primary auditor should consider qualifying his report.

Appendix

Definition of terms

Associated company:	a company as defined by SSAP 1, paragraph 13.
Holding company:	a company having interests in one or more subsidiary companies as defined by the Companies Act.
Primary company:	a company which is required to produce group (normally consolidated) financial statements which may incorporate amounts taken from the financial statements of subsidiary or associated companies.
Secondary company:	a subsidiary or associated company which is audited by a secondary auditor.
Subsidiary company:	a company as defined by the Companies Act.

21.4.4   Review of group financial statements

All the matters dealt with in Chapter 11 above are relevant to the review of the group financial statements. Some are matters that will be dealt with in the audit of individual group companies, others, like the going concern review, will need attention on a group basis.

21.4.5   Specimen consolidation questionnaire

As indicated in paragraph 14 of the draft Guideline in Section 21.4.3 above, it is customary for the primary auditor to obtain information and confirmation as to a variety of matters by means of a questionnaire.

A specimen form of questionnaire is given below:

CONSOLIDATION QUESTIONNAIRE

NAME OF GROUP   : ....

ACCOUNTING PERIOD ENDED : ....

NAME OF SUBSIDIARY   : ....

ACCOUNTING PERIOD ENDED : ....

AUDITORS OF SUBSIDIARY   : ....

ADDRESS   : ....

....

....

TELEPHONE NUMBER   : ....

CONTACT PARTNER   : ....

CONTACT MANAGER   : ....

Please sign below before returning this questionnaire to us, having been duly completed and supplemented by other appropriate information as required.

.... *Firm's Signature*

.... *Date*

INTRODUCTION

Auditors of subsidiaries are asked to provide the information requested in order to assist the primary auditors in forming their opinion on the group financial statements, with particular reference to:

(1) ascertaining the scope of the audit of subsidiary companies and the application of approved auditing standards;
(2) ensuring that consistent accounting principles and policies have been applied in group companies;
(3) ensuring that financial statements of group companies are consistent in their presentation.

The questionnaire is intended to meet these objectives whilst minimizing additional review work. Most of the questions may be answered 'Yes'/ 'No'/'Not applicable'. Where the reply to the question is 'No', an explanation should be given. Where the information required cannot be cross-referenced to the financial statements or the consolidation package where appropriate, the reply should be supplemented by explanatory notes or schedules.

Auditors of subsidiary companies are requested to complete all sections of the questionnaire and to use a separate questionnaire for each material company in the group which they audit. In the case of joint auditors only one questionnaire need be completed, but both auditors should insert their signatures on the front cover. Please return this questionnaire, duly signed (including additional schedules as necessary to complete the information required) with a copy of the final draft financial statements or the consolidation package (subject only to group policy decisions on group relief, dividends or major adjustments), including a detailed trading account. All enclosures, in addition to the questionnaire, should be initialled by yourselves for identification purposes.

If you have any queries or anticipate any difficulty in meeting the requested deadline please contact the partner or manager as indicated on the front cover.

Note: Where an asterisk is printed at the beginning of any question and the information required is fully disclosed in the financial statements, no further action is necessary except to write the word 'disclosed' in the comment column.

	YES	NO	N/A	COMMENT

1 GENERAL

1.1 Do you propose to issue an unqualfied audit report?

If not, please attach a copy of your draft report and describe the circumstances which give rise to the qualification.

1.2 Please explain:

(1) any material adjustments proposed but not yet agreed which could affect the financial statements, as drafted;

(2) any unsatisfactory matters which do not give rise to an alteration to your proposed audit opinion but which require to be reported at a group level.

1.3 Please give details of any restrictions on the scope of your audit which prevented you from complying with Approved Auditing Standards.

1.4 Are you satisfied that the going concern concept is appropriate? Please give any provisos.

1.5 Where there are standard group accounting policies, has the company complied fully with these requirements in its operations and financial reporting?

1.6 Are you satisfied that the financial statements or consolidation package comply with, and give the information required by, Statements of Standard Accounting Practice and the Companies Act 1985?

1.7 Please explain any other significant matters which you wish to bring to our attention but which are not covered elsewhere in this questionnaire.

1.8 Please submit to us a copy of the company's letter of representation on the financial statements and a copy of your management letter to the company.

	YES	NO	N/A	COMMENT
2 *Audit Planning and Control*				
2.1 Do your firm's audit planning procedures ensure that, at any early stage of the audit, staff are briefed and the company's interim results/management accounts are reviewed?				
2.2 Do you use a standard audit programme for transactions audit and balance sheet testing?				
2.3 Are all working papers reviewed by a manager and a partner?				
2.4 In the case of a joint audit does your firm have formal procedures to ensure that:				
(1) all material aspects of the business are covered;				
(2) the allocation of responsibility for different areas of the audit is rotated between firms from year to year;				
(3) that the results of each firm's work are thoroughly reviewed by the other?				
3 *Evaluation of Internal Control*				
3.1 Have you evaluated the adequacy of controls within the accounting system and ascertained the reliability of their operation?				
3.2 Where reliance was placed on internal controls did you:				
(1) perform compliance tests to ensure that the internal controls were operating as prescribed;				
(2) test to ensure the controls operated throughout the period;				
(3) report significant weaknesses in the system to management?				
3.3 Where little or no reliance was placed on internal control, please summarize the alternative audit procedures adopted.				

	YES	NO	N/A	COMMENT
3.4 (1) Is there an internal audit department?				
(2) Has any reliance been placed on the work of the internal audit department? If so please indicate the extent and how you satisfied yourselves as to its reliability.				
3.5 (1) Are any of the accounting systems, of audit significance, processed on computer?				
(2) If so, where you have not performed an audit review of the installation or systems, are you satisfied that there is an adequate system of manual control to compensate for any weaknesses which a detailed computer audit review may have brought to light?				
(3) Where an installation review has been performed have you considered the conclusions thereof and their impact on your audit approach, modifying audit programme where necessary?				
4 Review of Accounts				
4.1 Are the company's accounting policies in your opinion:				
(1) adequately disclosed;				
(2) appropriate to the company's business;				
(3) in compliance with group policies?				
4.2 Please give details of any material variances in sales, margins or expenses compared with previous periods, management accounts or budgets, and of any significant changes in balance sheet items.				
4.3 Please confirm that there were no material profits or losses of an exceptional or non recurring nature, apart from those disclosed in the accounts.				

	YES	NO	N/A	COMMENT
4.4 Please confirm that there has been no change in the nature or organization or level of activity of the business since the last audited period.				
4.5 *Have all comparative figures remained unchanged from those in the previous period? If not please give details of the changes together with the reasons.				
5. *General Matters*				
5.1 Does the company maintain satisfactory accounting records?				
5.2 Is all the information required by the Companies Act to be shown in the directors' report included, and is this information consistent with the accounts?				
5.3 Have the accounts been formally approved by the directors?				
5.4 Is the company's insurance cover for assets and other matters adequate? Please give details of any risk you consider under-insured.				
5.5 Have the directors made full disclosure of any interests in any transactions with the company or other group companies whether or not at arm's length or properly authorized?				
6 *Share capital, Reserves and Statutory Records*				
6.1 *Are all amounts and movements on share capital and reserves:				
(1) shown on the face of the accounts or by way of note;				
(2) in accordance with the articles of association and relevant statutory requirements?				
6.2 *Please give details of:				
(1) any movements of reserves not disclosed in the accounts;				

	YES	NO	N/A	COMMENT
(2) any options on unissued share capital.				
6.3 *Which reserves are free to be distributed (according to the definition in the Companies Act 1985)?				
6.4 Are there any unusual matters in the minutes which are relevant to the group accounts or any matters which require additional minutes?				
6.5 Has the share register: (1) been verified by share transfer audit or other means;				
(2) been agreed to the balance sheet?				
7 *Taxation* 7.1 Are you responsible for the tax computations? If not, how have you verified the figures?				
7.2 Please give the date up to which tax has been agreed with the Inland Revenue and details of any material points in dispute.				
7.3 Has full provision been made for all taxation liabilities by reference to tax assessments?				
7.4 Please give details of losses brought and carried forward, identifying losses available only against capital gains.				
7.5 Has the company disclosed the potential tax liabilities on unrealized surpluses brought into the accounts?				
7.6 (1) Are you satisfied that the deferred taxation accounts properly reflect full equalization of tax liabilities in the foreseeable future? Please give brief details of the composition of the account.				

	YES	NO	N/A	COMMENT
(2) If provision has not been made for any potential deferred taxation liability, please explain:				
(a) the basis for concluding that no liability will arise;				
(b) how you verified that conclusion.				
7.7 To what extent has the profit and loss charge for the period been affected by:				
(1) losses brought forward from prior periods;				
(2) group relief (UK companies only);				
(3) prior period adjustments or other abnormal items?				
7.8 Please provide a reconciliation between the actual tax charge and corporation tax at the current rate on profits for the period.				
7.9 Please confirm that corporation tax on gains arising on all disposals of chargeable assets has been duly provided for.				
7.10 Is all the advance corporation tax being carried forward recoverable?				
7.11 Has valid notice of group relief receipt or surrender been given to the Inland Revenue?				
7.12 Have all taxation matters which should be considered in a group context been brought to our attention?				
8 *Long- and Medium-term liabilities*				
8.1 Please provide details of borrowings including:				
(1) amounts outstanding;				
(2) repayment dates;				
(3) premiums on repayment;				
(4) rates of interest;				

(5) where secured wholly or in part (including securities over assets of and guarantees by group companies);

(6) conversion rights.

8.2 Are all borrowings within the limits set by:

(1) legal instruments covering the company;
(2) statute;
(3) internal company policies?

8.3 Did you obtain direct confirmation of all long- and medium-term loans?

8.4 Have there been any defaults in principal, interest or redemption provisions?

9 *Creditors*

9.1 (1) *Please give details of any unusually large or exceptional creditors at the balance sheet date.

(2) Please explain any material changes during the period.

9.2 Are all significant liabilities for future instalments under hire purchase and leasing arrangements disclosed in the financial statements?

9.3 Are amounts included in current liabilities payable wholly within 12 months from the balance sheet date?

9.4 Did you verify cut-off procedures at the balance sheet date?

9.5 Were all major trade creditors verified with statements or by circularization procedures?

9.6 Are all significant debit balances on the creditors ledger:

(1) satisfactorily explained;

	YES	NO	N/A	COMMENT
(2) recoverable in full;				
(3) included in debtors?				
9.7 Does the list of bought ledger balances agree with the nominal control account?				
9.8 Have you reviewed overhead expenditure levels to ensure that adequate accruals have been made?				
9.9 Does a right of set-off exist for all contra entries between debtor and creditor balances?				
9.10 Are you satisfied that the company, by its pattern of trading, does not have to rely on a limited number of suppliers?				
9.11 Have all provisions been applied for the purposes for which they were established?				
9.12 Have all material short-term loans been confirmed by certificates from the lenders?				
9.13 Are you satisfied that creditors are accurately disclosed in the accounts?				
10 *Fixed Assets and Depreciation*				
10.1 Were fixed assets physically verified and agreed to registers/accounting records within the last accounting period?				
10.2 Have all government grants been correctly accounted for and verified by yourselves?				
10.3 (1) *If any assets are shown at other than original cost please give full details of the allocation between cost and valuation.				
(2) If revalued during the period under review please furnish copies.				
10.4 Have intra-group transfers been recorded at original cost to the group together with accumulated depreciation? If not please provide details of the method used.				

554 de Paula's Auditing

	YES	NO	N/A	COMMENT
10.5 Have material profits and losses on disposals of assets been adequately disclosed and accurately calculated?				
10.6 (1) Are the bases and rates of depreciation the same as for the previous period?				
(2) Are those rates apportioned on acquisitions/disposals during the period?				
10.7 In the context of the business do you consider the bases and rates of depreciation to be:				
(1) reasonable;				
(2) appropriate;				
10.8 Are all depreciable assets in use or earning revenue?				
10.9 Have the following been accounted for in accordance with group policy:				
(1) assets purchased under hire purchase agreements;				
(2) assets acquired under financial lease-rental agreements;				
(3) intangible assets (classified as fixed assets)?				
10.10 Have all title deeds been verified by inspection or direct confirmation?				
10.11 Were all additions and disposals properly recorded and authorized?				
10.12 (1) Please outline what procedures were adopted to verify the existence and ownership of assets.				
(2) Please indicate the proportion of fixed assets verified by yourselves.				
10.13 Have capital and revenue expenditures been properly distinguished?				

		YES	NO	N/A	COMMENT
11	*Deferred Expenditure and Other Intangible Assets*				
11.1	*Please give details of any expenditure incurred on intangible assets during the period that has been carried forward and state the basis on which it is to be written off.				
11.2	*Please give details of any amounts written off during the period if not otherwise disclosed.				
11.3	Have the bases for carrying forward deferred revenue expenditure and calculation of goodwill been consistently applied?				
11.4	How has deferred revenue expenditure been treated for taxation purposes?				
11.5	Do you consider the bases of carrying forward and the writing off policy of deferred revenue expenditure and other intangible assets to be reasonable in the circumstances?				
11.6	Do you consider the carrying value of these items has been calculated correctly?				
12	*Investments and Investment Income*				
12.1	Are all investments held in the name of the company or subject to relevant deeds of trust and blank transfers?				
12.2	*Please furnish details of:				
	(1) substantial differences between book and market values;				
	(2) valuations incorporated in the accounts (including basis used; official responsible for valuation, etc);				
	(3) loans made to/from any company in which an investment is held;				
	(4) unlisted investments acquired or sold in the period.				

	YES	NO	N/A	COMMENT
12.3 Have all investments representing 20% or more of the equity voting rights of a company been treated as associated companies (and vice versa)?				
12.4 Have all material profits and losses on disposals of investments been disclosed?				
12.5 Has all investment income receivable been accounted for?				
12.6 Did you verify share certificates and blank transfers by direct confirmation or inspection?				
12.7 Was satisfactory evidence and authority seen to support the purchase and sale of investments?				
12.8 Did you examine the latest financial statements of unlisted investments to assess their earnings and net current values? Are you satisfied with the valuation?				
12.9 Are all investments free from any lien or charge?				
12.10 If any associated companies are not audited by yourselves please indicate how you ensured consistency of accounting policies and assured yourselves as to the adequacy of the audit?				
13 *Sub-subsidiaries*				
13.1 Please explain any significant sub-group consolidation adjustments that have been made for the first time.				
13.2 *Please give details of any accounting reference dates which are not co-terminous with that of the holding company.				
13.3 Please confirm that, if any sub-subsidiaries do not have co-terminous accounting reference dates, there were no intervening events which are relevant to the group's results.				

	YES	NO	N/A	COMMENT
13.4 Please explain any changes in the sub-group structure or composition during the period.				
13.5 Are the audit reports of sub-subsidiaries unqualified with respect to those companies' financial statements?				
13.6 Please indicate what procedures were followed to enable you to satisfy yourselves as to the consistent application of accounting policies and the adequacy of the audit for those sub-subsidiaries not audited by yourselves.				
14 *Intra-group Transactions*				
14.1 Have all balances with other group companies been independently confirmed and agreed in accordance with group instructions?				
14.2 Have all inter-company balances been disclosed separately?				
14.3 Are all inter-company transactions conducted on an arm's length basis which does not distort the results of individual group companies?				
14.4 Please give details of any unrealized inter-company profits which may require elimination on consolidation.				
14.5 If the accounting reference date is not co-terminous with that of the holding company please confirm that there were no material intervening events which were relevant to the group's results.				
14.6 *Please provide details of any set-offs within group balances and an analysis of inter-company balances.				
15 *Stock and Work In Progress*				
15.1 *Where practicable please give a breakdown of the value of stock and WIP under the appropriate headings.				

	YES	NO	N/A	COMMENT
15.2 Has stock and work in progress been physically verified during the period by actual count or perpetual inventory?				
15.3 Did you attend, and find satisfactory procdures being used during, the physical stock count or otherwise satisfy yourselves as to the adequacy of perpetual inventory?				
15.4 How did you satisfy yourselves as to the existence and ownership of stocks and work in progress?				
15.5 Have all major discrepancies between physical and book stocks, including their valuation, been satisfactoriy dealt with?				
15.6 Were the group instructions as regards cut-off:				
(1) adequate to ensure accuracy of stock and work in progress figures;				
(2) adequate to ensure correct treatment of goods on consignment, stocks on loan or sale on return?				
15.7 Please give details of:				
(1) stocks at the company's premises excluded as a result of sales invoices raised in advance of the year end;				
(2) methods of accounting for forward purchases and sales;				
(3) stocks purchased from group companies.				
15.8 Are the bases of valuing stock and work in progress:				
(1) appropriate to the company's business;				
(2) consistently applied?				

	YES	NO	N/A	COMMENT
15.9 Please specify what costs and overheads are included in the valuation above.				
15.10 Does the basis of valuation ensure the exclusion of any:				
(1) irrecoverable expenditure in work in progress;				
(2) unrealized profits?				
15.11 Has the company identified and satisfactorily valued obsolete, slow-moving and damaged stocks?				
15.12 All all formulae/percentages used to calculate provisions, consistent with previous periods?				
15.13 If stocks are stated at standard costs have the values been adjusted for major variances between actual and standard other than those caused by abnormal levels of operation or inefficiencies?				
15.14 Has provision been made against possible losses on orders accepted but not executed?				
15.15 Have you obtained direct confirmation of stock held by third parties?				
15.16 Has your work covered the following, with satisfactory conclusions:				
(1) pricing;				
(2) attributable overheads;				
(3) cut-off;				
(4) arithmetical accuracy;				
(5) realizable value?				
15.17 Has satisfactory provision been made against losses on forward purchases and sales?				

	YES	NO	N/A	COMMENT
15.18 Can you confirm that no stocks are in excess of current trading requirements?				
16 Contract Work In Progress				
16.1 How is the value of completed work ascertained and certified?				
16.2 Please summarize the methods of assessing the:				
(1) state of completion;				
(2) anticipated results;				
(3) total costs of contracts.				
16.3 Have you carried out site visits to verify the physical status of contracts?				
16.4 Please describe the method of accounting for:				
(1) profits and losses on contracts;				
(2) progress payments on account of work in progress;				
(3) claims receivable and payable (whether or not agreed).				
16.5 Are you satisfied that all work in progress is for current contracts?				
16.6 Did you obtain independent confirmation of the value of work completed on contracts to date?				
16.7 Has credit been taken for cost claims receivable only when agreed by purchaser?				
16.8 Have you reviewed the value of work completed against invoices rendered to ensure that income has not been duplicated in the accounting records?				
16.9 Have you reviewed all significant contracts to ensure that profit is taken according to the state of completion?				

	YES	NO	N/A	COMMENT
16.10 Have all sums due under contract clauses been brought into account?				
16.11 Has adequate provision been made against: (1) all costs in respect of penalties, rectification work and guarantees; (2) all anticipated losses on contracts?				
16.12 Were all contracts which were incomplete at the previous period end, either completed in the period at a profit or still carried forward (i.e. all foreseeable losses had been previously provided for)?				
16.13 Are the bases of valuation, including the recognition of profits and losses, appropriate to the company's business and consistently applied?				
16.14 Please confirm that no contracts have been accepted which give rise to exceptional burdens through fixed price clauses or performance undertakings.				
17 Debtors				
17.1 Did you examine an aged summary of debtor balances at the end of the period as part of your review?				
17.2 Please give brief details of: (1) any large or exceptional debtors; (2) any long term debtors (if not disclosed in the accounts); (3) material movements in total debtor balances during the period.				
17.3 Have all credit balances on the debtors' ledger been classified with creditors?				
17.4 Are all major credit balances on the debtors' ledger satisfactorily explained and payable in full?				

	YES	NO	N/A	COMMENT
17.5 Please give full details of the amounts and accounting treatment, of long-term and deferred debtors (including hire purchase or instalment debts).				
17.6 Are the bad and doubtful debt provisions: (1) specific; (2) calculated on bases consistent with previous years?				
17.7 Do you consider the credit control system, including the approval of credit notes, to be satisfactory?				
17.8 Do you consider that proper provision has been made for all bad and doubtful debts?				
17.9 Does the company maintain credit insurance in respect of trade debtors?				
17.10 Has provision been made against discounts allowable and other credits not yet credited to debtors?				
17.11 Are you satisfied that no provisions are necessary where debtors have been subject to factoring or other discounting arrangements?				
17.12 Are there any loans, quasi-loans, credit transactions or guarantees entered into by the company on behalf of directors or connected persons or officers of the company which were not fully disclosed in the financial statements, in accordance with the Companies Act 1985?				
17.13 Did your procedures cover the following: (1) sales cut-off at the end of the period; (2) debtors' circularization? If so please indicate results and follow up action necessitated;				

	YES	NO	N/A	COMMENT
(3) scrutiny of after-date credit notes to ensure matching against relevant sales revenue;				
(4) agreement of the total of the debtors' balances to the control account?				
17.14 Have all material loans and floats been confirmed in writing by the borrowers?				
17.15 Are all amounts not receivable within 12 months excluded from current assets?				
17.16 Does a right of set-off exist for all contra entries between debtor and creditor balances?				
17.17 Do you consider that the company is not exposed in its trading pattern by undue reliance on a limited number of principal debtors or customers?				
17.18 Are you satisfied that the debtors disclosed in the accounts are accurately stated?				
18 *Bank Balances and Cash*				
18.1 Are bank reconciliations for all bank accounts:				
(1) prepared regularly;				
(2) reviewed independently?				
18.2 Have bank borrowings been netted off against balances in hand only where there is a legal right of set-off?				
18.3 Please give details of the amounts and renewal dates of available bank facilities and open lines of credit.				
18.4 Please give details of all secured bank borrowings.				

564 de Paula's Auditing

	YES	NO	N/A	COMMENT

18.5 Please give details of any bank (including loan and currency) accounts which cannot be withdrawn in less than 6 months or which are blocked in any way.

18.6 Have you obtained direct confirmation for all bank accounts?

18.7 Have all outstanding payments and receipts been satisfactorily accounted for?

18.8 Have all material cash funds and advances been counted and verified at the balance sheet date?

18.9 Are you satisfied that bank borrowings are correctly disclosed according to repayment terms?

19 *Bills of Exchange*

19.1 Please give details of all bills receivable which have been discounted with, or for, group companies.

19.2 Please give amounts and provisions made against any overdue or doubtful bills.

19.3 Have you inspected or obtained confirmation of all bills receivable?

19.4 Are you satisfied that no liabilities or contingencies should be accounted for in respect of bills discounted?

19.5 Has adequate provision been made against doubtful bills receivable?

20 *Other Matters*

20.1 *If the accounts do not include a funds statement or a statement of changes in financial position please give details of:

(1) proceeds of sale of fixed assets;

	YES	NO	N/A	COMMENT
(2) tax paid during the period;				
(3) any other factors involving the source and application of funds which are not apparent from the balance sheet or the profit and loss account.				
20.2 Is the liability to value added tax regularly agreed with the Customs & Excise authorities and paid over at regular intervals?				
20.3 Please confirm that in relation to post balance sheet events, otherwise than indicated in the financial statements, there were no:				
(a) material post balance sheet events that required changes in the amounts included in the accounts where:				
(1) it was an 'adjusting event' or,				
(2) it indicated that the application of the going concern concept was not appropriate.				
(b) material post balance sheet events that should be disclosed where:				
(1) it was a non-adjusting event of such importance that non-disclosure would affect the user's understanding of the true position, or,				
(2) it was the reversal or maturity after the year end of a transaction primarily entered into to alter the appearance of the company's balance sheet ('window dressing').				
21 *Profit and Loss Account*				
21.1 Does the company prepare regular management accounts and budgets?				

	YES	NO	N/A	COMMENT
21.2 Has the profit and loss account been arrived at on a basis consistent with the previous period?				
21.3 Please give details of all directors' emoluments.				
21.4 Please confirm that there are no leases or equipment rental contracts of such nature that they ought to be disclosed in the accounts but have been excluded.				
21.5 Is there adequate disclosure of all revenue items subject to statutory regulation?				
21.6 Have you applied analytical review techniques to confirm that the trading profits are materially correct?				
21.7 Has any dividend been paid out of distributable reserves (if public—distributable assets), as per definitions incorporated in the Companies Act 1985?				
22 Contingencies and Commitments				
22.1 Are the amounts and descriptions of all material contingent liabilities, which have not been specifically provided for by the company, shown as a note to the accounts?				
22.2 Please indicate whether any contingent liability involves another member of the group.				
22.3 Have all contingencies been quantified where possible?				
22.4 Are the amounts or estimated amounts of material future capital expenditure not provided for shown by way of a note to the accounts under the following headings:—				
(1) authorized and contracted for;				
(2) authorized but not contracted for?				

	YES	NO	N/A	COMMENT

22.5 If any of the capital commitments are with other group companies please give details.

22.6 Please confirm that:

(1) there were no other unusual commitments;

(2) there were no commitments of a revenue nature which in your opinion merit separate mention in the accounts.

22.7 Have you obtained details from the company's solicitors of any outstanding claims or suits against the company or pending litigation including any unbilled costs incurred by the solicitors on behalf of the company?

23 *Overseas Funds and Exchange Translations*

23.1 Please give details of regulations preventing the free remittance of funds to the United Kingdom, and state the amounts involved.

23.2 Please give details of additional taxes which would be payable if the retained earnings were to be paid over to the holding company.

23.3 Please give details of the bases and rates of exchange used for translating financial statements denominated in foreign currencies into sterling to the extent not already disclosed in the accounts.

23.4 Can you confirm that all local legal and accounting regulations have been complied with?

23.5 If a sub-consolidation incorporates a foreign subsidiary, are you satisfied that the method of translation is in accordance with currently acceptable best accounting practice?

	YES	NO	N/A	COMMENT

24 *Current Cost Accounting* (if applicable)

24.1 Are you satisfied that the current cost operating profit is the surplus arising from the ordinary activities of the business after allowing for the impact of price changes on the funds needed to continue the existing business and maintain its net operating assets?

24.2 (1) If indices have been used to calculate the adjustments needed to arrive at CC operating profit, do such indices closely reflect the actual changes in input prices experienced by the company?

(2) If so, please provide details of the evidence you have to support this conclusion.

24.3 Please provide details of:

(1) price change information used in the calculation of the cost of sales adjustment;

(2) the method used to calculate the cost of sales adjustment.

24.4 Are you satisfied as to the validity of the method adopted in 24.3 (2) above?

24.5 Is the purchasing pattern of the company free from severe seasonal fluctuation?

24.6 If the averaging method has been used, please provide details of the average age of each category of stock that makes up the opening and closing stock figures and also how this has been computed.

24.7 If there are significant write-downs of stocks:

(1) is such stock stated in the CC balance sheet at its recoverable amount;

	YES	NO	N/A	COMMENT
(2) is the averaging calculation (if this method was used—if not, provide details) based on the recoverable amount?				
24.8 Is there inter-company buying or selling on a significant scale? If so, provide details of amounts purchased or sold and the names of the group companies involved in each type of transaction.				
24.9 If the company has any long-term contract work in progress please provide complete details as to how these items have been treated in the current cost accounts.				
24.10 Are items included in monetary working capital restricted to: (1) trade debtors, prepayments, trade bills receivable;				
(2) stocks not subject to a cost of sales adjustment;				
(3) trade creditors, accruals and trade bills payable?				
24.11 If any other items, particularly bank balances or overdrafts, have been included in monetary working capital, please provide details of the amounts included and the justification for this inclusion.				
24.12 (1) What price change information has been used to calculate the MWCA?				
(2) Are you satisfied that this information acccurately reflects the 'cost' changes during the period?				
24.13 (1) Have debtors and creditors been aged?				
(2) If so, please give details of average age of debtors and creditors and method of calculation.				

	YES	NO	N/A	COMMENT
24.14 Have you reviewed the asset lives and depreciation rates and satisfied yourselves as to their validity?				
24.15 (1) Are all fixed assets which are still in use brought into account both in the balance sheet valuation and the additional depreciation charge?				
(2) Please indicate the historical cost amount of fixed assets which are still in use but written-off.				
24.16 (1) What price change information has been used to restate fixed assets in the current cost balance sheet and to calculate the depreciation adjustment?				
(2) Are you satisfied as to its validity?				
24.17 Have significant profits and losses on the disposal of fixed assets been recalculated to give CC profits or losses?				
24.18 Please provide details of how all exceptional and extraordinary items and prior year adjustments have been dealt with in the CC accounts.				
24.19 Are you satisfied that the current cost information provided by the company is fairly presented and complies with the requirements of SSAP 16?				

21.5 The audit report

The audit report on the group financial statements follows the same principles as the report on those of a single company.

Matters peculiar to groups are:

(*a*) Consideration as to whether any qualifications in subsidiary company audit reports need to be reflected in the group report. Such qualifications need not automatically be repeated, because something highly material to a small subsidiary may be insignificant in the context of the large group of which it forms part.

(b) The need for qualification if material amounts are included from the financial statements of subsidiaries which have not been audited, unless the primary auditor has personally carried out sufficient work on the subsidiaries' records and financial statements to confirm that they show a true and fair view.

(c) Whether the financial statements comply in all respects with the provisions of the Companies Act 1985 and SSAPs concerning groups.

21.6 Summary

The Companies Act 1985 requires a company with subsidiaries to prepare group accounts which the auditor is required to report on. SSAP 14 makes further provisions regarding group accounts.

The audit of group accounts consists of five stages:

(a) obtaining preliminary information;

(b) checking of consolidation working papers;

(c) review of secondary auditors and their work—covered by an Auditing Guideline;

(d) review of group financial statements;

(e) consideration of the audit report.

The review of the secondary auditors frequently includes the use of a detailed questionnaire.

Progress questions

Questions	Reference for answers
(1) What are the circumstances giving rise to the holding company/ subsidiary relationship as defined in S736?	Section 21.1
(2) What exemptions from S736 are established in S229?	Section 21.1
(3) SSAP 14 provides for different treatment for each of four situations in which subsidiaries are excluded from consolidation. What are the four situations and how are they to be treated?	Section 21.2
(4) List the five main stages of the work of auditing group accounts. Give details of the work to be done in each stage.	Sections 21.4 and 21.5
(5) The review of the secondary auditors and their work frequently involves the use of a questionnaire. Explain the main headings likely to be found in such a questionnaire.	Section 21.5

22 Auditing current cost accounts

22.1 Introduction

In 1985 the ASC announced that SSAP 16 would cease to be mandatory and that a new exposure draft, probably allowing more flexibility, would be introduced in 1986.

In 1980 the APC issued a Guideline entitled 'Auditors' reports and SSAP 16 'Current cost accounting', which is currently under review.

At the time of writing the future of current cost accounting, and therefore its audit, is uncertain.

22.2 The audit of current cost accounts

If an audit of the current cost accounts is carried out, the following programme will be appropriate.

Reference should be made to SSAP 16 and the guidance notes issued by the ASC. Before commencing audit work establish with the client whether the audit report will be 'true and fair' or 'properly prepared in accordance with . . .'. This may influence the volume of checking required. Concentrate on those areas which may have a material bearing on the current cost accounts.

Suggested audit tests

INDICES AND ARITHMETIC
(1) Review and record indices used in calculation of depreciation adjustment, cost of sales adjustment (COSA) and monetary working capital adjustment (MWCA), and ensure that:

(a) they are appropriate to the nature of business;
(b) they have been correctly extracted.

(2) Where 'in-house' indices are used, check underlying calculations. Ensure method used is appropriate to the business.

(3) Where current indices are not available, establish that any estimates made are fair and reasonable.

(4) Carry out extensive checks to arithmetic.

FIXED ASSETS AND ADDITIONAL DEPRECIATION CHARGE

(5) Confirm that *all* fixed assets in use are brought into the balance sheet (including assets written off in historical-cost (HC) accounts).

(6) Where indices are used to calculate net current replacement cost and current cost (CC) depreciation charge, check underlying calculations. Confirm calculation of backlog depreciation. Ensure that revaluation surplus (net of backlog depreciation) is taken to credit of current cost reserve.

(7) Review asset lives and depreciation rates used and establish that they are appropriate for current cost accounting (CCA) purposes. Has proper consideration been given to 'future economic lives of assets'?

(8) Obtain copy of any professional valuations used to restate assets. In case of property, ensure that valuation is on basis of open market value for existing use. (If net building replacement cost exceeds existing use value, depreciation should be calculated on full existing use value.)

(9) Where adjustments are made to valuations produced in earlier years, review for reasonableness in light of general market conditions.

(10) Is there any evidence of substantial technological change, so that use of indices is not appropriate?

(11) Consider need for revaluation of balance sheet values to the recoverable amount to take account of permanent diminution of value.

STOCKS AND COST OF SALES ADJUSTMENT (COSA)

(12) Check calculation of COSA, ensuring that indices applied to opening and closing stocks relate to the average date of acquiring those stocks.

(13) Review valuation of closing stocks for CC balance sheet purposes. Compare with HC valuation to ensure that items stated at their recoverable amounts (net realizable value) have been treated consistently.

(14) Where special items of stock (e.g. long-term contracts) are treated as monetary working capital, ensure that they are included in the calculation of the MWCA.

(15) Review treatment of progress payments, which should be related to stock on a contract-by-contract basis. (Ensure that the excess of any progress payment over its related stock value is treated as a liability for MWCA purposes.)

MONETARY WORKING CAPITAL ADJUSTMENT (MWCA)

(16) Review MWCA calculation in light of CCA rationale. Ensure that the

calculation only includes those items used in day-to-day operations (including VAT and the fluctuating part of bank balances and overdrafts).

(17) Review basis of selection of intervals over which calculations have been made. Where trade is subject to seasonal fluctuations, ensure that methods used to calculate COSA and MWCA are compatible.

(18) Where monetary working capital is a net liability, and that liability exceeds the value of stock, ensure that the excess is *excluded* from the MWCA calculation and *included* in the gearing adjustment. (In these circumstances MWCA would cancel out COSA.)

GEARING ADJUSTMENT

(19) Review basis on which average net borrowing and net operating assets during the period have been calculated. (Net operating assets should normally include share capital, reserves (including revaluation surpluses and curent cost reserve), proposed dividends, and minority interests. Deferred taxation (calculated in accordance with SSAP 15) should be included as a liability.)

Note: If monetary assets (other than included in MWCA) included in calculation exceed monetary liabilities (other than included in MWCA) no gearing adjustment is made.

(20) Confirm that gearing adjustment is also applied to the CC adjustment relating to significant disposals of fixed assets.

(21) Are there assets surplus to operating requirements and in excess of borrowing? If so, do the accounts show the change in effective purchasing power of this surplus?

(22) Where HC accounts include surpluses on property revaluations, gearing adjustment may be applied to too low a figure of supplementary depreciation. If this distortion is material, ensure that appropriate adjustment is either made or noted in the CC accounts.

OTHER MATTERS

(23) Review *inter alia* the following matters to ensure that their treatment accords with CCA rationale:

(*a*) elimination of intra-group profits (as restated on a CC basis);

(*b*) interests in and share of profits/losses of associated companies;

(*c*) the restatement of any purchased goodwill retained in HC consolidated accounts. (*Note:* Where goodwill is carried at an amount established prior to introduction of SSAP 14, it should be reduced to the extent that it represents revaluation surpluses relating to assets held at the date of acquisition);

(*d*) differences arising on exchange translation;

(*e*) valuation of interests in wasting assets and intangible assets.

(24) Confirm the taxation (and deferred taxation) charge and the dividends payable are consistent with HC accounts.

(25) Review presentation of CC accounts and notes in the light of the recommendations that they should:

(a) be informative;

(b) contain sufficient information to explain the basis on which they have been prepared;

(c) contain a reconciliation between HC and CC operating profit (including extraction of interest from HC accounts);

(d) contain an analysis of current-cost reserve and indicate amounts realized and unrealized at balance sheet date;

(e) contain the current cost earnings per share based on the CC profit attributable to equity shareholdings before extraordinary items, and that this basis is explained in the notes;

(f) contain comparative figures. Where these figures are adjusted to a common price basis with the period's results, check calculations and confirm explanatory note. Where 5/10 year statements are provided, check calculation of common price basis.

(26) Is the audit report appropriate to the work carried out?

OVERVIEW

Partner to review the CC statement as a whole to confirm reasonableness from own knowledge of client comparison with previous year's figures, bearing in mind rate of inflation, and from level of adjustments made by other companies in the same trade.

CONCLUSIONS

Are you satisfied that:

(a) the current cost accounts are drawn up in accordance with SSAP 16 and, together with the notes, provide a true and fair view; are properly prepared to give the current cost information required by the Standard;

(b) there is adequate evidence on file to support this conclusion?

22.3 Summary

The audit programme for the current cost accounts will deal with:

(a) indices and arithmetic;

(b) review of fixed assets and depreciation charge;

(c) stocks and cost of sales adjustment;

(d) monetary working capital adjustment;

(e) gearing adjustment.

Progress questions

Question	Reference for answer
Draw up a suitable audit programme for current cost accounts.	Section 22.2

23 Special types of audit

23.1 Introduction

In one sense every audit is 'special' because every company has its unique features. What is meant here is, of course, specialized undertakings calling for special knowledge from the auditor, or for which there are special accounting or auditing requirements.

23.2 Solicitors

23.2.1 Introduction

The classic 'special audit' is the work necessary to enable an accountant to report as to whether solicitors have complied with the Solicitors' Accounts Rules 1975.

The work does not constitute a full audit, since the object is to enable the accountant to confirm that the solicitors have kept clients' monies at all times separate from their own, and that adequate records are maintained of clients' transactions. The reporting accountant is not required to examine the records of the solicitors' own transactions, except to ensure that clients' money has not been paid into an office account.

23.2.2 The Solicitors' Accounts Rules 1975

The main requirements of the rules are:

(a) The solicitor must maintain a 'client account' at a bank into which all clients' money is promptly paid.

(b) The solicitor must maintain a ledger of clients' accounts showing separately the transactions for that client dealt with by him.

(c) Money may only be drawn from the client account at the bank:
  (1) to make a payment properly required on behalf of a client;
  (2) on the client's authority;
  (3) to pay a debt due from the client to the solicitor. If this relates to costs the payment may only be made after a bill of costs has been

submitted to the client. The withdrawal in this case must be by means of a cheque drawn in favour of the solicitor or by transfer to a bank account in the name of the solicitor.

(d) No drawing from a client account can exceed the money held on behalf of that client (otherwise the funds of other clients would be used to finance the withdrawal).

(e) At intervals not exceeding three months a bank reconciliation must be prepared to agree the balance at bank on client account with the clients' cash book (the balance of which in turn will agree with the total of the balances in the clients' ledger).

23.2.3 The Accountants' Report Rules 1975

Every solicitor who handles clients' money is required under these rules to appoint a qualified accountant who reports to the Law Society, the governing body for solicitors, as to whether the solicitor has complied with the Solicitors' Accounts Rules 1975.

The Accountants' Report Rules lay down a detailed 'audit programme' which the reporting accountant must follow. Rule 4, which contains these requirements, is reproduced below:

(1) For the purpose of giving an Accountant's Report, an accountant shall ascertain from the solicitor particulars of all bank accounts (excluding trust bank accounts) kept, maintained or operated by the solicitor in connection with his practice at any time during the accounting period to which his Report relates and subject to paragraph 2 of this Rule make the following examination of the books, accounts and other relevant documents of the solicitor:

(a) So examine the bookkeeping system in every office of the solicitor as to enable the accountant to verify that such system complies with Rule 11 of the Solicitors' Accounts Rules 1975, and is so designed that:

—an appropriate ledger account is kept for each client;
—such ledger accounts show separately from other information particulars of all clients' money received, held or paid on account of each client;
—transactions relating to clients' money and any other money dealt with through a client account are recorded in the solicitors' books so as to distinguish such transactions from transactions relating to any other money received, held or paid by the solicitor.

(b) Make test checks of postings to clients' ledger accounts from records of receipts and payments of clients' money and make test checks of the casts of such accounts and records.

(c) Compare a sample of lodgments into and payments from the client account as shown in bank statements with the solicitor's records of receipts and payments of clients' money.

(*d*) Enquire into and test check the system of recording costs and of making transfers in respect of costs from the client account.

(*e*) Make a test examination of such documents as he shall request the solicitor to produce to him with the object of ascertaining and confirming:

(1) that the financial transactions (including those giving rise to transfers from one ledger account to another) evidenced by such documents, are in accordance with the Solicitors' Accounts Rules 1975; and

(2) that the entries in clients' ledger accounts reflect those transactions in a manner complying with the Solicitors' Accounts Rules 1975.

(*f*) Extract (or check extractions of) balances on the clients' ledger accounts during the accounting period under review at not fewer than two dates selected by the accountant (one of which may be the last day of the accounting period), and at each such date:

(1) compare the total as shown by such ledger accounts of the liabilities to the clients, including those for whom trust money is held in the client account, with the cash book balance on client account; and

(2) reconcile that cash book balance with the client account balance as confirmed direct to the accountant by the bank. (If the clients' account records are mechanized or computerized, this requirement is modified so that only a test check is necessary provided that a satisfactory system of internal control is in operation.)

(*g*) Satisfy himself that reconciliation statements have been kept in accordance with Rule 11(4) of the Solicitors' Accounts Rules 1975.

(*h*) Make a test examination of the clients' ledger accounts in order to ascertain whether payments from the client account have been made on any individual account in excess of money held on behalf of that client.

(*i*) Peruse such office ledger and cash accounts and bank statements as the solicitor maintains with a view to ascertaining whether any clients' money has not been paid into a client account.

(*j*) Ask for such information and explanations as he may require arising out of sub-paragraphs (*a*) to (*i*) of this paragraph.

(2) Nothing in paragraph 1 of this Rule shall require the accountant:

(*a*) to extend his enquiries beyond the information contained in the relevant documents relating to any client's matter produced to him supplemented by such information and explanations as he may obtain from the solicitor;

(*b*) to enquire into the stocks, shares, other securities or documents of title held by the solicitor on behalf of his clients;

(*c*) to consider whether the books of account of the solicitor have been properly written up in accordance with Rule 11 of the Solicitors' Accounts Rules 1975, at any time other than the time as at which his examination of those books and accounts takes place.

(3) If after making an examination in accordance with paragraphs 1 and 2 of this Rule it appears to the accountant that there is evidence that the Solicitors' Accountants Rules 1975 have not been complied with, he shall make such further

examination as he considers necessary in order to complete his Report with or without qualification.

(4) Except where a client's money has been deposited in a separate designated account, nothing in these Rules shall apply to any matter arising under Section 33 of the Solicitors Act 1974, or the Solicitors' Accounts (Deposit Interest) Rules 1975, notwithstanding any payment into client account of a sum in lieu of interest.

(5) In this Rule the expression 'separate designated account' shall have the same meaning as in Rule 2 of the Solicitors' Accounts (Deposit Interest) Rules 1975.

23.2.4 The accountant's report

On completion of the work outlined in Section 23.2.3, the accountant is in a position to sign his or her report to the Law Society which confirms:

(a) that all work called for by Rule 4 has been carried out;
(b) that the requirements of the Solicitors' Accounts Rules 1975 have been complied with, apart from trivial breaches due to clerical errors which have been rectified and which caused no loss to clients;
(c) that the clients' accounts, clients' cash book and client bank account were all in agreement at two dates as required in Rule 4(1)(f)—see Section 23.2.3.

If the accountant is unable to confirm that the requirements of the Solicitors' Accounts Rules have been met, or there have been material breaches of them, the report must give full details.

23.2.5 Solicitors' Accounts (Deposit Interest) Rules 1975

If a solicitor holds money on behalf of a client in circumstances in which it would be fair to the client for the money to be placed on deposit to earn interest, the solicitor must either so deposit the money and account to the client for the interest or pay the equivalent sum out of his own pocket to the client.

The Rules cite as an example of a sufficient amount to justify this procedure a sum of £500 likely to be held for at least two months.

23.3   Estate agents

23.3.1   Accounting

The provisions of the Estate Agents Act 1979 came into effect in 1982 and lay down rules broadly similar to the Solicitors Accounts Rules to safeguard clients' money.

'Clients' money' is defined as any money received by way of:

a pre-contract deposit or

a contract deposit

in connection with the acquisition of land in the UK. (A pre-contract deposit is one paid before an enforceable contract to acquire the land exists and a contract deposit is one paid after such a contract has been entered into).

Any such money received must be promptly banked into an account at a recognized bank which effectively separates it from any funds belonging to the agent. The name of the account must include the word 'client'.

As the estate agent is normally liable to account for interest on individual amounts of £500 or more, it may be convenient to open separate accounts for such amounts.

23.3.2   Audit requirements

The reporting requirements are basically similar to those of the Solicitors' Rules, but the Estate Agents Act and the Agents Regulations under the Act refer to an auditor's report rather than an accountant's report.

First of all, the auditor must be *qualified* (same requirements as S389).

The scope of the audit is limited to aspects relating to clients' money—there is no requirement for an audit of an estate agent's own affairs. This should be interpreted as including compliance with the rules regarding accounting for interest on deposits.

Unlike the Solicitors' Rules, the Estate Agents Rules do not set out a detailed programme of audit work. The Rules simply require the auditor to:

(1) ascertain particulars of all bank accounts kept, maintained or operated by an estate agent (or an employee) in respect of estate agency work at any time during the accounting period to which the report relates; and

(2) so examine the accounts and records of an estate agent as to enable him or her to verify whether they comply with the requirements of Regulation 6 (accounts and records relating to clients' money). In doing this, the auditor may ask for such further information and explanations as he or she may consider necessary.

The audit report is addressed to the estate agent personally, not to a regulating body as is the case with solicitors.

23.4 Chartered surveyors

The Accounts Regulations of the Royal Institution of Chartered Surveyors, issued in 1977, closely follow the Solicitors' Accounts Rules. They require broadly the same form of report, a copy of which must be sent to the Institution not, as with estate agents, merely to the estate agent concerned.

23.5 Insurance brokers

Insurance brokers (other than Lloyd's brokers who have their own regulatory system) operated under the rules laid down by the Insurance Brokers' Registration Council, set up by the Insurance Brokers (Registration) Act 1977.

Under the rules, brokers must submit audited accounts to the Council within six months of the end of each accounting period. The audited accounts must be accompanied by an accountant's report confirming that the broker has complied with the following rules during the period:

(a) maintained adequate working capital with a solvency margin of at least £1000;

(b) held all insurance monies at approved banks in an account designated 'Insurance Broking Account'.

23.6 Pension schemes

23.6.1 Introduction

Much of the contents of this section first appeared in an article by Neil Stein in the *Certified Accountants Students' Newsletter*.

Statement of Recommended Practice 1 (SORP 1) dealing with the accounts of pension schemes, proposes a format for their annual reports and suggests that there should be:

(a) Trustees' report;
(b) Audited accounts;
(c) Actuary's statement;
(d) Investment report.

The primary addressees of the report should be the members of the scheme (beneficiaries) and participating employers.

The ASC considers that it should not seek to introduce a standard on the subject of pension schemes and that the issue of a SORP embodying current best practice is to be preferred. Note that compliance with SORPs is not obligatory. Let us consider the proposed elements of the annual report in detail.

23.6.2 Trustees' report

This is a review of the general development of the fund to date, covering in particular:

(a) Membership statistics and major changes in benefits, constitution or legal requirements,

(b) The financial growth of the scheme as disclosed in the accounts,

(c) The actuarial position as reported on by the actuary,

(d) The investment policy and performance of the fund.

23.6.3 Audited accounts

These should consist of a revenue account and a net assets statement (balance sheet) and should normally be prepared annually on the accruals basis with the intention of showing a true and fair view of the financial transactions of the period. Investments should normally be valued at current market value or trustees' valuation rather than at cost. Property should be valued on the basis of existing use and should be revalued *annually*, not necessarily by a qualified valuer, but with valuation by a qualified valuer at least every five years. The accounts are essentially a stewardship report covering the immediate past. They need to be viewed in conjunction with the actuarial report, which deals with the present state and future viability of the scheme.

The accounts should contain the following details where material:

Revenue accounts
Contributions receivable
Investment income
Other income
Benefits payable
Other payments   SORP 1 gives many
Administrative expenses

                                         subheadings for each

Net assets statement
Investment assets   of these main headings.
Fixed assets not held
primarily as investments
Long-term borrowings
Current assets and liabilities.

The accounts should include a reconciliation of the net movement in the total value of the fund with the net additions less withdrawals from the fund but this may be incorporated in the revenue account or the net assets statement. In other words, a separate funds flow statement is not a requirement.

Accounting policies, and any changes in them, should, of course, be disclosed.

23.6.4   Actuary's statement

The actuary's statement is based on the actuary's investigation, and report on the ability of the present fund to meet accrued benefits and the adequacy of those funds and future contribution levels to meet promised benefits when due.

23.6.5   Investment report

This should give reasonable details of investments held and explain the investment policy and performance. The totals should, of course, be capable of reconciliation with the amounts shown in the accounts.

The investment report may be combined with the trustees' report and is intended to provide a greater analysis of the investment portfolio and income than is disclosed in the accounts.

The analysis suggested in SORP 1 is:

(a) analysis of investments by industrial sector
(b) analysis of investments by geographical sector
(c) details of the 10 or 20 largest investments
(d) details of investments which represent 5 per cent or more of any class of shares of any company
(e) details of the extent to which properties are subject to rent reviews.

23.6.6   Special points

(a) *Self-investment* (Investment by the scheme in the employing company). Any self-investment in excess of 5 per cent of the value of the assets should be disclosed by note.

(b) *Concentration of investment.* Any investment in a single enterprise exceeding 5 per cent of the total assets should be disclosed by note.

(c) *Insurance policies.* If insurance policies form a material part of the net assets, their main characteristics (e.g. whether with or without profits) should be disclosed by note.

(d) *Group accounts.* In principle, a pension scheme with investments in the nature of subsidiary or associated companies should prepare group accounts. Separate accounts for each entity in the group are not required.

(e) *Accounting for additional voluntary contributions* (AVCs). AVCs are additional payments *by members* (beneficiaries) made to secure additional benefits. These should be disclosed separately under the heading of contributions receivable from members in the revenue account, and the assets acquired with them should be included in the net assets statement. If AVCs are separately invested so that the proceeds from the investment determine the benefits, they should still be accounted for within the accounts of the scheme or notes thereto.

23.6.7 The audit of pension schemes

There is no statutory requirement for the audit of all pension schemes, but the Occupational Pensions Board requires audited accounts of contracted-out self-administered pension schemes to be filed with them annually. In addition, of course, many pension scheme trust deeds specify an audit. Legislation making an audit compulsory for all schemes is long overdue but is now in prospect.

In an insured scheme the principal asset of the pension fund will be the group pension policy, but there will be other investments, some representing temporary investment of funds pending payment to the insurance company. In a self-administered scheme the fund owns the investments directly and thus the verification problem is more extensive.

All the normal factors common to all audits are appropriate:

(a) Engagement letter
(b) Review of control procedures
(c) Compliance and substantive tests on transactions
(d) Verification of assets and liabilities
(e) Review of financial statements.

Points of relevance for pension schemes in particular are:

(a) Obtain a copy of the pension scheme trust deed and become familiar with its requirements.

(b) Confirm that the scheme has Inland Revenue approval and, if contracted out, OPB approval.

(c) Verify receipts and payments

(1) Test correctness of amounts received as members' contributions with membership records.

(2) Test correctness of amounts received as employer's contributions.

(3) Vouch transfer payments received (payments from other schemes when a new employee joins the scheme).

(4) Vouch repayments in respect of members leaving the scheme including tax deductions therefrom.

(5) Confirm that additional voluntary contributions (AVCs) received from members have been correctly calculated and, if separate investment is required, that they have been duly invested according to the rules of the scheme.

(6) Test authorization for initiation of benefits paid.

(7) Test calculation of benefits paid (lump sums and pensions) in accordance with the rules.

(d) Taxation.

(1) Check repayment claim for tax suffered on investment income.

(2) Vouch payments in respect of tax deductions from pension payments made.

(e) Verification of assets.

This will follow the normal procedures explained in Chapter 10.

(f) Insurance policies.

(1) Vouch premiums paid.

(2) Confirm receipt of bonus and other income from policies.

(g) Review the actuarial valuations and discuss them with the actuary.

(h) Confirm whether there is a deficiency on the immediate discontinuance basis, and if so confirm that adequate arrangements have been made to eliminate it, and that disclosure is made.

(i) If the scheme is contracted out, confirm that the annual statement required by the Occupational Pensions Board (OPB) has been lodged.

(j) Consider the effect of changes in the scheme or in asset values since the last actuarial valuation which might affect the solvency of the scheme or the computation of costs.

(k) Review the extent of any self-investment by the pension scheme.

(l) Consider the propriety of any 'related party' transactions by the pension scheme involving the company or its directors.

(m) If the company makes payments outside the scheme, perhaps on an *ex gratia* basis to past employees, confirm the authorization of such payments and confirm the company's system of control ensuring that payments do not continue after the death of the intended recipient.

23.7 Building societies

23.7.1 Introduction and legal background

Building societies exist to lend money on mortgage to members for the purchase of freehold or leasehold property (heritable property in Scotland). The funds to finance the lending are raised by taking deposits from members.

A building society is therefore undertaking two distinct operations which may overlap in the sense that a member may have a mortgage loan from the society while also maintaining a completely separate deposit account (normally a 'share' account).

Building societies are not companies but are governed by the Building Societies Act 1962.

23.7.2 Accounting requirements of the Act

Under S76, every building society is required to:

(a) Maintain proper books of account with respect to its transactions and its assets and liabilities as are necessary to give a true and fair view of the affairs of the society and to explain its transactions.

(b) Establish and maintain a system of control and inspection of its books and accounts and a system for supervising its cash holdings and all receipts and remittances.

(c) Establish and maintain a system to ensure the safe custody of all documents of title belonging to the building society, and of the deeds relating to property mortgaged to the society. This system must be such that the consent of the board or directors, or of a person authorized by the directors, is necessary before a document of title is released from the custody of the society.

Under S27, a building society must maintain a *record of advances* showing the value placed on each property mortgaged to the society and the name of the valuer, together with particulars of any additional security taken.

Building societies must submit annual returns to the Chief Registrar of Friendly Societies. The annual return includes the audited accounts of the society.

23.7.3 The requirement to appoint auditors

Every building society is required to appoint auditors. Their qualifications, rights and duties are broadly as under the Companies Act 1985, with the additional duty to report on whether the society has maintained a satisfactory system of control over its transactions and records, especially those pertaining to the system for supervising cash holdings and cash receipts and payments. The duties are contained in S87 of the Building Societies Act 1962.

23.7.4 Auditing procedures

In 1982 the APC issued an Auditing Guideline entitled 'Building Societies'. Paragraphs 13 to 56 of the Guideline relate to auditing procedures and these are reproduced below along with Appendix 3. The original paragraph numbers are retained to facilitate internal reference.

Auditing

Key audit areas
(13) This section of the Guideline comments on matters peculiar to building societies. It does not comment on key areas which are common to audits of other types of entity.

Systems of control, supervision and inspection
(14) Fundamental to the auditor's approach is the legal requirement that a society shall establish and maintain systems of control, supervision and inspection (s.76). The auditor's additional reporting requirements under s.87, compared to those under the Companies Act, will require him to ensure that the scope of his audit includes a full review of these systems. The auditor will take into account the results of this review in determining the extent to which he wishes to place reliance on internal controls and hence the level of substantive and other tests required to reach his opinion on the financial statements. Three essential points must be recognised by the auditor:

(*a*) in the case of most building societies, the volume of transactions is so great that the auditor cannot express an opinion without obtaining considerable assurance from adequate systems of control, supervision and inspection;

(*b*) in the case of most commercial organisations, most movements of cash are the result of an equivalent movement of goods. Certain audit assurance can therefore be obtained by reference to this relationship. This is not applicable, however, in the case of building societies and similar financial organisations. Assurance must therefore be provided by adequate systems of control, supervision and inspection, particularly over the handling of cash; and

(*c*) because transactions are cash based and there are large volumes of similar transactions, accounting systems frequently involve the use of computers. The auditor will need to have, or be able to call upon, the necessary expertise to satisfy himself that he fully understands the systems in operation, firstly in order to comply with Section 87(4), and secondly so that he can justify from his written record of the systems and his compliance tests the reliance he has placed on its internal controls.

The auditor should also recognize that most directors are non-executive and the day by day management of the society is delegated to one or more full time executives. The auditor will need to be aware of this delegation, the way in which it is defined and the supervision exercised by the board in order that he can assess the effect upon the overall controls of the society.

This topic is dealt with in detail in paragraphs 22 to 32 of this guideline.

Branches

(15) Many building societies operate a network of branches. The auditor's approach to such branches will principally be determined by the degree of head office control over the accounting function, and the effectiveness of the society's own inspection visits. Where the branches maintain separate accounting records, the extent of audit visits will be further influenced by the assets and liabilities involved at each branch. Where the accounting records are maintained at head office rather than at the branches, the auditor should make sufficient branch visits to provide himself with reasonable assurance that the systems of control, supervision and inspection are operating satisfactorily. Particular attention should be given to exceptions to the society's normal control procedures caused by the staffing levels at smaller branches, e.g.: the greater difficulty of ensuring adequate separation of duties, and to the consequent need for an increased level of supervision.

Agencies

(16) Most building societies operate a network of agencies, and the auditor will need to establish the powers and responsibilities of each agency. The systems of control and supervision over such agencies must be established and maintained as with other systems, and in particular should ensure prompt returns from the agency of its receipts. It can be more difficult for a society to monitor whether or not the systems are adhered to by an agent than by a branch, as an agent is not an employee of the society operating from the society's premises. Normally an auditor would not expect direct contact with an agent but, in case he should ever consider that it is necessary, the agency agreement should permit access by the society and its auditor to the agent's records, so far as they relate to the society's affairs (see s.87(5)).

Advances and repayments of mortgages

(17) The auditor must carry out appropriate audit tests in order to satisfy himself that the systems provide that:

(a) all advances are to bona fide borrowers, have been made in compliance with the system of internal control, and are properly secured on the title of the property;

(b) security continues to be maintained, including guarantees, endowment policies, insurance cover;

(c) all arrears in the repayment of advances are monitored to ensure that they represent nothing more significant than delays in repayment by bona fide borrowers, and are not due to misrecording or defalcation by employees of the society; and

(d) all redemption monies have been properly accounted for in the society's records.

The auditor must also satisfy himself, for the purpose of reporting on the annual return, that the society is properly identifying arrears over 12 months and recording special advances as defined by section 21 of the Building Societies Act 1962 and subsequent orders.

Deeds

(18) The auditor has a statutory obligation to report where the society has failed to establish and maintain a system to ensure the safe custody of all documents of title relating to property belonging to the society, and of deeds relating to property mortgaged to, secured to or additional security taken by the society (s.87(4)). Consequently, appropriate compliance tests should be carried out to enable the auditor to satisfy himself that an adequate system is in operation. Normally, the auditor will only need to be satisfied that deeds are prima facie valid, but should he need to establish more positively the legal validity of particular deeds, it would be appropriate to seek the advice of a member of the legal profession.

Investors' accounts

(19) Certain accounts need special attention such as where:

- (a) the investor cannot be traced;
- (b) passbooks are held by the society;
- (c) requests for non-communication have been received;
- (d) fixed amounts are held for a long period; or
- (e) there are exceptions to the society's usual procedures.

The auditor must ensure that the society's procedures control all types of account and prevent unauthorised access to the accounting records and pass books.

Communication between society and investors/borrowers

(20) It is an important feature of a system of internal control within a building society that the society should communicate with its investors and borrowers in a proper and timely manner, and that all queries from investors and borrowers which relate to the accounting function are properly monitored and resolved. The auditor should therefore take steps to satisfy himself that this aspect of the society's systems is operating adequately. The system of control should ensure that the statements are sent out in accordance with the society's policies. The statements issued by many building societies ask the recipient to send any queries direct to the external or internal auditor. This enables the auditor to judge the nature and significance of any discrepancies and to assess the system in operation for the resolving of such queries. It must, however, be stressed that it is the society's responsibility to issue statements and to process any queries arising therefrom. It must also be stressed that the monitoring by the external auditor of the system of communication is not necessarily a substitute for the positive circularisation of a sample of investors and borrowers, whether by the internal or external auditor.

Investments held by a society

(21) Significant amounts of the society's funds held as investments are often under the control of a very limited number of individuals. Special care must therefore be taken by the auditor when examining the systems of control, supervision and inspection in this area and, where considered necessary, the auditor should extend the

amount of substantive testing. It is also necessary for the auditor to satisfy himself that all investments are authorised by the current Building Societies Authorised Investments Orders, and that the society has established and maintained a system to ensure the safe custody of documents of title relating to investments (s.76(3)).

Systems of control, supervision and inspection

(22) Directors of building societies are responsible in a similar way to directors of other organisations for such matters as setting the objectives of the society, deciding its policies and procedures, controlling and maintaining custody of its assets, and meeting its liabilities. In addition, s.76 sets out a requirement that building societies establish and maintain systems of control, supervision and inspection. It is because a building society is in a special position of trust that the particular requirements are laid down by statute to ensure that directors take the necessary steps to carry out their responsibilities to secure compliance by the society.

(23) Auditors have a specific responsibility under s.87 to report if the requirements of s.76 have not been met. Auditors must therefore consider whether appropriate systems have been established and whether they have been maintained. Also the auditors' reports on the annual return under the 1981 regulations includes a report on part 13 which is a statement by the Board as to the 'date(s) of meeting(s) (if any) at which the board of directors considered the requirements of s.76 of the Building Societies Act 1962 and the evidence of the manner in which the society complied therewith'.

(24) It is important to recognise that the statutory requirement implies two levels of control; a primary system of control and supervision over records, cash transactions, assets, security, etc., and a secondary system of inspection to see that primary controls are operating. The systems required are a combination of all types of control as set out in the auditing guideline 'Internal controls'. With the particular emphasis placed on supervision and inspection, the objectives of internal audit and the responsibilities of directors and management should be clearly established.

(25) In addition to controls common to other businesses, e.g. control over purchases or payroll, there are certain aspects of control of particular relevance to building societies. In establishing and monitoring the systems of control, the society should, *inter alia*, consider the following aspects, taking into consideration such matters as the size of branches and the numbers of staff:

(a) *Receipts*

    (i)   immediate recording in books and records and passbooks;
    (ii)   dual control over the opening of mail;
    (iii) security procedures over tills and safes, and computer terminals;
    (iv) prompt and intact banking;
    (v)   daily balancing of tills and investigation of variances;
    (vi) regular bank reconciliations;
    (vii) control over opening accounts.

(b) *Withdrawals*

    (i)   evidence of identity, e.g. passbook, signature, authority;
    (ii)   evidence of sufficient balance;

       (iii)   authorisation of cheques independent from counter cashiers;

       (iv)   restrictions on access to inactive accounts, lost passbook accounts etc.;

       (v)   control over permanent information amendments.

(c) *Passbooks*

       (i)   records dealing with ordering, receipt and issue;

       (ii)   replacement for lost passbooks;

       (iii)   procedures for cancellation in the case of closed accounts;

       (iv)   controls over used and unused passbooks in the custody of the society.

(d) *Advances*

       (i)   offer according to society policy, board approval procedures and legal requirements;

       (ii)   valuation, security documents, solicitor's report on title checked;

       (iii)   independent preparation of cheques for advances;

       (iv)   control over permanent information amendments;

       (v)   adequate insurance cover;

       (vi)   regular review of arrears of repayments;

       (vii)   redemption only on full repayment of capital and interest.

(e) *Deeds*

       (i)   all movements of deeds recorded;

       (ii)   all deeds checked on receipt for legal requirements and for agreement with accounting records;

       (iii)   investigation of reasons if deeds not received when due;

       (iv)   strict security of deed room;

       (v)   deeds released only on proper authority;

       (vi)   matching of deeds held with accounting records.

(f) *Investments*

       (i)   investment in accordance with society policy, board approval procedures, and legal requirements;

       (ii)   custody of title documents;

       (iii)   receipts and calculations of income independently checked;

       (iv)   regular review of portfolio.

(g) *Branches and agencies*

       (i)   acting within limits of authority;

       (ii)   prompt banking and reporting to head office;

       (iii)   control over exceptions to standard procedures, e.g. caused by less segregation of duties;

       (iv)   supervision.

(h) *Computer processing*

       (i)   restrictions on access to operational areas, hardware, terminals, documentation, programs, and data;

       (ii)   controls over application development;

       (iii)   authorisation and testing of program changes;

       (iv)   authorisation of amendments to data files;

       (v)   ensuring systems software is properly installed and maintained;

(vi)   keeping proper documentation;
(vii) ensuring continuity of operation;
(viii) authorisation and checking of input of completeness and accuracy;
(ix)   controls to ensure the completeness and accuracy of processing;
(x)   maintenance of master files and standing data files;
(xi)   prompt review of control account agreements, exception reports, and error/rejection/suspense items.

(*i*)   *Other matters*

(i)   insurance indemnity levels;
(ii) control of interest calculation and payment.

(26) The systems of inspection should include procedures for:

(*a*) the recording and review of systems of control and supervision;
(*b*) the reporting of financial and other information to enable review of operations;
(*c*) the review of the operation of important controls;
(*d*) the review of the treatment of unusual/exceptional/special transactions; and
(*e*) the reporting and review of inspection arrangements including internal audit activities.

(27) Where the society is unable to establish a full-time inspection or internal audit department in conjunction with its other review procedures, it must set up an adequate alternative comprising one or more of the following:

(*a*) the use of a competent independent person on a part-time basis;
(*b*) consortia arrangements with other societies;
(*c*) the use of independent accountants or other external suitably qualified persons; and
(*d*) detailed work by one or more directors with relevant experience.

In addition to delegated inspection procedures, the directors may need to carry out some review procedures themselves. The auditor will need to be satisfied that the society overcomes the disadvantages inherent in the above alternatives to a full-time system.

(28) The auditor should consider the adequacy of the inspection procedures on a similar basis to that set out in the paragraphs on internal audit in the Auditing Guideline 'Internal controls'. The auditor must remember that he is required by law to report if the systems are inadequate, and must recognise that this is a major difference from a trading company. Key questions that the auditor should consider regarding the system of inspection include:

(*a*) is the system structured so that it can perform an independent appraisal function?
(*b*) is the organisation and staffing adequate?
(*c*) is the work adequately planned and controlled?
(*d*) are the inspection techniques used satisfactory?
(*e*) are adequate procedures employed for reporting?

Irrespective of the system of inspection, many societies will extend their internal audit programmes beyond inspection, and those procedures will need to be assessed in order to determine how much reliance can be placed on internal audit in forming an opinion on the accounts, in accordance with the Auditing Guideline 'Internal controls'.

(29) Particular consideration must be given to inspection/internal audit reporting procedures, especially where there is a senior official able to influence the operation of control overall or in particular parts of the society's operations. In such a case, reporting should be direct to the board and not just to that official. The board should approve the systems of control, supervision and inspection, regularly review their adequacy and review inspection/internal audit reports, and it may set up a committee with responsibilities, inter alia, for this area of the board's functions. The auditor should review these board procedures as part of his review of the inspection and internal audit, particularly considering the technical qualifications and experience available.

(30) In forming his opinion on the adequacy of the systems, the auditor must have regard to the need for audit evidence to support his conclusions, and the Guideline on audit evidence should be followed. For example, evidence of the establishment of systems is much greater if procedures manuals are prepared, if the directors approve new procedures which materially affect the control system, and if they minute any regular review of procedures. Evidence of the maintenance of inspection systems could be provided by proper documentation of inspection programmes, work carried out, conclusions reached and reports made.

(31) It is important to recognise that the external auditor is giving an independent opinion. Consequently he must consider very carefully his involvement in matters on which he is required to give that independent opinion. Where a society does not have the necessary expertise available amongst its directors, it may call on its external auditors for advice. The giving of advice on the procedures for establishing and maintaining systems or on the design of systems, or on the interpretation of reports from inspection/internal audit does not necessarily conflict with the giving of an opinion. If auditors are asked to assist in carrying out the inspection procedures, they must consider whether such assistance could result in a loss of objectivity, and thus independence, in giving their opinion on the maintenance of systems of inspection.

(32) No legal interpretation is available as to what procedures would satisfy the requirements of the 1962 Act, and the external auditors must exercise their judgement in the particular circumstances. The important factors are:

(a) that the society must establish and maintain the systems, which include a review of the results of inspection; and

(b) that such inspection is independent, evidenced, and sufficiently comprehensive and continuous to ensure that the directors are made aware of material weaknesses in internal control, and their potential or actual effect irrespective of the statutory work of the external auditor.

Should the auditors be in doubt as to the adequacy of the system, they should discuss the matter with the directors of the society, and if agreement cannot be reached, then they should advise the directors to refer the matter to the Chief Registrar in accordance with the advice of the Chief Registrar in his letter of 9 June 1978 to building society chairmen (see Appendix 3).

Operational guidelines

The following procedures are complementary to those given in the Operational Guidelines referred to in the preface to this Guideline.

Planning, controlling and recording

When planning the audit of a building society, the auditor should particularly consider the following:

(a) the requirements of the 1962 Act so far as they affect the audit and the accounts;

(b) the requirements of any relevant regulations issued under statutory instrument;

(c) any relevant Building Societies Association circulars;

(d) any guidance notes issued by the Chief Registrar of Friendly Societies;

(e) the rules of the building society;

(f) key audit areas (see paragraphs 13 to 21);

(g) any request from the society that the scope of the audit be expanded;

(h) the timing and nature of the audit work to be carried out to enable the auditors' report to be signed within a short period of time after the end of the accounting period;

(i) the use of staff with adequate training and experience.

There is no special considerations in relation to the controlling and recording of the audit work.

Accounting systems

(35) The Auditing Guideline 'Accounting systems' draws the attention of auditors of enterprises such as building societies to the need to consider their specific duties relating to accounting records. The auditor should follow the Guideline 'Accounting systems' in carrying out these specific duties.

Audit evidence

(36) To obtain adequate audit evidence, the auditor must:

(a) record the systems of control, supervision and inspection;

(b) assess those systems;

(c) carry out appropriate compliance tests to establish that the systems are operating effectively in all material respects; and

(d) carry out whatever substantive tests are necessary to enable him to express an opinion on the accounts.

(37) The level of substantive tests will be determined by reference to the auditor's judgement of the sufficiency of audit evidence required to enable him to express an opinion on the accounts. This judgement will be based on the evaluation of the system of control, the results of the compliance tests and the assessment of materiality

in the particular audit area concerned. The major substantive tests should be designed to confirm:

(a) investor's and borrowers' balances;

(b) existence of deeds;

(c) existence, ownership, and value of premises, equipment, vehicles, investments and cash; and

(d) interest received and paid.

(38) Certain factors to be considered when establishing a level of materiality in relation to the audit of building society accounts are different, at least in emphasis, from those for the audit of other enterprises. Building societies exist not to generate profits, but to provide savings facilities for individuals and loans for house purchasers. Indeed the auditor is required to report on income and expenditure, not surplus. Essentially building societies are based on the concept of mutuality. Important measures of their success and financial position are the increase in their assets, the level of reserves, advances made and the liquidity position, rather than the ability to pay dividends as in a trading company. The auditor should therefore consider materiality in relation to these matters.

(39) In some areas, such as interest received and paid, analytical review procedures can help to achieve a significant level of audit confidence, thus enabling the auditor to reduce the level of substantive tests. Similarly, management expenses can be reviewed by procedures such as comparison with the previous year's accounts and budgets and management accounts for the year under review.

(40) Regularly published statistics indicating trends within the building society movement as a whole should also be examined, and any variations from the trend should be investigated. These statistics are the product of regular (principally monthly) returns of financial information made by each society. This information is provided to the Registry of Friendly Societies, the Building Societies Association, the Central Statistics Office and the Department of the Environment. The auditor should be aware of these returns and refer to the information contained therein where appropriate.

Internal controls

(41) The Auditing Guideline on 'Internal controls' has particular relevance to the audits of building societies. The requirements of s.76, as discussed in paragraphs 22–32 (systems of control, supervision and inspection) should result in not only a strong system of internal control, but also good inspection and often broader based internal audit procedures. Because of the special considerations relating to building societies discussed in this guideline, the auditor should be able to place considerable reliance on internal audit in forming his opinion on the accounts, as well as carrying out his other duties and responsibilities under s.87. The auditor should therefore closely follow the Auditing Guideline 'Internal controls', in conjunction with the comments in paragraphs 22 to 32.

(42) Attention is particularly drawn to the comments in the Auditing Guideline 'Internal controls' on 'management responsibility' and 'limitations on the effectiveness of internal controls'. In a building society, controls such as segregation of duties, control account reconciliations, supervision and the delegation of authority are of considerable importance. Often the chief executive is, or individual managers are, in a position to override controls, as well as being able to exercise close control through

their detailed personal knowledge and contact within the organisation. The supervisory and inspection activities of the board over the actions of management to whom the board delegates authority and responsibility are therefore particularly important. The smaller the society, the more likely that control procedures will rely extensively on the chief executive, and the auditor will need to consider carefully how the board exercise their responsibility.

Review of financial statements

(43) The auditor should consider whether the accounts comply with all statutory requirements and other regulations. The majority of the requirements are contained in the Building Societies (Accounts and Annual Return) Regulations, 1981. The format of the accounts set out in Schedule 1 to that statutory instrument should be adhered to, unless to do so would not present a true and fair view of the state of the society's affairs and/or its income and expenditure. The auditor must also consider whether the accounting policies adopted are such as will enable him to express an unqualified opinion on the accounts.

(44) Statement of Standard Accounting Practice (SSAP) No.2 requires accounting policies to be disclosed. The S.I. 1981 regulation 4(1) requires this disclosure to be in separate notes. Particular policies, disclosure of which may be necessary to the accounts of building societies are those concerning:

(a) income tax: the basis of calculation of the charge in the Revenue and Appropriation Account, and of the current liability for the current tax year shown in the balance sheet, must be clearly explained (S.I. 1981—reg. 6(1)(e));

(b) corporation tax, including deferred tax (S.I. 1981—reg. 6(1)(f) and 10(1)(g and h));

(c) investments: the basis of valuation of investments—cost, market value, etc.—should be disclosed. It is common practice not to provide for the difference between cost and market values because the maturity value of the investments, if held for redemption, will be greater than cost;

(d) accruals for interest liabilities on shares and deposits; it should be clear whether contingent liabilities are accrued or only noted;

(e) losses on advances;

(f) the accounting treatment of unions of societies and transfers of engagements;

(g) property revaluations;

(h) depreciation; (S.I. 1981—reg. 6(1)(c and d));

(i) repairs and renewals: there can be a relationship between (h) and (i) since societies may write off some fixed assets in the year of acquisition in view of their immateriality. Exceptionally large acquisitions—a new head office or a computer, for instance—can force a change in this policy. Unusual capitalisation policies and any change in such policies must be clearly explained.

It should be noted that certain of the headings are set out in part 12 of the Annual Return contained in the 1981 regulations.

(45) The statement of source and application of funds is commonly in the form of a 'movement of funds' statement in the Directors' Report, following the model layout in the 'Guide to Building Society Finance' (second edition). This layout differs from that recommended in SSAP 10 and the auditor should review it carefully to ensure that it includes material information called for in SSAP 10.

(46) In reviewing the financial statements, the auditor should consider the following points, *inter alia:*

(*a*) building society accounts are used widely for statistical purposes. In this connection, the auditor should be aware that societies supply, amongst others, the Chief Registrar and the Building Societies Association with monthly financial statistics. While having no reporting responsibility in relation to such statistics, the auditor should ensure that infrequent or unusual receipts or payments (by type, timing or amount) are properly and consistently treated in the financial statements (on which he is reporting) in relation to income and expenditure for the accounting period;

(*b*) depreciation: many building societies do not depreciate their freehold properties. The auditor will have to assess whether such a policy (s.7 defines powers in relation to land) is material in relation to the income and expenditure of the society for the year and to the balance sheet. He must take into consideration the condition and location of the properties, whether the balance sheet value includes any items that will have a shorter life than the building as a whole (e.g. counters, lifts or air-conditioning) and whether the building has been revalued;

(*c*) income tax: the auditor should consider carefully the effect of the society's accounting policy in relation to income tax, in giving a true and fair view of its expenditure and liabilities. When payment is due soon after the balance sheet date, it is the usual practice to base the charge in the accounts for income tax in respect of interest on shares and deposits wholly on the current tax year. The alternative is to compute it using a proportion of the current tax year and a proportion of the previous tax year to coincide with the society's own financial year. The auditor should also recognise that income tax arrangements are liable to change. When checking the computation of a society's liability to taxation, it is useful to have to hand an up-to-date copy of 'Guide to Building Society Taxation' obtainable from the Building Societies Association. Also essential would be a copy of the current year's arrangements entered into by the Board of Inland Revenue and the building society. In addition, the circulars issued periodically by the Buildings Societies Association to building societies include details of agreed changes in taxation practice and these should be scrutinised;

(*d*) transactions near the balance sheet date: the auditor should have regard to the requirements of SSAP 17, and in particular should examine transactions which have the effect of showing as on the balance sheet date a state of affairs (particularly the society's liquidity) which is materially different from that during the year and shortly after. In addition to such matters as tax or interest payments soon after the balance sheet date, items requiring particular attention are:

(i)   large deposits received shortly before the year end and repaid shortly after;
(ii) large loan repayments received shortly before the year end and readvanced on the same property shortly after;
(iii) unusual delay until after the year end in making payments in accordance with applications received before the year end for withdrawals of shares or deposits;
(iv) an abnormal year end accumulation of commitments for advances followed by the making of the advances shortly after the year-end;
(v)   significant items in bank reconciliation statements.

(47) A building society's trustee status is related to arithmetical criteria which are

contained in the Building Societies (Designation for Trustee Investment) Regulations 1972, as subsequently amended. Whilst the auditor has no direct responsibility in this area, he should ensure that the presentation of the accounts does not distort in any material way the figures used for that purpose.

(48) The auditor will have to give special consideration to what constitutes a true and fair view where the society has been a party to a union or transfer of engagements during the year, or the society's operations have been restricted under s.48.

Reporting

Financial statements to members

(49) The auditor's report must be addressed to the members of the society. The matters on which the auditor must report are set out in s.87. As is the case with all auditor's reports, it should clearly indicate those areas of the financial statements on which the auditor is reporting. It is usual to deal with this by stating the page numbers of the financial statements in the report. It is becoming more common for the statement of source and application of funds (often called the movement of funds statement) to be included as a separate item in the financial statements. Many societies, however, still include this statement as part of the directors' report. In these circumstances, it will be necessary for the auditor's report to refer specifically to that statement.

(50) Set out below is a form of unqualified auditor's report:

AUDITOR'S REPORT TO THE MEMBERS OF . . . BUILDING SOCIETY

I/We have audited the financial statements on pages ... to ... (and the statement of source and application of funds (movement of funds statement) in the directors' report) in accordance with approved Auditing Standards.

In my/our opinion the financial statements [together with the statement of source and application of funds (movement of funds statement)] which have been prepared under the historical cost convention (as modified by the revaluation of land and buildings), give a true and fair view of the state of the society's affairs at ... and of its income and expenditure and source and application of funds (movement of funds) for the year then ended, and are drawn up in accordance with the Building Societies Act 1962 and the regulations made thereunder.

The above words in brackets should be deleted or included as appropriate.

Annual return

(51) The matters on which the auditor must report are set out in s.91. The auditor is required to report on, *inter alia*, any advances to directors or officers of the society or to companies in which they have a financial interest. The auditor will normally have to rely on information given to the society by the directors and officers as required by Section 89. In these circumstances, the auditor should make this clear in his report. However, the auditor should give careful consideration as to whether he can give an opinion on the amount outstanding at the end of the year on such advances which are now to be disclosed under the 1981 regulations.

(52) Set out below is a form of unqualified auditor's report on the annual return subject to the reservation referred to above:

AUDITOR'S REPORT ON THE ANNUAL RETURN OF THE ... BUILDING SOCIETY FOR THE YEAR ENDED ...

I/We have examined the foregoing annual return for the year ended ... in accordance with approved Auditing Standards, with the exception of the information contained in Part ... with which I am/we are not required to deal and which accordingly my/our report does not cover.

In my/our opinion the annual return (as far as I am/we are required to report on it), which has been prepared under the historical cost convention (as modified by the revaluation of land and buildings), is drawn up in accordance with the Building Societies Act 1962 and regulations made thereunder, is in agreement with the books of account and records of the society and gives a true and fair view of the matters to which it is addressed. In relation to Section B of Part 9, I/we have no information other than that disclosed by the directors and officers in accordance with Section 89(2) of the Act.

Claims by society under Option Mortgage Scheme

(53) The auditor is required to report on the annual statement claiming the final payment of the amount due to the society under the terms of the Option Mortgage Scheme.

The wording of the auditor's report has been agreed with the Department of the Environment as follows:

I/We have examined the above statements and the particulars given in the attached schedule. I/We have also examined the books, records and procedures of the applicant and have obtained such explanations and carried out such tests as I/we considered necessary.

On the basis of my/our examination and of the explanations given to me/us, I/we report that in my/our opinion (subject to the reservations set out in the attached letter dated ...) for the purpose of the Option Mortgage Scheme proper records have been maintained by the applicant in accordance with the Secretary of State's directions and the particulars and amounts referred to in paragraphs 2 to 5 above are in accordance with those records.

In a similar manner, an auditor will now normally have to report on advances made under the terms of the Home Purchase Assistance and Housing Corporation Guarantee Act 1978. The appropriate wording for this report is set out in form HPA 7, which is the standard annual return to be made by building societies concerning the home purchase assistance scheme.

Qualified opinions

(54) The areas where qualification may be considered which are peculiar to building society audits relate to systems:

(a) of control and inspection;

(b) for supervising cash holdings and receipts and remittances; and

(c) to ensure the safe custody of documents of title.

The responsibilities and requirements of auditors and directors in these areas were emphasised in letters to all building society auditors in 1978, from the accounting bodies specified in s.161 of the Companies Act 1948. It must be remembered that a lack of comment by the auditor in his report will be regarded by a user of the accounts as confirmation that the matters about which the auditor must satisfy himself are indeed satisfactory.

(55) Where the auditor is of the view that a qualified report may be necessary, he should discuss the matter fully with the directors of the society. Should agreement not be reached, or where it is agreed that the auditors will qualify their opinion, the auditor should advise the directors to discuss the matter with the Chief Registrar as referred to in the letter from the Registrar to all building society chairmen dated 9 June 1978 (see Appendix 3). Should the auditor wish to discuss a potential qualification (or other audit problem) with the Registrar, then he should normally first advise the directors of the society of his intentions.

Reporting to management and directors

(56) The Auditing Guideline on 'Internal controls' emphasises the importance of reporting significant weaknesses in internal controls to management. In a building society because of the particular requirements relating to systems of control, supervision and inspection, the auditor should also ensure that non-executive directors are aware of reports made by the auditors to management. Arrangements for each society will be different, but such awareness can best be achieved by the auditor attending a board meeting (or committee of the board) and explaining any matters from his audit.

Appendix 3: Letter dated 9 June 1978 from the Chief Registrar of Friendly Societies to all building society chairmen

Dear Sir

In September 1976 following the discovery of defalcations in the Wakefield Building Society I wrote to all Chairmen of building societies to draw attention to the responsibilities expressly imposed on directors by section 76(1)(b) and (5) of the Building Societies Act 1962, and to the consequent need for directors to satisfy themselves that the system of control, inspection and supervision required to be maintained in accordance with section 76(1)(b) were effective. The deficiency recently disclosed in the Grays Building Society makes it necessary for me to write again on this subject.

I am aware from the responses to my earlier letter that the advice which that letter contained was superfluous in the case of some societies. But the Grays affair has demonstrated how the consequences of failure may be of direct interest and concern to all societies in one way or another, and I am therefore sending this present letter to all societies.

As you may know, I have appointed Inspectors to inquire into the affairs of the Grays Building Society. When, in due course, the Inspectors have made their report to me it will no doubt be possible to examine more fully the lessons to be drawn from the failure in that society. In the meantime there is some positive action which should be taken.

Appraisal of a society's systems of control, inspection and supervision as provided for by section 76(1)(*b*) ought to be a continuing process. In the first place therefore, if your Board has not recently carried out a reappraisal of these systems it ought to do so now with a view to satisfying itself that they are effective to prevent irregularities in the society's books of account and in the handling of cash. The systems should be such that if irregularities do occur, despite the systems, they will be brought to light in the shortest possible time.

Professional advice should be sought if directors are in any doubt about the effectiveness of their systems. If in the end directors are not satisfied that their systems can be made continuously effective within the society's present capacity, they must draw what seems to me the inevitable conclusion and seek a merger with another society in which their members' funds can be properly safeguarded.

In the second place I must ask you, as I did in my letter of September 1976, to draw your fellow-directors' attention to the point that they should not consider that section 76(1)(*b*) has been complied with merely because the society's auditors have not reported to the contrary. Under the terms of the Act it is for the directors positively to satisfy themselves that the section has been complied with.

Thirdly, it is my view that directors ought to ensure, so far as lies in their power, that audits are fully effective for all purposes. In the Registry we shall seek to extend the use of checks designed to test the accuracy of the accounts and returns submitted to use. Also as a result of recent events it is to be expected that auditors will pay closer attention to the maintenance by societies of the systems of control, inspection and supervision mentioned in section 76(1)(*b*). If they are of the opinion that the systems are inadequate, they will qualify their report accordingly. You will appreciate that when confronted with a qualified report it may well be necessary for me to take some appropriate action in the case of the society concerned. You will also understand how damaging to confidence and to the society's future such a qualified report of itself could be. If, therefore, you ever have reason to think that your auditor may be considering qualifying his audit report I would ask you to let me know without delay.

No doubt you will bring this letter to the attention of your Board, and if there are any comments or any points arising I should be glad to hear from you.

23.8 Banks

23.8.1 Introduction and legal background

Banks will generally be companies registered under the Companies Acts. There are special provisions exempting them from some of the disclosure requirements of Schedule 4, but the clearing banks have voluntarily waived their right to limit disclosure in this way.

The exemption available allow the banks to omit certain details of fixed assets, the market value of investments and some details of movements on reserves.

23.8.2 Internal controls in bank branches

The highest standard of internal controls must be present in view of the large amounts of cash present, and possible opportunities to manipulate accounts if controls were absent. The following controls are necessary:

(a) *Custody controls*. Restrictions on access to vaults and other stores frequently require the presence of two designated bank officials to open them, and strict records are kept of the issue and receipt of cash and securities.

(b) *Segregation of duties*. Most banks now maintain a central computerized accounting system. Accounts are updated without directly involving branch staff.

(c) *Authorization*. Procedures must be established governing the granting of overdrafts and the monitoring of balances. Limits are normally set on the local manager's authority. Beyond that level authority from regional offices will be required.

(d) Regular *review* of accounts of bank staff. This is to detect unusual movements possibly indicative of involvement in fraud.

(e) Active *internal audit*. Typically, teams of internal auditors (normally referred to in banking as inspectors) make surprise visits to branches to count cash and securities and review the correct operation of other branch controls.

(f) There should be procedures for handling customer complaints so that tellers (counter staff) are not involved.

(g) Reconciliation of accounts with other banks.

(h) Reviews of securities held for loans and overdrafts, to confirm their continuing adequacy.

23.8.3 Audit procedures at branches

Work will be coordinated with the bank's inspectors, and branches will be visited on a rotational basis.

In view of the absolute need for the highest standards of internal control, the auditor's review of the system must be rigorous. Overdraft authorizations will be reviewed for compliance with the bank's procedures and for adherence to limits.

The adequacy of the provision for irrecoverable balances will be an important area for the auditor.

23.8.4   Audit procedures generally—head office and review of financial statements

Tests outlined in Chapter 13 will be carried out on the computerized records.

The Bank of England relies on the audited accounts of the banks as part of its role as supervisor of banking in the UK under the Banking Act 1979.

Verification of assets and liabilities and review of financial statements will follow the general lines explained in Chapters 10 and 11.

The review of the financial statements needs to cover the bank's exposure to risk of default on overseas government loans, or indeed on any large debts, and this is critical to the assessment of the bank's profit.

23.9   Insurance companies

23.9.1   Introduction and legal background

Insurance companies are subject to the Companies Act but are exempt, like banks, from some of the accounting disclosure requirements. They are also subject to the Insurance Companies Act 1982 and sundry regulations made under that Act.

Insurance companies engage in 'long-term' and 'short-term' business. Long-term business consists mainly of life assurance and pensions schemes; short-term business covers property insurance, motor insurance, marine insurance and indeed nearly all the other types of business carried on by insurance companies except life assurance and pensions.

The nature of long-term insurance business is that income flows in from premiums over a long period, and ultimately a payment is made on the eventual death or retirement of the policy-holder. Even in the case of short-term businss the premiums are received annually in advance. The result is the build-up of very substantial sums which are invested by the insurance companies in equities, Government securities, property and mortgage loans.

The Insurance Companies Act 1982 requires insurance companies to maintain separate revenue accounts for long-term and short-term business, and to maintain separate insurance funds, represented by various investments, for the two types of business in the balance sheet. Thus funds held for long-term purposes cannot be used for short-term claims.

23.9.2 The audit of an insurance company

(a) Features common to other audits

Insurance companies have features which are common to other audits. The verification of most assets, for example, will present no unusual problems, apart from the scale of the operation.

Apart from investment income, the main source of income will be premiums receivable, often collected through branches and agents. That necessitates a strong system of controls over cash handling, but presents no unique problem.

The premium income is normally received in advance and the calculation of the unearned portion to be carried forward to the next period will need to be checked.

(b) Special features

The three special features which present problems are

—treatment of claims (short-term business)
—premium deficiency
—evaluation of profit on long-term business in conjunction with the company's actuaries.

(1) Claims

In some insurance areas it may take several years before claims are settled, and there may also be delay before the claim is formally lodged with the company.

The liability for claims must reflect all events that have occurred up to the balance sheet date, whether or not the claim has actually been made at that time. The liability for claims will therefore consist of three elements:

—Claims agreed but not yet paid. This is clearly an easily quantified amount.
—Claims received but not yet agreed. Post balance sheet settlement, and discussions with claims managers after reviewing the files, will be the basis for the auditor's assessment of the reasonableness of the amount included as a liability.
—Claims not yet received. These claims incurred but not reported are even more difficult to evaluate than the previous category. The audit approach must include an appraisal of the company's procedures for identifying such claims, including statistical information relating to past experience. Once again, post balance sheet developments and discussions with the company's officials are the basis for the auditor's assessment.

(2) Premium deficiency

If insurance business is entered into on an annual basis, as is usual, the insurance company has, at the balance sheet date, an obligation to continue the insurance until the renewal date. If the claims experience before the balance sheet date is bad, it may be that further claims are to be anticipated before the expiry of the policy. Provision may thus be necessary on a minority of policies for the 'premium deficiency' that has arisen.

The adequacy of the provision made for these policies needs to be reviewed in the light of statistics covering past experience and, of course, post balance sheet events.

(3) Profit on long-term business

The auditor has to report in 'true and fair' terms on the insurance company's position, and this must include a review of the actuary's report on the viability of the long-term business, and confirmation that any profit taken on long-term business which is treated as distributable has been properly calculated.

The audit work to be carried out in this area is:

—Confirm that the actuarial data used in the calculation is consistent with that in the accounting records.
—Discuss with the actuary the processes used in preparing the actuarial valuations.
—Ensure that the actuary has been made aware of recommendations the auditor has made to the company's management in connection with the administrative systems, and confirm with the actuary that none of these matters would affect the actuary's certificate.
—Confirm that the actuary has given, or is prepared to give, the necessary certificate that the liabilities relating to long-term business do not exceed the figure at which they are stated in the balance sheet.
—Read any formal reports made to the directors on the financial condition of the long-term funds, including any relating to the determination and allocation of surplus. Discuss with the actuary any aspects of those reports which are relevant to the adequacy of the provision made for long-term business liabilities.
—In the light of these formal reports, enquire of the actuary as the auditor considers necessary about the object of any full or estimated valuation of the liabilities, and about the main assumptions made therein. Ask whether any alteration in bases or assumptions since the previous valuation amount to a change in approach to the assessment of the liabilities, and ascertain the reasons for any such change.
—If a surplus has been determined ascertain the principles governing the amount of the surplus, its relation to the previous surplus, and the extent to which the surpluses may have been affected by material releases from or additions to provisions or reserves (for example, following a change in the

valuation approach). Ask about the implications of such releases or additions for the future emergence of surplus.

—In the case of a proprietary company (one owned by its policy-holders), discuss with the actuary whether any distribution of surplus made by the directors complies with the provisions of the Insurance Companies Act 1982.

—Discuss with the actuary the provisions made for activities on which up to date information was not available at the time of the valuation.

—Read, and discuss with the actuary, any correspondence relating to the company between the company or the appointed actuary and the Department of Trade or the Government Actuary's Department.

23.10 Charities

The audit of charities is the subject of an Auditing Guideline issued in 1981.

For the purposes of the Charities Act 1960 a charity is any institution, corporate or not, which is established exclusively for 'charitable purposes'. These are defined as:

(*a*) The relief of poverty;
(*b*) The advancement of education;
(*c*) The advancement of religion;
(*d*) Other purposes beneficial to the community not falling under any of the preceding heads.

In the UK, charities are regulated by the Charity Commissioners. Only a charity registered by them may claim the taxation reliefs extended to charities.

There is no automatic audit requirement, except of course for charities registered as companies. The Charity Commissioners have the power to require a charity's accounts to be audited.

Paragraphs 15 to 69 of the Guideline relate to accounting and auditing of charities, and these are reproduced below. The original paragraph numbers are retained to facilitate reference.

Accounting

Purpose of financial statements—stewardship
(15) Charities exist not to generate profits but to meet an identified objective; consequently their performance is often measured in financial terms, not by the surplus of income over expenditure, but rather by the size of the income and the way in which it has been spent. Thus the primary purpose of the annual financial statements of a charity is to account for the stewardship of the funds entrusted to it by the public, the state and others. Financial statements may also be necessary for other

reasons. For example, in the case of a corporate charity, financial statements must be prepared in a manner to comply with statutes.

Form of financial statements

(16) Under section 32 of the Charities Act 1960, charities are required to keep proper books of account and to prepare consecutive statements of account. Where a charity is subject to other statutory regulations, there may be a requirement in these for proper accounting records.

The financial statements usually comprise:

(a) a revenue account, which in many cases provides considerable detail; normally this will take the form of an income and expenditure account, but occasionally it is described as a 'statement of transactions or operations';

(b) a balance sheet, or more than one if considered appropriate for specific funds;

(c) a statement of source and application of funds;

(d) notes to the accounts.

(17) However, the financial statements of small charities are often a simple document such as a receipts and payments account and a concise statement of assets and liabilities.

Accounting policies

(18) It is essential that the financial statements of all charities should include a statement of the main accounting policies in accordance with SSAP 2. The disclosure of significant accounting policies assumes a greater importance than for other enterprises in the absence of specific guidance from the accountancy bodies on the application of Statements of Standard Accounting Practice to not-for-profit organisations and charities in particular. The most important accounting policies for a charity will probably include:

(a) the basis on which income has been taken to the credit of the revenue account (for example, accruals or cash basis, policy with regard to legacy income, gross or net profit from trading activities);

(b) the basis on which expenditure has been charged to the revenue account (for example, accrual or cash, costs including VAT);

(c) the accounting treatment of fixed assets and investments, including donated assets;

(d) the presentation of the special funds and the movements thereon;

(e) the treatment of branches.

Statements of Standard Accounting Practice

(19) Many charities are subject to a statutory or constitutional requirement for their financial statements to give a true and fair view and in many other cases it is clearly desirable that a true and fair view should be given. As indicated in the explanatory foreword to Statements of Standard Accounting Practice, SSAPs apply to all financial statements intended to give a true and fair view of financial position and profit or loss.

(20) However, the explanatory foreword recognises that 'there may be situations in

which for justifiable reasons accounting standards are not strictly applicable because they are impracticable or exceptionally, having regard to the circumstances, would be inappropriate or give a misleading view'. In considering the appropriateness of particular SSAPs to charities, it must be remembered that SSAPs have been prepared primarily with business enterprises in mind, whereas charities are not-for-profit organisations. As a result it is important for the auditor to use his judgement as to the appropriateness or otherwise of an SSAP to the individual circumstances of the charity concerned. If any specific accounting guidance is issued on the application of SSAPs to charities, the effect on this Guideline will be considered following publication of that guidance.

Some areas of activity requiring special attention

(21) *Included and excluded activities.* It is often difficult to decide where the charity's activities stop and a third party takes over. The criteria are:

(a) does the charity have control?
(b) is the activity undertaken by a body with a separate constitution?

It is sometimes necessary for a charity to take legal advice to determine which activities form part of the stewardship of the main charitable body and should be accounted for in the financial statements.

(22) *Cash income.* In practice a charity may find it difficult to institute procedures to ensure that all cash collections, often by volunteers, are properly accounted for in the books of account.

(23) The cut-off date for the cash income of some charities is not always the year-end date, a later date sometimes being adopted because of the importance of accounting for income collected but not yet remitted by voluntary supporters.

(24) *Donations in kind.* Charities are sometimes reluctant, or find it impracticable, to bring donations in kind into their books at their market value.

(25) *Legacies.* Because legacy income fluctuates considerably, charities frequently employ a Legacy Equalisation Account. Some problems of auditing legacy income are dealt with in paragraphs 33 and 35.

(26) *Specific funds.* (See also paragraph 60.) Charities may produce separate accounts to detail movements in certain funds for which they act as trustee or which represent monies raised for specific projects. Categories of specific funds include designated, restricted and endowment funds.

(27) *Central and local government grants and loans.* (See also paragraphs 34 and 57.) Charities can be eligible for a number of grants and loans, which can create problems in respect of:

(a) knowing of the existence of the grant or loan scheme and the right to claim;
(b) using the money for the correct purpose.

(28) *Other areas.* The following are considered elsewhere in this Guideline:

(a) overseas activities (paragraph 36);
(b) branches (paragraphs 35 and 58);
(c) depreciation (paragraph 59).

Auditing

Scope

(29) The scope of the audit will depend on the status of the charity and the form of report to be given. The charity may have been constituted:

(a) by trust deed;
(b) as an unincorporated association;
(c) as a company limited by guarantee under the Companies Acts;
(d) under the Acts relating to friendly or industrial and provident societies;
(e) by Royal Charter; or
(f) by special Act of Parliament.

(30) Where the charity is a company, a friendly or an industrial and provident society or in many cases where it is incorporated by special Act of Parliament, the minimum audit requirements are laid down by statute. In other cases, the constitutional documents should be examined to determine audit requirements and discussions held with the trustees of the charity. Even in cases where the audit requirements are well defined, the trustees should be consulted, as they may wish to expand the scope of the audit to cover, for example, specific instructions for the auditors to look for fraud. Once the scope of the audit has been established, it should be defined and explained in a suitably worded letter of engagement.

Key audit areas peculiar to charities

(31) *Donations and fund-raising.* It may be difficult to ensure the completeness and accuracy of recording of income from donations and fund-raising activities. Donations can also take the form of capital gifts such as shares or property, which require to be valued.

(32) Sources which may require the special attention of the auditor include:

(a) postal receipts;
(b) deeds of covenant;
(c) flag days and door-to-door collections;
(d) functions and meetings;
(e) other fund-raising events;
(f) donations in kind.

(33) *Legacies.* These may give rise to problems of completeness where, for example, they involve reversionary gifts. The auditor's review procedures should confirm that, where possible, the charity has followed up legacies.

(34) *Central and local government grants and loans.* The auditor should be familiar with the workings of the grant or loan system and the accepted ways of treating grants or loans in the financial statements.

(35) *Branches.* Some charities regard a voluntary organiser in a particular areas as a branch, while others only confer branch status on a local office. It can thus be difficult to decide the status of a branch, and whether its transactions and balances should or can be included in the main financial statements. This is a matter which might usefully be dealt with in a letter of engagement. Where a branch has its own separate constitution which is quite different from that of the main charity, its transactions and

balances will properly be excluded from the financial statements of the charity. Where the branch is so independent that it cannot be required to submit independent returns it may not be possible to include its transactions and balances. Where branches are excluded, it is essential that adequate disclosure is made in the financial statements, and consideration given as to whether the auditor's report should be suitably amplified or qualified. There may also be a problem for the auditor in forming an opinion on branches which do not have proper accounting disciplines.

(36) *Overseas activities.* Where records are maintained overseas and the amounts are material, the auditor should give consideration to a local audit. If remittances to overseas branches are treated as an expense when made, evidence of receipt will be required.

(37) *Specific funds.* Tests will need to be designed to confirm that these funds have been correctly accounted for and applied.

(38) *Grants to beneficiaries.* The auditor should confirm that the bona fides of the recipient have been established. For example, the auditor will look for evidence of the payment and bona fides of a sample of grants made by the charity, and scrutinise all grants of an unusual size or nature.

Procedures

(39) Paragraph 1 of 'The auditor's operational standard' states that

'This Auditing Standard applies whenever an audit is carried out.

The application of Auditing Standards is no more onerous in the case of charities than in the case of other organisations.

(40) The following procedures amplify those given in the operational guidelines which support 'The auditor's operational standard'. They do not impose on the auditor any additional requirements. For example, the internal controls operated by some charities, particularly small ones, whilst adequate for their own purposes, may not be sufficient for the purposes of reliance by the auditor in arriving at his opinion. In such cases the auditor would choose a substantive route and not rely upon controls which may exist.

(41) In all audits, the scope will be determined by, and the audit procedures used will vary in accordance with, the terms of the auditor's appointment. The level of audit evidence to be obtained will be a matter of judgement for the auditor in each individual case.

Planning

(42) When planning the audit of a charity the auditor should particularly consider the following:

(*a*) the scope of the audit (see paragraph 29);

(b) recent recommendations of the Charity Commissioners or the other regulatory bodies;

(c) the acceptability of accounting policies adopted;

(d) changes in circumstances in the sector in which the charity operates;

(e) changes in the scale or nature of the charity's operations;

(f) past experience of the effectiveness of the charity's accounting system;

(g) key audit areas (see paragraphs 31 to 38);

(h) the amount of detail included in the financial statements on which the auditor is required to report.

Accounting systems

(43) Some of the areas of activity requiring special attention when reviewing a charity's accounting system are listed in paragraphs 21 to 28.

Audit evidence

(44) When designing substantive tests for charities the auditor should give special attention to the possibility of:

(a) understatement or incompleteness of the recording of all income including gifts in kind, cash donations, and legacies;

(b) overstatement of cash grants or expenses;

(c) mis-analysis or misuse in the application of funds;

(d) mis-statement or omission of assets including donated properties and investments;

(e) the existence of restricted or uncontrollable funds in foreign or independent branches.

(45) The extent of testing required will depend on the scope of the audit. For example, the auditor may be required to report on financial statements which include considerable detail. Similarly, while the level of audit testing would provide reasonable expectation of detecting material mis-statements resulting from fraud, the charity may seek further assurance that fraud has not taken place.

(46) Normal analytical review procedures as applied to a commercial enterprise, including the comparison of one year's financial statements with another, may need to be modified in the case of a charity. Particular consideration should be given to the relationship between appeals income and related expenses, and investments and the income from such investments. A comparison of the funds raised by particular branches from one period to the next should also be carried out and explanations obtained for significant differences.

Internal controls

(47) The auditor will have to consider whether there are any internal controls on which he may wish to rely, or whether he will need to carry out extensive substantive testing. Large charities should have the internal controls appropriate to any large enterprise, and the auditor should look for and encourage the charity to implement normal internal controls and reporting systems in keeping with the scale of operations.

(48) Small charities will generally suffer from internal control weaknesses common to small enterprises, such as lack of segregation of duties and use of

unqualified staff. Shortcomings may arise from the staff's lack of training and also, if they are volunteers, from their attitude, in that they may resent formal procedures. The auditor will have to consider particularly carefully whether he will be able to obtain adequate assurance that the accounting records do reflect all the transactions of the enterprise. Adequate control may often be available in a small charity by means of increased review and authorisation procedures by the trustees or other officials of the charity.

(49) In considering internal controls the auditor should bear in mind any related reporting requirements. For example, the Friendly Societies Act 1974 requires the auditor to state in his report if a satisfactory system of control over transactions has not been maintained.

(50) Generally, the auditor will hope to be able to rely on the internal controls of the charity in one or more key areas wherever the volume of transactions makes this reliance desirable. For example, the auditor might wish to rely on the charity's system of authorising and controlling grants payments by the grants committee. His compliance tests might include checking with the minutes concerned and other documentation.

(51) Some indication of the internal controls which might be expected to be present in most charities is given in paragraphs 52 and 62 below. Other areas where the auditor might seek to rely on internal controls are dealt with in the Auditing Guideline, 'Internal controls'.

(52) *Donations—collecting boxes and tins*
(*a*) Numerical control over collecting boxes and tins.
(*b*) Satisfactory sealing of boxes and tins so that any opening prior to recording is apparent.
(*c*) Regular collection and recording of proceeds from collecting boxes.
(*d*) Dual control over counting and recording of proceeds.

(53) *Donations—postal and cash*
(*a*) Dual control over the opening of mail.
(*b*) Immediate recording of donations on opening mail or receipt of cash.

(54) *Deeds of covenant*
(*a*) Regular checks and follow up procedures to ensure due amounts are received.
(*b*) Regular checks to ensure all tax repayments have been obtained.

(55) *Legacies*
(*a*) Comprehensive correspondence files maintained in respect of each legacy, numerically controlled.
(*b*) Search agency reports of legacies receivable.
(*c*) Regular reports and follow-up procedures undertaken in respect of outstanding legacies.

(56) *Fund-raising activities*
(*a*) Records maintained for each fund-raising event.
(*b*) Comparable controls maintained over receipts as for normal donations.
(*c*) Comparable controls maintained over expenses as for administrative expenses.

(57) *Central and local government grants and loans*

(a) Regular checks that all sources of income or funds are fully exploited and appropriate claims made.

(b) Ensuring income or funds are correctly applied in accordance with the terms of the grant or loan.

(c) Comprehensive records of applications made and follow-up procedures for those not discharged.

(58) *Branches*

(a) Any branch, office or individual representative of the charity should make regular reports or returns to the charity, and checks should be made to ensure that all these are received.

(b) Any reports of the misuse of the charity's name should be promptly investigated.

(c) Wherever the trustees of the charity have direct control over the branches, internal controls should be of equivalent standard to that of the main charity.

(d) Consideration of an accounts manual and the standardisation of procedures at all branches.

(e) Proper acknowledgements of remittances to and from abroad.

(59) *Fixed assets and depreciation*

(a) A register of fixed assets maintained including donated assets.

(b) Assets vested in the Official Custodian, where appropriate.

(c) Donated assets recorded at approximate market value, where appropriate.

(d) Depreciation calculated and recorded as for commercial enterprises, where the accounting policy requires.

(60) *Specific funds*

Records maintained of:

(a) separate revenue and assets accounts;

(b) terms controlling application of fund monies;

(c) application of fund monies.

(61) *Grants to beneficiaries*

(a) Records maintained of all requests for material grants received and their treatments.

(b) Checks made of the bona fides of applicants for substantial grants, and that amounts paid are *intra vires*.

(c) Minutes maintained of all Grants Committee meetings with record of decisions made.

(d) Adequate documentation given to Committee for them to base their decision on the accurate facts.

(62) *Bank records*

In small charities the following controls will have particular significance:

(a) prompt banking of receipts:

(b) independent agreement of banking records to receipts records;

(c) regular bank reconciliations;

(d) scrutiny of returned cheques for unusual or frequent endorsements;

(e) adequate arrangements for bank signatories.

Review of financial statements

(63) The auditor must consider carefully whether the accounting policies adopted are appropriate to the activities, constitution and objectives of the charity, and are consistently applied, and whether the financial statements adequately disclose these policies and fairly present the state of affairs and the results for the accounting period.

(64) In particular the auditor should consider the basis of:

(a) disclosing income from fund-raising activities (for example, net or gross);
(b) accounting for income and expenses (accruals or cash);
(c) the capitalising of expenditure on fixed assets;
(d) apportioning administrative expenditure;
(e) recognising income from donations and legacies;
(f) treating exceptional and extraordinary items.

(65) In determining whether the financial statements comply with all relevant statutory requirements and other regulations, it is necessary to take account of the legal framework within which a particular charity operates.

(66) In determining whether proper disclosures have been made, the auditor should consider the presentation of:

(a) special or irregular income or expenditure;
(b) specific funds;
(c) net surplus/deficit for the period;
(d) allocation of funds;
(e) movements on particular funds;
(f) statements of source and application of funds;
(g) realised and unrealised surpluses/deficits on disposal or revaluation of assets;
(h) branch accounts;
(i) detailed analysis of income and expenses.

(67) Charities without significant endowments or accumulated funds will often be dependent upon future income from voluntary sources, in order to meet the financial commitments arising from the continuation of their activities. In these circumstances, the review of the financial statements may lead the auditor to question whether a going concern basis of accounting is appropriate. He should therefore, in forming a conclusion on the matter, take account of the amount of, and trends in, income and expenditure since the accounting date, any forecasts and representations by management as to future income and expenditure and (where relevant) the market value of the charity's tangible assets.

Reporting

(68) Where the auditor is to express an opinion on financial statements intended to give a true and fair view this Guideline should also be read in conjunction with the Auditing Standards. 'The audit report' and 'Qualifications in audit reports' together with the Auditing Guideline 'Audit report examples'.

(69) The form of auditor's report and the persons to whom it will be addressed will depend on the constitution of the particular charity concerned. For example, the auditor's report on the financial statements of a charity registered under the

Companies Acts is determined in accordance with the provisions of those Acts and addressed to the members or appropriate governing body. The auditor's report on the financial statements of a charity registered under the Acts relating to friendly or industrial and provident socieities will be in another form and addressed to the charity itself. In other cases, where charities are not governed by statute, the auditor's report will be determined in accordance with the terms of the auditor's appointment. For example, it may be appropriate for the auditor to report only that the financial statements have been prepared in compliance with regulations governing the charity's operations.

23.11 Trade unions and employers' associations

23.11.1 Introduction

The Trade Union and Labour Relations Act 1974 (TULRA) requires all trade unions and employers' associations (referred to collectively below as trade unions) to submit audited accounts to the Certification Officer for Trade Unions and Employers' Associations (the Certification Officer).

In 1984 the APC issued an Auditing Guideline entitled 'Trade unions and employers' associations'. Relevant extracts from this Guideline are reproduced below.

23.11.2 Accounting requirements

Section 10 of the Act requires every trade union (except one which consists wholly or mainly of representatives of constituent or affiliated organizations) to:

(a) establish and maintain a satisfactory system of control of its accounting records, its cash holdings and its receipts and remittances; and

(b) keep proper accounting records with respect to its transactions, assets and liabilities.

These records must be such as to give a true and fair view of the trade union and to explain its transactions.

Under S11(2) of the Act every trade union to which S10 applies is also required (unless it has been in existence for less than 12 months) to submit an annual return, relating to its affairs, to the Certification Officer. Schedule 2 of the Act requires the annual return to be for a calender year and to be filed by 1 June, except where the Certification Officer directs that it should be for a different period and amends the time limit for filing.

Under the Act, the responsibilities of trade unions and employers' associations include preparing revenue and other accounts and a balance sheet which give a true and fair view of the matters to which they relate (Schedule 2 of the Act). In this context, it is preferable for a trade union working through branches to include the transactions, assets and liabilities of all the branches unless the accounts relating to certain branches are included in, or covered by, separate annual returns. It should also include those transactions, assets and liabilities relating directly to the rules or objects of the trade union, even where they are dealt with by way of a separate entity such as a limited company or a registered friendly society.

Schedule 2 of the Act also requires the revenue accounts to be prepared on an income and expenditure basis and not on a receipts and payments basis. The accounting records of the trade union should therefore be maintained in such a manner as to enable the revenue accounts to be produced on the basis laid down in the Act. This would involve the inclusion of members' contributions in arrears except where, after any necessary provisions for contributions which are not considered to be collectable, the amount is immaterial.

23.11.3 Appointment of auditor

Section 11(3) requires every trade union to appoint an auditor to audit the accounts contained in its annual return. Schedule 2 of the Act prescribes who may be appointed and provides that the auditor of a trade union should make a report to the trade union on the accounts audited by him or her and contained in its annual return. This report should state whether in the opinion of the auditor these accounts give a true and fair view of the matters to which they relate.

The auditor also has a duty to carry out such investigations as will enable him or her to form an opinion on whether proper accounting records have been kept, whether a satisfactory system of control over transactions has been maintained and whether the accounts are in agreement with the accounting records. If these statutory requirements have not in the auditor's opinion been satisfied, or if he or she fails to obtain the necessary information and explanations, this fact must be stated in the report.

Schedule 2 of the Act provides the auditor with the following rights:

(*a*) the right of access at all times to the accounting records of the trade union including those of branches dealt with in its annual return, and to all other documents relating to its affairs;

(*b*) the right to require from officers of the trade union, or of any of its branches, such information and explanations as he or she considers necessary;

(*c*) the right to attend general meetings of members or of delegates of members and to receive due notices of such meetings;

(*d*) the right to be heard at such meetings on any part of the business which concerns the auditor.

Schedule 2 of the Act also requires the trade union rules to contain provision for the appointment and removal of auditors and also prescribes both the scope of the audit and the terms of the auditor's report on the accounts included in the annual return. The auditors' responsibilities in connection with the annual financial statements may not be specifically covered in the trade union rules regarding audit ('audit rules') on such matters as:

(*a*) The scope of their audit;
(*b*) to whom they are reporting; and
(*c*) the terms of their report.

Problems can also arise where the audit rules provide that the auditors' responsibilities will be determined by the executive committee or senior officials.

23.11.4 Auditing procedures

The following procedures are supplementary to those given in the operational Auditing Guidelines.

(a) Planning

Because of the problems indicated above, auditors should pay particular attention to the wording of the audit rules and to minutes recording decisions regarding audit made by the executive committee. They should send an engagement letter to the executive committee to confirm their understanding of the terms of their appointment. The letter should indicate that they are required to state whether in their opinion the accounts contained in the annual return give a true and fair view. It should also indicate the matters which they are required to state in their report on the annual financial statements. In most cases, these will include their opinion on whether these statements give a true and fair view. The auditors should also use the engagement letter to exclude any requirements which they cannot reasonably fulfil, such as a requirement for them to 'certify' the annual financial statements as being 'correct'. Where the rules provide that the auditors should report in terms such as 'the financial statements are in accordance with the books and records', the auditors should bear in mind their statutory obligation to report in true and fair terms on the accounts contained in the annual return.

The engagement letter should deal with the treatment of branch funds within the annual return and the annual financial statements and the extent to which such branch funds are included within the scope of the auditor's responsibilities. It should also clarify the scope of the audit in respect of any activities where the connection with the rules or objects of the trade union is in doubt.

Auditors will need to consider the extent to which it is necessary to visit and examine the records maintained at branches. They will take into account the manner in which head office exercises its responsibilities for control and supervision over the accounting records maintained at branch level and whether separate branch auditors are appointed.

Branch financial statements are frequently audited by individuals or firms other than the auditors of the trade unions themselves. Such branch auditors may be either professionally qualified or unqualified. Trade union auditors, however, are responsible for reporting on the accounts contained in the annual return and/or the annual financial statements prepared by the trade union and, if these incorporate branch transactions, the auditors should take this matter into account when planning their audit. They will need to consider the extent to which they can rely on other auditors.

The trade union auditors should consider preparing a standard form of audit programme which could be used by branch auditors and requiring it to be completed, signed and submitted direct to themselves, together with any questionnaire which they might think is appropriate. This does not, however, relieve the trade union auditors from the need to consider the adequacy of audit arrangements and to communicate further with branch auditors to the extent they consider necessary.

When planning the audit of a trade union the auditors should also consider:

(1) The need, when reporting on the accounts contained in the annual return, to carry out investigations to enable them to form an opinion as to whether the trade union has maintained a satisfactory system of control over its transactions;

(2) The degree of reliance that they may wish to place on internal controls in order to arrive at an opinion on the accounts contained in the annual return and/or the annual financial statements;

(3) The amount of detail included in the financial statements on which the auditors are required to report;

(4) Decisions of the annual conference or executive committees of the trade union which affect the audit or the matters upon which the auditors are required to report;

(5) Any comments made by the Certification Officer following the submission of the previous year's annual return;

(6) The reports issued by the Certification Officer and the guidance notes contained within the form of annual return for the current year;

(7) Any changes which might have taken place in the law relating to trade unions and employers' associations.

(b) Accounting systems

Paragraph 8 of the Auditing Guideline 'Accounting systems' states that 'the auditor will need to obtain an understanding of the enterprise as a whole and how the accounting system reflects assets and liabilities and transactions'. In connection with this requirement, a trade union auditor will have to examine the system whereby branches within the scope of the audit account for trade union contributions and other items of income and expenditure administered on behalf of the trade union. This will involve the auditor in assessing the adequacy of periodic returns from branches as a basis for the preparation of accounts. If a branch does not submit periodic returns, the auditor should ascertain whether or not the excluded branches are submitting their own annual returns to the Certification Officer. He or she should also examine the rules and any supplementary decisions made under the rules to ascertain the rights and responsibilities of the branches concerned and the degree of their accountability to head office.

Members' contributions represent the largest source of income for most trade unions. It will therefore be necessary for the auditors to obtain an understanding of the accounting system in respect of contributions. In order to make an assessment of its adequacy they will have to consider its completeness. This will involve their examining the methods for updating membership and contribution records, the procedures for ensuring that all contributions due (including those collected by employers) are properly received and the arrangements for ensuring that all contributions are banked promptly and intact. They should also examine the systems dealing with arrears of contributions.

In particular, where there are delays between the date of collection and remittance to the trade union, the auditors will need to satisfy themselves as to the appropriateness of the method of determining arrears and the reasonableness of the figures produced.

(c) Audit evidence

Two important sources of audit evidence are the trade union rules and minuted decisions. Areas in which these sources are likely to be important are:

(1) Contributions (including political fund contributions) and entrance fees.
The auditors will have to consider whether contributions and entrance fees
have been collected at the correct rates.

(2) Fines and special levies receivable. The auditors will have to consider
whether the trade union has power to enforce fines and certain special levies.

(3) Benefits payable. Most benefits are recurring expenditure for which the
trade union rules lay down the basis of entitlement, the scales of benefit and
the terms and conditions of benefit. One of the principal conditions is usually
that the applicant is not in arrears with his contributions.

(4) Travel, subsistence and attendance payments and allowances. Apart
from day-to-day travel and subsistence of officials or employees in the course
of trade union business, payments are frequently made in connection with
attendance at conferences, negotiating committees and fraternal delegations.
The auditors will have to consider whether such payments made are in
accordance with agreed scales.

(5) Dispute payments and receipts. Industrial disputes sometimes involve
payment of dispute benefit (strike pay) and related expenses, and occasionally
involve the receipt of donations at local or national level. Although these
situations are usually referred to in the trade union rules, they are normally
too infrequent and the circumstances too varied to warrant detailed
treatment. The conduct of such disputes is accordingly usually determined by
decisions of the appropriate executive committee. The auditors should,
therefore, take note of the detailed proposals for the conduct of the dispute
as expressed in the relevant minutes or be satisfied that decisions taken are in
accordance with properly delegated authority. They should also devise tests
to check whether receipts and payments are in accordance with properly
delegated authority and also whether they are in accordance with the system
laid down and are properly evidenced.

(d) Requirement to maintain adequate internal controls

The Auditing Guideline 'Internal controls' has particular relevance to the
audit of trade unions. This is because of:

(1) The specific requirement (see Section 23.11.2 above) on most trade unions
to establish and maintain satisfactory systems of control over their
accounting records, their cash holdings, receipts and remittances;

(2) The duties (see Section 23.11.3 above) on auditors reporting on accounts
contained in annual returns to carry out investigations into, and where
necessary, to report on such systems.

Large trade unions should have the internal controls appropriate to any
large enterprise, and the auditors should look for and encourage such unions

to implement normal internal controls and reporting systems in keeping with the scale of operations. Small trade unions and branches, even those of large trade unions, will generally suffer from internal control weaknesses common to small enterprises, such as lack of segregation of duties and use of unqualified or part-time staff. Shortcomings may possibly arise in the implementation of formal procedures from the staff's lack of training, particularly if they are volunteers. Adequate control may often be available by means of increased review and authorization procedures by committee members or other officials of the trade union.

(e) Types of internal control

In addition to the controls necessary in most organizations and covered in earlier chapters, the following are the specific controls which should be present where relevant in trade unions:

(1) Financial organization
—Preparation and appraisal of budgets.
—Comparison of actual performance against budgets.
—Monitoring in detail by specific committees or officers of expenditure incurred.

(2) Contributions (including political fund contributions) and entrance fees
—Regular checks to ensure that the membership and contribution records are being kept up-to-date.
—Ensuring that contributions and entrance fees are collected at the appropriate rates.
—Reconciliations between contributions and entrance fees received and the membership and contribution records.
—Investigation of arrears by officials. Where possible, these officials should not be responsible for collecting or handling contributions or entrance fee moneys.
—Checks to ensure that any amounts accounted for by branch officers or other persons collecting contributions are in accordance with agreed rates and any deductions for collecting commissions or locally incurred expenditure are properly controlled.

(3) Fines and special levies receivable
Regular checks to ensure that fines and special levies receivable are properly imposed and recorded, and are in accordance with agreed rates.

(4) Benefits payable
—Regular checks to ensure that benefits payable are properly recorded.

—Checks to ensure that applicants fulfil all conditions necessary before receiving benefit.

(5) Travel, subsistence and attendance payments and allowances
—Regular checks to ensure that claims are bona fide.
—Ensuring that payments are made in accordance with agreed scale rates.
—Checks to ensure that claims for loss of earnings are properly supported.

(6) Dispute payments and receipts
—Ensuring that dispute payments and receipts are properly recorded.
—Checks to ensure that dispute payments and receipts are dealt with in accordance with the trade union rules, minuted decisions or decisions made by officials with appropriate authority.

(7) Separate funds
Checks to ensure that income and expenditure, assets and liabilities and numbers of members contributing are properly identified and recorded in respect of each separate fund.

(8) Cash and bank
—Prompt banking of receipts.
—Independent agreement of banking records to receipt records.
—Regular bank reconciliations.
—Adequate arrangements for bank signatories.
—Periodic checking of petty cash by an independent official.

(9) Investments
—Ensuring that investments are properly recorded.
—Periodic checks to ensure that all investment income due is in fact received.
—Proper authorization of purchases and disposals of investments.
—Regular checking of the register of investments with evidence of title.

(10) Properties
—Ensuring that all property transactions are properly authorized.
—Ensuring that all properties are properly recorded and that all rental income due is in fact received.

(f) Presentation and disclosure

In connection with the presentation and disclosure, the auditor should consider whether:

(1) the treatment of transactions, assets and liabilities relating to the rules and objects of the trade union, is appropriate;

(2) the treatment of branch funds is appropriate;

(3) there has been proper disclosure of separate funds, including any political funds set up in accordance with the Trade Union Act 1913;

(4) there has been appropriate disclosure of the allocation of the income and expenditure between funds and of any transfers between funds;

(5) a single statement of source and application of funds is appropriate where there are several revenue accounts produced, each covering separate activities of the trade union.

Where the annual return is completed some considerable time after the auditor has signed the audit report on the annual financial statements, the auditor should update the review of events after the balance sheet date and consider the effect that this might have on the report on the accounts contained in the annual return. The review should cover the period to the date of the report.

In reviewing the accounts contained in the annual return and/or the annual financial statements to ensure compliance with requirements the auditor should consider:

(*a*) the trade union rules and if relevant, delegated decisions; and

(*b*) the Act and any regulations made thereunder.

(g) The audit reports

(1) The audit report on the accounts in the annual return

The audit report on the accounts contained in the annual return is required to be in 'true and fair' terms, and should, of course, be dated.

Auditors should also state expressly in their report whether:

—the accounts have been audited in accordance with approved Auditing Standards;

—in their opinion, the accounts give a true and fair view of the state of the trade union's financial affairs, transactions, and where applicable, source and application of funds.

Under Schedule 2 of the Act, auditors must also state the fact in their report, where in their opinion:

—proper accounting records have not been maintained;

—a satisfactory system of control over its transactions has not been maintained;

—the accounts are not in agreement with the accounting records;

—they have not obtained the necessary information and explanations that they require.

In these circumstances auditors should include in their report a separate 'explanatory' paragraph outlining the facts giving rise to qualification. They are not required, however, to state in their report whether the accounts contained in the annual return comply with the Act.

(2) The audit report on the annual financial statements
The audit report on the annual financial statements should identify the members of the trade union as the persons to whom it is addressed, unless the trade union rules require it to be addressed to other persons such as the 'Executive Committee'. It should also identify the financial statements to which it relates.

The terms of the audit report will depend on the requirements set out in the trade union rules as confirmed in the engagement letter. In most cases, however, the audit report will be required to be in true and fair terms. Consequently regard will normally have to be paid to the Auditing Standards 'The audit report' and 'Qualifications in audit reports' and the Auditing Guideline 'Audit report examples'.

23.12 Friendly societies and industrial and provident societies

23.12.1 Introduction

We must begin by defining exactly what on earth 'friendly' societies are. In origin they, and the industrial and provident societies, were small-scale insurance companies, offering benefits to members in sickness, old age, widowhood, etc. Working men's clubs may offer such benefits as well as social facilities and may thus be registered as friendly societies. A few friendly societies have grown in size and offer insurance services to members invited from the public at large. They are governed by several statutes, which require them, among other things, to keep proper accounting records and to appoint auditors.

23.12.2 The relevant statutes

(a) The Friendly and Industrial and Provident Societies Act 1968 (FIPSA).
(b) Friendly Societies Acts 1974 and 1984 (FSA).
(c) Industrial and Provident Societies Act 1965 (IPSA).

IPSA sets out the general rules governing industrial and provident societies.

FIPSA and FSA set out the accounting and auditing requirements for industrial and provident societies and friendly societies respectively.

23.12.3 The accounting requirements of FIPSA and FSA

Societies registered under these Acts must:

(*a*) keep proper accounting records
(*b*) maintain a satisfactory system of internal control
(*c*) prepare annual accounts showing a true and fair view
(*d*) submit an annual return to the Registrar of Friendly Societies which must include audited accounts.

23.12.4 The auditing requirements of FIPSA and FSA

(*a*) Provisions governing the auditor

The provisions governing the appointment, qualifications and removal of the auditor of a society are broadly the same as those of the Companies Act 1985.

(*b*) Provisions governing the audit

The auditor is required to report in true and fair terms on the balance sheet and revenue account.

Some friendly societies engage in activities in the nature of insurance. Although the auditors are not specifically required to deal with the question of actuarial solvency, disclosure of actuarial information in relation to the solvency of the society is an essential requirement of the true and fair view.

23.13 Housing associations

23.13.1 Introduction

A Housing association is a non-profit-making organization which exists to construct houses and other accommodation.

If they are to receive certain loans, grants and subsidies payable under the Housing Acts they must register with the Housing Corporation, which was formed by the Housing Act 1964 and given additional powers by the Housing Acts 1974 and 1980. The Housing Corporation may only register housing associations which are also friendly societies (see Section 23.12 above) or charities (see Section 23.10).

In 1984 the APC issued an Auditing Guideline entitled 'Housing associations'. The notes which follow are an abridged version of this Guideline.

23.13.2 Accounting requirements

Housing associations are required to lodge copies of their audited accounts with the Housing Corporation within six months of the end of the period to which they relate.

Housing associations which are friendly societies will also lodge their accounts with the Registrar of Friendly Societies.

Housing associations which are charities will, if required by the Charity Commissioners, have to file their accounts with the Commissioners.

Housing associations which are companies will have to comply with the requirements of the Companies Act.

The accounts lodged with the Housing Corporation must consist of:

(*a*) balance sheet
(*b*) income and expenditure account
(*c*) statement of source and application of funds
(*d*) property revenue account and a statement of housing administration costs (not required for co-ownership societies)
(*e*) for co-ownership societies, a housing cost and finance statement.

The accounts must comply with relevant SSAPs.

23.13.3 Auditing requirements and procedures

The Auditing Guideline contains a great deal of detail reflecting the specialized nature of the operations of housing associations and their varied legal background. Much of this material is not thought to be of examination significance and is accordingly not covered here in full. Readers interested in pursuing the subject further should refer to the full text of the Guideline.

Two areas are singled out as of examination importance:

—factors to be considered in designing tests
—internal controls peculiar to housing associations.

(*a*) Factors to be considered in designing tests

The Guideline suggests that the auditor should give special attention to the possibility of:

(1) understatement or incompleteness of the recording of income including

rents, service charges and where appropriate rates from tenants, proceeds from the sale of properties, gifts in kind and cash donations;

(2) grants claimed being disallowed after the balance sheet date;

(3) payments made for repair work, when no work has in fact been carried out;

(4) prohibited payments made not being disclosed;

(5) housing land being sold or otherwise disposed of without the consent of the Housing Corporation;

(6) housing accommodation being misstated or omitted;

(7) loans incurred not being recorded;

(8) rents in respect of development schemes not being properly accounted for between capital and revenue. (Under the Housing Association Grant system, parts of the rents received during a development period should be capitalized if the scheme exceeds fifty units.)

(b) Internal controls peculiar to housing associations

(1) Rents
—Periodic checking (by an official other than a rent collector) of notification of voids, of rent registrations and of changes in the housing stock to the rent ledger and tenants' rent books;
—Reconciliation of rents receivable to the number of units, registered rents and the incidence of voids;
—Rotation of collectors and comparison of their performance;
—Arrears procedures by a person who is not responsible for collecting or handling rent monies;
—Regular comparisons between the rent ledger and the banking records.

(2) Service charges and, where appropriate, rates
—Reconciliation of service charges receivable with the number of units, the service charges determined by the rent officer and the incidence of voids;
—Arrears procedures by a person who is not responsible for collecting or handling service charge or rate monies;
—Procedures to ensure that rate refunds are obtained for void periods and that nil assessments are obtained when the property is uninhabitable.

(3) Property development
—Proper tendering procedures (e.g. procedures in accordance with 'Housing Corporation Schemework Procedure Guide');
—Involvement of the managing body in the appointment of consultants;

—Authorization procedures, involving the management body, before properties are purchased;
—inspection and approval procedures before payment.

(4) Disposal of housing land
—Authorization procedures, involving the managing body;
—Scrutiny by an independent official to ensure that, where appropriate,
Housing Corporation consent has been obtained, and that disposal
proceeds have been properly received and accounted for.

(5) Grants and loans
—Regular checks that all sources of income or funds are fully utilized and
that appropriate claims have been made;
—Procedures to ensure that income or funds are correctly applied in
accordance with the grant or loan;
—Controls over application for grants and loans;
—Reconciliations between property costs and property mortgages.

(6) Housing accommodation
—Controls to ensure that all housing accommodation is recorded and to
ensure that all changes are reflected in the records.

(7) Repairs
—Procedures for obtaining tenders or quotations, particularly in respect of
major repair work
—inspection and approval procedures before payment
—comparison of repair costs against budgets.

23.14 Share transfer audit

It is part of the normal process of the audit that the issued share capital and
debentures shown in the balance sheet will be agreed with the total of the
balances in the share register or register of debenture-holders.

In the course of checking, the auditor will record any major transfer of
shares which may change the control of the company, or exceed a limit
relevant for disclosure or accounting treatment.

The detailed checking of the share transfers is not part of the normal audit,
however, and this will only be done if specially requested. A separate fee
would be quoted for a share transfer audit, and it would not form part of the
audit fee reported in the accounts.

A suitable audit programme for a share transfer audit is given below:

1. Review internal control procedures in the registration department, paying particular attention to:

(*a*) controls over unused share certificates, including adequacy of custody and authorization procedures;

(*b*) system of routine checking of transfers before processing:

    (i)   names and addresses

    (ii) description and number of shares

    (iii) signature

2. Compliance tests to confirm satisfactory operation of controls.

3. Substantive tests:

(*a*) Check transfers with the transfer register, making certain that transfers have been properly signed and stamped, and check the distinctive numbers of the shares into the register. Thereafter, cancel the transfer with the auditor's stamp. If the shares have been converted into stock, there will, of course, not be any distinctive numbers to check.

(*b*) Verify a proportion of the signatures of transferors with shareholders' previous transfers, application letters, or dividend instructions.

(*c*) Check old certificates with transfers, and thereafter cancel the certificates.

(*d*) Check entries in the transfer register to the credit of the transferor's account in share ledger, seeing that the transferor has the shares and checking the distinctive numbers.

(*e*) Check entries in the transfer register to the debit of the transferee's account in the share ledger.

(*f*) Check and initial new certificates, and if the transferor has not sold the whole of his or her shares, check and initial balance certificates issued.

(*g*) At subsequent audits, see the directors' minute passing the transfers previously checked.

(*h*) Count the number of transfers, and see that the whole of the transfer fees, if charged, have been accounted for.

23.15 Auditors' reports to trustees under debenture and loan stock trust deeds

It is normal practice for the auditors of a company which has issued debentures or loan stock to be asked by the company to furnish to the trustees for the stockholders a certificate or report confirming that any restriction on the company's total borrowings imposed by the trust deed has been observed.

The scope of the report will be determined by the trust deed and the auditor should obviously read it with care and report only in strict accordance with its terms.

The circumstances in which auditors are likely to be required to report are now reviewed.

(a) Unsecured loan stocks

(1) Most unsecured loan stock trust deeds contain an overall limit on the borrowings of the company, or of the company and its UK subsidiaries, or of the company and all its subsidiaries—'the overall borrowing limit'. The overall borrowing limit is usually a multiple of the adjusted capital and reserves of the company and its UK subsidiaries or the company and all its subsidiaries, based on a consolidation of their latest available audited balance sheets.

(2) In addition, some trust deeds contain a more restrictive limit ('the inner limit') on the total of the secured borrowings of the company and of any guaranteeing subsidiary, and all borrowings, whether or not secured, of non-guaranteeing subsidiaries. These borrowings rank ahead of the unsecured loan stock, and this is the justification for a more severe restriction.

(3) Both the overall and the inner limits are usually running limits, i.e. the limits have to be satisfied at all times whilst the stock is outstanding. Typically the borrowing limit is established when the audited accounts are available and becomes effective as of that date, remaining unchanged until the next audited accounts except for specified adjustments such as subscriptions of additional capital. Trustees are frequently entitled to request a report from the auditor as to the borrowing limits and borrowings at a date during the year. However, in order to save costs for the company, trustees will usually ask for the report to be given as at the end of the company's financial year when the state of affairs is, in any event, being examined by the auditor for the purpose of the annual accounts. Where the trustees think the company may be getting close to or may have exceeded its limits, the trustees may require a report at other times.

(b) Secured debenture stocks

(1) These stocks are secured by a floating charge on the undertaking and assets of the company and sometimes also of some of its subsidiaries. The trust deed will often confer upon the company a right to create further stock, and upon the company and the charging subsidiaries a right to create certain charges ranking ahead of the floating charge securing the stock, or other charges ranking alongside the stock, provided that the capital and income cover requirements specified by the trust deed will be met immediately afterwards.

(2) The usual capital cover restriction is that the stock and the secured

borrowings ranking ahead of or alongside the stock will not exceed some specified percentage of the 'adjusted capital and reserves' of the companies which have given charges to secure the stock. There may be a further more restrictive limit on borrowings ranking ahead of the stock (priority borrowings). The income cover requirement is usually that the interest payable on the stock and other secured borrowings ranking alongside, or ahead of it, will not exceed some specified proportion of the profits of the companies securing the stock, averaged over a period, often three years.

(3) The deed usually makes it a precondition of any such further charge that an auditor's report confirming that the capital and income cover will be met immediately after the issue of the new stock is given to the trustees shortly before the transaction.

(4) The foregoing cover requirements are usually not running limits, but are formulae which have to be satisfied only on the occasions the particular transaction concerned is undertaken.

(5) There are also certain transactions which are usually restricted unless the specified cover will be met immediately after they are completed, e.g. the transfer of assets from the charging companies to a non-charging subsidiary. An auditor's report is not always made a precondition for such a transaction; but even where it is not, the company or the trustees may require such a report in order to establish that the transaction will not be in breach of the trust deed.

(6) The auditor should also be aware of the existence and the effect of clauses in the trust deed that restrict the disposal of specified classes of assets, such as freehold land and buildings, to a fixed percentage of the company's total assets. Such clauses are designed to protect the quality of the assets held by a company. The restriction normally operates cumulatively from the date of the trust deed, and is therefore not limited to any one financial year.

(7) In addition, *debenture stock* trust deeds sometimes contain an overall borrowing limit, established on an annual basis, on the same lines as those found in *unsecured loan stock* trust deeds. These are usually running limits, and the trustees may therefore require periodic reports to check compliance.

(c) Mortgage debenture stocks

(1) These stocks are usually secured by mortgages over immovable property. They sometimes contain provisions under which further stock can be issued to rank alongside the existing stock if certain capital and income covers will be achieved immediately after the issue. The capital cover will normally be a requirement that the value of the property in the security should exceed by some multiple the amount of the stock it will secure. The income cover requirement will usually be that the net income of the property within the security should exceed by some multiple the interest payable on the stock it secures.

(2) In order to establish compliance with these covers, the trust deed will normally make it a condition for the issue of further stock and certain other transactions that professional valuers should report on the value of the property to the trustees. Sometimes trust deeds require valuers to report on the net income of the properties, and sometimes they require the auditors to report on it.

23.16 Summary

23.16.1 Solicitors

Solicitors are required by the Solicitors' Accounts Rules 1975 to maintain separate records for the accounts of each client and to keep clients' money in a separate bank account.

The Accountants' Report Rules 1975 require them to appoint a qualified accountant to inspect their clients' records and report to the Law Society on their compliance with the Accounts Rules.

23.16.2 Estate agents

The Estate Agents Act 1979 came into force in 1982 and requires estate agents to follow broadly the same rules as solicitors in their handling of clients' money. A qualified accountant is required to inspect the records to confirm compliance, but no report has to be submitted to a regulating body.

23.16.3 Chartered surveyors

The Accounts Regulations of the Royal Institution of Chartered Surveyors (RICS) closely follow the Solicitors' Accounts Rules and an accountant's report as to compliance must be sent to the RICS.

23.16.4 Insurance brokers

Insurance brokers must submit annual audited accounts to the Insurance Brokers' Registration Council. There must also be an accountant's report confirming solvency and that all insurance monies are held at approved banks in an account designated 'Insurance Broking Account'.

23.16.5 Pension Schemes

Statement of Recommended Practice 1 (SORP 1) proposes that pension scheme accounts should consist of:

(a) trustees' report;
(b) audited accounts;
(c) actuary's statement;
(d) investment report.

Full details of the development of the fund and of the assets held should be given.

There is no statutory requirement for the audit of pension schemes but many pension scheme trust deeds require one. When there is an audit, apart from the normal matters of verifying income, expenditure, assets and liabilities, the auditor will need to consider the viability of the scheme in association with the advising actuaries.

23.16.6 Building societies

Building societies are not companies but are governed by the Building Societies Act 1962 which imposes broadly the same accounting and auditing requirements on them as those in the Companies Act 1985.

The audit of building societies is covered by an Auditing Guideline issued by the APC in 1982.

Audit procedures may be divided into two to reflect the two aspects of a building society's work:

(a) deposit taking
(b) lending on mortgage.

23.16.7 Banks

Banks, as companies, are subject to the requirements of the Companies Act 1985 as to accounts and audit. They are exempt from some of the accounting disclosure requirements, though the clearing banks have for some years waived their right to the exemptions.

Audit work may be divided into work on branches, which will be visited in rotation and in coordination with the work of internal auditors, and work at head office or the centralized computer accounting system.

The nature of the business means that the highest standards of internal control must operate.

Provisions for doubtful debts, both at branch level and in the bank's international operations, if any, need special attention.

23.16.8 Insurance companies

Insurance companies are subject to the Companies Act 1985 and to the Insurance Companies Act 1982. Although they are exempt, like banks, from some of the Companies Act disclosure requirements, the Insurance Companies Act 1982 requires greater disclosure than for companies in other areas, notably in the analysis of investments held and the separation of long-term and short-term business.

Special features in the audit of insurance companies are the adequacy of provisions for claims, some of which take several years to settle and may thus be extremely difficult to quantify, and the need to work closely with the advising actuaries in assessing the valuation placed on long-term assets and liabilities.

23.16.9 Charities

The audit of charities is covered by an Auditing Guideline issued by the APC in 1981. There is no automatic audit requirement but the Charity Commissioners, who are responsible for the registration and supervision of charities, have the power to order a charity's accounts to be audited. In addition, of course, the constitution and rules of the charity may require an audit.

The audit programme calls for routine verification of income and expenses, assets and liabilities.

Special points of concern to auditors are:

(*a*) possible weaknesses in internal control procedures resulting from the use of voluntary assistants;

(*b*) compliance with the rules of the charity in the disposition of money raised.

23.16.10 Trade unions and employers' associations

These bodies are governed by the Trade Union and Labour Relations Act 1974 (TULRA), which requires them to submit audited accounts to the Certification Officer for Trade Unions and Employers' Associations.

The accounting and audit requirements broadly follow those of the Companies Act.

The detailed audit requirements are covered in an Auditing Guideline issued by the APC in 1984.

23.16.11 Friendly societies and industrial and provident societies

These societies are governed by several statutes which impose broadly the same accounting and auditing requirements on them as the Companies Act 1985 does on companies.

In addition to the routine work of verifying income and expenses, assets and liabilities, the auditor may be involved in consultations with the society's advising actuaries if insurance business is transacted.

23.16.12 Housing associations

Housing associations are required to lodge copies of their audited accounts with the Housing Corporation set up under the Housing Acts 1964 to 1980.

The audit of housing associations is covered by an Auditing Guideline issued by the APC in 1984.

23.16.13 Share transfer audit

Although some work on the share register is necessary as part of the statutory audit of a company, this does not include the detailed checking of the share transfers. An audit of these transactions forms a separate appointment for a share transfer audit.

23.16.14 Reports under debenture trust deeds

Auditors may be asked to report to the trustees under debenture and loan stock trust deeds to confirm that the company has not exceeded any limitations placed by the deed on its borrowings.

Progress questions

Questions	Reference for answers
(1)(a) What is the primary purpose of the Solicitors' Accounts Rules 1975?	Section 23.2.1
(b) What detailed requirements do the Rules lay down to achieve this purpose?	Section 23.2.2
(2) What work is required of the accountant reporting under the Accountants' Report Rules 1975 applicable to solicitors?	Section 23.2.3
(3) What is the primary purpose of the rules governing estate agents and surveyors set up in: (a) the Estate Agents Act 1979;	Section 23.3.1
(b) the Accounts Regulations of the Royal Institute of Chartered Surveyors?	Section 23.4
(4) What matters must be covered in the Accountant's Report on the accounts of insurance brokers under the Insurance Brokers (Registration) Act 1977?	Section 23.5
(6)(a) In the accounts of a pension scheme what are the four main reports as recommended in ED 34?	Section 23.6.1
(b) Give a brief indication of the contents of each.	Sections 23.6.2– 23.6.5
(c) What special points should also be disclosed?	Section 23.6.6
(7) Set out a suitable audit programme for a pension scheme.	Section 23.6.8
(8) How do the accounting requirements for building societies under the Building Societies Act 1962 differ from those of the Companies Act 1985?	Section 23.7.2
(9) List the main internal controls needed in a building society.	Section 23.7.4: Guideline paragraphs 25–32

Questions	Reference for answers
(10) List (a) internal control procedures (b) audit procedures, likely to be encountered in a bank audit.	Section 23.8
(11) What three areas need special attention in the audit of an insurance company?	Section 23.9
(12) List the key audit areas peculiar to charities.	Section 23.10: Guideline paragraphs 31–38
(13) What internal controls should be present in a large charity?	Section 23.10: Guideline paragraphs 47–67
(14) In the case of trade unions and employers' associations (a) list the areas in which evidence in the form of rules and minuted decisions will be especially important; (b) state the areas in which internal controls should be present.	Section 23.11.4(c) Section 23.11.4(d) and (e)
(15) Summarize the legal requirements relating to accounting and auditing for friendly societies and industrial and provident societies.	Section 23.12
(16) What matters need special attention in the audit of housing associations?	Section 23.13.3
(17) Give an audit programme for a share transfer audit.	Section 23.14
(18) Why may an auditor be asked to report to the trustees under debenture and loan stock trust deeds?	Section 23.15

24 Investigations

24.1 Types of investigation

One major non-auditing task carried out by accountants is the *investigation*
—examining the affairs of an organization for some special purpose. Possible
types of investigation are:

(a) business purchase;
(b) prospectus reports;
(c) profit forecasts;
(d) in connection with a proposed loan;
(e) fraud;
(f) under the Companies Act 1985.

The end-product of an investigation is usually a *report* of some kind.
Before we begin our detailed coverage it will be useful to take a look at
report-writing techniques, and this we do in Section 24.2.

24.2 Some hints on report-writing

24.2.1 Terms of reference

In any relationship with professional advisers it is essential that all parties
have a clear understanding of what the client wants and what the adviser will
provide. In an audit, the letter of engagement spells out the precise nature of
the work to be undertaken. In an investigation there must also be a clear
statement of what is required. This could be written by the client, or written
by the accountant for the client to agree.

We normally refer to such written indications of the scope of an
appointment as the 'terms of reference'. Everything in the investigation report
should be within and relevant to the terms of reference.

24.2.2 The sections of the report

A typical report will consist of three main parts:

(a) an opening paragraph which incorporates the terms of reference

(b) a brief summary of work done, with detail given in appendices

(c) a clear statement of conclusions and recommendations. The natural place for these is towards the end of the report, but it may be useful to the reader to state the final conclusion in brief form near the beginning of the report, perhaps immediately after the opening paragraph.

The language of the report should be appropriate to the *reader's* background and understanding of accounting, not the writer's. This is true in practice and in the examination, where questions may refer to the limited accounting knowledge of the recipient. In such a case you will be penalized for writing an answer containing technical jargon that only another accountant would understand. The examiner is testing your ability to explain concepts clearly in language that a layman can follow—an essential skill for practising accountants! If some technical terms are unavoidable, provide clear definitions. Do not clutter the main body of the report with detail. It is convenient for you in answering questions, and good reporting technique, to use appendices for detailed calculations and supporting information.

There are several schools of thought about the precise format—headings and so on. In particular, should we frame the report as a letter or should we simply put a heading? There is no need to be over-worried about this. Either should be acceptable.

Be prepared to use numbered paragraph headings. In practice, these would be listed at the front of the report. If you want to use this technique, leave a half page of space at the appropriate point and enter paragraph headings or appendix titles as you use them.

24.3 Stages of an investigation

The stages of an investigation will be:

(a) Obtain and agree instructions from the client (terms of reference).

(b) Communicate with the auditors of the company to be investigated. This is necessary both as a matter of professional etiquette and because the investigating accountant will probably wish to obtain information from the auditors.

(c) Plan the work of the investigation:
  (1) staff to be involved;
  (2) sources of information;
  (3) timing of work and of delivery of report (to be agreed with the client);
  (4) need to visit offices of company under investigation.

(d) Collect necessary information and documents.

(e) Make necessary adjustments to information obtained to eliminate inconsistencies (as for example when past financial statements are being summarized, and accounting policies have changed during the period under review).

(f) Draft the report.

(g) Submit the report to the client.

(h) Meet the client to discuss the report's conclusions.

24.4 Business purchase

Business purchase investigations may concern the acquisition of a sole trader's business, a share in a partnership, or a major or controlling shareholding in a company. These different types of investigation have many factors-in common, but naturally there are also special features in each of them.

The objective of the investigation is to advise the prospective purchaser on the financial, and possibly other, implications of the purchase.

We shall approach our study by considering how to deal with the purchase of a company, and then consider the special features relevant for sole traders or partnerships. Parallel studies of share valuations (financial accounting) or sources of finance (financial management) may help you formulate your answer.

24.4.1 Factors to be considered

The factors that need to be considered in our answer can be expressed in the form of a grid:

	Past	Present	Future
Financial factors	1	2	3
Non-financial factors	4	5	6

Our answer should say something about each of these six matters, unless the question asks us to consider financial factors only, or limits its scope in some other way.

As accountants, we shall naturally tend to concentrate on the financial angles, but the non-financial ones should not be overlooked. A ratio of about two-thirds financial to one-third non-financial should be about right.

The temptation is to work mainly in box 1, and analyse past financial data. This may be a useful *start*, but it should always be remembered that a purchaser is buying the *future* of the business, not its past, and our objective must be to use historical infomation as a basis for statements about the future, not as an end in itself. Let us enlarge our diagram by identifying the detailed contents of each of the six fields in our grid:

Financial factors

Past	Present	Future
Basic financial information		
Previous financial statements	Current balance sheet and asset valuations Management accounts	Orders and enquiries Sales forecasts Cash flow forecasts Budgets Corporate plans Sensitivity analysis
Special problems		
	Pension scheme liabilities Deferred taxation Contingent liabilities	Capital commitments
Ratio analysis Past, present and projected future trends of: —gross and net profit on sales —return on capital employed —liquidity ratios —stock/turnover		
Capital		
	Capital structure and gearing	
Accounting systems		
	Quantity and quality of accounting information available	
Financial effects of acquistion		
	Methods of financing	Costs and benefits

Non-financial factors

Past	Present	Future
Business generally History of business and of personnel connected with it	Present state of business	Expected future trends for: —world economy —UK economy —important overseas markets —industry concerned
Labour force History of labour relations	Current labour relations	Future labour relations Other factors affecting availability of labour
Management Past management structure	Contracts currently held by senior management: —period covered —level of remuneration —taxation costs	Continuity of key management personnel
	Competence of management	Review of problems and costs in removing unwanted staff
Marketing Products Markets Market share Compositions	Past, present and projected future trends analysed	
Research and development	Projects currently in hand	Future plans

Past	Present	Future
Production		
	Condition and modernity of plant	Planned plant replacement and expansion
Legislation		
	Current problems being experienced	Possible effect of existing or planned future legislation affecting the company's operations (for example, pollution control, prohibition of use of products like medical drugs)

Political stability
Past, present and projected future developments affecting the company's operations at home and abroad.

These are rather long-winded charts. It would be impossible to deal adequately with all these points in the time allowed to answer an examination question, if indeed a question of acceptable length could contain all the necessary information.

Nevertheless, you need to know these headings, as examination questions often ask for an indication of the headings of a report rather than for an actual report.

24.4.2 Using the financial information

The ultimate objective of our report is probably to indicate a range within which the value of the company lies. A potentially important element in that value is goodwill, which in turn depends on the projected futue profit level.

It is not difficult to imagine, then, that the seller may be tempted to massage the figures a little. The investigating accountant must therefore do more than meekly accept profit figures supplied by the company. All the many ways in which the profit may be inflated must be reviewed.

Possibilities include:

(*a*) inflating sales figures by adding cash to takings;

(b) manipulating cut-off;
(c) overvaluing stock;
(d) suppressing purchase invoices or major expense accounts;
(e) failure to write-off as bad major irrecoverable debts;
(f) deferral of necessary maintenance expenditure;
(g) capitalizing expenditure normally classified as revenue expenditure;
(h) suppressing liabilities;
(i) failing to disclose contingent liabilities.

The fact that the figures have been audited does not necessarily mean that no investigation or adjustment is required. It could be, for example, that accounting policies followed by the company, while acceptable in themselves, do not accord with those of the purchasing company.

It may very difficult to guard against all possible manipulations. One possibility is to agree a purchase price conditional upon profits for the year following the takeover reaching a defined level, with a percentage of the payment deferred until the first accounts are prepared.

Ratio analysis may help us to detect manipulation. It may be possible to see as time in the past when the previous trend in the ratios changed. That might have been the time the existing owner decided to sell!

Care must be taken in extrapolating trends of profit. Consider the graph shown here.

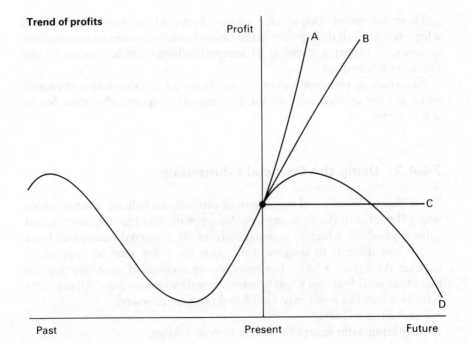

Trend of profits

Profits have previously shown a cylical pattern, but what is going to happen in future? Lines A, B, C and D indicate four possibilities.

For more on using the financial information, pick up ratio analysis and share valuations from your accounting texts.

24.4.3   Purchase of shares

It is possible to acquire a substantial interest in a company without acquiring it outright—in other words the acquisition is of a substantial shareholding.

It is important then to consider the legal and effective rights which attach to the percentage acquired. For example, a holding of more than 25 per cent would enable a special resolution to be blocked, and would normally mean in the case of a corporate holder that the company became an associated company.

The articles of association must also be consulted to discover additional rights, obligations or restrictions attaching to the shares.

Once again we are straying off into areas covered in your accountancy studies.

24.4.4   Purchase of a sole trader's business

All the points mentioned in Section 24.4.2 are relevant, except those few specifically relating to a company situation.

The additional factors to be considered stem from the fact that the purchaser will probably be looking to the business to provide his or her livelihood. The two vital questions to be added are:

(*a*) Does the purchaser have the expertise to run the business successfully?

(*b*) Can the business generate enough income to support proprietor and family?

Such a business may have succeeded because of the personal goodwill built up by the seller. We must also ask whether the seller plans to set up business again elsewhere. A reasonable limitation on such competition should be included in the contract.

It must be remembered too that such a business carries unlimited liability.

24.4.5   Purchase of an interest in a partnership

Once again most of the general points in Section 24.4.2 apply. Additional points for consideration are:

(*a*) the terms of the existing partnership agreement, and any changes in it thought necessary to safeguard the interests of the new partner, in particular the clauses which set out what is to be done if things go wrong, or if the new partner dies.

(b) equity of proposed profit sharing arrangements

(c) equity of formula for calculating goodwill

(d) possible clashes of personality with existing partners

(e) taxation considerations resulting from the change

(f) recognition that a partner has unlimited liability. In the case of a professional partnership the adequacy of professional indemnity insurance needs to be looked at.

24.5 Prospectuses

24.5.1 Introduction

A prospectus is an invitation to the public to subscribe for, or to purchase, shares or debentures in a company. The nineteenth century history of frauds in connection with prospectuses led to strict controls on them, by statute (now Schedule 3, Companies Act1985) and by the Stock Exchange for issues to be listed or in the Unlisted Securities Market (USM).

A prospectus may be necessary for:

(a) an issue by a company applying for admission to the Stock Exchange Official List

(b) an issue into the USM

(c) an issue into one of the over-the-counter markets

(d) an issue under the Business Expansion Scheme.

Statutory requirements and those of the Stock Exchange frequently entail an accountants' report either by the auditors of the company orby another independent accountant, on the following:

(a) Latest audited balance sheet of the company, normally made up as at a date not more than six months before the date of the prospectus (nine months for USM). If no such balance sheet is available it will normally be necessary to prepare and have audited suitable interim accounts. The balance sheets at the end of each of the five preceding years are also usually required.

(b) for the previous five years:

(1) profit and loss accounts

(2) statements of source and application of funds

(3) earnings per share and dividends paid

(4) movements in reserves

(c) statement of accounting policies used

(d) notes to the documents in (a) and (b) above

(e) details of borrowings by the company including contingent liabilities 'as at the most recent practicable date'.

(*f*) Any other matters which the reporting accountants consider relevant.

The report must give the reporting accountants's opinion as to whether the financial information gives a true and fair view.

Additional matters which must be dealt with by the reporting accountants though not included in the published document, are:

(*a*) *Statement of adjustments.* A statement detailing any adjustments made by the reporting accountants in preparing the prospectus report must be available for public inspection.

(*b*) *Working capital.* The Stock Exchange requires that the directors of the company state that in their opinion the company's working capital is sufficient for the requirements of the business. Although this is the directors' sole responsibility it is customary for the directors to ask the reporting accountant to review and report on the cash flow forecast prepared for this purpose, and this may include a request for a commentary on the assumptions on which it is based.

24.5.2 The reporting accountants' work

The stages of the reporting accountants' work will be:

(*a*) Agree terms of engagement and prepare an engagement letter. The engagement letter will cover:

(1) the form of report required;

(2) any audit work which may be necessary;

(3) the nature of any confirmations required from the directors concerning working capital, borrowings, or other financial information (comfort letters);

(4) whether a review of profit forecasts is necessary (see Section 24.6 below);

(5) an explanation of the reporting accountants' need to attend meetings at which the prospectus is drafted, and to approve the final published form and context of the accountants' report.

(6) agreed timescale for preparation and publication of the prospectus

(7) the reporting accountants' need to communicate with the company's auditors and other professional advisers.

(*b*) Carry out any necessary audit work, which will be required if, for example, interim accounts are to be prepared. Such work needs to be planned, controlled and recorded like any other audit.

(*c*) Review the audit working papers for the period covered, to detemine whether any further work is necessary.

(*d*) Review financial statements to determine whether any adjustments are necessary (see Section 24.5.3 below)

(*e*) Consider the effect of any previous audit qualifications

(*f*) Review appropriateness of accounting policies

(*g*) Study the remainder of the prospectus to confirm that the context in which the accountants' report is to be presented is acceptable, and provide a letter of consent agreeing to the issue of the prospectus

(*h*) Submit the report, which will be addressed jointly to the directors of the company and to the merchant bank, issuing house or stockbroker sponsoring the issue. See the specimen form of report in Section 24.5.4 below.

24.5.3 The statement of adjustments

Adjustments to previously reported figures should only be made:

(*a*) to ensure that the financial information for all the years reported on is stated on a consistent basis. This should normally be done by adjusting past figures to reflect current accounting policies.

(*b*) if necessary to prevent distortions resulting from changes in group structure;

(*c*) to correct fundamental errors.

24.5.4 The reporting accountant's report

The following form of wording may be appropriate for the introductory and opinion sections of the report. It includes an example of an unqualified opinion.

'We have examined the audited financial statements of X .... plc and its subsidiaries (the Group) for the five years ended ....

We have acted as auditors of the Group throughout the period covered by this report.

No financial statements have been prepared for the Group in respect of any period subsequent to ....

The financial information set out in paragraphs ..... to ..... below is based on the audited financial statements of the Group after making such adjustments as we considered appropriate.

Our work has been carried out in accordance with approved Auditing Standards.

In our opinion, the financial information, which has been prepared in accordance with the historical cost convention, as modified by the revaluation of land and buildings, gives a true and fair view of the profit and source and application of funds of the Group for each of the five years ended on .... and of the state of affairs of the Group at the end of each of those years.'

The report should be qualified if the reporting accountants have any material reservations. It should be dated as at the date the directors approved the prospectus.

24.6 Profit forecasts

24.6.1 Introduction

Profit forecasts may be required for a prospectus or in a bid situation. It is a requirement of the Stock Exchange in the case of prospectuses, and of the Panel on Takeovers and Mergers in the case of bids, that the auditors or an independent accountant should review and report on the accounting policies and calculations underlying the forecasts. The forecast will normally cover the remainder of a current accounting period, plus the next following accounting period if a significant part of the current period has already elapsed.

24.6.2 Review of a profit forecast

In carrying out their review, the main matters to which the reporting accountants will direct their attention are as follows:

—the nature and background of the company's business;
—the accounting practices normally followed by the company;
—the assumptions on which the forecasts are based;
—the procedures followed by the company for preparing the profit forecast.

(a) The nature and background of the company's business

The reporting accountants will wish to review the company's general management and recent history, with reference to such matters as the general nature of its activities and its main products, markets, customers, suppliers, divisions, locations, labour force and trend of results.

(b) The accounting policies normally followed by the company

The reporting accountants will wish to establish which accounting policies have been adopted by the company in published financial statements so as to ensure that they are acceptable and have been consistently applied in the preparation of interim accounts and the profit forecast.

(c) The assumptions on which forecasts are based

It is the responsibility of the reporting accountants to determine that the profit forecast is consistent with and has been properly compiled on the footing of the given assumptions. The reporting accountants have no specific responsibilities for and are not required by the regulations to report on the assumptions. However, in the course of their work on the accounting policies and calculations, they will need to consider the assumptions on which the profit forecast has been based. They should not allow an assumption to be published which appears to them to be unrealistic (or one to be omitted which appears to them to be important) without commenting on it in their report.

(d) The procedures followed by the company for preparing the profit forecast

In carrying out their examination of the accounting policies and calculations for the profit forecast, and the procedures followed by the company for its preparation, the main points which the reporting accountants will wish to consider include the following:

(1) whether the profit forcast under review is based on forecasts regularly prepared for the purpose of management, or whether it has been separately and specially prepared for the immediate purpose;

(2) where profit forecasts are regularly prepared for management purposes the degree of accuracy and reliability previously achieved, and the frequency and thoroughness with which estimates are revised;

(3) whether the profit forecast under review represents the management's best estimate of results which they reasonably believe can and will be achieved as distinct from targets which the management has set as desirable;

(4) the extent to which profit forecast results for expired periods are supported by reliable interim accounts;

(5) the details of the procedures followed to generate the profit forecast and the extent to which it is built up from detailed profit forecasts of activity and cash flow;

(6) the extent to which profits are derived from activities having a proved and consistent trend and those of a more irregular, volatile or unproved nature;

(7) how the profit forecast takes account of any material extraordinary items and prior year adjustments, their nature, and how they are presented;

(8) whether adequate provision is made for foreseeable losses and contingencies and how the profit forecast takes account of factors which may cause it to be subject to a high degree of risk, or which may invalidate the assumptions;

(9) whether working capital appears adequate for requirements; normally this would require the availability of properly prepared cash-flow forecasts; and where short-term or long-term finance is to be relied on, whether the necessary arrangements have been made and confirmed;

(10) the arithmetical accuracy of the profit forecast and the supporting information and whether forecast balance sheets and sources and applications of funds statements have been prepared—these help to highlight arithmetical inaccuracies and inconsistent assumptions.

24.6.3 The accountants' report

The accountants' report will be addressed to the directors and will normally include statements dealing with the following matters, so far as appropriate:

(a) specific identification of the profit forecast and documents to which the report refers;

(b) the fact that the directors are solely responsible for the profit forecast;

(c) the fact that the reporting accountants have examined the accounting policies and calculations used in arriving at the profit forecast;

(d) if, as will frequently be the case, the reporting accountants have not carried out an audit of results for expired periods, a statement to that effect;

(e) whether in the opinion of the reporting accountants the profit forecast so far as the accounting policies and calculations are concerned has been properly compiled on the footing of the assumptions made by the board of directors, as set out in the document, and is presented on a basis consistent with the accounting policies normally adopted by the company.

The report should be qualified if, *inter alia,* the reporting accountants:

(a) have reason for material reservation about the accounting policies or calculations for the profit forecast;

(b) have reason to consider the accounting policies and calculations to be inconsistent with the stated assumptions;

(c) have not obtained all the information they consider necessary (for example the fact that they were unable to review the profit forecasts of material subsidiary or associated companies or because of unduly restrictive time limits).

If any of the assumptions which are to be published appear to them to be unrealistic, or if any assumption is to be omitted which appears to them to be important, they should include an appropriate comment in their report.

24.6.4 Specimen report

An accountants' report might, in appropriate circumstances, where there are no grounds for qualifications, read as follows:

'To the directors of X Limited

We have reviewed the accounting policies and calculations for the profit forecasts of X Limited (for which the directors are solely responsible) for the periods...set out on pages...of this circular. The forecasts include results shown by unaudited interim accounts for the period... In our opinion the forecasts, so far as the accounting policies and calculations are concerned, have been properly compiled on the footing of the assumptions made by the Board set out on page...of this circular and are presented on a basis consistent with the accounting practices normally adopted by the company.'

24.6.5 Profit forecast checklist

The following checklist may be a useful aide-memoire to auditors dealing with a profit forecast:

Preparation

(1) Obtain written instructions from the client for the review of the profit forecast. Where this is not practicable, it is suggested that a letter recapitulating the verbal instructions received from the client should be sent by the reporting accountant.

(2) Obtain a statement of assumptions used in the forecast.

(3) Ensure that all personnel working on the profit forecast review are instructed:

(a) to list all documents and bases on which they are prepared, and to ensure that copies of all important documents are obtained and filed;

(b) that in all cases where information is obtained verbally from any official, indication is given in the relevant part of the review of the name and position of the official and the date the information was given.

Nature and background of the company's business

(4) Attach brief notes of the history of the company.

(5) Attach notes of the general nature of the company's activities.

(6) Attach notes with regard to the following:

(a) the main products;

(b) the main markets;

(c) the principal customers;

(d) the principal suppliers;

(e) the production capacity of the factories (where relevant in relation to forecast turnover);

(f) the labour force (where relevant in relation to forecast turnover);

(g) the organization of the company;

(h) the office and factory locations;

(i) the trend of results over a period of years and explanation of any fluctuations or special factors affecting the results.

Note: In connection with (a) to (d), the intention is that areas of the company's business which are of particular importance to the results of the company can be readily identified.

Accounting procedures normally followed by the company and followed in the forecasts

(7) Obtain from the company a statement of the accounting procedures normally adopted.

(8) Where not otherwise included, make notes on:

(a) the methods followed, and the nature of overheads included in determining the amount to be carried forward for stock and work in progress, and the identification, judgement and accounting treatment of obsolete and slow-moving items;

(b) the bases adopted for recognizing profits and providing for losses on long-term contracts;

(c) the bases for calculating depreciation charges;

(d) the accounting treatment of research and development expenditure;

(e) the accounting treatment, and adequacy of disclosure, of exceptional items;

(f) the accounting treatment of taxation, and government grants.

(9) Examine specifically, note and comment on the bases used in the forecast as follows:

(a) the method of arriving at turnover and verification carried out;

(b) the gross margins on products and the methods used in their determination;

(c) give consideration to reliability of (a) and (b) by comparison with previous years' figures, interim or management accounts, etc.;

(d) the method of valuing stock and the method and dates on which physical stock was last taken;

(e) consider the impact of obsolete and slow-moving stocks on all the forecasts.

(10)   Identify any unduly conservative or optimistic principles where the effect has been to depress materially or inflate disclosed profits.

(11)   Ensure that the arithmetic is checked for the forecast, together with any supporting documents.

(12)   Examine, generally, accounting procedures adopted and note any which:

(*a*)   have not been applied consistently during the forecast period/periods under review;

(*b*)   are not normally acceptable;

(*c*)   are known to differ from those adopted by the other party to the takeover or merger.

Note: In the case of a merger it may be essential that there should be no significant differences in procedures between the parties arriving at their respective forecast profits and to ensure that the published documents disclose the effect of any change in principle during the periods under review, and, where known, any principles which might be changed on completion of the takeover or merger so as to materially affect the results subsequently disclosed.

(*d*)   consider the impact of unrealized profit on intra-group stock on profits reported for the purposes of the forecast, and ensure that this has been dealt with where appropriate;

(*e*)   examine the bases adopted for assessing profit and/or losses on long-term contract and ensure that bases are consistent with those previously used;

(*f*)   depreciation:

(i)   examine bases for calculation of depreciation charges and ensure that bases are consistent with those previously used;

(ii)   examine treatment of surpluses or deficits arising on revaluation of disposals of assets and possible effects on depreciation charges;

(*g*)   obtain a schedule showing main items of interest receivable and payable and examine and indicate *all* items relating to group companies. Consider effect of new borrowings in current year;

(*h*)   where appropriate consider:

(i)   how items of a revenue nature actually arising in a period but reasonably attributable to the year as a whole have been dealt with, e.g. advertising expenditure;

(ii)   how income and expenditure of a substantially seasonal nature has been dealt with;

(*i*) where appropriate:
(i) consider and note exchange rates used;
(ii) consider effect of overseas Exchange Control restrictions on remittances of profits.

(*j*) confirm that consideration has been given to bad debts and provision made. Note any large items for which no provision has been made but which might be described as doubtful;
(*k*) taxation:

(i) examine basis of provision;
(ii) ensure that any necessary adjustments are made if alternations are effected to income or expenditure figures during the course of the review;
(iii) in the case of United Kingdom companies, compare written-down values with net book values of appropriate fixed assets and comment on deferred tax implications.

Note: Forecasts are normally of profits before taxation. However, it is necessary to examine the recent taxation history in order to ascertain whether there are special features of the taxation position relevant to the validity of the forecast as a guide to distributable profits.

(*l*) examine all prior-year adjustments and exceptional or extraordinary items;
(*m*) consider the effect on forecasts of any acquisition or disposals of investments in companies or trades. Note treatment of pre-acquisition profits and consider whether apportionment should be on a time basis or any other basis (e.g. seasonal factors);
(*n*) inquire as to the last date of agreement of intra-group balances;
(*o*) inquire as to unprovided contingencies, e.g. open positions on forward dealings in foreign exchange or commodities, forward option dealings in securities, guarantees, litigation and other claims, including taxation, and note all significant items;
(*p*) scrutinize minutes for any matters which might affect forecasts;
(*q*) in the case of United Kingdom companies, accounting treatment of investment or other government grants and ensure that method is consistent with that previously used;
(*r*) if a forecast balance sheet has been prepared as at the end of the review period, compare with the last audited balance sheet and the last balance sheet prepared from the books of account, note significant differences and consider effect on profits forecast;
(*s*) note and consider effect on forecasts of any other matters not specifically dealt with above.

Assumptions on which the forecasts are based

(13) Note assumptions made (including commercial assumptions) and determine whether the forecasts have been properly compiled on the footing of the assumptions. Ensure that (where appropriate) they have been correctly applied to accounting bases and calculations.

Note: Assumptions made by the board might include that:

(*a*) profit margins generally during the remainder of the financial year will continue at the levels shown by the latest management accounts;

(*b*) there will be no changes in rates of exchange during the remainder of the year;

(*c*) there will be no significant change in interest rates during the remainder of the year;

(*d*) the results will not be materially affected by industrial disturbances or by supply interruptions attributable to other causes;

(*e*) there will be no significant variation in taxes and duties wherever imposed;

(*f*) there will be no change in the basis of accounting hitherto applied in the company and its subsidiaries for a company subject to a takeover;

(*g*) there are not other unforeseen factors which might affect the turnover, profits and assets of companies in the group.

(14) Consider what other assumptions of significance *have been made in fact* for the purpose of the forecasts but not included above.

(15) If further assumptions noted have a material affect on the figures, ensure that these are included in the board's assumptions.

Procedures followed by the company for preparing forecasts

(16) Are profit forecasts under review based on forecasts regularly prepared for the purpose of management, or have they been specifically prepared for the immediate purpose? Are these forecasts best current estimates as opposed to desirable targets?

(17) Obtain from the company:

(*a*) a manual of accounting procedures or, where one is not in use, a description of the methods used in preparing its financial and management accounts;

(*b*) a reconciliation of the last published audited accounts with the management accounts covering the same period of trading;

(*c*) the working papers supporting those accounts.

(18) Compare the forecast with any earlier forecast made in respect of the same period and obtain explanations for any material change.

(19) Compare the results shown by the most recent management accounts with the forecast (if any) originally made for that period and obtain explanations for any material difference:

(a) In order that an examination may be made of the trend of past results and of the company's success in predicting those results, obtain from the company a comparison of the detailed results and forecasts for the past three completed years;

(b) If practical, where the level of activity fluctuates, whether for seasonal or other reasons, the examination should be extended to past periods equivalent to the completed part of the current year;

(c) The details required will depend on the size of the company or group under review but will normally include, at least on a test basis, a review of the main items of income and expenditure.

(20) Where the forecast results differed materially in the past from the actual results achieved inquire whether any alterations have been made to the forecasting procedures which should help to reduce any differences which might arise on the forecast profits for the period under review.

(21) Specific note should be made where the achievement of the forecast is subject to a high degree of risk. Examples of such situations are:

(a) businesses where sales levels are difficult to predict;

(b) long-term contracts at fixed prices;

(c) new or unproven products or processes.

(22) Inquire as to the adequacy of working capital and obtain from the company:

(a) a cash-flow forecast for a period not less than that covered by the profit forecast or, if different, the period covered by the directors' comments on working capital. (*Note:* It is desirable that the review should extend beyond the period reported on so as to ensure that account is taken of any relatively large payments, e.g. taxation falling due soon after the date specified.) The statement should be prepared on a monthly or quarterly basis so that seasonal fluctuations are shown;

(b) a forecast balance sheet as the end of the review period and at any interim periods if available.

The cash-flow forecast and projected balance sheet should be carefully examined to establish whether:

(a) the cash forcasts are reconciled with profit forecasts regularly prepared for management purposes;

(b) the cash-flow forecast for the period is reconciled with the profit forecast and closing balance sheet;

(*c*) compare cash-flow forecasts made in the past, if available, with the ultimate out-turn indicate weaknesses in the forecasting procedure;

(*d*) the forecasts prepared by subsidiaries are based on the same assumptions as those on which the results forecast are based.

Final points on the forecast

(23) Procure and file copies of up-to-date *written* assurances from management:

(*a*) that the figures contained in actual and forecast accounts are based on the same accounting principles as those applied in the audited annual accounts of the previous year;

(*b*) that all items of an exceptional or non-recurring nature (actual or expected) have been disclosed either in the actual or forecast accounts or by report and comment thereon (including such items as material contingent liabilities and capital losses or profits not normally dealt with in the profit and loss account);

(*c*) that management is at the present time aware of no reason why the estimated results (state amounts) are unlikely to be achieved.

(24) Check that the forecasts of trading subsidiaries or branches which have been the subject of detailed examination have been correctly included in the consolidated forecast.

(25) Test the arithmetical accuracy of the consolidation working papers.

(26) Consider whether any adjustment to the forecast is necessary on account of the reviews made and reported on by other firms.

(27) Ensure that detailed examination has been made, and letters of representation received, in respect of all companies, branches or divisions which contribute materially to the forecast.

(28) Ensure that the results have been adjusted for intra-group transactions and unrealized profits.

(29) Ensure that the forecast together with the assumptions on which it is based is formally adopted by the board of directors who should also take sole responsibility for it.

24.7   Investigations on behalf of a prospective lender

The considerations for a prospective lender are an abridged version of the points discussed in Section 24.4 above for a business purchase, plus attention to the matters of direct concern to a lender:

(a) the solvency and going concern status of the borrower;

(b) the purpose for which the loan is required, and the ability of the proposed investment, or the company's general operations, to generate funds sufficient to repay the loan;

(c) the need for and adequacy of any proposed security;

(d) the acceptability and feasability of proposed repayments.

24.8 Fraud

24.8.1 Introduction

In the types of investigation we have been looking at so far, the target of the work was the financial statements. We now turn to a completely different area—an investigation to discover the nature and extent of fraud. This may be needed for a variety of reasons, perhaps to support an insurance claim under a fidelity policy, or to enable better internal controls to be established to prevent a recurrence. Another possibility is an investigation by accountants other than the auditors in connection with a claim for negligence against the auditors.

The normal situation is that it is known that a fraud has been perpetuated, but the full extent is not known.

Possible types of fraud are:

(a) defalcation of cash, perhaps by teeming and lading (see Sections 10.7.1(b), 10.8.1(c) and 10.8.3);

(b) defalcation of stock or other assets

(c) manipulation of accounts to inflate profit, leading to inflated payments of commission, etc.

24.8.2 Stages of a fraud investigation

(a) *Briefing by client, followed by letter of engagement detailing the initial scope of the work.* It is important to realize, and for the client to realize, that the extent of the work may increase as the extent of the fraud is revealed by investigation.

(b) *Communication with other parties involved.* This can include the external auditors, if the investigation is not being conducted by them, internal auditors, if any, the audit committee, if any, and the client's accounting staff.

(c) *Determining the extent of the fraud.* The accuracy with which this can be determined will depend on the type of fraud, the areas of responsibility of the known perpetrator, and the extent to which he is providing information about the fraud.

(*d*) *Interviewing the defrauder.* This should happen at an early stage of the investigation if possible. It may be useful to ask the person to prepare a statement explaining his actions and indicating exactly what has been done.

(*e*) *Investigating the known area with detailed audit tests.* If all that is known is that a fraud has occurred somewhere in the area under review, it may be necessary to conduct exhaustive checks, concentrating perhaps on the larger items at first.

The most likely areas for defalcations are cash handling, wages, stock and debtors. If fraud is known or suspected in any of these areas the investigator's approach will be to apply normal substantive audit tests, as outlined in earlier chapters, but on an intensive basis. The use of ratio analysis may enable the invesigator to see, with hindsight, when the fraud must have begun. For example, if in a chain of supermarkets one store begins to show a lower gross profit percentage than all the others, a fraud dating from this time would be an obvious possible cause.

In the case of debtors, a circularization of customers may provide useful evidence.

(*f*) When the investigator believes that all possible areas have been covered to a suitable extent, he or she will report to management on the findings, with copies to other interested parties (external auditor, internal auditor, audit committee).

The report should detail:

(1) the circumstances which led to the investigation;

(2) the frauds which have been discovered, and their extent;

(3) the identity of the defrauder;

(4) effects on the reported profits of past periods;

(5) effects on the financial statements of the current period;

(6) internal control weaknesses which allowed the fraud, and recommendations for eliminating them;

(7) report of any interviews with the defrauder, including offers of restitution, etc, which may be relevant to management in deciding what action, if any, they should take against him or her.

(8) If there is a suggestion that the external auditor has been negligent, and the investigation is being conducted by an independent accountant, the extent to which a claim against the auditor could be justified, subject to legal advice.

24.9   Investigations under the Companies Act 1985

24.9.1   Introduction

The Companies Act 1985 lays down several ways in which inspectors may be appointed to investigate the affairs of a company. The procedure is for the

Department of Trade and Industry (DTI) to appoint the inspectors, on its own initiative; because required to do so by the court; or because requested to do so by a number of members.

24.9.2 Appointment of inspectors

(*a*) The DTI *must* appoint inspectors if the court so orders (S432(1))

  (*b*) The DTI *may* appoint inspectors if there are circumstances suggesting:

  (1) that the company's affairs are being or have been conducted with intent to defraud creditors, or otherwise for a fraudulent or unlawful purpose, or in a manner which is unfairly prejudicial to some part of its members;

  (2) that some proposed future act would be prejudicial to members;

  (3) that the company was formed for a fraudulent or unlawful purpose;

  (4) that persons connected with the company's formation or management have been guilty of fraud, misfeasance or other misconduct;

  (5) that the members have not received all reasonable information as to the company's affairs (S432(2)).

(*c*) The DTI *may* appoint inspectors on application from:

  (1) not less than 200 members, or holders of not less than 10 per cent of the issued share capital

  (2) in the case of a company not having a share capital, 20 per cent in number of the members

  (3) the company itself. (S431).

24.9.3 Expenses of investigation

When an inspector is to be appointed under Section 24.9.2(*c*) above, the DTI may ask for security, normally up to £5000, to cover the costs of the investigation.

On the completion of the investigation the following persons may be liable to make payments to the DTI to cover the expenses in whole or part:

  (*a*) any person convicted on a prosecution instituted as a result of the investigation;

  (*b*) the body corporate in whose name any action is brought, to the value of any property recovered by it;

  (*c*) the applicants, if under S431 (i.e. those in Section 24.9.2(*c*) above).

24.9.4 Powers of inspectors

Once appointed, inspectors have wide powers. They may:

(a) Extend their investigation into the affairs of any subsidiaries or holding company of the company initially being investigated (S433).

(b) Require officers, or other persons not officers with information about the company, to:

(1) produce documents;
(2) attend before the inspectors;
(3) give all necessary assistance (S434).

Failure to comply may be treated as contempt of court (S436).

(c) Examine directors' bank accounts for evidence of improper receipts (S435).

(d) Enter and search premises (S448).

(e) Bring civil proceedings on the company's behalf (S438).

24.9.5 The inspector's report

The inspector's report is made to the DTI. If the initial appointment was on the order of the Court, a copy must be furnished for the Court. A copy will also normally be sent to the company and supplied on request to any member, any person whose conduct is referred to in the report, any creditor, and to the auditors.

The DTI may also order the report to be published (S437).

24.9.6 Other investigations

The investigations dealt with above were all into the affairs of the company, and related acts by officers and others.

The DTI also has the power, under S442, to appoint inspectors to investigate the true ownership of the company and, under S446, to investigate share dealings by directors and their families in contravention of the 'insider dealing' provision of SS323 and 324 and Schedule 13.

24.10 Summary

24.10.1 Reasons for investigations

Investigations may be undertaken for the following reasons:

(a) business purchase;
(b) prospectus;
(c) profit forecasts;
(d) proposed loan;
(e) fraud;
(f) under the Companies Act 1985.

24.10.2 Report writing

The end-product of the investigation will normally be a report. This should:

(a) refer to the terms of reference;
(b) state conclusions and recommendations clearly;
(c) be written in language appropriate to the recipient's powers of understanding .

24.10.3 Stages of an investigation

(a) Obtain instructions and prepare letter of engagement.
(b) Plan work to be done and timing.
(c) Collect necessary information.
(d) Make necessary calculations.
(e) Formulate conclusions.
(f) Draft and submit report.
(g) Discuss findings with client.

24.10.4 Business purchase

Business purchase investigations will involve financial and non-financial factors. Accountants will be concerned with the financial factors but must allow in their report for the non-financial factors also.

The investigating accountant must be on guard for manipulation of the figures and will carry out a critical review to detect any such possibilities.

24.10.5   Prospectuses

A prospectus investigation has to cover the previous five years and will deal with:

(a) balance sheets;
(b) profit and loss accounts;
(c) statements of source and application of funds;
(d) supporting material.

The report on all this information is addressed jointly to the directors and the sponsors.

24.10.6   Profit forecasts

An accountant's report on a profit forecast may become necessary in a bid situation or because a profit forecast is to be included in a prospectus. The main matters to be reviewed are:

(a) the nature and background of the company's business;
(b) accounting practices normally followed by the company;
(c) the assumptions on which the forecasts are based;
(d) the procedures followed by the company for preparing the profit forecast.

24.10.7   Investigations on behalf of a prospective lender

The considerations here are an abridged version of those applicable for business purchase, with special emphasis on the following points:

(a) solvency and going concern status of borrower;
(b) purpose of loan;
(c) ability of borrower to repay;
(d) need for security.

24.10.8   Fraud

A fraud investigation may involve simple defalcations of cash or goods or the manipulation of accounts to inflate profits. The stages of a fraud investigation will be:

(*a*) initial briefing and formulation of terms of reference;

(*b*) communication with other interested parties (external auditor, internal auditor, audit committee, senior accounting staff);

(*c*) determining the extent of the fraud;

(*d*) interviewing the defrauder;

(*e*) applying detailed and extensive checks to suspect areas;

(*f*) reporting.

24.10.9   Investigations under the Companies Act 1985

Inspectors may be appointed by the Department of Trade and Industry to investigate a company's affairs:

(*a*) by the DTI on its own initiative

(*b*) when ordered to do so by the Court

(*c*) on the application of a number of members

(*d*) on the application of the company itself.

Inspectors have powers to require officers of the company to produce documents, attend for interview, and give all necessary assistance. They may examine directors' bank accounts for evidence of improper payments and enter and search premises in the course of their duties.

They may also bring civil proceedings on the company's behalf. The inspector's report is made to the DTI, who will supply copies to interested parties and may order the report to be published.

The DTI also has the power to appoint inspectors to investigate:

(*a*) the true ownership of the company

(*b*) share dealings by directors and their families.

Progress questions

Questions	Reference for answer
(1) What are the main purposes for which accountants will conduct investigations?	Section 24.1
(2) What three sections will a report typically contain?	Section 24.2.2
(3) What are the stages of an investigation?	Section 24.3
(4) List twenty matters requiring attention in a business purchase investigation.	Section 24.4.1
(5) How might a seller try to manipulate figures to inflate the profit of his company?	Section 24.4.2
(6) What special factors need to be considered in the following situations: (a) purchase of shares (less than 100 per cent); (b) purchase of sole trader's business; (c) purchase of share in partnership?	Section 24.4.3 Section 24.4.4 Section 24.4
(7) When will it be necessary for a company to issue a prospectus?	Section 24.5.1
(8) What matters must be included and reported upon in the accountants' report in the prospectus?	Section 24.5.1
(9) What is a statement of adjustments?	Section 24.5.3
(10) Draft a suitable form of unqualified accountants' report on figures in a prospectus.	Section 24.5.4

Questions	Reference for answer
(11) What matters need to be investigated in an accountant's review of a profit forecast?	Section 24.6.2
(12) What is the maximum time into the future that an accountant's report on a profit forecast can normally cover?	Section 24.6.1
(13) What special factors need to be considered in an investigation on behalf of a prospective lender?	Section 24.7
(14) What possible types of fraud may be the subject of an investigation?	Section 24.8.1
(15) What are the typical stages of a fraud investigation?	Section 24.8.2
(16) What will a report following a fraud investigation probably cover?	Section 24.8.2(f)
(17) Who may initiate the appointment of the inspectors under the Companies Act 1985?	Section 24.9.2
(18) What powers do inspectors have?	Section 24.9.4
(19) What other matters, apart from the company's affairs, may be investigated by inspectors appointed under the Companies Act?	Section 24.9.6

Appendix: Auditing Standards and Guidelines, and other professional pronouncements

The Standards and Guidelines issued by the Auditing Practices Committee since 1980 form essential study material and now cover most of the central features of auditing.

All of them are included in this book. The table below shows where to find them. Other professional pronouncements reproduced are also listed, with an indication of their source.

We are grateful to the Auditing Practices Committee and the Institute of Chartered Accountants in England and Wales for permission to reproduce all this material.

Date of issue	Title	Section reference
	(A) The auditor's operational standard	
	(1) *Operational Guidelines*	
April 1980	(a) Planning, controlling and recording	4.1
		4.5
		4.6
	(b) Accounting systems	6.2
	(c) Audit evidence	8.4
	(d) Internal controls	
	—main text	7.2
	—Appendix 1	5.2
	(e) Review of financial statements	11.2
	(2) *Detailed operational Guidelines*	
June 1982	(a) Bank reports for audit purposes	10.8
November 1982	(b) Events after the balance sheet date	11.10

Date of issue	Title	Section reference
November 1982	(c) Amounts derived from the preceding financial statements	11.15
July 1983	(d) Representations by management	10.12
October 1983	(e) Attendance at stocktaking	10.6
May 1984	(f) Engagement letters	3.3
June 1984	(g) Auditing in a computer environment	13.4
November 1984	(h) Reliance on internal audit	5.4
February 1985	(i) Quality control	4.8
June 1985	(j) Financial information issued with audited financial statements	11.16
June 1985	(k) Auditors' considerations in respect of going-concern	11.9
May 1986	(l) Reliance on other specialists	8.8
	(3) *Exposure drafts*	
May 1985	(a) Reliance on the work of other auditors	21.4
May 1985	(b) Reports to management	14.6
July 1985	(c) Fraud and other irregularities	19.3
	(B) Reporting Standards and Guidelines	
April 1980	(a) The audit report	14.2
April 1980	(b) Qualifications in audit reports	14.3
April 1980	(c) Audit report examples	14.4
October 1980	(d) Auditors' reports and SSAP 16 (summarized)	22.2
	(C) Auditing Guidelines— Industries	
October 1981	(a) Charities	23.10
	(b) Building societies (summarized)	23.7
August 1984	(c) Trade unions and employers' associations (summarized)	23.11
November 1984	(d) Housing associations (summarized)	23.13

Index

Index